The Art of

Theatre

Dennis J. Sporre

Ball State University

Prentice Hall, Englewood Cliffs, New Jersey 07632

Library of Congress Cataloging-in-Publication Data

Sporre, Dennis J.
    The art of theatre / Dennis J. Sporre.
        p.   cm.
    Includes bibliographical references and index.
    ISBN 0-13-052291-0
    1. Theater.   I. Title.
PN2037.S66   1993
792--dc20   92-24835
                                                       CIP

Production Editor: *Shelly Kupperman*
Acquisitions Editor: *Steven Dalphin*
Editor-in-Chief: *Charlyce Jones Owen*
Development Editor: *Ronald Librach*
Marketing Manager: *Chris Freitag*
Copy Editor: *Judy Ashkenaz*
Interior and Cover Designer: *Amy Rosen*
Prepress Buyer: *Kelly Behr*
Manufacturing Buyer: *Mary Ann Gloriande*
Supplements Editor: *Sharon Chambliss*
Editorial Assistants: *Caffie Risher/Asha Rohra*
Photo Editor: *Lorinda Morris-Nantz*
Photo Researcher: *Cindy Joyce*
Design Director: *Florence Dara Silverman/Anne T. Bonanno*
Cover Photo: *Phantom of the Opera. Clive Barda/Woodfin Camp.*

 © 1993 by Prentice-Hall, Inc.
A Simon & Schuster Company
Englewood Cliffs, New Jersey 07632

Printed in the United States of America
10 9 8 7 6 5 4 3 2 1

ISBN   0-13-052291-0

Prentice-Hall International (UK) Limited, *London*
Prentice-Hall of Australia Pty. Limited, *Sydney*
Prentice-Hall Canada Inc., *Toronto*
Prentice-Hall Hispanoamericana, S.A., *Mexico*
Prentice-Hall of India Private Limited, *New Delhi*
Prentice-Hall of Japan, Inc., *Tokyo*
Simon & Schuster Asia Pte. Ltd., *Singapore*
Editora Prentice-Hall do Brasil, Ltda., *Rio de Janeiro*

Contents

Preface   viii

Diary of a Production: Ghetto   1

JUDY E. YORDON: ARTISTIC DIRECTOR   2
DAVID C. SHAWGER, JR.: SCENIC DESIGNER   4
KATHLEEN M. JAREMSKI: COSTUME
DESIGNER   7
DENNIS J. SPORRE: LIGHTING DESIGNER   9
JUDY E. YORDON: DIRECTOR   11

Chapter 1

What Are the Arts?   15

THE WORK OF ART   16
  The Humanities, Humanity, and the Arts   17
  Profile Richard Mayhew (I): The Artist
  & His Audience   18
  What Are the Arts? What Is Art?   20
THE FUNCTIONS OF ART   24
  Entertainment   24
  Political and Social Commentary   25
  Therapy   27
  Profile Richard Mayhew (II): The Artist
  & His Medium   28
  Art as Artifact   29
THE ARTS AND LIFE   29
SUMMARY   30

Chapter 2

What Is Theatre?   33

THEATRE AS ART   35
  The Production   35
  Profile Tennessee Williams (I): The
  Timeless World of a Play   36
  Profile Arthur Miller (I): The Thought
  of Henrik Ibsen   40
  The Process of Theatre   42
  Theatre as Experience and Response   43
  Profile Tennessee Williams (II): The Tragic
  Tradition & Moral Values   45

HOW THEATRE FUNCTIONS   51
  Theatre as Entertainment   52
  Theatre as Therapy   52
  Theatre as Social and Political Weapon   53
  Theatre as Artifact   54
  Profile Arthur Miller (II): The Playwright
  as Individualist   55
SUMMARY   56

Chapter 3

Understanding and Evaluating Plays and Performances   59

APPROACHING THE PLAY   60
UNDERSTANDING BEYOND THE FIRST
EXPERIENCE   61
  Understanding Characters   61
  Understanding the Facts of the Play   64
  Understanding Setting   66
  Understanding the Play and Its Parts   66
  Finding the Play's Personality   72
  Profile Philip Radcliffe (I): Skills, Values,
  and Judgments   73
CRITICISM   81
  What Is "Criticism"?   81
  Profile Philip Radcliffe (II): Missionary
  Zeal   82
  Profile Critics: The New York Voices   86
  Types of Criticism   87
  Making Judgments   89
SUMMARY   90

Chapter 4

Types of Plays   93

PLAYWRIGHTS AND PLAYWRITING   94
PLAYS: SIX TYPES   95
  Tragedy   95
  Profile Arthur Miller: Tragedy
  and the Human Animal   98
  Comedy   100

Profile Edward Albee: The Laughter
in the Dark   102
History Plays   107
Tragicomedy   110
Melodrama   110

Profile Lorraine Hansberry: Heroes,
Realism, and Melodrama   114
Musicals   116
SUMMARY   117

Chapter 5

The Audience: Expectation, Perception, and Response 119

Profile Mrs. Trollope (I): "Domestic
Manners" in the Frontier Theatre   121
THE AUDIENCE: FIVE HISTORICAL
PERSPECTIVES   122
Ancient Greece   122
Ancient Rome   124
Elizabethan England   125
The English Restoration   128
Modern Times   128
THEATRE AND COMMUNICATION   130

Profile August Wilson: The Audience
Outside the Mainstream   131
Proximity: Physical and Personal Space   132
THE AUDIENCE EXPERIENCE
AND RESPONSE   133
Willing Suspension of Disbelief   133
Aesthetic Distance   134

Profile Theatre Space and Fantasy:
The Phantom of the Opera   136
Attention   136

Profile Mrs. Trollope (II): "Domestic
Manners" in the Bowery   138
Sympathy and Empathy   139
ENHANCING PERCEPTION   140
Variety   140
Focus   141
THE AUDIENCE: INDIVIDUAL AND GROUP
REACTIONS   143
The Audience: Experience
and Motivation   144
SUMMARY   146

Chapter 6

Theatre Forms and Architecture 149

GENERAL CONSIDERATIONS   151
Vision   152

Profile Nicola Sabbatini (I): What to Do
Before the Prince Arrives   153
Acoustics   156
Distractions   156
Safety   157
Seating Comfort   157
GENERAL REQUIREMENTS
FOR PRODUCTION TYPES   158
TYPES OF ACTOR—AUDIENCE SPATIAL
RELATIONSHIPS   158
Arena   162
Thrust   163

Profile Tamara: Theatre as
"Environmental Escapade"   164
Proscenium   164
Open Stage   166
THEATRE SPACES AND PRODUCTION
PRACTICALITIES   168

Profile Nicola Sabbatini (II): Protocol
for Ladies Day   170
OPTIONS WITHIN FORMS: MULTIPLE, UNIT,
AND SIMULTANEOUS SETTINGS   171
Multiple Settings   172

Profile George Tyspin: Interior
Architecture   173
Unit Settings   174
Simultaneous Settings   175
SUMMARY   176

Chapter 7

Producing Organizations and the Production Team 179

THE PRODUCING ORGANIZATION   181
The Broadway or Commercial Theatre   183

Profile Joseph Papp (I): The Democratic
Producer   185
The Not-For-Profit Regional
Theatre   186
The Noncommercial Theatre   187

THE PRODUCTION TEAM 189
The Playwright 189
Profile Gordon Davidson: How to Give
Good Meeting 190
The Producer 191
Profile Joseph Papp (II): Off Broadway
on Broadway 193
Profile Hal Prince (in the Company
of Stephen Sondheim) 194
The Director 194
The Actors 195
The Scenic, Costume, Lighting,
and Sound Designers 196
The Nonartistic Staff 196
The Technical Director 198
The Construction Head 198
The Property Head 198
The Business and House Managers 199
SUMMARY 199

Chapter 8

Directing 203

HISTORY: THE EMERGENCE OF THE
MODERN DIRECTOR 204
PERSPECTIVES ON THE DIRECTOR'S ROLE 206
Profile Duke of Saxe-Meiningen: The First
Director 207
THE DIRECTOR'S RESPONSIBILITIES 208
The Director's Concept 208
Collaborating with Other Theatre
Artists 209
Profile Elia Kazan (I): Finding the Play's
Style 210
Auditioning and Casting Actors 211
Rehearsing Actors 214
Profile Elia Kazan (II): "Stella!" 216
HOW DIRECTORS WORK IN TIME
AND SPACE 218
Profile Ariane Mnouchkine:
The Anti-Director 219
Composition and Time 226
Design and Variety 226
THE DIRECTOR AS MANAGER 226
EVALUATING THE DIRECTOR'S WORK 228
SUMMARY 229

Chapter 9

The Acting 233

ACTING IN LIFE AND ART 234
The Actor as Interpreter 236
The Actor as Stylist 236
APPROACHES TO ACTING 237
Acting Based on Mechanical Principles 238
Acting Based on Psychological Principles 238
The Stanislavski Method 239
Profile Lee Strasberg and the Actors
Studio 241
Holistic and Interaction Approaches 242
CREATING A ROLE 242
Analyzing a Role 242
Profile Elia Kazan: Phrasing Blanche's
Spine 243
Preparing Mentally 245
Movement 247
Stage Business 248
Rehearsals 250
THE ACTOR'S EQUIPMENT 252
Mind 252
Body 252
Profile Jessica Tandy: Star of Stage
and Screen 253
Voice 255
Profile Lawrence Olivier a.k.a. Sir Larry 256
SOME READINGS FOR CLASSROOM
EXERCISE 259
SUMMARY 262

Chapter 10

Scene Design 265

SCENE DESIGN TRADITIONS
IN THE THEATRE 266
Profile Sebastiano Serlio: The Renaissance
Perspective 272
The Scene Designer's Role 274
The Designer's Artistic Tools 274
Profile E. Gordon Craig: The Design
of a New Drama 275
The Designer's Employment
and Responsibilities 276
THE DESIGN PROCESS 278
Profile Jo Mielziner: The Poetic Realist 280

Scene Painting 284

Profile Bertolt Brecht: Scene Design
as "Individual Handwriting" 288
SUMMARY 291

Chapter 11

Technical Production 295

STAGE SCENERY 297
Characteristics 297
TYPES OF SCENERY UNITS 299
Two-Dimensional Units 300

Profile Joseph Furttenbach: Floors
for Swallowing Up Godless People, Etc. 304
Three-Dimensional Units 306
Sculptured Effects and Textures 310
Properties and Furniture 311
Decor Items 314
THE SCENE SHOP 314
Basic Shop Requirements 314
Space Areas 315
Tools 315
MATERIALS 316
SHIFTING SCENERY 318

Profile Les Misérables: Designing
the Human Spectacle 319
SUMMARY 321

Chapter 12

Costumes and Makeup 325

STAGE COSTUMES IN HISTORY 326
WHAT IS A STAGE COSTUME? 328
THE FUNCTIONS OF STAGE COSTUME 328
THE DESIGN PROCESS 331
Play and Character Analysis 331
Production Conferences 331
Research 333

Profile Susan Hilferty: You Don't Have
to Draw Like Michelangelo 334
Translating Ideas into Pictures 335
MAKING THE COSTUME 339
PRODUCTION ORGANIZATION 341
Dress Parade 342
Dress Rehearsals 343
THE COSTUME SHOP 343
STAGE MAKEUP 344
Purpose and Analysis 344
SUMMARY 347

Chapter 13

Lighting and Sound 351

THE DEVELOPMENT OF MODERN
LIGHTING DESIGN 352
FUNCTIONS OF STAGE LIGHTING 354
Selective Visibility 354
Rhythm and Structure 356
Mood 356
Motivation and Illusion 358
THE PROPERTIES OF LIGHT 359
THE DESIGN PROCESS 360
Analyzing the Script 361
The Production Conference 361

Profile Jean Rosenthal: A Bloody
Electrician with Notions 362
The Light Plot 364
Cues 367
LIGHTING INSTRUMENTS 368
LIGHTING CONTROL 371
Evaluating a Lighting Design 371
SOUND DESIGN 372
SUMMARY 372

Chapter 14

Asian Theatre 375

THE THEATRE OF CHINA 376
Drama and Religion 376
The Development of Theatre 377
Dramatic Forms 378
Elements of Performance 380
The Physical Theatre 382
Costumes and Makeup 384
THE THEATRE OF JAPAN 386
Drama and Religion 386
Dramatic Forms 386
Elements of Performance 388
The Physical Theatre 389

Profile Sergei Eisenstein: A Grand Total
Provocation of the Human Brain 390
Costumes and Makeup 395
THE THEATRE OF INDIA 397
Drama and Religion 397
Dramatic Forms 399
Elements of Performance 400
The Physical Theatre 402
Costumes and Makeup 403
SUMMARY 404

Chapter 15

Western Theatre from Ancient Greece to the Middle Ages 407

ANCIENT GREECE 408
Production and Style 408
The Tragedians 409
Profile Aristotle: The Form of Tragedy 411
Comedy 413
Costumes 414
The Theatre Facility 414
The Hellenistic Period 416
ROME 417
Dramatic Forms 419
Playwrights 420
The Theatre Facility 420
THE MEDIEVAL PERIOD 422
Evidence of Medieval Theatre 424
Liturgical Drama 425
Profile The Representation of Adam: "Paradise Shall Be Situated in a Rather Prominent Place" 426
Production Practices 427
SUMMARY 430

Chapter 16

Western Theatre from the Renaissance to Romanticism 433

THE RENAISSANCE 434
New Dramatic Forms 434
The English Renaissance 436
Profile Margaret Webster: Shakespeare Our Contemporary (I) 438
The Playhouses 440
THE BAROQUE PERIOD 445
French Neoclassicism 445
French Neoclassic Production 448
Italy 449
The English Restoration 449
Restoration Production 450
Profile Harold Child: Shakespeare Our Contemporary (II) 452
THE ENLIGHTENMENT 455
English Sentimental Drama 455
America 458
France 460
Germany 461
Profile Voltaire: Shakespeare Our Contemporary (III) 462
THE ROMANTIC ERA 465
Plays and Playwrights 466
Melodrama 467
Audiences 468
Repertory Companies 469
SUMMARY 472

Chapter 17

The Modern Theatre 475

REALISM AND NATURALISM 476
Plays and Playwrights 476
Profile Robert Lewis (I): You Can't Play Anything if You Can't Play the Piano 480
ANTIREALISM AND THEATRICALISM 486
Antirealism: The New Stagecraft 486
Profile Robert Lewis (II): There Must Be Something Different About the Way Jackson Pollack Throws the Paint 490
Major Antirealist Movements 491
Profile August Strindberg: From Naturalism to Expressionism 493
Pluralism 500
Profile Sam Shepard: Varieties of the Real 501
Profile Jan Kott: Shakespeare Our Contemporary (IV) 504
Profile Martha Clarke: From the Dance to the Visual Image 508
Profile David Rabe: Everybody Is Sane in Realism 510
SCENIC DESIGN SINCE WORLD WAR II 513
SUMMARY 517

A Timeline: Theatre and General World Events 518
Glossary 522
Further Reading 526
Photo and Figure Credits 528
Index 529

Preface

The purpose of this book is to nurture informed and perceptive theatre audience members and practitioners. In order to achieve that purpose, this text strives to illustrate how theatre functions as a means by which we come to know human reality, to show how theatre artists work to develop a portrait of that reality, to describe the media that theatre artists use in that portrayal, and to provide a taste of theatre history. Mastery of such subject matter should allow us both to respond as fully as possible to the messages that plays bring to us and to understand the processes by which theatre productions are brought from ideas to finished products. This text is an *introduction:* It is aimed at individuals with little or no knowledge of the theatre arts.

I have tried to assemble information about theatre as an art, its production, and its history. The text is straightforward, descriptive, and practical. The book itself is not a course. It is a *reference* upon which a course can be built. No textbook can be relied upon to answer all the student's questions and include every key point. A good text can only *suggest* the breadth of the offerings available.

We begin with a "Diary of a Production" in order to provide a very concrete "feeling" for the technicalities and nuances of a production without using synopses or other literary apparatus. Chapter One provides information usually not found in introductory theatre texts—that is, an introduction to the arts in general. Theatre, after all, is part of a broader context—the arts—that has a unique viewpoint on perceiving and reflecting human experience. Because introductory courses in theatre normally fulfill a "general studies" function, I find it important to introduce theatre by placing it in its broader context—along with painting, sculpture, music, dance, and architecture—as a form of artistic activity.

Organization

The first section of *The Art of Theatre* treats the fundamentals of theatre and introduces broad issues of theory and principle, as well as some basic concepts about the nature of theatre, criticism and analysis, genres, theatre forms and architecture, and audience. The material in these chapters constitutes a foundation that assists the student in understanding the parameters of theatre art and the workings of play productions. These chapters also provide information about what it means to be an audience member and why, when one attends a production, audience and stage spaces appear as they do. All of the concepts and vocabulary included in this group of chapters constitute essential "touchstones" to which the rest of the text relates. Theatre history and practice makes no sense at all if one does not understand how a play works, why certain conventions exist, and what one should expect when one goes to the theatre. In fact, this material ought to stimulate a sound answer to the basic question of why we attend the theatre.

The second section of *The Art of Theatre* explains contemporary production practice by discussing who makes theatre and how they make it. Although this material is fairly standard for an introductory theatre text, I have expanded somewhat the coverage normally devoted to the elements of the *mise-en-scène*. Audiences always find the "technical" elements of a production fascinating—if not mysterious. Knowing a bit more about scenic, lighting, sound, and costume design and technical production can only enhance the satisfaction derived from a production. Fundamentally, my approach in the second section of the book is to give relatively equal treatment to all of the production team members, thereby giving a clear signal that theatre is a composite of important functions rather than one or two important and several subsidiary ones. Some productions may emphasize one or more functions over the others, but that is a matter of choice and not implicit ordination.

The third section of *The Art of Theatre* concerns the practice of theatre throughout history, from its beginnings in the Western tradition in ancient Greece until the present time. I have chosen to include information about theatre in the Eastern traditions—China, Japan, and India—because I believe that we need to understand human activity in a variety of cultures. Our surveys of theatre programs indicate that although many instructors see the study of non-Western cultures as desirable, most do not include—and feel uncomfortable in their expertise concerning—non-Western cultures. My inclusion of a small amount of Eastern materials is my way of saying, "Here is material which, if you do not wish to use it, will not make the rest of the book unusable. If you do wish to use non-Western materials, these should be helpful. Finally, if you are ambivalent, the presence of this material might be tempting enough to give it a try."

I hope that those who use this text will see it as a compendium of materials sufficient to build a foundation for appreciation, perception, and participation and will use that foundation for a lifetime of involvement with the theatre: to attend the theatre, to participate in theatre production, to describe and analyze what theatre artists try to accomplish, and to seek to understand how we relate to creative expression in terms of our own perceptions of human reality.

Features

This text contains several special features. First is an extensive illustration program. As much as possible the illustrations serve the text. I have attempted, for example, when referring to a play, to include a visualization of a production of that play. We have paid close attention to and invested in color illustrations to create interest and give a better picture of theatre performance. Color is critical in theatre production, and the illustration program for this text tries very hard to acknowledge that fact. A second special feature is the frequency of plot synopses. Regardless of the topic discussed, specific plays are noted. However, merely noting a play does not assist a student who is coming at this material for the first time. The instructor, of course, understands what *Oedipus* is and *why* it might represent "tragedy," but for the beginning student, the mere citation of a play's title will mean little. Consequently, I have wherever possible added plot synopses for the plays noted. The synopses are short enough that they do not disrupt the train of development but full enough to give the student some idea of what the reference is all about.

Finally, a word of appreciation needs to be given to the many colleagues and friends who have assisted in so many ways in the preparation of this book. Those who contributed their production photos are credited in the text. The many teachers and fellow artists with and from whom I have learned enough over the years to attempt this book need acknowledgment, but remain too numerous to list here. Robert C. Burroughs, my friend and co-author of *Scene Design in the Theatre*, needs to be credited, almost as a co-author on this project, because I have drawn upon *Scene Design in the Theatre* in many instances in the preparation of this book.

In reviewing the manuscript in various stages, the following colleagues have added invaluable information and honed its presentation: Jackie Bromstedt, University of Texas; Richard A. Davis, Western Oregon State College; Ramon L. Delgado, Montclair State College; Ann Crawford Dreher, University of South Carolina; Jeffrey Fiske, Montclair State College; Michael J. Hood, University of Alaska—Anchorage; Jack Hrkach, Ithaca College; Joe Karioth, Florida State University; Joy Harriman Reilly, Ohio State University; Bradley W. Sabelli, George Washington University; and James Wallace, Normandale Community College.

My wife, Hilda, as always, has functioned nobly in her role as advisor, editor, and research assistant. I also owe a great debt to the professionals at Prentice Hall, where I would like to acknowledge the following people: Charlyce Jones Owen, Editor in Chief, Social Sciences; Ray Mullaney, Editor in Chief, College Book Development; Ann Marie McCarthy, Senior Managing Editor, Social Sciences; designer Amy Rosen; Lorinda Morris-Nantz, Manager, Photo Archives; and photo researcher Cindy Joyce. The production of this book was supervised by Shelly Kupperman. Steve Dalphin, Executive Editor, Social Sciences, encouraged and oversaw this project from inception to publication. Senior Development Editor Ron Librach is due profound thanks for his erudition, penetrating questions, and expert editing.

Dennis J. Sporre

New York Times Program

THE NEW YORK TIMES and **PRENTICE HALL** are sponsoring a **A CONTEMPORARY VIEW:** a program designed to enhance student access to current information of relevance in the classroom.

Through this program, the core subject matter provided in the text is supplemented by a collection of time-sensitive articles from one of the world's most distinguished newspapers, **THE NEW YORK TIMES**. These articles demonstrate the vital, ongoing connection between what is learned in the classroom and what is happening in the world around us.

To enjoy the wealth of information of **THE NEW YORK TIMES** daily, a reduced subscription rate is available·in deliverable areas. For information, call toll-free: 1-800-631-1222.

PRENTICE HALL and **THE NEW YORK TIMES** are proud to co-sponsor **A CONTEMPORARY VIEW.** We hope it will make the reading of both textbooks and newspapers a more dynamic, involving process.

Preface

Diary of a Production

Ghetto

Joshua Sobol

Adapted by Jack Viertel

Ball State University Theatre

Artistic Director	*Judy E. Yordon*
Musical Director	*Jeanne Henderson Everett*
Choreographer	*Ya'akov Eden*
Scene Designer	*David C. Shawger, Jr.*
Costume Designer	*Kathleen M. Jaremski*
Lighting Designer	*Dennis J. Sporre*
Sound Designer	*Michael Lamirand*
Makeup Designer	*Kerry McDonald*

*T*his is the story of a university production of Joshua Sobol's *Ghetto,* as told by some of the artists involved. The people quoted are real, and the circumstances occurred as they report them. The first series of color plates illustrates the settings, costumes, and actions of the production.

Judy E. Yordon

Artistic Director

My relationship to Joshua Sobol's play *Ghetto* began when I saw the play performed at the National Theatre in London. I had no way of knowing that someday I would direct a production of the play, but the production lingered in my memory. Originally, I suggested that one of my colleagues direct the show, and when he did something else instead, I began to entertain the idea of directing it myself. Before that, I had never seriously considered it because I remembered that the script was complex, the technical demands heavy, the costumes specialized, and the properties in the hundreds. As if this weren't enough to dissuade me, or at least make me hesitate, the play's subject matter—the Holocaust—was certainly not the easiest topic for me to tackle. I'm Jewish myself. But one day at a Play Selection Committee meeting, without knowing that I was going to do so, I heard myself say that I wanted to direct *Ghetto.* My colleagues concurred. When the designers read the play, they were as enthusiastic as I was, although equally humbled and frightened by the demands of the script.

I ordered and read a copy of the script, translated by David Lan and used for the National Theatre production. It was even more complex than I remembered, and I was genuinely frightened. The language was formal, not the least bit conversational, and the fourteen songs were appended to the back of the script with the note that "The songs can be sung in different sequence for different productions." I panicked.

Then a student came to me with an anthology called *Plays from the Holocaust,* which contained a translation by Jack Viertel that was more colloquial and easier to understand. In this edition the placement of the songs and directions as to who was to sing them were clearly marked. I relaxed a bit, and the designers were also relieved by the ease with which they were able to read the new translation. We easily obtained the rights by writing to Mr. Sobol's agent and then to the publisher of the anthology with the Viertel translation. The publisher gave us permission to copy the script directly from the anthology. But, new problems were about to arise.

For one thing, we had a script but no music. *Ghetto* is basically a tragedy with music, so the music is essential. But at this point all we had were the lyrics—lyrics that were different from those in the first translation,

Diary *of a* Production

which at least contained the music for the melody lines—but no orchestrations. We began a desperate search for music that would go with the translation we were using. Mr. Sobol's agent could furnish only music to go with the first translation. I advertised for a composer and got two volunteers.

Finally, we contacted Gary Friedman, the composer of the music for the Mark Taper Forum production of *Ghetto*. From him we obtained the original piano-reduction score and a tape of a live recording of the Los Angeles production. However, because the music for those from the Mark Taper production had been lost, and we were left with the task of transcribing the various instrumental parts. Our budget would not pay for an outside professional to score the parts, and so our musical director did the work herself. She wrote parts for every musician, worked out their schedules, and helped me figure out how to place them on stage. Because the musicians were to be integrated into the stage action rather than placed in the orchestra pit, the demands on them increased. They had to attend extra rehearsals and learn stage movements as well as the music. They had to become "characters"—relating to the other actors, attending costume fittings and makeup calls, and—most important—memorizing their music. Finding musicians who would agree to do all of this proved very difficult. The musical director, Jeanne Henderson Everett, made hundreds of phone calls before finding six musicians who would accept the assignment.

I spent approximately three months reading and rereading the script in order to (1) understand it and (2) devise a production concept. In our production, Srulik, the narrator of the play, would be appearing at Ball State University to give a speech about his experiences in the Vilna Ghetto during World War II. The play begins with his appearance in the present. Then, as he remembers the war years, the curtain opens and we see parts of his past life dramatized. The play's basic theme is apparent: We must remember—this must never happen again. But the structure of the play is complicated because it's based on Srulik's memory. There is a logical relationship between actions *within* each scene, but most scenes follow one another simply because they form the next moment that the narrator remembers. This makes transitions between scenes difficult; one episode may directly follow another when, in reality, it took place six months later. (The play covers approximately two years.) Another tricky problem is trying to decide which scenes are intended to be rehearsals—the ghetto residents are forced to form a theatre company—and which are real-life scenes of ghetto life. Sobol doesn't make this clear in the script—the lack of clarity on this point may be one of the messages in the play—but at the very least, the decision still has to be made for the benefit of the actors and the lighting designer.

Then there were two related problems in understanding the script and the working of Srulik's mind: you needed to become a quasi-expert on the Holocaust in order to understand the historical significance of the play, and we had to translate and pronounce the German, Yiddish, and French terms, lines, and songs. Sobol's play is theatricalized history. Four of the characters

GHETTO is basically a tragedy with music. . . . Sobol's play is theatricalized history.

that appear in the play were real people whose lives needed to be studied and understood. To get the help I needed, I contacted a rabbi in Chicago and sent him a list of the Yiddish terms. I called a Jewish woman in Muncie to help me with the pronunciations. I talked to an English teacher in Muncie who was teaching a seminar on "Literature of the Holocaust," and she agreed to help act as dramaturg and speak to the cast about the play's historical significance. I called a foreign-language teacher to help with the French song. I called an opera teacher who had spent years in Germany to help with the German and Yiddish songs.

Production meetings began in the early summer. The production concept was clarified. Decisions were made and revised, technical problems discussed, costume decisions made, and preliminary drawings for the set created. Meanwhile, I divided the play into "French scenes" (short scenes that change each time a character enters or leaves the stage), and I decided exactly how many actors I would need and how many different characters each would have to play. The ultimate decision was that I would need a cast of twenty-nine—eight women (one woman had to be tiny and athletic in order to play a ventriloquist's dummy) and twenty-one men. Several actors would have to play more than one role—the costume designer needed to know how this broke down.

David C. Shawger, Jr.

Scenic Designer

From the very first moment that I became familiar with *Ghetto*, I knew it was an important play that I somehow needed to undertake, both personally and professionally. When Judy Yordon proposed to direct the production, I jumped at the opportunity to design the scenery. My initial reaction to the script, however, was a sense of depression. To think that people had to endure such treatment in an atmosphere of hate and malevolence left my own emotions drained. It became the design's intent to support the theme of people living in total despair. I decided that the setting should reflect an environment forced upon the Lithuanian Jews by external circumstances.

Most of my design was formulated early on in the production process. I'd say that it was influenced mainly by aesthetic judgments from the production's artistic staff. In June, some four months before the first performance, I had a gut feeling about what the visual production should look like. The very first meeting with the director and costume designer helped reinforce my mental image. We discussed the script and production goals and talked at length about literature from the period. We talked about the Holocaust. Even though we never mentioned specific staging possibilities, many images kept running through my mind. It was interesting to view actual photographs of the Vilna ghetto and depressing to see pictures recording the genocide. I suggested projections, but the idea was rejected. Judy reported at length about the London production of *Ghetto* that she'd seen. She felt that walls and doors all askew were important visual elements. A mound of clothing located in the middle of the ghetto was also essential. As the meeting progressed, the production concept seemed to evolve. It was to be an abstract, theatricalistic view—which I liked. Perhaps the play's visual environment would have an eastern European feel. We decided to place less emphasis on realism and to concentrate on the mood of the play.

By the time of the second meeting two weeks later, I'd done only one small pencil sketch for my own purposes, but I had a very strong mental image of the production. I can attribute this directly to my early feelings and to the private discussions that I had with Kathy Jaremski, the costume designer. She did most of the research for the production and shared it with me. Instead of sketching, Kathy made a wonderful Xerox collage from photographs of actual ghetto residents during the Nazi occupation of Lithuania. I could never put into words what she created, but I fed off her work. We even had refreshing arguments about artistic points and the show's possibilities. Our discussions were the nucleus for the entire visual design that we later shared with lighting designer Dennis Sporre during the second meeting.

It was at this point that the director gave me a Xerox of a Jozef Szajna stage setting that reflected what she thought the set should look like. The picture (from a Czechoslovakian production) represented an abstraction of horizontal, vertical, and diagonal stairs, ramps, and so on. It helped me to determine that my image and hers were similar.

We finally got around to talking specifics. The director wanted the set to suggest people living in a ghetto, one on top of another. She wanted the image of many doors, exposed lighting, and a raked stage (the stage floor higher in the rear than in the front). It was all food for thought. As we discussed potential ideas, most of the staff felt that the idea of using only black and white was fitting. The only colors that Judy wanted were the red of the banners and the yellow stars. In my mind, however, a black-and-white scheme was not ideal. I felt that dark, grimy browns and grays would be more appropriate and still give her the foreboding, menacing feel she wanted.

The final color scheme for the setting was born with little further deliberation. Other specifics surfaced:

1. The hanging scene had to be as realistic as possible.

2. The library had to be a massive collection of books that would dominate the stage.

3. The gallows and library units had to move on and off from the wings.

It was interesting to view actual photographs of the Vilna ghetto and depressing to see pictures recording genocide. I suggested projections. The idea was rejected.

4. The set had to stop at the act curtain line with a trapdoor in the stage apron floor.

It took very little time to put together a rough model based on my initial response to the meetings and readings. At this point, I also kept in constant contact with Kathy in the costume shop. For the third meeting, in early August, I presented a finished model to the artistic staff. The design called for a multilevel setting that was ten feet tall at its highest point. Stage right and left featured platforming that resembled door units and levels built on top of one another. The general discussion centered around form and mass. Judy like the overall design but felt it was a little too "planned"—a little too symmetrical. She suggested some changes that seemed reasonable. At this point, my assistants and I again suggested using projections in the manner of 35 mm slides. Although the idea had been rejected earlier, everyone now thought that slides could enhance the mood of what was happening on stage at any given moment. Persistence had paid off. I also presented the director with a color chart ranging from dark brown to gray. We talked about color and finally settled on one particular color that seemed most appropriate. The setting was to have a very depressing, monochromatic scheme of subdued browns that reflected the utter despair of the ghetto environment.

Two days before the fourth meeting, I met privately with the director to go over all the revisions I'd made in the model. For the most part, they were accepted. At the next design meeting, I presented the "final" painted and textured model. Although there'd been quite a bit of compromise on both our parts, the director and I felt good about the design. Our communicative process had worked.

I could now consult with the technical director about further drawings. I presented him with the ground plan and other drawings, and by mid-August the setting was well on its way to being realized. During this time, I also had several meetings separately with the lighting designer, Dennis Sporre. He wanted to do justice to the setting while I felt it was important for him to feel completely free to interpret and create. Dennis appreciated the angles and recesses within the setting. We discussed many aspects of the production, especially the character of the show's multiple levels of reality. Indeed, the three designers—scenery, lighting, and costume—really kept the lines of communication open. We relied on each other for opinions and insights as well as moral support throughout the production.

At the very first rehearsal, Kathy and I presented our designs to the cast. We all agreed with Judy that it was important for everyone to know what the visual elements would look like. By this time, almost all my drawings were already in the technical director's hands, and the scenery was under construction. It was my job to look out for any problems that we hadn't foreseen or expected. Some minor revisions in the ground plan were made, and the cast and I were able to adjust. I became more involved

Diary *of a* Production

personally with the 35mm slide project. I was particularly concerned about the projections. It wasn't until opening night that I was fully satisfied with the brightness and clarity of the slide images.

Throughout the rehearsal period, there were several other frustrations, many of which were beyond my control. It seems a truism in the theatre that scenery never gets built fast enough to suit the director, the choreographer, and the actors. Even with the model on hand for rehearsals and the setting taped out on the stage floor, getting comfortable with the space and the levels remains elusive until everything's in place. For example, "knowing" from ground plans and models that they'd be ten feet in the air didn't lessen the actors' shock the first time they actually stood on the platforms at that height. As familiarity with the finished setting increased, however, anxiety lessened.

For me, the most enjoyable phase of the design process came during the painting and texturing of the set. I really love to express my design ideas through the medium of paint. Texture helped create the appropriately seedy, run-down environment for the ghetto. We were able to create in paint, lumber, and metal a visualization of the abstract theatrical feelings that we'd discussed four months earlier.

Kathleen M. Jaremski

Costume Designer

My initial reaction to the first reading of *Ghetto* was "let's do it." I knew that this show was going to be difficult, but I had no idea *how* difficult. I started my research by collecting as many books as I could on the Jewish ghettos because I knew that this would be primary research material, and I wanted the look of the costumes to come as close to reality as possible. I also started reading several books about life in the different ghettos and diaries of people who wrote about their own lives in these ghettos.

My approach to the design of the show was to be as realistic as possible in choosing colors, textures, and lines for the actors' clothing. I wanted nothing to stand out as a "costume" except for those things the director and I agreed should look like costumes. This idea of what constituted a "costume" and what should be "clothing" varied from production meeting to production meeting until we actually thought about how these people would have obtained the type of clothing needed for a scene. We finally decided that virtually everything would come from the pile of clothing that was on stage at all times. This pile represented those articles that were discarded by the Germans as too useless, ripped, or out-of-style to be of any use to anyone but the Jews living in the ghetto.

Ghetto also called for a hanging to take place on stage and for over-sized costumes during the last musical number. Both of these requirements presented problems beyond the usual costume dilemmas associated with a play. The design team debated whether or not we should simulate an actual

This idea of what constituted a "costume" and what should be "clothing" varied from production meeting to production meeting until we actually thought about how these people would have obtained the type of clothing required for the scene.

hanging. If we did, three men had to be "rigged." We decided that the play demanded this type of action. Never having built a "hanging" harness, I worked with my assistant to design a pattern we figured would work. Then we contacted a local harness maker, who went to work creating three strong leather harnesses that we prayed would save the lives of our actors. With minor modifications, the harnesses worked beautifully.

Surprisingly, the oversized clothing proved to be more troublesome. The director originally wanted the actors simply to hold up large-sized clothing that was already in our storage closets. But the choreographer had other ideas, and so ultimately we needed to create skirts, pants, and jackets that would hide the actors' heads and hands. Shop time for this preparation wasn't scheduled because the oversized clothing wasn't finally decided on until about two weeks before the opening. We also had no budget for buying all the fabric and accessories we needed. Two prototypes were made so that the actors could work with them to see if they could execute the choreography in oversized clothing. Only after we'd assured ourselves that the concept would work did we commit the shop to making fourteen costumes. This set back the shop schedule, but the costumes did work, even though the actors weren't able to rehearse in them until the last technical rehearsals.

Military uniforms proved to be another cost- and time-consuming series of costumes. I'm not well-versed in various types of German uniforms, and so I went to the library for another series of books that would give me the documentation I needed to make the uniforms. I wanted them accurate at least to the point of believability. Although I took a few liberties with things like insignias, on stage, to the audience, I think they did look authentic.

Several people approached me with things like belt buckles to get the authentic look of Nazi uniforms. However, these people failed to deliver the items they promised. Fortunately, having learned from experience to take all such offers with a grain of salt, I had proceeded to get what I needed on my own. I try never to borrow or rent if I don't have to, because too many problems can arise when you're responsible for someone else's property.

During production meetings, the question of using blood arose, and we finally decided that it would be a nice touch if we used stage blood. At first, I thought the actors could use blood capsules in their mouths, but it became clear that the effect wouldn't carry to the audience. The solution was for the actor to break a blood pack in the hand and smear it on the face discreetly at a convenient point in the action. This worked very well. A blood bag was needed for the knifing, and with some rehearsal this worked well, too.

Overall, this show was both exciting and demanding. It involved some special effects which I hadn't dealt with before but which worked out quite well. Both the director and the choreographer were satisfied. The show was costly to costume: thirty-five actors, each playing multiple roles, and each role requiring a costume.

Dennis J. Sporre

Lighting Designer

My sense of the play, its meaning, moods, and dynamics grew out of my first readings of the script and were underscored at production meetings. The old song title "Body and Soul" kept going through my mind. In addition to the horrific comment about the brutality of the historical situation, I believed that this was a play about trying to keep your soul alive despite the environment forced on you by external circumstances. Other people can destroy your body but not your soul. So for me, the operating principle was to create a lighting design that clearly separated the Jewish people from their oppressive environment. The set design offered a host of opportunities for making that concept come to life, and some difficulties as well. I wanted to light the set so that it would appear inhospitable and "cold" while the ghetto residents were three-dimensional and "warm." I wanted the fire and spirit of the ghetto inhabitants to stand out, through color, in contrast to the setting, which would be depressing in tone. This meant keeping all the warm-colored light that would fall on the actors from illuminating the setting, which would be lit in blue tones. Fortunately, the setting design, with its monochromatic, dark, and foreboding color scheme and its variety of levels, angles, and recesses, helped immensely. In addition, the character of the show itself, with its multiple levels of reality, allowed me the luxury of not having to light every area on stage with light that seemed to come from "realistic" sources. As a result, I could direct light from whatever angles would allow the actors to be lit without having the light strike the set. I chose high angles of incidence—that is, I wanted to put the lighting instruments in positions from which the light would strike the stage at angles from 55 to 85 degrees in elevation. This had the added artistic effect of creating deep shadows under the actors' eyebrows, cheeks, and chins, so that the actors, while being warm in color, would also look gaunt. I did need to check with the costumer to be sure that she didn't plan to costume any characters in hats with broad brims. In that case, the high-angle lighting would place the face totally in shadow—an unacceptable condition. As I watched the actors rehearse, I was able to determine that keeping the light away from the setting—which meant occasionally lighting actors only from one side or from the back—didn't create any situations that interfered with an actor's need to draw focus by being fully visible from the front.

The height of the set created some potential problems. For example, an actor standing on the front edge of one of the high platforms could not be lit above the waist because the edge of the platform was downstage of the first lighting position behind the proscenium arch and because the arch itself interfered with light from the front-of-house positions. At the same time, in two or three scenes the director had important characters on the front of the platform, and they had to be lit from the front. We decided, however, that nothing would be lost artistically if the actors sat, rather than stood, on the

The old song title "Body and Soul" kept going through my mind. In addition to the horrific comment about the brutality of the historical situation . . . this play was about trying to keep your soul alive despite an environment forced on you by external circumstances.

front of the platform; that allowed me to get light under the proscenium arch to illuminate them.

In another scene, an actor needing focus was placed on one of the high upstage platforms, and I simply couldn't get light on her face without illuminating the set behind her. The director asked that I light the front of the actor, but I couldn't convince her that the halo effect created by strong backlighting actually gave the actor a tantalizing and dramatic focus that fit the scene. Because the character was singing while the remainder of the cast danced below, I reasoned that there really was no need to see the actor's face clearly. The contrast between the way the single actor and the rest of the cast was lit created its own form of interest and separation for the scene while, again, maintaining my vision of keeping character and environment separate. Fortunately, the actor had lovely medium blonde hair and a dress with golden patches—colors that picked up the amber in the backlight and made the effect even more dramatic. All in all, the scheme worked very well, and the variety of angles and planes in the setting gave me the opportunity to create fascinating highlights and shadows for the environment, which was lit in blues, while creating equally poignant highlights and shadows on the actors, who were lit in amber.

Another challenge was the need to create a sense of change as scenes took the characters to supposedly different locations while the set remained the same. I also had to create a sense of change when the Jewish acting troupe were "performing" their play-within-the-play. The script itself didn't clarify these different locations and occasions. I tried to make the changes apparent in several ways. First, I changed intensity; the brightness of the overall light was higher or lower for one location than for another location. Second, I changed color. When the Jewish "actors" were doing their play, it wasn't necessary to reinforce the warmth of their normal characters and "souls." So I lit those scenes with uncolored light—"white" light. This was noticeably different from the "warm" amber light I used when the Jews were "themselves." Because the play-within-the-play scenes dealt with "characters" who were not "real," I further emphasized the difference between the play-within-the-play and the regular scenes by changing the angle of the light to straight-on, which made the players appear more two-dimensional than the lighting used for normal scenes, which came more from the sides.

There were also night scenes and day scenes and interior scenes and exterior scenes that depended on lighting to make the changes clear to the audience. When these variations were added to all the others, I was glad that we had a modern, well-equipped lighting system and inventory of instruments. The computer control board proved very helpful in making subtle changes in light levels and in adding a lighting instrument or two for changes in blocking that I hadn't anticipated or that had occurred between the time I attended rehearsals and the beginning of final technical rehearsals. (During our second dress rehearsal, the computer started acting up, and occasionally cues didn't execute properly. That kind of failure can place a production in jeopardy. In the long run, however, that's the trade-off you make for flexibility and accuracy in cue execution when the system is operating properly—as it is most of the time.)

Lighting design involves the added responsibility of trying to emphasize the play's dynamic structure. In addition to having to create a variety of ideas, moods, and location shifts, I began to wonder just what else I could add in order to help the audience recognize the structural progress of the play. The director and I decided that the play and the characterizations were sufficiently strong to carry this by themselves. So the lighting design, with its mood creation for each scene and its "message" of separating the warm "soul" of the characters from the cold reality of the physical environment, was freed from any added responsibility in this regard. Nonetheless, through angle and intensity I tried to create a kind of picture that gave the audience a sense of a scene's importance in the overall scheme of the play. In the last scene, in which a German officer kills all the ghetto inhabitants, I backlit the scene with red light. The actors did not appear "red" because the light came from behind them, but the added intensity and symbolism of the color as it illumined the floor were clear to the audience.

Judy E. Yordon

Director

By the time of auditions, I had a firm idea of cast requirements, a rehearsal schedule, a French-scene breakdown, a "final" set design, a list of discussion questions to give the cast, and many articles and videos for them to read or view. Approximately 120 people went through general auditions, and I called 60 back to read directly from the script. On the basis of the callback, I had a tentative cast list. The problem now was that four shows were being auditioned simultaneously, and students couldn't be in two plays at the same time. The four directors had to get together and barter for cast members. I ended up making concessions on some roles, but I got my first choices for all the major parts.

The first *unexpected* problem occurred when the choreographer became ill and couldn't work on the show. The new choreographer who was brought in at the last minute wasn't privy to many of the discussions that had already taken place. This meant that hours had to be spent going back over basic material.

Meanwhile, the properties master quit to direct a community production. Eventually, I'd go through two more prop masters before my stage manager, her assistant, various cast members, and I actually managed to accumulate more than a hundred props.

Rehearsals began on August 27, 1991. On that night, the costume designer talked to the cast, the set designer showed a model of the set, the dramaturg spoke to the cast, and we read through the script to define terms

I asked the cast if they would wear their yellow stars on campus. . . . This was the best way I could think of to get the students to discover what it might feel like to be treated the way the Nazis treated the Jews. . . . This young cast could never really know, but they got some idea during those weeks.

and clarify pronunciations. The next night, we viewed videos and looked at handouts on life in Vilna, notes from Sobol about the play, and biographical information on the four "real" people depicted in the show. We devoted the following six days to learning the songs and choreographing the six dance numbers. The next rehearsal was on a Sunday. The cast arrived at 2:00 P.M., and we spent three hours discussing the show and sharing the answers that the cast members had prepared on discussion sheets that I'd passed out during the first rehearsal. Over pizza, the cast shared their newly created "character histories," which often involved the death of both parents and other horrible deprivations. (These, of course, were invented by the actors to help them create a sense of life for their own characters.) That night and the next six nights were devoted to setting actor movements. Our only guides were tape marks on the stage floor to show where the units of the setting would eventually be. The choreographer had some trouble reading the space, and so when the setting was in place three weeks later, all the dances had to be altered or redone.

Meanwhile, the cast was starting to live the play day and night. Rehearsals went on seven nights a week, an average of four hours per night. The women in the show decided that they would no longer shave their legs. The whole cast decided to have a slumber party, where all 29 people would sleep together in a small space to get some idea of what it might have been like to live 13 in a small room, as was historically the case in many ghettos. In addition, I asked the cast if they would wear their yellow stars on campus—the Jews had been forced by the Nazis to wear these stars as a means of identification. I did not force anyone to wear them, but most people wanted to. I explained that when the cast members were asked why they were wearing the stars, they could just tell people that it was a form of advertising for a play. Yom Kippur, a major Jewish holiday, occurred at the same time so many of the cast members didn't have to explain anything. However, little did the 29 non-Jewish cast members realize how much discrimination they would encounter. Racial slurs were spit at them, they were demeaned and stared at, and one even had his life threatened. This was an eye-opening experience for many of the students, who had never known discrimination and didn't think it existed in Muncie, Indiana. This was the best way I could think of to get them to discover what it might feel like to be treated like the Nazis treated the Jews. I realized that this young cast could never *really* know, but they got some idea during those weeks.

Rehearsals were long and draining. Actors cried; even audience members cried. Musicians were there for only approximately five rehearsals, which made explaining things to them quite difficult. Hours of discussion with the cast and crew ensued, during which new discoveries were made and old ones reformulated or revised. As more of the set, with its slanting floor, high platforms, and numerous stairways, materialized, more adjustments and changes became necessary. The actors began to wear their costumes and establish their characterizations. Deeper insights were polished nightly.

One Saturday night following a four-hour afternoon rehearsal, the cast asked if they could convene in an hour at my house for another discussion. That night, we clarified some of the questionable moments and decided exactly where scenic and temporal changes should occur. Excitement was high that night, and the spirit of community and cooperation that had prevailed throughout the rehearsal period was apparent.

The following Sunday, the lighting designer, the stage manager, and I met in the afternoon to write in light and slide cues. Monday through Thursday were run-throughs during which more and more spectacle elements were added. On Friday night, October 4, we had a cue-to-cue rehearsal, in which the stage manager called the cues and we just ran the show from one sound, light, slide, and curtain cue to the next. This went very smoothly, and spirits ran high.

The remaining technical and dress rehearsals also went well as moments were polished, makeup designs realized, costumes tried/adjusted/readjusted. One scene in the play involves three cast members in a hanging that necessitated special leather harnesses and rigging in a gallows unit. The scene was rehearsed over and over again until everyone felt confident.

Meanwhile, no one could have anticipated the media circus that the production would generate. The *Indianapolis Star* put the story of the cast's experiences with discrimination on the cover of its edition of Wednesday, October 9—opening night. That morning, a reporter from an Indianapolis television station called to ask me if she could drive up to Muncie with a crew and interview me and any available cast members. Another reporter, from a different Indianapolis station, called to see if the station could videotape scenes from the show and interview two cast members on a Friday afternoon show. We were also informed that we had made the CNN newscast that evening. The editor of the *Jewish Press* in Indianapolis called for an interview the next day. The cantor of the Indianapolis Hebrew Congregation called to ask if as many of the cast and crew as possible could come to the synagogue in Indianapolis to share their experiences with the congregation. Editors of university newspapers all over the United States called me or the Department of Theatre and Dance Performance for interviews or comments.

Fortunately, the cast didn't let all this attention distract them. They maintained their focus on what needed to be done on opening night. That night there was a full house that included four Holocaust survivors who had driven up from Indianapolis. Although there were some unexpected laughs and some unexpected silences, the audience response was wonderful. The reviews praised the production as "touching" and "powerful," and the show was completely sold out by the second night.

On Friday, October 11, two adjudicators attended. The production was entered as a full, participating entry in the American College Theatre Festival. The two adjudicators led a critique of the show following the viewing. The critique was quite favorable. They saw "no weak links." It was an uplifting evening, and even though it was sad as we all realized that our familial intimacy would soon be dissolved, we were all relieved to see that our sense of accomplishment was shared by professionals in the field.

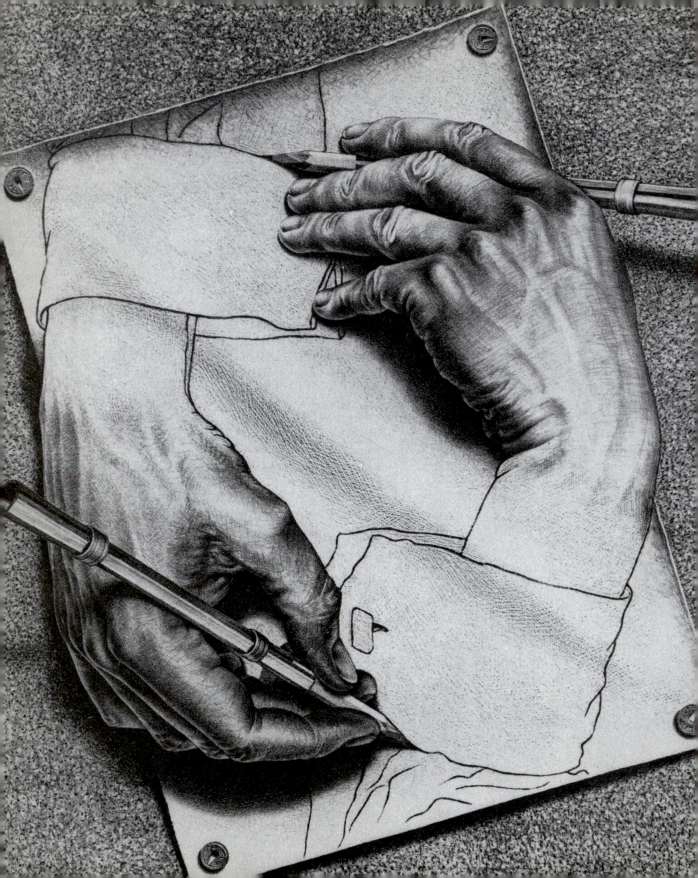

Chapter 1

What Are *the* Arts?

After studying this chapter,
you should be able to:

- Describe what constitutes a *work of art* and the ways in which it *communicates* its ideas.
- Discuss the *arts* as a field of the *humanities*.
- Explain the arts as *processes, products,* and *experiences*.
- Characterize art as a *human enterprise* and a *medium of expression*.
- Define the *symbol* and discuss the ways in which it can communicate.
- Identify and describe the major *functions* of art.

Drawing Hands, ©1948 M.C. Escher/Cordon Art, Baarn, Holland.

15

*W*e say that *theatre* is an *art,* and so as we proceed with our examination of the art of theatre, we can benefit by beginning with a general understanding of the broader context that aligns theatre with visual art, music, dance, architecture, film, and the other arts. As the title of this chapter suggests, we begin by drawing a brief general picture of the arts themselves. When we have finished this chapter, we will have a clearer sense of how theatre relates to human understanding and the ways that artists go about communicating that understanding.

The Work *of* Art

In order to function in the complex human relationships in which we find ourselves, we must bring a certain understanding to them. To develop our understanding of human relationships, we can approach human existence from a variety of vantage points. For example, when we meet people, we can choose several vantage points for perceiving and relating to them: We can see a person as an organized system of chemical components, as a bundle of interacting psychological and social experiences, as a spiritual entity, or as a combination of these factors. How well we perceive and respond to these vantage points requires the development of certain skills. In a sense, these vantage points and skills are ways of knowing human reality or the human condition. Humans have organized these ways of knowing into categories generally called science, technology, social science, humanities, and fine arts. No distinct boundaries separate these categories from each other. In simple terms, however, we may say that *science* seeks empirical truths about the physical universe—things that can be examined rationally. *Technology* uses the discoveries of science to create physical applications or tools for making life better. *Social science* studies how people behave, both individually and collectively. The *humanities* and *fine arts* try to comprehend humankind—that is, to describe what kinds of creatures we are and how we got to be this way. Specifically, the arts try to understand the human condition by drawing on creative impulses that sometimes communicate through mysterious channels.

Often, the boundaries between science, technology, social science, and the humanities and fine arts are indistinct. For example, the scientist, while supposedly dealing with facts, often depends on intuition to suspect or imagine that there is something calling out to be discovered. When Sir Isaac Newton was hit on the head by a falling apple, he needed to use his creative intuition to deduce that he could apply scientific methodology to that phenomenon and thereby prove the existence of gravity. This kind of creative intuition is much the same as the force experienced by an artist who, having sensed some truth about human life, may need to invent a technology capable of translating that

What Are *the* Arts?

insight into a painting, sculpture, musical composition, or theatrical artwork that can convey it to someone else. Nonetheless, the curiosity of the scientist, the technologist, and the social scientist is driven by a perceptibly different expectation of outcomes than the curiosity that drives the artist. For example, although the outcomes of science—demonstrable facts—seem very different from the swirling globs of paint in a painting by Jackson Pollock (Fig. 1.1), the Pollock painting, at least for some people, may portray some universal truth more effectively than a scientific fact that could be proved inadequate tomorrow. In the end, these different approaches let us enjoy different ways of understanding our world.

THE HUMANITIES, HUMANITY, AND THE ARTS

humanities The field of study concerned with the expression and perception of human thought and interaction

Both the **humanities** and that field of the humanities called the *arts* seek to understand what *humanity* is all about. Who are we as human beings, and how did we get this way? How do we relate to powers greater than ourselves? *Are* there powers greater than ourselves? How do we relate to each other? How do we behave and what do we believe? Sometimes artworks try to answer such questions directly; sometimes they generate responses that indirectly reveal conditions of human existence when viewers or listeners question why they responded to an artwork in the way they did. For example, is your reaction to the Pollock painting in Figure 1.1 a positive or negative one? Do

Figure 1.1 Jackson Pollock, One (Number 31, 1950). *Oil and enamel paint on canvas, 8' 10" × 17' 5/8". Collection, The Museum of Modern Art, New York. Gift of Sidney Janis.*

Richard Mayhew (I): The Artist & His Audience

The recipient of numerous grants and awards, Richard Mayhew is a painter with an eye for multimedia expression. Among the key challenges for the contemporary artist, he says, are the challenges of "science" in his art form and "making a contribution in his society."

WHAT DO YOU STRIVE TO ACHIEVE AND WHAT DO YOU FEEL YOU ACCOMPLISH IN YOUR ART? Many of us in exchanges with each other constantly review that kind of question—that is, what are we striving for? For myself, and in these discussions, a lot of different attitudes come out. There wasn't an intent involved in the beginning, when I started as an artist. There was a need to create, which now I can evaluate on the basis of a need for survival. As the years went by there was more dependence on the area of multimedia as I got involved with theatre and music. The various challenges through the years continued to build; in the beginning it was just a matter of mirroring or reflecting objects and the challenge of mastering technique. In the course of time it kept building, because new challenges

> *. . . In the beginning it was just a matter of mirroring or reflecting objects and the challenge of mastering technique. In the course of time it kept building, because new challenges kept coming up . . . such as . . . the science of the art itself.*

kept coming up, such as the use of color, the understanding of space, and the science of the art itself. There is a continuation through the years; nothing was ever solved, because it kept building with new challenges developing. As a youngster I started to paint a pond in my back yard. Philosophically, it must have dropped a pebble in the pond, and the ripples have been going out since then. The development from that beginning point to where I am now is unbelievable, I guess. That identity in itself is like something on the other side of the mountain, or of thinking of Rembrandt or someone else in a particular field and striving to compete at that level. One would never feel that one could achieve it.

DO YOU FEEL THAT THERE IS A CONSCIOUS EFFORT ON YOUR PART TO COMMUNICATE SOMETHING TO A RESPONDENT? Again, this is a question debated in conversation with other artists. Is one painting for an audience or painting for himself? I guess many artists paint for an audience out of survival, in terms of protecting their creative existence, because it is very difficult to survive as an artist, composer, or whatever. There isn't a subsidy for that kind of function in our society. So there are many artists who compromise their values on the basis of catering to a particular public which is not necessarily reflective of their image or impression, and so there is a prostitution of their art somewhere along the way in doing that. I haven't compromised my particular values because there is a dedication to a constant challenge of science in the art. In the course of this how does one communicate with the public? I found myself being involved with a lot of art programs within the various communities in making the community aware of the arts. There is a problem in that the public is not educated to the degree to comprehend what the artists are doing. There is difficulty there. There is a need to communicate, and there is certainly a joy if someone understands and appreciates what one does. But to directly appeal to a particular public is difficult because what you are doing is unique, and if you compromise for a dictation of, let us say, the art market or a general public, you stagnate in development.

BUT HOW IMPORTANT IS IT TO YOU THAT A RESPONDENT RECEIVE WHATEVER MESSAGE YOU MAY FEEL, AS AN INDIVIDUAL ARTIST, YOU HAVE PUT INTO A WORK? There is a certain satisfaction that the artist is making a contribution in his society. Now,

again, there is the commitment to what one is doing and the feeling that one has an influence in subliminal contributions to persons' development. If you are a dedicated artist there is a profound element in your work which is very strong, and anyone exposed to it is influenced by it. There are those who are very deliberate in their control over it, using subject matter and the manipulation of the science to control the viewer where there is a popular subject matter, and also manipulating them in control of the geometry or physics of the composition.

you feel comfortable with it? Does it say anything to you, or is it just an incomprehensible swirl of colors and dots? Do you understand *what* the painting has done to you to make you feel the way you do about it? Do you understand *how* the painting has done whatever it does to you? The revelations created by artworks do not fall into neat packages that can be examined under a microscope or duplicated in a test tube. Those insights, however, although far less tangible, may still be more or less accurate. As long as humans have existed, we have used artworks both as means of answering life's questions and for revealing and communicating life's realities. Artworks may involve rituals, drawings, stories, dances, and songs—and thus become paintings, plays, novels, ballets, and symphonies. Remarkably, although the first forms of expression are of course older than the second, they deal with the same issues that face us today. When Ice Age humans painted scenes on the walls of caves 15,000 years ago (Fig. 1.2), they were probably responding to

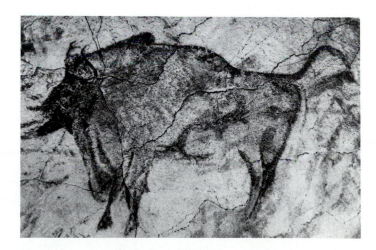

Figure 1.2 Bison, c. 14,000–10,000 B.C. *Paint, 8′ 3″ (2.5 m) long. Altamira, Spain.*

What Are *the* Arts?

the same basic concerns and questions that we have about our existence. When, in the fourth century B.C., Sophocles wrote a tragedy about a mythic king named Oedipus who tried to escape the prophecy that he would kill his father and marry his mother (see synopsis in Chapter 3), the dramatist was undoubtedly dealing with the same questions about human relationships that we face today with our parents, brothers, sisters, friends, and lovers: our desire to understand and perhaps control the forces that we find around us and our doubts as to whether we are the masters of our own fates or merely the pawns of some higher power. Whether capturing a bison in paint or dramatically portraying human actions in the Oedipus story, our predecessors used art to try to express or deal with human concerns about the extent of our control of ourselves and the universe around us.

WHAT ARE THE ARTS? WHAT IS ART?

All this brings us back to the title of this chapter: "What Are the Arts?" In a broad sense, the arts are processes, products, and experiences that communicate aspects of the human condition in a variety of means, many of which are nonverbal. *Processes* are the creative thoughts, materials, and techniques that artists combine to create *products*—the artworks themselves. *Experiences* are the human interactions and responses that occur when other humans meet the artist's vision in the artwork. We will have more to say on these topics as we proceed through this chapter.

We have just noted, very briefly and broadly, some characteristics that identify "the arts" as opposed to "science," "technology," and "social science" as vantage points that humans use to understand reality. But when we try to get more specific, we may arrive at a thornier pathway, because this need for specificity leads us to the question: *What is art?* Attempts to answer *that* question have ensnared scholars, philosophers, and aestheticians for centuries without yielding many clues about how to escape. The late pop artist Andy Warhol reportedly said that "art is anything you can get away with" (see Fig. 1.3). Perhaps we should be a little less cynical—and a little more specific. Let's avoid the question "What is art?" and ask instead, "What is a work of art?" Here is one possible working definition: A **work of art** is one person's vision of human reality expressed in a particular medium and shared with others. Let's explore the terms of this definition.

work of art The *process, product,* and *experience* in which one person's perception of human thought and interaction is expressed in a particular medium and shared with others

nonrestrictiveness A definition of art that includes among artworks anything that tries to communicate a perception of human thought and interaction through means traditionally associated with the arts

Nonrestrictiveness In the first place, this definition is sufficiently **nonrestrictive**: It defines an artwork as anything that attempts to communicate some vision of human reality through some means traditionally associated with the arts—that is, drawings, paintings, prints, sculptures, and works of music, dance, literature, and theatre. That is to say, if the originator *intends* it as a work of art, it is a work of art. Whether it is good or bad, sophisticated or naive, well or poorly made, profound or inconsequential matters little in terms of its acceptability as an artwork. For example, a drawing in which a child intended to show some feeling about mother, father, and home would be as

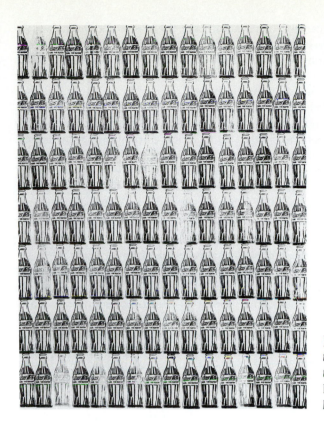

Figure 1.3 Andy Warhol, *Green Coca Cola Bot-tles*, (1962). *Oil on canvas. 82 1/2″ × 57″. Collection of Whitney Museum of American Art, New York. Purchase, with funds from the Friends of the Whitney Museum of American Art. 68.25.*

much an artwork as Michelangelo's Sistine Chapel frescoes. Although the *qualities* that we might ascribe to them would probably be different, the music of the Grateful Dead and the music of Mozart would both qualify as artworks under our definition. (We will discuss criticism and qualitative or *value* judgments in Chapter 3.)

Human Enterprise The second implication of this definition is that art is a *human* enterprise: Whenever you experience a work of art, you are coming into some form of contact with another human being. However, if works of art are expressions of other human beings, they can demand a certain intimacy that can be risky and even intimidating. After all, to some extent, we all build walls to protect ourselves from being hurt, threatened, or challenged. And yet, whereas some of us are uneasy about letting another person close to us, others dare to be vulnerable. In part, people tend to behave differently toward other people because opening ourselves to the vision of someone who sees a different reality than we do can be either intensely frightening or very stimulating. In either case, we experience the same kind of human contact in works of art because, as we will see, artworks are intended to engage us and to encourage our desire to respond. Those who produce theatrical performances, for example, do everything they can to entice us into the theatre. Once there, we are exposed to a variety of visual and aural stimuli that attempt to make us feel, think, or react in harmony with the goals that the artists have set for the production.

At the same time, our working definition of a work of art is still not entirely nonrestrictive: The fact that art is a human enterprise places a certain restriction on it. For example, it eliminates objects in nature that may produce profoundly *aesthetic* experiences—that is, experiences relating to the artistic or beautiful. Sunsets, oceans, mountains, clouds, and rocks may produce a significant experience of beauty and move us deeply, but they are not produced by a human being intent upon sharing a vision of human reality—unless, of course, one wishes to apply such intentions to some greater power that created rocks, mountains, seas, and so forth. It is easy to see why theology and philosophy have historical connections to art.

medium of expression
The vehicle, such as painting, sculpture, music, literature, or the theatre, through which the artist expresses a perception of human thought and interaction

Medium of Expression   Art also involves a **medium of expression.** Indeed, one of the problems that people may have with a given instance of artistic expression is the rejection of the artist's medium. For example, we can readily accept the traditional media of the arts—painting, traditional sculpture, music (using traditional instruments), theatre (using a script and performed in an auditorium), and so on. Sometimes, however, the medium tends to baffle us. When a medium of expression does not conform to our expectations or experiences of art, we may reject the work as a work of art. For example, Figure 1.4 shows an 18-foot-high by 24-mile-long fabric fence created by the artist Christo. For Christo, this work—which existed for only two weeks—was an artwork. For some other people, it most definitely was not. Our working definition, however, would allow it: Even though the medium

Figure 1.4   Christo, *Running Fence, Sonoma and Marin Counties, California, 1972–76. Woven nylon fabric and steel cables, height: feet 18, length: 24 1/2 miles. September 1976, two weeks.*

What Are *the* Arts?

was unconventional and the work itself transitory, the *intent* of the work was clearly artistic.

Communication   Artworks involve a **communication** or *sharing* process. The common factor in all artwork is a *humanizing* experience. That experience needs a **respondent**—another human being with whom the artist shares a perception of human reality. When an artwork comes into the presence of other humans, human interaction results, with its wide variety of possibilities. The interaction may be casual and fleeting, or there may in fact be little actual interaction, as in the first meeting of two people, one or both of whom may not be interested in interaction. Similarly, the artist may not have much to say and may not say it very well. For example, a play that deals with a trite topic—"Do unto others . . ."—and shows little skill in its writing or production does little to engage the audience. In similar fashion, the respondent may be ignorant, self-absorbed, preconditioned, or distracted. For example, an audience member whose preconceptions are not met by the production or an audience member who is preoccupied with events that may have occurred outside the theatre will find it nearly impossible to perceive what the production offers. In such circumstances, the artistic experience fizzles. At the opposite end of the spectrum of experience, all conditions may be optimum and a profoundly exciting and meaningful experience may occur: The play may treat a significant subject in a unique manner; the acting, directing, and design may be excellent; the audience member may be receptive and aware of what to look and listen for. Any given interaction is likely to fall somewhere between these two extremes. In any case, it is a human experience and one that is fundamental to art.

In discussing art as communication, we need to note in passing one important term, and that is *symbol*. A simple definition will suffice for the moment. A **symbol** is a thing that *represents* something else, often using a material object to suggest something less tangible or less obvious. *Symbols* differ from *signs,* which suggest the presence of a fact or condition. Signs are what they denote, whereas symbols carry deeper, wider, and richer meanings. Look at Figure 1.5. What do you see? In one case, you might identify this figure

communication The process through which the artist *shares* a perception of human thought or interaction with a *respondent*

respondent Any person with whom the artist enters into communication for the purpose of sharing a perception of human thought and interaction

symbol A thing, often an object, that *represents* some other thing, whether an object, a quality, or a process, whose *meaning* is abstract or not immediately apparent

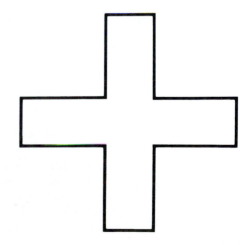

Figure 1.5   Signs and Symbols. *The figure illustrated here might be either a sign or a symbol. In the first case it could be seen as a plus sign, indicating the fact or condition of addition. In the second case it could be a Greek cross, symbolizing not only Christianity and its beliefs, but also a particular branch of Christianity with all of its cultural and theological implications.*

as a sign. It looks like a common "plus" sign, indicating the fact or state of addition in arithmetic. In that sense, it is what it seems to be. On the other hand, it might be a Greek cross. In this case, it becomes a symbol because it suggests a wide variety of images, meanings, and implications involving Christianity. Because artworks use a variety of symbols to convey meaning, they can relay, in limited time and space, a wealth of meaning that goes well beyond the apparent surface of the work to offer glimpses of human reality that cannot be sufficiently described in any other manner. Symbols help to transform artworks into doorways through which we travel in order to experience more of the human condition than we could in the same length of time and in the same place without the artwork at hand.

The Functions *of* Art

Art can *function* in many ways—as entertainment, as political and social weapon, as therapy, as artifact. No one function is inherently any more or less important than any other. Nor are these the only possible functions of art. Rather, these four functions serve as indicators of how art has functioned in the past and can function in the present. Like the genres or types of plays that we will examine in Chapter 4, these four functions present the artist with options, depending on what he or she wishes to do with an artwork. Moreover, these functions are not mutually exclusive; a single artwork can pursue any or all of them. In Chapter 2, we will return to these functions, applying them directly to theatre. The discussion here will be brief and will serve only as a broad introduction.

ENTERTAINMENT

entertainment The *function* of art that offers a means of escape from everyday activities or concerns; the artistic function of amusing or giving pleasure to respondents

When plays, paintings, concerts, and so on fill an **entertainment** function, they provide escape from our everyday cares, treat us to a pleasant time, and engage us in social occasions. However, works of art that entertain us may perform other functions as well. Through the visions of artists who primarily entertain us, we can gain insights into the human experience, glimpse the conditions of other cultures, or find healing therapy. Indeed, the primacy of any one function may depend on the individual respondent. An artwork in which one individual sees only entertainment may function as a profound social and personal comment for another person. A Mozart symphony, however, can be relaxing and allow us to escape our cares. For some listeners, it may also provide a sophisticated comment on the life of its composer and/or on conditions in 18th-century Austria. Grant Wood's *American Gothic* (Fig. 1.6) can amuse us and/or give us a detailed commentary on 19th-century America and/or move us deeply on an emotional level. The result depends on the artist, the artwork, and the respondent.

Figure 1.6   Grant Wood, *American Gothic*, 1930.   *Oil on beaver board,* 29 7/8" × 24 7/8". *Friends of American Art Collection. Courtesy of Art Institute of Chicago.*

political (or social) commentary The *function* of art that encourages political change or the modification of social behavior

POLITICAL AND SOCIAL COMMENTARY

When art is used to bring about political change or to modify the behavior of large groups of people, it can be said to make **political** or **social commentary**. In ancient Rome, for example, the authorities used music and theatre to keep masses of unemployed people occupied in order to quell urban unrest. At

What Are *the* Arts?

the same time, Roman playwrights attacked incompetent or corrupt officials. In ancient Greece, the playwright Aristophanes (see Chapter 15) used comedy in such plays as *The Birds* (Fig. 1.7) to attack the political ideas of the leaders of Athenian society. In *Lysistrata*, for example, he attacks war by creating a story in which all the women of Athens go on a sex strike until Athens is rid of war and those who would engage in it. In Scene I, the Commissioner argues the point with Lysistrata:

COMMISSIONER: All this is beside the point.
                    Will you be so kind
              As to tell me how you mean to save Greece?

LYSISTRATA: Of course.
              Nothing could be simpler.

Figure 1.7 Aristophanes, *The Birds*, 414 B.C. *Adapted by James Patterson. Director, Sandra Langsner-Crews; scenic designer, Rick Clark; lighting design, Ron Shaw; costume designer, Lisa Martin. An innovator in his own time because of his playful use of exaggerated language and often vicious attacks, through parody and satire, on a variety of topical practices, Aristophanes continues to inspire freewheeling adaptations that capture the quality of his theatre rather than the specifics of his content. As a master of the classic "Old Comedy" of ancient Greece, Aristophanes is discussed more fully in Chapter 15.*

What Are *the* Arts?

COMMISSIONER:	I assure you, I am all ears.
LYSISTRATA:	Do you know anything about weaving? Say the yarn gets tangled: We thread it this way and that through the skein, up and down, until it's free. And it's like that with war. We'll send our envoys up and down, this way and that, all over Greece, until it's finished.
COMMISSIONER:	Yarn? Thread? Skein? Are you out of your mind? I tell you, war is a serious business.
LYSISTRATA:	So serious that I'd like to go on talking about weaving.
COMMISSIONER:	All right. Go ahead.

LYSISTRATA:	The first thing we have to do
	is to wash our yarn, get the dirt out of it.
	You see? Isn't there too much dirt here in Athens?
	You must wash those men away.
	    Then our spoiled wool—
	that's like your job-hunters, out for a life
	of no work and big pay. Back to the basket,
	citizens or not, allies or not,
	or friendly immigrants.
	    And your colonies?
	Hanks of wool lost in various places. Pull them
	together, weave them into one great whole,
	and our voters are clothed for ever.*

Similarly, in late 19th-century Norway, Henrik Ibsen used *An Enemy of the People* as a platform for airing an issue of social consciousness—whether a government should ignore the pollution in a resort town's waters when acknowledging the problem would destroy the livelihood of the town's residents. (See playwright Arthur Miller's comments on Ibsen's play—which he adapted in the 1950's—in Chapter 2.)

THERAPY

therapy (or psychodrama) The *function* whereby such artistic activities as role playing are used to treat or communicate with individuals suffering from a variety of physical and mental illnesses

    In its therapeutic function, art can be and is used as **therapy** for individuals with a variety of illnesses, both physical and mental. Role playing, for example, is used frequently as a counseling tool in treating dysfunctional family situations. In this context, often called **psychodrama,** mentally ill patients act out their personal circumstances in order to find and cure the cause of their illness. The focus of this use of art as therapy is the single individual. In a much

* Aristophanes, *Lystrata,* translated by Dudley Fitts, in *Great Farces,* edited by Robert Saffron (New York: Collier Books, 1967), p. 34.

Richard Mayhew (II): The Artist & His Medium

The artist, says Mayhew, must be more than a "technician": He finds his subject matter through continuous experimentation.

WHAT ARE THE MOST CHALLENGING ASPECTS THAT YOU FIND IN THE MEDIA WITHIN WHICH YOU WORK, SPECIFICALLY? That is a very difficult question because everything about it is extremely difficult yet extremely enjoyable. Nothing ever seems to be resolved if one is a dedicated artist. If one is just a technician he masters technique, media, procedure, and image. As a result, it's just a performance which has determined what the end result would be. If one is really freely involved with the experimental, creative process, there is no mastering the media, the direction, or the future. It's always that elusive area. Actors walk out on the stage and there is a moment of truth. They know their lines well, and if they go out and perform like a puppet, they do it in a very sterile way. Painting is the same thing: When you are painting a painting, in the course of the painting there is a whole new moment of truth. If that is predetermined and controlled, it is limited. Many of us do stagnate: Even though we may remain technicians, we cease to make a contribution.

Actors walk out on the stage and there is a moment of truth. . . . if they go out and perform like a puppet, they do it in a very sterile way. Painting is the same thing. . . .

IN YOUR OWN PERSONAL WORK DO YOU FIND ANY PARTICULAR WAYS IN WHICH IDEAS COME TO YOU FOR A PARTICULAR WORK? Everything being visualized, that one sees or comes in contact with, is potential subject matter. So it is impossible ever to paint all the things you want to paint, to meet all the challenges you would like to meet; there is never enough time; life is just too short to do it, especially if there is complete dedication to it. It is constantly elusive: It's like in a dream, trying to hold on to a doorknob, and you can't quite get the grip of it, and it always keeps changing and moving. When you do open the door there is another one beyond it that you have to open.

ONCE YOU DECIDE ON A SUBJECT OR A TREATMENT, DO YOU CONCEIVE OF THE TOTAL PAINTING BEFORE YOU BEGIN, OR IS IT A DEVELOPMENTAL THING AS YOU WORK? In the early stages I was working directly from subject matter as a landscape painter; I was apprenticed, very young, to an illustrator and Hudson Valley painter. At the time I didn't realize the value of it. When I started painting, the fascination of the medium came from picking up color from blobs on a palette and transferring it over to the canvas. Pictures came out of the end of the brush. It was unbelievable fascination—magic. One does not have control over it. No matter how well you plan that image, it evolves and changes because of an intuitive extension which you cannot predetermine. Many writers talk about the world beyond, that marvel of consciousness that they have planned, that keeps changing.

What Are *the* Arts?

broader context, however, art acts as a healing agent for more general societal illnesses. Artworks illustrate a society's failings and excesses in hopes of saving us from disaster. In a very specific sense, the laughter caused by comedy is therapeutic because laughter releases endorphins, chemicals produced by the brain (and by exercise) that strengthen the immune system.

ART AS ARTIFACT

artifact The *function* of art as the product of the ideas and/or technology of a specific time and place

Art also functions as an **artifact:** As a product of a particular time and place, art represents the ideas and technology of that time and place. As we look back over history, we find in art striking and, in some cases, the only tangible records. Such revealing artistic artifacts as paintings, sculptures, poems, plays, and buildings records of some peoples—give us insights into various cultures, including our own. Artworks as artifacts connect us to our past and to human relations that may be as old as humanity itself.

In whatever way art functions, it has the potential to affect and effect human response. Sometimes that response is superficial, sometimes profound. In either case, the function of the artwork depends on numerous complex interactions among artist, artwork, and respondent.

The Arts *and* Life

Sometimes the arts are seen as "frills," as peripheral to real life. This may not be the place to debate the centrality of the arts in society, but it is a proper place to suggest that the arts are things with which we live in a daily fashion. The difficulty that many people experience in seeing the arts as important components of life results in part from a lack of familiarity. That unfamiliarity has perhaps been fostered by people both within the arts and without who have tried to make the arts elitist enterprises and have maintained art gallery, museum, concert hall, theatre, and opera house as privileged institutions open only to the knowledgeable and "sophisticated." Nothing should be further from the truth. The arts are elements of life to which we can and must respond in the course of our everyday lives. We live *with* the arts because the principles of artistic activity are everywhere in our lives. The use of artistic principles and elements of composition, whether visual or aural, governs the appeals to our senses and psyches in the products that we buy, the advertising that we see and hear, and the attitudes that we take or others would have us take. Line, form, color, and sound are used to attract us, calm us, enervate us—manipulate us—so that we do what others would have us do. Equally importantly, the artistic experience is a way of knowing and communicating. It can form a significant part of being human and can make the world around us a more interesting and habitable place.

SUMMARY

- As a field within the *humanities,* the *fine arts* are one of the vantage points from which we perceive and respond to our experiences as human beings who interact with other human beings. Other such vantage points include *science, technology,* and *social science.*

- As the name of the field implies, the *humanities* try to understand what "humanity" is all about. Artworks ask people to consider the same question by questioning their *responses* to different kinds of works. Even the earliest *forms of expression*—rituals, drawings, stories, dances, and songs—were inspired by the same questions that are still raised by plays, paintings, novels, ballets, and symphonies.

- "The arts" can be characterized as (1) *processes*—the creative thoughts, materials, and techniques combined by artists to create artworks; (2) *products*—the actual works created as a result of the artistic process; and (3) *experiences*—the human interactions that occur when other human beings *respond* to the artistic process revealed in the artistic product.

- In order to answer the question "What is art? " we can apply a four-part definition: (1) *nonrestrictiveness*—the artwork is anything that tries to communicate something about human reality through means that we associate with the arts (drawings, plays, and so forth); (2) *human enterprise*—the experience of an artwork is a form of contact with another human being; (3) *medium of expression*—the artist chooses a form of expression, whether conventional or unconventional, through which to communicate with respondents; and (4) *communication*—as "humanizing experiences," all artworks require the interaction of artist and respondent.

- *Symbols* are a form of communication in which certain "things" *represent* other things in order to suggest a wide variety of meanings. Art asks respondents to question the meaning of symbols in order to explore meanings that cannot be expressed on the surface of the work.

- Although the arts can have as many *functions* as there are interactions between artists and respondents, four general functions reflect the traditional ways in which art has functioned in the past and continues to function today:

  (1) as *entertainment*—art can provide an escape from everyday activities, and it can amuse us or respond to our interest in another time or place;

  (2) as *political and social commentary*—art can seek to encourage political change or to modify social behavior;

(3) as *therapy*—in such activities as role playing, art can be used to treat or communicate with both individuals and groups suffering from illnesses both physical and mental;

(4) as *artifact*—art can introduce us to or teach us about the ideas and technology of other times and other places.

Chapter 2

What Is Theatre?

After studying this chapter,
you should be able to:

- Describe the relationship of *theatre* to the wider context of the humanities and fine arts.

- Define the word *theatre* and discuss how the word identifies important characteristics of the art of theatre.

- Understand how theatre operates as an *interpretive art* in relaying the ideas of the *playwright* through the other artists involved in a theatre production.

- Explain theatre as a *communications model* and discuss how important concepts such as *production, product,* and *experience* relate to theatrical activity.

- Identify and discuss the important functions of theatre and how they contribute to our understanding and enjoyment of the theatrical experience.

- Identify and discuss the parts of a theatrical production, such as *plot* and *character*.

Kirmes. *Herzog Anton Ulrich-Museum Museumsfoto*: B. PI Keiser.

*I*n Chapter 1, we discussed very briefly the wider context of human experience, understanding, and communication of which the humanities and the fine arts form a part. We drew this wide context in order to show how the art of theatre relates to other human endeavors. In this chapter, we will expand upon some of the basic concepts and broad issues discussed in Chapter 1 and apply them directly to an understanding of theatre itself. In doing all this, we are painting with a broad brush. The issues of what constitutes art and what constitutes theatre can be quite complex—certainly more complex than our brief treatment may make them seem at first glance. Nonetheless, introducing theatre by first introducing the arts should not intimidate us. Rather, it should suggest to us that there *are* broader and deeper issues involved.

Before progressing in our discussion, let's note a quick definitional difference between *theatre* and *drama*—two words that sometimes seem interchangeable. Drama comes from the Greek word *dran* and means "to do" or "to act." *Drama* could thus be defined as a collection of words that have potential to come alive in action. Drama, therefore, consists of the printed words of a play—that is, its *dialogue*—the words spoken by the actors. *Theatre*, on the other hand, is drama put into production: It is drama combined with actors' movements, costumes, lighting, sound, and settings in a formal performance before an audience.

We will pursue an understanding of theatre by discussing theatre first as art and then as a communication model consisting of *product, process,* and *experience*. Finally, we will expand on the *functions of art* noted in Chapter 1 by applying those functions directly to the theatre. Before we move to those areas, however, let's begin by examining the word *theatre*. Where did it come from, and what does it imply about the art form that we are studying?

Our word *theatre* comes from the Greek *theatron*—that portion of the Greek theatre building where the audience sat. Its literal meaning is "a place for seeing." The Greeks' choice of this word suggests how they may have perceived an important aspect of the theatre as they understood it—that is,

Figure 2.1   *Sophocles,* Ajax *(ca. 455* B.C.*). National Theatre of Greece, Dodona Festival, 1963. According to Aristotle, Sophocles (see Chapter 15) introduced not only painted scenery to classical Greek production but a third major actor—an innovation that enabled him to develop more complex, character-oriented plots. A synopsis of Sophocles' greatest play,* Oedipus the King, *can be found in Chapter 3.*

theatre *Aesthetic communication* through and experience of the art, process, and production of works of dramatic expression

theatre is to a large extent a *visual* experience. (Figure 2.1 shows a modern production of Sophocles' *Ajax* [440 B.C.] at the restored ancient theatre at Dadona.) In addition to the words of the script, provided by the playwright, and the treatment of those words by the actors, the theatre artwork—that is, the *production*—also involves visual messages. These include *actor movement, costume, setting, lighting,* and the *physical relationship of the playing space to the audience.*

Theatre *as* Art

Like the other performing arts, theatre is an *interpretive* discipline. Between the playwright and the audience stand the director, the designers, and the actors. Although each functions as an individual artist who adds a specific form of artistic communication to the production, each also serves to communicate the playwright's vision to the audience. Sometimes, the play becomes subordinate to the expressive work of its interpreters. Sometimes, as we will see in Chapter 8, the concept of director as "master artist" puts the playwright in a subordinate position. Nonetheless, mounting a production requires the interpretation of someone's concept through spectacle and sound by theatre artists.

Theatre is *aesthetic* communication through the manipulation or design of time, sound, and two- and three-dimensional space using the live performer. First and foremost, theatre is art, and as such it conforms to the characteristics of artistic expression that we discussed in Chapter 1. Theatre represents an attempt by humans to reveal some vision of human life, through use of the live performer, time, sound, and space to a live and present audience. Because theatre gives us flesh-and-blood human beings involved in human action, we must occasionally remind ourselves that the dramatic experience remains only an imitation of reality. No matter how graphic the action appears, these are only actors on a stage employing the tricks of the theatre. What we encounter in the theatre is not reality itself but rather an *imitation* of reality acting as a *symbol* to communicate a group of artists' perceptions *about* human experience.

In a sense, then, theatre is make-believe: Through gesture and movement, language, character, thought, and spectacle, theatre imitates action. We can see clearly how, by its use of other human beings (actors) as a medium of expression, theatre is in part an imitation of life—that is, a copy of what goes on around us day by day. If theatre consisted of nothing more than that, however, we would not find it nearly as captivating as we have for more than 2500 years.

THE PRODUCTION

production The actual *theatre artwork* that combines *script, character, thought,* and *visual* and *sound elements* into a finished single entity

As we shall see, theatre consists of a complex combination of elements that form a single entity called a performance or a **production**—the actual

Tennessee Williams (I): The Timeless World of a Play

Along with Arthur Miller, Tennessee Williams (see Chapter 17) helped to define the American theatre during the two decades between the mid-1940s and mid-1960s. Although he took full advantage of the technical possibilities of the modern stage, he also tried to combine the poetic intensity of classical drama with the immediacy of modern life. Here, he argues that classical tragedy has long revealed the larger-than-life dimensions of all human experience.

The classic tragedies of Greece had tremendous nobility. The actors wore great masks, movements were formal, dance-like, and the speeches had an epic quality which doubtless were as removed from the normal conversation of their contemporary society as they seem today. Yet they did not seem false to the Greek audiences: The magnitude of the events and the passions aroused by them did not seem ridiculously out of proportion to common experience. And I wonder if this was not because the Greek audiences knew, instinctively or by training, that the created world of a play is removed from that element which makes people *little* and their emotions fairly inconsequential. . . .

A play may be violent, full of motion: Yet it has that special kind of repose which allows contemplation and produces the climate in which tragic importance is a possible thing, provided that certain modern conditions are met. . . .

. . . I wonder if . . . Greek audiences knew . . . that the created world of a play is removed from that element which makes people little and their emotions fairly inconsequential.

In a play, time is arrested in the sense of being confined. By a sort of legerdemain, events are made to remain *events,* rather than being reduced so quickly to mere *occurrences.* The audience can sit back in a comforting dusk to watch a world which is flooded with light and in which emotion and action have a dimension and dignity that they would likewise have in real existence, if only the shattering intrusion of time could be locked out. . . .

About their lives people ought to remember that when they are finished, everything in them will be contained in a marvelous state of repose which is the same as that which they unconsciously admired in drama. The rush is temporary. The great and only possible dignity of man lies in his power deliberately to choose certain moral values by which to live as steadfastly as if he, too, like a character in a play, were immured against the corrupting rush of time. . . .

theatre artwork—in the same sense that a finished painting or a musical performance is an artwork. (We will discuss this concept in more detail in Chapter 3.) Our understanding of the theatre production as a work of art can be enhanced if we have some specific tools for approaching it. These tools come to us from theatre's distant past. Writing 2500 years ago in his *Poetics*, Artistotle argued that *tragedy* (a type of theatre that we will discuss in Chapter 4) included *plot, character, diction, music, thought,* and *spectacle*. We can use and expand upon Aristotle's terminology to describe the basic parts of a production and to give ourselves a useful set of tools for understanding all theatrical productions. We can think of these terms as "can openers" that help us to get into the "container" called a production and enjoy its contents. We will modify Aristotle's terms to reflect our own times and usage, and we will also note that although Aristotle placed more importance on some parts than others, these six parts—and their descriptive terminology—still cover the entire theatrical product and help us approach it, even if a specific production minimizes or lacks entirely one or more of these "parts." In the paragraphs that follow, we will take Aristotle's terms and reshape them in language more familiar to us, explain what the terms mean, and learn how we can use this understanding to identify certain things to look and listen for in a production. In our treatment of this material, we will first examine the *script* and include in that discussion Aristotle's concepts of *plot* and *diction*—which we will call *language*. Next we will examine *character*, then *spectacle*—which we will call *visual elements*. Next we will briefly discuss what Aristotle called *music* and what we will call *aural elements*. Finally, we will examine Aristotle's concept of *thought*—that is, *themes* and *ideas*.

The Script   A playwright creates a written document called a **script,** which contains the dialogue used by the actors. Although Aristotle called the words written by the playwright *diction,* we will use a more modern term and refer to this part of a production as its **language.** The playwright's language tells us at least part of what we can expect from the play. For example, if he has written in a manner that seems like everyday speech, we generally expect action that will exhibit high **verisimilitude**—a strong resemblance to everyday truth or reality. Poetry, on the other hand, usually indicates a lesser degree of verisimilitude and, perhaps, stronger symbolism. In the play *Fences*, for example, playwright August Wilson (see the interview in Chapter 5) uses contemporary realistic language to bring the characters to life, to give us a sense of their individuality, and to bring home the context of the times. Set in 1957, *Fences* is the story of Troy Maxson's struggle with his circumstances and himself and the effect of that struggle on those around him:

(Act I, Scene iii. Troy is talking to his son, Cory)

Like you? I go out of here every morning . . . bust my butt . . . putting up with them crackers every day . . . cause I like you? You about the biggest fool I ever saw.

(Pause)

It's my job. It's my responsibility! You understand that? A man got to take care of his family. You live in my house . . . sleep you behind on my bedclothes . . . fill you belly up with my food . . . cause you my son. You my flesh and blood. Not 'cause I like you! Cause it's my duty to take care of you. I owe a responsibility to you! Let's get this straight right here . . . before it go along any further . . . I ain't got to like you. Mr. Rand don't give me my money come payday cause he likes me. He gives me cause he owe me. I done give you everything I had to give you. I gave you your life! Me and your mama worked that out between us. And liking your black ass wasn't part of the bargain. Don't you try and go through life worrying about if somebody like you or not. You best be making sure they doing right by you. You understand what I'm saying, boy?

Compare that language with the poetry used by Pierre Corneille in *Le Cid* to create a mythical hero who is larger than life and more a type than an individual. In Act III Scene iv, Rodrigue (the Cid) is confronted by Chimene, his fianceé, whose father he has just killed in response to his insult to Rodrigue's own father. The conflict is that between duty and honor—and love:

RODRIGUE: I'll do your bidding, yet still do I desire
     To end my wretched life, at your dear hand.
     But this you must not ask, that I renounce
     My worthy act in cowardly repentance.
     The fatal outcome of too swift an anger
     Disgraced my father, covered me with shame.
     You know how a blow affects a man of courage.
     I took that blow upon me, sought its author,
     And finding him, restored my father's honor.
     Were it to do again, then I would do it.
     'Tis true, against my father and my honor,
     My love fought hard and long; O wondrous power,
     That I could hesitate to take my vengeance.
     When such an offense had touched me, I was bound
     To make you hate me, or to suffer insult,
     And so I thought my hand too swift, too eager,
     Accused myself of too much violence;
     And thus your beauty would have won the day,
     But for the thought, still stronger than your charms,
     That no man, once dishonored, could deserve you.

In either case, we must seek the relationship of the language to the overall presentation of the play; using its tone to help determine how much more the words imply than what meets the ear. Language, then, helps reveal the overall tone and style of the play. It also can reveal, for example, character, theme, and level of verisimilitude. In a sense, language is the playwright's road map—directions that we can use to find meaning.

  The skeleton of the script is the *plot*, which comprises the structural elements called *exposition, complication,* and *denouement,* as well as momentary elements like *discovery, foreshadowing, crisis, point of attack, climax,* and *reversal.* Figure 2.2 illustrates how these parts of plot relate to each other. Because each of these terms is defined and described in Chapter 3, we will not redefine them here. We should note, however, that plot comprises the shape

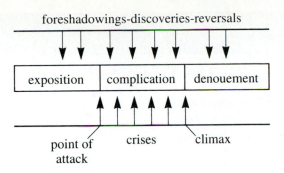

foreshadowings-discoveries-reversals

| exposition | complication | denouement |

point of
attack   crises   climax

Figure 2.2   *Parts of the Plot.*

that the playwright gives to the action as it moves forward from beginning to end.

character The
psychological
motivations of the
persons of the play

Character   The playwright also outlines another important part of the play, namely, **character**—the psychological motivations of the persons of the play. In most plays, the audience focuses on why individuals do what they do, how they change, and how they interact with other individuals as the plot unfolds. Notice that we have used the word *character* in a very specific way here—to mean *psychological motivation.* That is what Aristotle meant by *character,* and it is a different meaning of the word *character* than the meaning that identifies a particular individual in the play. For example, the role of Troy Maxson can be identified as a "character" in the play *Fences.* When we use the term in that manner, we are referring to Troy Maxson as an individual or person in the play. But Troy Maxson also has a particular set of motivating psychological forces that make him react the way he does when faced with particular circumstances. Those motivating psychological forces constitute Troy's "character" in the Aristotelian sense. Thus, we could correctly say that every character (person) in a play also has an individual character (motivating psychological forces).

Plays reveal a wide variety of characters—both persons and motivating psychological forces. In every play, we will find characters who fulfill major functions and on whom the playwright wishes us to focus. We will also find minor characters—those whose actions may interact with those of the major characters and whose actions constitute subordinate plot lines. We will find a variety of psychological makeups: misers, misanthropes, egotists, enablers, and so on. As we just noted, much of the interest created by the drama lies in the exploration of how persons with specific character motivations react to circumstances. For example, when Rodrigue discovers that his father has been humiliated, what is it in his character that makes him decide to avenge the insult even though it means killing the father of the woman he loves and thereby jeopardizing that love? Such responses, driven by character, are the choices that, in many cases, drive plays forward.

thought The aspect of
the *theatre artwork* that
communicates its
intellectual content—its
themes, ideas, and
perceptions about
human experience

Thought   In order to describe the intellectual content of the play, Aristotle uses the term **thought**—a term that we will use to refer to themes, ideas, and perceptions about human experience that the play communicates. In Lanford Wilson's 1987 play *Burn This,* for example, a young dancer named Anna

Arthur Miller (I): The Thought of Henrik Ibsen

Like Tennessee Williams, Arthur Miller has incorporated strong autobiographical elements into his plays; unlike Williams, however, Miller has also displayed an abiding interest in themes of "social consciousness." In 1951, he took the unusual step of adapting a play by another great playwright, Henrik Ibsen's An Enemy of the People. *In his preface to this adaptation, Miller expressed his admiration for Ibsen's intellectual forthrightness. (The work of both Ibsen and Miller is discussed in Chapter 17.)*

> It is his insistence, his utter conviction, that he is going to say what he has to say, and that the audience, by God, is going to listen.

There is one quality in Ibsen that no serious writer can afford to overlook. It lies at the very center of his force, and I found in it—as I hope others will—a profound source of strength. It is his insistence, his utter conviction, that he is going to say what he has to say, and that the audience, by God, is going to listen. It is the very same quality that makes a star actor, a great public speaker, and a lunatic. Every Ibsen play begins with the unwritten words: "Now listen here! " And these words have shown me a path through the wall of "entertainment," a path that leads beyond the formulas and dried-up precepts, the pretense and fraud, of the business of the stage. Whatever else Ibsen has to teach, this is his first and greatest contribution. . . .

I believe Ibsen's *An Enemy of the People* could be alive for us because its central theme is, in my opinion, the central theme of our social life today. Simply, it is the question of whether the democratic guarantees protecting political minorities ought to be set aside in time of crisis. More personally, it is the question of whether one's vision of the truth ought to be a source of guilt at a time when the mass of men condemn it as a dangerous and devilish lie. It is an enduring theme—in fact, possibly the most enduring of all Ibsen's themes—because there never was, nor will there ever be, an organized society able to countenance calmly the individual who insists that he is right while the vast majority is absolutely wrong.

The play is the story of a scientist who discovers an evil and, innocently believing that he has done a service to humanity, expects that he will at least be thanked. However, the town has a vested interest in the perpetuation of that evil, and his "truth," when confronted with that interest, must be made to conform. The scientist cannot change the truth for any reason disconnected with the evil. He clings to the truth and suffers the social consequences. At rock bottom, then, the play is concerned with the inviolability of objective truth. Or, put more dynamically, that those who attempt to warp the truth for ulterior purposes must inevitably become warped and corrupted themselves. This theme is valid today, just as it will always be, but some of the examples given by Ibsen to prove it may no longer be. . . .

lives in a Manhattan loft with two gay roommates, Larry and Robby. As the play opens, we learn that Robby has been killed in a boating accident; Anna has just returned from the funeral and a set of bizarre encounters with Robby's family. Larry, a sardonic advertising executive, and Burton, Anna's boyfriend, maintain a constant animosity. Into the scene bursts Pale, Robby's brother, a threatening, violent figure. Anna is both afraid of Pale and irresistibly attracted to him; the conflict of their relationship drives the play forward to its climax.

This brief description summarizes the *plot* of the play. But what this play is *about*—that is, its *thought*—remains for us to discover and develop. Some people might say that the play is about loneliness, anger, and the way "not belonging" manifests itself in human behavior. Others might focus on abusive relationships. Still others would see in the constant sexual references, both hetero- and homosexual, a thought content dealing with those conflicts and issues. Whatever the case, the process of coming to conclusions about meaning moves through several layers of interpretation. One layer involves the playwright's choice of how to interpret the ideas themselves through the characters, language, and plot. A second layer of interpretation lies in the director's decisions about what the playwright has in mind—which will be balanced by what the director wishes to communicate, either because of or in spite of the playwright. Finally, we must interpret what we see and hear in the production along with what we may perceive independently from the script, in order to find meaning for ourselves. Interestingly enough, even when there appears to be disagreement among the various layers of meaning, the process still has value. The knowledge that I have taken a different meaning from the play than what I find the director and the production have had to say means that I have been able to discern more than one point of view. That discernment means that my perception is acute and that the issues have been sifted through my own critical thinking.

Visual Elements   The director takes the playwright's language, plot, and characters and translates them into action by using, among other things, what Aristotle called *spectacle* but which we can simply call the **visual elements.** The visual elements of a production include, first of all, the *physical relationship established between the actors and the audience.* As we will see in detail in Chapter 5, the actor–audience relationship can take any number of shapes. For example, the audience might sit surrounding the stage, or perhaps on only one side of it. The visual elements also include *stage settings, lighting, costumes,* and *properties,* as well as the actors and their movements. Whatever the audience can *see* contributes to this part of the theatrical production.

Aural Elements   What we *hear* also contributes to the production. Aristotle's term for the aural elements of a production is *music,* but that term, too, means something quite different from our normal associations. Let's simply understand that **aural elements** (or **sound**), whether the actors' voices, the background music, or the clashing of swords, is an important part of the theatrical production. How a production sounds—and looks, and feels, and reads—represents a series of conscious choices on the part of all the artists involved: playwright, director, actors, and designers. Just as a composer of a

visual elements That aspect of the *production* that communicates through what the audience sees, including stage settings, lighting, costumes, and properties, as well as the actors, their movements, and the *physical relationships* between the actors and the audience

aural elements (or **sound**) That aspect of the *production* that communicates through what the audience hears, including music, actors' voices, and sound effects produced both on and off the stage

musical piece creates harmonies, dynamics, rhythms, and melodies, so the director, working with the actors and the sound designer, makes the production develop in an aural sense so that the audience is put into the proper mood, drawn in the proper emotional direction, and captured by the proper attention points.

The previous discussion illustrates a very important consideration regarding the nature of a theatrical production—the creative choices and interplay that exist among individual production artists. As an interpretive discipline, theatre allows the artistry of an individual playwright—who has made conscious, creative choices in putting together the script—to be enhanced or altered by directors, actors, and designers as they make their own creative choices in how to translate the playwright's contribution into the actual production. In reality, what the audience sees and hears is a marvelous interplay of creative interpretations originating in the work of the playwright, even though the playwright's work may in some cases become secondary to the interpretations of those who bring it to sight and sound.

Breaking a production down or examining it by applying the concepts that we have just enumerated helps us to understand what the production is and what it does. Every play is unique in the way it explores plot, character, language, thought, sound, and visual elements. Every play is unique in terms of which of these concepts it emphasizes. As we noted earlier, some plays may dispense with one or more of these elements altogether. We can use these concepts, however, as tools to understand how the play works, whether the play is, say, a Greek classical tragedy, a Japanese Noh drama, or a modern comedy.

communication model
A model of theatre that emphasizes the *process* of *experience* and *response* on the part of the audience that comes into contact with the production

We can learn more fully what theatre is by examining it as a **communication model.** In such a model, we have a creative *process* engaged in by an artist that yields a particular *product* called an artwork—a production; that artwork generates an *experience* and *response* for those who come into contact with it. We have just examined the production or product part of the model. Let's continue by examining the artist's process and then the audience's experience and response.

THE PROCESS OF THEATRE

Theatre also is a *process:* That is, the production itself must come together from a variety of ideas, crafts, materials, and activities. As noted in the production diary chapter at the beginning of this book, months of planning, rehearsals, building, and painting are necessary before opening curtain. What happens between the time a script is conceived by the playwright and the opening night of a production constitutes the process of theatre. After a script is chosen for production, and before rehearsals begin, the director and the designers work together to analyze the script, setting goals and mapping strategies to bring it to life. Throughout this part of the production, ideas are exchanged continually. The participants refine their understandings about the play, and their discussions about meaning and bringing it to life play an ongoing role in the process. In addition, settings, costumes, and lights must be coordinated, both with each other and with acting style and movements. The director must cast the play carefully so that each role can be expressed with voices and bodies that will help the audience find meaning. Over a six- to eight-week rehearsal period before opening night, directors and actors strive to create an atmosphere of teamwork and togetherness so that the performance product will be credible and unified. A small army of craftspeople—carpenters, electricians, painters, seamstresses, and running crews—work to bring settings, costumes, and lighting designs to life. During the final rehearsals, stage, lighting, makeup, and costume crews rehearse their roles together with the actors so that scenery changes efficiently, lighting and sound cues run smoothly, actors dress properly, and hair and faces look appropriate. Throughout the preparation time, business managers purchase equipment, materials, and supplies so that the various crews receive the resources they need at the time they need them. Theatre, then, is a process consisting of the emerging ideas and physical structures that come together to form the performance or production.

THEATRE AS EXPERIENCE AND RESPONSE

Most importantly, theatre performance is an *experience* to which an audience responds. When the process becomes a production in the presence of a live audience, miraculous things occur: People often experience more of life in the time it takes for the production to run than they could ever hope to experience in that same time span outside the theatre. It is quite difficult for us to experience a theatre performance without responding in some manner. Some productions, for example, invite us to become involved in the experience so that we respond with warm affinity for the characters and their actions. In other cases, the experience may try to create distance or "alienation" in us in order to cause us to respond with detached objectivity to the characters and situations. A predictable experience and response on the part of the audience constitute a goal that the artists try to achieve. The choices that are made in putting the production together all aim at experiential results. Even in a still photograph from a production of Brecht's *Mother Courage*, for instance (Fig. 2.3), we can sense the straightforward theatricality and audience confrontation in the eye contact and gestures of the central character and the projected background.

> During the Thirty Years' War Mother Courage makes her living by selling goods to both armies. She is a survivor who makes her way through cunning and guile. However, when both her son and daughter are killed in the war, she is left alone with only her wagon and her wares. As one who profits from war, she is partly to blame for the deaths of her children, for war, and for all evil in the world. Nonetheless, she learns nothing and merely continues on with her existence.

The kind of experience and response intended by this production is one that keeps us from becoming emotionally involved. We are held at arm's length and

Figure 2.3   *Bertolt Brecht,* Mother Courage *(1937). Ball State University Theatre, 1979. Director, Don Heady; scenery and lighting, David C. Shawger. Brecht's contributions to modern theatre are discussed in Chapter 17.*

asked to give rational thought to the conditions that caused these circumstances. As neutral bystanders, we are then supposed to go out and work to eliminate such conditions in society.

The specific treatment given to each element of the production stimulates us in a particular manner. We respond to the play's structure and how it works—that is, we respond to its dynamics. We are stimulated by the language and movements and speech of the actors. Our response is shaped by the relationship of the stage space to our own and by the sets, lights, properties, and costumes. All these elements bombard us simultaneously with complex visual and aural stimuli—sights and sounds. *How* we respond—and how *much* we are able to respond—determine our ultimate reaction to and experience of the production.

Physical Response: Empathy   Perhaps the theatre is unique in its ability to stimulate our senses, because only in the theatre is there a direct appeal to our emotions and intellect through the live portrayal of other individuals. Such an experience is difficult to equal. The term we use to describe our reaction to and involvement with what we experience is **empathy**: our immediate emotional and physical response to the events that we witness.

empathy Our immediate emotional, mental, and physical *response* to events that we witness or situations in which we are not direct participants

To a certain degree and in certain circumstances, empathy is involuntary—we see and, involuntarily, we react. Empathy causes us to cry when individuals, whom we know to be actors become involved in emotional situations; empathy makes us wince when one actor slaps the face of another. In fact, we may respond physically, just as the affected stage character might. In the musical *Carnival,* for example, an orphan named Lilly comes to a seedy carnival looking for a friend of her deceased father. The friend, however, has also died, and Lilly, a vision of loveliness and innocence, finds herself alone among the rough and worldly roustabouts and performers. Eventually, she falls in love with Marco the magician, a manipulative womanizer; meanwhile, Paul—a former dancer, a wounded war hero, and now a puppeteer for whom

Tennessee Williams (II): The Tragic Tradition & Moral Values

The playwright, Williams contends, must understand crucial things about the "modern condition of his theater audience": Dramatic traditions developed as means of putting entire lives into perspective, especially in demonstrating the relationship between "human sympathies" and "moral values."

Plays in the tragic tradition offer us a view of certain moral values in violent juxtaposition. Because we do not participate, except as spectators, we can view them clearly, within the limits of our emotional equipment. These people on the stage do not return our looks. We do not have to answer their questions nor make any sign of being in company with them, nor do we have to compete with their virtues nor resist their offenses. All at once, for this reason, we are able to *see* them! Our hearts are wrung by recognition and pity, so that the dusky shell of the auditorium where we are gathered anonymously together is flooded with an almost liquid warmth of unchecked human sympathies, relieved of self-consciousness, allowed to function. . . .

Men pity and love each other more deeply than they permit themselves to know. But so successfully have we disguised from ourselves the intensity of our own feelings, the sensibility of our own hearts, that plays in the tragic tradition have begun to seem untrue. For a couple of hours we may surrender ourselves to a world of fiercely illuminated values in conflict, but when the stage is covered and the auditorium lighted, almost immediately there is a recoil of disbelief. "Well, well! " we say as we shuffle back up the aisle. . . .

> *So successfully have we disguised from ourselves the intensity of our own feelings . . . that plays in the tragic tradition have begun to seem untrue.*

As soon as we pass beneath the marquee, we have convinced ourselves once more that life has as little resemblance to the curiously stirring and meaningful occurrences on the stage as a jingle has to an elegy of Rilke.

This modern condition of his theater audience is something that an author must know in advance. The diminishing influence of life's destroyer, time, must be somehow worked into the context of his play. Perhaps it is a certain foolery, a certain distortion toward the grotesque, which will solve the problem for him. Perhaps it is only restraint, putting a mute on the strings that would like to break all bounds. But almost surely, unless he contrives in some way to relate the dimensions of his tragedy to the dimensions of a world in which time is *included*—he will be left among his magnificent debris on a dark stage, muttering to himself: "Those fools. . . ."

Lilly has gone to work—falls in love with her. At the climax of this stormy love triangle, a frustrated Paul slaps Lilly. The slap shocks Lilly, and it does the same to the audience members, whose involuntary gasps often fill the theatre. Empathy, then, is our mental and physical reaction to situations in which we are not direct participants. (Incidentally, Paul and Lilly realize in the end that they love each other, and the play ends happily.)

Sensory Response: Language   In the theatre, our sense response is triggered in a number of ways. For example, in productions with minimal scenery and language of high poetic value, what we hear becomes especially important. This is often especially true in plays written for theatre conditions that de-emphasize the **mise en scène**—that is, the setting and arrangement of all the visual elements of the production. The playwright can set the time, the place, and the atmosphere in the dialogue. Shakespeare, who wrote for just such a theatre, gives us many such descriptive details—for example, in the opening scene of *Hamlet*. As the play opens, we find Bernardo and Francisco, two guards. The hour is midnight; it is bitter cold; they are on guard; we are in Denmark; later, a ghost appears in "warlike form." How do we know all of this? The playwright gives us all this information in the dialogue:

mise en scène The setting and arrangement of all the *visual elements* of the production

(Act I, Scene 1)

BERNARDO: Who's there?

FRANCISCO: Nay, answer me. Stand and unfold yourself.

BERNARDO: Long live the king!

FRANCISCO: Bernardo?

BERNARDO: He.

FRANCISCO: You come most carefully upon your hour.

BERNARDO: 'Tis now struck twelve; get thee to bed, Francisco.

FRANCISCO: For this relief much thanks. 'Tis bitter cold, and I am sick at heart.

BERNARDO: Have you had quiet guard?

FRANCISCO: Not a mouse stirring.

BERNARDO: Well, good night. If you do meet Horatio and Marcellus,
The rivals of my watch, bid them make haste.

Enter Horatio and Marcellus

FRANCISCO: I think I hear them. Stand, ho!
Who is there?

HORATIO: Friends to this ground.

MARCELLUS: And liegemen to the Dane.

FRANCISCO: Give you good night.

MARCELLUS: O, farewell, honest soldier! Who hath relieved you?

FRANCISCO: Bernardo hath my place. Give you good night. [*Exit.*]

MARCELLUS: Holla, Bernardo!

BERNARDO: Say—
What, is Horatio there?

HORATIO: A piece of him.

BERNARDO: Welcome, Horatio; welcome, good Marcellus.

HORATIO: What, has this thing appear'd again to-night?

BERNARDO:	I have seen nothing.
MARCELLUS:	Horatio says 'tis nothing but our fantasy,
	And will not let belief take hold of him
	Touching this dreaded sight, twice seen of us;
	Therefore I have entreated him along with us to watch the minutes of this night,
	That, if again this apparition come,
	He may approve our eyes and speak to it.

Shakespeare wrote for a theatre that had no lighting instruments except the sun. As far as we know, his theatre probably used no scenery. The costumes were the street clothes of the day; the theatrical environment was the same whether the company was playing *Hamlet, Richard III,* or *The Tempest.* Play-

Figure 2.4 William Shakespeare, Hamlet (1601). *Royal Shakespeare Company, 1984. Director, Ron Daniels; scene designer, Maria Björnson. Although sometimes criticized for devoting too much of its energy to developing its "crude" source in the Elizabethan "revenge tragedy," Hamlet is also recognized as a powerful combination of psychological, philosophical, and dramatic themes. One eminent student of the classical drama has summarized as follows the points of similarity and difference between Hamlet and the classic Greek tragedies that we introduce more fully in Chapters 4 and 15:*

> *. . . Greek tragedy presents sudden and complete disaster, or one disaster linked to another in linear fashion, while Shakespearean tragedy presents the complex, menacing spread of ruin. . . . At least one explanation . . . is that the Greek poets thought of the tragic error as the breaking of a divine law . . . while Shakespeare saw it as an evil quality which, once it has broken loose, will feed on itself and on anything else that it can find until it reaches its natural end.*

Compare this interpretation with Aristotle's description of Greek tragedy in Chapter 15.

What Is Theatre?

wrights writing for conditions like these needed to use language to create many of the effects that we might expect scene, costume, and lighting designers to provide. Language thus became a source for creating sensory response through the imagination of the audience. (Shakespeare and the English Renaissance theatre are discussed more fully in Chapter 16.)

Sensory Response: Visual Stimuli   We also respond to what we see. For example, a sword fight performed with elaborate action, swift movements, and great intensity may set us on the edge of our seats. Although we know that the action is staged and the incident fictitious, we can easily be caught up in the excitement of the moment. We respond in many different ways to events of quite different dynamic quality: The intense but subtle movements of the actors, pulling us here and pushing us there emotionally, may cause us to leave the theatre feeling as if a rock were resting in our stomach. Although we cannot illustrate physical action in a textbook figure, even in a still photograph like the one in Figure 2.5, we find ourselves beginning to respond as the two bound prisoners struggle forward before the dagger. In this illustration, the careful arrangement of the actors evokes a response from us—the director has chosen to create a diagonal line, a device that generally evokes a response of motion and action.

In Figure 2.6 the platforms zigzag backward to create depth of space and to suggest formality and universality by their openness and lack of specific location. The play illustrated here is Henrik Ibsen's *Peer Gynt*—a blend of reality and fantasy about a man who avoids life's decisions by skillfully skirting issues. Although the play is a satire of Norwegian life, the choice of a nondepictive setting suggests that there is more to be seen here than a story about a particular man in Norway. We are invited to respond to this set of visual stimuli with an understanding that would allow the play to suggest a larger reality than the mere facts of its story.

Another way that visual stimuli evoke responses is through the relationship between the size of the settings and the height of the actors. In Figures 2.7A–2.7D (pages 50 and 51), for example, we find different relationships among actors and settings in terms of *scale*—that is, the relationship of the size of the set to the size of the human form. Each of these factors helps to place the actors in a different relationship with their surroundings. Those examples in which the settings tower over the actors suggest to us that humankind exists in a subordinate positon to the rest of the world. Those in which humans seem larger than life suggest that very conclusion—that humanity is the significant force in the universe. Neutrality of scale may suggest neutrality of relationship. These are the images chosen by artists, and we are invited to respond to their ideas.

The central question here is: *How* do visual stimuli translate into specific kinds of sensory and emotional responses? Unfortunately, that question does not have a concise or a scientific answer. Much of the stimulus–response activity that the production attempts to foster is based on generalized common experience. Such common experience concludes, for example, that curved lines evoke a "softer" response than straight lines, and that reds, yellows, and

Figure 2.5 *Shakespeare,* Titus Andronicus (1593). *Adams Memorial Shakespearean Theatre, 1990. One of Shakespeare's earliest (and bloodiest) tragedies,* Titus Andronicus *is often considered rather "crude" by certain standards. It was, however, quite popular among Shakespeare's own audiences, and as is evident in Jan Kott's essay on "Shakespeare Our Contemporary" in Chapter 17, its combination of effects and defects has appealed to such influential contemporary interpreters of Shakespeare as Peter Brook.*

Figure 2.6 *Henrik Ibsen,* Peer Gynt (1867). *University of Arizona Theatre. Scene design by Robert C. Burroughs. The importance of Ibsen to the modern theatre, which is discussed more fully in Chapter 17, is evident in the thoughts about his play* An Enemy of the People *expressed by playwright Arthur Miller in this chapter.*

Figure 2.7A *Aeschylus,* The Eumenides. *Scene design, C. Ricketts. The* Eumenides *is part of a three-part tragic trilogy called the Oresteia (ca. 458 B.C.), which is summarized in Chapter 5. Aeschylus is discussed in Chapter 15.*

Figure 2.7B William Shake-speare, Richard II (1595), Act II, Scene 2: Entrance into St. Stephen's Chapel. *London,* 1857. Producer, Charles Kean; design, William Telbin. *A synopsis of* Richard II *can be found in Chapter 4. For more on Kean's famous mid-19th-century productions of Shakespeare, see Chapter 16, especially at Fig. 16.18; certain excesses of Shakespearean production during the era are chronicled in Harold Child's essay in that chapter.*

What Is Theatre?

Figure 2.7C *Shakespeare,* Hamlet. *Charles Fechter's revival, Lyceum Theatre, London, 1864. Design by William Telbin.*

Figure 2.7D Oscar Wilde, The Importance of Being Earnest *(1895). University of Arizona Theatre. Director, William Lange; costume designer, Helen, Workman Curie; scenic and lighting designer, Dennis J. Sporre. A synopsis of* The Importance of Being Earnest *can be found in* Chapter *3.*

oranges evoke "warmth" while blues and greens evoke "coolness." These are situations that artists sense, and the results depend heavily on the respondent. For our purposes here, perhaps the best we can do is to raise this theoretical issue and be aware that what happens visually in the performance does have an effect on us and is designed to help us respond in the way the artists desire.

How Theatre Functions

In Chapter 1 we examined four of the *functions* of art. Now that we have examined theatre as an entity—what the word means, theatre as a form of art, and the theatre as a communication model—we can elaborate on its functions. Although we can point specifically to this function or that, probably no art-work—theatre included—functions strictly in any one category. We can isolate the functions of entertainment, social awareness, therapy, and/or artifacts, but we do so mostly for convenience and for introductory purposes. As we speak of entertainment, however, we will discover that "teaching" about life can also occur; and when we discuss a theatre work as an artifact, we see that "teaching" can again take place. Therefore, although we highlight specific functions in the next section, you should be alert to the fact that highlighting specific functions does not imply that they are mutually exclusive or that they occur in isolation from one another. A play produced to function primarily as entertainment, for example, may teach serious lessons about life and at the same time function as an artifact that tells us something about the changing nature of human behavior and human society.

THEATRE AS ENTERTAINMENT

The function that we find most familiar is that of entertainment. On first reading, some people may find the term *entertainment* troublesome because the word has come to mean something less than profound or lacking in seriousness. It is often associated with popular culture—films, rock concerts, television, and other outlets to which we turn for the light diversions traditionally called "entertainment." In the theatre, musicals and light comedies might seem to meet such an expectation. Nonetheless, theatre, including its serious, "higher" genres, has traditionally upheld its purpose "to teach and to entertain"—by which practitioners usually mean to teach *through* entertainment.

Theatre, of course, is more than a lecture: It teaches us about life, and does so effectively—because its *form*—everything that goes into the theatre production and experience as we have described them—is entertaining. At the risk of sending mixed messages about quality in theatrical artworks, we should thus remind ourselves that even the most serious students of the theatre recognize that some productions are more profound than others. Some plays, of course, are entertaining without offering much substance about human behavior. At the same time, although such an assertion might lead us to question what we really mean by "entertainment," some profound plays, classic tragedies as well as contemporary comedies, also entertain us. *Entertainment* is a broad enough term to include all types of theatre, including tragedies or dramas that treat unpleasant subjects. These types of plays can also entertain us—not in the sense of giving us a frivolous time but, rather, by engaging us and simply keeping us *interested*. When we are engaged and interested, we *are* entertained. Good productions of all types of theatre can and do meet such a definition.

THEATRE AS THERAPY

To understand theatre as therapy, we need to decondition ourselves from the conventional implications of the word *therapy*. Although the therapeutic function of theatre does have clinical implications, that function has further ramifications as well. In such a situation, called *psychodrama,* theatre functions as a device whereby mentally disturbed patients can act out personal problems and relationships in order to find the root of their illness. But, a broader application of the concept of therapy is also available. Moving slightly

What Is Theatre?

away from clinical applications, theatre can be, and often is, used as a specific therapy for its participants. For the playwright as for all artists, involvement in the theatre can be a means of coping with personal difficulties. In fact, art as a release from personal illness has a long history quite apart from that of art as a release for the respondent. For example, many people take up painting, music, sculpture, ceramics, and so on as "release valves" for the stress of everyday life, much as people do who exercise as a stress-reducing therapy. As respondents, however, we can also gain from the health-giving nature of theatre. Aristotle notes in the *Poetics,* for example, that tragedy has the power to purge the soul of pity and fear—aspects of mental health that affect even modern people. By witnessing the tragedies of kings and heroes, the audience could supposedly be healed of these troubles. (Aristotle's thoughts on the form of tragedy are presented more fully in Chapter 15.) How this healing occurs—and the conditions of drama that cause it—may be debatable on a theoretical level, but common experience again indicates clearly that there are circumstances in the theatre that can cause us to come away with a sense of refreshment and restoration. Comedy, likewise, theoretically has the potential to heal us through the lighthearted revelation of our personal and social foibles. Of course, laughter can be present in comedy, drama, tragedy, or any of theatre's many types. Thus we have a healing—therapeutic—function present on many levels: patient, artist, and audience.

THEATRE AS SOCIAL AND POLITICAL WEAPON

Throughout history, theatre has been used as a social and political weapon. Rather than—or in addition to—teaching us to see reality more clearly, theatre can take on an *advocacy* function. Sometimes, that position means stirring the audience to strong social and political action outside the theatre. Sometimes, it means fostering awareness of or sympathy for a cause or condition. Although the propagandistic theatre of various cultures can be seen as a social and political weapon, the use of theatre as a weapon is not limited to those circumstances. In a play like Clifford Odets' *Waiting for Lefty,* for example, the theatre becomes a platform for support of the New York taxi strike in the 1930s (see Chapter 17 for a plot synopsis). The play was written to stir a response to a current event, and it did so effectively. Although written for a specific occasion, however, Odets' play also retains the capacity to incite an audience today. I have seen several productions of this play, and in almost every case, the audience has responded to the outrages described by joining the actors in shouting "STRIKE! STRIKE! STRIKE!"

Bertolt Brecht's "Epic Theatre" (see Chapter 17) purposely tries not to entertain but rather to "alienate" audiences so that they will view the production experience objectively and without emotional involvement and will be moved to respond "properly" outside the theatre. In 18th-century England, John Gay's *Beggar's Opera* (1728; Fig. 2.8)—a story about common thieves and their hero—satirized the upper classes (who were just as crooked but did not suffer the same punishments). It pointed such an accusing finger at the

Figure 2.8   John Gay, The Beggar's Opera (1728). *Cambridge Drama Festival at Sander's Theatre, Harvard University, 1953. See also Chapter 16, especially at Fig. 16.12.*

British Prime Minister that it proved at least a partial factor in stimulating Parliament to pass the Licensing Act of 1737, which effectively censored all professional theatre productions in London for almost a century (see Chapter 16).

THEATRE AS ARTIFACT

Finally, theatre may also function as a doorway to other times and other cultures. For example, when we witness the production of a play written in a time or place other than our own, our initial response is contemporary—the play speaks to *us* in *our* present circumstances: It reveals to us aspects of human behavior that enable us to grow, to understand, and to become more human. The experience is, so to speak, in the "present tense." Theatre, however, can also function as a lesson in history and culture. It can provide us with an important understanding of our place in history at the same time that it teaches us about history.

In *Everyman,* an example from the Middle Ages (see Chapter 15), Everyman, summoned by Death to his final judgment, asks Fellowship, Cousin, and Goods to accompany him. They all refuse. He also enlists Good Deeds, who is too weak from neglect. After seeking the counsel of Knowledge, Everyman does penance—an act that revives Good Deeds. Along the way, Strength, Discretion, Beauty, and the Five Wits also desert Everyman. The rejuvenated Good Deeds, however, remains steadfast to the end. From plays like *Every-*

Arthur Miller (II): The Playwright as Individualist

In adapting An Enemy of the People *some 80 years after it was first written, Miller argued the need to interpret Ibsen's social and moral thought in terms of the history that his own audience had actually experienced—the thought that the audience, too, would bring to the theatre.*

There are a few speeches [in *An Enemy of the People*], and one scene in particular, which have been taken to mean that Ibsen was a fascist. In the original meeting scene in which Dr. Stockmann sets forth his—and Ibsen's—point of view most completely and angrily, Dr. Stockmann makes a speech in which he turns to biology to prove that there are indeed certain individuals "bred" to a superior apprehension of truths and who have the natural right to lead, if not to govern, the mass.

If the entire play is to be understood as the working-out of this speech, then one has no justification for contending that it is other than racist and fascist—certainly it could not be thought of as a defense of any democratic idea. But, structurally speaking, the theme is not wholly contained in the meeting scene alone. In fact, this speech is in some important respects in contradiction to the actual dramatic working-out of the play. But that Ibsen never really believed that idea in the first place is amply proved by a speech he delivered to a workers' club after the production of *An Enemy of the People.* He said then: "Of course I do not mean the aristocracy of birth, or of the purse, or even the aristocracy of the intellect. I mean the aristocracy of character, of will, of mind—that alone can free us."

I have taken as justification for removing those examples which no longer prove the theme—examples I believe Ibsen would have removed were he alive today—the line in the original manuscript that reads: "There is no established truth that can remain true for more than seventeen, eighteen, at most twenty years."

> . . . *The line in the original manuscript . . . reads: "There is no established truth that can remain true for more than seventeen, eighteen, at most twenty years."*

In light of genocide, the holocaust that has swept our world on the wings of the black ideology of racism, it is inconceivable that Ibsen would insist today that certain individuals are by breeding, or race, or "innate" qualities superior to others or possessed of the right to dictate to others. The man who wrote *A Doll's House,* the clarion call for the equality of women, cannot be equated with a fascist. The whole cast of his thinking was such that he could not have lived a day under an authoritarian regime of any kind. He was an individualist sometimes to the point of anarchism, and in such a man there is too explosive a need for self-expression to permit him to conform to any rigid ideology. It is impossible, therefore, to set him beside Hitler. . . .

Throughout the play I have tried to peel away its trappings of the moment, its relatively accidental details which ring the dull green tones of Victorianism, and to show that beneath them there still lives the terrible wrath of Henrik Ibsen, who could make a play as men make watches, precisely, intelligently, and telling not merely the minute and the hour but the age.

Figure 2.9   *Henrik Ibsen,* A Doll's House, *New York Shake-speare Festival, 1975. Director, Tormod Skagestad; scenic design, Santo Loquasto; costume design, Theoni V. Aldredge. Sam Waterston as Torvald and Liv Ullman as Nora. First produced in 1879, A Doll's House dwelt on the themes of individual freedom of expression and social conformism in the story of a young wife who succumbs to various forms of enslavement—financial, intellectual, emotional—to the men in her life. The character of Nora retains as much relevance as she did when the play was first produced and touched off the heated controversy over "Ibsenism" and the theatre as a venue for social criticism.*

man, we learn about the spiritual concerns of the Middle Ages and the medieval Christian view of worldliness, good, and evil. In *A Doll's House* (Fig. 2.9), the actions of Ibsen's heroine reveal in graphic detail the role of women in the late 19th-century Europe, as Nora struggles to become more than just a "doll"—a role that she has fulfilled for both her father and her husband. A past indiscretion—forging her husband's name to a loan application and thereby saving his life—places her in a position from which she must decide whether to continue in her previous role or leave her husband and strike out on her own. In productions of plays from historic times and different cultures, the performance acts as an *artifact*—as an object that we can examine as a product of its time and by which we come to know that time and, perhaps, to know our own more fully as well.

SUMMARY

• Because theatre is a branch of the *humanities* and a form of the *fine arts*, it can be described in terms of the creative processes and functions of both. In this sense, *theatre* is *aesthetic communication* through the art and production of dramatic expression. The Greek *theatron* means "a place for seeing," and the theatre experience is largely a *visual experience*.

• Theatre is an *interpretive discipline:* Between the playwright and audience are individual artists—actors, directors, designers—who contribute to the communication of the playwright's *script* through specific artistic activities. Theatre is thus *aesthetic communication* that uses primarily the *live performer* to "design" time, sound, and three-dimensional space into a *production*.

• The *production* is the actual *theatre artwork* that has been constructed by a group of artists using certain "tools." In the *Poetics*, Aristotle first identified those tools as *plot, character, diction, music, thought,* and *spectacle.* As a contemporary treatment of these terms, this book defines them as follows:

> The *script* (Aristotle's "plot") is the text through which the playwright uses language to communicate a play's structure and meaning; the script is generally written and should not be equated with the *theatre artwork. Language*—through which the playwright initially communicates such things as style, theme, and character—is an aspect of the script.
>
> *Character* refers to the psychological motivations of the persons introduced into the play through the script; note that this is not the same sense in which, conventionally, one refers to a "character" as a particular individual who appears in the play.
>
> The "intellectual content" of the play, which includes its themes, ideas, and perceptions about human experience, is its *thought;* "thought" is what the play is *about;* it can generally be considered to originate with the playwright, but it is interpreted in production by everyone involved in creating the theatre artwork.
>
> The production's *visual elements* (Aristotle's "spectacle") include everything that the audience sees—settings, lighting, costumes, and properties; the actors and their movements, as well as the *physical relationships* established between the actors and the audience, also function as visual elements; what Aristotle called "spectacle" is also sometimes called *mise en scène*—that is, the setting and arrangement of the visual elements of a production.
>
> *Aural elements* (Aristotle's "music") are the different *sounds* that are arranged in the production; they consist of everything the audience hears, including background music, actors' voices, and sound effects.

• Understanding what a "production" *does* means understanding that it results from the creative choices of numerous artists who constantly exchange ideas; that is why a *script* can remain essentially the same while every *production* differs in the way the play's elements (script, character, and so on) are interpreted. Theatre can thus be regarded as a *communication model* if we emphasize that it is a *process* of *experience* and *response* on the part of the audience that comes into contact with the finished theatre artwork.

• The goal of the theatre *process,* which includes the numerous activities that go into the production, is a reasonably predictable *experience* and *response* on the part of the audience. *Physical response* includes *empathy*—an emotional and mental, as well as physical, response to situations in which the audience members are not direct participants. *Sensory response* can be response to both language and *visual stimuli.*

• As a form of artistic expression, theatre performs the same functions as other *media of expression:* as *entertainment, therapy, social and political weapon,* and *artifact.*

Understanding *and* Evaluating Plays *and* Performances

***A*fter studying this chapter, you should be able to:**

- Explain the basic principles for organizing your *analysis* and *judgment* of an artwork in the theatre.

- Identify *characters, facts, setting, parts,* and *personality* as aspects to consider beyond your *first impressions* of a play.

- Identify *plot, character, language, thought,* and *aural and visual elements* as the principal *parts* of a play.

- Explain the difference between *plot* and "story line" and describe the ten elements that constitute plot.

- Understand what is meant by the *style* or *personality* of a play and describe *classicism, romanticism, realism,* and *expressionism* as some of the important stylistic types in the theatre.

- Define *criticism* and discuss the important functions of criticism in the theatre.

- Discuss certain *criteria* for making *judgments* about your experience with artworks in the theatre.

Le Principe du Plaisir, 1937. *Sotheby's.*

*I*n this chapter, we will look in greater depth at how plays and productions are put together, how we can use the tools described in Chapter 2 to understand plays and productions and their parts, and how we can approach plays and productions so that, ultimately, we can evaluate them. First, we will discuss several factors that help us to approach the play—factors such as understanding our first impressions and going beyond them, understanding the facts of the play, understanding the play's setting, understanding the play and its parts, and finding the play's personality. Then we will discuss the process of critical evaluation and value judgment.

Approaching *the* Play

Our experience of theatre and drama comes in two forms. The first is that prompted by a *production*. In this capacity, we must pay attention to all of the elements that make up the production—plot, character, language, thought, and aural and visual elements. We may also approach a play through its script—that is, by *reading* a play. In doing this, of course, we must use our own imaginations to supply the aural and visual elements. We are also free to place our own interpretation on the playwright's work—something that the director does for us in the production. Moreover, whereas we have the advantage of applying critical analysis to the script because we can pause and reflect, the play in production—though illuminated by the director's vision—passes by us in an instant. Approaching the script, therefore, is often easier because we are less dependent on our perceptual skills and better able to find literary nuances: We can reread a passage that may seem obscure or look up an unfamiliar word in the dictionary—a luxury that we do not have when viewing a production.

We can approach both the script of a play and its production in such a way as to identify just about every aspect of our immediate, "gut" reactions to technical requirements, mood, time, place, structure, and style. In fact, our initial reaction may be the most important response that we have to a play. In that experience, what the play is and what we are combine to create a unique set of impressions. Only when we consciously ask questions about the play and try to answer them do we go beyond our first response and begin the process of analysis.

Natural response and conscious analysis, of course, are not totally separate processes. In fact, people with extensive background and experience in the arts still usually begin the process of analysis with their first experience, even if they try consciously to avoid doing so. For thorough analysis, then, it is important that we approach the play on first experience with an open mind, trying temporarily to put aside any analytical judgments. It is important to try to capture our first impressions of a play and to hold on to them for later use in developing *formal* analysis. When we have completed reading a play, or when a production ends, we need to take time to examine what we *feel* about it. We should ask ourselves: Did I like the play? Did I find it dull or exciting or just so-so? *Why* did I feel that way? Was I amused or depressed? Was I truly interested in the outcome, or was that less important than the believability of the characters? Did I feel that I know people like these, or did I find them larger than life—*types* rather than individuals? Were the issues raised by the play outside my range of experience? Asking questions like these can put us in touch with first impressions that remain just that—*first* impressions: They should be developed through more reading and more thought and, however vivid they may be, by *analysis*.

When we conduct analysis, we modify our natural responses and find more complex meanings in plays. We also discover the sort of details that make possible useful and accurate criticism. Both first impressions and analysis are important. We must learn to appreciate both, to store each while dealing with the other, and to recall both vividly when we are ready to prepare our final criticism.

Understanding Beyond *the* First Experience

Going beyond first impressions involves several considerations: first, understanding our reactions to the *characters* in the play; second, understanding the *facts* of the play; third, understanding *setting;* fourth, understanding the *play and its parts;* and, finally, understanding the *personality* of the play.

UNDERSTANDING CHARACTERS

Our natural response to a play usually involves our attitude toward the *people* in that play—generally toward some character on whom we are led to focus. Do we like that person? Do we like other people in the play? The important question is: Do we like the character more or less significantly than his or her actions and motivations warrant? Some of the best-drawn and most important characters in plays are villains—for example, Iago in Shakespeare's *Othello.* Iago, Othello's supposed friend and confidant, is jealous of Othello's love for Desdemona. With evil guile, he manipulates the people around him and makes it appear that Desdemona has been unfaithful. He thus plays upon Othello's weakness—*his* jealousy—and creates the circumstances in response to which the previously noble Othello (Figure 3.1), in a rage, kills his wife. As evil as Iago is, his character is a fascinating one, and we are drawn to it regardless of our feelings about him as a person. We may dislike Iago on a moral level, but we appreciate him as, artistically, a fully realized character. The same may be said for another of Shakespeare's characters—Macbeth

(Figs. 3.2A–3.2C). Here we have a central figure whom we follow throughout the play and whose character is terribly flawed. His murderous acts to gain the throne and his manipulation by his ambitious wife, Lady Macbeth (Fig. 3.2D), show us his lack of moral courage. Despite the fact that Macbeth is less than admirable, our interest in his complex character—the motivating forces that cause him to act as he does in these specific circumstances—draws us to him with fascination. The same may be said for our fascination with Lady Macbeth. Her evil ambitions, overpowering compulsions, and ultimate destruction

Figure 3.1   *James Earl Jones as Othello and Diane Weist as Desdemona in a 1981 production of William Shakespeare's Othello (1604). In addition to Othello, Jones has played Macbeth and King Lear for the New York Shakespeare Festival. The question of Othello's race has, of course, been addressed by every generation of the play's critics and producers. Margaret Webster (see Chapter 16), herself a lifelong interpreter of Shakespeare both on stage and in print, has argued that "Othello is the most human of [Shakespeare's] four great tragedies. There are no ghosts, no inexplicable convulsions of nature. . . . There is human passion . . . raised to its highest pitch and forged to a white heat of dramatic action."*

Figure 3.2A   *Scene design for Macbeth, Royal Shakespeare Company, 1982–83. Director, Howard Davis; scenic designer, Chris Dyer; costume designer, Peggy Mitchell.*

Figure 3.2B   *Shakespeare,* Macbeth (1606): The Three Witches. *Utah Shakespeare Festival, 1989. Director, Howard Jensen; scenic designer, Ron Ranson, Jr.; costume designer, Rosemary Ingham.*

Figure 3.2C   *Shakespeare,* Macbeth: The Setting. *Utah Shakespeare Festival, 1989. Director, Howard Jensen; scenic designer, Ron Ranson, Jr.*

Figure 3.2D   *Ellen Terry as Lady Macbeth. The most popular English actress of her day, Terry (see Fig. 9.9) was noted for the complete naturalism that she brought to a variety of Shakespearean roles. In making two vicious murderers husband and wife, Shakespeare goes a long way toward humanizing the main characters of* Macbeth *by focusing on the psychological motivations behind utterly evil actions performed by two people mutually committed to a fiendish pact. Characterized alternatively as a malevolent visionary and the pawn of a remorseless fate, Lady Macbeth is easily one of Shakespeare's most coveted female roles.*

give us powerful reasons to sympathize with her even as we despise her actions. On first impression, we may tend to like such figures more than their actions and motivations warrant because their characters are so skillfully drawn.

UNDERSTANDING THE FACTS OF THE PLAY

Analysis must also illuminate the *facts* of the play—that is, the literal facts from which the play was constructed. In one sense, we can call the facts of the play its "story." "Facts" are not the plot, which is far more complex than

Figure 3.3　Oscar Wilde, The Importance of Being Earnest. *Utah Shake-spearean Festival, 1990. Director, Malcolm Morrison; scenic designer, John Iacovelli; costume designer, James Berton Harris.*

the storyline and which makes up the *structure* of the play. But we must know the facts of the story in order to understand fully *how* the playwright has developed the plot. Consider, for example, some of the facts that make up the story of Oscar Wilde's *The Importance of Being Earnest* (see Fig. 3.3 above and synopsis below):

The Importance of Being Earnest

OSCAR WILDE

A handsome young man is leading a double life. In London, he calls himself Ernest; in the country, Jack. At his country estate, where the play is set, he is the austere and proper guardian of an attractive young lady named Cecily. In London, however, he is involved with and proposes marriage to Gwendolyn. A friend of our hero comes to the country, falls in love with Cecily, and proposes to her. When Gwendolyn arrives at the country house, both she and Cecily complicate the lads' lives when they insist that they can only marry a man named Ernest. Through the interference of Gwendolyn's mother and the confessions of a former nanny, the true pasts of all parties are revealed, and the play ends happily.

Although the facts summarize for us what happens and who is involved, they tell us virtually nothing about the way the play is structured or how the playwright works the revelations and crises into a perfectly arranged pyramidal structure that rises from exposition to climax and tapers down through the denouement. Without knowing the facts, however, we would be hard-pressed to find the proper character relationships and to identify the central character who drives the plot.

UNDERSTANDING SETTING

setting As a *fact* of the play, the playwright's use of time and place to communicate theme and tone through the play's environment

Playwrights normally give careful attention to *time* and *place,* the two elements of **setting.** We must thus be sure that we understand the ramifications of what may seem at first like a straightforward extension of what we have just described as the "facts." Setting is more than that. Time and place, for example, often support important, although sometimes subtle, themes. Some playwrights are explicit about setting; others are noncommittal, leaving it almost entirely up to the ingenuity of the designer or director. As audience members, however, we have a need to know: The nature of the setting tells us something not only about the people who inhabit it but also about the nature of the production itself. For example, in a highly *realistic* setting such as Peggy Kelner's design for Rudolf Besier's *The Barretts of Wimpole Street* (Fig. 3.4), we sense the formality and order of the family, their social class, and the historical period in which the play is set. In turn, that understanding implies certain expectations of behavior from the characters: People behaved differently then than they do now. If we look carefully at the setting for Arthur Kopit's *Indians,* illustrated in Figures 3.5A and 3.5B, we discover quite a different set of circumstances. To begin with, although the setting does not depict a particular place, it does suggest a general theme and tone. *Where* we are in this play about Buffalo Bill is far less important to the audience's perceptions than the *feeling* that the audience has about the environment in which the action takes place. Furthermore, there is nothing in this setting to help the audience understand the background and motivation of the major character. What is important is the setting's statement about the *style* of the production.

UNDERSTANDING THE PLAY AND ITS PARTS

In Chapter 2, we introduced six parts of a play and/or production to use as a tool for understanding: *plot, character, language, thought, aural elements,* and *visual elements.* Because they give us a basic outline that we can use to structure our understanding of a play or production efficiently and effectively, we will now look at them in more detail. They offer touchstones to help us see and hear what is happening in a script and/or on stage. Let's examine each of these parts in order.

Figure 3.4   *Rudolf Besier,* The Barretts of Wimpole Street. *University of Arizona Theatre. Director,* Peter R. Marroney; *scenic and costume designer Peggy Kellner; lighting designer, Jeffrey L. Warburton.*

Figure 3.5A   *Arthur Kopit,* Indians *(1968). University of Arizona Theatre. Director, Robert C. Burroughs; scenic designer, Dennis J. Sporre; costume designer, Helen Currie; lighting design, John Lafferty.*

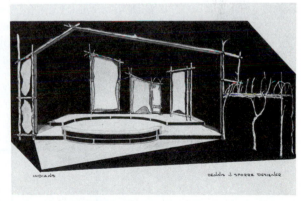

Figure 3.5B   *Kopit,* Indians. *University of Arizona Theatre. Scenic design rendering by Dennis J. Sporre.*

Understanding *and* Evaluating Plays *and* Performances

plot The *structure* of the play, which determines its story movement, its conflict development, and its resolution

Plot Simply put, **plot** is the *structure* of the play. As noted earlier, it includes but is far more than the *story line*. We might think of plot as the "skeleton" of the play—the element that gives it shape and on which the other elements hang so as to flesh out the final creature. The nature of the plot determines how a play *works*—how it moves from one moment to another, how conflicts are structured, and how the experience finally comes to an end. We can think of plot as consisting of ten elements:

1. *exposition,*
2. *point of attack,*
3. *complication,*
4. *inciting incident,*
5. *denouement,*

6. *crisis,*
7. *climax,*
8. *foreshadowing*
9. *discovery,* and
10. *reversal.*

We will define each of these terms in the sections that follow.

We can examine the workings of plot by seeing the play as a timeline that begins as the script or production begins and ends at the final curtain or the end of the script. At this point, however, let's think of this diagram as a sort of road map of a journey that has a beginning, a middle, and an end. At any point in the play, we should have a sense of how things are working out. We know where we started, where we are going, and where in the journey we are at any given moment. In many plays, plot tends to operate as a climactic pyramid (Fig. 3.6). In order to hold our attention, the dynamics of the play will rise in intensity until they reach the ultimately intense crisis—the *climax*—after which moment they will relax through a resolution called the *denouement* to the end of the play.

Depending on the playwright's purpose, plot may be shaped with or without some of the features to be noted here. In some plays, plot may be so deemphasized that it virtually disappears. When we evaluate a play critically, however, the elements of plot give us things to look for—sometimes if only to note that they do not exist.

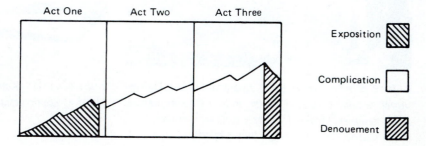

Figure 3.6 Hypothetical dynamic and structural development of a three-act play.

Understanding *and* Evaluating Plays *and* Performances

exposition Aspect of *plot* in which the playwright provides background information

Exposition   **Exposition** is that part of a play in which the playwright provides necessary background information: It introduces the people of the play, their characters, relationships, backgrounds, and present situation. Although different playwrights use different devices for providing exposition, it is frequently a recognizable section at the beginning of the play. Exposition can be presented through dialogue, narration, setting, lighting, costume, or any other device that the playwright or director chooses.

At some point in the play this background material must give way to the story. The point at which the playwright choose to enjoin the story is called the **point of attack.** The amount of exposition depends on where the playwright takes up the story. A play that is told chronologically, like many of Shakespeare's plays, may need little expository material. On the other hand, Greek tragedies require a good bit of summary before the current story can be engaged.

point of attack Aspect of *plot* in which background *exposition* gives way to the development of the story

Complication   Drama is *conflict*. Although not every play may satisfy that definition, conflict of some sort is a fundamental and effective dramatic device if a play is to interest an audience. At some point in the play, the normally expected course of events must be frustrated. Such frustration generally gives the audience a reason to be interested in what transpires. At a specific moment, the playwright provides an action or a decision that upsets the current state of affairs. That moment, sometimes called the **inciting incident,** opens the middle part of the plot—the *complication*. The **complication** is the meat of the play, comprising a series of conflicts or *crises* that rise in intensity until they reach a turning point—the *climax*—that constitutes the end of the complication section.

inciting incident Moment in the *plot* at which an action or decision upsets the current state of affairs

complication Part of the *plot* comprising a series of conflicts or *crises* that increase in intensity

Denouement   The **denouement** is the final resolution of the plot, which can take various forms and occupy various lengths of time. The denouement is the period of time during which the audience is allowed to sense that the action is ending; it is a period of adjustment, downward in intensity, from the climax. Ideally, the denouement brings about a clear and ordered resolution.

denouement Final resolution of the *plot*, lower in intensity than the *climax*

Exposition, complication, and denouement make up the timeframe within which the remaining parts of the play operate. Before we continue, however, we need to understand that the neat structural picture of plot described by this discussion of exposition, complication, and denouement will not be so neat in many plays. However, the fact that a play does not conform to this particular plot structure does not mean that it is poorly constructed or of inferior quality. Nor does that fact negate the usefulness of understanding and using these concepts as a means for describing and analyzing how a play is put together.

crisis Point in the *plot* at which events or forces require of characters that decisions be made or actions taken

Crisis   As we have seen, drama can be seen as conflict: Throughout the play there occur events or forces that disrupt the flow of action. Normally, these events or forces put one or more characters into situations in which decisions must be made or actions taken. The moment when such a circumstance occurs is a **crisis.** There may be any number of crises, and taken together, they make up the *complication section*.

Climax   At some point, of course, all these crises must come to a halt: The audience cannot handle any more conflicts, and the play, after all, must end. This ultimate crisis, which puts the disruption to an end in one way or another, is called the **climax.** It is the peak of the action, the pinnacle of the pyramid in Figure 3.6.

Foreshadowing   Preparation for subsequent action helps the audience to understand clearly where they are at all times. That preparation is called **foreshadowing,** and it operates in several ways. First, it provides credibility for future events by keeping the action logical and avoiding confusion. Second, foreshadowing builds tension and suspense: The audience is allowed to sense that something is about to happen, but because they do not know exactly what or when, anticipation builds suspense and tension. In the movie *Jaws,* for example, a rhythmic musical theme foreshadows the presence of the shark. Then, just when the audience has become comfortable with that device, the shark suddenly appears without the musical motif. As a result, tension and uncertainty as to the next shark attack are heightened immensely. Third, foreshadowing moves the play forward by pointing toward events that will occur later.

Discovery   Discovery is the revelation of information about characters, their personalities, relationships, and feelings. In *Oedipus the King* (summarized later in this chapter), when Oedipus discovers the truth about himself, that discovery motivates his final actions; in *Tartuffe* (see summary on page 87), the other characters, especially Orgon, discover the truth about the character of Tartuffe; in *The Importance of Being Earnest,* everyone discovers everything about everybody else. In fact, discovery through the resolution of mistaken identity provides the thread on which numerous plays are hung. This is especially true in comedy, although tragedy also uses the device—for example, in Aeschylus' *Libation Bearers,* when Electra recognizes her brother by a lock of hair and matching footprints. Hamlet discovers from his father's ghost that his father was murdered by his uncle Claudius and is urged to avenge the killing— a discovery without which the play cannot proceed. The skill of the playwright in *structuring* the revelation of such information in large part determines the overall impact of the play on the audience.

Reversal   Reversal is any turn of fortune. For example, Oedipus falls from power and prosperity to blindness and exile; King Lear goes from monarch to madness. In comedy, reversal often changes the roles of social classes, as peasants jump to the upper class and vice versa.

Character   As we noted in Chapter 2, the term **character** can mean a number of different things. We generally call the individuals of the play its "*characters.*" We can also think of character as including the social and physical aspects of the people in the play. Then there are *stock characters*—character types like tragic heroes, witty servants, and braggart soldiers, to name just a few. In addition, of course, plays have "major" characters and "minor" characters. Thus, the word *character* can be applied to the people of the play in a variety of ways. However, perhaps the most significant of these applications

climax End of the *complication* and turning point in the series of *plot crises* so that conflicts come to an end

foreshadowing Preparation for subsequent action that keeps the audience clear about *plot* development

discovery Aspect of the *plot* in which information is revealed about characters, their relationships, and so forth

reversal Any turn of fortune during the development of the *plot*

character Aspect of the play consisting of the psychological motivations of the persons in it

refers to the motivating psychological forces of the people of the play. In this sense, character is what makes people tick; it causes them to react as they do when faced with a crisis. That, in essence, is what theatre is all about: examining why people make the choices they make in a variety of circumstances. For example, if we should find a bag of money on the sidewalk, our "character" will dictate whether we keep it or turn it over to the police. "Character" determines whether we accept the failure that accompanies our lack of preparation for an exam or whether we cheat. Drama deals with choices made in conflict; as different motivations drive different people to different paths of response, character is the key factor that we examine in order to learn lessons about human lives like our own.

In analyzing a play, we isolate the central motivating force of the persons in the play and describe and analyze what decisions they made, why they made them, and how those decisions shaped both the forward progress of the play and the decisions of other persons. Whose character is dominant? Whose play is it? Is the play's action and environment shaped by the character of one person or another? As we noted in Chapter 1, we must recognize that even though the people in a play may look, act, and sound like real individuals, they are not "real" people: They are *imitations* of people, and their characters are *imitations* of human character. Human character is far too complex to be portrayed realistically on stage. No audience could follow the intricacies of motivation and the complexities of psychological make-up possessed by real people without some form of shaping and focusing. Playwrights thus shape human character into a form which is appropriate to their purposes and which is simple enough for an audience to comprehend it in performance.

thought Aspect of the play that communicates its intellectual content—its themes, ideas, and perceptions about human experience

Thought   As used here, **thought** comprises the playwright's ideas or the intellectual content of the play. Thought, however, goes well beyond the play's basic moral arguments and general thematic material. A playwright may very well have a particular thesis in mind and may use the play as a vehicle for arguing or proving a point, just as the medieval morality play *Everyman* makes the point, in the title character's last dance with death, that the Christian would do well to have more to lean on than worldly goods and relationships: Only good deeds, enlivened by repentance, will bring him to salvation. *Everyman* is an example of plays that are openly *didactic*—that seek to teach particular moral lessons, often in straightforward fashion. But however blatant or subtle a play's messages may be, ultimately the *thought* of the play is the insight that it gives us into our own condition in the larger realm of human behavior. Although the playwright's primary aim may be the illustration of an aspect of thought, the concept of thought also includes our own reactions to the play and conclusions about what it means. What both playwright and production artists seek to communicate often provides only a basic stimulus to *our* analysis, which opens much larger doorways of revelation to us.

Language   *Language* is the one of the vehicles of the playwright (see Chapter 4). What a playwright *does* with language provides a basic set of expectations for both the production artists and the audience. A play written in poetry, for example, will indicate a totally different set of expectations for the

language Aspect of the play through which the playwright communicates overall tone, style, and theme

audience than will one written in normal conversational style. In a very real sense, **language** is the playwright's sole vehicle for conveying the themes of the play: Plot, character, and thought are all conveyed through language. How—and how well—the playwright commands language can have a significant impact on the way the play is perceived. For example, language that is rich in imagery—that is, that contains several layers of meaning—may express thought with the potential for several layers of meaning. Indeed, theatre has throughout much of its history used poetry as its language. Because poetic language generally cannot be confused with everyday speech, the level of human reality to which the audience is asked to ascend is clearly beyond the commonplace. In the contemporary theatre, where realism abounds and "street speech" runs the gamut from colorful to disturbing, one of the questions we must ask is: How far beyond surface appearances does the playwright really wish us to go?

aural elements Aspect of the play consisting of everything that the audience hears, including music, actors' voices, and sound effects

Aural Elements   The **aural elements** of the play include the sound of the actors' voices, music, the clash of swords, the slamming of doors, the crack of hand against cheek. Whatever we hear is part of the *sound* of a production, and each and every one of those sounds must be carefully orchestrated for maximum effect. The rising and falling inflections of the spoken word and the range of voices in the cast—sopranos, altos, tenors, and basses—are as carefully chosen and rehearsed as a concert of fine choral music. Likewise, the *sound effects,* from telephone rings to pistol shots, are crafted to produce the perfect effect relative to the style and mood of the production. As we shall see in Chapter 13, the aural elements of a production require careful consideration and represent crucial choices made by the director and the sound designer. Together, all the sources of sound in a production weave a complicated fabric of tones and colors that help audience members direct their focus where they should in order to gain meaning from the play as a work of art.

visual elements Aspect of the play consisting of everything that the audience sees, including settings, costumes, and actors' movements

Visual Elements   Whether we call this part of theatre *spectacle* or concentrate on it as a complex of **visual elements,** it consists of *all* the things that the audience sees, including settings, costumes, and the physical actions of the actors. Each production reflects a decision about the importance of spectacle and about how each visual element should relate to the others, and we will discuss these items in considerable detail in Chapters 10, 11, 12, and 13. A wealth of creative choices present themselves to theatre artists in every production. Careful communication ensures that each of the visual elements complements the others: Actors' movements must be compatible with costume, which, in turn, must coordinate with scenery and lighting. When the visual elements of the production work together, the tapestry viewed by the audience is rich and meaningful.

FINDING THE PLAY'S PERSONALITY

The final aspect in the development of our understanding beyond our first impressions involves finding the style or personality of the play. Every play

Philip Radcliffe (I): Skills, Values, and Judgments

Philip Radcliffe, who has served as head of the Department of Communications at the University of Manchester, has been a long-time reviewer of both music and theatre for the London Sunday Times *and the* Daily Mail, *two of England's most widely circulated national newspapers. Review criticism, he stresses, combines the critic's experience and judgment with the reviewer's skills as a writer.*

WHAT DO YOU FEEL ARE THE PARTICULAR TOOLS OR SKILLS THAT ARE REQUISITE TO FUNCTIONING AS AN ARTS CRITIC? I think the problem is, as you get into the professional work as a critic, it's all too easy to be a critic of anything at any time at the drop of a hat. You do develop the professional skills, almost, of hack journalism. I think that is fairly inevitable. You just have to keep them under control. The skills required I find very difficult to identify because basically my view is that it just so happens that one is fortunate enough to be paid to do this work. I still consider myself very fortunate that people will pay me to go to the theatre to express an opinion, or go to a concert to express an opinion, and provide me, free of charge, the very best tickets. In addition, they actually pay me for doing so. It really is remarkable. The skills clearly have to be largely professional journalistic skills, in the sense that you have to be able to work within the disciplines of time: You may have to write a notice within a half-hour of leaving the event. You have to be able and prepared to work within the disciplines of space; the newspaper only allows you so much space, and you have to work within it. You have to be prepared to work within the disciplines of style: You must have a clear idea of the audience for which you are writing, depending on the newspaper for which you are writing. You have to be able professionally to combine these skills with a critical faculty, which is very indefinable, and an experience which produces value judgments that may be taken to be reasonable. So you are basing your judgment on something or other—probably a wide experience of having seen good performances and bad performances before. You have to have the facility to express yourself, to communicate your interest, enthusiasm, disappointment, or whatever, to the reader. So it is very much a combination of skills and interests which takes some time, I think, to come together.

You have to . . . combine skills with a critical faculty . . . and an experience which produces value judgments which may be taken to be reasonable. So you are basing your judgment on something or other—probably a wide experience of having seen good performances and bad performances.

YOUR EXPERIENCE HAS BEEN IN THE PERFORMING ARTS. DO YOU SEE A DIFFERENCE BETWEEN YOUR APPROACH OR TASK AND THAT OF A CRITIC OF THE VISUAL ARTS? I'm tempted to say yes, perhaps because I have not really had the experience of covering the visual arts. Therefore, something you haven't done you tend to think of as different. I suspect it may not be that much different, although there again, what you need to have is knowledge gained by experience. I spend a lot of time looking at paintings as a personal pleasure in various parts of the world, and so I might be able to have a go at some visual-arts criticism, I suppose.

However, nobody has ever asked me to do it. I think that what I would say which may be helpful is that there is a vast difference, I find, between writing criticism of music and writing criticism of theatre. Music is much more difficult to describe to a reader. To communicate sound through words is not that easy. With a play you start with a common language: You describe a story as well as a performance. Also, in the music field, almost by definition the level of performance is in a sense much less variable than the level of performance in the theatre. Most often one is listening to music that is well-established "classical music." Of course, one hears new works and has to assess those, but by and large one hears a standard repertoire and one hears constantly performers of international repute. Therefore, the demands on the music critic are much more keenly felt than the demands on the theatre critic.

and production has a distinct *personality*. In part, this personality comes from the playwright, especially through the use of language; in part, it comes from the treatment of the play by the director, actors, and designers in a particular production. Often, we call this distinctive personality the play's *style*—a term that can be used very loosely to mean a number of things. More often than not, when we refer to the "style" of a production, we cannot be very specific about what that style really is. Productions are so complex in their elements that they refuse to fall neatly into the kinds of categories with which we customarily identify the "style" of other artworks such as paintings, sculptures, works of architecture, and musical compositions and performances. Every play and every production has a style all its own, and that is in fact what the term **style** really means—"identifying characteristics." Whether or not the particular style of a play or production can be identified with a broader, widely recognized "style" such as "expressionism" or "postmodernism" remains for us to judge.

style The identifying characteristics in the manner of expression, design, or execution of an artwork

The various ways in which plays may be written or produced may also have something to do with specific artistic movements or philosophies of art. Most plays, for example, reflect cultural and historical contexts. Whether a play is produced as it might have been staged originally or is given a modern treatment, establishing the focus of a given play depends partly on understanding the characteristics of the style, movement, or philosophy of theatre that were prevalent or influential when the play was written or first performed. Understanding a playwright's approach in a given work can help us not only to understand its meaning more fully but also to evaluate both the playwright's intentions and perceptions of human reality and the appropriateness of the choices made by the director and designers for a specific production.

In Chapters 14, 15, 16, and 17, we will trace the history of theatre. Here, however, we will survey very briefly some important theatrical styles, philosophies, and movements in order to focus on the role of the play's "personality" in guiding us toward understanding. If we can understand more about the styles, philosophies, and movements that have been important in theatre history, we may be better able to identify the specific personalities of the plays that we read and see. In applying what we learn, as in applying the parts of the play that we studied earlier, we will find that whereas some plays or productions may fit categories nicely, in other cases a given play does not seem to fit any obvious category. When that happens, we *might* be seeing something totally original—a very special and exciting possibility. In any case, we can become more adept in our perceptions if we understand some of the ways in which artists choose to reflect human reality and what those specific treatments have been called.

When we describe, analyze, and evaluate the personality of a production, we should try to discover if all the elements are *consistent* in their treatment of the subject matter. For example, does the acting appear exaggerated while the settings look lifelike? Are the costumes lifelike but the setting exaggerated? Is the language poetic but all the other elements realistic? If so, what might that artistic choice mean?

Four styles that give us a broad picture of the variety of approaches available to the playwright and the production are *classicism, romanticism, expressionism,* and *realism.* These styles more or less exemplify polar points among which infinite variation may be possible. Classicism and romanticism, for example, represent differences in *appeal:* Classicism appeals to the intellect, romanticism to the emotions. Realism and expressionism represent differences in *point of view:* Whereas realism represents the viewpoint of objective observation, expressionism represents the subjective viewpoint that emanates from within an individual's personality. Along with the brief discussion of each style that follows there is also a synopsis of a play that exemplifies that style.

classicism Play and production *style* that focuses on intellect and structure and concentrates on restraint and control

Classicism   **Classicism** is a term that can be applied broadly to works of art that draw upon models from ancient Greece and Rome. Basically, classicism appeals to the intellect rather than to the emotions, and it regards elements of structure and form as primary. In the classical viewpoint, the element of plot, because it represents the structural aspect of a play, would be judged more important than character or the visual and aural elements. In addition, classicism pursues the ideal rather than the mundane and concentrates on restraint and control. In the theatre, productions of plays in the classical style often exhibit poetic language, symmetrical settings, and characters that are larger-than-life types rather than fully developed individuals. However, although classicism focuses on intellect and structure, emotional appeal can still be present. The focus is a matter of degree and emphasis. In classicism, emotion is often consciously restrained and subordinated.

Certainly, there is no lack of emotion in *Oedipus the King.* As we study the play further, however, we discover that emotion is secondary: The play conforms in every respect to classical characteristics. Its structure is well-defined, and its larger-than-life characters are representative of types rather than fully fleshed individuals. The play utilizes poetry, and its actions are restrained—all the mayhem takes place offstage. Even Oedipus' blinding is controlled and minimized, because the actors in ancient Greece wore masks (Fig. 3.7). The production elements, such as costumes and scenery, that we will discuss in Chapters 12 and 13 would have contributed further to the play's sense of idealism, restraint, and order.

Figure 3.7 *Sophocles,* Oedipus the King, *Stratford Shakespearean Festival, Stratford, Ontario, Canada, 1954. Director, Tyrone Guthrie; scenic designer, Tanya Moiseiwitsch. Behind the masks: James Mason as Oedipus, Eleanor Stuart as Jocasta.*

Oedipus the King (ca. 429 B.C.)
SOPHOCLES

Oedipus, king of the Greek city-state of Thebes, sends a messenger to the Oracle at Delphi to determine why a plague is affecting the city. The messenger reports that, according to the Oracle, the murderer of the previous king, Laius, has not been punished. Oedipus vows to find the murderer and punish him. When the blind soothsayer Teiresias accuses Oedipus of the crime, Oedipus rejects his accusations. Queen Jocasta pleads with Oedipus to disregard the Oracle because her own experience has proved the Oracle incorrect. According to Jocasta, the Oracle had predicted that Laius, her first husband, would be killed by his own son at a place where three roads intersected. According to Jocasta, that event did not come to pass. Jocasta then explains that she and Laius had put their son to death in order to thwart the prophecy. Oedipus, however, realizes that he himself had killed a man at a place where three roads met, and he reveals that he had escaped to Corinth precisely because of a prophecy that he would kill his father and marry his mother. Oedipus then learns that the man he believed to be his father has just died. He learns that he was not in fact the real son of the Corinthian king but had been taken to Cor-

inth by a shepherd from Thebes. Meanwhile, Jocasta realizes that Oedipus is indeed the son whom she had presumed dead and pleads with him to abandon his quest for the truth. Oedipus, however, driven by his pride, will not renege on his promise to the people of Thebes to find the murderer. Jocasta runs into the palace and kills herself. Shortly thereafter, Oedipus, having relentlessly pursued the matter, learns the truth about himself. He discovers Jocasta's body and blinds himself with her brooches. Urging Jocasta's brother Creon to care for his children by Jocasta, Oedipus leaves Thebes for a life of exile (Fig. 3.8).

Figure 3.8
Sophocles, Oedipus the King. *Guthrie Theatre, Minneapolis, Minnesota, 1972. Translator and adapter, Anthony Burgess; director, Michael Langham; scenic designer, Desmond Heeley. Len Cariou as Oedipus and Patricia Conolly as Jocasta.*

romanticism Play and production *style* that focuses on an appeal to emotion, experimenting with form and language and glorifying the individual

Romanticism Romanticism, which focuses on emotionalism, feeling, and an escape to the exotic—the faraway and long-ago—is largely the antithesis of classicism. A revolt against an 18th-century revival of classicism—called *neoclassicism* in theatre, painting, and sculpture, and classicism in music—romanticism flourished in the first half of the 19th century. In contrast to the classicists, who portrayed heroes who were larger than life, the romantics sought out eccentric protagonists. Rather than cultivating high poetry, they used the everyday speech of actual people. They experimented with form and language and often with taboo subjects. Romanticism glorified the individual, especially the outcast and the downtrodden. In many respects, the romantic movement has never ended.

Romanticism is such a large and encompassing style that any one example is likely to prove deficient. What Cyrano exhibits is the "romantic" side of romanticism—a flair for the emotions of passion and love. It is unrestrained in its tone and treatment: Cyrano's flowery speeches and the robust onstage action carry the play away from the careful control of the classical. Cyrano, although an exaggerated character, is nonetheless an individual, fully devel-

Cyrano de Bergerac (1897)

EDMOND ROSTAND

Cyrano, a poet/soldier, cannot reveal his love for Roxanne because he has a grotesquely large nose. When she falls in love with Christian, a handsome but shallow soldier, Cyrano decides to coach Christian in order to help him woo her. While Cyrano and Christian are away at war, Cyrano writes beautiful love letters expressing his own feelings in Christian's name. After Christian is killed in battle, Roxanne enters a convent. Cyrano visits her, but only when he is dying from wounds suffered in an ambush by his enemies does he reveal his love for her. She, in turn, realizes the nature of her own love: She loved the great soul and depth of Cyrano despite his disfigurement (Fig. 3.9).

Figure 3.9 *Edmond Rostand,* Cyrano de Bergerac *(Act 4). Denver Center Theatre, Denver, Colorado. Scenic design, Mark Donnelly.*

Understanding *and* Evaluating Plays *and* Performances

Death of a Salesman (1949)

ARTHUR MILLER

At age sixty, Willy Loman discovers that his life is barren and his expectations unmet. His son Biff, a popular athlete in high school, has turned into a chronically unemployed nonentity. At the same time, his neighbor's son Bernard, who was an unpopular nerd in high school, has become a successful lawyer. Willy reminisces about his past and his troubles with Biff, culminating in the moment when Biff found Willy with another woman. Unable to continue his own career and rejected by his sons, Willy commits suicide in a premeditated automobile accident so that Biff can have a start in business with his insurance money. At the funeral, his wife, Linda, and his sons try to find some meaning and value in Willy's life (Fig. 3.10).

Figure 3.10 *Arthur Miller,* Death of a Salesman, *1949. Director, Elia Kazan; scenic designer, Jo Mielzner. Lee J. Cobb (center) as Willy Loman, Arthur Kennedy (left) as Biff, and Cameron Mitchell as Happy.*

oped in his motivations. The settings are exotic, and the flavor of the play is designed to elicit an emotional response from the audience. Appeal to the intellect takes a back seat to appeal to the feelings.

realism Play and production *style* holding that art should depict life with complete honesty, trying to paint pictures of life as we actually experience it and emphasizing its commonplace, often brutal aspects

Realism   **Realism** holds that art should depict life with complete honesty. It focuses on verifiable details and strives for impersonal accuracy. In attempting to avoid idealism and romantic "prettifying," realists often emphasize the commonplace and brutal aspects of life. Contemporary realists try to paint a picture of life as we find it, not as we might hope it to be. This approach, however, does not mean that all contemporary realism is sordid or negative. In fact, the triumph of the human spirit often characterizes contemporary realism in the theatre. In the mid-20th century realism also witnessed a direction called *neorealism,* in which the precepts of realism were followed with an added debt to psychology. Neorealism is characterized by sensitive psychological studies of social misfits.

In many ways, *Death of a Salesman* represents the variety of directions that realism has taken in the 20th century. Even though the characters are drawn fully as individuals, the language reflects everyday speech and the situations depicted are commonplace, there are elements in the play that go beyond what can be called strictly realistic or can be objectively observed. As we noted earlier, contemporary realism explores the psychology of its characters, but in so doing, it opens them to even more objective examination. *Death of a Salesman* operates through a series of flashbacks, a technique characteristic of the cinema—perhaps our most realistic art form.

expressionism Play and production *style* that tries to evoke in the audience responses to experience similar to the artist's by expressing the underlying reality of the play's subject matter rather than its surface appearance

Expressionism   Expressionism was a movement, centered primarily in Germany in the first quarter of the 20th century, that attempted to express the underlying reality of its subject matter rather than reproducing its mere surface reality or appearance. Essentially, expressionism was a revolt against 19th-century realistic trends that expressionists believed to be superficially attractive but no longer true to human experience. For the expressionist, subject matter itself mattered little; what counted was the artist's attempt to evoke in the viewer a response similar to his or her own. For example, in Max Beckmann's painting *Christ and the Woman Taken in Adultery* (Fig. 3.11), the artist's revulsion against physical cruelty and suffering is transmitted through distorted figures crushed into shallow space; linear distortion, changes of scale and perspective, and a nearly Gothic spiritualism communicate Beckerman's reactions to the horrors of World War I. This same kind of distortion of prominent features, as well as the attempt to establish a joint artist–respondent reaction, also found an outlet in the theatre. Eugene O'Neill's *The Hairy Ape* provides an excellent example.

Eventually, the kinds of exploration and understanding discussed in this

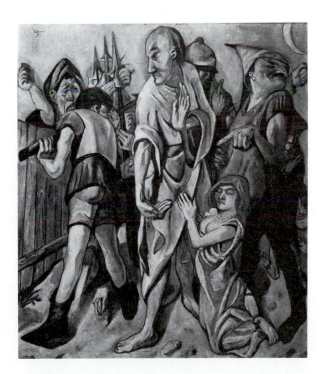

Figure 3.11   Max Beckmann, Christ and the Woman Taken in Adultery, 1917. *Oil on canvas,* 58-1/4″ X 49-1/8″.

[City Art Museum of St. Louis. Bequest of Curt Valentin.]

Understanding *and* Evaluating Plays *and* Performances

The Hairy Ape (1922)

EUGENE O'NEILL

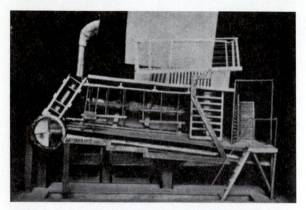

Figure 3.12 *Stage model for Alexander Tairov's production of Eugene O'Neill's* The Hairy Ape, *Moscow Kamerny Theatre, 1924. Compare this model with the constructivist set design for a production of O'Neill's* Dynamo *at Fig. 17.7.*

Yank, a ship's stoker, believes that he and his fellow stokers are the only humans who "belong" because they make the ship go and, thereby, make all the factories and machines of the industrialized world go as well (Fig. 3.12). Deluded by the boundaries of his self-perception, Yank cannot see that the world in which he lives—the bowels of a ship—resembles the steel framework of a cage, nor does he see that he himself resembles a Neanderthal man.

Meanwhile, Mildred Douglas, the ship-owner's daughter, leads a life apparently without purpose. She insists on seeing the stokehole in order to watch the men shovel coal. But when she sees Yank, the "hairy ape," she faints in horror. This episode has a profound effect on Yank's self-perception. He begins to question all his former beliefs and perceptions and comes to believe that everything, including what was previously familiar, is now alien.

On shore in New York, Yank walks up Fifth Avenue and is revulsed by the sight of the wealthy and powerful. He tries to gain their attention and is ignored. In frustration, he resorts to force and begins striking out physically. Even then, however, passersby remain oblivious to him as they give their full attention to a monkey-fur coat in a shop window. In the next scene, Yank is in jail ("the zoo"). He decides to seek revenge and, when he is released, offers to blow up the enemies (the wealthy shipowners) of the International Workers of the World. His offer meets only contempt, and he is thrown into the street. In the final scene, Yank goes to the zoo and sees a gorilla who seems to understand him. Yank frees the gorilla, who, in turn, grabs Yank, crushes him to death, and throws him into the cage. Yank's search for a place to belong ends, unfulfilled.

chapter lead us to the question of analysis and evaluation. The remainder of the chapter will take us through a process that we can use—in addition to those we have already discussed—for deeper understanding and enjoyment of the theatrical artwork and for a personal evaluation of what we experience in the theatre. That process is called *criticism*.

Criticism

WHAT IS "CRITICISM"?

One of the questions that everyone seems to ask about an artwork is, "Is it any good?" Whether it be rock music, a film, a play, a painting, or a classical symphony, judgments about the "quality" of a work often vary from one extreme to the other. Responses may range from "I liked it" (with no real understanding of why) and "interesting" (meaning, "I can't think of anything else to say about it, and don't ask me what 'interesting' means") to fairly concrete reasons why the various components of the work were effective or ineffective.

Because the word *criticism* itself implies many different things to many people, we must first come to some agreement about what it means here. First, let's be clear about what criticism is *not*. Criticism is not saying negative things about a work of art. All too often we think of "critics" as people who write or say essentially negative things about art in the newspapers or on television, where they give their opinions on the value of a theatre production, a concert, or an exhibition. Passing personal judgment on a work of art is not *criticism*. Judgment may result from criticism, but criticism is not just passing judgment.

criticism A detailed process of analysis performed in order to gain enhanced understanding and appreciation of an artwork in one or more of its aspects

Criticism is a detailed process of analysis performed in order to gain enhanced understanding and appreciation. Identifying the elements of an artwork—learning, for example, what to see and what to hear—is the first step in this analytical process. First, we describe an artwork by examining its many facets; then we try to understand how those elements work together to create some form of meaning or experience. Next we try to state what that meaning or experience is. Only when that process is complete does the critic offer judgments.

In order to make such judgments, the critic brings to the work some set of standards developed essentially from personal experience, and *the application of standards to actual works* is what makes value judgment so tricky. Our *knowledge* of an artform, for example, can be shallow. Our *perceptual skills* may be faulty. The range of our *experiences* may be limited. The application of standards may be especially tricky when we try to judge artworks as "good" or "bad" solely on the basis of preestablished criteria. For example, if someone believes that plot is the most important element in a film or a play, then any film or play that does not depend heavily on plot may be judged faulty despite any other qualities it possesses. Such preestablished criteria for "quality" account for much for the difficulty that new or experimental approaches to an art form often have in receiving critical acclaim. History is full of examples of new approaches that received terrible receptions from so-called experts whose ideas of what an artwork ought to be could not allow for experimentation or depar-

Philip Radcliffe (II): Missionary Zeal

"Credibility," says Radcliffe, comes from "a general background of knowingness," and for the critic, the purpose of knowing the arts is "to better the arts." He also has some ideas as to how the critic can help to better the arts.

DO YOU COMMUNE IN ART CIRCLES AND AMONG ARTISTS, OR DO YOU FEEL A NEED TO REMAIN SEPARATE FROM THEM, PERSONALLY, IN ORDER TO BE OBJECTIVE? Well, I think a bit of both in my own case. I live a normal, rounded life, I would like to think, because I do spend a lot of my time in this sense working in theatres and concert halls and whatnot. Inevitably, of course, I see a lot of artists and musicians, and talk with them. I think this builds up a general background of knowingness. I think, also, that any critic worth his salt really hopes that the people he is sitting in judgment upon not exactly value his opinion, but at least trust his opinion. I think that you need to have, for your own self-preservation, a credibility. Therefore, it's important to know as much as you can about the topic, even though you are judging a particular performance on a particular night and no more than that.

YOU SPOKE EARLIER OF MISSIONARY ZEAL. DO YOU EVER FEEL IN CONFLICT WITH YOURSELF IN YOUR ROLE OF A CRITIC AS OPPOSED TO AN APOLOGIST FOR THE ARTS? My missionary zeal relates to the context of one particular paper—that is, the context of writing for a paper with a general readership rather than a readership you know is already committed to an interest in the arts. That zeal would not lead me to give false judgment on any performance or event. I would express my opinion and would not change that opinion simply because it did not convince people that they ought to go to see it. That would be counterproductive, and

would spoil the missionary zeal when I really wanted to exploit it. I think my concern is really to better the arts and to make a contribution to the furtherance of the arts. One of the exciting things, really, would be the thought that one just might communicate to somebody who hasn't had that experience the possibilities held for them in terms of lasting pleasure in such things as paintings, music, and theatre. I think if a critic can do that while at the same time being constructively critical of what's happening, then I think that is a reasonable way to spend part of one's time.

One of the exciting things . . . is that one just might communicate to somebody who hasn't had that experience . . . in terms of lasting pleasure in such things as paintings, music, and theatre.

FROM YOUR POINT OF VIEW, WHAT DO THE ARTS NEED TO DO TO FULFILL THEIR ROLE IN SOCIETY? I find this very difficult because in the end the public is going to make up their own minds. I think what worries me to an extent, and links it to my missionary-zeal feeling, is that the arts are not so easily communicated in terms of the use of television. When you think about it, it is very rare for people to see through such a medium as television—although it is ideal for the job—the work of the artist or the workings of a musician. What I am trying to say, really, is that I would like to see the arts made more accessible to a wider public, because I suspect that as long as the arts seem to be a kind of elitist, intellectual preserve there are a lot of people who are missing a lot of pleasure. Anything the arts can do—I don't know what the answer is, really—to disassociate themselves from this mystique that they are terribly special things for terribly special people, the better. How you do it I don't know. Sometimes I think it works by, if you like, cheating slightly. Certainly, at home I know we had a very popular exhibition at an art gallery; it was an exhibition of Hollywood costumes from the movie houses in Hollywood, costumes worn in various movies by distinguished actors. That at-tracted people into the museum, into the art gallery, for the first time; many people had never been there before. If by chance a few of those, then, see enough while they're there to want to come again and look at the other things in the art gallery, then that's good. I think that's an idea: That one offers a temp-tation for people to come in who otherwise wouldn't come in. In any case I would like to see this mystique broken down.

tures from accepted practice. For example, in 1912, when Vaslav Nijinsky choreographed the ballet *Rite of Spring* to music by Igor Stravinsky, the departures from conventional music practice, as well as the dancing, which embodied Nijinsky's ideas about free-form expression, actually caused a riot: Audiences and critics could not tolerate the fact that *Rite of Spring* did not conform to accepted musical and ballet standards. Today, both the music and the choreography are considered masterpieces. Similarly, a play like Samuel Beckett's *Waiting for Godot* (1953) (Fig. 3.13) does not approach its plot, character, or thought in the manner of the Aristotelian model that was the standard of the late 19th century. Two tramps wait beside the road by a withered tree for the arrival of someone named Godot. They tell stories to each other, argue, eat some food, and are interrupted by a character named Pozzo leading a slave, Lucky, by a rope. After a brief conversation, Lucky and Pozzo leave. At the end of the first act, a boy enters the stage to announce that Godot

Figure 3.13   *Samuel Beckett,* Waiting for Godot. *Utah Shakespearean Festival, 1990. Director, Roger Bean; scenic designer, Roger Sherman; costume designer, Carol Wells-Day.*

will not come today. In Act Two, much the same sequence of events occurs. Now Pozzo is blind and led by Lucky. The tree has sprouted a few leaves. The play ends as the young boy returns to indicate that Godot will not arrive that day either. If your standards indicate that a good play must have a carefully fashioned plot with beginning, middle, and ending all wrapped around fully developed characters and a clear message, then *Waiting for Godot* can't possibly be a "good" play. But although some people would agree with that assertion, others would disagree vehemently. What are we to conclude? What happens if my criteria don't match yours? What if two "experts" disagree on the quality of a movie? Does that make any difference either to the movie or to our experience of it?

Although the easiest answer to such questions is that value judgments are intensely personal, such an easy answer is not a satisfying one. Some opinions *are* more informed than others and represent more authoritative judgment. In the case of *Waiting for Godot,* however, even knowledgeable theatre people disagree. Probably the best we can conclude is that, in the end, value *judgments* simply may not be important or essential. Disagreements about quality, however, can enhance the experience of a work of art when they lead to thought about why those differences exist. Then the judgments themselves come under scrutiny, and the result is a deeper understanding of the artwork. Nonetheless, criticism can be exercised quite thoroughly without involving any judgment. We can thoroughly dissect any play or production, describe what it comprises—what choices the artists have made—describe and analyze plot, character, language, aural and visual elements, and thought and how all these factors affect an audience and its response. As incomplete as it may seem, we can spend a significant amount of time performing such analysis and never pass a value judgment.

Does this mean that all artworks are somehow "equal" in value? Not at all. It means that in order to understand what criticism involves, we must separate the different parts of the critical process. We must distinguish between descriptive analysis, which can be satisfying in and of itself, and the act of passing value judgments. By itself, analysis necessarily leads us to enhanced understanding. Although we may not *like* the work that we've analyzed, at least we've understood something that we did not understand before. By contrast, passing judgment may play no role whatsoever in our understanding of an artwork.

Here is the crux of the issue: As an exercise in understanding, criticism is necessary: We must understand new things if we are to grow not only in learned knowledge but also in our knowledge of how to interact with other human beings and how to react to new experiences. In short, we must investigate and describe; if we are to have perceptions to share, we must experience the need to know something about the process, product, and experience of art. In fact, one important value of criticism is the sharing process itself: Our mutual agreement on any particular interpretation is less important than the enhanced perception that results from going through the critical process and sharing it with someone else.

Nevertheless, criticism without some form of summary judgment leaves many people feeling that the process is incomplete. Summary judgment, however, has many occasions and takes many forms. For example, a university art teacher must decide whether a performance, a painting, or a composition by a student has quality—and what kind of quality. For someone who wants to purchase a piece of art, perhaps as an investment or perhaps simply for love of the piece, the question is: Is its quality in keeping with its price? Finally, people who write reviews in the print and broadcast media may do so because their editors or producers and the public expect judgment calls from them.

Certain judgments require higher levels of expertise than others, and the results of some judgments have wider-reaching effects than others. Media reviewers, for example, may or may not have significant impact. Sometimes, the combined weight of several negative reviews spells doom for a production, with millions of dollars of investment lost as a consequence. Many plays and musicals, however, have had long runs despite uniformly poor reviews. At the grass-roots level, when a reviewer pans a production, the consequences are usually minimal: A few patrons might not attend a worthy exhibition or performance, a few egos might be assaulted, and those who worked hard and well and deserve recognition might not receive it—but that's about all. In the decision to buy a work of art or a ticket to a performance, one's knowledge or expertise may or may not be important. Of course, it would be a shame—perhaps even foolish—to pay several thousand dollars for an artwork of poor quality; but in the decision to spend money on art, other factors may be more important than quality or price—one might simply fall in love with a piece of art and decide that living with it on a daily basis is worth the price. The implications of quality judgments, then, can be minimal when compared with personal satisfaction. On the other hand, when applied to a student's work, a teacher's inexpert judgment could render an unfair grade or even affect graduation. The fact is, however, that judgment is usually fairly personal and limited in impact. In addition, it is probably not very important for us to worry about whether we can predict the impact of a work of art on future generations: We will not be around to see if we were right. Such an assertion does not mean to trivialize the impulse to make judgments but, rather, to suggest that, as students wanting to understand something about a particular art form, we should put greater emphasis on the descriptive and interpretive aspects of criticism.

On the other hand, we really ought to know the difference between trash and treasure. In our health-conscious age, some people have suggested that we are what we eat. We can expand that observation to note that we are also what we read and value: If we do not pursue the noble and uplifting, as the Apostle Paul suggests, then we may very well pursue—and become—the opposite. Sometimes, we need to know trash from treasure in order to avoid the trash; at other times, we need to know in order to choose where to invest our energy and resources. Sometimes, we need to know in order to protect ourselves from

Critics: The New York Voices

There are many stories in the theatre world about the power of New York reviewers to make or break Broadway productions. In fact, throughout this century, certain drama critics have indeed influenced the theatre-going public more than others. George Jean Nathan (1882–1958) was probably the most famous critic of his era. After a brief stint at the New York *Herald,* in 1905 Nathan was made drama critic for two magazines, *Outing* and the *Bohemian.* Two years later, he moved to the *Smart Set,* becoming in 1914 coeditor with H. L. Mencken. Quick to attack the shallowness of contemporary plays, Nathan, who saw the future of the theatre in new and more serious American dramatists, became the first powerful critic to champion Eugene O'Neill. In 1924, Nathan left the *Smart Set* to start another magazine with Mencken, the *American Mercury,* which the two coedited until 1930. Two years later, with O'Neill and others Nathan also founded the *American Spectator.* In addition, Nathan's reviews appeared in many other magazines and newspapers, thus ensuring their wide dissemination.

In contrast to the acerbic Nathan, Brooks Atkinson (1894–1984), the drama critic of the *New York Times* from 1924 until his retirement in 1960, was known for gracious and tolerant reviews. The paper's prestige, coupled with Atkinson's sense of fairness, made him highly respected by both the play-going public and theatre professionals. During his long tenure at the *Times*, Atkinson became one of the strongest supporters of the "musical play," the integration of song and story introduced by *Oklahoma!* in 1943.

Unlike Nathan and Atkinson, Harold Clurman (1901–1980) combined drama criticism with an active career in the theatre. In 1931, Clurman had been one of the founders of the Group Theatre, for which he directed *Awake and Sing!* (1935) and *Golden Boy* (1937). From 1949–1953, Clurman was drama critic for the *New Republic* and, subsequently, drama critic for many years at the *Nation.* In these two liberal magazines, Clurman supported American realist dramatists like Arthur Miller. The plays that he himself chose to direct during this period, such as *The Member of the Wedding* (1950) and *Bus Stop* (1955), reflected his commitment to American realism.

At present, Frank Rich (b. 1949) has seemingly inherited the mantle of most influential American theatre critic. Before becoming the *Times'* chief drama reviewer in 1980, Rich was movie critic for *Time* and the *New York Post.* His background in film has made Rich particularly sensitive to the cinematic techniques of innovative American theatre, such as the concept musicals of Steven Sondheim and Harold Prince.

manipulation, sometimes, merely for the joy of knowing that we know. This position is not intended to foster elitism or snobbery or to suggest that some approaches to art are implicitly better than others. Such judgments are often like comparing apples and oranges—praising or condemning one work simply because it is not another. Instead, we should put our efforts into knowing what constitutes an apple or an orange so that we can discuss the relative merits of examples of each in the midst of their own kin. The more art we see and hear, and the more we practice criticism—in all its parts—the more confidence we will have in making judgments and finding artworks and art forms that truly do have some impact on our experience and that of others. Although we all develop certain preferences, *preferences* should not be confused with *prejudices*. Our ability to savor delicacies like truffles need not preclude our love of hot dogs. The inability to distinguish one from the other, however, could lead to a number of unfortunate consequences, including social embarrassment and a large hole in the wallet for what should have been an inexpensive pleasure. We need, therefore, some way of enhancing our understanding of those things in which we will invest our time and, perhaps, our money.

Now that we have examined very briefly what criticism is and why we might want to do it, what *criteria* or approaches can we use?

TYPES OF CRITICISM

In general, we can do one of two things: We can either examine a single artwork at hand—this is called *formal criticism*—or we can examine the same work in the context of the events surrounding it and perhaps the circumstances of its creation—this is called *contextual criticism*.

formal criticism
Criticism that attempts to analyze an artwork with no external conditions or information applied to it

Formal Criticism   In the case of **formal criticism**, we are interested primarily in the artwork itself: We can allow the work to stand alone, with no external conditions or information applied to it. We can analyze the artwork just as we find it. If it is a painting, we look only within the frame. If it is a play, we analyze only what we see and hear in the production. As an example, let's conduct a very brief analysis of Molière's comedy *Tartuffe* (1664) (Fig. 3.14).

Tartuffe

Orgon, a rich bourgeois, has allowed a religious con man, Tartuffe, to gain a complete hold over him. Tartuffe has moved into Orgon's house and literally taken over. He tries to seduce Orgon's wife at the same time that he is planning to marry his daughter. Tartuffe is un- masked and Orgon orders him out. Tartuffe seeks his revenge by claiming title to Orgon's house and blackmailing him with some secret papers. At the very last instant Tartuffe's plans are foiled by the intervention of the king, and the play ends happily.

We have just described the *story*. If we were to go one step further and analyze the plot, we would look, among other things, for those points at which *crises* occurred and caused the characters to make important decisions. We would also want to know how those decisions moved the play from one point to the next, and we would try to locate the extreme crisis—the *climax*. Meanwhile, we would discover auxiliary parts of the plot like *reversals*—for example, the moment when Tartuffe is discovered and the characters become fully

Figure 3.14 Molière, Tartuffe (1664). *University of Arizona 1990. Director, Dianne Winslow; scenic designer, Charles Connor; lighting designer, Julie Mack.*

aware of the true situation. Depending on how detailed we make our criticism, we could work our way through each and every aspect of the plot—that is, the plot as we described it earlier in this chapter. We might then devote some time to describing and analyzing the driving force—the *character*—of each person in the play and how those people relate to each other. Has Molière given us fully developed characters? Are these people types, or do they seem to behave more or less like real individuals? In examining *thought,* we would no doubt conclude that the play deals with religious hypocrisy and that Molière had a particular point of view on that subject.

In summary, *formal criticism* approaches the artwork as an entity complete within itself. In this approach to criticism, information about the playwright, previous performances, historic relationships, and so on is basically irrelevant. This approach to criticism is thus useful for analyzing how an artwork "works" and why it produces the responses that it does. We can apply this form of criticism to any work of art and come away with a variety of often fairly sophisticated conclusions. Of course, the critical process is enhanced by knowledge about how artworks are put together, what they are, and how they stimulate the senses. If we did not know that we could look for plot, character, language, thought, sound, and spectacle, we might not know where to begin.

contextual criticism
Criticism that sees the artwork as the result of several forces and functions, including such related materials as the artist's biography and philosophy, prevailing social and political conditions, and so forth

Contextual Criticism The other general approach to criticism, called **contextual criticism,** seeks meaning by adding to the kind of analysis just mentioned an examination of numerous related materials: details about an artist's life; about his or her culture, social and political conditions, and philosophies; about public and critical reactions to the work; and so on. All this can be researched and applied to the work in order to yield enhanced perceptions—and increased understanding. This approach tends to view the artwork as an artifact generated from particular contextual needs, conditions, and/or attitudes rather than from artistic necessity: That is, it sees the artwork as the result of many forces and functions. For example, if we carried our critical approach to *Tartuffe* in this direction, we would note that certain historical events help to clarify the play. For example, the object of Molière's attention in

Understanding *and* Evaluating Plays *and* Performances

Tartuffe was probably the Company of the Holy Sacrament, a secret, conspiratorial, and influential society in France at the time. Like many fanatical religious sects—including those of our time—the society sought to enforce its own view of morality by spying on the lives of others and seeking out "heresies"—in this case, within the Roman Catholic Church. Its followers were religious fanatics, and they had considerable impact on the lives of the citizenry at large. If we were to follow this path of criticism, any and all such contextual matters that might clarify what happens in the play would be pursued.

MAKING JUDGMENTS

Now that we have defined *criticism* and noted two critical approaches that we might take in our efforts to understand and enjoy a play or a theatre production, let's move on to a final step—that of making *value judgments*. In this section, we will note two criteria—*craftsmanship* and *communication*—that we can use in making such judgments.

There are several approaches to the step in the critical process that calls for an act of judgment. There are, for example, certain basic assumptions about *quality* in works of art. Two characteristics, however, are inherent in all artworks: (1) they are *crafted* and (2) they *communicate* some vision to us about our experiences as human beings who inhabit a world with other human beings. Therefore, any judgment about the quality of an artwork should address each of these characteristics.

The Criterion of Craftsmanship   Is the work *well made?* In order to make this judgment, we need some understanding of the medium in which the artist works. For example, if the artist proposes to give us a realistic vision of a tree, does the handling of the paint yield a tree that looks like a tree? Of course, if **craftsmanship** depended only on the ability to portray objects realistically, judgment in this area would be quite simple. That is not the case, however, and we must remember first of all that judgments about the craftsmanship of an artwork require some knowledge about the techniques of its medium. Although we may not yet be ready to make judgments about all the aspects of craftsmanship in theatre or any other art form, we can try to apply what we do know. We can, for example, use *clarity* and *interest* as touchstones. We can ask ourselves whether the play was clear or confusing with regard to thought, character, and the other aspects of theatre that we have discussed. We can ask ourselves whether or not the play held our interest: If the answer is no, then we may wish to examine whether the fault lay in the play or in ourselves. Beyond that, we are left to learn that many lessons that the remainder of this book tries to examine. Each succeeding chapter will give us more pieces to use in evaluating the craft of the play or production.

The Criterion of Communication   Perhaps evaluating what an artwork is trying to "say" offers more immediate opportunity for judgment and less need for expertise. Johann Wolfgang von Goethe, a 19th-century poet, novelist, and playwright, set out a basic commonsense, three-step approach to the

criterion of craftsmanship
Criterion for *judgment* that focuses on how well the work is made as a touchstone for evaluating the success or effect of an artwork

**criterion of
communication**
Criterion for *judgment*
that focuses on the
interpretation of what
the artist is trying to
achieve and evaluating
the success of the effort

criterion of communication. In a general sense, because this approach provides an organized means for getting at an artwork's communication by progressing from analytical to judgmental functions, it gives us a helpful procedure with which to end our discussion of criticism and our chapter on understanding and evaluating plays and performances:

1. What was the artist trying to say?
2. Did he or she succeed?
3. Was the project worth the effort?

These principles focus on the artist's communication by making us focus, first, on *what* was being attempted and then on the artist's degree of success in that attempt. The question of whether or not the project was worth the effort raises other issues, such as the work's uniqueness or profundity. The third question asks us, in essence, to decide whether the communication was *important*—that is, was it worthwhile? Answering these questions may necessitate some contextual information, or, on the other hand, the artist's purpose may be quite clear in the artwork itself. For some people, that basic clarity itself functions as a fundamental criterion for quality.

SUMMARY

• We *approach* theatre and drama in two ways: as a *production* and as a play to be *read*. Critical analysis prompted by a production is different than analysis prompted by the *script*.

• Critical *approach* to the production can be broken down into a few key steps in *understanding* our experience. Our *first impressions* are natural responses that can be developed into formal analysis. Going *beyond first experiences* means considering five aspects of the production: the plays' *characters, facts, setting, parts,* and *personality.*

• In trying to understand *character,* we examine whether or not we like the people of the play in ways that are prompted by their actions or motivations. In trying to understand the *facts* of the play, we look for the details that make up the story and character interactions. In trying to understand *setting,* we examine how the choice of time and place communicates theme and tone.

• In trying to understand the *parts* of the play, we must consider six aspects of the play—the same six aspects that we discussed as parts of the *production* in Chapter 2:

> *plot:* the *structure* of the play;
>
> *character:* the psychological motivations of the people in the play;

language: the means by which the playwright communicates overall tone, style, and theme;

thought: the aspect of the play that communicates its intellectual content;

aural elements: everything in the play that the audience hears;

visual elements: everything in the play that the audience sees.

• *Plot* consists of ten elements: *exposition* (which ends with the *point of attack*), *complication* (which includes the *inciting incident*), *denouement, crisis, climax* (which concludes the *complication*), *foreshadowing, discovery,* and *reversal.*

• The final step in developing critical understanding beyond first impressions is finding the *style* or "personality" of the play. *Style* includes the "identifying characteristics" of the play, and various external factors can also influence the ways in which a play is written or produced—for example, the author's biography, certain movements in the arts, and the historical or cultural context in which the play was written.

• In order to get a broad picture of the various styles available to the playwright, we can define four that may help us to identify and describe others that we might encounter in the theatre:

classicism focuses on intellect and structure, restraint and control;

romanticism focuses on emotional appeal and experiments with language and form;

realism holds that art should portray life as we experience it and emphasizes its commonplace aspects;

expressionism tries to evoke audience responses similar to the artist's responses to the experiences depicted in the artwork.

• *Criticism* is detailed analysis aimed at understanding an artwork in one or more of its aspects. *Formal criticism* looks at an artwork without applying external information about it; *contextual criticism* applies such external conditions as the artist's biography or prevailing social and political conditions. Although criticism is a process of learning and sharing experiences, it is also often a matter of making *judgments;* the process of learning how to tell a "bad" artwork from a "good" one should emerge as part of the process of learning how to *interpret* an artwork.

• Two broad but useful *criteria* for judging artworks are *craftsmanship* (whether the work is sufficiently well made to be clear and interesting) and *communication* (whether the effort to interpret the work has been worthwhile in terms of what it helps us understand about our experience).

Chapter 4

Types *of* Plays

*A*fter studying this chapter,
you should be able to:

- Define the term *playwright* and explain how the playwright shapes the *script*.
- Identify and describe six of the major types of plays: *tragedies, comedies, history plays, tragicomedies, melodramas,* and *musicals*.
- Discuss several major plays as examples of particular play types.
- Characterize how, in Arthur Miller's view, tragedy can be applied to common as well as heroic events.
- Describe Edward Albee's approach to comedy.
- Describe Larraine Hansberry's concepts regarding A *Raisin in the Sun* as an example of melodrama.

William Faversham as Mark Anthony and Kenneth Hunter as Octavius in Julius Caesar.

We began this book with the assertion that a play—a work of art—was a vision of human reality manifest in a particular medium and shared with others. The way that a playwright perceives human reality often is described by the form or type of play through which that perception is presented: Words like *tragedy, comedy,* and *tragicomedy* describe the playwright's perceptions and help us to understand how we might respond to that perception—for example, is the play "serious," "satirical," or something else?

This chapter introduces us to some additional terminology fundamental to our understanding of the theatre. As the title of this chapter suggests, then, we are about to spend some time describing and giving some examples of a *few* of the many *types* or *forms* (I am using the terms as synonyms) of plays that we might someday experience—forms that have developed over the 2,500 years of recorded theatre history. Some types are as important as they were 2,500 years ago. Others have seen changes in the way playwrights use the approach. Still others have come and gone—in terms of the writing of new plays—although productions of such plays may still be mounted.

Playwrights *and* Playwriting

playwright Maker of plays; the theatre artist whose vision is transmitted through characterizations described by dialogue in a script

The term **playwright,** containing the term *wright,* suggests a *maker* of plays in the same way that *wheelwright* means a maker of wheels. One who makes plays is a person of the theatre, and the conditions of theatrical production impose themselves on the crafting of the play. The playwright's vision is transmitted through characterizations described by dialogue in a *script,* which others shape into a production (see Chapter 3). Since the nineteenth century, however, the playwright has been much further removed from the production of the play than in former times. For example, the Greek playwrights typically staged their own works; as we shall see in Chapter 16, Shakespeare and Molière both wrote for companies in which they held ownership shares and also acted.

With the exception of a brief period in the nineteenth century, and despite the conventions associated with some play forms, playwrights rarely craft plays according to specific formulas. They do, however, tend to adhere to broad theatrical *conventions*—otherwise, the audience could not comprehend what happens on stage. All in all, playwrights are free to range wherever and however they see fit. Ultimately, however, given the practicalities and conventions of the theatre, the *skill* with which playwrights craft their visions determines whether or not the play communicates to the audience. Left without the descriptive narrative of the novelist and faced with theatrical demands that do not necessarily occupy the poet, the playwright must use only his or her theatrical vision coupled with human dialogue to transmit a statement about human experience to the rest of us.

Plays: Six Types

Throughout history, playwrights have chosen a variety of forms or types of plays in order to reveal their vision of human reality. These forms have changed as society has changed. While many have passed out of existence, others are of recent derivation. In the remainder of this chapter, we will discuss a few major forms and some examples of each. We will discover that some forms can be represented by plays written in widely separated historical periods. Although tragedy and comedy are the oldest and may perhaps be called the "major" types of theatre, there are others, and we will take a quick glance at some of them as well. As we examine some of these forms or types, however, we must understand that they are not always as clear as the divisions or definitions in textbooks make them seem. Great variety exists within types, and many plays seem to defy categorizing altogether. There are many ways to organize an examination of play types. What follows is a more or less *generic* approach—that is, an examination organized by the common name of some of the more important types. We begin with tragedy, arguably the most significant of dramatic types, followed by comedy and then a few other types.

TRAGEDY

tragedy Complex theatre *type*, typically described as a play with an unhappy ending with a hero who makes a free choice that brings about suffering, defeat, and, sometimes, triumph as a result of defeat

We commonly describe a **tragedy** as a play with an unhappy ending. Tragedy is that and much more. The contemporary American playwright Arthur Miller describes tragedy as "the consequence of a man's total compulsion to evaluate himself justly, [and] his destruction in the attempt posits a wrong or an evil in his environment." In the centuries since its inception, tragedy has undergone many variations and definitional modifications as it served as a means by which playwrights made statements about human frailty and failing. Typically, tragic heroes make free choices that bring about suffering and defeat—and sometimes triumph as a result of defeat. Their struggles help us to find meaning in the pain and questions of our existence.

type Character who is larger than life—as opposed to a "real" or life-like individual

tragic flaw: Some defect that causes the hero of a tragedy to participate in his or her own downfall

The earliest tragedies were produced in ancient Greece, prior to the fifth century B.C. The name *tragedy* means "goat song," and several theories exist as to its derivation—for example, the chorus of the Greek tragedy may have dressed as goats (an animal sacred to the Greek gods). Another source may be Greek mythology, in which the god Zeus disguises Dionysus, the god of revelry and celebration, as a goat cared for by the daughters of Eleuther until Hera's jealousy subsides. In tragedy, the protagonist usually undergoes a struggle that ends disastrously. In Greek classical tragedy of the fifth century B.C. (see Chapter 3), the hero was generally a **type**—a larger-than-life figure—who gains a moral victory amid a physical defeat. The classical hero usually suffers from a so-called **tragic flaw**—that is, some defect that causes the hero to participate in his or her own downfall. In the typical structure of classical tragedies, the climax of the play occurs as the hero or heroine recognizes his or her role and accepts destiny.

Aristotle wrote in the *Poetics* that tragedy was "an imitation of an action" that concern the fall of a man whose character is neither too good nor too bad—that is, one who is capable of making an error—"whose misfortune is brought about not by vice or depravity but by some error or frailty." (Aristotle's famous discussion of the nature of the tragedy is excerpted in Chapter 15.) In the years from ancient Greece to the present, however, writers of "tragedy" have employed many different approaches in order to show the fall of an individual into misfortune. Shakespeare, writing in England in the sixteenth century, regularly mixed tragedy with comedy and poetic verse with prose.

In Shakespeare's *King Lear* (Fig. 4.1), the hero makes an unwise decision because of his own pride and shortsightedness. The consequences of that decision spin out in a downward spiral of destruction for all concerned.

Figure 4.1

Peggy J. Kellner, costume design for William Shakespeare's King Lear. *The Old Globe Theatre, San Diego. Because most people respond rather strongly to the play's darker side—its apparently overriding pessimism (indeed, nihilism)—it is often difficult to square* Lear *(1605) with Shakespeare's more orthodox religious morality in other plays. This same quality, however, has made* Lear *a favorite among 20th-century interpreters of Shakespeare, such as the producer-director Peter Brook (see Chapter 17), who poses as follows a few of the central questions raised by the play:*

So what does Shakespeare mean? . . . Does he mean that suffering has a necessary place in life and is worth cultivating for the knowledge and inner development it brings? Or does he mean us to understand that the age of titanic suffering is now over and our role is that of the eternally young? Wisely, Shakespeare refuses to answer. But he has given us his play, and its whole field of experience is both question and answer. In this light, the play is directly related to the most burning themes of our time, the old and the new in relation to our society, our arts, our notions of progress, our way of living our lives.

Types *of* Plays

King Lear *(ca. 1605)*

WILLIAM SHAKESPEARE

King Lear is a proud and arrogant old man who decides to divide his kingdom among his three daughters, with the largest inheritance going to the one who loves him the most. Two of the three flatter him with praise, but the youngest, Cordelia, who truly loves him, tells him the truth. In selfish anger, Lear rails against Cordelia, banishes her, and gives the entire kingdom to her sisters, Goneril and Regan. Now in control, the two eldest daughters proceed to strip Lear of all dignity and possessions: their true disaffection for their father shows itself openly. In his desperate state, while Lear gradually goes mad, he begins at the same time to know himself as a human being. In a subplot, meanwhile, the loyal Gloucester is also blind to the evil he has fathered in his illegitimate son Edmund. In a tragic action, Gloucester is physically blinded and in that state comes to "see" the truth about himself and his bastard son. Only through the actions of his son Edgar, who disguises himself as a madman, is Gloucester saved from despair and suicide. In the meantime, Lear and Cordelia are reunited and her love expressed and received. She dies in Lear's arms as he bemoans his fate.

Ghosts *(1881)*

HENRIK IBSEN

Mrs. Alving had married Captain Alving because he was a good match for her socially. Later, when she discovered that he was a philanderer, her Victorian sense of duty prevented her from leaving him. After their son was born, Mrs. Alving tried to escape the tangles of her marriage and its consequences by sending her son away to school so that he would not be corrupted by his father. After the Captain's death, she used his fortune to build an orphanage, thus preventing her son from inheriting "tainted" money while also protecting the Captain's reputation and hiding his true character.

At the beginning of the play, Mrs. Alving believes that she has finally laid to rest all of the ghosts of her past. Her son is about to return home to attend the dedication of the orphanage. As soon as the son arrives, however, the past begins to come to life. In imitation of his father, Oswald attempts to seduce one of the servants, who is actually his illegitimate half-sister. He then confesses to his mother that he is dying of syphilis, which he inherited from his father. His father's degeneracy and the true identity of the servant are revealed to him. Mrs. Alving reasons that death would be a merciful end for her son, but her maternal instinct will not allow her to commit the deed. As the play ends, the orphanage burns to the ground, and Mrs. Alving stands beside her muttering, insane son: His mind has turned to "cherry covered velvet," as he describes it—and he asks for "the sun."

Arthur Miller: Tragedy and the Human Animal

One of this country's foremost contemporary playwrights, Arthur Miller certainly understands the roots of both dramatic structure and tragedy in the classical theatre. He is, however, intensely aware of the "common" dramas enacted within the family under the pressures of modern life and argues here that not only genuine "tragedy" but also human fulfillment can result from the expression of "modest hope."

Our modern literature has filled itself with an attitude which implies that despite suffering, nothing important can really be learned by man that might raise him to a happier condition. . . .

Such a concept of man can never reach beyond pathos, for enlightenment is impossible within it, life being regarded as an immutably disastrous fact. Tragedy, called a more exalted kind of consciousness, is so called because it makes us aware of what the character might have been. But to say what a man might have been requires a soundly based, completely believed vision of man's great possibilities. As Aristotle said, the poet is greater than the historian because he presents not only things as they were, but foreshadows what they might have been. We forsake literature when we are content to chronical disaster.

Tragedy, therefore, is inseparable from a certain modest hope regarding the human animal. And it is the glimpse of this brighter possibility that raises sadness out of the pathetic toward the tragic. . . .

We forsake literature when we are content to chronicle disaster.

Tragedy arises when we are in the presence of a man who has missed accomplishing his joy. But the joy must be there, the promise of the right way of life must be there. Otherwise, an endless, meaningless, and essentially untrue picture of man is created—man helpless under the falling piano, man wholly lost in a universe which by its very nature is too hostile to be mastered.

In a word, tragedy is the most accurately balanced portrayal of the human being in his struggle for happiness. That is why we revere our tragedies in the highest, because they most truly portray us. And that is why tragedy must not be diminished through confusion with other modes, for it is the most perfect means we have of showing us who and what we are, and what we must be—or should strive to become.

In France during the seventeenth century, the neoclassicists Jean Racine and Pierre Corneille wrote under the strictures of "rules" for tragedy established and enforced by the French literary establishment. Modern playwrights, however, have exercised great freedom with regard to the treatment of "tragic" themes, characters, language, and situations. In our time more than any other, "ordinary" people have been portrayed as tragic heroes. Since the eighteenth century, the events of tragedies have increasingly centered on everyday situations, such as those that occur in Henrik Ibsen's *Ghosts* (Fig. 4.2).

Typical of the modern approach to tragedy is *Desire under the Elms* by Eugene O'Neill (Fig. 4.3). Here, the greed and self-absorption of the central characters create a web of conflict and sorrow out of which the characters climb in a final sort of victory—even in punishment.

Figure 4.2   *Henrik Ibsen,* Ghosts *(1881). Revival at the Empire Theatre, New York, 1935. Director, Alla Nazimova; scene designer, Stewart Chaney. Pictured: Nazimova as Mrs. Alving and Harry Ellerbee as Oswald. See the discussion of Ibsen in Chapter 17.*

Figure 4.3   *Set-design drawing for Eugene O'Neill's* Desire under the Elms, *1925. "The theatre," declared O'Neill,*

> should give us what the church no longer gives us—a meaning. In brief, it should return to the spirit of Greek grandeur. And if we have no Gods or heroes to portray, we have the subconscious, the mother of all gods and heroes.

Because the household stands at the center of Desire under the Elms, the Cabot house as depicted onstage must reflect the theme of a "real" family drama animated by the power of collective "subconscious" forces. Here, then, the Cabot house has been designed to suggest both the reality of the space inhabited by people on whom certain forces are closing in and a "theatrical" space— that is, the appropriate environment in which conflicting subconscious forces can be played out. Compare this design with the set design for O'Neill's The Hairy Ape at Fig. 3.12—an overtly expressionist play in which both depicted events and visualized scenic externals directly reflect the interplay of "subconscious" forces. See the discussion of O'Neill in Chapter 17.

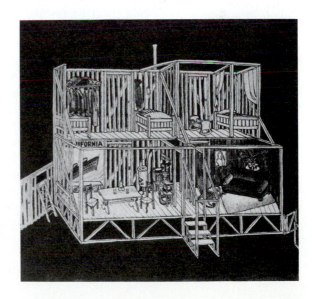

Types *of* Plays

Desire under the Elms *(1924)*

EUGENE O'NEILL

Ephraim Cabot is a stern and tyrannical New England homesteader. He is a widower who has lost two wives, and his three sons hate him. Two of them, Simeon and Peter, leave for the California gold rush, while the youngest, Eben, remains at home. Eben blames his father for his mother's death and considers himself the only rightful heir to the property and its brooding elms. While Eben presses his claim, Cabot marries for a third time. Abbie Putnam is a beautiful, sensuous young woman, and she seduces Eben so that she can have a child that Cabot will think his own and thus stake a claim to his property. Caught in their swirling passions and struggle for the farm, Abbie tries to prove her love for Eben by smothering the child. Shocked and repulsed by the crime, Eben rejects Abbie and reports her to the sheriff. He then changes his mind and confesses his part in the crime. They stand in torment but also in new-found human dignity as they accept their punishment.

COMEDY

comedy Highly complex play *type* embracing a wide range of theatrical approaches—from intellectual wit to slapstick

comedy of manners *Type* of dialogue-centered, "high" comedy popular in the 17th century and characterized by intellectual wit

low comedy Comedy that depends on action and situation, usually involving a trivial theme

farce Kind of *"low comedy"* involving exaggerated physical actions, mistaken identities, and pratfalls

In many respects, comedy is much more complex than tragedy and even harder to define. **Comedy** embraces a wide range of theatrical approaches, ranging from the intellectual wit of dialogue-centered "high comedy"—for example, the **comedy of manners** popular in the seventeenth century—to the slapstick, action-centered "low comedy" represented by a vast variety of plays from nearly every historical period. **Low comedy** may include a category that some theorists identify as a separate type: *farce.* **Farce** is typically a wildly active and hilarious comedy of *situation,* usually involving a trivial theme. It is the kind of comedy we associate with the Three Stooges—that is, exaggerated physical actions such as beatings, pies in the face, mistaken identities, and pratfalls. Whatever happens in a farce carries little serious consequence—at least within the play. For example, although violence occurs, no harm is suffered; adultery takes place, but no consequences result; brutality is perpetrated, but no one seeks revenge. Farce seems to provide an opportunity to act out deep and socially unacceptable desires without having to take responsibility for them. Thus, it seems that farce, though dealing with seemingly inconsequential matters in a superficial way, takes on a far more serious purpose in its wider consequences for an audience. Its differences from other varieties of comedy appear to lie in the method of its *treatment* of material rather than in its intent or *purpose.* Between the extremes just noted, for example, lies a variety of comic forms. One of these is the popular form called *domestic comedy,* in which family situations—such as those treated in many television "sitcoms"—form the focus of attention and in which members of a family and their neighbors find themselves in various complicated and amusing situations (examples in the theatre include Neil Simon's *Brighton Beach Memoirs* and *Broadway Bound*).

satire Use of derisive wit to attack folly or wickedness

In any case, comedy, defined in its broadest terms, may not even involve laughter. Many comedies employ stinging **satire** while others create an absorption in romance. We can probably say with some accuracy that "humor" forms the root of all comedy. In many circumstances, comedy treats a serious theme but remains, despite that seriousness, lighthearted in spirit. Characters, for example, may be placed in jeopardy, but not *too* seriously. To a large degree, comedy deals with the world as we find it and focuses on everyday people through an examination of the *incongruous* aspects of conduct and human relationships. Character and ideas are often the focus of comic plays. In the first instance, we focus on a person of eccentric character such as Molière's hypochondriacs, misanthropes, and misers. This technique relies on developing humor by contrasting the ways in which characters see themselves and are seen by others. In the second, we deal with a concept or a philosophy—for example, Aristophanes' satires on the political structures of ancient Athens, such as *The Frogs*, or George Bernard Shaw's *comedy of ideas*, such as *Major Barbara*, both of which are summarized in this chapter.

The idea that comedy ends happily is probably a common misconception—misconceived because of our expectations that, in "happy endings," all the characters are left more or less to do what they please. "Happy endings," however, can imply quite different sets of circumstances in different plays. Comedy appears to defy any such thumbnail definitions, and perhaps we should say that comedy can be defined as the sum of such partial definitions as "farce" and so on. In Renaissance England, for example, Shakespeare's plays *The Merry Wives of Windsor, The Merchant of Venice,* (see synopsis in this chapter), and *Twelfth Night* all have happy endings. As the literary theorist Northrop Frye points out, however, *happy* in these cases refers to forms of *plot resolution* and is underlain by a certain tone that is quite different, for example, from that of Shakespeare's "dark comedies," like *All's Well That Ends Well* and *Measure for Measure*. Similarly, the underlying tone in these plays is quite different from the characteristic and more bitter tone of Ben Jonson's comedies of the same period—for example, *Cynthia's Revels*—which rebuke human behavior and grant people a sort of divine parole if they'll shape up, reform, and contribute. These "happy endings" are purchased with the promise of human reconstruction, and often at the price of foregoing the sort of unbridled pursuit of human "happiness" that might be suggested by the term *happy ending* and seen in any number of other plays. All of our extensive categorizing may not mean much unless we are familiar with the actual plays suggested as examples. But it does further emphasize the point offered earlier that comedy is a deceptive form when it comes to creating a simple definition for it. For example, the Greek playwright Aristophanes (ca. 445-ca. 388 BC) fearlessly attacked Athenean life—its politics, poets, and religion—in his comedies. In *The Frogs,* the answer to his complaint that contemporary playwrights are inept is to bring back to life the old, dead ones. The play, a synopsis

Edward Albee: The Laughter in the Dark

Described by one critic as an exercise in "acute verbal sadism," Edward Albee's first full-length play, Who's Afraid of Virginia Woolf?, *was an immediate success despite its author's avowed principle that theatre should be "disturbing." Albee also believes that if theatre wants to change people, it must change itself, and one means toward that change, he feels, is to break free of conventional notions of what is "serious" and what is "humorous."*

Interviewer: The popular notion of Edward Albee is of a rather grim . . . .

Albee: Grim and humorless.

Interviewer: Yes, grim and humorless. From the beginning you have been labeled an "angry" playwright. Yet from the beginning there has always been a great deal of humor, especially through word play, in your work. . . .

Albee: . . . Humor—I've always thought that my plays were rather funny, and almost any work of art or play that has any merit or seriousness always has humor to it. I mean, well, there are exceptions. . . . I suppose there aren't too many jokes in *Oedipus*— one or two. But most art has a sense of absurdity—the laughter in the dark, be it what you will. And God knows, you better have it in the twentieth century.

Interviewer: Could you define what you mean when you refer to "serious? . . .

. . . Almost any work of art or play that has any merit or seriousness always has humor to it.

Albee: As opposed to frivolous? . . .

Interviewer: Yes, what do you mean by "serious drama"?

Albee: . . . Opposite of frivolous. Engagement rather than escapist. Involved rather than uninvolved.

Interviewer: And by definition, engagement can't really take us into lighter realms?

Albee: . . . I see no reason why it can't. Your true comedy which is not written by your gag writer—your true comedy is as instructive and useful as many other things.

Interviewer: *Virginia Woolf,* which a lot of people read as a very depressing play, seems to have a great deal of humor in it, again, especially the word play. Despite the fact that there is a great deal that is destructive about George and Martha, they seem quite admirable in many ways.

Albee: When I directed a revival in '76 . . . I tried to emphasize the fact that George and Martha enjoyed their verbal duels with each other, and while they were deadly serious, they were always at the same time in admiration of each other's skills. I wanted it to be clear that they were both using their minds very, very inventively throughout the play and that we would get some sense of the glee that they were having in what they were doing, and in that way reveal more of the humor of the piece. . . . I always thought I was a droll playwright. . . .

I'm interested in the fact that I write plays in such different styles from time to time. Different degrees of abstraction, that interests me. I'm not doing it to avoid, or to revenge, or to confuse, or to be fresh in my mind, even. I just do it because that is the way each one wants to be.

Interviewer: Would it be possible to abstract a definition of what drama means to Edward Albee?

Albee: I've written . . . what . . . nineteen plays out of the forty or so that I plan to write. And maybe when I am at the end of it, I may be able to say something comprehensive about the overall shape of it. But at this point, no. I just go on. I've got five plays in my head right now. One of them is about Attila the Hun, by the way, and four of them are not.

From Charles S. Krohn and Julian N. Wasserman, "An Interview with Edward Albee." In *Edward Albee: An Interview and Essays,* Julian N. Wasserman, ed. Houston: The University of St. Thomas, 1983, pp. 1–27.

of which follows, contains serious thought about victims of war as well as inventive comic fantasies—including dancing girls and a chorus of frogs (Fig. 4.4).

In another approach to comedy, Shakespeare uses a major character in

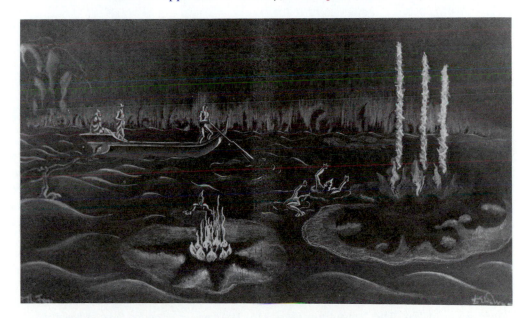

Figure 4.4 *Elemer Nagy, setting design for Aristophanes' The Frogs, Yale Dramatic Association, 1941. See the discussion of Aristophanes in Chapter 15.*

The Merchant of Venice (Fig. 4.5A), Shylock, whose dimensions certainly are not "comic" but whose behavior helps the playwright express his point of view within a comic framework. In this play, Shakespeare also uses a favorite device of comic playwrights—disguise: that is, the manipulation of the situation by creating confused or mistaken identity among the characters.

The French comic playwright Molière (who is discussed more fully in Chapter 16) tackles the subject of how to prevent a wife from being unfaithful. The way *not* to do it is tried by the central character of *The School for Wives* (see Fig. 4.6 and synopsis on page 106).

Another comic approach, heavy in the use of *irony* is that of George

Figure 4.5A   William Shakespeare, The Merchant of Venice (1596). *Oregon Shakespeare Festival, 1991. Pictured: Antonio and Portia.*

Figure 4.5B   *Sir Henry Irving as Shylock in Shakespeare's* The Merchant of Venice, *ca. 1880. Although happiness reigns for the Christian protagonists of Shakespeare's "comedy," the Jew Shylock, whose role is the most prized in the play, does not share in it; crucial elements of the play—namely, responses to this captivating figure—thus remain unresolved. A theatre manager as well as prestigious actor, Irving was knighted in 1895, the first English actor to be so honored.*

Figure 4.6   Molière, The School for Wives (1662) *Arena Stage, Washington, DC, 1992. Translator, Neil Bartlett; director, Kyle Donnelly. Pictured: Arnolph, Agnes, and Horace. See the discussion of Molière in Chapter 16.*

The Frogs *(405 B.C.)*

ARISTOPHANES

Dionysus (the god of wine and cult figure of an orgiastic religion celebrating the power and fertility of nature) is disgusted by the terrible state into which the writing of tragedy has fallen in Athens. As a result, he decides to go down to Hades and bring back the playwright Euripides. Remembering that his half-brother Heracles once went down to Hades to retrieve another dead soul, Dionysus disguises himself as Heracles by putting on a lion skin. Charon ferries Dionysus across the River Styx to the underworld where he is mistaken for Heracles and is both welcomed and attacked by the residents there. In order to escape those who wish to harm "Heracles" while benefiting from those who would welcome him, Dionysus makes his servant Xanthius wear the lion skin—depending on the circumstances. In the underworld,

Dionysus meets the older playwright Aeschylus, who demands that Dionysus take *him,* rather than Euripedes, back to Athens. At this point a battle ensues between the two playwrights to determine which was the better tragedian.

Here Aristophanes is using a satirical device to poke fun at what he considers the weaknesses and excesses of both playwrights. A series of contests is engaged, the climax of which has the two poets weighing their lines of poetry on a pair of scales. The humor of ultimately judging literary merit by the literal weight of the words reveals the playwright's more serious—and satirical—comment on the literary criticism and practice of the time. Dionysus finally chooses Aeschylus, and they return to Athens with the fond farewell of Pluto, god of the underworld.

The Merchant of Venice *(ca. 1596)*

WILLIAM SHAKESPEARE

Antonio, a merchant, borrows money from the Jewish moneylender Shylock in order to assist his friend Bassanio in the latter's courtship of the heiress Portia. Shylock (Fig. 4.5B), who has a simmering grudge against all Christians, demands that a pound of flesh be given as the penalty, in place of interest, if the loan is not repaid in three months. Antonio gives the money to Bassanio, and, with the 3,000 ducats now in hand, Bassanio and his loud friend Gratiano set off to woo Portia. In order to protect Portia from fortune-hunters, however, her father had decreed before his death that she would marry whoever rightly chose among three caskets—one of gold, one of silver, and one of lead. Portia truly loves Bassanio, and Bassanio proves his worthiness by distrusting

outward appearances and choosing the right casket. However, just as it seems that all will end happily, Antonio suffers a terrible business loss when his ships are lost at sea. He has no money and cannot repay the loan. Shylock—in a foul mood and more anti-Christian than ever because his daughter has just eloped with one—is disinclined to be generous and thus prepares to take his pound of flesh. Neither the Duke nor Portia, now disguised as a judge, can dissuade him. But Portia forbids him from shedding even one drop of blood in claiming his rights, and this strategy thwarts his intentions. Shylock is defeated and punished, and Portia mockingly tests Bassanio's love by tricking him into relinquishing his wedding ring as the play ends.

The School for Wives (1662)

MOLIÈRE

Arnolph, a wealthy middle-aged bourgeois, has remained unmarried because he is afraid of being betrayed (cuckolded) by a wife. In order to avoid such a state of affairs, he has raised his ward, Agnes, in complete isolation from and ignorance of the ways of the world. When she is of age, he plans to marry her. Agnes' innocence, however, proves to be the very cause of her interest in Horace, the son of an old friend of Arnolph's, whom she sees by accident over the wall of the garden in which she is literally held captive. Unaware of Agnes' relationship to Arnolph, Horace confides in Arnolph his feelings for Agnes and her return of his attention. Armed with Horace's confidence and ignorance of his true role and motives, Arnolph sets out to foil the relationship. His every effort causes the opposite effect from that intended, and in the end the young lovers overcome Arnolph.

Molière is employing here the convention of a series of *comic reversals:* The harder the character strives in one direction, the more his efforts cause him to go in just the opposite. In the midst of all these machinations, two comic servants, Alain and Georgette, constantly outwit their master as they bounce back and forth between his orders and Agnes' wishes. In this case, Molière employs yet another comic convention—that of mirroring the main plot in a subplot featuring characters of lower social class.

Major Barbara (1905)

GEORGE BERNARD SHAW

Salvation Army Major Barbara is the daughter of a munitions manufacturer, Undershaft, who considers poverty the worst possible evil. The play revolves around the conflicts between Undershaft and Barbara's scholarly suitor, who pretends to be interested in the Salvation Army in order to be near her. As the debate between the major characters rages, Barbara's sister and her boyfriend provide additional comedy through their obvious inability to understand what the others are discussing. Other characters represent working-class people and Salvation Army workers. The conventional Britisher, represented by Barbara's mother and brother, also bear the brunt of Shaw's comic invective. Eventually, Undershaft "wins" the debate by convincing Barbara that humankind's souls can be saved only if their stomachs are full; otherwise, they merely pretend to believe in Christianity in order to receive a bit of food.

Types *of* Plays

Figure 4.7   *George Bernard Shaw*, Major Barbara *(1905). Oregon Shakespeare Festival, Angus Bowmer Theatre, 1991. Director, Jerry Turner; scene designer, Richard L. Hay; lighting designer, James Sale; costume designer, Jeannie Davidson. See the discussion of Shaw in Chapter 17.*

irony Device, often in *plot*, marked by such a deliberate contrast that the apparent or literal meaning and the intended meaning are just the opposite of one another

Bernard Shaw (see Chapter 17). **Irony** is a device, often in plot, marked by such a deliberate contrast that the apparent or literal meaning and the intended meaning are just the opposite of one another, as in Shaw's play *Major Barbara* (see Fig. 4.7 and synopsis on page 106).

HISTORY PLAYS

History plays use history as source material and treat history in a serious manner. The form probably originated in medieval plays (see Chapter 15), which were very popular during the Elizabethan Renaissance. Shakespeare used the type extensively in plays that dealt with the lives of the English kings: *Henry IV, Henry V* (Fig. 4.8), *Henry VI, Richard II* (Fig. 4.9), *Richard III,* and *Henry VIII.* Shakespeare's *Julius Caesar* also falls into this category. The form is a broad one, including, perhaps, works as diverse as George Bernard Shaw's *Saint Joan* and Bertolt Brecht's *Galileo.*

Figure 4.8 *Shakespeare, Henry V (1599). Princess Theatre, 1859. Scene design by Thomas Grieve. Although the play itself is introduced by a chorus that speaks eloquently of national glory and heroism in war, Shakespeare's text actually calls for only brief onstage glimpses into the Battles of Harfleu, and Agincourt, where England's Henry V defeated the French in 1415. Shakespeare places epic historical events into highly personalized moral and psychological contexts.*

[Victoria and Albert Museum]

Figure 4.9 *Shakespeare, Richard II (1594). Contemporary watercolor by Thomas Grieve, London, 1857. Pictured: Act III, Scene 3—a broken man deserted by his supporters, Richard determines to confront Bolingbroke at Flint Castle in the aspect of a rightful king.*

[Victoria and Albert Museum]

Types *of* Plays

Richard II (ca. 1594)

WILLIAM SHAKESPEARE

Bolingbroke (later, King Henry IV), cousin of King Richard II of England, accuses Mowbray of plotting to kill the king's uncle. Richard decides to let Bolingbroke and Mowbray settle their dispute in a "trial by combat" at Coventry. Richard hopes that they will destroy each other and that he will then be rid of them both. However, he changes his mind and banishes them instead. On the death of John of Gaunt (Bolingbroke's father and Richard's uncle), Richard quickly appropriates Gaunt's property. When Bolingbroke hears of Richard's actions, he raises an army and returns to England to claim his rightful inheritance. While Richard is in Ireland, rumors of his death in combat reach his nobles, who desert him. He thus is forced to take refuge in Flint Castle, where he is discovered by Bolingbroke. By this point, although he retains his intelligence and sensitivity, Richard is a broken man. He is captured and forced to relinquish the throne to Bolingbroke at Westminister Hall. Deposed and weak, Richard is murdered by Exton, who believes that he is doing the new king a favor. Henry repents Richard's death and promises to do penance by visiting the Holy Land.

Saint Joan (1923)

GEORGE BERNARD SHAW

Figure 4.10 Katharine Cornell as Joan of Arc in George Bernard Shaw's Saint Joan, *Martin Beck Theatre, New York, 1936. Along with Lynn Fontanne and Helen Hayes, Cornell (1898–1974) was among the foremost actresses of the American theatre who rose to fame in the 1920s and 1930s. Noted for her ability to combine technique with intensity of performance, she was known popularly to many critics and audiences as "The First Lady of the Theatre."*

Shaw portrays Joan of Arc (Fig. 4.10) as a naive young woman in terms of politics and religious affairs even though she is a great military leader. She is a country girl who would be a foolish tomboy were it not for the dignity given to her by her profound faith. She is totally dedicated to France and honest in her dealings. The world she faces, however, is full of political intrigue and corruption. The people who take part in Shaw's great debate and Shaw's depiction of history are less than sublime. The Dauphin of France is childish and petulant; the generals are jealous of Joan's abilities; the archbishop fears the loss of his own political power. Joan's major military opponent, the Grand Inquisitor, balances her devotion with his own fanatical sincerity. In the end, Joan is the victim of the struggle between the medieval Church and the increasingly nationalistic European states. The play's epilogue is a dream sequence in which Joan learns that her honesty is just as untenable in the twentieth century as it was in the Middle Ages.

TRAGICOMEDY

tragicomedy Mixed *form* originally characterized as a serious play involving reversals, language appropriate to both tragedy and comedy, and ending free of disaster for the characters.

As the name suggests, **tragicomedy** is a mixed form that, like many other dramatic types, has been defined in different terms in different periods. Until the nineteenth century, the *ending* determined the necessary criterion for this form. In traditional tragicomedy, characters reflected diverse social standings—kings (as in tragedy) and common folk (as in comedy), and reversals went from bad to good and good to bad. Tragicomedy also included language appropriate to both tragedy and comedy. For the most part, tragicomedies were serious plays that ended, if not happily, then at least by avoiding catastrophe. In the last century and a half, the term has been used to describe plays in which the mood may shift from light to heavy or plays in which endings are neither exclusively tragic or comic. In Anton Chekhov's *The Three Sisters* (Fig. 4.11), for example, although nothing particularly terrible happens to the characters, they are trapped in an unfulfilling existence from which they cannot escape: They can only endure and survive. Samuel Beckett's *Waiting for Godot,* which we discussed in the last chapter, also represents this form in mixing humor and despair.

MELODRAMA

melodrama Mixed *form* characterized by stereotypical characters involved in serious situations portraying the forces of good and evil battling in exaggerated circumstances

Melodrama, another mixed form, takes its name from the Greek terms *melo,* meaning "music" and *drama.* "Melodrama" first appeared in the late eighteenth century, when the name implied a form in which the dialogue took place against a musical background. In the nineteenth century, it was used to describe serious plays without music. Melodrama uses stereotypical characters involved in serious situations in which suspense, pathos, terror, and occasionally hate are all aroused. This form portrays the forces of good and evil battling in exaggerated circumstances. As a rule, the issues involved in melodrama are in black-and-white terms—that is, simplified and uncomplicated: Good is good and evil is evil, with no ambiguous combinations.

Figure 4.11   *Anton Chekhov,* The Three Sisters *(1901). Curtain call at the Arena Stage, Washington, DC, 1984. Director, Zelda Fichandler; scene designer, Alexander Okum; costume designer, Ann Hould-Ward. See the discussion of Chekhov in Chapter 17.*

The Three Sisters (1901)

ANTON CHEKHOV

The three daughters of the commander of a local army post find their lives empty and without purpose. Their father has been dead for a year, and without his driving force in their lives, Olga, Masha, and Irina seek some substitute for the good times they formerly enjoyed. Olga turns to teaching but wishes for a home and family. Masha, unhappy in marriage to a boring schoolmaster, has an affair with a married colonel. Irina hopes to find her purpose in the "dignity of work" at the local telegraph office. More and more clearly, each sister realizes that her efforts are in vain and that her life is frustration. Their brother, meanwhile, marries a coarse peasant woman, whose presence in their home pushes the sisters even further into a sense of futility when even the solace of privacy is taken away. They dream of moving to Moscow to start new lives but cannot cope with the practicalities of making the change. Finally, when the army post is withdrawn from the town, they admit their hopelessness and, as the play ends, resolve to find some purpose and hope in life.

spectacularism Use of lavish settings and costumes to add sensational qualities to a dramatic production

Geared largely for a popular audience, melodrama concerns itself primarily with situation and plot. Conventional in its morality, it tends toward optimism—good generally triumphs in the end. Typically, the hero or heroine is placed in life-threatening situations by the acts of a villain and then rescued at the last instant. The forces against which the characters struggle are *external* ones—that is, caused by an unfriendly world rather than by inner conflicts. Probably because melodrama took root in the nineteenth century, at a time when scenic **spectacularism** was the vogue, many melodramas depend on "sensation scenes" for much of their effect. This penchant can be seen in the popular nineteenth-century adaptation of Harriet Beecher Stowe's novel *Uncle Tom's Cabin* (Fig. 4.12), as Eliza and the baby, Little Eva, escape from a plantation and are pursued across a raging, ice-filled river. These effects taxed the technical capacities of contemporary theatres to their maximum but gave the audience what it desired—spectacle. Perhaps the most extreme use of melodramatic spectacle came in the early-twentieth-century stage production of *Ben Hur,* wherein the famous chariot race was staged with two chariots and eight horses placed on two movable treadmills in front of revolving backdrops. Although not all melodramas use such extreme scenic devices, such use was so frequent that it has become identified with the type. Over its history, melodrama has encompassed a wide variety of plays, from those just mentioned to more restrained varieties like Lillian Hellman's *The Little Foxes* (1938) (Fig. 4.13) and perhaps Lorraine Hansberry's *A Raisin in the Sun* (1959).

Figure 4.12   *Production of* Uncle Tom's Cabin *(1852). Pictured: Simon Legree takes the whip to Uncle Tom. Although certainly triumphs of melodramatic "realism," both Harriet Beecher Stowe's immensely popular novel and the numerous stage adaptations that appeared during the year of its publication may also be considered drama as social and political weapon (see Chapter 2). One of the immediate effects of the sentiments expressed in* Uncle Tom's Cabin *was the call for Northern churches to defy the Fugitive Slave Act of 1850, and Abraham Lincoln is said to have addressed Stowe as "the little lady who made this big war." During the 1911–12 revolution in China, student productions of* Uncle Tom *were deemed appropriate weapons in the struggle for both social and literary change.*

Figure 4.13   *Lillian Hellman,* The Little Foxes *(1939). Ball State University Theatre, 1981. Director, R. Robbins; scene designer, Greg Haydock; lighting designer, D.C. Shwager; costume designer, Margi Deuhmig.*

Uncle Tom's Cabin (1852)

GEORGE L. AIKEN

(adapted from the novel by Harriet Beecher Stowe)

Uncle Tom's Cabin tells the story of slavery in the South with dramatic fury, fast action, and impressive scenery. When threatened with the prospect of being "sold down the river," the slave Eliza and the child, Little Eva, escape from the plantation. Pursued by slave hunters and bloodhounds, Eliza braves a perilous crossing over the ice floes on a raging river. The fabled Uncle Tom, who had earlier saved Little Eva's life and who is dearly loved by the slave owner's family, is nonetheless sold to the villain, the equally fabled Simon Legree, after Little Eva and her father die. The cruel Legree, despite the fact that Uncle Tom prays fervently for his conversion, ultimately beats Tom to death. The play is set in several locations in both the South and Vermont, where its comic character, Topsy, is taken after adoption by a Northerner. The final scene shows Uncle Tom rising into Heaven, where he is met by the angel Little Eva.

The Little Foxes (1939)

LILLIAN HELLMAN

Two brothers, Oscar and Benjamin Hubbard, and their sister, Regina Giddens, set out to raise money to build a cotton gin in their small southern town. Oscar's wife, Birdie, believes the family to be excessively greedy and tries to get Regina's daughter Alexandra to flee the family's plotting. Regina's husband, Horace, president of the local bank, is in a Baltimore hospital for treatment of a heart ailment. Nonetheless, when letters to Horace fail to yield the necessary dollars, Regina sends Alexandra to Baltimore to bring her father home. Though weak from the journey, Horace still refuses to come up with the money that his wife wants. Consequently, Benjamin and Oscar steal some securities belonging to Horace and decide to cut Regina out of her share of the scheme. When Horace tells his wife that her entire inheritance will be the stolen securities, she flies into a rage, revealing her true and malicious character. The discovery of his wife's true nature causes Horace to have a heart attack; he dies when Regina refuses to give him medication. Regina threatens to expose her brothers' theft and, in return for her silence, demands 75 percent of the cotton-gin business. Alexandra, who now cannot tolerate her family any longer, takes her aunt's earlier advice and leaves.

Lorraine Hansberry: Heroes, Realism, and Melodrama

The moment that Lorraine Hansberry's A Raisin in the Sun *opened on Broadway on March 11, 1959, she became one of America's preëminent black writers. The story of the Youngers, a black Chicago family,* Raisin *is a realistic play in three acts, all in one setting. The family is expecting a life insurance check, and while Mama wants to bring the family together in a home of their own, her son-in-law, Walter Lee, dreams of owning a business. Hansberry admits that although there is a "larger-than-life" element in the play, it is not necessarily simple melodrama. The interviewer is Chicago journalist Studs Terkel.*

Studs Terkel: Someone comes up to you and says, "A *Raisin in the Sun* is not really a Negro play. Why, this could be about anybody!" What is your reaction?

Lorraine Hansberry: What people are trying to say is that this is not what they consider the traditional treatment of the Negro in the theatre. They're trying to say that it isn't a propaganda play, that it isn't a protest play. They're trying to say that the characters in our play transcend category. However, it is an unfortunate way to try and say it, because I believe that one of the soundest ideas in dramatic writing is that in order to create the universal, you must pay very great attention to the specific. Universality, I think emerges from truthful identity of what is. . . .

Terkel: You've spoken of Walter Lee Younger, the focal character of the play, as an affirmative hero in contrast to many of the heroes of theatre such as we see today.

Hansberry: Walter is affirmative because he refuses to give up. There are moments when he doubts himself and even retreats. . . . There is a genuine heroism which must naturally emerge when you tell the truth about people. This to me is the height of artistic perception and the most rewarding kind of thing that can happen in drama.

Terkel: In your work, you showed Walter Lee's frailties throughout, and when he did emerge in that heroic moment, we *believed*.

Hansberry: That was the hope. That was the intent. What I do *not* believe in, to turn for a moment to technical dramaturgy, is naturalism. I think naturalism should die a quiet death. I *do* believe in realism.

Terkel: What's the difference?

Hansberry: There's an enormous difference. Naturalism is its own limitation—it simply repeats what *is*. But realism demands the imposition of a point of view. The artist creating a realistic work shows not only what *is* but what is *possible*—which is part of reality, too.

---

*So*ap opera implies melodrama . . . and melodrama has a classical definition. If you can prove that there are no motivated crises in the play, I would be astonished.

Terkel: But there is a great deal of poetry in *Raisin in the Sun*. A feeling that is larger than life. Isn't that what theatre should be?

Hansberry: Always. Always. There used be a ballet in this play. [Laughing.]

Terkel: There was a ballet?

Hansberry: That's right. The motifs of the characters were to have been done in modern dance. It didn't work! But I think that imagination has no bounds in realism—you can do anything which is permissible in terms of the truth of the characters. That's all you have to care about. . . .

I've been interested in some of the criticisms of the play—there was one let-ter in the *New York Times* from a very sophisticated young man who said he regarded it as a soap opera. Which amused me. Soap opera implies melodrama, of course, and melodrama has a classical definition. If you can prove that there are no motivated crises in this play, I would be astonished. Or a "happy ending"! If he thinks *that's* a happy ending, I invite him to come live in one of the communities where the Youngers are going! So I don't think the play qualifies as melodrama; it is legitimate drama.

It's very interesting to me that no one has picked out something that is a very genuine criticism of the play—that is that it lacks a central character in the true classical sense. There is a *pivotal* character. . . .

Terkel: Is this really a weakness? . . .

Hansberry: Well, obviously, when you start breaking rules you may be doing it for a good reason. But in my view of drama, the great plays have always had a central character with whom we rise or fall no matter what, from the Greeks through Shakespeare through Ibsen.

Excerpted by permission from Studs Terkel's interview with Lorraine Hansberry in the November 1984 issue of *American Theatre* magazine. Published by Theatre Communications Group.

opera comique Opera that, in addition to musical solos and ensembles, has dialogue that is spoken rather than sung

operetta Theatrical production that has many of the musical elements of opera, but is lighter and more popular in subject and style, and contains spoken dialogue

musical comedy Play in which dialogue is interspersed with songs and dances

musical Play in which dialogue is interspersed with songs and dances, but characterized by more serious subjects and treatments than "musical comedy."

The *musical* has a variety of applications, beginning, perhaps, with a type of opera called **opera comique**, which has spoken dialogue. As we think of it today, the form is probably an outgrowth of a musical form called **operetta**, which also has spoken dialogue but represents a lighter style of opera characterized by popular themes, a romantic mood, and an often humorous tone. The term *operetta* has slowly evolved into *musical*, with a stopover in the middle part of the twentieth century in the term *musical comedy*, which has been called the United States' unique contribution to the world of theatre. The **musical comedy** is characterized by the interspersing of dialogue and vocal solos, choruses, and dances, the ratio of dialogue to music varying widely from one musical to another. In many musicals, scenic spectacle plays an important role, in some cases—for example, *Starlight Express* and *Phantom of the Opera*—replacing the story and the music as a primary focus. The term *musical comedy* has now been replaced by the term **musical** because the form has increasingly treated serious and even tragic stories—for example, in *West Side Story, A Little Night Music, Cabaret,* and *Phantom of the Opera* (Fig. 4.14).

Figure 4.14 Phantom of the Opera (1987), Majestic Theatre, New York. Music by Andrew Lloyd Webber; director, Harold Prince; scene and costume designer, Maria Björnson.

SUMMARY

- The playwright is a "maker of plays" who transmits a vision through characterizations described by dialogue in a *script*.

- Among the choices made by the playwright are the various *forms* or *types* of plays in which a vision can be transmitted. We will experience many forms of plays as we attend the theatre. Among the more important of these are:

Tragedy: a complex form often described as a play with an unhappy ending; it is that and much more; typically, tragedies involve heroes who make free choices that bring about suffering, defeat, and, sometimes, triumph as a result of defeat; the struggles of tragic heroes help us to find meaning in the pain and questions of our existence.

Comedy: perhaps even more complex and difficult to define than tragedy, a form embracing a wide range of theatrical approaches ranging from intellectual wit to *slapstick*.

History play: a serious treatment of historical events in dramatic format.

Tragicomedy: a mixed form that has been defined differently in different periods: in its early forms tragicomedy was a serious play characterized by reversals, language appropriate to both tragedy and comedy, and endings free of disaster for the characters.

Melodrama: another "mixed form" typically using stereotypical characters in serious situations and depicting the battles between "good" and "evil."

Musical: a type of play characterized by the interspersing of dialogue with vocal solos, choruses, and dance.

Diary of a Production

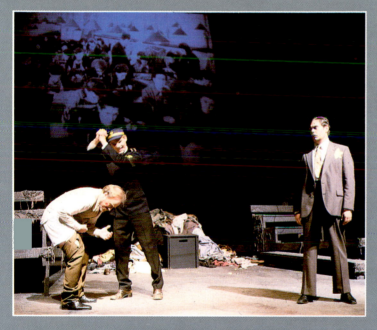

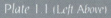

Plate 1.3 *(Above)*
Srulik's dummy comes to life as a figment
of a memory through which he can look back
at the Vilna ghetto from forty-five years in
the future.

Plate 1.1 *(Left Above)*
The warmth and human spirit of the Jewish ghetto pours forth in
the inhabitants' plaintive songs.

Plate 1.2 *(Left Below)*
The cold cruelty of Nazi oppression is reinforced by the lighting
designer's use of cold, flat light.

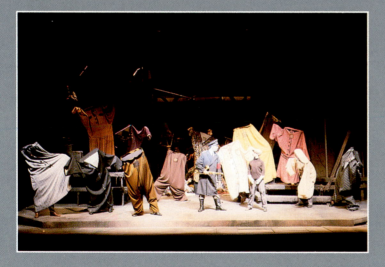

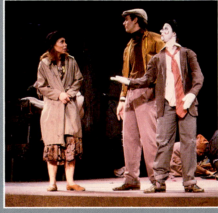

Plate 1.6 (*Above*)
Chaja, the singer, Srulik, and the Dummy draw focus downstage, as other ghetto residents go about their business in the background.

Plate 1.4 (*Left Above*)
As three young thugs smuggle a corpse into the ghetto, Kruk, director of the library, keeps a journal of ghetto activities and acts as a narrator for the play.

Plate 1.5 (*Left Below*)
"The Dance of the Clothes": Bathed in the garish white light of the ghetto theatre, the residents become oversized clothing—a symbol of their very existence.

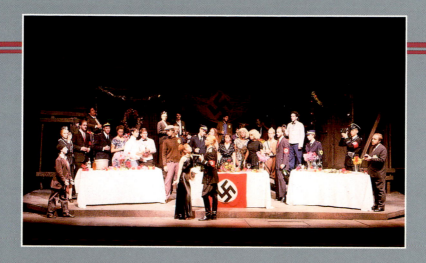

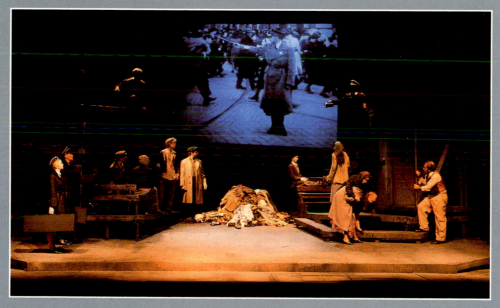

Plate 1.7 (Above)
A banquet for the residents — at which, for the first time, flowers are allowed in the ghetto — is arranged by the Nazi Kittle, Gens, the head of the Ghetto, and Weiskopf, the owner of the clothing factory. The occasion quickly becomes an obscene orgy because of the actions of the Nazis and the ghetto police.

Plate 1.8 (Below)
Color, actor arrangement, and front and back lighting combine to create a tableau in which the audience focuses on the projections depicting actual scenes from the Holocaust.

Plate 1.11 (Above)
As an old man, Srulik remembers the past and the people of the ghetto during those terrible years. He is isolated by a warm light that stands in contrast to the cool images of the past.

Plate 1.9 (Left Above)
Strong colors, high platforms, and careful arrangement of the cast create a dynamic scene embracing the residents of the Vilna ghetto.

Plate 1.10 (Left Below)
The SS officer Kittle—dangerous and ever-present—emerges even from a huge pile of clothing to menace the Jewish residents of the ghetto. To stay alive, the ghetto residents are put to work in a clothing factory to refurbish old clothing for the German army.

Chapter 5

The Audience

Expectation, Perception, and Response

*A*fter studying this chapter, you should be able to:

- Describe the communication process that transpires between a performance and the audience.

- Understand what it might have been like to be an audience member in the theatre at other times in history.

- Explain how physical *proximity* to the stage can effect audience response.

- Characterize how *attention* affects audience perception and performer action.

- Define the important concepts in audience response called *willing suspension of disbelief, aesthetic distance, sympathy,* and *empathy.*

- Identify and describe how *perception* is enhanced through *variety* and *focus.*

- Discuss the audience experience in terms of its *individual and group reactions, experience,* and *motivation.*

An Italian Comedy in Verona, 1772, by Marco Marcola. Oil on canvas, 115.3 × 84.2 cm. Courtesy of the Art Institute of Chicago. Gift of Emily Crane Chadbourne, 1922.4790.

*I*n 1830, Victor Hugo's play *Hernani* opened in Paris. In the audience were many theatre goers who believed that plays should conform to very strict rules governing language, plot, mood, and decorum. Also in the audience, however, were those who were tired of the old ways and restrictive rules. *Hernani* is primarily a melodrama with an unhappy ending. It is the story of a noble outlaw, Hernani, who, despite the opposition of the king and her guardian, wishes to marry Dona Sol. Eventually, Hernani wins the hand of Dona Sol, and the couple looks forward to a happy life together. However, Hernani is reminded that at one time, in a moment of crisis, he had pledged to Dona Sol's guardian that he would give his life if the guardian ever requested it. When the vengeful guardian decides to invoke the pledge, Hernani and Dona Sol commit suicide rather than choose dishonor.

The fact that, in this play, Hugo chose to fly in the face of tradition by using common language long considered beneath the dignity of tragedy, by changing locations and stretching the plot over an extended time period, by showing death and violence on stage, and by changing the mood frequently by mixing comedy and seriousness caused the audience to fly into a furor (see Fig. 5.1). Every night, violent arguments arose in the theatre between traditionalists and adherents of change. The commotion was so great that the actors could scarcely be heard. Such was the effect of one play on audience expectation, perception, and response.

Exploring the art of theatre requires that we spend much of our time

Figure 5.1

Albert Besnard, Premier d'Hernani, 25 February 1830. Although even the actress who played Dona Sol complained about the questionable taste of some of her lines, Victor Hugo's Hernani was a huge commercial success, with audience members often staying after the performance to debate its merits. Hugo's contribution to Romanticism in the French theatre is discussed in Chapter 16.

[Victor Hugo Museum, Paris.]

The Audience

Mrs. Trollope (I): "*Domestic Manners*" in the Frontier Theatre

Frances Trollope, the mother of the English novelist Anthony Trollope, visited America between 1827 and 1841 to take the social and cultural pulse of the new country. Her first three years were spent in Cincinnati, where she observed democracy and "domestic manners" on the "frontier," including a local performance by the distinguished touring actors Mr. and Mrs. Alexander Drake.

Men came into the lower tier of boxes without their coats; and I have seen shirt sleeves tucked up to the shoulders; the spitting was incessant, and the mixed smell of onions and whiskey was enough to make even the Drakes' acting dearly bought. . . .

The bearing and attitudes of the men are perfectly indescribable; the heels thrown higher than the head, the entire rear of the person presented to the audience, the whole length supported on the benches, are among the varieties that these exquisite posture-masters exhibit. The noises, too, were perpetual, and of the most unpleasant kind; the applause is expressed by cries and thumping with the feet, instead of clapping; and when a patriotic fit seized them, and "Yankee Doodle" was called for, every man seemed to think his reputation as a citizen depended on the noise he made.

The spitting was incessant. . . . Everyone agreed that the morals of the Western world would never recover the shock.

Two very indifferent figurantes, probably from the Ambigu Comique, or la Gaieté, made their appearance at Cincinnati while we were there; and had Mercury stepped down, and danced a *pas seul* upon earth, his godship could not have produced a more violent sensation. But wonder and admiration were by no means the only feelings excited; horror and dismay were produced in at least an equal degree. No one, I believe doubted their being admirable dancers, but every one agreed that the morals of the Western world would never recover the shock. When I was asked if I had ever seen any thing so dreadful before, I was embarrassed how to answer; for the young women had been exceedingly careful, both in their dress and in their dancing, to meet the taste of the people; but had it been Virginie in her most transparent attire, or Taglioni in her most remarkable pirouette, they could not have been more reprobated. The ladies altogether forsook the theatre; the gentlemen muttered under their breath, and turned their heads aside when the subject was mentioned; the clergy denounced from the pulpit.

examining what happens on the stage, why it happens, how it happens, and who makes it happen. We cannot forget, however, that everything and everyone concerned with the stage is there ultimately because of the group of people who come to the theatre to witness the production—that is, the audience. In this chapter, we will focus on some of the relevant factors concerning audiences: who we are, how we communicate, what we expect, how the production appeals to us, and how we respond to what we experience. When all is said and done, theatre artists want to say something to the audience, and they want the audience to respond in a particular manner. Just as in individual personal relationships, communicating and achieving desired results in the theatre requires as much knowledge as possible about those to whom we wish to communicate and whom we wish to motivate. In the same sense, communication and response, whether in individual relationships, or in the theatre, require that we know something about ourselves and why we are apt to act as we do when someone seeks to communicate with us in a particular manner.

The Audience: Five Historical Perspectives

Understanding the communicative process is essentially what this chapter is about, although for part of our examination I will transport us back to periods in the past to see how it might have felt to be an audience member at various other times. Although that discussion is historical, we include it here rather than in the chapters on theatre history because it can help us to understand our role and actions as audience members by comparing and contrasting the way we feel about theatrical production with the actions and expectations of other people at other times. Therefore, as a prelude to some of the weightier matters that are to come, let's travel back and attend some plays with people of different times. Although we cannot survey every place and time, we can sample a small variety of differing circumstances.

Ancient Greece

Let's step back 2,500 years and attend the opening of Aeschylus' *The Oresteia* in the theatre at Athens. As individuals, we would have come to the theatre as citizens, women, slaves, or foreigners. All classes and categories attended, and for citizens—that is, free males—attendance was more or less obligatory. It is a religious festival time, and we are going to the slopes of the Acropolis to the theatre of Dionysos (Fig. 5.2) to spend the entire day. *The Oresteia* is a trilogy of tragedies by Aeschylus—*Agamemnon, The Libation Bearers,* and *The Eumenides (The Furies)*—all of which will be performed today because they are among the winners of a yearly competition.

Figure 5.2   *Model of the Theatre of Dionysos at Athens, ca. 400 BC. The role of Dionysian worship in the development of Greek theatre is explained at Fig. 15.1.*

The Oresteia

In *Agamemnon*, King Agamemnon returns from the Trojan war with the captive Trojan princess Cassandra. His wife, Clytemnestra, and her lover, Aegisthus, murder Agamemnon and Cassandra. In *The Libation Bearers*, Orestes, son of Agememnon and Clytemnestra, returns home after many years. Met and recognized by his sister Electra, he is urged by her and the god Apollo to take revenge on his mother and her lover for the murder of his father. He does the deed, but is then pursued by the Furies (Eumenides) because he has committed matricide. Finally, in *The Furies*, (Fig. 2.8A), Orestes seeks sanctuary in Apollo's temple and appeals for help to the goddess Athena. Athena decides to put Orestes on trial and to act as judge in that trial. Apollo defends Orestes, and the Furies act as prosecutor. Twelve Athenian citizens form the jury. The jury vote is a tie, and Athena casts the deciding vote in favor of Orestes' acquittal. She then pacifies the Furies, who agree to act in a new role as benefactors of the city of Athens.

We are in high spirits, expecting to see the best of the best and preparing to witness a part of our strongly felt cultural heritage. Whatever our social standing, most of us know the story. As an important part of our cultural understanding, the mythological history of the House of Atreus, which the play is about, means as much to us as the stories of the Founding Fathers and the Revolutionary War will to an American.

Our way to the theatre takes us through the agora, the ancient market-place at the foot of the northeast corner of the Acropolis, that dramatic precipice which juts up out of central Athens. Atop is the Parthenon, the great Temple of Athena, patron goddess of Athens. As we wind our way up the lower slopes of the Acropolis, the Thysseon temple rises to our right, and we walk below a huge outcrop of rock where, 500 years later, the Apostle Paul will preach Christianity to the Athenians. As we work our way around the cliffs of the Acropolis, we come finally to the southwest corner and enter the large amphitheatre stretching up the slope. The cut-stone seats are filling up, and perhaps 20,000 of our fellow Athenians join us for the day's festivities. The plays that we are about to see represent our political and religious heritage, but even if the stories are well known to us, the playwright's treatment is not, and so we wait eagerly to see how Aeschylus will develop the familiar characters of Agamemnon, Clytemnestra, and Orestes. Perhaps we will get a novel glimpse of the dramatic conflict and better understand how it causes the characters to react. This experience is part of our education—indeed, part of our social responsibility. As we look at ourselves, we see our humanity as a complex experience in which training in science, the arts, philosophy, and athletics plays an essential role. For us, theatre is not entertainment—it is an experience in healthy living. We have a zest for living and thinking. Our quest for knowledge seems insatiable, and our tastes and expectations vary widely from tragedy to comedy.

ANCIENT ROME

Four hundred fifty years have elapsed, and we are wandering through the streets of Rome. Augustus is emperor, and the Roman Empire is at its zenith, stretching from the British Isles to the far reaches of the Middle East. In less than a century, rumblings from Judaea will carry the unsettling news of a new and rapidly spreading religion based on the teachings of Jesus of Nazareth, whom his followers are calling the Christ. Here in Rome, however, things are somewhat unsettled: As we walk along the Tiber river toward the theatre that sits on its banks, we are likely to pass performers presenting mimes and farces to large crowds of lower-class people, mostly the unemployed and hungry who have come to Rome from the conquered regions of the empire in hopes of finding some form of survival better than what they have left behind. Disappointed, they are kept entertained by actors, musicians, and all manner of performers. The whole spectacle is supported largely by the government to keep the people distracted. Like the Greeks, they are a cosmopolitan audience; in addition to the rabble, any number of other classes of individuals also pause to see what the actors have to present. Sometimes it is pretty strong stuff, with a corrupt local official or inept public servant being attacked through the vehicle of the drama. The audience is more like an unruly crowd. However, we have more important theatre to attend. Here, in the pleasant surroundings of a stone building, built with our comfort as an audience in mind, we will mingle with a better class of people—like ourselves, people well educated by our Greek slaves and reasonably secure in our financial and social positions. We will experience a variety of fare ranging from the comedies of Plautus, written over 200 years ago, to bawdy, lascivious mimes and pantomimes.

The Menaechmi

Twin brothers, Menaechmus I and Menaechmus II, were separated in childhood. Menaechmus II comes to Epidamnus in search of his brother, who has settled there and married. Everyone in Epidamnus, including Menaechmus I's wife,

Figure 5.3 *Interior of the Roman theatre at Orange. Compare this theatre with the Greek Theatre of Dionysos in Fig. 5.2. Although less sophisticated than the Greeks in both architecture and drama, the Romans were better engineers. For example, by reducing the orchestra to a semicircle and attaching it to the auditorium complex, they improved acoustics, and the regularly spaced doors above the auditorium, called* vomitoria, *made entry and exit into more convenient. By law, only spectators of privileged rank, who brought their own portable seating, could occupy the auditorium.*

mistress, and others, mistakes brother II for brother I. Confusion and mayhem result, but Menaechmus II does not catch on to the cause of all the calamity. Rather, he accepts it and, by so doing, unwittingly adds to the confusion. After a series of comic episodes based on mistaken identity, the brothers are reunited and all the confusions are explained.

Our expectations are much more superficial than those of our Greek neighbors of 475 B.C. As a result, the fare we witness is much less profound and includes more light comedies than serious works.

ELIZABETHAN ENGLAND

We are now standing on the banks of the Thames River, across from the City of London, in the early seventeenth century. We make our way along the footpath toward one of several theatres, mostly octagonally shaped buildings called the Globe and the Swan (Figs. 5.4A and 5.4B). Along with perhaps as many as 2,500 other souls, we will see a new comedy by Ben Jonson, *Volpone*.

Volpone

Volpone, a rich Venetian, cons other rich people into giving him their money by pretending to be on the verge of dying. With the help of the cunning servant Mosca, each victim is convinced that he or she is Volpone's sole heir. As these connivances evolve, Volpone finally undoes himself by attempting to rape a woman brought to him by her own husband. Having been discovered, Volpone ridicules his "heirs-to-be" and makes Mosca his beneficiary. The greedy Mosca takes over Volpone's house and eventually evicts Volpone. Everyone ends up in court, where Volpone and Mosca both receive their just punishments.

As members of the aristocracy, we will sit in the galleries surrounding the stage, above the pit where the common folk stand to see the performance. The emotional sense among the audience is one of lively expectation. We are an enthusiastic lot, all of us, and our interest in politics, language, literature, and music is keen. The age is one of intellectual ferment, and with the expanding wealth and size of the middle classes, this enthusiasm permeates society from top to bottom. We live in that time called the Renaissance, and the focus on human potential and achievement gives daily life a dynamic and positive cast.

Figure 5.4A The Swan Theatre, 1614. Although theories about the origin of the Elizabethan playhouse still abound, the Swan is often regarded as one of the best available models of the 16th-century English theatre. The Swan is said to have held about 3000 spectators, and reports of the neighbors' complaints about noise and traffic date from as early as 1597. The Elizabethan playhouse is discussed in more detail in Chapter 16.

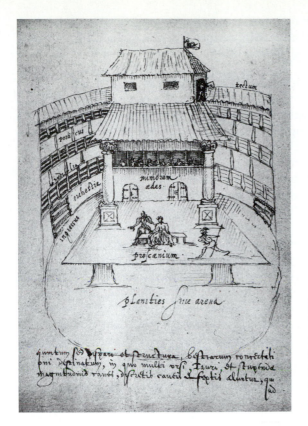

Figure 5.4B *Johannes DeWitt, interior of the Swan Theatre, ca. 1596. Because the Elizabethan playhouse was open, the English climate dictated the theatre season. Spectators could either stand on the ground floor, called the "pit" or the "yard," or sit in one of three tiers of balconies.*

[University Library, Utrecht]

The theatre gives us a window into our age, and professional theatre in London draws perhaps as many as 30,000 customers every week. Competition among the theatre companies creates lively theatre fare that provides a focus for social and intellectual life in this flourishing capital city. We desire pageantry, vitality, and action, and we find it in deeply probing dramas, comedies, and histories that have a magical appeal to all classes and intellectual tastes. Even the most common among us has a curiosity and love of our native language, and playwrights like Jonson, Marlowe, and especially Shakespeare, who can weave poetic tapestries in the language of his plays, gain easy popularity among us all. Of course, we want action as well as high ideas, and the dramatic fare of our theatre provides that as well. We marvel at the fast-paced action of these plays as they unfold in the various parts of the open stage before us. Scenes move from the main stage area to areas on a second level to the center and the sides. Thunder and music come from a gallery on the third level above the stage. Actors are revealed from behind curtained alcoves at the rear of the stage. It seems perfectly natural to us not only that the actors are in contemporary clothing but that all the women's parts are played by boys. There is no scenery except a few small set properties, and yet we feel ourselves fully a part of the action and the time of the plays. In fact, the action can be quite violent at times. Our diversity as an audience seems to stimulate our playwrights, and the plays that we admire appeal to a broad spectrum of taste as they reveal to us the world around us.

THE ENGLISH RESTORATION

As members of the aristocracy in England at the end of the seventeenth century, we have been riding an emotional high since 1660 when, after a terrible civil war, the monarchy was reestablished and Charles II returned to the throne from France, where he had lived in exile since the execution of his father and the institution of the Commonwealth. Now the theatre has become strictly a court activity, and when we attend, we are surrounded by fops, wits, prostitutes, and other court hangers-on. The audience is so small now that, despite the size of the city of London, only two professional theatres exist. For us, theatre is a fashionable outlet in which to see and be seen. The fare we watch is designed to reinforce our narrow world view and shield us from the realities of everyday life. Our favorite plays are social comedies dealing with the foibles of our fashionable peers. The most popular, however, are the satires of the Puritans, who made our lives miserable for twenty years before the Restoration of the king. The fact that we are so limited in numbers and perspective makes it rather easy for playwrights to fulfill our expectations. They write witty language, hurl invective at our enemies, and dwell on intrigue and manners. We love repartee and eloquence in dialogue. What we want as an audience is what we get in plays like William Congreve's *The Way of the World*.

The Way of the World

Mirabell, a reformed rake, loves Millamant, a beautiful young woman. However, his past includes an affair with Mrs. Fainall, now married to a gentleman of great wit. Using secrecy, disguise, and carefully planned misunderstanding, Mirabell pursues Millamant while interacting with individuals whose names reveal their characters—for example, Wishfort and Witwoud. Ever elusive, Millamant finally succumbs to Mirabell's proposal, and they plan a marriage that will create dignity and independence for both of them in the midst of a generally corrupt society.

MODERN TIMES

Today, we usually can find nearly any kind of theatre anywhere we look—a comedy produced by a local high school, a classic done by a community theatre group, an experimental production at a local college, or a Broadway musical done by a professional touring company. If we live in a large metropolitan area, we may have several professional companies from which to choose, plus a variety of amateur and educational productions. When we attend the theatre, we may be among our closest friends and relatives or in a diverse group of strangers. Often, we discover that the plays to which we respond well have quite a different effect on our parents or even our friends.

One of the things that makes our experience different from that of audiences of the past is the fact that we are free to choose what we will attend, and the plays available to us are not, for the most part, censored or sanctioned by any particular authority or point of view. We have a further advantage in the fact that, perhaps more than at any other time in history, the plays of the past are performed frequently as, or more frequently than, the plays of the present. Thus, we have the opportunity to view and respond to the widest possible array of the expression of "reality" as represented in the art of theatre. The influence and experience of our forebears from ancient Greece, for example, can in a current production affect us profoundly.

As audience members of the present, we recognize the diversity of approaches that theatre artists can use in staging a play. The "openness" of our aesthetic conventions and standards makes it possible for a production of, say, Shakespeare's *A Midsummer Night's Dream* to recreate the architectural stage environment of the Globe Theatre in the style of the original production; it might also be produced in the fully realistic style of the nineteen-century approach to Shakespeare; or it might even be produced in a novel and controversial style (Fig. 5.5). On the other hand, we might be seeing a controversial new play that makes us uneasy in our expectations of what theatre should portray—for example, a play like Henry David Hwang's *M Butterfly* (Fig. 5.6).

Figure 5.5 *Sally Jacobs, scene design for* A Midsummer Night's Dream, *Royal Shakespeare Company, 1970. Director, Peter Brook. Another scene from this well known production can be found at Fig. 8.4. Brook's contributions to contemporary interpretations of classic and modern play scripts are discussed in Chapter 17.*

M Butterfly

A French diplomat in Beijing, Gallimard, falls in love with a Chinese opera star, Song Liling. His love is so complete and so blind that he totally misses the fact that she is really a man. The affair lasts for twenty-one years, and during that time Gallimard passes diplomatic secrets to Song Liling. As a result, Gallimard is arrested, imprisoned, and disgraced. When he finally comes to the realization that his lover is really a male, he is unable to accept reality and retreats into madness.

Theatre *and* Communication

Any human communication requires three factors— a *sender*, a *medium of transmission*, and a *receiver*. For effective communication to occur, the sender must comprehend and place in usable syntax whatever message is to be sent. The medium must be free of unwanted distractions, and the receiver must invest the effort necessary to find meaning in the message. In the theatre as in life, our perception is enhanced if we have a reasonable grasp on who we are, how we tend to react in certain kinds of circumstances, and whether we can accept responsibility for our part in the communication chain. We all know, for example, how many understandings can occur in human communication. How far must the sender go to communicate in a language and a style appropriate to the situation and acceptable to the receiver? How far must the receiver go in order to be sure that the proper *interpretation* has been given to the message received?

We also know that who we are and how we are prone to perceive the world has a lot to do not only with *what* we communicate to those around us, but also with *how* we receive what they have to say. As theatre-audience members, we are subject to the same circumstances with regard to the mes-

August Wilson: The Audience Outside the Mainstream

Pittsburgh-born August Wilson, whose play Fences *won the 1987 Pulitzer Prize for drama, is one of America's foremost black playwrights. Although plays like* Fences *and* Ma Rainey's Black Bottom *have been highly successful both on Broadway and on tour, Wilson remains committed to communicating with an audience whose cultural experience informs his own perceptions and his own message.*

ONE OF YOUR CHARACTERS SAID, "EVERYONE HAS TO FIND HIS OWN SONG." HOW DO THESE PEOPLE FIND THEIR SONG?

They have it. They just have to realize that, and then they have to learn how to sing it. In that particular case, in *Joe Turner,* the song was the African identity. It was connecting yourself to that and understanding that this is who you are. Then you can go out in the world and sing your song as an African.

DO YOU THINK THOSE PEOPLE IN PITTSBURGH MUST FIND THE AFRICAN IN THEM OR IN THEIR PAST BEFORE THEY REALLY KNOW WHO THEY ARE?

Yes, they are African people. We are Africans who have been in America since the seventeenth century. . . . We have a culture that's separate and distinct from the mainstream white American culture. We have different philosophical ideas, different ways of responding to the world, different attitudes, values and linguistics, different aesthetics—even the way we bury our dead is different.

WHAT HAPPENS WHEN YOU GET IN TOUCH WITH THAT SENSIBILITY?

When white Americans look at a black, they see the opposite of everything that they are. This is what black means. We are a visible minority in this linguistic environment, and we are victims of that. It's not a question of going back to Africa. It's to understand that Africa is in you, that this is who you are and that there isn't anything wrong with being an African, even though the linguistic environment teaches that black is all these negative things.

We have different philosophical ideas . . . different attitudes . . . different aesthetics—even the way we bury our dead is different.

BUT IF BLACKS KEEP LOOKING FOR THE AFRICAN IN THEM, IF THEY KEEP RETURNING SPIRITUALLY OR EMOTIONALLY TO THEIR ROOTS, CAN THEY EVER COME TO TERMS WITH LIVING IN TWO WORLDS? AREN'T THEY ALWAYS GOING TO BE HELD BY THE PAST IN A WAY THAT IS POTENTIALLY DESTRUCTIVE?

It's not potentially destructive at all. To say that I am an African, and I can participate in this society as an African, is to say that I don't have to adopt European values, European aesthetics and European ways of doing things in order to live in the world. We would not be here had we not learned to adapt to American culture. Blacks know more about whites in white culture and white life than whites know about blacks. We *have* to know because our survival depends on it. White people's survival does not depend on knowing blacks.

YOU HAD A WHITE FATHER. AND YET YOU CHOSE THE BLACK ROUTE, THE BLACK CULTURE, THE BLACK WAY. . . . YOU DIDN'T MAKE A CONSCIOUS CHOICE, YOU DIDN'T SAY, "I'M GOING TO CHOOSE BLACK."

No, that's who I always have been. The

cultural environment of my life, the forces that have shaped me, the nurturing, the learning, have all been black ideas about the world. . . . In the '60s, you became temporarily a black nationalist.

I still consider myself a black nationalist and a cultural nationalist.

WHAT'S THAT?

That's a good question. I simply believe that blacks have a culture, and that we have our own mythology, our own history, our own social organizations, our own creative motif. That's what I mean when I say cultural nationalist.

From *Bill Moyers: A World of Ideas* by Bill Moyers. Copyright © 1989 by Public Affairs Television, Inc. Used by permission of Doubleday, a division of Bantam Doubleday Publishing Company.

sages of the theatre communicators (playwright, director, designers, actors) as we are in any other human situation. To be effective audience members, we must know who we are.

PROXIMITY: PHYSICAL AND PERSONAL SPACE

Each of us has a set of "baggage" that we bring with us to the performance and that we will shed only with great effort. Who we are dictates much of the potential for a performance to affect us. Some of us, for example, are highly protective of our physical space and reserved in our ability to come physically close to others. In that case, we might be threatened by a production in which the actors come into the audience space and interact with us. For example, in a production of Euripides' *The Bacchae* at the University of Illinois at Chicago Circle, the actors, dressed in body stockings (Fig. 5.7), climbed down into the audience from the balcony and crawled over audience members. This kind of proximity—actors hovering precariously overhead and mingling physically with the audience—created a striking effect—but it also made some people very uncomfortable. Similarly, if we come from a conservative religious

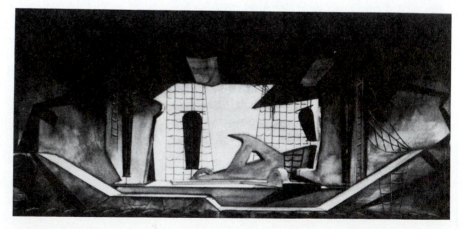

Figure 5.7 Dennis J. Sporre, *scene design for Euripides'* The Bacchae, *University of Illinois at Chicago Circle.*

The Audience

or political upbringing, we may be offended or disturbed by a performance that employs profanity or nudity. Part of our role as audience members is taking inventory of who we are and trying to understand why we might react in the way we do to events or devices used in a production. The theatre, as we have said before, provides an opportunity to grow, and understanding who we are in relation to the human situations that occur in our presence is one way to grow.

The Audience Experience *and* Response

Having sampled the experiences of audiences at different times in the past, and having noted a few characteristics of contemporary audience situations and human communication, let's examine some factors that affect us as audience members. Each of these elements relates to our perception: Some of them are manipulated by theatre artists to help us perceive the play in the way that those wish; some of them concern characteristics that we can control in order to get the most we can, as audience members, out of a performance.

One of my favorite exercises on the first day of class is to ask the class to draw a squirrel. Naturally, the initial response to that request is one of bewilderment, bemusement, and occasional frustration. When the class realizes that I'm serious, however, they usually undertake the task diligently. I can almost read the thoughts of some students: I can't draw—how can I draw a squirrel? Yet even those with some drawing ability tend to stumble.

The point of the exercise centers on *perception*. Drawing itself comprises little more than hand–eye coordination and a bit of spatial perception. What stands in the way of drawing an accurate representation of a squirrel is a lack of the perceptual *details* needed to draw one: Because most of us have never really perceived the details of a squirrel despite having seen squirrels thousands of times, the brain has few details from which to instruct the hand. Responding fully to the theatrical experience is very much like drawing squirrels: In order to respond, we must know what to perceive. What to perceive, of course, is what this book attempts to teach. Knowing what to perceive, however, stems from knowing both how to perceive and how perception works. Perception works in a number of ways that we now will examine in turn.

WILLING SUSPENSION OF DISBELIEF

willing suspension of disbelief Ability of an audience member to accept, without condition or distraction, the *conventions* and *artifices* of the theatrical environment

Our ability to perceive in the theatre depends to a fundamental degree on a factor called the **willing suspension of disbelief.** The theatre environment is an artificial one. The people who act the roles are not the people they portray; they may even be our relatives and friends. The scenery is make-believe: the trees are papier-mâché; the walls are canvas. Overhead, we can see lighting instruments, and if we are in an arena configuration, we see other audience members sitting on the opposite side of the stage. The actions that we witness

The Audience

are calculated: No one actually gets stabbed in the fight scenes in *Romeo and Juliet.* No one is hurt when the young prince hurls himself off the battlements in *King John,* and the actors in *Ghetto* are not killed by machine gun fire. Oedipus does not gouge out real eyes, regardless of how much blood we see. On a less obvious level, suspension of disbelief helps to transport us into imaginative circumstances and to accept the plausibility of what we experience. We do not dismiss out of hand the impossible world of Aristophanes' *The Birds,* even though we know that there is no place as Cloudcuckooland and no such thing as talking birds. We accept the logic of the playwright's tale and look for the human reality and message that it presents to us.

In addition, although we are quite aware of all these imaginative strategies, we can still be moved to tears, fright, and occasionally nausea. Why? When we enter the theatre, we accept the fact of its artificiality, and, in order to allow ourselves to become involved to the greatest degree possible, we *willingly suspend our disbelief.* This is one of the conventions of theatre and film: We accept the conditions of the art at face value and allow ourselves to go beyond the reality of the everyday world into the reality of the stage and screen world. During a filmed love scene on a deserted beach, for example, we do not pause to wonder where the orchestra is. We accept the background music as part of the *convention* of the art and dismiss it by suspending our disbelief. We allow our imaginations and our perceptual sensors to take over so that we can enjoy a satisfying experience. Our willing suspension remains one of those lovely childlike abilities that we may overlook or suppress from time to time but which, when we do use them, enrich us wonderfully. Willing suspension of disbelief has the power to transport us into fantasy worlds like the Never-Never land of James Barrie's *Peter Pan* and Shakespeare's magical island of *The Tempest,* with their mythical creatures and flying spirits. Suspending our disbelief in the theatre enhances our perception and experience in the world of the production.

AESTHETIC DISTANCE

aesthetic distance The proper *psychological and physical separation* between the audience and the action that enables the audience to become involved at a level appropriate for understanding and meaning

A second fundamental factor involving our ability to perceive the communication of a work of art is *aesthetic distance.* Simply put, **aesthetic distance** is the proper psychological and physical separation between us and the artwork that enables us to become involved in it at a level appropriate for understanding its meaning. Every work of art demands proper distancing between us and it. How far or how close is "appropriate" depends entirely on the specific artist, the artwork, and us. As we noted before, the distance is sometimes purely psychological or emotional, as when we read a novel or a poem. Ultimately, emotional distance is the more important. However, physical distance in the theatre is also important and can affect emotional distance.

Common experience in the theatre suggests that some relationship exists between physical distance and emotional distance. Certainly, one cannot draw sweeping conclusions: Aesthetic distance, like most other audience considerations, is highly personal. Nonetheless, every production seeks some specific

The Audience

relationship among actor, action, and audience. If the goals of the production call for emotional involvement by the audience, the production team may want the audience in close proximity to the stage space. At the same time, however, one may well sense that *too close* a physical proximity may create a distancing effect: We immediately erect psychological barriers and engage our defense systems when strangers invade what we consider to be our "personal space."

Obviously, that response is a *distancing* and not an *involving* response. Physically, then, the production team must determine how close is close enough and how close is too close. The theatre itself will often have some bearing on these decisions. For example, a large auditorium in which the last row of seats may be 100 feet from the stage makes physical intimacy impossible for all but the first few rows of seats. Indeed, intimacy, as a production goal, poses many problems in such circumstances. Many large auditoriums, as a partial solution, have curtains that can be drawn across the house to create a smaller place in which to perform.

Some theatre theorists maintain that any play can be performed in any space. Others disagree. Probably any play *can* be performed in any space, but certainly some are better suited to large theatres and vice versa. I am not sure that I would like either to stage or to see *The Gin Game*, an intimate, two-character drama about the lives of elderly people, in a 1,000-seat proscenium theatre, or the musical *The Phantom of the Opera*, with its elaborate visual spectacle, in a 100-seat arena theatre (Fig. 5.8). Of course, such conclusions are personal and debatable. However, the question of aesthetic distance for desired audience response is a vital consideration in production decision making in the theatre. As audience members, we gain or suffer from the results of these decisions, which attempt to place us at just the right degree of separation from the play and its action, thereby enhancing our ability to perceive whatever the production attempts to communicate to us.

Figure 5.8
Phantom of the Opera, *Majestic Theatre*, New York, 1983. Director, Harold Prince; production designer, Maria Björnson; lighting designer, Andrew Bridge.

The Audience

135

Theatre Space and Fantasy: *The Phantom of the Opera*

In the 1988 New York staging of the pop opera *The Phantom of the Opera,* with music by British composer Andrew Lloyd Webber, director Harold Prince, collaborating with the designer Maria Björnson, achieves in the view of many critics a tour de force of physical production. A retelling of the 1911 thriller by Gaston Leroux about a grotesque genius who, on becoming obsessed with a chorus singer, directs her career from the subterranean depths of the Paris Opera House, this beauty-and-the-beast story has become, in the hands of director and designer, an extravagant imaginative journey, tapping into the audience's desire for a transforming sensory and mystical experience.

Thus Björnson creates an underground lake that the Phantom rows across. The lake is lit by dozens of candelabra that rise and fall but remain magically unquenched. In another mysterious, logic-defying effect, the lagoon seems to be at the level of the Phantom's lair but is never flooded.

The staging also abounds with horror-movie special effects. The most noteworthy example is the near-to-the-floor plummet of a 1,500-pound ceiling chandelier. Other examples are the bolts of lightning and flashes of fire accompanying the Phantom's midair descent in a chariot.

ATTENTION

Without *attention*, perception is impossible. Within the theatre experience, then, both we and the artists must "pay attention." Try the following exercise. Find a place in which you can be free of external distractions—someplace private and quiet. Take a clean white piece of paper and make a dot in the center. Concentrate on that dot and see how long you can keep it as the sole focus of your attention. As soon as another thought comes into your mind, stop. How long were you able to give exclusive attention to the dot? If you managed one minute, you have extraordinary powers of concentration. Most of us probably managed only 20 or 30 seconds. Attention—or at least *concentrative* attention—is a very short-lived thing.

Attention and the Audience   We should remember this fact when we go to the theatre in order to perceive what comes to us through this medium of human expression: We must be willing to give the production an exceptional amount of attention. Theatre is a lot like music in the demands it makes on us. Unlike paintings or novels, theatre and music do not allow the respondent the luxury of reviewing or rereading the parts that do not immediately make sense. When we arrive at the end of the play, however, we are expected to remember important actions and dialogue that occurred at the beginning or in the middle of the play. If we have not been paying attention, we will miss these touchstones as they pass by, and when the puzzle eventually begins to come together, we may not have all the pieces (like the parts of the squirrel) and so will not be able to capture the meaning (or draw the picture). It is thus vital to understand that paying attention requires some effort and is critical to comprehending the production.

Attention and the Artist   All of the responsibility, however, is not in our hands. The artists who put the production together have a shared responsibility to assist us in paying attention. Because attention is fleeting, most productions do in fact try to achieve a structure in which the dynamics of the play ebb and flow and thus keep our interest *peaked* and *released* as the play moves forward. If we look at the chart of a hypothetical three-act play in Figure 3.6, we see that as the action rises at the climax, it does so in ascending dynamic peaks. These peaks would correspond to times of *crisis* in the plot and are structured to bring us to a moment of intense attention followed by a period of release and transition until the next intense point of attention. Because each point of attention tends to be slightly higher in dynamic and emotional value, when we reach the climax, we have arrived at the moment of highest dynamic and emotional value. This pattern of peaking and releasing serves the needs of human attention by keeping us from having to give maximum concentration throughout the performance—something very few of us could do.

Serving the needs of human attention thus serves the needs of human interest as well: By manipulating our attention, the production keeps our interest. It is interesting to speculate on how our attention may respond to stimulation and whether we have any particular expectations as to how a production should stimulate us. For example, have we—in whatever age group we may be—become accustomed to short bursts of intensity and rapidly paced changes in which our attention is constantly stimulated by such popular-culture genres as action movies, MTV, and so on? Do we then expect all "theatrical" genres to conform to such dynamic devices? Are we capable of staying alert and attentive when faced with slowly developing material? Naturally, our answers to such questions will be highly individual. Nonetheless, audience expectation and its effect on attention can affect the way that we experience and respond to plays that do not contain a lot of action and attention-stimulating devices. In the theatre, we must be prepared for an unfolding of a *variety* of effects and devices that attempt to stimulate and relax our attention.

Theatre artists may be tempted to employ devices for "grabbing" the audience that may be totally inappropriate for the play. As a result, the audience may miss the basic communication of the play because the presentation technique was totally at odds with its language, meaning, and structure. We must realize, however, that such an assertion contains room for what may be purely aesthetic disagreement between the vision of the production and the preestablished expectations of an audience member. It is easy to attack a novel approach to a play as "wrong for the play"—when, in reality, all that is at issue is a differing *aesthetic viewpoint* about what the play means and how best to transmit that to an audience.

Occasionally, however, we experience productions in which the gim-

Mrs. Trollope (II): "*Domestic Manners*" in the Bowery

In 1831, Mrs. Trollope made the rounds of the three theatres then established in New York, where she also discovered disconcerting patterns of informal behavior among audience members. (Roscius was one of the four great actor-managers of ancient Rome; Edwin Forrest was America's first great Shakespearean actor.)

The Park Theatre is the only one licensed by fashion, but the Bowery is infinitely superior in beauty; it is indeed as pretty a theatre as I ever entered, perfect as to size and proportion, elegantly decorated, and the scenery and machinery equal to any in London, but it is not the fashion. The Chatham is so utterly condemned by *bon ton,* that it requires some courage to decide upon going there; nor do I think my curiosity would have penetrated so far, had I not seen Miss Mitford's Rienzi advertised there. It was the first opportunity I had had of seeing it played, and in spite of very indifferent acting, I was delighted. The interest must have been great, for till the curtain fell, I saw not one quarter of the queer things around me; then I observed in the front row of a dress-box a lady performing the most maternal office possible; several gentlemen without their coats; and a general air of contempt for the decencies of life, certainly more than usually revolting.

At the Park Theatre I again saw the American Roscius, Mr. Forrest. He played the part of Damon, and roared, I thought, very unlike a nightingale. I cannot admire this celebrated performer.

. . . Till the curtain fell, I saw not one quarter of the queer things around me; then I observed in the front row . . . a lady performing the most maternal office possible.

Another night we saw Cinderella there; Mrs. Austin was the prima donna, and much admired. The piece was extremely well got up, and on this occasion we saw the Park Theatre to advantage, for it was filled with well-dressed company; but still we saw many "yet unrazored lips" polluted with the grim tinge of the hateful tobacco, and heard, without ceasing, the spitting, which of course is its consequence. If their theatres had the orchestra of the Feydeau, and a choir of angels to boot, I could find but little pleasure, so long as they were followed by this running accompaniment of *thorough base.*

micks seem to be there primarily for purposes of artistic display rather than as an enhancement of the ultimate meaning of the play. One can also make the case here for audience-stimulating gimmicks as a cover to make a bad script appealing to an audience. The most obvious recent examples of this debate probably involve the use of nudity and profanity. Nudity and profanity are nothing new in the theatre, and they are often part of the playwright's intention. On the other hand, let's suppose that a director decides that one of Shakespeare's comedies ought to be played partially in the nude. In that case, we have probably crossed over into controversial territory. Is the nudity a useful device for giving new meaning to this play, or is it purely a titillating gimmick? Of course, we can't answer such a question on the basis of a vague hypothetical example. When we participate as audience members, however, we must make such judgments about the devices that the production uses to capture our attention.

A less controversial and more mundane problem that often occurs in a production seeking to maintain audience attention lies in the use of *actor intensity*. We know, for example, that the volume level of our speech is an effective device for getting attention—that is why we tend to speak more loudly when we sense that our listeners are slipping away from us. In the theatre, the volume level of the actors can escalate in early scenes of conflict to a level that makes later scenes of more important conflict seem anti-climatic. At least, part of the issue of controlling audience attention, therefore, lies in the ability of the director and the actors to use devices that are carefully calculated not only to *capture* attention but also to *hold* it at the level proper for the part of the play in which it occurs. Our judgement, as audience members, must focus on the whys of the devices used to get our attention. Are they appropriate to the play as a whole, and are they appropriate to the part of the play in which they occur—that is, do they assist the play in moving to its required conclusions? *Appropriateness* is thus our watchword.

SYMPATHY AND EMPATHY

Some of our perceptions come to us through our ability to put ourselves in someone else's place—to gain a real sense of what they are going through and how they feel. Because theatre presents us with human situations that in some way explore character in crisis, we perceive the various levels of meaning explored in the play by our ability to sense the human situation portrayed. This sensitivity to others' circumstances is called **sympathy**—that is, our sensitivity to the condition of others in a deep and meaningful way. Although the terms are occasionally used as synonyms, sympathy is not the same as another quality, *empathy*. Whereas sympathy is passive and cerebral, empathy is active and physical: **empathy** is a psychophysical response to events to which we are witnesses but in which we are not direct participants. For example, during a stage fight—a "fight" that we know is not "real"—we find ourselves actually involved physically. We strain forward or to the side, ducking and dodging with the characters. In other words, we are physically involved even though we are safely distanced from and not at all entrapped by the action. Our emotional response has become physical. In a sense, we are "out of control." Similarly, when a character on stage slaps another character, some members of the audience may gasp loudly in response. That is empathetic response. If we have our sensors and spirit turned to the "expectation" mode, our empathetic sensitivity will enable us to respond in some fairly intense ways to various kinds of actions that occur on the stage.

sympathy Sensitivity to the condition of others in a deep and meaningful way

Empathy Psychophysical response to events to which we are witnesses but in which we are not direct participants

Enhancing Perception

VARIETY

variety Any *change* in the ordered presentation of the elements of a work of art

Our perception can be enhanced both by things that we bring to the production and by things that the production provides for us. In the latter case, our perception is enhanced when artists use a particular principle of composition called **variety**. Although attention depends on repeated stimulation, it also depends on stimulation that *changes*. Our attention, for example, may be caught by a sudden loud shout, but if that shout is repeated without some variation, its attention-getting capacity soon fades, and the intensity of volume will become an annoyance rather than a stimulator. Similarly, if the dynamic intensity of a production rises too high and/or too early, it has nowhere to go, and the resulting monotony will create not interest but boredom. Monotony in any of the many factors in a production can frustrate an audience, disrupt attention, and inhibit perception of meaning. In a production of Arthur Miller's *All My Sons,* for instance, the action revolves around a family involved in the production of aircraft engines (Fig. 5.9). The issue of the play is the question of morality versus pragmatism. The father, who is the head of the business, discovers cracks in the engines that he is providing to the Air Force. Because halting the shipment of the engines would mean bankruptcy, in the interest of his own financial survival, he ships the engines, ignoring the moral question involved in what might happen if they fail. The climax of the play is his discovery that one of his faulty engines has caused the death of his own son,

Figure 5.9
Arthur Miller, All My Sons (1947). American Playhouse Presentation 1991. *Compare the insistence upon moral conflict as a theme in* All My Sons *with Miller's comments on the moral realism of Ibsen's* An Enemy of the People *in Chapter 2.*

an Air Force pilot: In seeking to save his family, he has actually destroyed it by his moral weakness.

As this play unfolds in production, the early scenes involve family conflict. A careless production may allow the actors to use too much volume and intensity in these early but relatively unimportant scenes. As a result, the last three-quarters of the play will have to be played at fever pitch. That level of unbroken volume and intensity becomes monotonous, and when the really crucial revelation occurs, the audience is too bored and worn-out to care. Variety in pacing and intensity could save such a production. If variety is the spice of life, it certainly is the essence of art.

FOCUS

In perceiving and sorting out the various aspects of a theatre production, we must call on our ability to *focus* on those parts of the performance that are most important. Whether we see the production proceeding according to the pyramidal form that we studied in Figure 3.6, or see the play as an outline with its parts ranked in ordinal relationships—that is, I.A.1.a.1)a)—some parts are clearly more important than others. Part of our responsibility as an audience is to detect those important–less important relationships and, through them, meaning. The production team, of course, will help us in this respect by using a number of devices, both visual and aural, to separate the important from the less important. Focus, for example, can be achieved by contrasting important dialogue with casual dialogue through increased vocal emphasis; the speed or rate at which the dialogue is uttered also indicates focus. Just as we may slow down when we want to emphasize something important in conversation, an actor may do the same thing to help us focus on important lines. Dialogue uttered with greater vocal intensity or *force* also draws attention to itself and creates focus. Increased force may or may not include greater volume. Words whispered with great intensity often are more forceful in impact than shouted words.

Visual devices also create focus. For example, an actor placed *downstage-center* (see Chapter 8) will draw more focus than one placed *upstage-left*. An actor at the top of a stairway or on a platform will draw focus better than one at floor level. Bright colors in costume and colors contrasting with others in the same scene also create focus. We focus on the actor in Figure 5.10, for instance, because he stands in contrast to the barren stage environment. A similar condition occurs in Figure 5.11. Our focus on the character of Pippin occurs because he is more brightly lit than those who surround him. In addition, actors are often given focus by framing them with scenic elements like those illustrated in Figure 5.12. All these devices are the tools with which the production team communicates to tell us which parts of the performance are the keys to understanding the overall meaning of the play. If we can keep the *focal points* of the performance in mind as we move along during the play, we will have done much in our role as respondents to assist in the communication process of the theatre.

Figure 5.11   *Stephen Schwartz, Pippin (1972). Washington and Lee University, 1980. Director, Al Gordon; scenic designer, Tom Ziegler.*

Figure 5.12   The Torch Bearers. *Henry Street Play-house, Lexington, Virginia. Director, Rose Gordon; scenic designer, Skip Epperson.*

The Audience: Individual *and* Group Reactions

One thing that makes theatre quite different from the dramatic entertainment that comes to us in our living rooms over television is the curious interrelationships that we form not only with the live actors but with other members of the audience as well. The way we react as individuals can be affected significantly when we find ourselves among a group of strangers. We may even be somewhat intimidated, unsure whether to laugh or applaud, perhaps even fearful that we may react in such a way as to draw unwanted attention to ourselves. On the other hand, our reactions may be uninhibited because someone else in the audience responds freely to the play. In a comedy, for example, other members of the audience may often be enticed to respond to the play because the laughter of one member, at first drawing attention to itself, has the effect of "loosening up" everyone else. Soon, inhibitions are lowered all around and the audience as a whole is fully responsive to the actors.

In other situations, we may find ourselves swept up in the reactions we sense among those around us. Our sense of tragedy, for example, may be heightened when we hear or see others react to the play. In certain plays, the audience as a group becomes so swept away by the drama that it begins to

Figure 5.13 *William Calfee*, First Performance—Edwin Booth. *Oil on canvas, 10′ × 5′. Although forced to retire for a year after his brother, John Wilkes Booth, assassinated President Abraham Lincoln, Edwin Booth went on to become one of the foremost 19th-century American actors. Depicted here are the conditions under which American audiences were first introduced to theatre artists of their own, but by 1868, Booth was at home in his own fan-cooled New York theatre with three tiers of galleries and room for over 1700 in the pit. Ironically, students of American theatre history have suggested that the development of audience arrangements in the U.S. contributed to a sort of undemocratic theatre-going in which people tended to populate spectator space according to social standing.*

(Courtesy of The Section of Fine Arts, Public Buildings Administration).

function almost as if it were a mob. The range of possible responses that we face when we enter the theatre runs from the most intimate, private, and repressed to the most public, unrestrained, and involved. Who we are, the makeup of the audience, and the nature of the dramatic experience all play roles in shaping our response. The one inescapable fact, however, is the fact that the presence of other individuals, many of whom are strangers, does indeed affect us and our experience of the performance. Theatre is very much a group experience.

THE AUDIENCE: EXPERIENCE AND MOTIVATION

For over 2,500 years, people have found participating in theatre as audience members a worthwhile venture, one to which they look forward and, indeed, for which they sometimes spend considerable money. Just this morning as I came to my office at 7:30 A.M. on a chilly December 10, a line of nearly 100 students awaited the 8:00 opening of the auditorium box office for tickets to a road company production of *Cats*—a show that toured here less than two years ago. What accounts for this ability to command an audience? Certainly theatre is a *special occasion*. There is something inherently pleasurable and satisfying about going to the theatre as an audience member. It gives us the opportunity to do something different; we have to get up and go out. It is a special evening. We may combine it with dinner and friends, or we may extend the evening with a pretheatre party and a post-theatre dinner. Whatever the circumstances, going to the theatre forms the heart of something out of the ordinary. Although formal dress is no longer necessary in today's scheme of things, some people still like to don formal clothing and go to an opening-night performance. Thousands of people travel to New York, Chicago, and other metropolitan centers for no other purpose than "to see a show." No matter where you call home, there is something special about mingling with other members of an audience at a play.

The Learning Experience We also noted earlier that one of theatre's primary purposes is to *teach*. That means that audience members will *learn* something. Indeed, the theatre is for many people the optimum place to learn. The common conditions that we face in life, including the questions we seek to answer about our existence, have been with us since we first took human form in the dim recesses of the prehistoric past. They echo in the poetic tragedies of Aeschylus in Athens in the fifth century B.C., and they form the core of our existence today. Attempting to answer life's troubling questions about self-perception and relationships both to others and to higher powers provides us with our most awesome challenges. Looking at ourselves in the mirror can be a very threatening experience. Facing uncertainty and day-to-day trials can cause anxiety.

The theatre, therefore, gives us an opportunity to learn about these threats and dilemmas in a haven of relative safety. We can find ourselves revealed to us in the guise of a play's characters in ways that, though challenging and sometimes discomfiting, are nonetheless less threatening and devastating than they would be if they were revealed to us by either our friends or our enemies. We learn without question that the trials that we face are not ours alone but are in fact those of just about everybody—and have been for centuries. We can draw great comfort from that revelation. Learning thus forms the core of the theatrical experience. In a well-written play, every character is us— or at least a part of us. As symbols, the people of the play stand for the many sides of our characters, and we can recognize their conflicts as both the conflicts in our own souls and those that we may have with other people.

Escape: The Audience as Participant   Theatre also attracts an audience because it can be an *escape* from life's burdens. Much of what has graced the stage in the theatre's long and distinguished history has not been particularly profound—its appeal has been primarily that of escapism. However, great plays with profound meanings also can be entertaining and may provide escape for the viewer. Great art is not necessarily boring.

When we conclude that one of the reasons we attend the theatre is to escape, we focus on the drive of the *audience member,* not on the condition of the *production.* Seeking escape in an evening of theatre is a matter of our expectation, and that expectation can be fulfilled by either a meaningless piece of fluff or a profound masterpiece. One thing that we must understand when we undertake the theatrical experience is the role that *we* play and the conditions that *we* bring to that role: The way we experience a production often may depend more on what we bring to it than on what happens after we get there. Still, it is fair to say that escapism as a reason to attend the theatre remains a relatively noble one. Lifting one's burden for just a while can be a refreshment that is just as life-saving as a flash of deep insight.

Admiration: The Audience as Critic   Another reason we choose to become audience members is *admiration:* We go to the theatre to admire a well-crafted performance. We expect to see characters developed with plausibility and acted with believability. We look for depth of insight and can admire portrayals with which we can identify. We often go to the theatre for the express purpose of seeing how a particular actor handles a noted role. Sophisticated theatregoers come to a production to admire effective ensemble acting, skillful directing, effective interaction of actor and stage space, masterful playwriting in the use of language and storytelling, and superbly designed and executed scenery, costumes, and lighting. In the musical theatre, we expect to hear the best songs well sung and to see choreography that is engaging, energetic, well executed, and original.

Deciding to become an audience member, however, also places us in a precarious position: We cannot predict what the experience will bring us. It may be that for every satisfying experience of theatre, we may have to endure a half dozen or so mediocre productions—and even one or two outright turkeys. In life, the exceptional is not an everyday occurrence. When we have accumulated a large enough body of experiences, we will know the difference between the exceptional and the mediocre, and that knowledge will keep us from one of everyday life's tragedies—thinking that the mediocre is the best there is. Thus, unless we take the opportunities available to us, we rob ourselves of the chance to glory in the marvelous experiences that life and the theatre can bring us. Too many of us are impoverished by our lack of curiosity, fear of the unknown, and acceptance of the mundane.

SUMMARY

• We are able to experience theatrical performances because, ultimately, everything and everyone concerned with the stage is there because of the audience.

• Throughout history, audiences had markedly different *expectations* and *attitudes* with regard to attending the theatre:

In ancient Greece all classes of individuals attended theatre in what essentially was a religious-festival time.

In ancient Rome, street performers presenting mimes and farces attracted cosmopolitan crowds from the well-to-do to the lower-classes and the unemployed; however, in the more formal theatrical surroundings, accommodated by a stone building built with audience comfort in mind, a more well-educated audience experienced a broad fare of mostly comedies.

In Elizabethan England, the popular professional theatre provided its audiences a focus for social and intellectual life in the fast-paced, open-staged plays of Marlowe, Jonson, and Shakespeare.

After the Restoration, audiences in the English theatre comprised mostly the upper classes, engaged in a court activity and entertained by witty satires and social comedies.

As members of a modern audience, we can find any kind of theatre almost anywhere we look and find among those attending with us examples of every social class representing a diverse set of expectations.

• To understand fully our experiences as audience members, we must realize that theatre is a form of *communication*—consisting of a *sender*, a *medium of transmission*, and a *receiver*—all of whose parts must meet specific conditions:

Our ability to perceive and respond as a member of an audience depends on *proximity*—our physical and personal space and the way we regard it—and to a certain degree on our cultural or ethnic conditioning, as August Wilson indicates in dealing with "the audience outside the mainstream."

In our experience of the theatre, several factors affect us as audience members:

First, we must be aware of what it means to perceive;

Then we must understand how perception is affected by a factor called *willing suspension of disbelief*—the ability to accept without condition the conventions and artifices of the theatrical experience;

We must also attend to the effects of *aesthetic distance*—that is, the proper physical and psychological distancing that allow us to respond to the play in a manner compatible with the expectations of the artists;

Without *attention*, perception is impossible, and so for the maximum satisfaction of a theatrical performance, we must understand how attention works in the audience and how attention is stimulated by artists;

Finally, some of our perceptions come to us through our ability to put ourselves in someone else's place—abilities called *sympathy* and *empathy*.

• Getting the most out of a theatrical experience can be enhanced by things that the production provides for us. Two of these factors are *variety* and *focus:*

variety is a change in stimulation;

focus is the clear definition of relationships and meanings in the performance.

Clearly, one important characteristic of the live theatre is its involvement with the performance of the audience—as individuals and as a group. Being part of the latter has a definite influence on reactions of the former—and vice versa.

Chapter 6

Theatre Forms *and* Architecture

*A*fter studying this chapter,
you should be able to:

- Identify and describe the basic needs that must be met in order for a production to succeed.

- Describe the general requirements for theatre space required by various types of productions.

- Identify and explain various kinds of actor-audience spatial relationships such as *arena, thrust,* and *proscenium forms.*

- Explain some of the practical considerations that various *theatre spaces* cause in production.

- Define and explain the workings of the *multiple setting.*

- Identify and describe a *unit setting.*

- Discuss the characteristics and uses of *simultaneous settings.*

Setting for The Playboy of the Western World, *Harvard Dramatic Club, 1962. Des
Ramzi Mostafa. Loeb Drama Center, Harvard.*

*T*he material in this chapter describes some general conditions that relate to physical relationships between audiences and theatre spaces and the impact of various forms of theatre spaces on production. We have placed this material at this point in the text to suggest that it has a broad and fundamental character in addition to and apart from some of its more specific applications to production practice (Unit II) and theatre history (Unit III). Some information concerning theatre spaces is best left to a historical context (Chapters 14 through 17) and some to the scenic-design process (Chapter 10), and that is where we will deal with it. What I wish to discuss here, however, has a more general "background" purpose and is best treated in this unit on fundamentals. Later, when specific historical examples of architectural forms are mentioned or when design considerations (e.g., checking sightlines) are discussed, we can move along efficiently in our examination without pausing for elaborate definitions or explanations.

Whatever idealism theatre artists carry into the real world of the production, they quickly learn that the creative imagination can proceed only as far as the limitations of time, budget, staff, and physical space allow. First and foremost, men and women of the theatre are limited by the actual theatres in which they work. In this chapter, we will discuss the *physical theatre*—its types, potentials, and limitations, both practical and aesthetic. In reading what fol-

Figure 6.1 *Thalian Hall, Wilmington, North Carolina.*

Theatre Forms *and* Architecture

lows, you must use common sense to avoid drawing sweeping generalizations about specific observations. Every theatre building is unique. Vast differences exist among theatres that represent the same type, and often theatres of different types have much in common. For example, the Purdue Music Hall in West Lafayette, Indiana, seats 6,402, and Thalian Hall in Wilmington, North Carolina (Fig. 6.1), seats just over 600. Although both are examples of the *proscenium* theatre, in both aesthetic and practical terms they are quite different. All this must be kept in mind as you read the general comments in the next few pages.

General Considerations

Every theatre production begins with the artists thinking about the entire theatrical ambiance—that is, the general environment and atmosphere—appropriate for the planned production. The ambiance of a production embraces the actual theatre in which it is to occur. Certain general standards exist for what constitutes an ideal theatre facility, and a minimum of effort can often transform a less-than-ideal theatre into an ideal production environment. The scene design, for example, should not begin at the edge of the preestablished stage: It should begin at the edge of the street outside the theatre. (See the exterior and interior drawings of an eighteenth-century British playhouse in Figures 6.2A and 6.2B.) Although you may or may not be able to change the

Figure 6.2A   The Duke's Theatre, ca. 1665.   *The first theatre built after the Restoration of the British monarchy in 1660, The Duke's Theatre reflected the influence and popularity of baroque architecture. The ornamentation, although dramatic and spectacular, was also intricate, and complex design is restrained by attention to line, repetition, and balance. Compare the architectural values displayed by the building's exterior with those evident in its interior in Fig. 6.2B. The Restoration playhouse is discussed in further historical context in Chapter 16 (esp. at Fig. 16.11).*

[Harvard Theatre Collection]

Figure 6.2B The Curtain of The Duke's Theatre. *Fully rigged in the manner of the European baroque theatre, The Duke's Theatre was the first English theatre to introduce scenery. As in the typical Restoration theatre, however, most of the action was staged on a deep apron stage thrust forward from the central proscenium arch because English audiences preferred the intimacy carried over from the Elizabethan playhouse (see Fig. 6.16). Actors entered through the symmetrical arches at either side, above which are located additional boxes for spectators.*

[Harvard Theatre Collection]

auditorium in which you are required to work, that is nonetheless, the place where all production considerations begin. For audience members, awareness of production circumstances allows for a greater understanding of why the production takes the form that it does. For artists and audience members alike, certain basic needs must be met in order for the production to succeed. These needs are (1) *vision,* (2) *acoustics,* (3) *freedom from distractions,* (4) *safety,* and (5) *seating comfort.*

VISION

Our purpose in this book, of course, is not to teach you to design an auditorium; understanding certain principles, however, will help you to come to grips with the productions that you attend or work on. There is an important interrelationship between *practical* decision making in a theatre production and the *aesthetic* considerations that relate to specific theatres and the positions in which they place audiences relative to the stage action. If an audience is to gain the full benefit of a production, that production must use its

Nicolà Sabbatini (I): What to Do Before the Prince Arrives

Nicolà Sabbatini (1574–1654) was one of the foremost practitioners of scenic-design theory in the late Italian Renaissance. A true Renaissance man, Sabbatini was as practical and scientific-minded as he was artistically inclined (see Fig. 11.8), and the advice that he addressed to the theatre world of his day was both wide-ranging and attentive to detail.

First of all, when you are planning to give a performance, it is necessary to select as convenient and spacious a hall as possible; this must have behind, at the sides, above and under the backdrop and scenery, space sufficient both for the various machines employed to present heavenly, terrestrial, marine, and infernal apparitions and for such distant prospects and perspective views as may be deemed necessary. Take note that one must secure not only length but adequate height and depth as well (provided, of course, that one may have what one wishes). This brief reference to these things is obligatory because we recognize that they are all necessary or at least exceedingly useful in the arousing of wonder among the spectators, in the gaining of praise and in the imitating, so far as possible, of the natural and the real. After having made careful selection of the place where the play and the *intermezzi* are to be presented, the architect must go in person to inspect the site, taking with him good master masons and bricklayers in whom he has confidence, and diligently examine again the capacity of this place. After this the masons will look at the beams, the vaults and the roofs to see if they are sound and able to bear the weight of the stage floor, the machines and the spectators, and especially must this be done when princes are expected in the company.

Select . . . space sufficient . . . for the various machines employed to present heavenly, terrestrial, marine, and infernal apparitions.

When he has received the reports of the workmen, the architect will give order (should there be anything requiring remedy) to put matters to right, always maintaining a watchful eye himself and often going personally to supervise the work. He will show confidence in all, give good words to all, yet put complete trust in none, for often is one cheated either by the malignity of enemies or the ignorance of the incompetent.

From *Manual for Constructing Theatrical Scenes and Machines* (1638). *The Renaissance Stage,* edited by Bernard Hewitt, translated by A. Nicoll, J. H. McDowell, and G. R. Kernodle. Coral Gables: University of Miami Press, 1958, pp. 43–44, 96–97. Reprinted by permission of the University of Miami Press.

spaces so that ease of vision is accommodated. Even within a theatre type so seemingly arbitrary as the proscenium, much can often be done to ensure that the design and actors are not limited by unfavorable conditions caused by a poorly designed auditorium.

For example, many auditoriums, especially school auditoriums, were designed more as lecture halls than as theatres, and the seats at the extreme sides of the front row often make viewing the entire stage area impossible. When a production is staged in such a facility, those seats that do not offer an adequate view of the action should not be used. Otherwise, the resulting experience for certain audience members will be unsatisfactory. Consideration of audience vision must meet six basic principles, as follows:

1. A given audience member should be able to take in the full action on the stage without eye movement. To meet this need, the width of the stage action should not exceed 40 degrees of horizontal angle from any seat in the house (Fig. 6.3).

2. In order for objects and actors on stage to be perceived in the intended relationship to each other, no seat in the house should exceed 60 degrees of horizontal angle from the centerline (Fig. 6.4).

3. Audiences will not choose seats beyond a line approximately 100 degrees to the curtain at the proscenium. The shaded areas of Figure 6.5 illustrate undesirable seats.

4. Audience ability to recognize standard shapes is reduced significantly if the vertical angle of observation exceeds 30 degrees (Fig. 6.6).

5. An audience member cannot perceive facial expressions plainly at any distance exceeding 50 feet; any distance exceeding 75 feet for legitimate theatre is unworkable.

6. No member of the audience should sit directly behind another. Seats should be staggered as much as space will allow. Good vision cannot be maintained if an audience member's view of the stage is impeded by the head of the person in the row ahead.

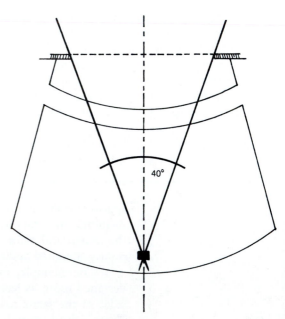

Figure 6.3 *Maximum Angle for Comfortable Vision.*

Theatre Forms *and* Architecture

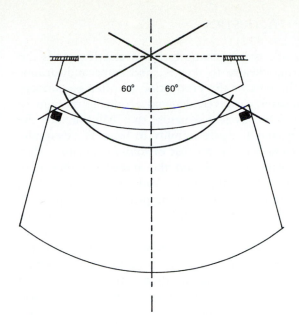

Figure 6.4 *Maximum Angle to Centerline.*

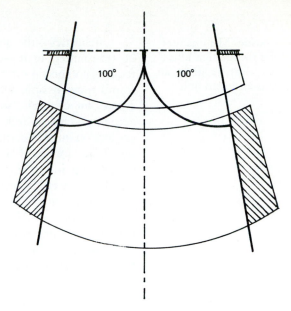

Figure 6.5 *Audience Choice for Desirable Seats.*

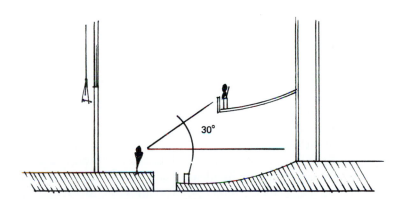

Figure 6.6 *Audience Ability to Recognize Standard Shapes.*

The implications of these principles are obvious for both theatre artists and audience members: When producing a play, eliminate the seats that fall outside these guidelines—or else be prepared to deal with unhappy patrons; if you are an audience member wishing to have good vision for a production, don't buy seats that are outside these guidelines.

ACOUSTICS

acoustics The qualities
of a theatre that affect
how clearly sounds can
be transmitted in it

Acoustics—the qualities of a theatre that affect how clearly sounds can be transmitted in it—vary from theatre to theatre, and some auditoriums require no special effort on the part of the production to offer satisfactory sound transmission. Other theatres, however, demand agonizing thought to create, for example, some kind of physical structure that will enhance the actor's projection and, thereby, the audience's ability to hear. For example, *ceilings* on interior settings became popular because of *sound reflection*—they direct the sound of actors' voices outward into the audience rather than straight up into the open space above the stage. Auditorium space, then, should be carefully considered in the design-planning process of the production so that sound can be enhanced in those theatres in which sound transmission is a problem. Whether the result of poor auditorium design, poor actor training, or some combination, it is a fact of contemporary theatre that it is more and more losing the qualities of the "live" performance—qualities that lie at its heart as an art form. Everywhere, it seems, there is the perceived need to amplify everything and everyone—wireless microphones, for example, have become a staple product in theatre productions. As audience members, our perception of a production's aural elements can be enhanced by subtle sound reinforcement manipulated by a skillful technician. We can also be *distracted* by amplification—for example, if the actor is standing on the right side of the stage and the sound comes to us from a speaker on the left side. Sound reinforcement that seems natural helps us hear clearly; sound amplification that sounds mechanical often inhibits our attention.

DISTRACTIONS

The previous discussion brings us to the next consideration—the audience's need to see and hear the production without distraction. This requirement includes everything from faulty amplification and noisy air conditioners and exhaust fans to scene shifting, actor entrances and exits in "blackouts," and noisy plumbing in adjacent rest rooms. Even the most famous of theatre buildings has its legendary physical idiosyncrasies that give rise to "production problems." My own experience as a theatre artist gives us a few examples to draw on. One theatre, for example, was on the direct flight line of a nearby Air Force base. When the wind was from the north, we could expect regular interruptions of the performance because the B-52 bombers on take-off would completely drown out all sound in the theatre. Another theatre was in a large classroom building, and a public hallway allowed nontheatregoers access to rest rooms that flanked the stage. Whenever a toilet was flushed, the sound carried clearly into the audience. Although signs were hung on the bathroom doors, that precaution did not stop the problem completely. Other theatres have had whining air conditioners. Whatever may be the case, a facility's

Theatre Forms *and* Architecture

idiosyncrasies affect an audience's attention and thus have the potential to distract from conscientious attention to the production.

Specifically related to the architectural point are aesthetic considerations involving theatre types in which act and scene curtains cannot be used to mask actors who must "appear" in place at the beginning of a scene or must be removed from view before the house lights rise. Granted, contemporary audiences have become accustomed to any number of "distractions" in the guise of *conventions*—for example, seeing a character who has just "died" rise and walk off the stage. Nevertheless, good production design can and should relieve the audience from distraction rather than strain its acceptance of conventions. For example, one highly problematical distraction caused or increased by careless design, especially in the open, thrust, and arena forms that we will discuss momentarily, is the **half-blackout**. In these circumstances, stage lights must be left on dimly so that actors who are still visible can get off and on stage without running into various obstacles. The result is a troublesome situation in which the mood and rhythm of the production are suspended. Few distractions are worse in disrupting production aesthetics. Simply put, the production must find a means for actors to negotiate on- and offstage movement in a manner appropriate to the demands of the play, with the physical circumstances of the theatre taken into account. Failure to meet this need can disrupt flow and plausibility in many plays.

half-blackout A convention indicating a break in the action—normally calling for all light to be extinguished on stage—in which stage lights are left on dimly so that actors and stagehands can see to move about the stage without running into furniture, and so forth

SAFETY

Although it may seem obvious, it must be stated that audience and actor safety are vital considerations in the configuration of stage and audience spaces. In their zeal to create a production ambiance that is novel and creative, many practitioners disregard safety. Such oversight especially plagues educational and community theatres, where fire and OSHA (Occupational Safety and Health Administration) inspections and regulations may be infrequent or even unknown. I have seen actors climbing down netting from the balcony, directly above audience members; lighting instruments hung above the audience without safety chains; inadequate marking of fire exits; inadequate aisle space for emergency exits; the use of real firearms with commercial "blank" cartridges (which can injure persons up to 20 feet away); the use of smoke effects without warning asthma sufferers that such effects were going to occur; and many more conditions that placed both actors and audience members in jeopardy.

SEATING COMFORT

Finally, considerations for the audience must allow members to sit in comfort. A certain degree of audience comfort relates to the *angles-of-vision perception* just noted. In addition, there are variations in audience seating to be found, for example, in innovative audience arrangements in nonstandard theatre facilities. The use of benches, folding chairs, or portable bleachers may seem like a brilliant seating strategy, but one must consider that the audience will contain the elderly, the infirm, and often the handicapped. These people, as well as the young and healthy, cannot tolerate two or more hours on a flat slab with no back support, or even on a folding chair with no padding or arms. What is appropriate for the gymnasium, where individuals can periodically stand or move around, will not work in a theatre in which decorum and, more importantly, attention rule. In the long run, solutions to production problems that leave even a part of the audience in discomfort are not acceptable. A physically uncomfortable audience member cannot give the production the attention that the theatre requires for a satisfactory experience.

General Requirements *for* Production Types

One of the major considerations that the theatre building forces on the production is the general appropriateness of a theatre form for a particular type of production. Although some theatre artists may fail to recognize that fact, every production is influenced by the specific theatre in which it will be executed; moreover, not all theatres are appropriate for all productions. The production process, then, begins with the choice of the play itself. If the play is inappropriate for the physical form of the theatre in which it must be produced, there is very little that directors or designers can do to save themselves from a variety of shortcomings caused by an inappropriate marriage of play and playhouse.

Here are some general descriptions of various types of productions in terms of theatre space and other related factors. Some of the types noted in the chart in Figure 6.7 do not fall within the coverage of this text, but they are familiar and may be helpful by comparison.

Types *of* Actor–Audience Spatial Relationships

theatre form The physical relationship of audience space to stage space

Throughout theatre history, the actor–audience spatial relationship has witnessed just about every conceivable arrangement. In our time, the wide variety of available artistic styles and performance aesthetics leaves open so many options that auditorium space becomes a critical factor in the production process. Because just about any auditorium form or type can be modified into at least the basic semblance of another form, the original construction of a theatre may not restrain the production. However, each basic **theatre form** has its own characteristics and aesthetics, its advantages and limitations. Not all will work well for every production format; likewise, not all theatre forms will work well for every play. Auditorium form, then, inescapably inserts itself into production considerations. In general, theatres may be divided into the following forms: arena, thrust, proscenium, or open stage.

Figure 6.7

Performance Type	Subject Matter	Visual Components	Auditory Components	Theatre Required
Legitimate Drama	Plays. Live shows employing all dramaturgical, artistic, and technical devices to persuade the audience to suspend disbelief and credit the characters and the story as presented.	The actor. Human scale used for all elements of production. Business realistic or in conformity with any other stylistic idiom. Costume appropriate to the character, situation, and production style. Visual elements of the production coordinated to achieve maximum dramatic impact. Lighting in conformity with style of production: provides visibility sometimes greater than that in nature.	Human voice in speech. Incidental sound to indicate locale, advance plot, create and sustain atmosphere and mood. Overture and entr'acte music from orchestra (by no means universal). Vocal, instrumental, or reproduced music as required within the play.	Most varied requirements of any theatrical type. Small enough so facial expression is significant, equipped for fast changes and effects. Specialized theatres (Shakespearian, Arena) limited in usefulness.

Musical
  Folk Opera
  Operetta
  Musical Comedy
	Line of demarcation between types not clear. Often the best in musical theatre. Reasonably simple story. Framework garnished with music and dancing. Book generally satirizes some current situation of general interest. Boy meets girls in fanciful rather than realistic surroundings.	Actor's business realistic or appropriate to script: conventionalized for musical numbers and dancing. Elaborate costumes harmoniously keyed to color scheme of the production. Scenery usually functional, decorative, stylized rather than realistic. Machinery for quick change and for effect. Lighting arbitrary and for novelty and visibility rather than for conformity with dramatic necessities. New production forms and techniques readily adopted. Pleasant eye entertainment.	Auditory component given appropriate importance relative to visual as dictated by necessity for achieving maximum total effect. Semi-classical and popular music (sweet, hot, and blue), sung by principals, occasionally with chorus and usually with pit orchestra accompaniment. Subject matter and personality of singer often more important than musical excellence. Noisy entra'acte, overture, and covering pieces played by pit orchestra (about 20 pieces). Spoken dialogue between songs. Ear entertainment.	High production costs necessitate a large theatre, though the importance of the individual performer and the required subtlety of effect rule out the grand opera house. Equipment similar to, but more than in, a good legitimate house. Large orchestra pit.

Figure 6.7 (cont.)

Performance Type	Subject Matter	Visual Components	Auditory Components	Theatre Required
Grand Opera	Classic tragedy, folklore, sagas, mythological tales, superheated passion, men vs gods. As currently produced, subject and story are of little importance.	Elaborate conventionalized pantomime by principals. Elaborate costumes, symbolic color. Occasional mass movement by chorus and ballet. Monumental settings (Valhalla, the bottom of the Rhine). Elaborate lighting. Technical tricks: appearances, magic fire, etc.	The world's best music sung by the most accomplished artists, accompanied by thoroughly competent orchestra and chorus. Soloists sing everything at relatively high intensity to achieve audibility and dominate orchestra.	In cities: A large theatre needed to pay high production and operating costs. Comfortable seats and lounges—the performance is often long. Opera houses being built into municipal arts centers. Summer opera can often do with a tent or shed.
Pageant	Incidents from history or local folklore having historical or religious appeal assembled into a plow boy's epic. Story oversimplified, direct, romanticized, salutes a glorious past, promises paradise as a just reward for something or other. No controversial matter included.	Realistic dramatic episodes acted or mimed. Period costumes. Mass movement. Ballet, folk dances. Marches. Permanent decorative backgrounds with movable scenic pieces. Scenery simple, suggestive rather than closely representational. Local geographic features included. Stage machinery in operation. Elaborate lighting. Steam and water curtains. Pyrotechnics. Display of technical virtuosity. Individual performer counts for little.	Music: symphonic, organ, choral. Synthesized descriptive score. Speech: narrator's principals'. Speech dubbed on pantomime scenes. Incidental sounds, descriptive effects. All sound amplified. Level often too high for comfort. Reproduction often less natural than in motion pictures.	Large open-air amphitheatre, stadium, or ball park.

Figure 6.7 (cont.)

Performance Type	Subject Matter	Visual Components	Auditory Components	Theatre Required
Vaudeville Revue	Vaudeville: Assorted songs, dances, dramatic episodes, blackouts, trained animals, acrobats, bell ringers, jugglers, magicians, ventriloquists, mind-readers, musicians, clowns: in fact any feat or phenomenon of man or beast (not excluding elephants) which can be gotten onto a stage and which is calculated to have sufficient audience appeal through uniqueness, novelty, skill, virtuosity, renown, or notoriety.	Performers principal visual element. Costumes bright. Scenic background unimportant except as it contributes necessary paraphernalia or adds flash to act. Lighting conventional; follow spots on principals; no illusion of time or place. All scenic elements combine to center attention on performer. Revue: Design unity sometimes runs through whole production. Much more elaborate and effective setting than in vaudeville.	Speech and music. Not subtle, high in intensity, aimed at the gallery. Popular and classical songs, instrumental and orchestral numbers. Revue has musical unity and balance.	Large enough to pay operating costs with ticket price below opera. Small enough so facial expression counts. Equipped for fast changes of simple scenes.

Harold Burris-Meyer and Edward Cole, *Theatres and Auditoriums,* 2nd ed. (New York: Van Nostrand Reinhold Company, 1964), pp. 2–5. Used by permission.

**arena form/
theatre-in-the-round**
A physical arrangement
in which the audience
completely surrounds
the stage or playing
area

The **arena form** or **theatre-in-the-round** (Fig. 6.8) surrounds the action with audience seating. This format is perhaps the oldest and most natural arrangement for viewing an event. Its proponents argue that the arena form (whether circular, ovoid, square, rectangular, or some other configuration) provides the most intimate kind of theatrical experience possible. This type of staging—sometimes called *central staging*—gained new popularity in the mid-twentieth century on university campuses and in community theatres. The University of Washington, for example, converted a large room into a theatre by placing a few rows of chairs around a central acting area. The economy and intimacy of this kind of arrangement seemed ideal for the production of small-cast, single-set, realistic plays. However, successful productions of larger-scaled plays by Margo Jones at her Dallas theatre in the 1950s led to a wider adaptation of play types to the arena format. The arena concept was expanded even further at the Arena Stage in Washington, D.C., a professional theatre facility seating 750 people and producing a wide variety of play types (Fig. 6.9).

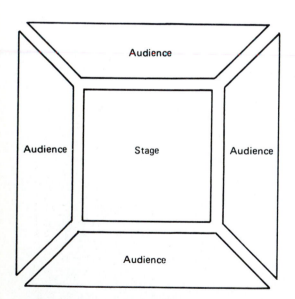

Figure 6.8 *Arena Theatre Form.*

Figure 6.9 *Set construction for a production of Anton Chekhov's* The Three Sisters, *Arena Stage, Washington, DC, 1984. A glimpse of the finished product can be found in Fig. 4.11.*

thrust/three-quarter stage A physical arrangement in which the audience encircles three sides of the stage or playing area, leaving one side open to act as a scenic background or entrance to backstage areas

A second actor–audience arrangement is the **thrust** or **three-quarter stage** (Fig. 6.10). With the three-quarter stage, the audience surrounds the stage on all but one side. The Tyrone Guthrie Theatre in Minneapolis, Minnesota, has an asymmetrical stage that juts out into the audience with steps leading down each side of the stage to the audience level (Fig. 6.11).

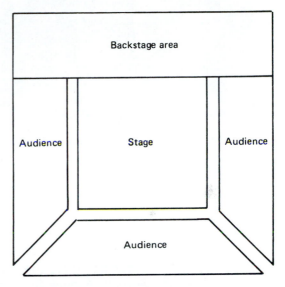

Figure 6.10 *Thrust or Three-Quarter Theatre Form.*

Figure 6.11 *Interior of the auditorium, The Guthrie Theatre, Minneapolis, Minnesota. The occasion is a 1978 production of Noel Coward's* Design for Living.

Theatre Forms *and* Architecture

Tamara: Theatre as "Environmental Escapade"

A combination drawing-room comedy and commentary on the rise of Fascism in Italy during the 1920s, the play *Tamara* by John Kritzanc turns the conventional actor-audience relationship upside down.

Called an "environmental escapade" by one critic and a "living movie" by its author, the New York production of *Tamara,* which opened in December 1987, converted 13 rooms of the Seventh Avenue Regiment Armory into the lavish villa of the Italian poet and soldier Gabriele d'Annunzio. Instead of sitting in their seats, the audience rushes from room to room in pursuit of fleet-footed actors. Scenes are performed simultaneously in various rooms as well as on staircases and passageways. In one room, a ballerina dances; in another, a maid hides a revolver. Throughout the nearly three hours of the performance, theatregoers choose the scene or character whom they wish to see. For instance, they can follow the actress playing Tamara de Lempicka, the Polish artist who has come to the villa to paint d'Annunzio's portrait. Or, they switch from following one character to sprinting after another.

Thus, *Tamara* does indeed resemble a movie in the cinematic swiftness with which actors and audience move from scene to scene. But it also resembles a living movie in that each member of the audience, by choosing what he or she sees, participates in "editing" his or her own version of the story.

The interactive nature of the production is also emphasized when audience members occasionally talk back to the actors—and by the actors responding in kind during intermission. In another gesture designed to make them feel part of the action, the audience is provided with champagne and canapes before the play begins—and during intermission, a buffet supper in d'Annunzio's dining room.

proscenium stage A physical arrangement in which the audience is placed on one side of the stage and views the action through an opening called a proscenium arch

proscenium arch An opening through which the audience, sitting on one side of the stage, views the action

PROSCENIUM

The **proscenium stage,** which has dominated theatrical production since the Renaissance, has the audience seated on one side of the stage while viewing the action through an architectural opening called a **proscenium arch** (Fig. 6.12). Because of the framing effect of the proscenium arch, this form of stage arrangement is often called a *picture-frame stage*. Its development followed the development of rational perspective in visual art in the Italian Renaissance and was the theatre's attempt to make the *mise en scène* look like a framed painting (Fig. 6.13). The development of the proscenium-theatre form in the Italian Renaissance is detailed in Chapter 16. (The famous Teatro Farnese is pictured in Figure 6.14.)

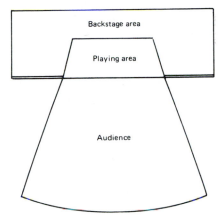

Figure 6.12   Proscenium Theatre Form.

Figure 6.13   *Sebastiano Serlio, setting for a comedy, from* De Architecttura *(1545). Serlio's conception of the model tragic setting can be found in Fig. 10.3B, which accompanies a brief essay on the role of perspective in Renaissance scenic design.*

Figure 6.14   Teatro Farnese, Parma, ca. 1630.   *The world's first proscenium theatre designed for movable scenery, Teatro Farnese boasts a spacious ballroom-arena that could actually be flooded with two feet of water when the spectacle demanded. Except for the influence of 16th-century theatres in England and Spain, European auditorium and stage design followed that of Teatro Farnese until well into the 19th century.*

Theatre Forms *and* Architecture

The **open stage** creates an actor–audience relationship in which the audience is placed on one side of the action but is not separated from the actors by an archway or by a raised stage. As you can see in the drawing for Figure 6.15A, although the stage space extends into the audience, because of the extensions of the stage to each side, the relationship is not three-sided, as in the thrust arrangement. (Figure 6.15B also is an open stage arrangement. This type of actor–audience arrangement, without a raised stage, was called for by the French producer-director Antonin Artaud (see Chapter 17) for his experimental productions in the mid-twentieth century. Artaud wanted to abolish formal stages that, he believed, created a barrier between actor and audience. He sought to create a single site, without any barriers, that could become a "theatre of action." He wished to abandon traditional theatre architecture and make it possible for any site to be a space for theatre production.

In a reconstruction of the second Globe Theatre from 1614 (Fig. 6.16), we can see how this type of theatre meets the definition of an open stage: On the yard or pit level, while the audience remains on only one side of the stage, the galleries wrap very slightly around the sides of the stage.

In the **extended stage** (Fig. 6.17), we have a variation of the open-stage or proscenium forms in which the action wraps around the audience. To a certain degree, this arrangement looks like a reversed thrust arrangement; that is, the stage space wraps around the audience.

The spatial relationships that we have just described are the major spatial relationships that occur between actors and audience in the theatre. Other relationships exist and are used often—for example, placing stage action in

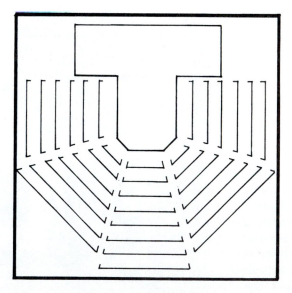

Figure 6.15A *Open-Stage Theatre Form 1.*

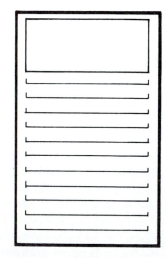

Figure 6.15B *Open-Stage Theatre Form 2.*

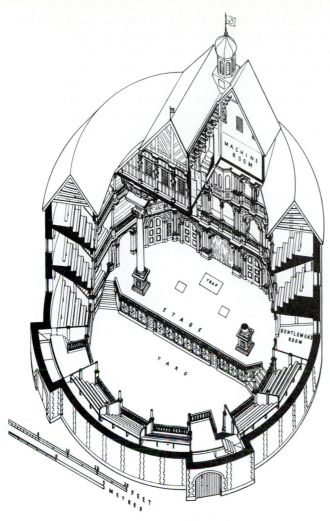

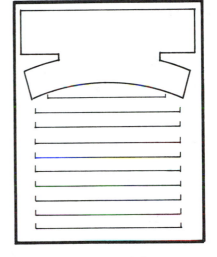

Figure 6.16 The second Globe Theatre, as reconstructed, ca. 1614. *The original Globe, built in 1599, burned to the ground in 1613—according to contemporary accounts, a stage-cannon blast during a production of Shakespeare's* Henry VIII *ignited its thatched roof. Another important Elizabethan theatre, the Swan, is pictured in Figs. 5.4A and 5.4B. The Elizabethan playhouse is discussed in further historical context in Chapter 16.*

Figure 6.17 *Extended-Stage Theatre Form.*

various "islands" amidst the audience or placing the audience in the middle of the "stage." In discussing the arrangements of audience and action, we should also understand that these types of relationships are not necessarily restricted to formal types of "theatres." For example, arrangements such as "arena" or "proscenium" can be established anywhere: Theatre is often produced in warehouses, civic arenas, sports arenas, tents, museums, and so on. The increasingly popular "black box" theatre—that is, a large open space designed for theatrical production and painted black—is usually designed so that it is flexible enough to accommodate any type of spatial arrangement: arena, thrust, proscenium, and so on. Thus, whether we consider traditional theatre spaces or untraditional spaces, the relationships possible in those spaces can encompass not only the arrangements discussed above but any others created by the artists of an individual production.

Theatre Spaces *and* Production Practicalities

Every form—and every theatre displaying every form—forces its own set of conditions on the plays produced in it. Some of the general claims made both for and against specific forms must be considered individually and/or applied to specific theatres. For example, the claim that the arena form is the most "intimate" simply does not hold true when an arena theatre seating 2,000 spectators is compared to a proscenium theatre seating 300. Likewise, the claim that a proscenium theatre offers greater "scenic potential" than other forms may be invalid if the proscenium stage has no space or mechanisms for storing and shifting scenery, especially when compared to arena and thrust theatres that are fully equipped with floor traps and the potential to "fly" scenery in and out using pulleys and wires (see Chapter 11). It probably does no good whatsoever to try to make wide-ranging claims or lists of positives and negatives for various forms. The only important factor regarding theatre form is the specific nature of the form in which the specific production must be executed. Of course, considerations such as the limitations on vertical scenic units in the arena and thrust forms can be acknowledged in a general sense. If the audience surrounds the acting area, obviously not much in the way of scenic background can be used—the audience's vision of the actors would be severely impaired. This fact might be considered a serious limitation for thrust and, especially, arena forms. However, some analysts and practitioners consider it a blessing because scenery is expensive and time-consuming to build. Although a stage empty of scenery in a proscenium form might appear inappropriate to the play, such absence is required in an arena form: Production budget and—some might argue—production aesthetics benefit greatly.

By contrast, some considerations regarding various forms are not so obvious and have driven even experienced directors and designers into awkward traps. The single most important consideration is the establishment of workable movement patterns for the actors. In the proscenium form, for example, the general tendency is to design movement flow that follows the natural horizontal configuration of the form. Very often, proscenium stages—especially those with troublesome sightlines from the side seats—force the director and designer into a shallow setting that leaves almost no possibility for upstage and downstage movement. If the stage space is shallow and wide, for example, then the theatre artist must take steps to ease the problem and create the impression—if not the reality—of nonhorizontal movement (Fig. 6.18). In thrust stages, which tend to be significantly longer than they are wide, a similar tendency for one-directional movement exists (Fig. 6.19). One way to create more flexible movement patterns is to design obstructions to the movement flow, thereby forcing actors to detour. Such devices can be counterproductive, however, if, in breaking one traffic pattern, one eliminates it entirely as an option. Careful discussion between the director and the designer regarding potential problems is an essential part of the planning process.

In the arena form, a major movement problem is the tendency to keep actors circling so that they can remain "open" to all parts of the audience as

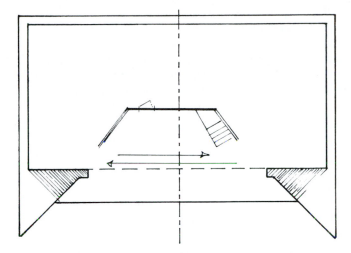

Figure 6.18 *Movement Patterns in a Shallow Proscenium Setting.*

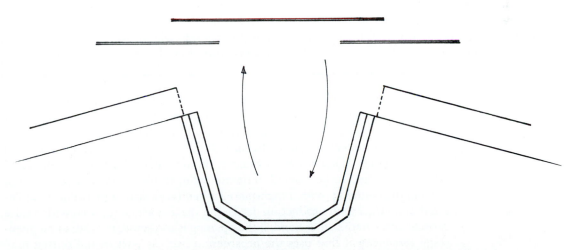

Figure 6.19 *Movement-Pattern Tendencies in the Thrust Theatre Form.*

Nicolà Sabbatini (II): Protocol for Ladies Day

Sixteenth-century Italian Renaissance treatises on scenic design ranged from such contingencies as the need to create believable water-spouting sea monsters to the use of substage chariots to move synchronously shifting flats. Sabbatini was also concerned with the particular comforts and distractions that might affect audience appreciation of the stagecraft before them.

> *The more elderly ladies should be seated in the last rows on account of the proximity of the men, so that . . . scandal may be avoided.*

The accommodating of an audience is a matter of much importance and trouble. Yet, at these performances there is never a lack of willing helpers, especially those who seek the job of showing the ladies to their seats. You must take care, however, to select for this purpose, persons of years of discretion, so that no suspicion or scandal arise. The ladies are to be placed in the orchestra, or as we say, in the third of the hall nearest the stage, taking care to place the least important in the first rows nearest the parapet and proceeding in the other rows according to rank. Care should be taken always to place the most beautiful ladies in the middle so that those who are acting and striving to please, gaining inspiration from this lovely prospect, perform more gaily, with greater assistance, and with greater zest.

The more elderly ladies should be seated in the last rows on account of the proximity of the men, so that every shadow of scandal may be avoided. Those who are responsible for seating the men should be persons of authority and, if possible, should be acquainted with all or at least part of them. In giving them the seats, it will be necessary to see that the common or less cultivated persons are set on the tiers and at the sides, since the machines give a less perfect appearance in these places, and because such people do not observe them minutely. The persons of culture and taste should be seated on the floor of the hall, as near the middle as possible, in the second or third rows. They will have the greatest pleasure there, since in such a position all the parts of the scenery and the machines are displayed in their perfection, and they will not be able to see the defects which are sometimes discerned by those on the steps or at the sides.

the play progresses (Fig. 6.20). Here again, recognition of potential problems leads the designer and the director to confront the situation and to adopt solutions appropriate to both the play and the specific production goals.

In the proscenium form, the size of the proscenium opening itself can create potential problems. For example, the designer who tries to "upscale" what is supposed to be a small, intimate room to fill a fifty-foot proscenium opening will wind up with a nightmare. When faced with a proscenium opening that is larger than production needs, the space must be reduced with a false proscenium. On the other hand, if the opening is too small, moving to an open-stage arrangement that uses the proscenium arch as part of the setting may solve the problem. In the setting shown in Figure 6.21, for example, the acting

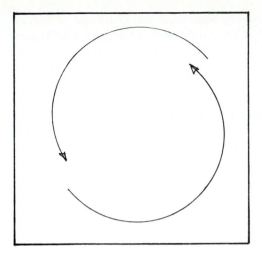

Figure 6.20   *Circular-Movement Patterns in the Arena Theatre Form.*

Figure 6.21   *Euripides,* The Bacchae *(ca. 405 B.C.). University of Illinois at Chicago. Director, William Raffield; scenic designer, Dennis J. Sporre.*

area was moved outside the proscenium arch (an opening of approximately 24 feet) immediately upstage of the ramps in the foreground). This solution created a stage area stretching from one wall of the auditorium to the other, kept the proscenium backstage area intact, and gave the production the scale that the play and style demanded. However, changing the size of the proscenium opening in an existing theatre also changes the angles of audience vision and thus creates the possibility for audience discomfort.

Options within Forms: Multiple, Unit, *and* Simultaneous Settings

Whatever its form, the specific characteristics of the individual theatre will ultimately force itself on the production, especially when plays of more than one scenic locale are produced. Whenever more than one scenic location is called for, the director and designer must face the challenge of solving aesthetic and practical problems. Previous productions of the play may suggest solutions, and still other solutions may be invented or combined to meet specific needs. Production goals and, perhaps, contemporary conventions may shape these decisions. For example, Elizabethan audiences watched Shakespeare's plays essentially without scenery in an architectural surrounding suggested by the reconstruction of the second Globe Theatre in Figure 6.16; Figure 6.22 shows the amphitheatre built for the Oregon Shakespeare Festival, which is internationally known for its Elizabethan-style productions of Shakespearean plays. In the nineteenth century, when scenic spectacle was the order of the day, both the audience and the current style required elaborate settings for each scene. Medieval productions used "simultaneous" settings to solve the problem of multiple-scene plays (see Figs. 10.2A and 10.2B). In the modern theatre, artists are free to choose one or all of these options to meet their needs.

MULTIPLE SETTINGS

multiple setting Scenic form in which complete separate sets are designed for different locations

In some cases, production needs can be met by the **multiple setting**, in which a separate and complete set is designed for each required location. Such a design calls into play a designer's creative understanding of how to shift scenery by a variety of means (see Chapter 11). Even if the theatre is well endowed with wing space and flying systems, an organization of designs that allows for rapid scenic changes is required. Often, the play itself is written in such a way as to suggest solutions. For example, many musicals are structured

Figure 6.22 *Auditorium and stage, Oregon Shakespearean Festival, Ashland Oregon. Founded in 1935, the Oregon Festival specializes in Elizabethan-style staging in an amphitheatre designed after the Shakespearean playhouse.*

Theatre Forms *and* Architecture

George Tyspin: Interior Architecture

Born in the Soviet Union in 1954, George Tyspin studied architecture and physics as well as literature before he turned to theatre design in 1984. His designs are often associated with the movement known as deconstructivist architecture, which prefers to represent fantasies of the mind rather than pursue traditional ideas of composition. Here he discusses a production of Jean Genet's absurdist fantasy The Screens, *directed by JoAnne Akalaitis at the Guthrie Theatre in 1990.*

What I am trying to do is explode the box. Usually the theatre model is in a box, but the box is irrelevant. In fact, you try to overcome the box whenever you design for the theatre. You design a world that is not in the box, that is much larger than the box. So I just got rid of the box.

I WOULD LIKE TO TALK ABOUT THE PRODUCTION OF *THE SCREENS* YOU RECENTLY DID WITH JOANNE AT THE GUTHRIE. I'D LIKE TO KNOW HOW THE TWO OF YOU APPROACHED THAT PLAY.

Although Jean Genet asks that his plays not be set in very specific locations, JoAnne decided to use Algeria in the late 1950s and early '60s for this production. . . . [so] JoAnne and I went to Morocco. . . . Some parts of Morocco are modern, of course, but we went specifically to look at the architecture in the medieval towns. And then we went into the desert.

What I am trying to do is explode the box. Usually the theatre model is in a box, but the box is irrelevant.

JoAnne really wanted to create an environmental event at the Guthrie. In fact, we were going to use another space run by the theatre, but then decided to do it at the Guthrie because it's right beside the Walker Arts Center. The museum is a center for Western art, and our major impulse was to have it clash with this unbelievable third-world culture. All of the lobby windows were painted with wild, violent drawings, so as you passed the Guthrie you were already pulled into the world of the play.

HOW DID YOU APPROACH THE THEATRE SPACE?

I wanted to get rid of all of the notions of Western theatre, and I had two ideas about how to do it. One was to take out all of the seats and make people sit on this desert-like yellow fabric. I thought it would work like an Arabic theatre, or like watching a spectacle in a marketplace.

My second idea was to continue the fabric up and over the audience to create another acting level. Within the structure of the play, these two worlds—the world of the living and the world of the dead—are very important. People die in the world of the living and then appear in the world of the dead.

But I couldn't do both. I couldn't take out all of the seats, which is labor intensive, and create this upper level for the world of the dead. So I decided to go with the world of the dead. I suspended a huge net over the stage. It wasn't supported in any way, but was stretched from many different points in the theatre. We had to hire an architect and go through walls to reach the main beams of the building. Even then we weren't sure that the tension would be great enough to sustain the weight of the actors.

But it worked. The image was like that of the desert. It was shaped like the desert.

And when the characters walked across the net, which they had to do slowly, in slow motion, they sank into it—like into sand. It was like they were weightless. It was very beautiful.

HOW DID YOU TREAT THE REST OF THE SPACE?

I covered the stage with yellow fabric, and then had lots of transparent screens which moved during the performance. The screens had different images on them, but the actors also drew on them during the show, so you had these many different layers of images.

From *American Set Design* 2 by Ronn Smith. Copyright © 1991 by Ronn Smith.

---

in-one technique
Method of changing scenes by shifting smaller or larger components of a single set to create multiple sets

so that the concept of the **in-one technique** is built into the play itself. In this case, scenes are arranged in progression from small to large. The production, then, begins with several sets in place, each inside a larger one. Shifting is executed by removing a smaller set, which then reveals a larger one. The shift is economical because the need to put a second set in place has been met ahead of time.

Of course, there are numerous means of shifting multiple settings by placing the units on wheels for rolling, picking them up and carrying them manually, or attaching them to cables running over pulleys above the stage and "flying" them (see Chapter 11). Shifts at scene breaks are much more critical than those at act breaks because scene-break shifts do not have an intermission to cover them.

In evaluating the effectiveness of multiple settings in a production, we look for two factors. First, was the *shift* from one scene to another quiet and efficient so as not to detract from the rhythmic flow of the production? Second, were the various settings reflective of the same *general style*—that is, did multiple settings help to *unify* the production visually?

UNIT SETTINGS

unit set A single setting that serves as a scenic location for a multi-scene play. It provides a means for staging the play without the need for shifting scenes

The **unit set** has become a practical solution for the multiscene play. It provides a means for staging the play without the need for settings for each different scene and the need to shift from one setting to another. Unit sets range from a single design that sustains itself and the play for the entire production to units that form a basic environment to which various elements are added to suggest various scenes. A unit set may be *conventional*—that is, *nonrepresentational*, like the Globe Theatre in Figure 6.16—or *illusionistic*, heavily suggesting time and place (for example, Figure 6.23). Of course, a unit set may occupy a middle ground, as does the setting for *Ghetto* discussed in our opening "Diary of a Production." In that case, although the setting was not immediately recognizable as a "place," it did attempt to show some realistic detail of the Vilna ghetto. In addition, a unit set may represent any style; also, it can be stationary or it can move. At its simplest—and perhaps best— the unit set can provide the perfect ambiance for plays whose language is so written that virtually nothing is required in the way of representational sugges-

Figure 6.23   *Proscenium setting for Stephen Sondheim's musical* Company. *University of Arizona Theatre. Director, Peter R. Marroney; scenic and lighting designer, Dennis J. Sporre. See the* PROFILE *on Hal Prince, Sondheim, and the making of* Company *in Chapter* 7.

tion for the audience. As we will see in Chapters 15 and 16, many great classical plays—many whose language is high and poetic—were produced in the simplest of unit settings.

In evaluating unit settings, we can look for three factors. First, did the setting provide appropriate *acting space?* Second, did it provide a *mood* appropriate to the production? Third, did the setting contain enough *visual stimuli* to sustain itself for the audience throughout the running time of the production?

SIMULTANEOUS SETTINGS

simultaneous setting
The provision, in one production, of several settings that remain totally within view of the audience at all times

Although **simultaneous settings** are not new in the theatre, they have gained in popularity in the last several years. The device itself dates back to Roman comedy and to medieval mystery, miracle, and morality plays. In the simultaneous setting, the designer creates two or more settings that remain totally within view of the audience and are united within an overall design picture. Many plays actually call for a simultaneous setting. For example, Neil Simon's popular play, *Brighton Beach Memoirs* (later made into an equally popular movie) calls for action to occur in various rooms of the family home in Brighton Beach, New York. To solve the need to move from one room of the house to another, the Broadway production placed the entire house on stage, sectioned through the middle to reveal living room, dining room, hallway, and

Theatre Forms *and* Architecture

175

upstairs bedrooms. As Simon traces the episodes of his youth, audience focus on the various parts of the house is controlled by action and lighting.

Two major limitations of the simultaneous setting are the *size* of the stage space and the *sightlines* of the theatre. A simultaneous setting that is not skillfully organized and carefully designed can end up with too little space for the necessary action. As a result, actors may move in fear of bumping against walls and furniture, and the director may not be able to use the kind of actor movement that is best for a scene. In addition, especially where a second level is used, it may be impossible for major portions of the audience to see anything but the downstage action or the upper bodies of the actors if great care is not taken in planning or if the theatre is not suited to elevated sightlines. In some theatres, a second level may drive the lighting designer to distraction because of limitations in the possible placement of lighting instruments or problems in lighting areas independently.

In evaluating a simultaneous setting, look for the same qualities noted in evaluating a unit setting plus the accuracy of *depiction of realistic details* and the adequacy of *stage space* in handling the movement needs of the actors and the vision requirements of the audience. Whatever the solutions, the options for multiscene productions are many. In every case, however, scenic options are closely tied to the facility—if, indeed, not dictated by it. The theatre artist who is in a situation in which the same theatre is used in production after production may be able to learn from mistakes, and the facility may become an ally rather than an adversary. But if one has no control over the physical facility and must take it as it stands, one will often need as much creativity in dealing with the theatre building as in dealing with all the other production factors combined.

SUMMARY

• The creative imagination involved in a theatre production can proceed only as far as the limitations of time, budget, staff, and physical space allow.

• The physical theatre—its types, potentials, and limitations, both practical and aesthetic—have significant impact on what can happen onstage in a theatre production. Every production has certain basic needs that must be met in order for the production to succeed; these are *vision, acoustics, freedom from distractions, safety,* and *seating comfort.*

• In meeting the needs of *vision,* the production must allow audience members to take in the full action on the stage without eye movement. To meet the needs of *acoustics,* the theatre must allow the audience to hear clearly. *Distractions* must be kept to a minimum. *Safety* concerns are always vital in considerations of stage and audience spaces. Seating *comfort* allows the audience to give the production the attention required for a satisfactory experience.

• In trying to understand the general requirements for production types, we must remember that every production is influenced by the specific theatre in which it will be executed—not all theatres are ideal for all productions.

• Many types of *actor/audience spatial relationships* exist. We can divide theatres into four general *forms:*

arena, in which the audience surrounds the stage;

thrust, in which the audience sits on three sides of the stage area;

proscenium, in which the audience views the action through an architectural opening called a *proscenium arch;*

open stage, in which the audience is placed on one side of the action but is not separated from the actors by an archway or, in some cases, by a raised stage.

• All of the theatre spaces discussed in this chapter have their own set of inherent production practicalities. However, sweeping generalizations about what may be possible in a particular theatre form prove to be less valid than specific conditions resulting from individual theatres—that is, although conditions such as "intimacy," scenic potential, and stage movement may be related to specific forms such as arena, thrust, or proscenium stages, they also relate directly to the size and equipment present in the specific theatre in which a production is to be mounted.

• Within each of the theatre forms we have discussed in this chapter, three additional options exist: *multiple, unit,* and *simultaneous settings:*

multiple settings create a separate and complete set for each required location;

unit sets provide a means for staging the play without the need for settings for each different scene;

simultaneous settings contain two or more settings that remain totally within view of the audience and are united within an overall design picture.

AS YOU LIKE IT

SHAKESPEARE

Chapter 7

Producing Organizations *and the* Production Team

After studying this chapter, you should be able to:

- Discuss how the process of collaboration and cooperation helps to create a theatre production.

- Explain how good communication enhances the development of a theatre production.

- Characterize the various types of producing organizations such as *commercial, not-for-profit, educational,* and *community* theatres.

- Define the term *professional theatre.*

- Describe how the *production team* functions in artistic and nonartistic decision making.

- Identify and describe the major areas of responsibility that make up a production team.

Cover of a program for As You Like It, *The Guthrie Theatre, 19th Season. The Guthrie Theatre.*

*I*n the chapters of the Introduction and Unit I—"The Fundamentals of Theatre"—we examined some of the theoretical and general background information that helps us to understand, for example, theatre's place in the artistic world, how to analyze and criticize a theatrical work, types of plays, factors that influence how and where performances are staged, and our role as audience members. In Unit II, we move to the actual making of theatre in order to understand how theatre artists work together to create a production. In this unit we will examine each of the artistic and craft positions in some detail—beginning in this chapter with the organizations that produce theatre and the organization of the team of artists who bring theatre productions to fruition. Thus, we will have a much better appreciation of the tremendous creative and human effort that goes into a production of a play.

Theatre is a cooperative art, and it cannot be created by a single artist. A play can be read, but it comes to life only in performance. A scene-design sketch cannot be considered a work of art because it only suggests the actual finished product on the stage. Collective wisdom states that for every actor who walks on the stage to perform, forty individuals work in various backstage capacities. Writers, designers, technicians, publicists, stage managers, dressers, electricians, and many others work together to present a single actor to an audience. Each of these individuals must function cooperatively in an organization dedicated to presenting a successful production.

Good communication is a vital factor in any producing company. Without it, no one functions well, and chaos reigns. With it, the varied talents of each participant grow and contribute to the success of the venture (see Fig. 7.1). Good communication requires a number of presentations, conferences,

Figure 7.1 John Steinbeck, Of Mice and Men. *Ball State University Theatre, 1984. Director, Allen English; scenic designer, D. C. Shawger; costume designer, C. Shawger; lighting designer, J. Koger. This particular production is high in realistic treatment of character, settings, and costumes. Notice the attention to detail in costume and scenery: Such unification of concept among all of the production elements requires thorough communication among director, actors, and designers.*

Producing Organizations *and the* Production Team

meetings, and discussions with the individuals who have responsibility in the creative development of the production. Every person must be aware of all the other personnel involved and must know the particular responsibilities of those personnel in order to secure the cooperation and assistance necessary to operate within the group successfully. In the "Production Diary" that begins this book, we find a group of artists meeting and working together over a period of months. Each new understanding in the play and each problem that arises requires that these individuals discuss the implications of those understandings and problems thoroughly so that the production can proceed smoothly and with everyone aware of what the others were doing. As you read each artist's perceptions of the performance in that diary, you notice how often "communication" with the other artists occurred and the important role it played in bringing the production to a successful opening night.

In this chapter we will gain an overview of the kinds of organizations that produce theatre and the working relationships among the various partners who make up the emerging production. Let's look first at an organizational chart of the various staff production assignments for a typical theatrical organization (see Fig. 7.2). This chart is a general one; structure will vary in size and complexity, depending on budget, schedule, and talent. However, this structure applies to most producing organizations, even though the purpose of the group may vary from profit-making to fun.

The Producing Organization

The basic intent or purpose of a producing organization is the criterion used to separate these organizations into several categories—*commercial, not-for-profit, educational,* and *community.* The term *professional* probably does not adequately describe a producing organization, inasmuch as the term has a number of arguable definitions and various kinds of applications to all theatre producing organizations.

Professional theatre can in fact be applied broadly to any producing organization that pays its staff, regardless of the amount. In the purest sense, however, many theatre professionals reserve this term for those agencies that have some formal relationship to **Actors Equity,** the national actors' union, and to United Scenic Artists, the national designers' union. The Broadway or commercial theatre most frequently comes to mind when one thinks of "professional theatre." On the other hand, many *regional* theatre organizations, which are generally not-for-profit, are also fully professional. In addition, some educational institutions have professional companies that use Equity actors but may pay less than union scale. The term *professional,* then, has many applications. Whether we apply the term broadly or with the restrictions just noted, we tend to assume that *professional* means receiving payment for *doing* the art. An additional connotation for the term comes from the *educational theatre.* Theatre teachers whose basic pay comes from teaching may also

professional theatre Any producing organization that pays its staff, usually those with some formal relationship to *Actors Equity* and United Scenic Artists

Actors Equity The national actors' union

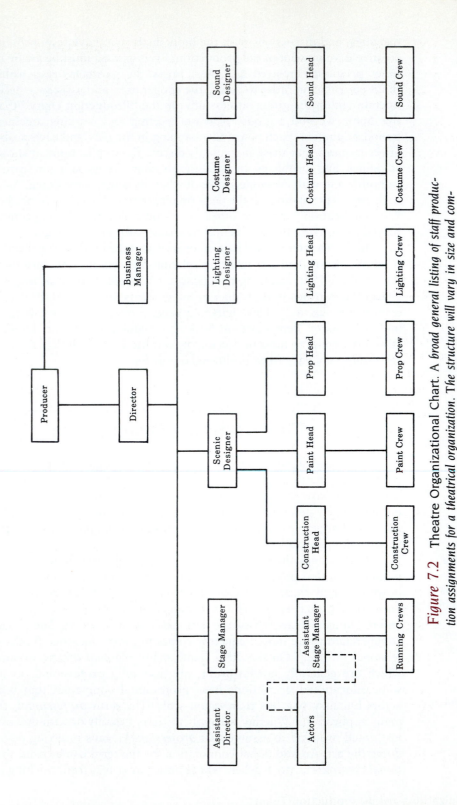

Figure 7.2 Theatre Organizational Chart. *A broad general listing of staff production assignments for a theatrical organization. The structure will vary in size and complexity, depending on budget, schedule, and talent.*

act, direct, or design as part of their employment responsibilities to the school. These individuals also think of themselves as "professionals"—that is, as gaining a livelihood from the making of theatre. All of the artists involved in the production of *Ghetto* that we studied in the "Production Diary" would fall into this category. The costume and scenic designers for this production have nearly their entire "teaching" load assigned to designing, and each is responsible for designing several productions a year. The director of the production *Ghetto* has most of her load assigned in teaching regular coursework—she directs one production each year. The lighting designer is a college dean who spends most of his time in administrative work but also designs one or two productions in a calendar year.

THE BROADWAY OR COMMERCIAL THEATRE

Most theatre artists consider the Broadway theatre the ultimate goal to be achieved in the profession. Actors, directors, playwrights, and designers all equate success with the commercial New York area. Much of this regard is reinforced by the theatre unions, which are most active in New York. Commercial theatre, whether it is in New York, London, or elsewhere, has fundamentally a business purpose that separates it from other kinds of production organizations. Commercial (Broadway) theatre is essentially a single-production business headed by a *producer* who is responsible for estimating the costs of production and for raising the money to achieve its presentation. After opening, box-office sales must cover weekly operating expenses and begin to repay the investors. The production runs for as long as it continues to turn a

Figure 7.3 Broadway opening, 1967. *Attendance at Broadway theatre productions in 1981–1982 was 6.6 million; for the 1991–1992 season, that figure had dropped to just over 4 million. In addition, the average cost of mounting a production rose about 10 percent between 1990 and 1992, with "straight" dramas costing an average of $1.3 million and musicals from $4 to $7 million. Produced by one of Broadway's most successful and celebrated entrepreneurs, David Merrick, I Do, I Do! was among the productions to open at what many observers believe to be the end of the "golden age" of the Broadway musical, and in the early 1990s, revivals seem to be less risky than original musicals.*

Producing Organizations *and the* Production Team

profit. This approach contrasts with the *limited-run* practice of other kinds of producing organizations. The producer is responsible for selecting the show's designers, sometimes with recommendations from the playwright and the director. Because the producer in the commercial theatre must first raise money from interested investors in order to produce the production, it is not unusual for the producer, even before establishing a cast—and sometimes even a director—to use the services of the designer to help raise capital on the basis of his or her sketches and models. The investor, then, can "see" how potentially attractive the show will be to an audience, as opposed to trying to judge the play's potential for success solely from the script or the producer's opinion. Many potential paths can lead to a commercial or Broadway production. For example, a new play may come to the attention of a Broadway producer through a production at a regional theatre. Its success there gives it stronger credence toward attracting backers than a new play that has never been produced. Often commercial productions in New York are imported from London, where they may have already earned commercial success. Many popular musicals are typical cases in point—for example, *A Chorus Line* (Fig. 7.4), *Jesus Christ, Superstar, Cats, Starlight Express, The Phantom of the Opera,* and *Aspects of Love.* Thus, the fundamental purpose of the commercial theatre is to make money for its partners or investors. This is the primary motivation for raising the millions of dollars that it typically takes to stage a commercial production.

Figure 7.4
Broadway's longest-running production, A Chorus Line, *prepares to close at the Shubert Theatre, 1990.* A Chorus Line *opened in April 1975 and closed after 6104 performances. In the interview in this chapter, producer Joseph Papp has a few words on the circumstances, both historical and critical, under which* A Chorus Line *originated.*

Producing Organizations *and the* Production Team

Joseph Papp (I): The Democratic Producer

Producer and impresario Joseph Papp (1921–1991) founded the New York Shakespeare Festival on a Central Park truck stage in the late 1950s; thirty-five years later, his innovative productions of Shakespeare have been seen by over three million people. In 1967 Papp renovated an old New York library building to house six theatres, rehearsal space, and offices for his new Public Theatre, which debuted with a curious and controversial hippie musical called Hair! *Papp's enterprise remained strongly rooted in the theatre culture of New York, whose organizations and audiences were always central to his various plans. The interview excerpted here was conducted in 1986.*

SOME OF YOUR CRITICS FIND IT HARD TO SEE A CONSISTENT GUIDING ARTISTIC VISION IN YOUR CAREER. THEY SAY YOU CHASE AFTER FASHIONS. . . . But I've had a very consistent vision! . . . It's been addressed primarily to reaching audiences, new audiences, people who can't afford to go to the theatre. . . . And I've always had a strong social base, always. You'll find that 80 percent of my plays deal with problems that are issues of today. Is that chasing after fashions? . . .

I do a lot more black and Hispanic works than anybody. Is that chasing after fashions? That's part of my artistic vision. These critics, they want an artistic vision where an individual is the director of a theatre that turns out only one kind of art, but I'm not that kind of person. . . .

I want lots of people to see my plays. I believe in a popular, democratic theatre. I want the theatre to reach great numbers. . . . I don't have just one single artistic thought or style. I want to do a great variety of plays to satisfy all kinds of audiences, not just some coterie. . . . And finding young writers, giving them a chance. That's my policy.

WHAT FASHION DO I FOLLOW? When I introduced *A Chorus Line*, there was no fashion for *A Chorus Line*. There was no fashion for *The Pirates of Penzance*. . . . Those critics, they weren't doing plays about Vietnam; I was doing plays about Vietnam. They weren't doing plays with blacks; I was doing plays with blacks. Who was doing the first plays about women? I was doing them. That's not fashion, that's tied in to what's going on with the world, so that the theatre has some life. . . .

The only difference now is that I have more power . . . more possibility of having an impact on the American theatre.

OKAY, LET'S MOVE . . .

In fact, I've made a complete circle. . . . I'm doing what I originally started out doing. . . . The only difference now is that I have more power, more clout, more prestige, more possibility of having an impact on the American theatre. Just changing the economics, to make it possible to do dramas on Broadway and open up four or five of those dark theatres and have lights in those streets—if I can do that, that would be amazing, because we're going against history. History is going to tear all those theatres down. . . .

Excerpted by permission from Ross Wetzstein's interview with Joseph Papp in the September 1986 issue of *American Theatre Magazine.* Published by Theatre Communications Group.

A word needs to be said here about art and commercialism. Although the vehicles chosen for commercial production are chosen almost solely for their ability to turn a profit, that does not mean that commercial productions are without artistic merit. Some may very well be, but the converse can also occur—and examples of either case will undoubtedly be arguable.

The Off-Broadway Theatre   Another form of producing organization is called the **Off-Broadway theatre.** The term refers to a geographical area of Manhattan anywhere outside the defined Broadway area, which is bounded roughly by Fifth and Ninth Avenues from 34th to 56th Streets or from Fifth Avenue to the Hudson River between 56th and 72nd Streets. Although the term Off-Broadway does have geographical parameters, its status as a producing organization has come to be defined by union rules. The Off-Broadway theatre was initially a reaction to the commercialism of the Broadway theatre in the 1950s and 1960s. Its purpose was to foster new plays and experimental productions and to produce the works of new playwrights. Originally established as low-budget showcase-theatre organizations, Off-Broadway theatres were eventually unionized, which increased production costs and encouraged commercialization. By union agreement, the seating capacity of an Off-Broadway house must be less than 499 seats. Today, however, the number of seats is not as important as the possible weekly gross of the theatre's box office ticket sales. The history of Off-Broadway theatres as producing organizations includes a lively record of important productions and persons, whose stories we will examine in Chapter 17. In this chapter we must limit ourselves to descriptions of categories, leaving the details for later.

The Showcase Theatre   Another type of production organization that operates close to the commercial theatre is the **Showcase Theatre.** This type of production organization operates in houses of under 100 seats and could originally operate without union employees. However, showcase theatres are now subject to jurisdiction by Actors Equity under the Showcase Code, which allows for audience contributions and/or limited ticket prices. The Showcase Theatre can opt for runs of 4 weeks, 8 weeks, 12 weeks, or 24 weeks, depending on box office sales.

THE NOT-FOR-PROFIT REGIONAL THEATRE

As early as the mid-1930s, decentralization of the professional, commercial theatre was encouraged by such organizations as the American National Theatre and Academy. This attempt to bring high-quality production to all parts of the United States was established by congressional charter—but without public funding. Nonetheless, by the early 1960s these **regional theatres,** as they were called, had developed sufficiently to exert an important influence in the American theatre scene. Theatres such as the Tyrone Guthrie Theatre in Minneapolis were employing some of the country's best actors, directors, and designers and producing outstanding productions of new plays and classics.

The early 1960s saw the formation of the National Endowment for the

---

Off-Broadway theatre
Collectively, professional producing organizations initially founded as a commercial and artistic alternative to the commercial theatre of Broadway

showcase theatres
Professional producing organizations operating in small theatres and generally offering limited-run productions

regional theatres
Professional producing organizations, usually repertory companies, located in and supported by local venues and groups

Figure 7.5 Actors Theatre of Louisville, Louisville, Kentucky. *Along with other noted regional theatres like Chicago's Steppenwolf, the Seattle Repertory Company, and Hartford Stage, the Louisville Actors Theatre supports such activities and soliciting new plays and subsidizing play development. The American Conservatory Theatre in San Francisco and the American Repertory Theatre in Boston are repertory companies, and permanent summer festivals are now held in such venues as Stratford, Ontario (Canada), and Ashland, Oregon.*

Arts, as well as a number of local arts councils, which contributed financial support with direct funding, grants, and contributions for struggling nonprofit resident theatres. As these theatres grew, they created and developed audiences in numbers and areas never before imagined. Because regional theatres were noncommercial, they were free to take greater risks with the shows they produced. Creativity, imagination, and originality abounded. This type of producing organization can be found in most of the major cities in the United States— Minneapolis, Dallas, San Francisco, San Diego, Louisville (Fig. 7.5), Milwaukee, Tucson, Los Angeles, Denver, Chicago, and Seattle, among many others. The regional theatre has given professional-quality theatre a broad base outside of Manhattan. In fact, the decrease in commercial productions on Broadway has led many theatre artists to seek assignments in the regional theatres. Because most regional theatres produce a season of plays, it is economically beneficial to establish repertory companies and resident designers— a practice that enables the artist to enjoy a more secure income for a longer period of time than does the commercial Broadway system of single-show productions.

THE NONCOMMERCIAL THEATRE

educational theatres
Producing organizations located at and sponsored by educational institutions, often with professional equity associations

The Educational Theatre The past twenty-five years have seen the **educational theatre** replace the private professional schools of the 1920s as training grounds for serious students of theatre arts. Universities such as Yale pioneered in the training of actors, directors, and designers for the commercial theatre. Their lead was followed by state universities such as the University of Iowa. Before 1950, for example, most scene-design students studied at private art schools, with occasional apprentice positions in summer stock or professional design studios. Productions in colleges and universities were considered extracurricular activities sponsored by honorary clubs and similar to athletic events. Slowly, however, the educational process was expanded, not only to degrees in music and the graphic arts but to drama and even dance.

The affluent 1960s also brought about the expansion of physical facilities until many campuses could boast theatre structures that far surpassed any commercial Broadway playhouse. Not only were theatre auditoriums built, but shops, storage areas, and rehearsal rooms were judged equally important. The new structures allowed for more intense training, more flexibility in presentation, and more inspiration in execution. The security of the teaching profession attracted talented and outstanding theatre artists, and many professional artists accepted short-term positions on university faculties in between professional engagements.

Many universities also have strong connections with professional Equity companies that give students added contact with the profession through association. Some professional actors, directors, and designers work as guest lecturers and/or professors in schools with professional programs—a combination that provides additional financial security as well as satisfaction in contributing to the development of young artists. As a result, this producing/training organization—the educational theatre—tends to select its plays with a mixture of objectives. For example, although most educational theatres are concerned with attracting audiences, they base their seasons more on the educational needs of students—for training and for exposure to the various periods and play types throughout history. Their missions in production encompass the direct nurturing of cultural values and education of audiences as well as the presentation of theatre art of high quality.

community theatres
Generally nonprofit local producing organizations staffed by nonsalaried amateurs and supported by local funding

The Community Theatre The **community theatre** is essentially a nonprofit urban project that involves enthusiastic but amateur artists. Beginning in the 1920s and 1930s, the community theatre has become a means of artistic expression for individuals who do not consider the theatre their profession but, rather, a responsible hobby. Reinforced by municipal funding, many organizations are contributing vitality and enthusiasm to a cooperative community activity.

Most of those involved are nonsalaried amateurs dedicated to producing plays and performing them for their local neighbors. The organization is generally headed by a board of directors who will hire at least two paid theatre artists, generally a managing director and a designer/technician. Community theatres usually operate under a seasonal plan of productions, and the paid staff will be hired by the season. Although some communities have their own theatre buildings, they are in a minority. More often than not, community theatres locate in temporary quarters such as stores, fieldhouses, ballrooms, and school or civic auditoriums.

Producing Organizations *and the* Production Team

The Production Team

As the opening chapter of this book—"Diary of a Performance"—suggests, a close and creative relationship exists among the individuals who work together to produce a play. We will discuss this intricate relationship in much more detail in the next few chapters as we examine more specifically each of the areas of theatrical production. In the next several pages, however, we will gain an overview of the organizational assignments that actually make up the production team. We will focus on the division of labor and note that the production team has a structure of its own, at the top of which are the creative decision makers.

Reporting to these individuals are other important team members who are responsible for carrying out the ideas of the creative team. In addition to the creative and crafts personnel, theatre productions also depend on business personnel who take responsibility for contracts, tickets, publicity, and house management. All of these individuals together form a production team, without which theatrical productions cannot come into being. Knowing what these individuals do and how they relate to each other helps us to gain a deeper understanding of the theatre and its relationship to us. We will begin our discussion of the production team by returning briefly to the playwright—an individual who is fundamental to the art of theatre but only occasionally involved in the actual production of theatre.

THE PLAYWRIGHT

According to tradition, Thespis was the first actor and playwright, winning the very first contest for tragedy in Athens in 534 B.C. Certainly "theatre" existed prior to that time, and it probably comprised performers acting spontaneously before an audience. At various times in history, theatre has been scriptless—for example, during the Italian Renaissance, when performances of a type of theatre called *commedia dell'arte* (see Chapter 16) used improvisation to create dialogue. Contemporary theatre has seen its share of advocates for a totally unscripted performance. Nonetheless, throughout its history theatre has depended on the playwright as its fundamental impetus. Whether or not the playwright functions as an active member of the production team, however, depends on a number of circumstances. Perhaps the most significant of these is whether or not the playwright is alive to be able to function as a member of the team. The bulk of contemporary theatre productions involve plays that are not by living playwrights. If the play is in its initial production, however, the playwright likely will play a critical collaborative role as a member of the production team. Very likely, the playwright's ideas, intentions, and visions act as a focus for the other creative artists. In a premier production the playwright acts in a responsive role to the other artists as well. If, in the view of

Gordon Davidson: How to Give Good Meeting

In 1964, Gordon Davidson (born 1932) helped to found The Theatre Group to bring socially committed culture to Los Angeles. A veteran of numerous theatre occupations, Davidson has for over twenty-five years been artistic director of the Mark Taper Forum in Los Angeles and a prolific director of both theatre and opera.

HOW HAVE YOU LEARNED TO COMMUNICATE, TO COLLABORATE WITH DESIGNERS?

When I was a young stage manager, I worked for Martha Graham. . . . I will never forget going to a preliminary design meeting about a new ballet that she was going to choreograph based on the Phaedra legend. She summoned Isamu Noguchi, who was going to do the set, Jean Rosenthal, the lighting designer, and me. Having attended a number of design meetings like that in the past, I expected a certain procedure to be followed. I had my pad ready, expecting to learn where the platform had to be, or the doors, or what have you. To my surprise, delight, puzzlement and amazement, they never talked about the ballet. We sat down in Martha's apartment on the East Side. She said, "I'm thinking of doing a new ballet based on the Phaedra legend." She reached over to the table and picked up a rock. She handed it to Noguchi. It was an interesting shape and he felt it. He gave it to Jean Rosenthal. She felt it. I looked at it and gave it back to Martha. And that was the end of the meeting. Noguchi went off and designed an extraordinary set. Jeannie lit it. It was a wonderful ballet. To this day, I still don't know how that happened, although sometimes I've experienced the kind of communication that happens among artists who have worked together over a long period of time.

I had my pad ready, expecting to learn where the platform had to be. . . .

The best work gets at the essence of something and defines it. Out of that emerges a design and, therefore, a concept. Of course, you can't make anything like that work every time. When creative people get together they don't always make it happen. The longer the gestation time, discussion time, the longer you have to live with it the better. Sometimes you can press the right buttons and release the right ideas, and other times you don't.

Excerpted by permission from the May 1988 issue of *American Theatre Magazine*. Published by Theatre Communications Group.

the producer, director, or designers, some part of the script does not work well, then the playwright may rewrite the troublesome portions. In fact, part of the playwright's contract with the producer will specify how responsive to requests for rewrite the playwright must be. Thus, when playwrights are present for the development process of a production, they do play a central collaborative role.

Figure 7.6   *The hands-on playwright: George Bernard Shaw rehearses a production of* Androcles and the Lion *at the St. James Theatre, 1913. Having subtitled his first play "An Original Didactic Realist Play," Shaw generally left little to chance in either the reading or production of his works. Most of his major dramas are accompanied by lengthy prefaces (the preface to* Major Barbara *begins with a "First Aid to Critics"), and his concern for psychological realism led him to take a hand in the stage direction of actors, including supporting players, whom he considered essential to communicating the fullness of his message. Shaw is discussed more fully in Chapter 17, and summaries of* Major Barbara *and* Saint Joan, *two of his most important works, can be found in Chapter 4.*

Whether or not the playwright participates personally as a member of the team, the playwright's script forms a core from which the production team works in bringing that script to the stage. In some cases the script forms an inviolable core. If the director views the script as the central part of the production, then careful research into the playwright's intentions and meaning will probably drive the decisions of the team. If the director views the script in a less central role, as we will see in Chapter 8, then the playwright's "involvement" lessens. Nonetheless, the playwright almost always has *some* presence in the deliberations of the production team, if only an ethereal one.

THE PRODUCER

producer Individual, usually in the commercial theatre, with varying degrees of authority in managing the overall project of mounting a production

We noted earlier that the **producer** organizes the production, beginning with making solicitations to investors, setting up budgets, and securing performance and rehearsal spaces. This person brings together the script, the theatre, the director, the designers, and the actors. He or she ultimately is responsible for the production's finances. Regardless of the production organization—whether commercial, not-for-profit, educational, or community—someone will fill this role, even though he or she may not carry the title. Even in the commercial theatre, the term *producer* emerged only recently. As late as the nineteenth century, productions were initiated and organized by "actor-managers" such as England's Charles Kean (Fig. 7.7) and Henry Irving (see Chapter 16). In educational theatres, for example, the chairman of the theatre department normally fulfills this function. In the community theatre the producer may be called a managing director. In the commercial theatre the producer may be anyone (preferably someone with strong business and artistic inclinations) who can negotiate the backing of financial investors and bring the play forward to production.

The producer's role as a member of the production team varies greatly among the various types of theatre organizations. The authority of the producer to effect changes in the directions of the artistic team may be by virtue of a contract, the power of individual personality, or both. In the commercial theatre producers exert tremendous authority. In business terms, the producer is usually the managing partner in a limited partnership corporation; that is, the other partners (those who have invested in the production) have agreed to give all decision-making authority to the managing partner. The producer, then, has sole authority to negotiate contracts with the playwright, the director, the designers, and the actors. Within the scope of those contracts, the producer may hire and fire at will. Some producers micromanage the artistic team, others function collaboratively, and still others leave the creative decisions to the creative artists.

Theatre, in a sense, is very much like any other organization: Its organizational interaction depends almost entirely on the personal characteristics of those involved in the specific production. Whether in the commercial, not-for-

Figure 7.7 *Charles Kean in August von Kotzebue's* The Stranger, *1849. The son of Edmund Kean, the greatest English romantic actor of the early nineteenth century, Charles Kean (1811–1868) was both a distinguished realist actor and theatre manager. Appointed the Queen's Master of Revels in 1848, Kean took over the Princess Theatre, which was noted for its Shakespearean staging, in 1850. In addition to Shakespeare, Kean produced melodramas like those of the German Kotzebue and the Irishman Dion Boucicault. Kean is credited with introducing limelight and curtain times.*

Producing Organizations *and the* Production Team

Joseph Papp (II): Off Broadway on Broadway

Among Papp's last projects—as yet unrealized—was a new approach to finding an "audience constituency" for quality production in New York. The key to the success of this project, according to Papp, is not simply encouraging better drama at lower prices, but creating an entirely "different kind of theatrical culture."

. . . This is what interests me now. *(He holds up an advance copy of a full page ad in the Sunday* New York Times.*)* A new play by a new writer, *Cuba and His Teddy Bear* by Ray Povod—I'm moving it to Broadway. I'm experimenting, taking the first step toward a low-priced theatre on Broadway. Not musicals, dramatic works. We have 250 seats at $10 a seat, with the rest of the house at regular Broadway prices.

YOU MEAN THIS ISN'T JUST A ONE TIME. . . .

Getting a new audience into the theatre—that's what I want. The Broadway houses will really be Off Broadway on Broadway. . . . I want to introduce the notion . . . that theatre people have to step back to make it possible to have a grace period of about 10 weeks where union conditions are very loosely applied in terms of salary, in terms of work, so that it'll be possible to charge very little money to be able to break even, to be able to perpetuate productions of plays. . . . I want a few hundred thousand people who will come to see four plays a season at one or two theatres.

HOLD IT, I HAVEN'T EVEN ASKED A QUESTION YET, AND ALREADY YOU'VE MENTIONED UNION NEGOTIATIONS AND AN EXPERIMENTAL PROGRAM FOR NEW PLAYS ON BROADWAY. . . . LET'S TAKE IT ONE STEP AT A TIME.

I want to produce low-priced plays with big stars every season in Broadway houses at low rent, or rent-free. My goal is to create a theatre constituency in New York for plays that have something to say, at affordable prices, and at Broadway houses that are

We're seeing the diminution of everything, even top tailors—because the whole industry has shrunk and its economic base is very small.

empty or threatened with demolition. The reason, the necessity to do this, is for a decent living for people in the theatre. In the non-commercial system, without government support, people cannot make a living. Under our program, during the 10-week grace period, the writer, for example, will get the highest salary, probably $1,000 a week, no royalties, no nothing. All the rest will get less. The stars, the unions, everybody. . . .

The idea is to get people of some reputation to appear in these plays, so that people who ordinarily don't go to the theatre—even those who *do* go to the theatre—have a reason to go aside from the play itself. Because dramas are dead now, they virtually disappear as soon as they arrive. . . .

To gain this new constituency I'm after, this new audience, you have to create a different kind of theatrical culture. . . . We're seeing the diminution of everythng, even top *tailors*—because the whole industry has shrunk and its economic base is very small. All you get are a few shows that try to become blockbusters, that try to attract audiences who don't have a stake in the theatre itself. So what you get is a constituency of people who are essentially credit card people, who do not establish a standard. In fact, by the high prices they're willing to pay, they encourage a certain kind of pure entertainment, and generally not very good entertainment at that—just a kind of theatrical product.

Excerpted by permission from Ross Wetzstein's interview with Joseph Papp in the September 1986 issue of *American Theatre Magazine*. Published by Theatre Communications Group.

Hal Prince (in the Company of Stephen Sondheim)

Harold (Hal) Prince (born 1928) is one of America's most influential producers and directors. Striking gold at the start of his career, he coproduced, with Robert F. Griffith and Frederick Brisson, the hit musical *The Pajama Game* in 1954, followed by *Damn Yankees* in 1955. With Griffith, he went on to produce such successes as *West Side Story* (1957) and *Fiorello* (1961) and then, on his own, *Fiddler on the Roof* (1964). Beginning with *She Loves Me* (1963), he both directed and produced a number of musicals. Prince is noted for his stage wizardry, but his most important contribution to the theatre has been a series of "concept musicals" in collaboration with composer-lyricist Stephen Sondheim. *Company* (1970) was the first of these joint productions. Instead of a plot, revue-like vignettes illustrate what Sondheim described as "the total possibility and impossibility of relationships on the isle of Manhattan.

A bachelor named Robert links the vignettes by visiting in turn five couples who, together, represent upper-middle-class Manhattan attitudes toward love and marriage. Whatever drama there is depends on whether, after observing his friends, Robert will choose to commit himself to a relationship, marry, or remain single. In his first "concept" score, Sondheim suggests traffic sounds and uses repeated busy signals and nervously abrupt rhythms to evoke the aural environment of Manhattan. To carry out the concept visually, Prince, among other things, imparted a swift tempo to the production that was emblematic of the pace of the city—a decision that also underscored how the characters are constantly on the run as a means of avoiding self-exploration.

profit, educational, or community theatre, the producer—or the person filling the role of producer—ultimately has responsibility for the production. That individual must be sure that the artistic, craft, and business needs of the production are met. In addition to acting, directing, and design, every theatre production involves ticket distribution, publicity, ordering supplies, and paying bills. The producer is responsible for the smooth operation of all of these aspects of a production.

THE DIRECTOR

The director controls the actors and, less directly, the designers, stage manager, and technical director. The amount of authority varies according to the organization and the personalities of the individuals involved. Educational theatre directors often exert more control in their instructive situation—with student actors—than is necessary in the professional theatre. However, ultimate decisions must sometimes be made by the director after careful consideration. The director does have authority over all aspects of the production, including the final designs for scenery, costumes, lighting, and sound. The effectiveness of the production team, to a very large degree, depends on each member's ability to work productively and creatively within a collaborative body that, ultimately, is hierarchical; that is, all its members are not equal. Final decisions on artistic matters rest in the hands of the director, and the director remains subordinate to the producer.

THE ACTORS

Strictly speaking, the actors are not part of the production team. Of course, in most productions, actors form the heart of the play. They are the principal means by which the playwright's script comes across to the audience. Although actors do not participate in meetings between the director and the designers, and so on, they are an important part of a team effort. Actors' needs must be communicated to the scenic, costume, and lighting designers, both directly and indirectly. Costume fittings, for example, involve direct communication between the actor and the designer. Difficulties with rehearsal clothing or with actual costumes need to be brought to the attention of the costume staff, either directly by the actor or through the director and/or the stage manager.

How the actors work within the production organization can vary from one circumstance to another. The level of independence afforded an individual actor relative to the ensemble and/or the director depends on the specific production. A play written for or centered on a "star" actor may give that person far more authority in the production scheme than a play in which all actors are part of repertory ensemble or one in which a name director controls

Figure 7.8 Ira Gershwin and George Kaufman, Of Thee I Sing. Henry Street Playhouse, Lexington, Virginia. Director, Al Gordon; designer, Kip Epperson. Here, the careful design of actor placement using levels and costume color to integrate with the color and line of the set requires careful working out of details between director and designers during the play's early production meetings.

Producing Organizations *and the* Production Team

a cast of lesser-known personalities. One may argue that in some modern musicals the actors are inconsequential in comparison with the settings. For the most part, however, actors are a primary element. Even though they may not sit in on artistic staff meetings, they are nonetheless influential in decisions made in those meetings, where their voice is that of the director and stage manager.

THE SCENIC, COSTUME, LIGHTING, AND SOUND DESIGNERS

stage manager
Technical staff member in control of all performance elements requiring the coordination of actors and production technicians

These artistic functions, sometimes fulfilled by a single individual, rest on an equal level in the organizational chart (Fig. 7.2) and employ many of the same procedures and tools. The scenic, costume, and lighting designers need frequent conferences to make certain that coordination exists among all the visual elements of the production. Each of the designers is dependent on the others, and a failure in concept, communication, and procedure by one can have disastrous effects on the others.

THE NONARTISTIC STAFF

cues Rehearsed signals, such as spoken dialogue, stage business, or lighting changes, by which the stage manager communicates to actors and technicians some transition in the production

The Stage Manager   In addition to those individuals we have just noted, whose responsibilities can be termed "artistic," numerous other individuals play vital roles in bringing productions to the stage and ensuring their smooth operation during performance. The **stage manager** has complete control of all elements of the performance. He or she is responsible for all the **cues,** which coordinate the actors and the production technicians. To accomplish this, the

Figure 7.9   *Peter Weiss,* Marat/Sade. *Northern Illinois University.* Director, Judy Lee Oliva; scenic designer, Scott Marr; costume designer, Jane Gilbert; lighting designer, Betsy Cooprider-Bernstein. Photo by George Tarbay. *The elaborate integration of actors, scene, costume, and lighting design seen in this production can come about only through extremely thorough understandings developed among the production artists throughout the production planning process.*

GHETTO MASTER CUES

CUE#	Page	Action
ACT I		
1	155	(When house opens) Preset Music On Preset Lights On House Up
5	155	(When Srulik enters House to half Spot On (Srulik) Warmers Out Preshow Music Out
10	156	(after "I don't want to talk about It) Cue Actors Spot Out House Out (When actors are in place) Set Light ON

Figure 7.10 From the stage manager's prompt book. *In this specially designed version of the production script, all actor blocking, prop notes, and light and sound cues are kept. The cue sheet tells the stage manager on which page of the script the cue is located, the cue number, the actual cue, and the action that should take place. The only thing that is transmitted to the operators are the commands, "warning for cue 1" and "Cue 1—Go."*

stage manager must have been associated with the production from the earliest meetings. In the professional theatre, the stage manager is a member of Actors Equity. As an Equity member, the stage manager is allowed to replace a cast member if an emergency should arise. The stage manager has complete authority over all backstage and onstage operations. After the opening performance, the professional stage manager is responsible only to the producer. A stage manager's **prompt book** is used to record script changes, shifting instructions, actors' stage movements, and light, sound, special effects, and activity cues (Fig. 7.10).

The role of the stage manager is probably the most pivotal role in ensuring a smoothly running preparation period and performance. The stage manager keeps careful notes during all rehearsals and transmits written directives to the designers regarding any needs or changes that may transpire during the rehearsal period. If the stage manager is careless or indecisive, chaos can result. During final rehearsals the entire production depends on the stage manager's abilities to organize the stage crews, interpret the wishes of the designers, and record and execute cues. The stage manager is responsible for starting rehearsals and performances on time. During the run of the show the stage manager's leadership skills keep the cast attentive to check-in times, the crews attentive to timely execution of scene shifts and properties placement, and the control board operators exacting in the execution of lighting and sound cues.

prompt book Stage manager's record of script changes, scene-shifting instructions, actor movements, and light, sound, and special-effects cues

Without a good stage manager, the best of artistic vision, skill, and intent cannot produce an excellent production.

THE TECHNICAL DIRECTOR

technical director Staff member responsible for all aspects of technical production, including budgets and schedules

We will examine the technical director's role in much more detail in Chapter 11. As a member of the production team, however, the **technical director** is responsible for supervising all aspects of the technical production, including budgets and schedules. The technical director directs assembly of all the elements, such as scenery, lights, and properties for the production. The actual responsibilities of the individual called the technical director, however, may vary significantly from one producing organization to another. In some organizations, the technical director functions as a production manager: As noted earlier, he or she is responsible for supervising the execution of all technical elements of the production. In that scheme of responsibilities, the technical director has authority for apportioning budgets among the technical departments and is responsible for ordering materials and maintaining the technical departments' budgets—in coordination with the financial office of the organization. In other theatre organizations, the technical director has authority only over the scenic, lighting, and sound departments. Here, again, oversight, ordering, coordination of schedules, and so on form the bulk of the responsibilities. In still other organizations, the technical director's duties are more those of a scenery shop manager who is directly subordinate to the set designer.

THE CONSTRUCTION HEAD

construction head (or **shop foreman** or **master stage carpenter**) Staff member responsible for scene construction, rigging, and assembly

The **construction head,** sometimes called the **shop foreman** or **master stage carpenter,** takes responsibility for construction, rigging, and assembly of all scenery. Order and safety are the watchwords for this job. A construction head also exists in the costume area. This person, who may hold the title of shop supervisor, has the responsibility for making sure that all of the costume designs are executed properly and on time.

THE PROPERTY HEAD

property manager/property head Staff member responsible for constructing and organizing all properties and items of scenic decor

Often referred to as the **property manager,** the **property head** assumes responsibility for constructing, assembling, and organizing all set properties, hand props, and decor items required by the script, the set designer, and sometimes the actors. This job also involves running the show during the performance and returning properties to lenders or storage when the run closes.

The Business and House Managers

house manager/business manager One or two individuals with managerial responsibility for all audience-related and business-office activities

Working closely with the producer, and through the producer with the artistic production team, numerous individuals in the business office take care of all legal aspects of the production; pay bills and salaries; manage the printing, sale, and distribution of tickets; and oversee the *front-of-house* operations—that is, all audience-related functions, including hiring and training ushers. Typically, these duties are supervised by a **house manager** and/or a **business manager.** These managerial-supervisory responsibilities may be executed by one or two individuals. During the run of a production, close communication between the house manager and the actors and stage personnel ensures a smoothly running performance. For example, if communication between backstage and front-of-house is uncertain or disrupted, the performance may start while scores of audience members are standing in the aisles or still in the restrooms. These team relationships, in some ways, are just as crucial as the creative relationships among the artistic and craft personnel.

As you examine the organizational chart in Figure 7.2, you will note that many other jobs exist in bringing a theatre production to the stage. You can imagine that some of the ones we have not described involve responsibilities comparable in another area to those that we have discussed. You also can imagine not only the ordinal but also the creative and decision-making relationship of one job to another, with the greatest decision-making and creative responsibilities occurring as one moves toward the top of the chart.

Theatre is a team effort, a cooperative and collaborative art. One might be hard pressed to prove that the most collaborative, communicative, and cooperative of circumstances have produced the best theatre productions in history. Legendary accounts circulate concerning remarkable productions emerging from stormy relationships. Nonetheless, theatre, of whatever quality, does depend on an interdependent working team of artists and craftspersons. Human nature being what it is, some interrelationships will be smooth and cordial, and from these may come both good and bad theatre. Some interrelationships will be story and fractious, and from these as well will come both good and bad theatre. The constant factor remains the *interrelationships*. When any one job area falls down, the production falters and may fail. When all excel, whether through democratic cooperation or autocratic control, the production succeeds.

SUMMARY

- Theatre is a *cooperative* and *collaborative* art that brings a play to life on the stage. Each of the individuals in the *production team* must function cooperatively in an *organization* dedicated to presenting a successful production.

- Good *communication* is essential to every successful theatre production.

- *Producing organizations* differ in their basic purposes, ranging from pure *commercialism* to amateur productions done strictly for the joy of participation in theatre.

- The *Broadway* or *commercial* theatre exists as a single-show business enterprise designed to make a profit for its *investor-partners*.

- Other producing organizations associated with the commercial theatre include:

   The *Off-Broadway theatre:* Originally a reaction to commercialism, it now is governed by union rules restricting size of house and ticket sales.

   The *Showcase theatre:* A small-house, limited-run organization regulated by union rules in conjunction with the commercial theatre.

- Outside the commercial theatre lies the *not-for-profit regional theatre*. Growing from roots established in the 1930s, this form of producing organization exists in major urban areas around the country and produces exceptional professional theatre productions.

- Another type of noncommercial theatre is the *educational theatre*, whose major mission is to function as a training ground for theatre personnel and to educate not only its trainees, but also its audiences. This type of theatre can also have ties to the professional theatre, perhaps supporting a professional company on the campus.

- The *community theatre* has become a means of artistic expression for individuals who do not consider theatre their profession but, rather, a responsible hobby.

- In understanding theatre we must grasp the interrelationships of the many jobs and skills—creative and otherwise—that go into the development of a theatrical production. These individuals and their responsibilities make up the *production team*.

- The *production team* divides the labor of the theatre and creates a framework for artistic decision making and cooperation necessary for the creation of a theatrical production:

   The *playwright* is the source of ideas, intentions, and visions for the other creative artists.

   The *producer* is the organizer and overseer of all aspects of the theatrical production.

   The *director* is the chief artistic and creative decision maker for the production.

The *actors* are the principal means by which the production team communicates to the audience.

The *scenic, costume, lighting,* and *sound designers* are the principal artistic and creative personnel for the creation of the visual and auditory environment of the production.

The *stage manager* is a member of the nonartistic staff whose responsibilities include running the production when it reaches performance.

The *technical director* is responsible for supervising all aspects of technical production, including budgets and schedules.

Other nonartistic staff include *the construction head, the property head,* and the *business* and *house managers.*

Chapter 8

Directing

*A*fter studying this chapter you should be able to:

- Describe how the role of the modern director emerged through history.
- Discuss the conceptual framework that defines the director's functions.
- Explain the role of the director as a *collaborative artist.*
- Characterize the director's role in *auditioning, casting,* and *rehearsing actors.*
- Explain some of the options available to directors as they work in time and space.
- Define and describe the *director's concept.*
- Identify the questions that we can ask in evaluating a director's work.

Jan Eliasberg directing The Diary of a Scoundrel, 1981. James Natchwey/Magnum.

*I*n Chapter 7 we discussed the director's leadership role in the production team. Such prominence, however, has not always been the case. In fact, the modern concept of the *director* emerged only within the last 150 years or so. In this chapter we will focus on some perspectives on the role of the modern *director* and then examine some of the director's responsibilities, such as the *director's concept; collaboration with other theatre artists;* and *auditioning, casting, and rehearsing actors.* Then we will examine how directors utilize time and space in creating an artistic vision. Finally, we will learn how we can evaluate a director's work. We begin, however, with history: how the modern concept of the director has emerged over the twenty-five hundred years of Western theatre history.

History: The Emergence *of the* Modern Director

The modern concept of the director and the specific functions resulting from that concept emerged from the late-nineteenth-century theory of the "organic" or totally integrated production, in which all elements of the production are coordinated to work together toward a common purpose. Prior to the rise of the organic theory and the development of the specific role of director, actors' movements were set by various individuals involved in the production. At one time or another in theatre history, for example, playwrights, leading actors, and/or company managers all created *blocking*—that is, actor movement.

To understand the forces that brought about the need for a director in the theatre, we must first turn to eighteenth-century aesthetic theory. Prior to the eighteenth century, history was deemed largely irrelevant to art. Although mythology might provide classical subject matter for artworks, the thought that an artist might somehow integrate mythological subject matter with any sense of historical accuracy simply did not exist. Of course, historical accuracy in any art form was probably out of the question anyway, because the research resources and techniques that we take for granted today also did not exist. Nor was such accuracy of much concern to anyone. Renaissance paintings, for example, portray biblical scenes in which characters like Jesus and the Apostles appear in contemporary Italian dress (Fig. 8.1). In a way, that was a device for making the Bible and religion relevant to the age; in another sense, however, it reflected the lack of information available to Renaissance artists concerning historical detail. With no practical resources to draw upon, aestheticians tended to sweep aside historicity or historical pictorializing as irrelevant to art.

The integration of history and production elements took the stage through a side door leading to the opera house. The German composer Richard Wagner sought to combine all elements of the opera into a unified production. He called his unification a *gesamtkunstwerk*—a German word

Figure 8.1 *Masaccio,* The Tribute Money *(ca. 1427). Fresco, S Maria del Carmine, Florence.*

[Scala/Art Resource]

meaning "totally integrated artwork." In Wagner's concept, opera formed a comprehensive work of art in which music, scenery, and poetry are all subservient to the central generating idea. For Wagner the total unity—that is, the *integration*—of all elements reigned supreme.

The emergence of a theatre producer-director, bringing similar concepts to the legitimate stage at about the same time, arguably may testify to the influence of Wagner in the work of Georg II, Duke of Saxe-Meiningen. As a producer-director, Saxe-Meiningen (see the PROFILE in this chapter) focused on ensemble acting and designed all the costumes, properties, and scenery for his historically authentic production style. In the "Theatre Duke's" company there were no stars, and herein lies the foundation for the creative authority in which the aesthetics of a complete production rest in one person's hands.

Throughout Europe and the United States in the mid-nineteenth century, the concentration of coordinating power in the theatre coalesced into the hands of the **actor-manager.** In many respects, these actor managers performed the same functions as the modern director. England's Charles Kean (see also Chapter 7) typified the actor-manager, and his attempts to produce historically accurate and spectacular revivals of Shakespeare illustrated the trend to integrate history into theatre production (Fig. 8.2).

The Duke of Saxe-Meiningen, as noted, pioneered ensemble acting, historical accuracy, and production unification in the theatre. Following in the directions he established came André Antoine in France and Constantin Stanislavski in Russia (see Chapter 9). Antoine and his Théâtre Libre in Paris and Stanislavski in the Moscow Art Theatre gave a strong impetus to moving

actor-manager
Nineteenth-century actors who performed the role of producer and director and from whose concentration of duties emerged the concept of the modern director

Directing

205

Figure 8.2 *William Shakespeare, Richard II. The Princess' Theatre, London, 1857. Producer, Charles Kean; set designer, Thomas Grieve. The director's intention is to teach a history lesson as well as to stage the production. So, in contrast to the simple, conventionalized, and architectural setting used in Shakespeare's time, director Charles Kean has carefully reproduced "realistic" historical settings for each scene of the play. Richard II is summarized in Chapter 4; both Kean and mid-nineteenth-century productions of Shakespeare are discussed more fully in Chapter 16.*

[Victoria and Albert Museum]

the theatre into a realistic acting style that was integrated with scenic elements and controlled by a single artistic vision. Their work formed the catalyst by which the role of the modern director assumed its current parameters. Thereafter, one individual, trained and knowledgeable in all the theatre arts, assumed responsibility for creating a totally unified artistic production.

Perspectives *on the* Director's Role

Perhaps the best way to understand the *functions* of a director is to see them in a broad conceptual framework defined by specific creative tasks. In the broad sense, the function of the director falls into one of three concepts of the director's role. The first of these sees the director as an *interpretive* artist who serves the playwright by faithfully translating the *script* (see Chapter 2) and the playwright's vision into theatrical form. This concept rests on the argument that the playwright's script is more or less sacrosanct. The director's role, then, is to actualize the script with a production that is as close to the playwright's original vision as is humanly possible. In this role the director is not a free and independent artist but, rather, an *actualizing agent* bound by the playwright's intent.

The second concept takes the opposite stand. Here the director functions as a *creative artist* free to develop every aspect of the theatre, including the script, to mold his or her own work of art. In this view, the script is a tool that may be changed by the director to suit whatever ends the production seeks.

A third concept takes a middle ground. In this view, the script remains the focal point of the production, and the playwright's intent plays a seminal role in the emerging work of art. The director, however, maintains the freedom

Directing

The Duke of Saxe-Meiningen: The First Director

George II, Duke of Saxe-Meiningen (1826–1914), made his court theatre into the most widely admired theatrical company in late-nineteenth-century Europe and is now widely regarded as the first modern theatre director. The Duke, who financed the Meiningen Court Theatre out of pocket, not only directed but also designed the costumes and scenery (see Fig. 8.3). After 1866, the actor Ludwig Chronegk (1837–1891) supervised and rehearsed the actors. The Meininger, as the company was known, pioneered ensemble acting, established the director's creative control over production, and insisted on historical accuracy in scenery and costumes ("Any helmet, not antique, worn by an actor, must be pulled down over the forehead," the Duke decreed, forbidding his actors to wear them in the popular but inauthentic "tenorstyle.") The Meininger Players were also famous for their lifelike crowd scenes, with each member assigned distinguishing individual traits and lines. Both André Antoine, founder of the Théâtre Libre in Paris, and Constantin Stanislavski (see Chapter 9), the Russian producer-theorist who founded the Moscow Art Theatre, saw the company on tour, and through these two great exponents of stage realism, the Meininger exercised a profound influence on twentieth-century drama.

Figure 8.3 *Sketch by the Duke of Saxe-Meiningen for Mark Antony's oration,* Julius Caesar, *1867. Among other innovations, the Duke (see* Profile *in this chapter) sought to vitalize his Shakespearean productions by making the crowd a character in the drama. Each member of the crowd was considered an individual actor, and, following the lead of Charles Kean (see Fig. 8.2), the Duke divided his crowds into smaller groups, each headed by an experienced actor responsible for seeing that the several groups coordinated their activities according to the director's overall concept of emphasis and movement.*

[Deutsches Theatermuseum, Munich]

or discretion to shape that script in whatever ways are necessary to actualize a meaningful production. Nonetheless, the director remains an interpreter and coordinating artist, much like a musical conductor who lacks the *total* creative freedom of the composer.

Regardless of which concept is employed, the general function of a director is somehow to translate the elements of theatre into an auditory and visual complex in such a way that each part of the production comes together into a coherent experience that communicates meaning to an audience.

The Director's Responsibilities

THE DIRECTOR'S CONCEPT

director's concept The director's overall vision of the play and the production—its meaning and goals

Contemporary theatre practice places the responsibility for overseeing the production in the hands of the director. The **director's concept** is the focus of that function. A theatre production, for example, completes the play; that is, the playwright's interpretation becomes a reality on the stage through the director's concept or vision. Each director finds in the playwright's script something important, either for himself or for the audience. In order to bring that "something" to the stage, the director must crystalize a unified expression called a **production goal:** an artistic vision involving not only the meaning of the play but also the visual and aural expression of that meaning in actors, scenery, costumes, and lighting.

production goal An artistic vision involving the entire production and its effect on an audience

Part of what makes theatre exciting is the possibility for many concepts within a single script. The same script staged by different directors will produce dramatically different results depending on the vision and skill of each director. No two productions will be the same even if exactly the same words are spoken by the actors. Like any work of art, theatre depends on both vision and technical skill. That is, the director may have an outstanding vision or concept for the production but may not have the skill of his or her craft to bring that concept to life on the stage. Conversely, a director with great skill may have a faulty concept of a particular play or production. Whatever the case, the director's concept is the first and most important problem to be resolved.

We must understand how the director's concept differs from that of the playwright. As we have noted, each is a vision of human experience and behavior. However, the skills and the medium required for the *expression* of that vision are entirely different. The playwright is adept at putting human thought, action, and a message into the script as we defined it in Chapter 3. The director is adept at turning a script into action. Although the content of both visions may be similar, the medium of expression and the skill and imagination required to turn a vision into an artistic product are quite different.

Figure 8.4   Sally Jacobs, scene design for A Midsummer Night's Dream. *Royal Shakespeare Company, 1970. Director, Peter Brook. The production is the same one depicted in Fig. 5.5. Brook's concept of the expanding role of the modern director—that is, director both as interpreter and as theatrical innovator—is discussed in Chapter 17, where some of his more ambitious projects are described at Fig. 17.14.*

COLLABORATING WITH OTHER THEATRE ARTISTS

production conferences
Meetings between the director and other members of the artistic, craft, and business staffs during which collaborative efforts affect decisions relating to the production

As we saw in Chapter 7, theatre is a collaborative art, and the collaboration from which a production emerges takes place through a series of production conferences. **Production conferences** comprise a series of meetings between the director and the designers and other unit heads, such as the stage manager, who are involved in the decision-making aspects of the production. Here individuals share ideas, solve problems, and agree on goals. The nature of the meetings generally depends heavily on the particular style of the individual director.

Directorial styles range across a wide spectrum from laissez faire—hands-off—at one end of the spectrum to absolute dictatorship at the other. Most theatre practitioners, of course, prefer to work with directors whose style falls somewhere in the middle of that spectrum.

The collaborative director uses the production conference as a forum in which ideas are discussed and the best visions of the group are enhanced and coordinated with the director's vision. However, one should not infer from these descriptions that democratic collaboration always produces the best theatre. When the collaborative process focuses on cooperation and facilitation, a fundamentally creative and comfortable working environment usually emerges. The *human* process of theatre thus forms a foundation for a joint project seeking excellence.

Elia Kazan (I): Finding the Play's Style

In 1947, Elia Kazan (b. 1909) directed Marlon Brando and Jessica Tandy in Tennessee Williams's A Streetcar Named Desire. *The impact of this play—reaffirmed in the 1951 film version in which Kazan directed Brando and Vivien Leigh—was immediate and powerful, and Kazan's subsequent staging of plays by Williams and Arthur Miller established him as one of the most important forces in American theatre at mid-century. While Brando's famous Stanley Kowalski was all uncultured sensuality, Blanche DuBois, as played by both Tandy and Leigh, was both a pitiable figure of genteel poverty and a representation of the world of imagination. As his* Streetcar *notebook indicates, Kazan regarded* style *as the key to expressing Williams's psychologically realistic examination of idiosyncratic characters in an exotic world.*

A thought—directing finally consists of turning Psychology into Behavior.

Theme—this is a message from the dark interior. This little twisted, pathetic, confused bit of light and culture puts out a cry. It is snuffed out by the crude forces of violence, insensibility and vulgarity which exist in our South—and this cry is the play.

Style—one reason a "style," a stylized production is necessary is that a subjective factor—Blanche's memories, inner life, emotions, are a real factor. We cannot really understand her behavior unless we see the effect of her past on her present behavior.

This play is a poetic tragedy. We are shown the final dissolution of a person of worth, who once had great potential, and who, even as she goes down, has worth exceeding that of the "healthy" coarse-grained figures who kill her.

All props should be stylized: they should have a color, shape and weight that spell: style.

Blanche is a social type, an emblem of a dying civilization, making its last curlicued and romantic exit. All her behavior patterns are those of the dying civilization she represents. In other words her behavior is *social*. Therefore find social modes! This is the source of the play's stylization and the production's style and color. Likewise Stanley's behavior is *social* too. It is the basic animal cynicism of today. "Get what's coming to you! Don't waste a day! Eat, drink, get yours!" This is the basis of his stylization, of the choice of his props. All props should be stylized: they should have a color, shape and weight that spell: style. . . .

The style—the real deep style—consists of one thing only: to find behavior that's truly social, significantly typical, at each moment. . . .

Stylized acting and direction is to realistic acting and direction as poetry is to prose. The acting must be styled, not in the obvious sense. (Say nothing about it to the producer and actors.) But you will fail unless you find this kind of poetic realization for the behavior of these people.

Reprinted with the permission of Macmillan Publishing Co. from *Directors on Directing: A Source Book of the Modern Theatre* by Toby Cole and Helen K. Chinoy. Copyright © 1963 by Bobbs-Merrill Publishing Co., an imprint of Macmillan Publishing Co.

Ideally, a production goal and style emerge from the early production conferences. The meaning of the play is agreed upon. Prior to conferences, each of the participants will have gone through a process designed to focus on the specific tasks of each indiviudal—sets and lights for the scenic and lighting designers, costumes for the costume designer, and so on. Decisions about *setting* will be made. The *facts* of the play as given by the playwright may or may not be those chosen for the production. Although William Congreve's *The Way of the World* was set in 1700 by the playwright, the director and designers may choose to set the production in contemporary times (Fig. 8.5) or no time in particular. Such are the decisions made in production conferences. Later conferences will focus on specifics: actual set and costume designs as well as technical requirements such as rain, snow, trapdoors, flying apparatus, vanishing actors, and so on.

Over a period of weeks, then, before rehearsals begin, the director, designers, and others meet together in collaboration to try to work out every aspect of the production. As time progresses, members of the production team will continue to meet to assess the progress of the play, discuss changes that need to be made, and arrive at strategies for getting what is needed where it is needed when it is needed. Collaboration during the production conferences functions as a vehicle for facilitating preparations. Even with careful and thorough preparation, however, oversights happen—at which time the production conference becomes a collaborative damage-control session. Whatever the reality of the process, the production conference provides a place for artists to talk to each other about their common purpose: meaningful theatre.

AUDITIONING AND CASTING ACTORS

Auditions and Casting   Actual auditions may or may not involve scenes from the play itself. In some cases, actors may secure copies of the script in advance and be asked to do specific scenes. During the tryout, actors may be

Figure 8.5 William Congreve, The Way of the World. *The Maryland Stage Company, 1989. Director, Xerxes Mehta; set designer, Richard Montgomery; costume designer, Elena Zlotescu; lighting designer, Terry Cobb. Photo by Edie Catto. In this production of a play written in 1700 (see the synopsis in Chapter 5), the director has decided on a "modernized" approach. Such decisions are part of the director's concept and determine the overall production style for the production.*

paired in order to provide contrasts in relationships to help the director create the right blend of individuals. In other cases, because access to the script may be impractical, the actor simply does an audition piece of a specified length of his or her own choosing.

casting The act of choosing actors to play specific roles in a play

repertory company A permanent acting company that prepares several productions during a yearly season

Casting for plays depends largely on the circumstances of the particular production. In some situations a **repertory company**—a permanent company that prepares several productions—may have a stable of actors who are hired to play particular types of roles in a season of plays; casting for individual roles draws from the company. Because a number of plays are to be staged, choosing actors for the company may involve several directors and executives from the producing organization. In some cases an executive casts the company, and directors are free to choose among preselected individuals. In these circumstances an actor's versatility or particular "type" may be more important than his or her suitability for a particular role.

Casting Criteria In the Broadway professional theatre, a "name" actor may be chosen for major roles in order to give the production the highest public relations visibility. Other roles may be cast by **open audition,** in which actors present a short audition piece and are then chosen by the director on the strength of that presentation, coupled with the strength of previous experience.

open audition Audition in which actors are chosen for roles on the basis of short presentations and prior experience

Although the open audition may be used at any level of production, one generally finds that the ability to work and acquaintanceship with a particular director often weighs heavily in the casting process, even in the educational theatre. The ability of a director to carry out his or her vision depends very heavily on the ability of the actor to transform that vision into a role. Few directors care to risk their artistic vision on unknown quantities, regardless of the strength of a particular audition piece.

Casting Types Casting, therefore, becomes one of the major steps in the development of a production. Beyond what we have just noted, directors often look for very specific characteristics in potential cast members. Certain physical types, for example, are very important: Because a play is an act of symbolic communication, in order to use every image possible to create meaning for an audience, a director must often call upon conventions and stereotypes to facilitate audience comprehension. Tall, handsome, rugged heroes, pixie-like ingenues, crotchety old women, and so on call to mind specific physical characteristics. Even the most unsophisticated theatregoer is familiar with the statement "He just did not fit the part" when someone evaluates a particular portrayal on the stage or screen. This kind of type-casting can cause particular problems for the director in the educational theatre, in which twenty-year-old actors must be asked to portray elderly people. Occasionally, especially when makeup and distance are optimum, the image can be convincing. Often, however, the audience must stretch its suspension of disbelief in order to accept the portrayal as credible.

Casting Voices In addition to physical type, directors also look for strong and well-moduated voices. An actor who cannot be heard, or whose voice does not match the physical image, will obviously cause difficulty in the director's efforts to communicate with an audience. Most directors also try to cast voices

Figure 8.6 John Wayne in Red River (1948). United Artists. *Perhaps more than any actor before or since, Wayne developed a character not only as a* persona—*a recognizable personality bound to but largely independent of the personality of the
actor—but as an* icon: *In numerous classic Western films,
Wayne portrayed a figure who represented a set of values—
physical courage and competence, stable (though sometimes stub-
born) moral forthrightness—that remained in fairly close orbit
around a core character. Those values were predictable in the
sense that the core character determined their application to dramatic situations that varied from film to film.*

ensemble effect Effect
of variety and
coordination achieved
by casting actors of
different but
complementary types or
voices

so as to create an **ensemble effect.** That is, in order to provide variety and
interest, the total cast approximates a mixed musical chorus, with basses,
baritones, tenors, altos, and a variety of sopranos, ranging from lyric to colora-
tura. When such casting is possible, the audience receives a rich tapestry of
sound rather than a dull monotone.

Casting for Physical Presence The director usually seeks cast members who
have a dynamic physical presence—actors who not only look the part but who
can generate attention and interest in an audience by lively bodily action and
masterful bodily control. We all know people who have a certain unexplain-
able quality about them—a charisma or a very real physical dynamism, a
"presence."

Directors seek such qualities because they give the actor the fundamental
ability to attract and hold an audience's attention. Their bodies do what they
are asked to do and maintain character physically even when no lines are being
spoken. The amateur stage provides innumerable examples of actors who
literally disappear whenever they have no lines to utter. Such people lack the
professional concentration, control, and energy to maintain a character's physical presence, and directors will generally avoid casting them regardless of the
quality of their voices or their physical type.

Just as an ensemble of voices may be sought by the director, so may an
ensemble of physicality be desirable. In the same sense that line and form may
be used by the set and costume designer, the director may seek round or

angular, vertical or horizontal actor shapes and sizes so as to create the desired stage picture—that is, a picture appropriate to the director's original understanding and concept of the play. Casting provides a vitally important step in realizing the concept basic to the production.

REHEARSING ACTORS

Directors who have done their homework come into the rehearsal period with a reasonably clear picture of how each character relates to the totality of the play and how the actors will be moved in time and space in order to actualize the overall concept. For example, part of the director's task is to plot climaxes, whether emotional, intellectual, or physical, and to work out the relationships of the characters, both to each other and to the physical space in which the action occurs. Before rehearsals begin, therefore, the director will have an active understanding of the flow of action—fast, slow, or medium— and where and how changes in that *pace* occur.

Analyzing Scenes   To assist in dealing with the unfolding of the drama, the director usually breaks the action into **French scenes,** a method of dividing the play into parts that change each time a person enters or leaves the stage. Because drama draws its life blood from the tensions that exist between and among human characters, each time a person enters or leaves the stage, a new set of tensions or relationships emerges. The director thus charts each of these changes and develops the dramatic tension of each scene individually, always keeping in mind how that particular scene fits into the whole. This is a task only the director can accomplish because, as skillful as each actor may be in developing and portraying his or her own character, only the director has the perspective of all the characters over the entire period of the play. Therefore, the director is able to guide the actors in tone, rhythm, force, and pace in order to keep each scene in its proper relationship to the whole. From this conceptual perspective, the director is able to help the actor shape individual interpretations of character.

Analyzing Action and Movement   Actually, the rehearsal period involves many things happening all at once. Actors, for example, involve themselves in learning physical actions—practicing subtle body actions as well as movements from one part of the stage to another, memorizing lines, shaping vocal presentations (pauses, inflectons rate, volume, etc.), and polishing dialect if necessary. The first rehearsal is usually a simple read-through, with director and actors seated in a circle and concentrating on the script (Fig. 8.7).

Blocking   Next comes *blocking,* the rehearsed placement of actors in relation to each other and the set. Every director has an individualized approach to teaching blocking. Some directors come to the rehearsal with every movement and physical action charted. All that remains is to transfer specifics from director to actors. Some directors bring to the rehearsal a generalized sense about blocking and allow the specifics to take shape as the rehearsal period progresses. Final decisions are reached late in the rehearsal period.

French scenes A method of dividing the play into parts that change each time a person enters or leaves the stage

The Art of Scene and Lighting Design

Plate 2.3 (*Above*)
Pavel Kusnezov, color rendering for the front curtain of the ballet *The Firebird*, by Igor Stravinsky.

Plate 2.1 (*Left Above*)
Heidi Landesman's Tony Award-winning set design for *The Secret Garden*, St. James Theatre, New York, 1991. Note the strong use of warm colors and elaborate detail in the design.

Plate 2.2 (*Left Below*)
Leon Bakst, design for the ballet *Schéhérazade*. Pay particular attention to the scale of the setting relative to the dancers; note, too, the strong use of bright, contrasting colors. The details of the setting clearly locate the scene in time and place.

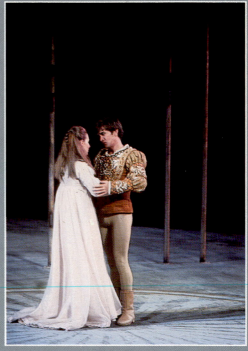

Plate 2.6 (Above)
Romeo and Juliet, New York Shakespeare Festival, Delacorte Theatre, 1968. Director, Joseph Papp; costume designer, Theoni V. Aldredge. Pictured: Martin Sheen and Susan McArthur. Simple suggestive elements characterize Ming Cho Lee's setting for the "balcony scene"—without the balcony—in this production of Shakespeare's tragedy. See the PROFILE of Joseph Papp in Chapter 7.

Plate 2.4 (Left Above)
Big River, Eugene O'Neill Theatre, New York, 1985. Director, Des McAnuff; scenic designer, Heidi Landesman; lighting designer, Richard Riddell; costume designer, Patricia McGourty. Clutter, detail, and costume combine to reflect character and atmosphere.

Plate 2.5 (Left Below)
Les Misérables, Broadway Theatre, New York, 1987. Directors, Trevor Nunn and John Caird; scenic designer, John Napier; costume designer, Adreane Neofitou. Powerful rear illumination heightens the sense of dramatic tension in lighting designer David Hersey's interpretation. See the PROFILE of the production of *Les Misérables* in Chapter 11.

Plate 2.7 (Above)
Edwin Drood, New York Shakespeare Festival, Delacorte Theatre, 1985. Director, Wilfrid Leach; scenic designer, Bob Shaw; costume designer, Lindsay W. Davis. Paul Gallo's dramatic lighting intensifies the atmosphere of this 1985 production.

Plate 2.8 (Right)
Sunday in the Park, Booth Theatre, New York, 1984. Director, James Lapine; costume designers, Patricia Zipprodt and Ann Houldward. This detail from scenic designer Tony Straiges' setting combines a skillful arrangement of painted background and live actors to duplicate faithfully Georges Seurat's famous painting *Sunday Afternoon on the Grande Jatte.*

Plate 2.9 (*Left Top and Below*)
City of Angels, Shubert Theatre, New York, 1990. Director, Michael
Blakemore; lighting designer, Paul Gallo; costume designer, Florence
Katz. In Robin Wagner's Tony Award-winning design, elaborate
detail complements large scenic scale to create atmosphere and
suggest the scale of this Broadway production. The design also makes
use of a *simultaneous setting* to reveal two rooms in adjacent stage
space.

Plate 2.10 (*Above*)
Cats, Winter Garden Theatre, New York, 1982.
Director, Trevor Nunn; scenic and costume designer,
John Napier. Special technical effects like the
celebrated flying-tire enhance the setting of this
extremely popular musical.

Whatever the director's method, actors record blocking instructions in their scripts so that they can learn their movements as they learn their lines. The final authority for checking blocking is usually the stage manager's *prompt book* (see Fig. 7.10). Failure to keep abreast of blocking can have serious consequences, especially in a show in which lighting changes occur when actors move to different parts of the stage: If an actor moves or fails to move to areas predesigned for a lighting change, he or she may end up in the dark and the scene may be ruined. Even during the rehearsal period, oversights and failures to record blocking create loss of time, break the rhythm of the rehearsal, and occasionally fray tempers. In rehearsing actors, the director must ensure that careful notes are kept in order to avoid problems like those just mentioned.

Guiding Actors Each and every rehearsal must be well planned, with specifically articulated goals and means for reaching them. Actor morale, for example, can be enhanced if the rehearsal period is organized by French scenes,

Figure 8.7 and Figure 8.8
Rehearsal and production of Moss Hart's comedy You Can't Take It with You, *1937. Note the creation of realistic effect through the accumulation of detailed properties that must be coordinated both with actor movement and blocking in what is, overall, a busy mise-en-scène.*

Directing

Elia Kazan (II): "Stella!"

"[Brando's] 'Stella!' " observes one contemporary critic, "echoes down from 1951 to the present, bringing with it the powerful contrast between fame in American theatre and the more lucrative, widespread fame in Hollywood." Although the international recognition accorded both the director and the star of A Streetcar Named Desire *does indeed derive more from the 1951 film than from the 1947 theatre production, Kazan and Brando's Stanley Kowalski was always more an inhabitant of the theatre than the soundstage, and Kazan hastens to point out that when he adapted the play to film, he basically shot the play itself. (For Kazan's notes on the character of Blanche DuBois, see Chapter 9.)*

Spine—keep things his way (Blanche the antagonist).

The hedonist, objects, props, etc. Sucks on a cigar all day because he can't suck a teat. Fruit, food, etc. He's got it all figured out, what fits, what doesn't. The pleasure scheme. He has all the confidence of resurgent flesh. . . .

Why does he want to bring Blanche and, before her, Stella *down to his level?* It's as if he said: "I know I haven't got much, but no one has more and no one's going to have more." It's the hoodlum aristocrat.

Choose Marlon's objects . . . the things he loves and prizes: all sensuous and sensual—the shirt, the cigar, the beer (how it's poured and nursed, etc.). . . .

Stanley has got things his way. He fits into his environment. The culture and the civilization, even the neighborhood, etc., etc., the food, the drink, etc., are all his way. And . . . God and Nature gave him a fine sensory apparatus . . . he enjoys! The main thing the

> *Choose Marlon's objects . . . the things he loves and prizes: all sensuous and sensual—the shirt, the cigar, the beer (how it's poured and nursed, etc.).*

actor has to do in the early scenes is make the physical environment of Stanley, the *props* come to life. . . .

Stanley is interested in his own pleasures. He is completely self-absorbed to the point of fascination.

To physicalize this: he has a most annoying way of being preoccupied—or of busying himself with something else while people are talking with him, at him it becomes. . . .

Stanley is supremely indifferent to everything except his own pleasure and comfort. He is marvelously selfish, a miracle of sensuous self-centeredness. . . . It really doesn't work . . . because it simply stores up violence and stores up violence, until every *bar in the nation is full of Stanleys ready to explode.* He's desperately trying to drug his senses . . . overwhelming them with a constant round of sensation so that he will feel nothing else.

In Stanley sex goes under a disguise. Nothing is more erotic and arousing to him than "airs" . . . she thinks she's better than me . . . I'll show her . . . Sex equals domination . . . anything that challenges him—like calling him "common"—arouses him sexually.

In the case of Brando, the question of enjoyment is particularly important. Stanley feeds himself. His world is hedonist. But what does he enjoy? Sex equals sadism. It is his

thus eliminating the need for actors to sit around during long rehearsals of scenes in which they are not needed. Actors also need concrete suggestions that help to turn their characterizations into physical action. Many directors develop concrete thumbnail sketches for each character that can be summed up in terms of an action verb. Actors generally can play an *action:* Being told to *do* such and such is infinitely more helpful than being told to *be* such and such.

Guiding actors usually means that a director must maintain a sense of equanimity toward the actors as an ensemble. The director must be sure that actors adhere to company rules, keep deadlines, and arrive at rehearsals on time. At the same time, the director must be sure that a sense of freedom exists for the actors—within a disciplined environment. In order to accomplish these ends, directors also must learn how to deal with change and flux. Human emotions are complex, and the director must be prepared to deal tactfully and decisively with the actors (and all production personnel) in order to keep the rehearsal schedule moving apace with the inexorable march toward opening night.

Familiarizing Actors with the Physical Environment Rehearsing actors efficiently and effectively requires rehearsal spaces as close as possible to actual stage space, size, and dimension. To assist actors in familiarizing themselves with spacial parameters, the director normally has the ground plan for the setting taped to the rehearsal room floor so that actual spatial relationships can be felt immediately. Rehearsal furniture and clothing must be provided—especially if actors must wear period clothing of unfamiliar cut and feel (for example, hoop skirts, large headdresses, and swords). Anything that requires the actor to adapt needs to be present as early as possible during the rehearsal period. Effective communication between the director and the costume designer, scene designer, technical director, and/or property master is essential so that the director can meet actors' needs in a timely manner.

The Time Process for Rehearsing the Actors In an overview, the actual time period of the director's rehearsals with the actors breaks into a five-phase process. In the first phase, a series of readings occurs in which the actors familiarize themselves with the play, the director's concepts, and production goals. The second phase comprises memorization of lines and the creation of the stage picture through blocking. In the third phase of the rehearsal period, the director helps the actors to polish each aspect of their work. Precision comes to line delivery, blocking is solidified, and characterizations come to life. In the fourth phase the director coordinates the actors and their needs and goals with the other elements of the production—costumes, lighting cues, scene changes, sound cues, special effects, and so on—to create a unified and smoothly operating whole.

In this fourth phase tensions reach their peak. In the fifth and final phase the director oversees the actors and all other production elements as finishing touches are added to the production in what is called the dress rehearsal period. Here the production comes as close to actual performance as can be managed. Occasionally an invited audience attends in order to give the actors a sense of what the real performance will be like. In rehearsing the actors at this point, the director needs audience reactions, especially laughter, so that the overall timing of the actors' lines can set. Last-minute feedback from uninvolved persons may be used to give final polish to the actors' portrayals and to the production as a whole.

How Directors Work *in* Time *and* Space

Whatever the director's preference for beginning the rehearsal period, he or she must eventually work out of the dramatic structure of the play *in phsyical space and over time*. The logic of actors moving as their characters dictate is not enough in itself to create overall meaning for the audience. The purpose of a theatre production is not simply the re-creation of life as we find it—at least not in terms of superficial details.

Design and Meaning   A play is an *abstraction*, a search for or *vision* of reality that must reflect a higher or deeper level of perception than the obvious. Therefore, what each actor portrays realistically (if that is the style of the production) must be shaped and blended both with other actors and with the stage space itself so that every aspect of the production says what the play needs to say to the audience. The moment-to-moment design of the visual picture, including the actors, must reveal the play's deeper, complex effort to communicate.

In simplest terms, working in time and space means putting together a visual pantomime that can carry meaning even without the words of the script. Anyone who has had the opportunity to see an excellent production of a play in a language that he or she does not understand understands this point. In such an experience, although we can infer some information through tone, volume, intensity, rate, and so on, the words themselves carry virtually nothing in the way of meaning. Nonetheless, we discover that we can discern much meaning from what we see of the actors' physical relationships, actions, and sequences, as well as from costumes, settings, and lighting. All of this conveyance of meaning through design of space and time must be worked out carefully by the director. The audience must be able to *see* conflict, change, and resolution.

Design and Communication   Designing the visual elements of a production also means controlling the audience's attention so that they see what is

Ariane Mnouchkine: The Anti-Director

The avant-garde French theatre director Ariane Mnouchkine (*b.* 1934) is famous for her use of *creátion collective*—collaboratively devised productions—as well as for the concept of shared responsibility within her theatre group, the Théâtre du Soleil, which she founded in 1964. Influenced by the radical theorist Antonin Artaud (see Chapter 17), Mnouchkine sought to explore the whole range of expression available to theatre, but like the German playwright-theorist Bertolt Brecht (see Chapter 17), she was also interested in an idiom capable of encompassing both private drama and social process. Her production of British dramatist Arnold Wesker's *Kitchen* (1967) clearly represented an attempt to wed the two modes, but after the French student revolts of 1968, she realized that to achieve her goals, the Théâtre du Soleil would have to create its own plays collectively. The company achieved this goal in plays like *1789* (1970), *1793* (1972), and *L'Age d'Or* (*The Golden Age,* 1975).

After these productions, Mnouchkine made the extraordinary film *Molière,* dealing with the experience of a theatre group committed to living and creating together. She then returned to the theatre, adapting Klaus Mann's *Mephisto* (1979), which was followed by a cycle of Shakespearean plays: *Richard II* (1981), *Twelfth Night* (1982), and *Henry IV Part 1* (1984)—in which Oriental theatre methods were used to create new insights into both the plays themselves and contemporary reality. The next work by the Théâtre de Soleil, Hélène Cixous's epic play *Norodom Sihanouk* (1985), continued in the same direction, also borrowing from Oriental theatre to make a statement about present-day life.

important at any given moment (see Fig. 8.9). In film and television, for example, a director can control audience perception of visuals through the use of camera angle, close-up, image, cutting, and so on. The theatre director, however, has no such tools: The audience's field of vision is the entire stage space, and only the skill of the director can cause an audience member to focus where focus is needed (see Fig. 8.10). Unlike the movie screen, which can be filled with a single small object such as an actor's eye, the theatre stage and all its furniture, people, walls, trees, or whatever remain in full view of the audience at the same time that the director wishes the audience to focus on, for instance, an actor's facial expression. What can the director do?

Obviously, a director can do anything that his or her imagination inspires relative to a particular circumstance. For our purposes, however, we can de-

Figure 8.9   Samuel Beckett, Waiting for Godot. Ball State University Theatre. Director, James Hardin; *scene designer, D. C. Shawger; costume designer, C. Shawger; lighting designer, michael Lamirand. The director has focused the audience's attention on one character by moving that character downstage of the others into a stronger stage position, and by encircling the actor with the other actors. Further strength is added to the focus by having actors not in focus point toward the actor in focus. See also Fig. 3.13. An undisputed masterpiece of absurdist theatre, Waiting for Godot is summarized in Chapter 17.*

Figure 8.10   Howard Richardson and William Berney, Dark of the Moon. *University of Arizona Theatre. Director, Peter R. Marroney; scene designer, Robert C. Burroughs; costume designer, Helen Workman Currie; lighting designer, John E. Lafferty. Notice how the director leads the audience to focus on the central actor in this scene consisting of many actors. Notice the contrast between the costume of the central actor and the others. Also notice how the line produced by the grouping of actors parallels the line produced by the outline of the church and the curvature of the foliage borders.*

scribe a few devices and general principles to illustrate some key points and to form a basic foundation for directing *practice*. First, let's look at some general concepts.

Stage Space   In working in time and space, the director must pay attention to the *floor space* of the stage itself. *In general,* the stage has six areas, each of which appears to have a **strength of focus** relative to the rest, as diagrammed in Figure 8.11. Stage directions stem from these areas. Those areas along the front half of the stage and nearest the audience are called **downstage areas;** those along the rear of the stage and farthest from the audience are called **upstage areas.**

The part of the stage that in some theatres extends out in front of the curtain line is called an **apron.** For reasons that are not entirely clear, common experience tells us that **downstage center** seems to be the strongest area on stage. The terms "house right" and "left" and "audience right" and "left" refer to right and left as one faces the stage from the audience or "house." "Stage right" and "left," then, are the *actor's* right and left as he or she faces the audience. (The terms *upstage* and *downstage* derive from the historic proscenium theatre, in which upstage was physically higher than downstage; that is, the stage floor slanted or was *raked* upward from apron to backstage wall.)

The strength of downstage center and its appeal to both actor and audience still can be seen in the staging of some operas and musical comedies: When important arias or songs are sung, the actor moves to downstage center and stays there throughout the number, to be replaced when the next performer has a song to sing. This practice is an awkward but durable convention from theatre's less "realistic" past, and the modern director must often work

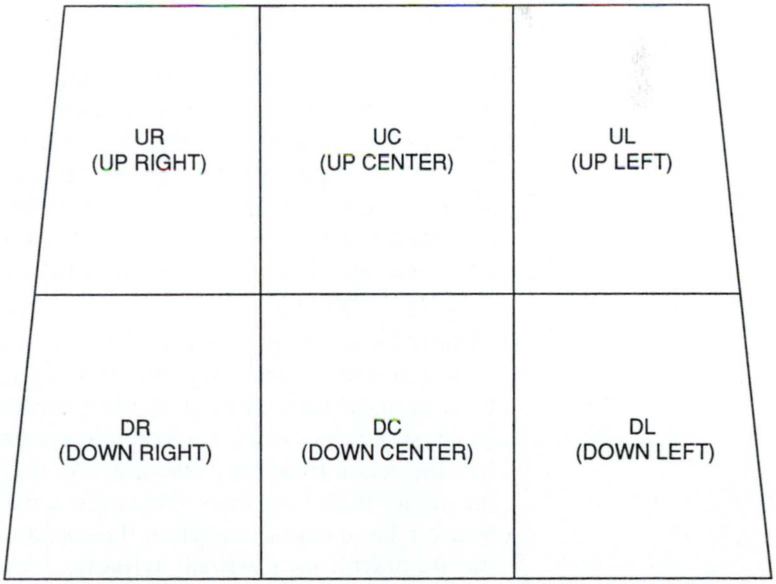

strength of focus The relative ability of a character to draw the attention of the audience

downstage areas Those parts of the stage closest to the audience

upstage areas Those parts of the stage furthest from the audience

apron The part of the stage that extends out in front of the curtain line

downstage center The center portion of the stage closest to the audience

UR (UP RIGHT)	UC (UP CENTER)	UL (UP LEFT)
DR (DOWN RIGHT)	DC (DOWN CENTER)	DL (DOWN LEFT)

Figure 8.11
Diagram of the stage and its six areas.

Directing

to avoid the tendency to place all important action in this dominant but uninspired position.

The remaining five stage areas move from strongest to weakest successively as follows: down-right, down-left, up-center, up-right, to up-left. If the stage floor, for example, were always flat, focus and dominance might be fairly straightforward matters. However, the introduction of three-dimensional scenic pieces, platforms, and stairways gives the director other tools with which to create visual design. For example, because an actor who is physically higher than another assumes a stronger position, the director and the designer come into a close and important relationship in creating additional spatial opportunities for focus and visual relationships, all of which must be carefully thought out in terms of the progress of the play over time. Occasionally, great restraint must be employed so as not to lessen the effect of a later and more important scene by the use of some part of the set in the early moments of the play. This is especially true of dramatically designed and elevated spaces. When we experience a play as audience members, we must be alert to all of the subtle cues and clues that the director gives us visually, storing them up as the production proceeds and relating them to each other in order to see the meaning that unfolds through them.

We can draw a good example of how directorial, visual composition works by examining one of the world's most familiar paintings, Leonardo da Vinci's *The Last Supper* (Fig. 8.12). This is, in a two-dimensional composition, a dramatic and theatrical portrayal whose devices are used by virtually every competent theatrical director. The scene is the last supper taken together by Jesus and his disciples. The climactic moment of the portrayal is Jesus' announcement that one of the disciples will betray him. The setting is theatrical—on a stage. Notice that none of the personages has his back to the audience—that is, to the viewer. Each of the disciples is identifiable, and groupings portray relationships described in the Bible. We can discern from the body language and physical placement who relates to whom and the quality of each relationship. Like a skillful stage director, Leonardo causes us to move our attention from one individual to another and from one grouping to another. Although we take in each and every response, no matter where we start our looking, we are eventually led back to the central figure of Jesus. An arm, an angle of a head, a glance, a color—everything at the artist's disposal moves the eye along. Even the lines of the room (stage setting) direct our eye to the central focus. A stage director turns the play into many such compositions to show us the play's meaning.

Theatre Form   Theatre forms also have a definite effect on directorial actions in time and space. The characteristics of theatre form noted in Chapter 5 apply here. In one theatre form or another, certain devices by which directors create emphasis may not exist. For example, spatial relationships for an audience that sees the action from only one direction may disappear when the audience sees the action from four sides. Thus, the actual form of the actor–audience relationship has a major impact on the choices that the director must make. Some theatre practitioners actually reject the idea of a single focus for each scene or

Figure 8.12 *Leonardo da Vinci, "The Last Supper," ca. 1495–1498. Mural painting. Santa Maria della Grazie, Milan. The figure of Christ achieves focus by having all other elements of the painting emanate outward from or lead inward to it. The same compositional devices are used by the stage director to achieve focus on the stage, even though the play is constantly in motion. In another context, it is also interesting to compare the composition of figures in this famous painting with the composition of characters in the production of Eugene O'Neill's* The Iceman Cometh *at Fig. 11.3: Leonardo's depiction of Christ and his disciples has entered the repertory of images available to artists in a variety of modern media, and the composition in the O'Neill production goes a long way toward reflecting the playwright's thought—that is, his desire to give greater, perhaps even* symbolic *meaning to the lives of characters who can at least seek "communion" in basic human interaction.*

subscene. Whether focus is singular or multiple, however, choices must be made and devices employed.

Composition and Movement   In addition to considerations of stage areas, several other devices for achieving focus or emphasis assist the director. *Height,* for example, gives the director a means by which to place one actor in a more dominant position than another: Elevation usually equals emphasis. In addition to the use of stairs and platforms, the director may also juxtapose actors in standing, sitting, and/or kneeling positions or vary the heights of actors in any one of those positions.

Movement also places focus on an actor relative to those who remain motionless. The eyes of the audience are drawn quickly to motion, and this phenomenon occasionally works to the consternation of the director when an undisciplined actor moves a hand or shifts a stance in the middle of someone else's scene. The result, of course, is an audience whose focus is interrupted and drawn to an inconsequential piece of action.

Body position also creates focus or emphasis. Onstage, we refer to actors as being *open, half, closed,* and *three-quarters.* These references usually correspond to the stage area as well, as illustrated in Figure 8.13. An actor can be positioned "three-quarter right," "one-quarter left," "closed," "open," and so on. The more open the actor, the more emphasis the director achieves.

Spatial relationships also give the director choices by which to indicate focus. When this device is used, both grouping and isolation play key roles. A sure way for the director to draw focus to an actor is to separate him or her from a grouping of several authors. Whereas the eye is drawn to the person apart, grouping tends to blur the identity of the individuals.

Because they can draw upon color and other design compositional elements to attract the eye, *scenery, costumes,* and *lighting* prove powerful devices by which the director can choose to create emphasis. Perhaps the most useful of these design options is color. By careful selection of hue and value, the director can make actors stand out or recede in contrast with each other and the setting. For example, bright and high-value colors such as orange and yellow create strong emphasis; their eye-attraction value is nearly overpowering. Of course, the most effective device for creating emphasis is light: When one lights the desired focal object and darkens the rest of the stage, focus results automatically.

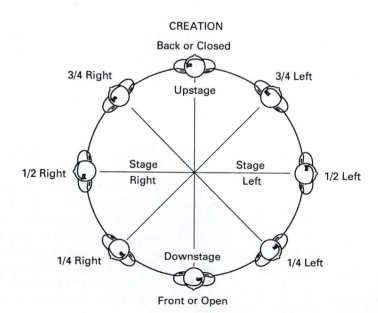

Figure 8.13 *Diagram of actors' body positions. Clockwise, from the top: closed, three-quarter left, one-half left, one-quarter left, open, one-quarter right, one-half right, and three-quarter right.*

Directing

Figure 8.14 *Jim Jacobs and Warren Casey,* Grease. *Northern Illinois University.
Director, Timothy Mooney; scene designer, Alexander F. Adducci; costume designer, Lili
La Tourette; lighting designer, Betsy Cooprider-Bernstein. Photo by George Tarbay. All
the visual elements making up this scene suggest action: the upraised hands of the
actors, the intensity of their expressions, and the strong diagonals of the setting.*

Movement   Earlier we mentioned *movement* as a device that a director can
use to create focus or emphasis (see Fig. 8.14). Used in the design of time and
space, movement has four primary characteristics:

1. Movement That Is Appropriate to Character. To create a specific visual
image, movement can be used to affect the age of a character—old people,
after all, move differently than young people. Movement can also be used to
reinforce character through what is known as **stage business:** Actions such as
smoking a cigarette, filling a pipe, and so on give clues to character.

stage business Actor
movements used to
reinforce character

2. Movement That Is Appropriate to Situation. Situations of strong emotion
require movement of a considerably different quality than situations of calm-
ness. People under emotional strain gesture more broadly, rapidly, and with
less fluidity than people at peace. The director must be sure that actor movement fits the emotional situation.

3. Movement That Is Appropriate to Genre or Style. Classical tragedies demand
broader and more controlled gestures than do farces. The director who
chooses inappropriately in this circumstance can mislead the audience in its
expectations—and can appear downright ignorant if the actors' movements do
not correspond with conventions of style.

4. Movement That Is Appropriate to the Play's Development. Movement in this consideration must fit the level occurring in the play's dynamic development. For example, movement of excess vitality in a play's early moments can cause the climax to lack intensity and power.

COMPOSITION AND TIME

Because theatre is *action,* however important the visual or spatial designs of a production may be, those designs have very little value until they relate to each other in some sense of time. Captivation of an audience and, ultimately, the meaning of the play depend on movement forward in time. In the normal plot structure, anticipation precedes action; action builds through crisis, finally reaching a climax, and resolves to a conclusion. All these considerations are elements of time, and the director must shape and manage actors, sound, lights, settings, and costumes so that what is revealed over time leads the audience to understand the basic concept or vision behind the production.

DESIGN AND VARIETY

As time progresses and devices are employed, directors must concern themselves with *variety,* which is one of the most important concepts and choices in any artistic work. In the theatre, changes of pace, force, pitch, dynamics, and so on keep audience attention from flagging as the play moves forward. However, designing action and variety in time is a subtle and complicated task: With too little change, the audience becomes bored, as happens when we listen to a monotone; too much change and we become confused.

The director must have an intuitive sense about these things. In fact, the director must be both artist and ideal or objective audience. In the theatre, as in dance and music, what transpires in time must be made clearer to the receptor (the audience) than might be necessary in such arts as painting or sculpture. Assuming that it is doing its fair share, an audience must be able to grasp important points in a moment and retain them for reference to other passing moments. The theatre does not afford the luxury of rereading or studying until meaning becomes clear—meaning must be clear immediately, or it is lost. The director's job is to make time work toward meaning. Every actor on stage and every other element visible or audible to the audience must be carefully designed and controlled to effect maximum communication.

The Director *as* Manager

One final aspect of the director's work in time and space has a different thrust from what we mean by the time and space that is designed between the opening and the closing curtain of a production. Theatre productions have a finite time and space, prior to opening night, in which they emerge. Opening night is an established date and hour, and the production will be mounted in a specific theatre. Directors must work within the confines of the time allotted between the beginning of preparations and opening night. The director must be able to take his or her artistic vision or concept and bring it into realistic conformity with the circumstances allowed the production by rehearsal time, size and equipment of the stage, the type of stage, availability and skills of designers and crews, budgets, and the skills and needs of the actors available. That is, the director must be a manager.

Sometimes, for example, the director's concept is far too elaborate for the realities of available time and space. Failure to recognize that fact can lead to a horrendous experience for all concerned. In addition, control and authority also mean responsibility, and the director must assume the responsibility for misjudging the relationship between concept and practicality. This judgment also includes the ability to sense when a designer's concept is more than can be delivered. Most of all, management of time and space means attention to details, making sure that all the necessary elements for a production are in place when they are needed, and passing judgment on each of these items, including sets, costumes, make-up, and properties.

Some theorists have ventured the opinion that the stage director is a "master artist" to whom all other elements or participants in the production are subordinate (see Fig. 8.15). As distasteful as that concept may be for some theatre practitioners, it remains essentially true. Someone must take ultimate responsibility for the production: Although theatre may be a collaborative art, it is not a democracy. One overall vision and authority must guide the production, and that vision and authority belong to the director.

Figure 8.15 Bertold Brecht, The Good Woman of Setzuan. *University of Arizona Theatre. Director and designer, Robert C. Burroughs; costume designer, Helen Workman Currie; lighting designer, John E. Lafferty. The particular stylistic difficulties of Bertold Brecht's "epic theatre" demand a strong directorial control. In this production the director also has designed the scenery, thus giving the production a totally unified vision and giving the director complete control of the production's concept. Brecht is discussed more fully in Chapter 17. His thoughts on scene design in the "epic theatre" can be found in an essay excerpt in Chapter 10.*

Directing

Evaluating *the* Director's Work

A director's work is difficult to judge accurately. All too often, while what is wrong with a production becomes the director's fault, credit goes to designers and actors. As in any corporate model, the difficulty rests in deciding how much credit or blame goes to the chief executive officer when his or her subordinates either succeed or fail. The fact that one can or cannot find a discernible overall "hand" or "stamp" in a production may be a mark of directorial success or failure. The point is that, except in perhaps the most extreme of circumstances, the director's task remains somewhat elusive when it comes to evaluation.

Perhaps the only way to judge directorial efforts is to experience a number of projects and try to discern whether a noticeable style emerges from a body of work. Because this is a tricky business, outside of some general evaluative considerations applied to the performance as a whole, there emerges few dependable criteria for judging a director's work. If the production warrants praise, then the director has succeeded; if not, the director has fallen short. Ultimately, the best test of a director's job is audience reaction.

Figure 8.16   Alan Ayckbourn, Woman in Mind. *Oregon Shakespeare Festival, Ashland. Projecting the image of the character: Left to right—Caroline Shaffer, Don Burroughs, Mikel MacDonald, and Fredi Olster. Director, Cynthia White; scenic designer, Carolyn L. Ross; costume designer, Frances Kenny; lighting designer, James Sale.*

More specifically, as audience members we can ask several questions about the production. A yes response indicates some degree of success for the director; a no response, the opposite.

1. Is the play's central action clear?

2. Does the production make clear what the play is about?

3. Do the settings and costumes contribute to the production?

4. Is the setting an integral part of the action, as opposed to being an empty envelope providing little besides a background? For example, does the director utilize every opportunity the setting provides? If the set is large, with numerous levels, and yet the actors seldom seem to stray from downstage center, then something is wrong directorily.

5. Are the actors visible in light?

6. Do the costumes indicate relationships clearly and reflect time and place accurately?

7. Can the actors be heard clearly? Coaching voices is a fundamental function of the director.

8. Is action purposeful?

9. Are the actors credible?

SUMMARY

• The modern concept of the director and the specific functions resulting from that concept emerged from the late-nineteenth-century theory of the totally *integrated production*. Among those whose work led to the modern director were Richard Wagner; Georg II, Duke of Saxe-Meiningen; Charles Kean; André Antoine; and Constantin Stanislavski.

• The role of the director, or the *director's function*, exists within a conceptual framework that allows for three possibilities: (1) the director an *interpretive* artist, (2) the director as a free *creative* artist, and (3) a middle ground between these two extremes.

• The director's responsibilities include (1) developing an overall *concept* for the production; (2) *collaborating* with other theatre artists; and (3) *auditioning, casting,* and *rehearsing actors.* Casting actors includes consideration of:

Casting criteria

Casting *types*

Casting *voices*

Casting for physical presence

Rehearsing actors includes:

Analyzing *scenes*

Analyzing *action and movement*

Guiding *actors*

Familiarizing actors with *the physical environment*

The overall time process for rehearsing actors

• The director's work involves putting the dramatic structure of the play *in physical space* and *over time.* In this process the director must put together a visual pantomime that can carry meaning even without the words of the script.

• The director must control the audience's attention so that they see what is important. This means employing design and communication devices that include:

Stage space and the utilization of its various areas, such as upstage, downstage, and so on

Visual composition

Theatre form

Composition and movement—including *body position* and *spatial relationships*

• *Movement,* as a device by which the director can meet artistic goals, has four characteristics:

Movement that is *appropriate to character*

Movement that is *appropriate to situation*

Movement that is *appropriate to genre or style*

Movement that is *appropriate to the play's development*

• Ultimately the value of a director's design choices must relate to each other in some sense of *time*—the unfolding of the production from beginning to end.

• One of the most important concepts and choices available to the director is that of *variety*—the changes of pace, force, pitch, dynamics, and so on that keep audience attention from flagging.

• In *working* in time and space, the director finally must be *a manager* who is responsible for working within the practical realities that affect the production.

• Our enjoyment of a theatrical production is enhanced if we can employ some standards by which we can evaluate a director's work. Questions we can ask address the clarity of the play's central action and message, the contributions of the costumes and settings, the appropriateness of the lighting, the accurate reflections of time and place by the costumes, the clarity of actors' speech, the purposefulness of the action, and the credibility of the actors.

Chapter 9

Acting

**After studying this chapter
you should be able to:**

- Discuss the relationship between acting in life and art and the role of the actor as *interpreter* and *stylist*.

- Describe several approaches that have influenced the development of acting.

- Characterize how *analysis*, *mental preparation*, *movement*, *stage business*, and *rehearsals* operate in an actor's *creation of a role*.

- Explain the role of *facts*, *spine*, *relationships*, *style*, *subtext*, and *integration* in the actor's process of analysis.

- Define *gesture*, *facial expression*, *posture*, and *body tone* and explain how actors use these parts of their equipment.

- Identify and describe the five qualities of vocal expression used by an actor.

Sir Lawrence Olivier as Romeo; Vivian Leigh as Juliet. Vandam Collection, New York Public Library.

*T*he essence of theatre is the live actor performing before a live audience, and the circumstances created by the potential for immediate interchange between artist and respondent make theatre different from film, television, and the visual arts. Needless to say, our response to actors' performances is immediate; and, whatever our level of theatrical sophistication, we have a pretty good sense of when the art is done well or poorly. In this chapter we will focus on four aspects of acting as a theatrical art and craft, and thus will add to our own repertoire of understandings that enable us to respond more fully and to enjoy more deeply the performances we experience. First, we will discuss "acting" as it relates to life and art. Second, we will note some approaches to acting with a brief historical context. Third, we will examine the actual preparation of a role and, finally, the "equipment" actors use in character portrayal.

Acting *in* Life *and* Art

Actors bring plays and characters to "life." In a very real sense, acting is an extension of human life. In fact, "acting out" may be the most normal of human traits. As children we played imitation games such as "house" or "cops

Figure 9.1A
William Macready as Macbeth, ca. 1820.

[Courtesy of the Lilly Library, Indiana University, Bloomington Indiana]

Figure 9.1B Edwin Forrest as Richard III, ca. 1830. Known for a sober intellectual temperament and a mannered, often subdued style, Macready (1793–1873) was one of England's foremost Shakespearean actors in the early nineteenth century. Meanwhile, Forrest (1806–1872) emerged as America's first great tragedian about a decade later. Noted for the passion of his performances, Forrest encountered resistance from English audiences, who preferred the more measured style of Macready, when he toured Europe in the 1830s, and when Macready ventured on to the U.S. stage in the late 1840s, American audiences voiced their preference for their homegrown "star": At one performance in New York, 22 people died during a riot.

[Courtesy of the Lilly Library, Indiana University, Bloomington, Indiana]

and robbers" in which we acted various roles. In fact, every human uses acting in many ways each and every day. We play roles at home, at work, in school, and at parties; whether with ourselves or with others, we constantly live in a state of role playing. We could say that, in life, each of us seeks through role playing to do exactly what the actor does—to discover the essence of a "character" and to portray that character so that the audience not only sees and hears what the actor wishes it to see and hear but *believes* what the actor wishes it to believe about the character. To the extent that an actor can discover *character*—who someone *is*—and can transmit the essence of that character to others—whether an audience, friends, family, or strangers—one can conclude that successful acting has been achieved.

But acting, of course, is different from real life. Like all art, acting is removed from life: If stage characters were as complicated as real-life characters, audiences would never be able to understand them in two hours. Furthermore, actors are not the characters they portray (although confusion may occasionally exist). Finally, acting in the theatre—as opposed to the acting we do in real life—has a completely different purpose: For an actor, who is imitating in order to be observed, "selling the character" seeks practical ends far less profound than "selling ourselves" in the roles we play in daily life.

THE ACTOR AS INTERPRETER

The actor functions in a unique way. Like any other artists in the theatre, the actor is an *interpreter* of the director's concept, the playwright's vision, and the actor's own understanding. At the same time, however, the *instrument* used by the actor for interpretation is not paint and canvas, paper and pencil, or other human beings: The actor's instrument is the actor himself. This situation creates an awkward circumstance for the actor because—unlike scene, costume, and lighting designers, unlike the director or the playwright—the actor can neither observe the *product* of his or her art nor evaluate it by stepping back and changing perspective. Although an actor can watch the videotape of a performance, even that is one step removed from witnessing the actual art itself.

THE ACTOR AS STYLIST

Actors are also captives of the *styles* of the pieces in which they appear and the conditions of the theatres in which the production is staged. An actor in a touring company, for example, may have to adjust his performance on a nightly basis. On one evening, he may have to convey character to an audience in an intimate theatre seating 100 or so; the next evening, the same character may have to be conveyed in the space of a huge auditorium seating 2,000. An actor in a repertory company may play in the poetic and theatrical style of a Shakespearean comedy one night and the ultrarealism of a contemporary drama the next. No rigid formula can be applied to all conditions or to the preparation required for those conditions.

Thus we find in acting important linkages to everyday life—certain common experiences and purposes. Nonetheless, however similar and familiar the conditions may be, acting in the theatre goes far beyond what happens in life. Art may appear to imitate life, and life may seem, occasionally, to resemble art, but ultimately the two are quite different (Fig. 9.2).

Figure 9.2 *Thornton Wilder,* Our Town. *Oregon Shakespeare Festival. Director, James Edmondson; scenic designer, William Bloodgood. Using such devices as a stage manager-character to narrate the action, the representation of imagined as well as real events, and minimal scenic elements on a bare stage, Wilder managed to apply experimental technique to subject matter that usually lends itself to much more conventional means of expression: the celebration of life in small-town America.*

Approaches *to* Acting

Until the twentieth century, actors developed their art in the simplest of all circumstances: They acted. They developed as actors through observation and experience. They watched the leading actors of their times and emulated them as best they could. In order to gain experience and recognition by those who could cast them in roles, actors began as apprentices, doing menial tasks around the theatre and taking nonspeaking roles. Through diligence and opportunism, they grasped the first speaking role they could and tried to prove to producers and managers that they could handle roles of increasing importance. The surest way into the upper echelons of the acting profession was—and still

Figure 9.3A   *Henri-Louis Lekain as Genghis Khan in* Voltaire's Orphan of China, *1761.*

[S. B. Lenoir, Comédie-Française, Paris. Performing Arts Research Center, New York Public Library at Lincoln Center]

Figure 9.3B   *Friedrich Schroder as Falstaff, 1780. By the end of the eighteenth century, several countries in western Europe would boast theatre "stars," many of whom rose to prominence as interpreters of the great dramatic writers of the age. Lekain (1729–1778), for example, was trained in a private theatre built for him by Voltaire in the great philosopher-satirist's own home. Schroeder (1744–1816), noted as Germany's first great interpreter of Shakespeare, was influenced by the contemporary dramaturgy of the poet Johann Wolfgang von Goethe and specialized in the works of the dramatic and social critic Gotthold Lessing. As three of the major figures in European drama in the eighteenth century, Voltaire, Lessing, and Goethe are discussed in some detail in Chapter 16.*

[Performing Arts Research Center, New York Public Library at Lincoln Center]

is—personal contact with working professionals. The luckiest—and perhaps the best—young actors became protégés of the leading actors or managers of the day and gained not only additional opportunity but also some important tutelage.

For the most part, however, aspiring actors had to learn by their wits and be powered by their own imaginations. Actors learned that success lay in doing what the public desired, and many of the great actors of history began as dismal failures while they were learning their craft. Rarely did the actor find a self-help book to assist in the task. Although some observations occasionally found their way into print, they were rare and the quality of the observations questionable. Experience, insight, adaptability, and persistence were the great actor-preparers of history.

ACTING BASED ON MECHANICAL PRINCIPLES

In the nineteenth century, a system of acting based on mechanical principles arose. The Frenchman François Delsarte, for example, devised a detailed scheme of gestures, zones, and vocal mechanisms which, when mastered, supposedly gave the actor a stock of expressions applicable to every situation in role creation. In the Delsarte school, then, acting became a memorization of lines and techniques. The result was a fundamentally *external* approach to acting. Even in modern times the external approach to acting has proved particularly appropriate for certain genres, such as farce and musical comedy, and can be very helpful in the preparation of plays from pre-nineteenth-century periods.

ACTING BASED ON PSYCHOLOGICAL PRINCIPLES

The nineteenth century, however, also discovered a deep interest in psychology. Coupled with the emerging styles of realism and naturalism, that interest led to a different approach to acting. In opposition to the external approach exemplified by Delsarte, this new school focused on the *inner* life of the character and saw character as a complex interaction of *contextual conditioning*: That is, in pursuit of the new theory of behavior as environmentally conditioned, the theatre began to focus on character as a complex relationship of psychological and physical factors.

At the Théâtre Libre in France, for example, André Antoine recognized the need for a new approach to acting in order to give the emerging realistic and naturalistic drama a production style suitable to the style in which plays were being written. Antoine insisted that his actors become immersed in their roles, and he introduced stage mannerisms totally unconventional at the time: Actors turned their backs on the audience, spoke in natural tones, and used restrained, realistic gestures. To a large extent, the psychological approach to acting has become the modern norm, and the bombastic and affected style of acting has largely disappeared.

THE STANISLAVSKI METHOD

The new approach to acting found its most prominent supporter in Constantin Stanislavski of the Moscow Art Theatre. As the founder and manager of a theatre, Stanislavski was in a position to put his theories into practice at all levels. His theory, developed during the first decade of the twentieth century, was published in three books, *My Life in Art*, *An Actor Prepares*, and *Building the Character*. Teaching his method to actors studying at the Moscow Art Theatre, he put theory, training, and practice together in productions in which he himself both acted and directed (Fig. 9.4). Stanislavski's students became teachers, and the "Stanislavski method" spread throughout the Western world.

Stanislavski wanted an approach in which actors could follow a regimen in order to gain complete mastery over their bodies and emotions. That is, he wanted to develop a method by which actors could make their bodies and emotions react precisely as they wished, given the requirements of the character. By so doing, Stanislavski believed, they would be best prepared to bring meaningful interpretation to their roles and to the play. Discipline formed an important foundation for the Method. Its object was a correct "state of being" on the stage. Such a state of being was the normal state of a human being in life. To attain such a difficult condition, the actor needed to be "physically

Figure 9.4 Anton Chekhov's Uncle Vanya *performed at the Moscow Art Theatre, 1899. Chekhov is one of the most important of all modern playwrights, and Stanislavski, in addition to being one of the theatre's great modern theorists, was Chekhov's first and foremost interpreter. A synopsis of Chekhov's* Three Sisters *can be found in Chapter 4, and Chekhov's unique contributions to realism in the modern theatre are described in more detail in Chapter 17.*

free"—in control of his body—and to have "limitless attention." In order to be able to communicate with other actors on stage and to "accept the given circumstances of the play completely," the actor needed to see and hear as he or she does in real life.

Stanislavski suggested a series of exercises to develop such qualities. He wanted the actors to do these exercises every day, just as a singer or a pianist does scales and arpeggios.

Stanislavski distinguished between "inner psychological actions" and "outer physical actions," both of which he believed made up the "correct actions in the progressive unfolding of the play." When such a distinction was mastered, actors achieved the correct state of being on stage. He intentionally separated actions into psychological and physical, in the belief that such a separation made it easier for him to communicate with the actors during rehearsal. He emphasized that every physical action is caused by an inner psychological action. "And in every psychological inner action there is always a physical action which expresses its psychic nature; the unity between these two is organic on the stage." The unity of psychological and physical action was defined by the play's theme, its idea, its characters, and the given circumstances. Actors must place themselves into the given circumstances by saying to themselves, "What would I do *if* all that happens to this character happened to me?" Stanislavski characterized this creation of hypothetical circumstances as the "magic *if*"—a device that helped the actor "to begin to *do* on the stage." He instructed his actors to learn to act from themselves, to define the differences between their behavior and that of the character. He wanted them to find all the reasons and justifications for the character's actions, and then to go on from that point without thinking where their own personal actions ended and the characters began. Stanislavski believed that if actors did as he suggested, then their actions and the actions of the character would fuse automatically

Figure 9.5 *Inner emotions are outwardly expressed as Lucy (Caroline Shaffer, right) thinks her mother Susan (Fredi Olster, left) is the most wonderful person in the world and can do anything in Alan Ayckbourn's* Woman in Mind *at the Black Swan Theatre at the Oregon Shakespeare Festival (1991). Director, Cynthia White; scenic designer, Carolyn L. Ross; costume designer, Frances Kenny; lighting designer, James Sale.*

Acting

Profile

Lee Strasberg and the Actors Studio

One of America's most famous—and controversial—acting teachers, Lee Strasberg (1901–1982) revolutionized American acting by becoming the leading exponent of the so-called "Method" based on the theories of Constantin Stanislavski.

Beginning in 1950, when he became its director, Strasberg achieved his influence at the Actors Studio, a workship for professional actors founded four years previously by several members of the Group Theatre. As taught by Strasberg, the Method encouraged actors (1) to have an almost mystical belief in the power of truth in acting; (2) to probe fearlessly their own inner feelings in order to discover a character's psychological truth; (3) to improvise during rehearsals in order to keep their acting spontaneous; (4) to engage only in psychologically sound stage behavior; (5) to reproduce recognizable reality based on acute observation of the external world; and (6) to use objects for their symbolic and real value ("There are times when you pick up your shoes," Strasberg has observed, "and see through them your whole life").

Although some critics of the Method have contended that it created self-indulgent actors deficient in technique, the list of performers who either attended classes at the Studio or studied privately with Strasberg reads like a who's-who of American acting. Included are James Dean, Marlon Brando, Marilyn Monroe, Paul Newman, Joanne Woodward, Shelley Winters, Al Pacino, and Geraldine Page.

During Strasberg's tenure, the Studio initiated a number of workshop plays, some of which became Broadway successes. Perhaps the most celebrated of these was *A Hatful of Rain* (1955) by Michael Grazzo. In 1962, a grant by the Ford Foundation enabled the Studio to establish the short-lived Actors Studio Theatre. One of its most noted productions, a version of Chekhov's *The Three Sisters* directed by Strasberg himself in 1964, seems (depending on the observer) to have displayed the primary virtues (e.g., "memorable performances") or the nagging weaknesses (e.g., "overacting") of the Method approach.

Strasberg (third from left) is pictured above with Actors Studio cofounders Rip Torn, Geraldine Page, and Cheryl Crawford.

(Fig. 9.5). He went on, however, to emphasize that accurate character analysis was essential—as was "a good appearance, clear and energetic diction, plastic movement, a sense of rhythm, temperament, taste, and the infectious quality we call charm."

Acting

HOLISTIC AND INTERACTION APPROACHES

Other approaches to acting have emerged, some quite recently. Contemporary psychology continues to form a focal point for dealing with acting, and two such concepts, for example, are those of Robert L. Benedetti and Eric Berne. Robert Benedetti has tried to adapt to acting a psychological theory that emotion follows action—the principle, for example, that we are afraid because we run away as opposed to running away because we are afraid. In following the course of this theory—as applied to acting—Benedetti uses a holistic approach to the person. In other words, he tries to involve all of the inseparable ways in which actions create feelings. In a second new approach, theatre practitioners call upon the work of the Canadian psychiatrist Eric Berne, who suggests that humans develop systems of interacting because we have a basic need to interact with other humans. As a result, play analysis, role development, and rehearsals use game-playing techniques (from Berne's book *The Games People Play*) in order to give actors a sense of the needs and relationships of the characters in the play.

Creating *a* Role

Although there may be different approaches to acting, the fact is that when actors create a role, a fairly straightforward process emerges. In the next few pages we will follow that role creation process by examining how an actor analyzes a role, prepares mentally for the role, establishes the character's movements, decides on "stage business," and rehearses the role.

ANALYZING A ROLE

The actor's first step in creating a role requires the same process that every other theatre artist employs—*analysis*. When specifically applied to character, analysis means isolating several layers of information.

Facts   First are the *facts* about the personage—physical size, profession, social class, economic status, family background, and so on. Each of these facts can be found in the script.

spine The single drive that motivates the character in making decisions and taking action

The Spine   Second is the **spine** of the character—the single drive that motivates this person to do what he or she does, decide issues, meet crises, and so on. In determining the spine, the actor must find the general attitudes, likes, dislikes, and general psychological profile and distill all of these into a single action verb that can be woven into all of the actions and relationships throughout the play. The spine of a character is basic to the play's meaning and essential to the actor's portrayal. For example, let's examine the character of Blanche DuBois in Tennessee Williams's *A Streetcar Named Desire*. Her name, "Blanche," is French for "white," and she has a dreamer's view of the level of

Elia Kazan: Phrasing Blanche's Spine

The role of Blanche DuBois in Elia Kazan's 1947 production of Tennessee Williams' *A Streetcar Named Desire* made a star of Jessica Tandy (see the PROFILE in this chapter). As is clear from Kazan's notes on the character of Blanche—a neurotically naive schoolteacher cast out of a world of Southern gentility into a world of social and sexual squalor—Tandy encountered in her director a collaborator who expected the actress to become a student of human nature in a form that was both symbolic and subtle.

Spine—find Protection: the tradition of the old South says that it must be through another person.

Her problem has to do with her tradition. Her notion of what a woman should be. She is stuck with this "ideal." It is her. It is her ego. Unless she lives by it, she cannot live; in fact her whole life has been for nothing. . . .

Because this image of herself cannot be accomplished in reality, certainly not in the South of our day and time, it is her effort and practice to *accomplish it in fantasy.* Everything that she does in *reality* too is colored by this necessity, this compulsion to be *special.* So, in fact, *reality becomes fantasy, too.* She makes it so!

The variety essential to the play, and to Blanche's playing and to Jessica Tandy's achieving the role demands that she be a "heavy" at the beginning. For instance: contemplate the inner character contradiction: bossy yet helpless, domineering yet shaky, etc. . . .

There is another, simpler and equally terrible contradiction in her own nature. She won't face her physical or sensual side. She calls it "brutal desire." She thinks she sins when she gives in to it. . . . So she is constantly in conflict, not at ease, sinning. *She's still looking for something that doesn't exist today, a gentleman,* who will treat her like a virgin, marry her, protect her, defend and maintain her honor, etc. . . .

> *Even as frantic and fantastic a creature as Blanche is created by things you have felt and known, if you'll dig for them and be honest about what you see.*

An effort to phrase Blanche's spine: to find *protection*, to find something to hold onto, some strength in whose protection she can live, like a sucker shark or a parasite. The tradition of *woman* (or all women) can only live through the strength of someone else. Blanche is entirely dependent. . . .

Blanche—Physically. Must at all times give a single impression: her social mask is: *the High-Bred Genteel Lady in Distress.* Her past, her destiny, her falling from grace is just a surprise . . . then a tragic contradiction. But the mask never breaks down.

The only way to understand any character is through yourself. Everyone is much more alike than they willingly admit. Even as frantic and fantastic a creature as Blanche is created by things you have felt and known, *if you'll dig for them and be honest about what you see.*

perfection that everything and everyone should possess. We find this reflection in her imaginary flights of fancy regarding her childhood home, "Belle Reve" ("Beautiful Dream"). She seems to be driven by a desire to make the world pure and clean, and she wants to see people in that light as well. Her major obstacle, of course, is her brother-in-law, Stanley Kowalski, a brooding, macho slob. It is possible that an actress seeking Blanche's spine could find those "cleaning" characteristics to be Blanche's driving force and conclude that her spine is "to clean." (Spines usually take the form of action verbs so that actors can easily transform the spine of the character into physical action: The actress playing Blanche can "clean" everything she comes near—furniture, herself, other people. Or—as was the case in the 1947 Broadway production—Blanche's spine could be "Find Protection.") Without a clearly conceived spine, the portrayal will prove ambiguous and unconvincing. Once the spine is decided upon, it must be applied to each and every scene and to each and every relationship within scenes. Elia Kazan, who directed the Broadway debut of *Streetcar* in 1947, kept careful notes on the characters of both Blanche DuBois and Stanley Kowalski; his notes on Blanche are excerpted in this chapter.

Relationships   Third, the actor must understand the play's *relationships*. In addition to determining the way his or her character relates to others, the actor also must see the character's relationships from the point of view of each of the other characters: How do the other characters view his character? Here the actor's analysis steps outside the perceptions of his character and finds the broader perspective, which itself is helpful in adding depth to the portrayal (Fig. 9.6).

Style   Fourth is the character's relationship to the play and its *style*. Acting is not "becoming a character": That is too limiting a viewpoint. The actor must always understand the goals of the production and how the character relates to and can be portrayed within those broader issues. For example, a

Figure 9.6   *Actor interaction and relationships. The characters witness and respond to the conditions surrounding them in a scene from the Southern Utah University production of Bernard Pomerance's moving drama,* The Elephant Man. *Directed by Roger Bean, with Richard Bugg as Dr. Frederick Treves and Brian Vaughn as John Merrick.*

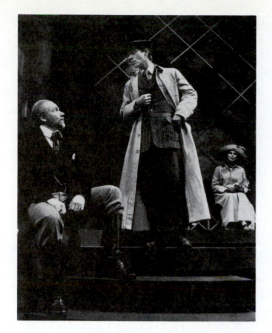

Figure 9.7 Realism in playwrighting and in acting style emerged in the late nineteenth century, especially in the works of the British playwright George Bernard Shaw. Here the style, with costumes, scenery, and acting appropriate to the time, is reflected in a contemporary production with Dan Kremer as Andrew Undershaft, Mark Murphey as Adolphus Cusins, and Sandy Kelly Hoffman as Lady Britomart in Shaw's Major Barbara (which is summarized in Chapter 4) in the Angus Bowmer Theatre of the Oregon Shakespeare Festival at Ashland (1991). Director, Jerry Turner; scenic designer, Richard L. Hay; costume designer, Jeannie Davidson; lighting designer, James Sale. Shaw's unique combination of realism and intellectual comedy is discussed in more detail in Chapter 17.

play whose style departs from strict realism requires that the actors understand the level of departure and adapt their portrayals accordingly (Fig. 9.7)

subtext The meaning that lies beneath the actual dialogue

Subtext Fifth, the actor must find the **subtext.** Art comprises surface and "essence." Although communicating the surface is, of course, important, communicating the essence is even more so. In a pictorial sense, the difference between surface and essence is equivalent to the difference between illustration and art. In the former, the picture looks accurate but is just a picture. In the latter, the picture looks accurate, conveys further meaning, and encourages a more complex experience. Subtext for an actor embraces the meaning that lies beneath the lines: unstated motivations, relationships, and ideas that may not be explicitly stated but are implied and are essential to the overall meaning (Fig. 9.8).

Integration Finally, the actor must find a *gestalt,* a totality, a whole: Everything pertinent to the role must ultimately be integrated into an organic whole with every other aspect of the production.

PREPARING MENTALLY

Creating a role also requires emotional and psychological *preparation* that allows actors to imagine themselves as characters, to project themselves into the environment and conditions of a play, and to respond to the guidance of the director.

Observation Through *observation* the actor seeks to understand the essences of behavior and movement appropriate to a role. Observation must be

Figure 9.8 *Actors reveal relationships, play style, and subtext in Tennessee Williams'* The Glass Menagerie *(1945). Ball State University Theatre. Director, Judy Yordon; scene designer, D. C. Shawger; costume designer, Kathy Jaremski; lighting designer, Lisa K. Murphy. For further comments on Williams, see Chapter 17. Williams himself explains his thoughts on the fate of tragedy in the modern theatre in an essay excerpt in Chapter 2. In this chapter, excerpts from the notebooks of Elia Kazan chronicle the efforts of one major director to come to grips with the characters in Williams' best-known play,* A Streetcar Named Desire.

sophisticated and thorough. Playing the role of an elderly individual, for example, depends not simply on aping stereotypical behavior and movements, but also in knowing what those movements and behaviors look like in a variety of individuals and, further, knowing *why* they occur. One can merely observe, for instance, they many elderly people have a shuffling gait. In reality, this behavior bears little resemblance to the bent-over, tight-kneed caricature that most young and inexperienced actors think portrays old age. The credible and accurate portrayal of such a role results only after careful observation of the movements of many elderly individuals and some understanding of the effect on movement caused by inflexible muscles, painful joints, and a fear of missing one's step because one cannot clearly see the ground.

Sensibility Creating a role, mentally, requires an actor to feel the emotions and reactions of a character. *Sensibility* or sensitivity to the human condition certainly is an important personal characteristic for an actor and an essential tool in preparing mentally. In some cases an actor can call upon personal memory in order to understand how a character might respond to circumstances. When an actor has experienced a similar condition, accurate recall of emotions provides a good basis for character response. Often, however, the role lies outside the actor's personal experience; even with careful observation, little clue may exist to how the character actually feels or expresses that feeling physically. To deal with such cases, actors need a keen ability to sense what it is like to be in someone else's condition.

Figure 9.9 Ellen Terry as Portia in *The Merchant of Venice*, 1875. *The dominant actress of the English stage for an entire generation, Terry (1847– 1928) was ultimately renowned for her flexibility in adapting her popular personality to the sensibilities of a wide variety of characters. Associated with the successful actor-manager Henry Irving from 1878 to 1902, she excelled not only in Shakespeare but also in comedy and sentimental drama. By the 1890s, George Bernard Shaw was pronouncing Terry the prime example of an actress capable of combining naturalistic technique and intellectual insight into the kind of performance demanded by the emerging "modern" theatre.*

[Courtesy of Lilly Library, Indiana University, Bloomington, Indiana]

MOVEMENT

In Chapter 8 we discussed the "blocking" that creates a visual picture to enhance meaning for the audience. We tend to think of pictures as primarily static, and some directors visualize the progress of a play as the *movement* from one "frozen moment" or picture to another. However, movement may be conceived by the director, its meaning and incorporation into the role is an important part of an actor's role creation.

For the most part, although the director may have some specific purpose for a movement that does not directly stem from what actors call their "motivation," movement corresponds to some basic character motivation. The type of movement involved can indicate to the audience a variety of meanings and can assist both the actor and director in creating the right appearance for the scene. As simple as it sounds, actor movements, like the concept of line in a designer's composition, are either curved or straight.

Straight movements—that is, movements in which an actor moves directly from one place to another—tend to indicate strong and simple motivations. Such directness is particularly useful in indicating important moments. It suggests a forceful motivation and intensity of purpose that gives the audience the message "pay attention to this." Strong movement demands audience attention. Thus, when this kind of direct motivation and strength of purpose and intent is called for, actors will choose straight-line movements.

Acting

When less compelling motivations need to be portrayed, *curved movements* are chosen. By using curved movements, actors can portray, for example, the fact that they are unsure of their relationships or have negative relationships with other characters. The path across the stage may be free of obstacles, but, in order to show an aversion to another character, an actor may cross in an arc so as to put as much distance as possible between himself and that character. The message to the audience has been suggested, if not made absolutely clear. Curved movements can also give the actor a greater sense of grace than do straight-line movements. When such a characteristic needs emphasis, curved rather than straight movements are a good choice. Finally, in a more practical sense, a curved movement gives the actor an opportunity to end the movement facing in any desired position. A straight movement often requires a turn at the end, thus creating a potentially awkward situation.

Straightness and curvedness are *qualities* of movement, and the quality of movement we perceive on stage yields a wealth of clues about the relationships portrayed. Actors who move directly toward one another, for example, reveal the attractive quality of the relationship. If the movement separates persons, then the opposite quality may be indicated. If ambivalence prevails, we may see actors making sideways or arcing movements around each other. Whatever the movement may be, we can rest assured that is has some purpose stemming from the goals and needs of the production and relates directly to choices made by the actor in developing the role (Fig. 9.10).

In a well-directed and well-acted performance, motivation can be a clear clue for the perceptive audience member. For example, emphasis results when an actor makes a long movement. Aggressive movements indicate strength; retreating movements reveal weakness. Choices involving degrees of strength and weakness can be reflected in *degrees* of curvature in a move: Because straight movements reveal strength, the deeper the curve of a movement, the greater the weakness—all of which *should* have direct bearing on character and meaning and should be part of the actor's conscious preparation for the role (Figure 9.11). Usually, the most effective transmission of meaning resembles an exclamation point coming at the end of the movement: Again, the stronger the ending, the greater the indication of strength and emphasis. In sum, all these considerations form the reservoir of available choices made by actors and directors in the process of developing the role and understanding the relationship of the role to the play as a whole. The desired result is the clearest meaning possible for the audience.

STAGE BUSINESS

To expand upon the comments made about stage business in Chapter 8, we need to focus on how business relates to meaning in the actor's portrayal and the development thereof. *Business* is any detailed activity done by the actors—lighting a cigarette, twirling a fan, taking a drink, and so on. Often employing some stage property, it includes but goes beyond movement.

The establishment and working out of business is another important part

Figure 9.10   *Movement and positioning indicate strength and relationship between characters in Henrik Ibsen's* Hedda Gabler *(1890). Hedda's upright posture gives her strength and solidity in conrast with the subordinate positioning and distancing shown in the diagonal lines created by the posture of her husband, George. Ball State University Theatre (1980). Director, Edward Strother; scenic designer, D. C. Shawger; costume designer, C. Shawger; lighting designer, E. Morrell. This play is among Ibsen's greatest, Hedda among the most coveted women's roles in the modern theatre. George Bernard Shaw has summed up Hedda's complex character as follows:*

> *Hedda Gabler has no ethical ideals at all, only romantic ones. She is a typical nineteenth-century figure, falling into the abyss between the ideals which do not impose on her and the realties she has not yet discovered. The result is that though she has imagination and an intense appetite for beauty, she has no conscience, no conviction: with plenty of cleverness, energy, and personal fascination, she remains mean, envious, insolent, cruel in protest against others' happiness, fiendish in her dislike of inartistic people and things, a bully in reaction from her own cowardice.*

The importance to Ibsen of the moral component of character is clear also in Arthur Miller's comments, in Chapter 2, on Ibsen's An Enemy of the People.

Figure 9.11   *Response and reaction coupled with physical action suggest meaning in the University of Arizona Theatre production of Rudolf Besier's* The Barretts of Wimpole Street. *Director, Peter R. Marroney; scenic and costume designer, Peggy Kellner; lighting designer, Jeffry L. Warburton.*

of role development, and it takes place during the rehearsal process. Some stage business is absolutely required by the script and must be included in the actor's understanding of the character. For example, a whole scene of dialogue is written in and around the sword fight between Tybalt and Mercutio in Shakespeare's *Romeo and Juliet*. Because staging the play without that scene would be virtually impossible, the business of a sword fight remains an integral part of the actors' action. Although how the sword fight is staged affords many options, the fight itself is obligatory. In pursuit of these actions, we have business for the actor. Later in *Romeo and Juliet,* when Romeo must fight Tybalt, *how* he comes by a sword is the *source* of business—a kind of business that may be described as *incidental.*

When stage business involves groups of actors or occurs for the purpose of establishing the production's style, actors must find ways to incorporate such external causes comfortably into their individual roles. For example, many plays have scenes involving eating and drinking. *How* the actors go about that business is worked out with other actors, but the *way* individual aspects of these activities occur must be consistent with the attitudes and other characteristics of the specific character. Stage business also allows the director to provide helpful foreshadowing that prepares the audience for later action when such preparation does not occur in the dialogue. Business also can add meaning to exposition. In all these cases business helps make the characterizations clear to an audience—to clarify motivation, to emphasize, and to enrich. Incorporating all business into expressions consistent with character forms an important part of role creation.

REHEARSALS

We discussed the rehearsal period in Chapter 8, but it also is relevant to an actor's creation of a role. The rehearsal period is a period of approximately four to six weeks during which the actor's role creation takes the final form leading up to its ultimate goal, the performance. The stages of rehearsal for the actor are exactly the same as they are for the director. The actor, of course, is less concerned than the director with the totality, although, as we have noted, such concern is crucial to proper role creation. The actor concentrates primarily on making his or her own character come alive within the parameters of the production and in relationship to the other actors.

The major thrust of the rehearsal period is the cementing of basic factors in role creation—for example, basic movements, actions, vocal patterns, and understandings, as well as such mundane matters as line memorization—so that the performance has a sense of completion and confidence. At the same time, the rehearsal period should not develop role creation to the point of mechanization. The actor's role must maintain a sense of spontaneity. Part of this is good acting technique: making a line that you have spoken a thousand times appear to the audience as if it just occurred to you. Part of it, however, is concentration and alertness so that little nuances that occur on a given evening both between audience and actor and between actor and actor can be

Figure 9.12 *Concentration and alertness portray nuances between audience and actor and actor and actor in order to give the production spark, freshness, and enhanced meaning, nightly, through the Bishop, General, Judge, and Chief of Police in Jean Genet's* The Balcony *(1956) at the Maryland Stage Company (1988). Director, Xerxes Mehta; set designer, William T. Brown; costume designer, Elena Zlotescu; lighting designer, Terry Cobb. Peopled by social outcasts (the inhabitants of the brothel) whose entire theatrical environment is a fantasy world,* The Balcony *is an often grotesque parable about power-seeking in which the idea of "domination" is never very far from its sexual connotations. The theatre of Genet (1910–1986) is an example of absurdist drama (see Chapter 17) that is often taken to aggressive extremes in its efforts to view the world by turning it inside-out: In a world in which one can no longer assume intrinsic order, a brothel may be an appropriate mirror on a world obsessed with power.*

drawn upon to give the performance a new spark and enhanced meaning (Fig. 9.12).

Because this part of role creation is a public event, the rehearsal period places significant demands on an actor. This does not mean that an audience is present, but it does mean that as the actor struggles with his role, he does so amid other people. At the end of an evening's rehearsal, the director and other actors make suggestions and offer criticism. Often, especially in the educational theatre, the greatest growth in the role during the rehearsal period occurs in the self-concept of the actor. Many acting teachers emphasize getting to know oneself as, in fact, the first and most important step in creating a role.

Throughout the rehearsal process, with all its struggles, frayed nerves, self-doubt, and self-growth, a sense of ensemble emerges among the actors. The creating of a role thus moves beyond an individual activity and becomes, like the rest of theatrical production, a collaborative effort. Arguably, the best theatre productions are those in which the actors work with and respond to each other—not as separate individuals pursuing a common goal but as individuals formed into a mysterious single organism. Each actor comes to understand his own strengths and weaknesses and how those can be used in conjunction with the strengths and weaknesses of the other actors in the interest of the production. A spirit of willingness to submit to the good of the production pervades, and the self-serving desire to be the center of attention recedes.

The Actor's Equipment

Finally, in our discussion of acting, we need to identify and analyze the tools actors use to bring their roles to life. Designers use paint, fabric, and light; directors use actors; all theatre artists use their minds and sensibilities. Actors, of course, use their minds and sensibilities, too, but they also use two additional pieces of equipment—their bodies and their voices. Like any artist, the actor must master his or her medium of expression in order to convey meaning to an audience. A sculptor must have the skill to put chisel to stone in order to communicate her vision. Even if you or I could envision a magnificent portrayal of the human figure as Michelangelo's *David,* which of us has developed enough skill to attack a block of marble and make the finished work appear? Actors need no less skill in handling their equipment in order to make their finished work appear. Mind, voice, and body are the chisels, hammers, paint, and fabric that actors use with consummate skill to form a mental image of character and transform it into something visible and audible. An actor whose mind, body, and voice will not do what needs to be done is like a speaker who cannot conceive the words, control the trembling of his knees and the cracking of his voice, or articulate his words so that he can be understood.

MIND

In order to understand who and what a certain character is, how that character thinks, and what the driving force of that character comprises, an actor needs a well-developed intellect and sensibility. Earlier we discussed the application of such mental characteristics to role creation. These characteristics form one part of the actor's equipment; they can be enhanced by study and observation, but they also are innate and intuitive.

BODY

In the case of the body, actors, of course, can come in any shape and size. As we saw in Chapter 8, some body types seem better suited for some roles than others because of the natural stereotypes audiences apply to physical structure and stature. As we will see in Chapter 12, some physical features may be overcome or changed by the costume designer or makeup artist so as to transform the natural body and facial type of the actor to meet the require-

Jessica Tandy: Star of Stage and Screen

Jessica Tandy (*b.* 1909), one of America's greatest living actresses, made her Broadway debut in 1930 in *The Matriarch.* Among her later roles were Ophelia to John Gielgud's *Hamlet* (1934) in her native England and Blanche DuBois in the Broadway production of *A Streetcar Named Desire* (1947), in which Marlon Brando also played the brutish Stanley Kowalski. Tandy's performance as the tormented Blanche made her a star.

In 1942, she married actor Hume Cronyn and became an American citizen in 1954. The couple has performed together in seven Broadway productions: *The Fourpost-er* (1951); *The Physicists* (1964); *A Delicate Balance* (1966); *Noel Coward in Two Keys* (1974); *The Gin Game* (1977); *Foxfire* (1982), and *The Petition* (1986). For her portrayal of an elderly widow who communicates with her dead husband in *Foxfire,* Tandy earned a Tony Award. "Everything about the character," one critic noted, "is played with crystalline expressiveness and excitingly precise detail."

Tandy and Cronyn have appeared regularly in American regional theaters, most notably at the Tyrone Guthrie. There she has played a wide variety of roles, including Linda, the wife in Arthur Miller's *Death of a Salesman,* and Gertrude in *Hamlet.* In 1990, Tandy won an Oscar as best actress for her role as a flinty Southern Jewish widow in the movie *Driving Miss Daisy.*

---

ments of the role. Regardless of the appropriateness or inappropriateness of an actor's natural appearance, the fundamental fact about the actor's body is that it must remain under absolute control at all times.

Because the actor's body is part of the instrument that he or she plays, that body must be as carefully conditioned and fully responsive as the fingers of a pianist. Every movement must have purpose and meaning. The pianist who can conceive the proper volume, phrasing, and emotions of a piece but cannot execute them physically on the keyboard is ineffective as an artist. The actor who cannot make his or her body perform with the subtlety, expression, power, or dexterity required by a role likewise fails. As we shall see, having such complex mechanism under absolute control requires conditioning and training.

As we have said, the theatre is a place for seeing, a physical place, and the eyes of the audience focus first on the actor's physical presence, which imparts so much meaning to what is also heard. In Figure 9.13 actor Brian Vaughn portrays John Merrick, the "Elephant Man," with nothing more than suggestive movements of his own undeformed body. Through the body, actors illustrate the essential meaning of the role. When, accompanied by different sets of

Figure 9.13 *Bernard Pomerance, The Elephant Man. Southern Utah University. Director, Roger Bean. Actor Brian Vaughn portrays John Merrick, the "Elephant Man." In this production no attempt is made to realistically show the deformities of elephantiasis, with anything other than the actor's suggestive movements of his own undeformed body.*

gesture Hand and arm movements

facial expression Use of facial muscles and features to convey meaning

physical behavior, for example, speech can have completely different sets of meaning. The actor learns to employ the body and its various parts to impart precise meaning through, essentially, four modes of expression: *gesture*, *facial expression*, *posture*, and *body tone*. **Gesture** includes primarily hand and arm movements. For example, calling upon gestures that suggest openness or self-protection, the actor may illustrate the mind of the character behind the lines of the text, as we noted earlier in our discussion of *subtext*. **Facial expression**—that is, the use of facial muscles and features—makes every part of the face from forehead to chin a communicator of meaning (Fig. 9.14). As we know

Figure 9.14 *Thornton Wilder, Our Town (1938). Oregon Shakespeare Festival, 1991. Director, James Edmondson; scenic designer, William Bloodgood; costume designer, Claudia Everett; lighting designer, Robert Peterson. Photo by Christopher Briscoe. Dawn Lisell-Frank as Emily Webb exclaims, "Oh, earth, you're too wonderful for anybody to realize you." The joy and excitement of the line are carried to the audience not only by the actor's voice, but also through her body language and facial expression.*

posture The manner in which the body is carried by the actor.

body tone The energy conveyed by the body and its movements

from daily life, the expression on the face of those with whom we communicate has much to do with the meaning we receive in their conversation. **Posture,** the manner in which the entire body is carried, conveys a clear picture of character. A rigid, militaristic posture conveys quite a different picture of character than the bent posture of old age or the slouching posture of the reprobate. Likewise, **body tone,** the energy conveyed by the body and its movements, conveys important messages. High-energy people cause different reactions in us than do low-energy people. Body tone gives the actor one more choice in making the role come alive.

The hundreds of variations on these four themes give the actor an arsenal from which to choose the exact tool appropriate to a specific role. When, through physical conditioning and practice, the actor's body is capable of using these tools effectively as parts of the portrait executed precisely night after night, he or she can visually transmit meaning to the audience (Fig. 9.15).

VOICE

However well trained and finely tuned the body may be, an actor with an inadequate voice still falls short of the ability to create a credible role. His or her native equipment may preordain an actor to certain types of roles. Al-

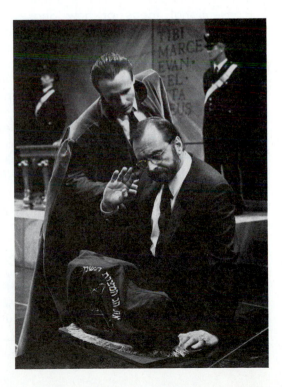

Figure 9.15 *William Shakespeare.* The Merchant of Venice. *Oregon Shakespeare Festival, Ashland (1991). Director, Libby Appel; scenic designer, William Bloodgood; costume designer, Deborah M. Dryden; lighting designer, Robert Peterson. All of the actors' attention is focused and bodies are physically controlled as Shylock (Richard Elmore, seated) confers with his attorney (Dennis Rees). In the background, Benjamin Livingston and Philip Hubbard focus their attention and do not "hear" the conversation because of the conventions of the theatre that allow "private" conversation that the audience can hear but other characters on stage cannot. A synopsis of* The Merchant of Venice *can be found in Chapter 4; the production concept here, of course, is very much different from the one reflected in Fig. 4.5A.*

Profile

Laurence Olivier a.k.a. Sir Larry

Nearly universally regarded as the century's greatest English-speaking actor, Sir Laurence Olivier (1907–1989) began his stage career playing Katharina in a school production of *The Taming of the Shrew*. A natural talent, Olivier excelled in an exceptionally wide range of roles: comedy, classical as well as contemporary drama, action/adventure, romantic hero. His daring and quick intelligence as an actor was noted when he alternated with John Gielgud (along with Ralph Richardson, Olivier's other great contemporary) the parts of Romeo and Mercutio in *Romeo and Juliet*. Directed by Gielgud, this production (1935), largely due to performances in which Olivier emphasized virility and physical agility rather than perfect verse-speaking, upset conventional ideas of how Shakespeare should be performed. Fresh from this triumph, Olivier joined the famous Old Vic Company in 1937. In a display of the stamina that became a professional trademark, in his first season he played various Shakespearean leads: Hamlet, Macbeth, and Henry IV, and in his second he took on the roles of Iago and Coriolanus.

In 1939, Olivier entered a new phase, appearing as the romantic hero in such films as *Wuthering Heights* and *Lady Hamilton*. With these performances, he became an international film star and subsequently alternated between films and the stage.

In 1944–1945, Olivier returned to the Old Vic, where he and Richardson divided leading roles. There, Olivier's performances as Richard II, Oedipus, and Astrov in Chekhov's *Uncle Vanya* were widely regarded as acting of the highest order. In the postwar years, Olivier, increasingly disenchanted with a theatre that he considered outdated, turned to films, partly as an escape. His revolutionary version of *Hamlet* (1948), which he directed and starred in, brought him fresh acclaim. Here for the first time was a flesh-and-blood prince mass movie audiences could relate to: bold, athletic, and, in the age of Freud, a son with possibly incestuous desires for his mother.

While Olivier's attention was focused on films, a new generation of British dramatists had barely begun to surface. In 1957, Olivier allied himself with them by appearing as the down-and-out comic Archie Rice in John Osborne's *The Entertainer*. Appointed to the directorship of the new National Theatre in 1962, Olivier battled against building delays, cancer and other illnesses, and a government that doled out money frugally. Despite his physical limitations Olivier continued to challenge himself, giving his characteristically risky and courageous performances as, among other classic figures, Othello (1964) and James Tyrone in Eugene O'Neill's *Long Day's Journey into Night* (1971). In 1970, he became the first actor to receive a lifetime peerage. After being replaced as director of the National Theatre, Olivier appeared until his death in films and on television.

In 1960, Olivier shared his thoughts about acting with an interviewer: "An actor gets the right thing by doing it over and over. Arguing about motivations and so forth is a lot of rot."

Figure 9.16 *Sarah Bernhardt in Victorien Sardou's Cleopatra, 1890. Her unconventional personality (she slept in a coffin) made Bernhardt (1844–1923) the best known theatrical figure of her age, but it was her voice more than any other single attribute that characterized Bernhardt's performances. "In your throat, you possess a natural harp," she wrote in her 1923 treatise on acting,* The Art of the Theatre, *in which she devotes considerable attention to voice training and arguments for voice as the key to dramatic character.*

though training can effect some change in the basic voice, very little can be done to change the fundamental *pitch range* and *tonal quality* of the voice with which we were born. Making that basic voice work in the theatre, however, requires extensive training and understanding. Making artistic choices in creating a role means manipulating five qualities of vocal expression: *pitch, rate, timbre, inflection,* and *force.*

pitch The measurable frequency of sound

Pitch is the measurable frequency of sound. In the human voice, we describe pitch as the "highness" or "lowness" of the voice. In general, women have higher voices than men; that is, the normal pitch range of the female voice is higher than that of the male voice. Each of us comes equipped with a voice whose basic pitch we can do little about. A voice whose basic pitch is in the tenor range, for example, will likely never be able to sound like a deep, booming bass. More important to an actor, however, is the *variety* of pitch that he or she can develop within that natural range. With practice and care, every voice can be expanded several notes above and below the natural range; and when variety of pitch is employed, the voice takes on an expressive quality that is essential to quality performance.

inflection A change of pitch on a single syllable

Variety in pitch usage also applies to a characteristic called **inflection**— the change of pitch that occurs on a single syllable. The most subtle shades of meaning come from the use of inflection. Consider the word "no." It can carry certain emphasis and potential meaning when said on a single pitch, and that meaning or emphasis can shift slightly if the pitch is high, medium, or low. However, when the word "no" is said beginning on a high pitch and sliding to a low pitch, meaning shifts again. If the pitch reverses with a slide from low to high, an entirely different meaning results.

rate The speed at which speech is uttered

Rate is the speed at which speech is uttered. Here again, the key to success is variety. An actor who maintains a constant and unvaried rate runs the risk of losing audience attention in the same sense as an actor who speaks in monotone. Rate provides a tool for actors to create emphasis as well. Listen to effective speakers—they tend to slow their rate when they wish to communicate the most important parts of their speeches; they speed up through less important material. Good actors work the same way. Consider the various effects of changing rate in Macbeth's soliloquy:

Is this a dagger which I see before me,
The handle toward my hand? Come let me clutch thee.
I have thee not, and yet I see thee still.
Art thou not, fatal vision, sensible
To feeling as to sight? Or art thou but
A dagger of the mind, a false creation,
Proceeding from the heat-oppressed brain?
I see thee yet, in form as palpable
As this which now I draw.
Thou marshall'st me the way that I was going,
And such an instrument I was to use.
Mine eyes are made the fools o'th'other senses,
Or else worth all the rest. I see thee still;
And on thy blade and dudgeon gouts of blood,
Which was not so before. There's no such thing.
It is the bloody business which informs
Thus to mine eyes. Now o'er the one half-world
Nature seems dead, and wicked dreams abuse
The curtained sleep; witchcraft celebrates
Pale Hecate's offerings; and withered murder,
Alarumed by his sentinel the wolf,
Whose howl's his watch, thus with his stealthy pace
With Tarquin's ravishing strides, towards his design
Moves like a ghost. Thou sure and firm-set earth,
Hear not my steps, which way they walk, for fear
Thy very stones prate of my whereabout,
And take the present horror from the time,
Which now suits with it. Whilst I threat, he lives.
Words to the heat of deeds too cold breath gives.
    [*A bell rings within*]
I go, and it is done. The bell invites me.
Hear it not Duncan, for it is a knell
That summons thee to heaven, or to hell.
    Macbeth II.1

timbre The tonal color or identifying characteristics of a single voice

Timbre is also called tonal color. Each of our voices has a unique color. We are able to tell who is speaking to us because of timbre. When a friend calls us on the phone, we know who is talking because we "recognize the voice": What we really recognize is the individual timbre of that person's voice. It may be described as full, rich, bright, breathy, and so on, and we have certain predispositions and expectations attached to certain vocal timbres. Certain full timbres we might call "cultured"; certain breathy types might be thought of as "sexy." Changing the natural timbre of the voice thus gives the actor a means by which to describe character. The hoarse quality of Marlon Brando's voice in *The Godfather,* for example, did as much to establish that character as did virtually any other tool in the vast array of his acting arsenal.

force The intensity of sound, regardless of its volume

The last vocal characteristic that we need to examine, **force**, sometimes is confused with "volume." Although *volume,* or *loudness* and *softness,* can be a peripheral result of force, force encompasses much more. Force can be best explained as *intensity.* When produced with great intensity or force, a vocal tone might be either loud or soft. In fact, soft volume produced with great force often is more demanding and expressive than loud volume produced with the same degree of force. During the first night of the 1991 Persian Gulf War, for example, a team of CNN newsmen broadcast from a Baghdad hotel. As trained newspeople, they tried to keep their voices at a volume level compatible with their sound equipment; at the same time, they had to speak softly because of the fear of discovery by Iraqi authorities. Nonetheless, their adrenalin was so high that the effective force of their delivery conveyed the fear and excitement to us—thousands of miles away and over phone lines—despite the low volume of their delivery. Thus, when an actor puts vocal tools such as these to work with a highly trained voice, meaning can be vividly communicated to the audience.

Some Readings *for* Classroom Exercise

Use the following readings to analyze style and meaning and to coordinate body and voice in order to project that meaning. Try various approaches to gesture, facial expression, pitch, rate, intensity, and so on to effect changes in your presentation—and try to determine how these changes affect the meaning of the piece.

*Sophocles, Oedipus the King: Exodos**

OEDIPUS: Do not counsel me any more. This punishment
That I have laid upon myself is just.
If I had eyes,
I do not know how I could bear the sight
Of my father, when I came to the house of Death,
Or my mother: for I have sinned against them both
So vilely that I could not make my peace

*Translated by Dudley Fitts and Robert Fitzgerald in *Tragedy: Ten Major Plays* by Robert O'Brien and Bernard Dukore, eds. Copyright © 1968. Published by Harcourt Brace Jovanovich, Inc.

By strangling my own life.
>   Or do you think my children,
Born as they were born, would be sweet to my eyes?
Ah never, never! Nor this town with its high walls
Nor the holy images of the gods.
>   For I,
Thrice miserable!—Oedipus, noblest of all the line
Of Kadmos, have condemned myself to enjoy
These things no more, by my own malediction
Expelling that man whom the gods declared
To be a defilement in the house of Laios.
After exposing the rankness of my own guilt,
How could I look men frankly in the eyes?
Nor, I swear it,
If I could have stifled my hearing at its source,
I would have done it and made all this body
A tight cell of misery, blank to light and sound:
So I should have been safe in my dark mind
Beyond external evil.
>   Ah Kithairon!
Why did you shelter me? When I was cast upon you,
Why did I not die? Then I should never
Have shown the world my execrable birth.

Ah Polybus! Corinth, city that I believed
The ancient seat of my ancestors: how fair
I seemed, your child! And all the while this evil
Was cancerous within me!
>   For I am sick
In my own being, sick in my origin.

O three roads, dark ravine, woodland and way
Where three roads met; you, drinking my father's blood,
My own blood, spilled by my own hand: can you remember
The unspeakable things I did there, and the things
I went on from there to do?
>   O marriage, marriage!
The act that engendered me, and again the act
Performed by the son in the same bed—
>   Ah, the net
Of incest, mingling fathers, brothers, sons,
With brides, wives, mothers: the last evil
That can be known by men: no tongue can say
How evil!
>   No, For the love of God, conceal me
Somewhere far from Thebes; or kill me; or hurl me
Into the sea, away from men's eyes for ever.

Come, lead me. You need not fear to touch me.
Of all mean, I alone can bear this guilt.

Christopher Marlowe, Doctor Faustus, Act V, scene 2

FAUSTUS: Ah Faustus,
Now has thou but one bare hour to live,
And then thou must be damned perpetually.
Stand still, you ever-moving spheres of heaven,
That time may cease and midnight never come.
Fair nature's eye, rise, rise again, and make
Perpetual day; or let this hour be but
A year, a month, a week, a natural day,
That Faustus may repent and save his soul.
O *lente, lente currite noctis equi!**
The stars move still; time runs; the clock will strike;
The devil will come, and Faustus must be damned.
O, I'll leap up to my God! Who pulls me down?
See, see, where Christ's blood streams in the firmament!
One drop would save my soul, half a drop! Ah, my Christ!
Rend not my heart for naming of my Christ!
Yet will I call on him. O, spare me Lucifer!
Where is it now? 'Tis gone. And see where God
Stretcheth out his arm and bends his ireful brows.
Mountains and hills, come, come, and fall on me,
And hide me from the heavy wrath of God.
No, no!
Then will I headlong run into the earth.
Earth, gape! O no, it will not harbor me!
You stars that reigned at my nativity,
Whose influence hath allotted death and hell.
Now draw up Faustus like a foggy mist
Into the entrails of yon laboring cloud,
That when you vomit forth into the air,
My limbs may issue from your smoky mouths
So that my soul may but ascend to heaven.

(*Thunder, and enter the Devils.*)
   My God, my God, look not so fierce on me!
Adders and serpents, let me breathe a while!
Ugly hell, gape not! Come not, Lucifer!
I'll burn my books! Ah, Mephistophilis!

* O slowly, slowly; run you horses of night.

Tennessee Williams, The Glass Menagerie, Scene 7**

(*Tom's closing speech is timed with the interior pantomime. The interior scene is played as though viewed through soundproof glass. Amanda appears to be making a comforting speech to Laura, who is huddled upon the sofa. Now that*

**From THE GLASS MENAGERIE by Tennessee Williams. Copyright 1945 by Tennessee Williams and Edwina D. Williams; renewed 1973 by Tennessee Williams. Reprinted by permission of Random House, Inc.

we cannot hear the mother's speech, her silliness is gone and she has dignity and tragic beauty. Laura's dark hair hides her face until at the end of the speech she lifts it to smile at her mother. Amanda's gestures are slow and graceful, almost dancelike, as she comforts the daughter. At the end of her speech she glances a moment at the father's picture—then withdraws through the portieres. At the close of Tom's speech, Laura blows out the candles, ending the play.)

TOM: I didn't go to the moon, I went much further—for time is the longest distance between two places—Not long after that I was fired for writing a poem on the lid of a shoebox. I left Saint Louis. I descended the steps of this fire escape for a last time and followed, from then on, in my father's footsteps, attempting to find in motion what was lost in space—I traveled around a great deal. The cities swept about me like dead leaves, leaves that were brightly colored but torn away from the branches. I would have stopped, but I was pursued by something. It always came upon me unawares, taking me altogether by surprise. perhaps it was a familiar bit of music. Perhaps it was only a piece of transparent glass—Perhaps I am walking along a street at night, in some strange city, before I have found companions. I pass the lighted window of a shop where perfume is sold. The window is filled with pieces of colored glass, tiny transparent bottles in delicate colors, like bits of a shattered rainbow. Then all at once my sister touches my shoulder. I turn around and look into her eyes . . . Oh, Laura, Laura, I tried to leave you behind me, but I am more faithful than I intended to be! I reach for a cigarette, I cross the street, I run into the movies or a bar, I buy a drink, I speak to the nearest stranger—anything that can blow your candles out! (*Laura bends over the candles.*)—for nowadays the world is lit by lightning! Blow out your candles, Laura—and so good-bye. . . .

SUMMARY

- The essence of theatre is the live actor performing before a live audience.

- Stage acting is an extension of human life, in which we "act out" various characters and relationships. Stage acting, however, goes beyond the acting that occurs in life, and involves the actor as an *interpreter* of the director's concept, the playwright's vision, and the actor's own understanding.

- The actor also functions as a reflector of the *style* of the production.

- Across history, a number of approaches to acting have developed. Among these are:

  Acting based on mechanical principles, such as the approach of François Delsarte

  Acting based on psychological principles, such as grew out of the new styles of *realism* and *naturalism,* particularly in the work of André Antoine and the Théâtre Libre

The *Stanislavski Method*

Holistic and *interaction* approaches

• Although there are many approaches to acting, when actors *create a role,* a fairly straightforward process emerges. The process of *creating a role* includes:

Analyzing a role and determining its *facts,* the *spine* of the character, *relationships,* the *style* of the production, the *subtext* of meaning, and *integration* of the role with all other aspects of the production

Preparing mentally through *observation* and *sensibility*—sensitivity to the human condition

Movement—using straight and curved movements to convey attitudes and relationships

Stage business—the detailed activity done by the actors

Rehearsals—the period of time during which the actor's role creation takes its final form leading up to its ultimate goal, the performance

• Like any artist, the actor must master his or her medium of expression in order to convey meaning to an audience. In so doing, actors make use of their "equipment"—that is:

mind, their abilities to analyze and use their sensibilities

body, which consists of:

gesture, primarily hand and arm movements

facial expression, the use of facial muscles and features

posture, the manner in which the body is carried

body tone, the energy conveyed by the body and its movements

Voice—including the characteristics of:

pitch, the measured frequency and natural range of the individual voice

inflection, changes of pitch on a single syllable

rate, the speed at which speech is uttered

timbre, the natural "tonal color" of the voice

force, the intensity of sound, regardless of its volume

Acting

Chapter 10

Scene Design

After studying this chapter
you should be able to:

- Describe the traditions of *scenic design* as they have occurred in theatre history.

- Discuss the *designer's role* in theatrical production.

- Identify and explain the designer's artistic tools.

- Describe a scene designer's employment and responsibilities.

- Explain the *scene design process*.

- Comment on the art of *scene painting* and its history in the theatre.

Jo Meilziner, (R) at Studio Alliance workshop where sets for Annie Get Your Gun *were built. Ann Roesener/Pix Inc.*

*F*our horses pulling two chariots raced side by side in front of a revolving panorama. The horses ran on two treadmills that were adjustable so that either chariot could move ahead of the other as the race progressed. That spectacle represented part of the scene design for the stage play *Ben Hur* as it was produced in the early years of the twentieth century. Often our enjoyment of a play rests on the visual environment that the scene designer provides for us. Contemporary musicals like *Les Misérables* and *Phantom of the Opera* may be more about scenic design than plot or character. Whatever kind of play we see, and whatever importance the production places on scenery, *every* production has some kind of visual environment; the creation of that visual environment is the task of the scene designer. In this chapter we will examine some scenic design traditions in the theatre, the role of the designer, the designer's employment and responsibilities, the designer's artistic tools, the design process, and the art of scene painting. All this discussion has at its heart the men and women who are scene design artists and the variety of choices that they must make in order to bring the visual scene alive on stage for the audience. As one veteran designer has put it, "actors are the primary element, the given quantity, but designers are the craftsmen embedded in the workings of stage creation." Design, suggests Howard Bay, is a "visual progression of a dramatic event." Simply put, **scene design** is the art of creating the proper visual environment for a play. Design involves not only scenery, but also considerations of overall form—that is, the total actor–audience physical relationship.

The insert on "The Art of Scene and Lighting Design" offers several full-color illustrations displaying the end product of the scene designer's work.

scene design The art of creating the proper visual environment for a play

Scene Design Traditions *in the* Theatre

A scenic environment occurs wherever theatre takes place. Sometimes scenic artists design "scenery" specifically for a single production; sometimes, however, theatre artists choose an existing location as a scenic environment. Arguably, any physical surrounding for a production is a scenic design because someone made an artistic choice in its selection. In the long history of the theatre, the scenic environment emerged as a result of many differing philosophies and approaches. In ancient Greece all productions took place in front of a simple architectural façade that remained constant regardless of whether a play was a comedy or a tragedy (Fig. 10.1); the same was true of the Elizabethan theatre of Shakespeare's time (see the drawings of the Swan theatre in Figs. 5.4A and 5.4B). During the Middle Ages scenery was both more complex and more realistic, although it still remained constant from play to play (Figs. 10.2A and 10.2B). Scenery designed for individual types of productions took the form of elaborate technical displays and the adaptation of architectural principles during the Italian Renaissance (Figs. 10.3A and 10.3B) before reach-

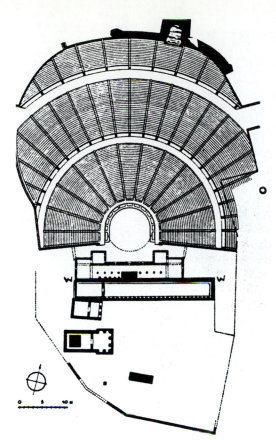

Figure 10.1 *Plan of the classical Greek Theatre. The classical (or Athenian) theatre (ca. 450–350* B.C.*) allowed for the performance of all types of performances (see the model of the Theatre of Dionysos at Athens, ca. 400* B.C.*, in Fig. 5.2A). From about 350 to 320* B.C.*, the Hellenistic theatre lent itself to more realistic staging, as Greek drama grew away from its roots in ritual. The development of the Greek theatre facility is discussed in more detail in Chapter 15.*

[From Oscar G. Brockett, *History of the Theatre*, 6th ed. Copyright © 1991 by Allyn and Bacon, Inc. Reprinted with permission.]

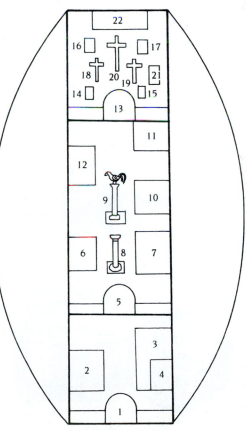

1. First door
2. Hell
3. Garden of Gethsemane
4. Mount Olivet
5. Second door
6. Herod
7. Pilate
8. Pillar of scourging
9. Pillar for cock
10. Caiaphas
11. Annas
12. Last Supper
13. Third Door
14. 15. 16. 17. Graves
18. 19. Thieves crosses
20. Cross
21. Holy Sepulchre
22. Heaven

Figure 10.2A *Plan of a medieval* mansion stage, *showing the series of* mansions—stations used as backgrounds for individual scenes or episodes—in the Donaueschingen Mystery Play, Germany. See Chapter 15 for more information on the configuration of the mansion stage throughout Europe, particularly the increasing attention paid to the station designed to represent the spectacular horrors of Hell.*

[From Dennis J. Sporre and Robert C. Borroughs, *Scene Design in the Theatre* © 1990, p. 11. Prentice Hall, Englewood Cliffs, New Jersey.]

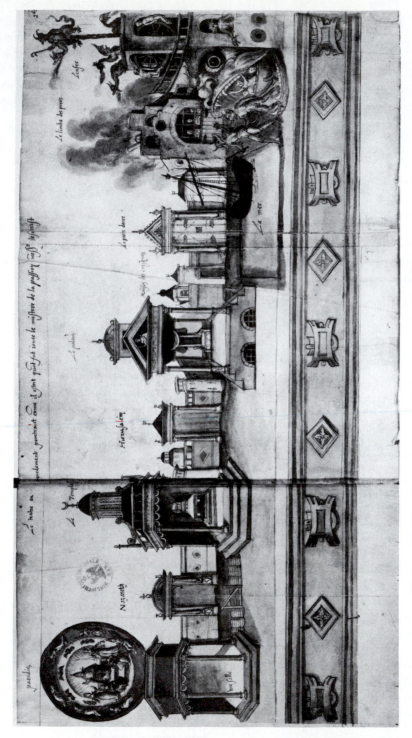

Figure 10.2B *The configuration of the mansions for the Valenciennes Mystery Play, France. Miniature by Hubert Cailleau, 1547. Featured stage left is an enormous dragon's head spitting real fire, as befits the representation of Hell. Ships, lakes, and castles separate Hell from Heaven, stage right. An excerpt from the oldest known French mystery play,* The Representation of Adam, *can be found in Chapter 15.*

[From Dennis J. Sporre and Robert C. Burroughs, *Scene Design in the Theatre,* © 1990, p. 12. Prentice Hall, Englewood Cliffs, New Jersey.]

Figure 10.3A   *Baldessare Peruzzi, stage design, probably for* La Calendria, *1514. Usually performed at court, Italian drama of this era featured elaborate trappings and echoed the painterly principles characteristic of the High Renaissance.*

[Scola/Art Resource]

Figure 10.3B   *"Tragic" setting, Sebastiano Serlio, 1545. The first few feet of the stage on which Serlio worked were flat, with the rest of the floor receding at a gentle rake. Typical until the Victorian age, this arrangement probably gave rise to the terms* upstage *and* downstage. *Serlio's conception of the model comic setting can be found at Fig. 6.13.*

[Molinari, *Theatre Through the Ages,* p 128, by permission of F. Arborio Mella, Studio dell'illustrazlone, Milano.]

ing even more lavish heights during the seventeenth through nineteenth centuries (Figs. 10.4A–10.4C). In many cases, however, scenery was not typically "designed" for each specific production, and often the "scene designer" remained anonymous. Nonetheless, records of design artists and scene painters exist from earliest times, and the names of great designers—for example, the names of Sebastian Serlio (Fig. 10.3B) and the Bibienas (Fig. 10.4B) are often more prominent than those of the playwrights and actors of the period. Yet, only since the nineteenth century have individual settings designed specifically for single theatre productions become commonplace (Figs. 10.5A and 10.5B).

Figure 10.4A *Giacomo Torelli, stage set for Pierre Corneille's* Andromède. *Engraving by F. Cheveau, 1650. Torelli (1608–1678) developed his craft in Italy, where audience enjoyment of elaborate scene changes required ingenious technical solutions. Ingenuity was important to the staging of plays like those of Corneille, who tried to satisfy his own audience's desire that Aristotelian unity of action be complemented by "less perfect" actions that helped build "suspense."*

[The Metropolitan Museum of Art, Elisha Whittelsey Fund, 1951. (51.501.5779).]

Figure 10.4B *Giuseppe Galli da Bibiena, design for an opera, 1719. Contemporary engraving. The influence of the Bibiena family, who began work in Italy, spread throughout Europe in the eighteenth century. By dispensing with the single vantage point characteristic of designers like Serlio (see Fig. 10.3B), they made use of vanishing points at either side of the stage, breaking down rigid symmetrical designs through the application of principles based on multiple perspective.*

[The Metropolitan Museum of Art, Elisha Whittelsey Fund, 1951.]

THE "CORSICAN BROTHERS." ACT II. THE MASKED BALL.

Figure 10.4C Drawing of a production of Dion Boucicault's The Corsican Brothers, 1852. With the demand for greater spectacle by the middle of the nineteenth century, scene designers became more important to successful stage production. In mounting popular plays by writers like Boucicault, Victor Hugo, and others, actor-managers like Charles Kean, Mme. Vestris, and Henry Irving called upon designers as John Philip Kemble and Tom Robertson to develop innovations that included gaslight, the simultaneous set, and stage traps.

[Courtesy of the Lilly Library, Indiana University, Bloomington, Indiana.]

Figure 10.5A Erwin Piscator's production of Ernst Toller's Hurrah, We Live!, 1927. A practitioner of expressionist drama (see Chapter 17), Toller (1893–1939) appealed immediately to the audience's visual sense rather than its intellect by employing symbolic images to project—express—abstract ideas and psychic development. Here as elsewhere, Piscator (1893–1966) used large cartoon-like drawings, projections, treadmills, and abstract scenic architecture to capture Toller's largely comic sense of internal human dramas acted out before the audience's eyes.

Scene Design

Sebastiano Serlio: The Renaissance Perspective

Influenced by the Roman architect and engineer Vitruvius Pollio, the Italian architect and painter Sebastiano Serlio (1475–1554) expressed the fundamentals of Renaissance thinking about scenery and stage space in his book De Architecttura *(1545). Serlio's work was the first of the period to discuss the art of designing for the theatre, and his treatise on the relationship between design and such theatre modes as the Tragic, Comic, and Satyric became influential throughout Europe. Assuming theatres to include a special orchestra area designed for various dignitaries, Serlio described scenic perspective according to a stage placed at eye level from the seats of "lords, dukes, grand princes, and particularly kings."*

The Tragic scene is for the representation of tragedies (see Fig. 10.3B). In this setting the houses must be those of great persons, because amorous adventures, sudden accidents, and violent and cruel deaths such as we read of in ancient and modern tragedies alike have always taken place in the houses of lords, dukes, grand princes, and particularly kings. Therefore, as I have said, you must introduce here none but stately houses such as those indicated in the following figure [Fig. 10.3B]; you must note, however, that, because of the limitations of space, I have not been able to sketch those grand edifices of kings and lords that I could show in more ample space. The architect concerned with these things needs no more than a suggestion of the general method, which he may adapt according to the setting and subject called for. As I have said in the section on the comic scene, the builder must take care to arrange the parts of his setting in such a way as to give the best impression to the spectators, placing, for instance, a small building in front of a higher one.

I have made all my scenes on flat frames. Since these sometimes fail to appear convincing, it is necessary to avail oneself of wooden relief—as in the building on the left side of the stage, the pillars of which rest on a base with several steps. In this case the base must be made of low relief raised above the floor, and upon it are set two frames, one facing the audience, the other in perspective. They extend upwards only to the top of the parapet which runs above the first arches. Now because the second arches are set back so as to make room for this parapet, the two upper frames also must be set back so as to produce the effect desired. What I say of this building applies also to others which have certain parts set back—especially to the houses near the front of the stage. If the house is set very far to the back, however, one frame will be sufficient, so long as all its parts are skillfully designed and painted. . . .

> *The houses must be those of great persons, because amorous adventures . . . and violent and cruel deaths . . . in ancient and modern tragedies alike always take place in the houses of lords, dukes, grand princes, and particularly kings.*

All the superstructures on the roofs, such as chimneys, belfries, and the like, although they are not indicated on the illustration, are to be made of thin board and cut in profile and drawn and colored with skill.

Similarly, statues supposed to be of marble or bronze will be made of thick cardboard or even thin wood, cut to size, and shadowed. They are to be so placed in the distance that the spectators cannot see them from the side.

Some artists are in the habit of painting supposedly living characters in these scenes—such as a woman on a balcony or in a doorway, even a few animals. I do not recommend this practice, however, because although the figures represent living creatures they show no movement. On the other hand, it is quite appropriate to represent some person who sleeps, or some dog or other animal that sleeps, because no movement is expected here. I can recommend painting on the back shutter statues or similar objects supposedly of marble or of other material, as well as scenes of history and legend. Concerning the representation of living things having motion I shall speak at the end of this book; there I will tell how this is to be accomplished.

From *De Architecttura* (1545). *The Renaissance Stage,* edited by Bernard Hewitt, translated by A. Nicoll, J. H. McDowell, and G. R. Kernodle. Coral Gables: University of Miami Press, 1958, pp. 29–32. Reprinted by permission of the University of Miami Press.

Figure 10.5B   *Josef Svoboda, set design for a production of Sophocles'* Oedipus the King, Prague National Theatre, *1963. An innovator in the use of design technology, Svoboda (b. 1920) created a broad single-flight, semitransparent staircase rising from the bottom of the orchestra pit and up through the proscenium to the grid. The musicians were underneath the staircase, in which perforations allowed the music to be heard. The staircase itself suggested an infinite incline as a concrete representation of Oedipus's great struggle with his fate, with both lighting and music suggesting the mysterious but often beautiful forces at work in his universe. (See the synopsis of* Oedipus the King *in Chapter 3.)*

Whether scenery was conventional and simple like that of the Greeks or the Elizabethans, or representational and elaborate like the designs of the eighteenth and nineteenth centuries, audiences have been fascinated by the visual and technical displays created by the artists and craftsmen responsible for "designing" scenic backgrounds and elements. Even in ancient Greece, audiences were captivated by a wide variety of machinery that complemented the simple architectural backgrounds of the scenic environment by flying gods and revealing tableaux. All these scenic devices existed to make the play more effective in presentation and audiences more appreciative. Those who designed these scenic trappings may not have been scene designers as we know them today, but their artistry and creativity served an important function in theatre production.

THE SCENE DESIGNER'S ROLE

In the contemporary theatre scene designers function as creative partners (see Chapter 7) in determining the direction and "look" of a theatre production. Their basic role is to design an environment appropriate for a specific production. In order to create a proper environment for a play, the designer must be able to analyze the writing, including the author's intent and purpose, discover suggestions and descriptions in the script, understand the director's approach, and coordinate all this with the work of the various other technical departments—scene construction, costumes, and lighting. The designer must have a knowledge of mechanical drawing, freehand and mechanical perspective, and painting.

Designers use the playwright's eyes and insights as the basis for their vision. Ultimately, however, the design must have something of its own to say to the audience. An understanding of a given play, coupled with training and creativity, should give the designer something important to say. Beyond that, the designer's message depends on his or her ability to put thoughts into a *form* that adequately reflects them. Designers must first of all be able to make *visual images* from creative insights. The workings of the designer's translation from insight to image can be seen clearly in the process described in "The Diary of a Production" at the beginning of this book. From the designer's description of ideas and creative and practical choices, we gain a clear picture of a fairly typical process leading to the creation of a scenic design.

THE DESIGNER'S ARTISTIC TOOLS

However else we may view stage design, it is first and foremost a visual art. Although stage design serves the theatre and conforms to the aims and necessities of theatre art, we cannot escape the fact that its roots and guiding principles are those that underride the visual arts—that is, the two-dimensional arts of painting, drawing, printmaking, and photography and the three-dimensional arts of sculpture and architecture.

E. Gordon Craig: The Design of a New Drama

Edward Gordon Craig (1872–1966) was an English director and stage designer whose visionary designs and theories have had a lasting influence on modern theatre. Influenced himself by the symbolists (see Chapter 16), he directed and designed at the turn of the century a number of highly praised productions, including several operas as well as Henrik Ibsen's *The Vikings* (1903), before going to Germany. There, he designed productions for the legendary actress Eleonora Duse, influenced the director Max Reinhardt (see Chapter 17), and began his personal and artistic relationship with the American experimental dancer and choreographer Isadora Duncan.

In "The Art of the Theatre" (1905), his first and most famous essay, Craig argued that the theatre must become, like music or poetry, an art form in which neither the play, actor, scene, nor dance predominates: All must be unified through the efforts of the director. He also suggested the establishment of an English National Theatre. From 1908 to 1929, Craig disseminated his views through *The Mask,* a theatre journal that he founded and largely wrote pseudonymously (see Fig. 17.6). In its pages, he attacked conventional acting and realism (the task of theatre is "not to *produce* nature, but to *suggest* some of her most beautiful and living ways") and advocated instead an abstract and ritual theatre.

The new drama, according to Craig, was to be based on light and rhythmic movement. For example, he envisioned a flexible stage on which an infinite variety of architectural shapes could be created. In one variation on this idea, Craig invented movable screens to substitute for scenery. These were first used by the poet-playwright William Butler Yeats at Dublin's famed Abbey Theatre in 1911, and a year later by Craig himself in the celebrated *Hamlet* which he directed for Stanislavski's Moscow Art Theatre. After this production, Craig directed only one other play, Ibsen's *The Pretenders* (1928) in Copenhagen, and completed only a single set of designs, for a 1928 production of *Macbeth* in New York. Thus, it was mainly through his writings that Craig achieved his considerable impact on the practice of modern stage production.

The fundamental artistic tools of the scene designer are those of the visual artist—in essence, elements and principles of composition. They are bodies of knowledge and training that organize a visual design so that it "speaks" what the artist intends in a language that the audience can comprehend. Using elements and principles—for example, color and focus—designers create mood, establish historical period, control our vision, and ultimately establish meaning in the mind of the audience. These principles and elements are present in every visual picture—they are how we perceive objects and create meaning from them. As a result, they are the elements and principles that the designer must manipulate in order to allow us to see what he or she wishes us to see relative to the production.

THE DESIGNER'S EMPLOYMENT AND RESPONSIBILITIES

Working as a scenic designer requires a variety of preparations. Whereas the commercial theatre tends to rely on breadth of hands-on experience, the educational theatre, for example, tends to emphasize academic training and degrees. However, most of the active designers on Broadway possess advanced university or college degrees. As we suggested in Chapter 7, much of theatre production, especially commercial theatre production, is accomplished within guidelines established by various unions: All the various artistic professionals discussed in this section of the book—producers, directors, actors, and designers—have governing unions and professional organizations that develop and maintain guidelines for working in the theatre. The paragraphs that follow describe in general some of these conditions as they relate to designers. Similar organizations exist for other theatre artists, even though we do not discuss them here.

Most theatre artists consider the Broadway theatre to be their ultimate professional goal. In order to work in the Broadway theatre, the scenic designer must be a member of the designer's union, the United Scenic Artists of America (USA), local #829, which is affiliated with the Brotherhood of Painters, Decorators, and Paperhangers of the United States and Canada, AFL-CIO. Its members are scenic, lighting, and costume designers; diorama and display designers; television and motion picture art directors; mural artists; costume stylists; and theatre, motion picture, and television artists. Membership is restricted by complicated and costly examinations and limited employment opportunities. The union sets minimum wage scales and fees, worker responsibilities, and working conditions for its members. Besides New York, the USA maintains offices in Chicago and Los Angeles, and members frequently transfer membership from one local to another depending on residence. Local #829 works with the League of New York Theatres and Producers, Inc., to set minimum pay scales, including fee rates for additional settings for single productions, for single-unit settings for multiscene plays, and for bare-stage productions. As with any contract, there can be additional benefits such as weekly royalties, incidental expenses incurred in designing, and other related expenditures.

The specific services required of the scene designer are carefully described by the union. They include:

1. Providing a complete working model of the settings or complete sketches and working drawings for construction
2. Creating color schemes and color sketches for painting contractors

3. Designing and/or selecting and approving properties, draperies, and furniture
4. Designing and/or supervising special scenic effects (including projections)
5. Supplying specifications for construction
6. Supervising the building and painting of settings and properties
7. Providing estimates available for discussion sessions
8. Attending the beginning pre-Broadway setup, the Broadway setup, all dress rehearsals, the first public performance, out-of-town openings, the first New York public performance, and any scenic rehearsals as needed.

The International Alliance of Theatrical Stage Employees (IATSE) represents stage carpenters, stagehands, electricians, property personnel, audiovisual personnel, light board operators, follow-spot operators, sound technicians, pin-rail personnel, rigging personnel, loaders, and unloaders. The IATSE, like the USA, is affiliated with the AFL-CIO.

The number of workers for each job assignment depends on the type and size of the production and the landlord's agreement with the local union office. The union is responsible for setting a minimum wage scale and the fees for each of the specific categories, as well as for the workers' responsibilities in each category. The union also will specify safety measures and conditions involved in work areas. For example, the minimum call for a show is three or four hours at a set minimum fee—that is, the minimum that the worker is to be paid hourly. The union requires lunch and dinner breaks; and any work after midnight, no matter what the starting time, requires time-and-a-half payment.

Applications for membership require the unanimous vote of the active members. An examination in each area of expertise must be passed before an applicant is accepted as an apprentice member—that is, a learning, beginning member working at the lowest pay level. After an established length of time, a journeyman's membership (full membership and benefits) can be awarded.

New York designers must be prepared to accept the fact that they are temporary employees who are hired for one job at a time and who will need to supplement their incomes with additional income, perhaps from outside the profession. Faced with the costs of setting up a single business office/studio, a number of professional artists have recently begun partnership arrangements similar to those of law and architectural firms.

New designers with little or no professional background can begin or reinforce careers by working as assistants to established designers. Most Broadway designers have supplemented their early training in this fashion. It is always good for the beginner to view first hand how professional designers handle the actual business of designing and, specifically, how established artists approach their work creatively. These positions are usually secured by recommendations from other designers and/or by individual interviews reinforced by a strong portfolio and references.

Designers' assistants may be required to draft, work on models, and do research for particular projects. Other assignments may include securing samples of materials, searching for set props, and checking progress at scene shops. An assistant's weekly payments and length of service on a New York theatrical production can be negotiated with the management of the designer's design contract; all details must meet USA approval before any work begins.

The Design Process

Just as directors and actors develop their artistry through processes and procedures, designers develop their creative products through a progression of analyses, sketches, models, and renderings. A designer's analysis of a script parallels that of an actor or director. After analysis and preliminary meetings with the director and other designers, the scene designer begins to draw and paint. First come *thumbnail sketches,* which are followed by *presentation sketches, color renderings,* and *models.* The designer is also responsible for creating a series of drawings called *ground plans, sightline drawings, front elevations,* and *paint details.*

Thumbnail Sketches   The thumbnail sketch represents a shorthand method by which the designer commits his or her first visual ideas to paper. **Thumbnail sketches** are rough, rapidly drawn, basic conceptions, concerned more with feelings than with details. They also are *progressive*; that is, they provide a means to work quickly through an emerging set of ideas toward a finished product.

thumbnail sketches
Rough, rapidly drawn, basic conceptions concerned more with feelings than details

One technique of developing thumbnail sketches involves dividing a page of sketchbook paper into a series of small rectangles whose proportions represent, roughly, the proscenium opening (see Chapter 6) (or the frame of visual reference for the audience, if production format entails some other form or environment) (Fig. 10.6). After dividing the page, the designer begins in the upper left rectangle with some simple concepts of line and form. He then moves to the next box and refines these. Next the designer adds more detail or reworks the sketch entirely. He may, for example, wish to develop alternative approaches to the scenic needs of the play so that they can be compared side by side. Normally, the original sheet of paper will be filled quickly, and many pages and sketches are exhausted as ideas become clearer and more refined. Ultimately, the designer will reach a point at which he feels comfortable that the last sketch fairly represents his ideas about the dynamics, mood, basic forms, unity, and production needs of the design (Fig. 10.7). When he reaches the point at which the thumbnail sketches have served their purpose, he is ready to move on to a more finished sketch that can be shown to the director and other designers.

Presentation Sketches   The designer must remember always that what is shown in public is a reflection of her professionalism, skill, and overall competence as a designer. Everything presented to the director should be as complete,

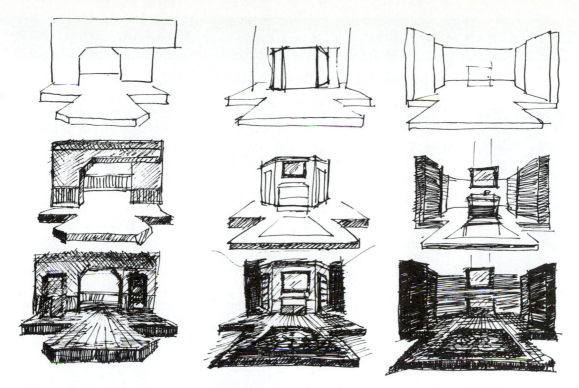

Figure 10.6 *Format for the thumbnail sketch.*

[Dennis J. Sporre and Robert C. Burroughs, *Scene Design in the Theatre*, © 1990, p. 125. Prentice Hall, Englewood Cliffs, New Jersey.]

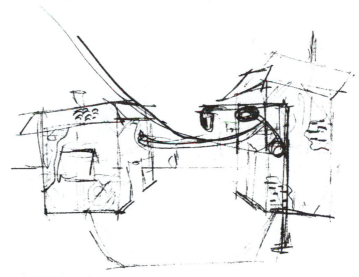

Figure 10.7 *Thumbnail sketch,* The Liar *by Carlo Goldoni, Hilberry Repertory Theatre. Designer, Tom Macie.*

[Dennis J. Sporre and Robert C. Burroughs, *Scene Design in the Theatre*, © 1990, p. 126. Prentice Hall, Englewood Cliffs, New Jersey.]

Jo Mielziner: The Poetic Realist

Jo Mielziner (1901–1976) was the leading American lighting and set designer of his era. His first professional work in the theatre was as an actor and designer. He then worked at the New York Theatre Guild beginning in 1924, and over the next fifty years, he designed sets— and often the lighting—for more than 400 Broadway productions, including nearly every major American drama and musical after 1930.

At the beginning of his career, Mielziner showed his complete mastery of then fashionable detailed realism in sets for Elmer Rice's *Street Scene* (1929) and *For Thee I Sing* (1931). Later, however, he abandoned realism, as well as the voguish expressionism of other popular designers, for more suggestive, stripped-down, evocatively lit settings. Employing scrims and a painterly style, Mielziner visually reflected the poetic realism of plays like Tennessee Williams' *A Streetcar Named Desire* (1947) and Arthur Miller's *Death of a Salesman* (1949) (Fig. 10.8). In these legendary sets, the scrims (together with fragmented scenes) permitted a cinema-like change of scene through the manipulation of light rather than through a conventional shifting of scenery.

Collaborating with Edward K. Kook,

Mielziner also designed many improvements in stage lighting instruments. In addition, he worked as a theatre designer and consultant on many theatres, including Lincoln Center's Vivian Beaumont Theatre. Among Mielziner's most famous sets are those for such Broadway successes as *Pal Joey* (1940), *The Glass Menagerie* (Williams, 1945), *Annie Get Your Gun* (1946), *Mister Roberts* (1948), *South Pacific* (1949), *Guys and Dolls* (1950), *The King and I* (1951), *Cat on a Hot Tin Roof* (Williams, 1955), and *Gypsy* (1959).

Figure 10.8 *Jo Mielziner, sketch for the opening set of Arthur Miller's* Death of a Salesman, *directed by Elia Kazan, New York, 1949. One of the modern theatre's most celebrated simultaneous settings, Mielziner's conception expresses a strong poetic component in its rendering of a common man's common dwelling as a construct of skeletal scenic forms perceived through a liberal use of scrim and gauze. (See the synopsis of* Death of a Salesman *in Chapter 3 and the discussion of Arthur Miller in Chapter 17.)*

clear, and professionally rendered as possible. The designer is not only an artist but a salesperson of ideas. Presentation sketches are the initial opportunity for the designer to make her way in the production. Well-executed sketches can

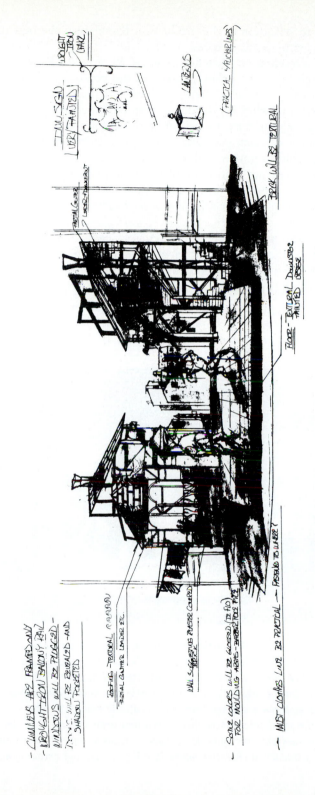

Figure 10.9 *Presentation sketch, The Liar by Carlo Goldoni, Hilberry Repertory Theatre. Designer, Tom Macie.*

[Dennis J. Sporre and Robert C. Burroughs, *Scene Design in the Theatre*, © 1990, p. 127. Prentice Hall, Englewood Cliffs, New Jersey.]

281

help to sell ideas to the production team. Even the best design ideas can be crippled by poor sketches.

Presentation sketches (Fig. 10.9) are black-and-white sketches large enough in scale to show clearly all the necessary details of the design. They must carry sufficient clarity of detail for the director and other designers to understand what is intended and to make accurate decisions about their acceptability. Because discussions about color and texture will take place at this stage, the designer may also wish to supplement the presentation sketches with some color samples and fabric swatches, for example. Verbal discussions about color are highly imprecise: One person's impression of "institutional green" may not be someone else's impression of the same term, and discovering that fact after spending a dozen or so hours on the color rendering can be a frustrating experience.

Although presentation sketches need not take a great deal of time to prepare, they must be sufficiently complete for everyone to be confident that the next step—color renderings—will meet the director's expectations.

Color Renderings The **color rendering** is, perhaps, the most familiar part of the process of scene designing. It is, however, only one step in the entire design process. It is important in showing what the finished setting will look like under *production conditions* (Fig. 10.10). The color rendering is usually

presentation sketches Black-and-white sketches large enough in scale to show clearly all the necessary details of the design

color rendering A colored, perspective drawing showing what the setting will look like under production conditions

Figure 10.10 *Production photograph,* The Liar *by Carlo Goldoni, Hilberry Repertory Theatre. Designer, Tom Macie. Note both the costume and scenic design in this production of a late commedia dell'arte (see Chapter 16). In writing for the traditional commedia, Goldoni (1707–1793) was nevertheless influenced by the movement in the eighteenth-century European theatre to reflect the interaction of human nature and the social order. In addition to insisting upon the use of written instead of improvised scripts, Goldoni thus strove for a modest "realism" by telling contemporary stories, eliminating traditional character masks (see Fig. 16.1), and encouraging less stylized settings.*

the device from which the director can see what the completed set will convey in terms of mood, color, and atmosphere. The color rendering is used not only by the director but also by the costume and lighting designers for the visual information that will aid them in their work—specifically, to be sure that their use of color and style, for example, do not conflict with the scene designer's.

As we have noted, the designer usually draws a very simple thumbnail sketch followed by a presentation sketch early in the design process. These sketches are useful in consolidating ideas and in preliminary discussions. In certain stock companies, however, as well as in some educational theatres and in television designing, a simple pencil sketch may be substituted for an elaborate color rendering. Such practices are acceptable only when time does not permit the execution of a color rendering. Some designers can execute a workable design in as little as two hours; others will require as long as thirty hours, depending on the particular style of rendering. Because the length of time devoted to the execution of a drawing generally has very little bearing on its excellence as a stage design, the student of design learns to work as rapidly as possible, using as many acceptable shortcuts as possible, all the while keeping in mind the fact that the completed rendering must have a professional quality.

models
Three-dimensional replicas of the stage setting

Models   Some directors prefer **models** to sketches because they believe they can visualize the finished setting more easily from a scaled, three-dimensional replica. At the same time, compared to a water-color rendering, accurately detailed models involve three or four times the amount of work to execute.

However, because a model gives both the designer and the director a definite picture of such areas, models are very useful for settings requiring many platforms and levels (Fig. 10.11). Sometimes, designers believe they can

Figure 10.11   *Scenic model. Edmond by David Mamet, University of North Carolina at Wilmington. Designer, Tom Macie.*

Scene Design

express the design better in a model than in a two-dimensional rendering, but either format is generally acceptable to a producer or director. Models can be made in almost any scale, but ½ inch = 1 foot is preferred.

ground plan (or floor plan) A scaled drawing showing the dimensions and placement of the setting as seen from above

Ground Plans   The **ground plan** (or **floor plan**) shows the dimensions and placement of the setting as seen from above. It is a scaled, mechanical drawing (Fig. 10.12) and must be executed carefully to show the position of all walls or units, all backings, dimensional thickness, hangings, ground rows, platforms, steps, ramps, and furniture. The plan must also show the relationship of the set to certain physical aspects of the stage, such as the proscenium opening, the apron, and the back wall. This plan, of course, cannot be carried out if the setting is designed with no particular stage in mind or if the production intends to tour.

sightline drawings Scaled drawings showing the horizontal or vertical plan of the theatre and projecting imaginary lines from the furthest seats right or left to the back of the setting

Sightline Drawings   The plan also includes **sightline drawings,** which must take into consideration any problems that may be involved with sightlines (see Chapter 6). Horizontal sightlines can be checked easily by using a horizontal plan of the theatre and projecting imaginary lines from the furthest seats right or left to the back of the setting (Fig. 10.13A). Vertical sightlines are checked by using a vertical-section drawing of the theatre and stage (Fig. 10.13B).

front elevation A scaled drawing designed to show the actual details of the audience side of scenic units

Front Elevations   The **front elevation** of a setting is designed to show the actual details of the *audience side* of scenic units (Fig. 10.14). It is executed in scale, usually ½″ = 1′, and shows the position and design of such units as doors, windows, fireplaces, moldings, and other details. These drawings establish exact dimensions of all of the units of the scene design and allow the technical director to determine precisely how to build each unit (see Chapter 11).

paint details Scaled drawings designed specifically for scene painters and presenting the units as they will be painted

Paint Details   **Paint details** are designed specifically for scene painters or paint crews. Unlike water-color sketches, they present flats or units as they will be painted—without the benefit of stage lighting or the illusion of distance. The paint detail is like the front elevation except that it is colored and frequently includes color formulas for mixing paint. The objective of the paint detail is to provide an accurate color guide for painting the scenery itself. When the paint detail is finished, the entire board is covered with cellophane to protect it from being soiled in the paint shop.

SCENE PAINTING

scene painting The art of theatrical painting by which two-dimensional surfaces are transformed into representations—for example, of wood, brick, foliage, and so on

One of the most fascinating aspects of scene design is the art of **scene painting.** Through this art, two-dimensional surfaces are transformed into representations of everything from wood and brick to foliage. The scene designer must have a thorough knowledge of scene painting in order to *execute* the design accurately. In fact, most professional designers are excellent scenic artists because of their training and apprentice work in the field; and, barring union regulations, practically all designers, professional or otherwise, function as scene painters on their own sets. Professional scene painters can be scarce, if

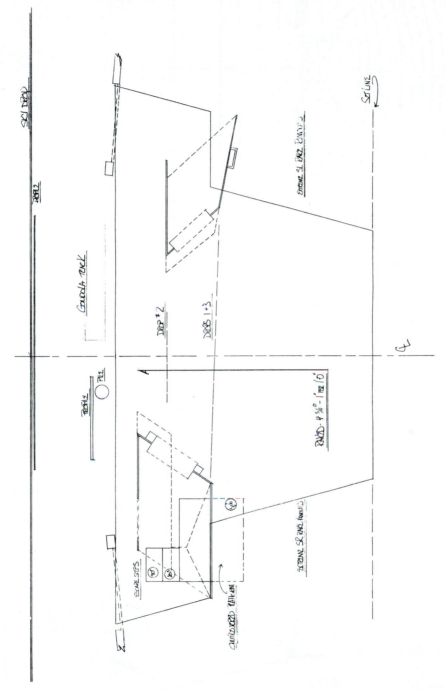

Figure 10.12 *Ground plan, The Liar by Carlo Goldoni, Hilberry Repertory Theatre. Designer, Tom Macie.*

[Dennis J. Sporre and Robert C. Burroughs, *Scene Design in the Theatre,* © 1990, p. 136. Prentice Hall, Englewood Cliffs, New Jersey.]

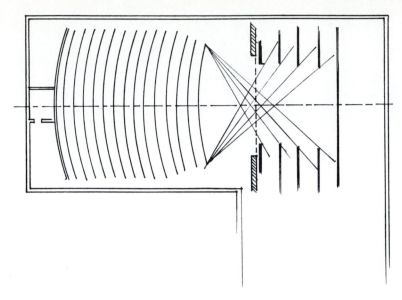

Figure 10.13A *Sightline drawing from horizontal plan.*

[Dennis J. Sporre and Robert C. Burroughs, *Scene Design in the Theatre,* © 1990, p. 136. Prentice Hall, Englewood Cliffs, New Jersey.]

not prohibitively expensive, and a good designer needs to be careful about trusting inexperienced personnel to produce desired effects. Even in the educational theatre, where the development of student talent is important, the designer must carefully supervise the execution of painting in order to ensure accuracy and quality.

Part of the problem arises from the fact that scene painting requires skill in a number of specialized techniques not found in other painting forms. For example, because details must carry to the audience, most stage designs are larger than life in color, line, and mass. When compared to those used in other forms of graphic art, the techniques and scale of scene painting can be described as broad. Anyone who wishes to become a proficient scene painter

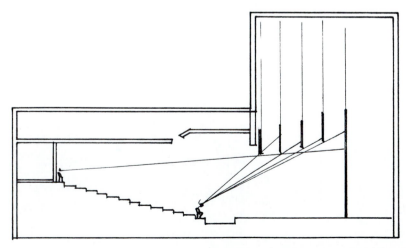

Figure 10.13B *Sightline drawing from vertical plan.*

[Dennis J. Sporre and Robert C. Burroughs, *Scene Design in the Theatre,* © 1990, p. 137. Prentice Hall, Englewood Cliffs, New Jersey.]

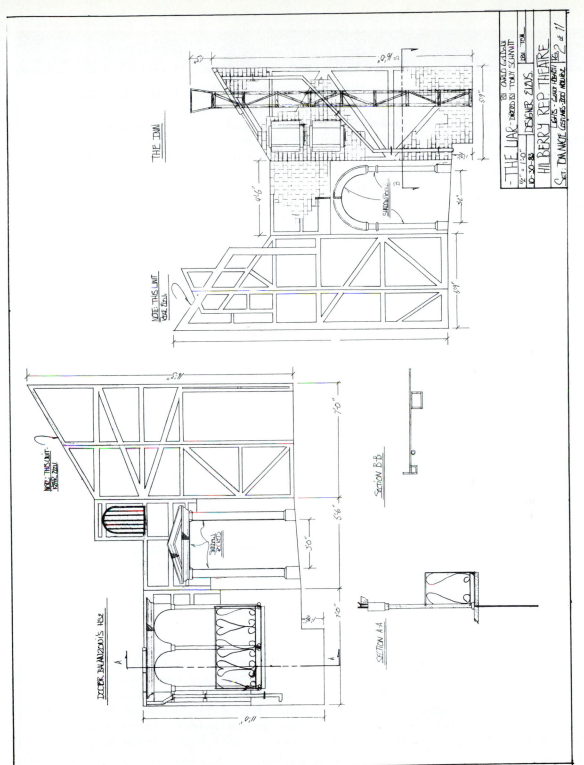

Figure 10.14 Front elevation drawings. *The Liar by Carlo Goldoni, Hilberry Repertory Theatre. Designer, Tom Macie.*

[Dennis J. Sporre and Robert C. Burroughs, *Scene Design in the Theatre,* © 1990, p. 138. Prentice Hall, Englewood Cliffs, New Jersey.]

Bertolt Brecht: Scene Design as "Individual Handwriting"

The work of the German playwright and drama theorist Bertolt Brecht (1898–1956) is discussed more fully in Chapter 17. Here he expresses some of his ideas on the nature of set design as required by the "epic theatre" and applauds the contribution of the designer Caspar Neher, who created the settings for most of Brecht's productions prior to 1933 (see Fig. 10.15). For Brecht, the scene designer's art, like that of the playwright, was not the art of "reproducing" a factual reality but, rather, that of capturing the social history of concrete objects and the people who lived with and through them. The designer's collaboration with the playwright is successful when his objects allow the characters to embody the historical, economic, and emotional conditions that the playwright has taken as his subject matter.

His sets are significant statements about reality. He takes a bold sweep, never letting inessential detail or decoration distract from the statement, which is an artistic and an intellectual one. At the same time everything has beauty, and the essential detail is most lovingly carried out.

. . . And it all helps the playing. One chair will have short legs, and the height of the accompanying table will also be calculated, so that whoever eats at it has to take up a quite specific attitude, and the conversation of these people as they bend more than usual when eating takes on a particular character, which makes the episode clearer. . . .

[The] small objects which he puts in the actors' hands—weapons, instruments, purses, cutlery, etc.—are always authentic and will pass the closest inspection; but when it comes to architecture—i.e. when he builds interiors or exteriors—he is content to give indications, poetic and artistic representations. . . . There is no building of his, no yard or workshop or garden, that does not also bear the fingerprints, as it were, of the people who built it or who lived there. He makes visible the manual skills and knowledge of the builders and the ways of living of the inhabitants.

[Stage designs should] arouse the spectator's imagination, which perfect reproduction would numb.

In his designs our friend always starts with "the people themselves" and "what is happening to or through them." He provides no "décor," frames and backgrounds, but constructs the space for "people" to experience something in. Almost all that the stage designer's art consists in he can do standing on his head. . . . He is a great painter. But above all he is an ingenious story-teller. He knows better than anyone that whatever does not further the narrative harms it. Accordingly he is always content to give indications wherever something "plays no part." At the same time these indications are stimulating. They arouse the spectator's imagination, which perfect reproduction would numb.

He often makes use of a device which has since become an international commonplace and is generally divorced from its sense. That is the division of the stage, an arrangement by which a room, a yard, or a place of work is built up to half height down-

should realize that this skill will require a good deal of practice and experimentation before success can be expected.

A Short History of Scene Painting   The art of scene painting reached rather astonishing heights during the nineteenth century, when theatre artists

Figure 10.15   *Bertolt Brecht, The Threepenny Opera. Empire Theatre, New York, 1933. The set design, by Cleon Throckmorton, closely followed that of Caspar Neher for the Berlin premier in 1928. Note, for example, the exposed lights and scenery and the various printed mottoes. For Brecht, each of the elements of the production— music and choreography as well as decor—were to augment the "text" of the play rather than simply "repeat" it. Ideally, like the individual scenes of which the whole play was constructed, the objects and other background material supplied by the designer should communicate something of significance even if removed from the production as a whole.*

began competing with two-dimensional landscape artists. For example, much use was made of painted perspective to give a three-dimensional effect to standard wing and drop settings (Fig. 10.16). Because stage lighting was lim-

Figure 10.16 *Clarkson Stanfield, design for* Henry V, Battle of Agincourt, *early nineteenth century. Although almost the whole of* Henry V *is set during a time of war, very little of the fighting actually takes place onstage—certainly not the climactic Battle of Agincourt, which is depicted here as a product of the nineteenth-century imagination. The play is presented by a Chorus which declaims about battlefield valor and national glory but also "apologizes" for the theatrical shortcomings built into Shakespeare's script:*

> . . . *But pardon, gentles all,*
> *The flat unraised spirits, that hath dared,*
> *On this unworthy scaffold, to bring forth*
> *So great an object. Can this cockpit hold*
> *The vasty fields of France? or may we cram*
> *Within this wooden O the very casques*
> *That did affright the air at Agincourt?*

The author's apology, however, is at least partly ironic: Although Shakespeare was well aware of the limitations of Elizabethan stagecraft, he was also advising his audience that through characterization and language, he intended his appeal to their imagination to be anything but "flat" and "unraised."

[Victoria and Albert Museum, Art Resource]

ited to general illumination until after the turn of the century, the scenic artist was relied upon to paint shadows and highlights on two-dimensional, flat

Scene Design

surfaces. Conversely, contemporary designers must take into consideration effects achieved by highly developed stage-lighting techniques. Despite the increasing importance of three-dimensional scenery, there remains a need to make frequent use of the illusionary elements of perspective to trick the vision of the audience.

For a long time, scene painting was a rather mysterious art that remained a highly specialized field. Because the craft was closely guarded by a relatively small number of skilled artisans, early books on stagecraft and design gave very little information on the various techniques and materials of scene painting. Practically no information on the use of analine dyes for drop painting appeared in textbooks until the 1960s, even though such dyes had been used to great effect in England and Europe for a number of years. Today, most professional productions, including television and motion pictures, employ the services of a scenic studio equipped with all the necessary tools, materials, and space necessary to reproduce a variety of designs.

Not unlike typing or the technical part of playing the piano, scene painting is essentially a developed skill. Scene painting requires an understanding of the characteristics of scenic paint materials, the paints to be used, the application, and the reproduction of the color elevations. As with any skill, devoting a reasonable amount of time to the actual practice is essential.

SUMMARY

• Often enjoyment of a play rests on the *visual environment* that the scene designer provides for us.

• *Scene design* is the art of creating the proper *environment* for a play and involves not only scenery, but considerations of overall form—that is, the total *actor–audience physical relationship*.

• A *scenic environment* occurs wherever theatre takes place: Any physical surrounding for a production is a scenic design because someone made an artistic choice in its selection.

• In the contemporary theatre, scene designers function as creative partners in determining the direction and "look" of a theatre production.

• The designer must be able to:

    Analyze the writing, including the author's intent and purpose;

    Discover suggestions and descriptions in the script;

    Understand the director's approach;

    Coordinate with the various other technical departments.

- Ultimately, the scene design must have something of its own to say to the audience.

- Stage design is first and foremost a visual art, and the fundamental artistic tools of the scene designer are those of the visual artist: the *elements and principles of composition,* such as color and focus.

- In order to work in the Broadway theatre, the scenic designer must be a member of the designer's union, whose membership is restricted by complicated and costly examinations and limited employment opportunities.

- Specific services required of the scene designer are:

  Providing a complete *working model* of the settings or complete *sketches* and *working drawings* for construction;

  Creating *color schemes* and *color sketches* for painting contractors;

  Designing and/or selecting and approving *properties, draperies,* and *furniture.*

  Designing and/or supervising *special scenic effects;*

  Supplying specifications for construction;

  Supervising the building and painting of settings and properties;

  Providing estimates available for discussion sessions;

  Attending various rehearsals, setups, and opening performances.

- Just as directors and actors develop their artistry through processes and procedures, designers develop their creative products through a progression of analyses, sketches, models, and renderings, including:

  Thumbnail sketches;

  Presentation sketches;

  Color renderings;

  Models.

- Other drawings for which the designer is responsible include:

  Ground plans;

  Sightline drawings;

  Front elevations;

  Paint details.

• One of the most fascinating aspects of scene design is the art of *scene painting*, by which two-dimensional surfaces are transformed into a variety of representations.

Technical Production

*A*fter studying this chapter,
you should be able to:

- Describe the characteristics of *stage scenery*.
- Discuss the role of *working drawings* in the building of stage scenery.
- Identify and describe various types of *stage scenic units*.
- Characterize how *properties and furniture* assist in creating an artistic scenic effect.
- Explain how *sculptured effects and textures* are achieved and how they contribute to an artistic design.
- Describe the qualities that must be present in a *scene shop*.
- Identify and explain tools and materials and their contribution to technical production.
- Discuss the three basic concepts on which all *scene shifting* is based.

Phantom of the Opera. *Photograph: Bob Marshak.*

ecall the scene that we described at the beginning of Chapter 10: two chariots pulled by four horses racing on treadmills in front of a revolving scenic background. Imagine yourself as a director or a designer for whom that scenic effect formed a vital part of your concept for the production. Now consider your reactions if the person responsible for building the scenery informs you that this important effect cannot be constructed. All the creative imagination of the director and scenic designer comes to naught without equally creative expertise in those artists and craftspersons responsible for a play's technical production—that is, the translation of the scenic designs into actual settings. The work of the technical director is illustrated in several of the production shots in the color insert entitled "The Art of Scene and Lighting Design."

technical production
The craft of turning the *scene design* into reality

Technical production, then, is the craft of turning the scene design into reality. Fundamental to every scenic design is a thorough appreciation of the practicalities involved in executing the design. It does little good to design a stage setting that cannot be built or to victimize the actors because the wrong materials were chosen. If one cannot translate into space, time, budget, personnel, tools, and details the design envisioned and sold to the director, then the

Technical schematic showing the elaborate planning and apparatus necessary to stage "The Robber Chief's Banquet" in The Miracle, *London, 1911. Drawing by J. Duncan.*
[Victoria and Albert Museum, London]

design is virtually worthless, no matter how good it looks in the rendering or model. This chapter examines the principles, materials, and standard techniques for translating the scenic design from rendering to actual stage scenery. First we will discuss in detail stage scenery itself: its characteristics, the working drawings used for construction, types of scenic units, properties and furniture, and sculptured effects and textures. Second, we will examine the scene shop in which scenery is prepared, including a general description of the tools and materials used for making stage scenery. Finally, we will describe the methods available to the technician for shifting scenery when a play calls for more than one setting.

Although some of the material in this chapter may seem technical and isolated from the art of theatre we have focused on thus far in the book, it nevertheless forms an important piece of our ability to understand the complex choices, relationships, and processes that make theatre production satisfying for us. The excitement we experience from visual spectacle cannot occur without the minute details of technical production. The aesthetic goals of a production cannot be met without knowledge of arcane materials and processes. Thus, our understanding of the art of theatre must take us—at least partially—into some of its hidden qualities.

Stage Scenery

CHARACTERISTICS

In general stage scenery has nine characteristics

1. Scenery is constructed to be used for a comparatively short time.
2. Scenery must be planned for rapid construction.
3. Scenery is often planned for possible alteration and reuse.
4. Scenery is usually built in one place and used in another.
5. Scenery is constructed in easily portable units and assembled onstage by temporary joining.
6. Scenery is generally finished on one side only.
7. Scenery must be light in weight and capable of compact storage.
8. Scenery must be strong enough for safe use and handling.
9. Scenery must be constructed as inexpensively as possible and still comply with the foregoing requirements.

Working Drawings Stage scenery cannot be built without a plan to follow. Thus, the first task of the technician is to transform the elevational drawings of the scene designer (see Chapter 10) into a *back view* showing how each unit will be constructed, including lumber, hardware, and covering material (Fig. 11.2).

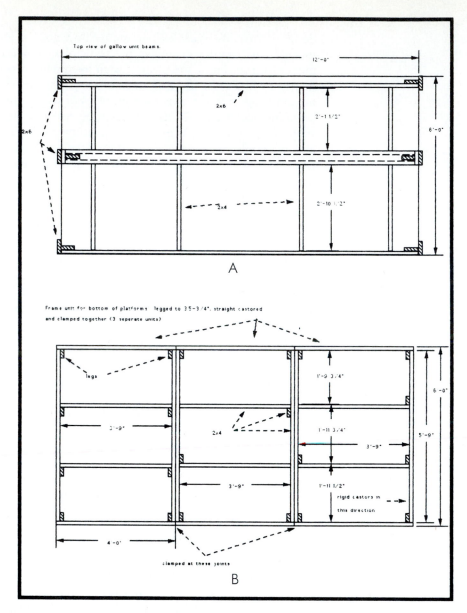

Figures 11.2A–11.2C *Technician's working drawings. This series of technical drawings (drawn on a computer) show the construction of a rolling platform and superstructure for the Ball State University production of* Ghetto *chronicled in the Production Diary at the beginning of this book. The three separate views indicate the "top view of gallow unit beams" (Fig. 11.2A); "frame unit for bottom of platform" (Fig. 11.2B); and "front elevation of center gallow beam unit" (Fig. 11.2C). The information transmitted by the drawings tells the carpenters how to build the unit—that is, (1) what materials to use; (2) how to place these materials; (3) the actual dimensions of each part of the unit; and (4) specific construction notes on how to join the units together, how to face the casters, and so on.*

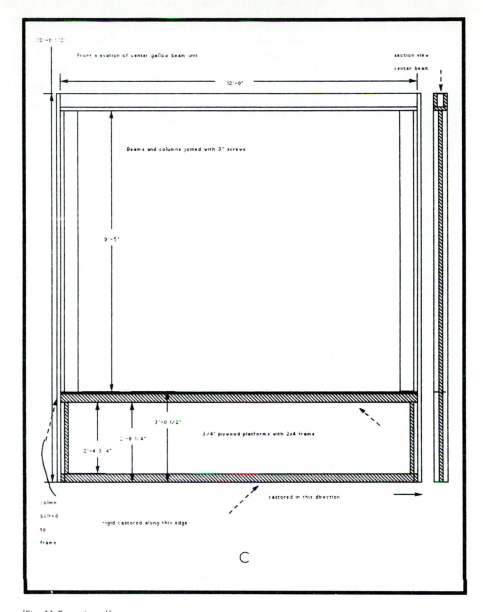

13'-0 1/2"

Front elevation of center gallow beam unit

section view

center beam

12'-0"

Beams and columns joined with 3" screws

9'-5"

3'-0 1/2"

2'-8 1/4"

3/4" plywood platforms with 2x4 frame

2'-4 3/4"

castored in this direction

column

bolted

to

frame

rigid castored along this edge

C

[Fig. 11-2 continued]

Types *of* Scenery Units

Stage scenery can be divided into two categories, two-dimensional and three-dimensional units. The first category includes framed and unframed scenery; the second category includes weight-bearing and non-weight-bearing structures. Part of the magic of theatre that gives us enjoyment as an audience is the ability of the scenic technician to turn wood, metal, and cloth into objects that can be built quickly and inexpensively and look like rocks, trees, mountains, skies, walls, and earth. Deciding which type of unit to construct depends on whether the unit must be used by the actors or can stand in the background. Sometimes scenery units combine types—for example, a unit that appears to the audience as a large rock may be weight-bearing only on a small part of its surface. Thus, an actor who walks where he is not blocked may fall through the unit.

Two-Dimensional Units

These units are vertical and horizontal: Thickness is not generally important. They can be framed for support or left unframed, as will be noted.

framed scenery
Two-dimensional scenic units constructed with rigid supporting members

Framed Scenery   Framed scenery consists of several variations of a standard piece of construction called the *plain flat*. All these can be constructed in a well-organized scene shop with proper materials and advance planning. There are many ways of achieving the final product, and today's technological advances have relaxed a number of methods previously used as rigid guidelines for construction. A number of solutions always exist for any problem advanced by the design.

plain flat (or flat) The basic unit of *two-dimensional, framed scenery* for the theatre

Flats   The **plain flat** (or just **flat**) is, essentially, a lightweight screen constructed of lumber and covered with cloth. A variation of the flat is a screen that can be taken apart and rolled up for easy storage. Flats should be light enough to be lifted by a single stagehand and no wider than the usual width of scenic muslin or canvas adjusted for shrinkage—that is, approximately 5′9″. The height or length of a flat is usually governed by the length that can be accommodated by available transportation or access doorways. In general terms, 18′0″ is the maximum height for a single flat. If a unit is constructed in place—that is, on stage—and there are no plans for storage after the production, these limitations obviously do not apply.

Because the finished product must be straight and without knots and defects that would interfere in the alignment of the unit with other units, lumber for constructing the flat frame must be selected with care. A select grade of white pine is the most suitable for scene construction, and the ideal size is the standard 1″ × 3″. The bottom and top boards of the frame are called the *rails,* and vertical boards on the right and left sides of the frame are called the *stiles*. The *toggle bars* are the horizontal boards that keep the stiles the same distance from each other across the length of the flat. Diagonal braces are on the same side of the frame and prevent the frame from warping (Fig. 11.4).

Corner blocks cut from ¼″ plywood into right triangles with 10″ sides are attached ¾″ from the outside edge of the flat frame to reinforce the butt joints. For maximum strength, the grain of two of the layers of the plywood should run across the butt joint. *Keystones* are pieces of three-ply cut in 3″ × 8″ rectangles and used to attach the toggles to the stiles. They must also be placed ¾″ from the outside edge of the stile. Keystones are used also to secure the two diagonal braces for the flat.

Figure 11.3

Eugene O'Neill, The Iceman Cometh. In this 1946 production, the simple painted-flat scenery serves O'Neill's deceptively complex blend of realism and expressionism. Written in 1946 and based on the playwright's own experiences some thirty years earlier, when he over-frequented a Greenwich Village saloon popularly known as the "Hell Hole," The Iceman Cometh is both a study in psychological realism and a drama of grand illusions reduced to distinctly common, if somewhat shabby, realities. Compare this composition with the iconography established in Leonardo da Vinci's The Last Supper at Fig. 8.12. The importance of O'Neill to the modern American theatre is discussed in Chapter 17.

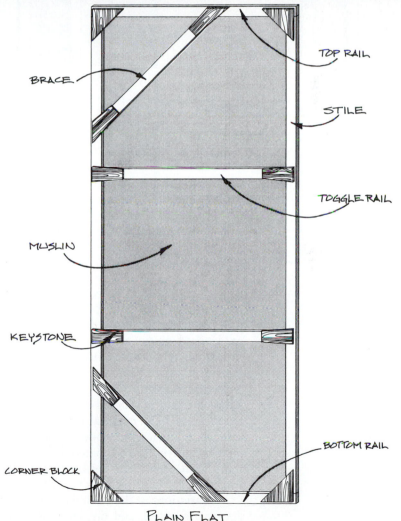

BRACE

TOP RAIL

STILE

TOGGLE RAIL

MUSLIN

KEYSTONE

CORNER BLOCK

BOTTOM RAIL

PLAIN FLAT

Figure 11.4   *The Plain Flat.*

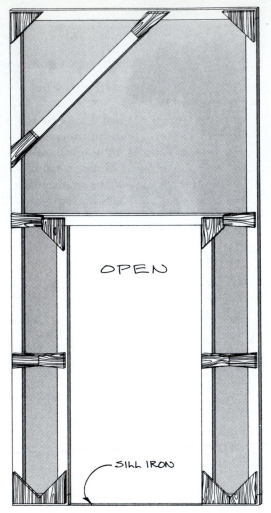

OPEN

SILL IRON

Figure 11.5 Door Flat.

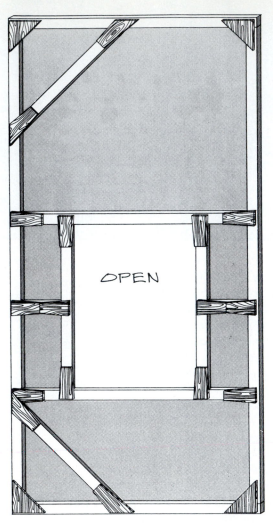

OPEN

Figure 11.6 Window Flat.

After the flat frame is assembled, the covering of lightweight canvas or unbleached muslin is measured for attachment to the frame. The material should extend over the outside edges of the frame by at least 1″. The material is then attached to the frame on the inner edge of the stiles and rails by staples or tacks placed approximately 18″ apart. The material is then folded back, and an adhesive of either watered-down polyvinyl glue or animal glue is applied to the wood frame. The material is pressed against the adhesive on the frame and smoothed with a small wooden block. After a reasonable drying time (approximately eight hours), the material is trimmed to the edge of the flat frame with a sharp knife. Before the finished flat can be painted, it must be sized to tighten the fabric so that it accepts the scene paint more evenly.

Variations of the plain flat include flats with openings such as windows, doors, bookcases, and fireplaces (Figs. 11.5 and 11.6). The construction of

Technical Production

such units uses rails, stiles, toggles, and diagonal braces in essentially the same manner as in a plain flat, with allowances for modifications to accommodate the openings.

profile flat A version of the *plain flat* with irregular edges added

Another variation of the plain flat is the **profile flat,** which is a plain flat with irregular edges added. Used primarily as wings, unusual borders, and ground rows, these flats employ the same construction techniques as the standard plain flat to which additional framing of 1″ × 2″ or 1″ × 3″ lumber is appended.

ceiling units Large, *framed scenic units* designed to form a ceiling over an interior setting

Ceiling units, which are less common today than in the past because of the trend away from realistic settings, comprise very large, framed units that are not unlike the standard flat. The ceiling unit uses 1″ × 4″ framing for strength because it must be suspended above the stage. Muslin or canvas is attached only to the stiles of the ceiling unit so that it can be dismantled and rolled up for storage. The unit suspends from ceiling plates attached to an overhead batten. Sometimes the unit is divided into two pieces hinged together to allow the ceiling to fold in half for storage in the flies when not in use. This is called a *book ceiling* (Fig. 11.7).

Unframed Scenery Unframed scenery comprises drops and curtains. A drop, however, can be framed, in which case it can be considered framed scenery.

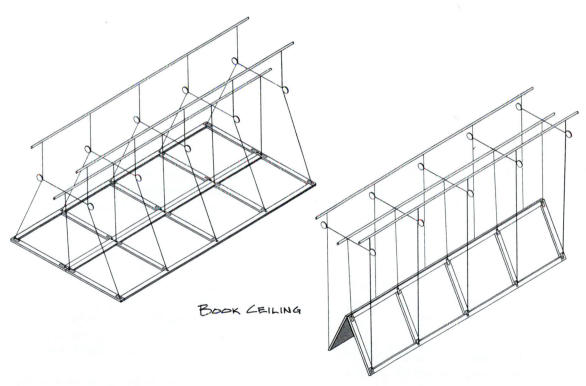

BOOK CEILING

Figure 11.7 *Book Ceiling.*

Joseph Furttenbach: *Floors for Swallowing Up Godless People, Etc.*

A German working in Italy during the seventeenth century, Joseph Furttenbach (1591–1667) enjoyed the bounties of a theatre culture in which, as he himself acknowledged in his late discourse, The Nobel Mirror of Art *(1663), it was not generally necessary to spare expense. An early innovator in lighting, he was among a group of several designers and architects who had the freedom to experiment with the means to satisfy the fascination of contemporary audiences with special-effects ingenuity of all kinds (see Fig. 11.8).*

MACHINES FOR BRINGING OBJECTS FROM THE GROUND AS WELL AS FOR LETTING OBJECTS DOWN FROM THE SKY In the presentation of the play of the prophet Jonah when he prophesies the fall of the city of Nineveh, there was need to show a gourd vine that suddenly grew from the ground and later suddenly withered and then disappeared. For this a vine is cut out 7' high and 4' wide. Behind it is a bench as a seat for Jonah. When the time comes for the vine to grow from the ground, a two-foot-wide trap door in the floor is let down on two iron hinges, just like the lid of a trunk, and the vine is suddenly shoved up. It is painted with live green vines on one side, but the other side is painted as withered and dead. When the time comes for the vine to wither, the whole vine is quickly turned around by means of a four-foot handle set into the middle of the base. Then just as suddenly it is pulled down under the stage and disappears. The trap is closed again. Such a trap may serve for many other uses.

The audience, glad to be rid of such arrant sinners, will take this inexpensive spectacle to its heart.

A FLOOR THAT LETS GODLESS PEOPLE BE SWALLOWED UP In another scene in the play when Core, Datan, and Ibirim were to murmur against Moses, the earth was to open and swallow them up with all their houses and people. For this action a section of boards in the floor of the stage is left free, but suspended as a platform by four ropes at the corners where it is cut across. These ropes go through small round holes above the stage and back through holes in the platform itself, and from there are wound on two windlasses under the stage. When the time nears that Core, Datan, and Ibirim are to be swallowed in the earth, they stand close together on this trap. Of course the audience is not aware that the floor is cut. Then when Moses calls down curses on them, the windlasses are turned loose and the platform with the men sinks slowly under the stage. They disappear with a great cry before the eyes of the audience. When at the same time the moans and wailings from the hell are heard and smoke and flames come from the hole, the spectator's heart will throb and his eyes fill with tears. The audience, glad to be rid of such arrant sinners, will take this inexpensive spectacle to its heart.

How such fires are prepared will be explained in the next chapter. By the first kind of platform, fastened by hinges, Lucifer would be brought on quickly from hell and let down again amidst flames and smoke. Especially when the lights are dimmed for night, this gives quite a terrifying effect. Such a platform next to the rear shutters would serve as the river Jordan when the godless Pharaoh has the innocent child thrown between the small waves.

HOW FLAMES AND LIGHTNING ARE MADE In the palm of the right hand, in a well-shaped piece of tin to keep the hand from being burned, is put a quantity about the size of a hazelnut of *colofonio* or Greek pitch. This is a fine meal-like powder of a beautiful yellow color like resin, sifted through a hair sieve. A lighted wax candle is held between the four fingers of the same hand, so that the flame is scarcely a half inch from the [pitch]. Then the whole arm is extended and the meal is thrown through the light. It makes a long bright flame in the air like lightning. This flame can be used from under the stage to show hell, or above between the clouds to represent lightning. It will not set anything on fire or cause any damage; moreover it leaves a pleasant odor behind.

From *The Noble Mirror of Art* (1663). *The Renaissance Stage*, edited by Bernard Hewitt, translated by A. Nicoll, J. H. McDowell, and G. R. Kernodle. Coral Gables: University of Miami Press, 1958, pp. 203–4. Reprinted by permission of the University of Miami Press.

drop Scenery, framed or unframed, equipped with a bottom weight for raising and lowering

draperies Large pieces of fabric hung to mask the backstage areas from the audience's view

Drops   **Drops** usually employ a weight at the bottom, either a pipe or heavy chain. Loose edges use webbing for reinforcement and are pierced by metal grommets so that the drop can be laced to a frame or batten with cotton rope. Canvas or muslin drops are seamed horizontally for smooth hanging. Gauze and scrim drops do not normally have seams.

Draperies   **Draperies** function primarily to control what the audience sees: They define the edges of the performance space and conceal the off-stage space from audience view. While performing such functions, draperies can also provide an attractive stage decoration. Depending on their principal purpose, stage draperies can be made of many different fabrics or materials. Durability, decoration, masking, and expense must all be considered in selecting the weave, texture, and color of drapery fabric.

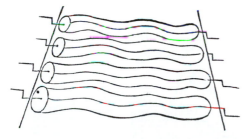

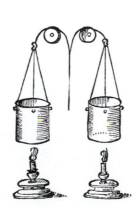

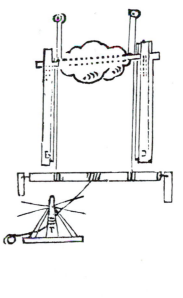

Figure 11.8   In *his* Manual for Constructing Theatrical Scenes and Machines (1638), *Nicola Sabbatini (see Chapter 6) described some of the favorite devices of Renaissance stagecraft. On the right, for example, Sabbatini has drawn the "cloud machine," adapted from Greek technicians required to present the appearance of gods or the ascension of mortals into heaven; Sabbatini and his colleagues would use the same capstan-rope apparatus to manipulate the flight patterns of angels. Center is a system for dimming lights by lowering cylinders over candles. The crank-turned rollers above were serviceable for producing waves.*

Technical Production

platform *A three-dimensional scenic unit* designed to raise floor areas of the stage

Weight-Bearing Structures **Platforms** The most important and most used structure for the stage is the **platform,** which is used to elevate stage areas for more interesting visual effects. The *folding platform* comprises one type of platform, called a *parallel*. It consists of a platform top with cleats that sits on a base that can fold for storage. The base has four sides held together by hinges and constructed much like a flat. When set in place, the top, which is the cleat side, prevents the unit from folding. The hinges on the platform base must be specifically placed to allow the base top to fold for storage (Fig. 11.9).

Rigid platforms (Fig. 11.10) can be constructed of a ¾″ plywood top supported by 2″ × 4″ legs and frame. Rigid platforms are usually both heavy and strong and can present problems in moving and shifting. Platform legs can

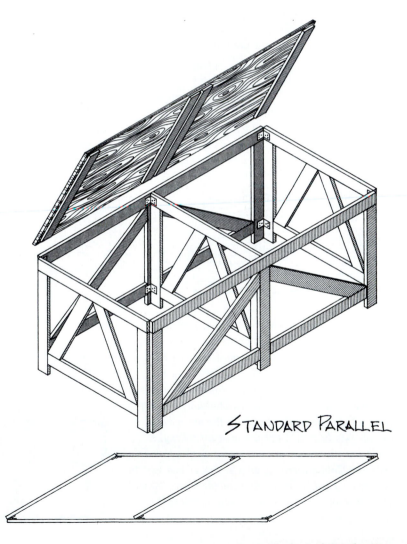

STANDARD PARALLEL

Figure 11.9 *The Standard Parallel.*

Figure 11.10 *The Rigid Platform.*

be secured by nails, screws, or bolts. Bolts and wing nuts allow the legs to be removed easily, without damage to the structural members. However, wood can splinter, and bolt holes enlarge with use, so the length of service of the rigid platform is limited. Perhaps a more efficient method is the use of pipe or preformed steel for supporting legs. Welded frames are the best for weight, strength, and durability. Although the expense is greater, the practicality is superior. Construction of this type of platform requires proper welding equipment and an experienced welder. One-and-a-half inch black steel pipe with flanges and pipe clamps can also be used to support platform tops. Most platforms comprise rectangular shapes, but pipe construction can be adapted easily to irregular or even curved shapes. These units can be disassembled and stored when not in use.

Other flexible systems of metal platform construction can be used. The first employs slotted angle iron with perforated slots and holes. The pieces of angle iron can be joined together with bolts and are easily cut with special cutting tools. A second type employs Unistrut channel—that is, steel pieces made with special channels and grooves that hold spring-held nuts bolted to special fittings. A third system uses lengths of steel tubing logs formed in squares that can fit into each other, so that the tubes can telescope (Fig. 11.11). This system allows for flexibility in platform height. The legs can be attached to a plywood top whose support frame consists of slotted angle metal.

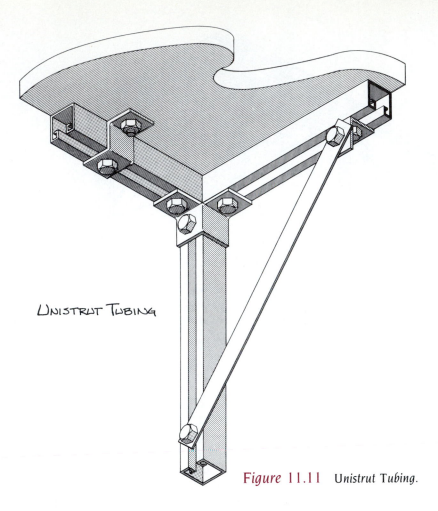

UNISTRUT TUBING

Figure 11.11 *Unistrut Tubing.*

wagons *Platforms*
mounted on wheels

Wagons Wagons are simply castered platforms. They can be of standard platform sizes, such as 4′0″ × 8′0″, or they can be as large as a full-stage acting area, thereby moving an entire setting and making possible a quick scene shift of a very large setting. Rubber-tired casters from 3″ to 6″ in diameter provide the best support for wagons. Casters come in three types: *rigid*, which move back and forth in one direction only; *swivel*, which can move in any direction; and *brake*, which allow the caster to lock into position.

To reduce noise caused by footsteps, platform and wagon tops should be covered with padded material. Carpet padding covered with heavy canvas or muslin can be painted as desired.

Steps and Stairs Steps and stairs, another type of three-dimensional unit, consist of three sections: (1) the *carriage*, which provides the fundamental support; (2) the *tread*, which is the horizontal surface of the step; and (3) the *riser*, which is the vertical facing separating the treads. The height and depth of the tread will depend on the type and size of the unit; however, steps with riser

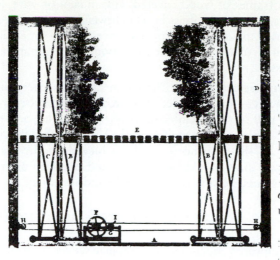

heights of over 7″ present problems for short actors. In addition, the tread must be deep enough to accommodate the actor's foot comfortably (Fig. 11.13).

Non-Weight-Bearing Structures Non-weight-bearing three-dimensional scenery, such as rocks, trees, ceiling beams, fireplaces, and pillars, is usually

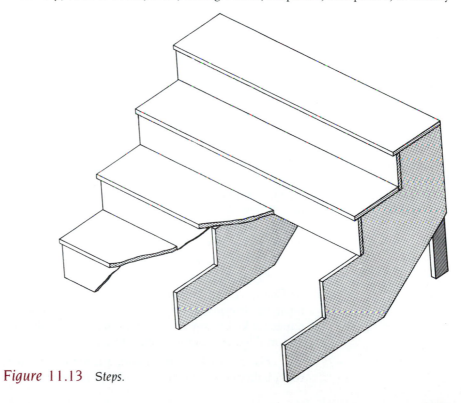

Figure 11.13 *Steps.*

built on frames of wood covered with muslin or wire and muslin to provide contours. These units must be as lightweight as possible. Additional materials can be used to establish a proper surface effect—for example, different sizes of mesh wire, corrugated cardboard, wooden strips, papier-mâché, Celastic, and fibreglass.

Architectural Units   Three-dimensional scenery units attached to or inserted in flats—for example, doors, windows, and archways—give the appearance of reality and architectural style. The technician stays in close contact with the designer when making such choices so that precisely the right effect—as seen by the audience—can be achieved. Archways conform to various shapes and sizes. Bookcases, niches, and fireplace units are constructed in a fashion similar to that of doors and window units.

SCULPTURED EFFECTS AND TEXTURES

Sculptured effects and textures give scenery a professionally finished look and thus enhance the audience's perception, appreciation, and enjoyment of the play. Some of the many choices for the technician include *wooden trims, appliqué, papier-mâché, plastic foam,* and *vacuum-formed plastics.*

Wooden Trims   Architectural trim on scenery gives dimension and interesting highlights and shadows to the setting. Beginning with profile frames, wooden moldings, and thin and narrow strips of lumber, additional decor can be added using cardboard, wooden blocks, plastic forms, and fiberboard or cardboard attachments. Cornices, moldings, rails, paneling, fireplaces, doors, doorways, and other trims can be constructed for heightened visual effects and a strong sense of professional finish. Application of these technical effects springs from the desire for aesthetic results related to the scene designer's impression of how these details will affect the audience, which rises in turn from overall production goals established between the director and the designers.

Appliqué   Dimensional effects are sometimes required to give the appearance of stone, brick, rough plaster, and other surfaces on flat areas. Burlap, pieces of Styrofoam, sawdust, padding, newspaper, and the like can be glued or pasted to specific areas and covered with muslin or cheesecloth dipped in a heavy size-water solution and molded around forms. After drying, the surface can be painted as desired. Sawdust, cork, or ground Styrofoam can be mixed with the size-water or sprinkled on the surface while wet and allowed to dry before the base coat is applied.

Papier-Mâché   A commercial preparation called Instant Papier-Mâché or Celluclay can be applied to a surface and molded by hand. The mixture must be thoroughly dry before applying a base coat of paint. Small bits of paper soaked in water for a reasonable time also can be combined with paste and molded for dimensional effects.

Plastic Foams   Styrofoam, a trade name for polystyrene, is a rigid, porous, lightweight plastic. It can be purchased from local suppliers in a variety

The Art of Costume and Makeup Design

Plate 3.1 (Above)
Phantom of the Opera, Majestic Theatre, New York, 1983.
Director, Hal Prince; production designer, Maria Björnson; light-
ing designer, Andrew Bridge. Color and character typify the
costume designs for Andrew Lloyd Webber's popular musical.
See the PROFILE of Hal Prince in Chapter 7.

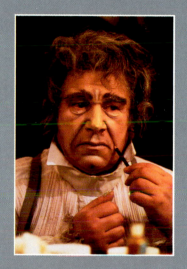

Plate 3.2 (Right Above)
Peter Ustinov applies makeup for his role in *Beethoven's
Tenth* at the Vaudeville Theatre, London, 1983.
This is an example of *straight makeup:* changes in
features are effected by painting highlights and
shadows directly on the face.

Plate 3.3 (Right Below)
William Thomas, Jr., and Gene Barry in *La Cage
aux Folles,* Palace Theatre, New York, 1983. Director,
Arthur Laurents; scenic designer, David Mitchell;
costume designer, Theoni V. Aldredge; hairstyles and
makeup, Ted Azar. Dramatic accessories like feather
boas round out some of the elaborate costumes
in this successful musical.

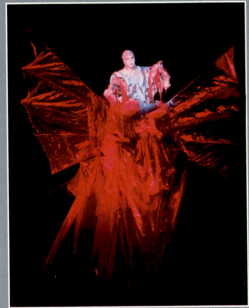

Plate 3.5 (*Above*)
Medea, New York Shakespeare Festival, Delacorte Theatre, 1986. Director, Yukio Ninagawa. Elaborate costuming characterizes the style of this all-male Japanese production of the classic Greek tragedy by Euripides.

Plate 3.4 (*Left Above and Below*)
Raul Julia and Meryl Streep in *The Taming of the Shrew*, New York Shakespeare Festival, Delacorte Theatre, 1978. Director and designer, Wilford Leach; costume designer, Patricia McGourty.
Tracy Ullman and Morgan Freeman in *The Taming of the Shrew*, New York Shakespeare Festival, Delacorte Theatre, 1990. Director, A.J. Antoon; scenic designer, John Lee Beatty; costume designer, Lindsay W. Davis. Historically accurate "period costumes" accentuate the NYSF's 1978 production, while the novel 1990 production opts for the playful world of rodeo fashion.

Plate 3.6 (Above)
C. Wilhelm's color rendering of costumes for four
fairies in Robert Courtneidge's production of
A Midsummer Night's Dream, Princess Theatre,
London, ca. 1900.

Plate 3.7 (Right)
Pablo Picasso, *Costume of the Chinese*, for Jean
Cocteau's surrealist ballet, *Parade*, Paris, 1917.
The music was by Erik Satie, the choreography
by Sergei Diaghilev.

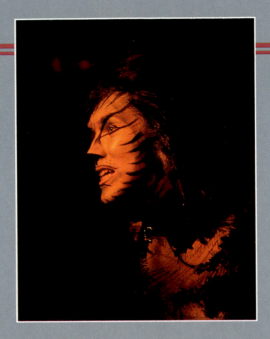

Plate 3.8 *(Above and Below)*
Cats, Winter Garden Theatre, New York, 1982. Director, Trevor Nunn. The elaborate creations
of scenic and costume designer John Napier are essential to the spectacular fantasy
world of this immensely successful production.

of sizes and shapes and can be carved into statues, trims, cornices, capitals, and bas-relief effects, and it is easily bonded, both together and to frames, with white glue or special Styrofoam glues available from hobby shops. It can be cut with knives, power saws, electric hot-wire cutters, soldering irons, and propane torches. It also can be sanded. Before basecoating, the plastic must be covered with cheesecloth dipped in glue. Flexible polyurethane is most useful as a molding and as a trim on curved units like columns, pillars, and cornices.

Vacuum-Formed Plastics   Shaped plastic sheets of high-impact polystyrene are commercially available at local home-decorating stores as well as theatrical and display suppliers. It is strong, flexible, and easily cut with ordinary scissors. It is especially useful when duplications of three-dimensional objects are needed. Brick or stone walls, involved lengths of intricate moldings, numerous carved panels, and other dimensional items are more easily achieved through the use of these molded sheets. Vacuum-form machines are expensive, however, and educational theatres often find it more economical to build their own.

PROPERTIES AND FURNITURE

Scenery frequently has been defined as the environment of the play, and so far we have been discussing backgrounds and dimensional units. Frequently, however, the actors need portable objects and articles to move around, use, and handle while telling the story. The selection of these elements, whether useful or ornamental, is the responsibility of the designer. One expects the designer of the scenery to devote the same energies, creativity, and expertise to researching, organizing, designing, and sometimes locating the proper furniture and other properties that he or she gives to the set design itself. Even at this level, artistic choices and insights relating to aesthetic goals of the production drive decisions.

properties Items used on stage that are not scenery or costumes

set properties A category of properties used as parts of the setting

hand properties A category of properties used by the actors

set decoration A category of *properties* used to dress the setting

Properties   Properties fall into four basic types or groups according to use. The first—the type most closely associated with the actual design—is **set properties,** which include furniture, rugs, stoves, sinks, free-standing cabinets, rocks, plants, logs, and other large items to be found in the setting itself.

Actors themselves use the second group, called **hand properties.** These are small items used by the play's characters as part of their stage business. They can be placed on the set before the production begins, or carried on stage by the actors. Hand properties might include luggage, guns, trays, dishes, glassware, books, canes, swords, banners, flags, signs, papers, letters, cigarettes, watches, and so on.

Properties in the third group comprise those items of **set decoration** that are not usually handled by the actors but add to the general atmosphere of the setting. They form an essential ingredient in the total visual effect of the scene and serve to integrate or unify the various areas of the setting, thus contributing to *aesthetic communication.* Such items usually consist of draperies, window treatments, tapestries, pictures, mirrors, clocks, side tables, decorative chairs, pillows, wall brackets, flower arrangements, and plants.

The final type of property—essentially everything not included in the first three categories—includes breakaway and trick effect items that have a performance purpose. These include breakaway objects like bottles, dishes, and crockery, as well as furniture, window panes, and so on. Usually, electrical devices or exploding and burning effects, which might fall into this category, are the responsibility of the effects technicians.

Properties Research   Research for properties generally requires searching out drawings and photographs in published materials available at local libraries. Books on decoration, design, architectural details, art masterpieces, historical manners and customs, stage and motion picture production histories, as well as magazine publications of the nineteenth and twentieth centuries, contain many photographs and drawings that will provide help in identifying the objects needed for the production. Museums are also excellent sources for property details, as are furniture stores, catalogues, antique shops, and secondhand stores. Most professional designers develop and maintain files, called *morgues,* for photographs, clippings, and back issues of publications for easy reference on properties.

Properties Lists   As is the case for the design in general, listing and assembling properties required for a particular production begins with several readings of the play to ascertain the atmosphere, period, style, and locale and to determine the specific technical requirements for each scene. A list is compiled from the author's scene description, any stage directions, any mention of properties in the dialogue, and any requirements that might be involved in the implied action.

Next comes a conference with the director to discuss his or her specific interpretation and wishes for staging the production. At this point, the initial list may be adjusted to satisfy the director's understanding, alterations, and suggested additions. The list must always be considered flexible, and occasional attendance at rehearsals allows discussion of particular problems that require solutions. When agreements are reached on property requirements, the designer must plan construction and acquisition schedules and coordinate them with rehearsals intended to deal with technical matters.

Obtaining Properties   Properties may be obtained in several ways. The theatre organization may possess a stock room of properties stored from previous productions. These can include furniture items, both period and contemporary, hand props, and set decor articles. If production budgets allow, a particular property may be purchased. In addition, properties may simply be borrowed from commercial businesses, antique dealers, and individuals. Renting may prove more economical for some pieces.

Certain properties that cannot be secured by other means must be constructed. Such properties include period furniture, hard-to-find and perishable items—for example, food to be consumed on stage by the actors—and properties that might be destroyed during each performance. Properties—including, for example, exotic period candle stands and furniture—that cannot otherwise be found must be designed by the designer and constructed in the theatre shop.

Furniture Furniture properties are usually identified by historic or cultural periods, and the designer must have a thorough knowledge of furniture styles. Although historical accuracy is important, however, it should not overshadow the creative artistry of the design. For example, an exquisite museum replica of an eighteenth-century drawing room may be historically accurate, but its colors, lines, and social status may be wrong for the characters who supposedly live there.

In general, furniture forms can be divided into three basic categories according to use: *tables, seating pieces,* and *containers.* Tables include desks, occasionals, dining tables, vanities, and the like; seating pieces include benches, stools, sofas, love seats, armchairs, lounges, straight chairs, settees, and so on. Containers are receptacles like chests, bookcases, buffets, sideboards, cabinets, dressers, and other storage items.

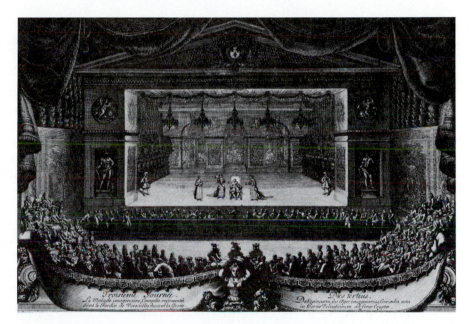

Figure 11.14 *Molière,* The Imaginary Invalid. *Engraving of a production at Versailles, 1647. Scene decor by Carlo Vigarani. Note the consistency of design between the set decor of the play and the proscenium architecture. When the great French writer Voltaire called Molière "the painter of France," he was referring to the extent to which the dramatist's work reflected the range of French aesthetic attitudes in his day. Designed at once to appeal to and to satirize the affectation and artificiality practiced by the aristocracy that made up Molière's audience, the decor of the play reflects an official preference for form over content, and formality defines the limits not only of decor but of speech, movement, and even behavior. (Both Molière, as a major figure in the French neoclassic theatre, and Voltaire, as one of the great writers of the Enlightenment, are discussed more fully in Chapter 16; Molière's* Tartuffe *is summarized in Chapter 3,* The School for Wives *in Chapter 4.)*

[Bibliotheque Nationale, Paris.]

Decor Items

Most unadorned stage walls need items of decoration such as pictures, hangings, wall sconces, bell pulls, shelves, and the like. These must be appropriate to the period, locale, and social status of the characters in the play. Walls, however, are not the only areas that can display decorative items. Tables, mantels, bookcases, shelves, and other units of furniture can also be used to hold set dressings.

Other important decor items include lighting instruments—chandeliers, candelabras, lamps, and wall sconces—that must all reflect the period and locale of the production. Ornamental vases, statuary, flower arrangements, clocks, plates, and other items complete a set's decoration and are chosen with an eye toward aesthetic impact on the audience in terms of the production's goals.

The Scene Shop

Creative thinking, artistic choices, careful planning, and aesthetic goals rest not only on the abilities of the artists and craftspersons involved in a theatre production but also on the space, materials and equipment in which those ideas are made into real stage scenery. The scene shop can be as important to the effect of a production on an audience as the actors' performances and director's concepts. Although a **scene shop** should be as carefully planned as any factory assembly plant, unfortunately, few are. Therefore, the designer and the shop technician must constantly adjust to less-than-efficient operational procedures. Not surprisingly, theatre building planners usually focus more attention on the auditorium and the public rooms than on the actual working areas. Although the stage area may be given consideration on the basis of presentation, the scene shop areas are seldom examined. As a result, most theatre shops are inadequate for the basic production requirements of many organizations.

scene shop A specially designed location used for the construction of *stage scenery*

Basic Shop Requirements

The size of the shop is directly related to the size of the theatre's performance areas. Scenic units must be constructed and assembled so that they will closely approximate their position and appearance on the stage itself. If the production requires more than one setting, shop requirements must allow for additional space to handle production demands.

Frequently, one shop area must serve several performance areas, and it is not unusual for two and even three productions to be in preparation at one time. A repertory program is certain to make additional demands on shop space ordinarily committed to a conventional program. The actual construction of scenery units requires reasonable and unencumbered floor space in addition and unrelated to space for assembled units for trimming and painting.

The location of the shop in relation to the other theatre areas is also an important consideration. For example, a shop attached to a rehearsal or performance area is bound to create major conflicts with rehearsal, performance, and shop schedules. The noise generated by shop activity will be in direct conflict with rehearsal, lecture, or performance activity: Soundproofing would be an absolute necessity. To allow for deliveries of materials and equipment, the shop also must be located adjacent to or at least close by the loading area. Because finished settings must be moved from the work area, it is advantageous to have the shop on the same level as the performance area to allow easy movement from one location to another. For maximum efficiency, storage spaces should be in close proximity to the shop.

In addition to space for actual set building for productions, educational theatre buildings also need space—and time—for teaching students of stagecraft and design. The number of workers who will use shop facilities needs to be considered carefully. For example, four full-time professional technicians will require a very different organizational and spatial plan than will fifteen amateur volunteers. Finally, consideration must be made of the type of productions planned—experimental, classic dramas, musical comedies, operas, or any or all of these. Planning should focus on the most demanding of production types, generally dependent on the amount and size of the scenery required. In other words, one should plan for the space needed to build and paint scenery for the most complicated productions.

SPACE AREAS

The various *functions* of the shop must be examined carefully in order to plan for efficiency. For example, an area sized for the reasonable construction of both two-dimensional scenery and three-dimensional units should be available. Once units are built, they must be assembled in trial setups similar to finished stage plans. The next step requires the painting of scenery, and those area requirements are vastly different from those of the construction space. Wall space, floor space, incandescent lighting, paint frames, plumbing, and paint storage are all special considerations for painting.

Storage areas for scenic elements, drops, properties, and electrical equipment must not be omitted; few theatrical organizations can afford to create everything new for each production. Property construction requires space for the building of small hand props and for larger items such as furniture and special units. Metalworking equipment and work with plastics make special demands on safety, ventilation, and storage.

TOOLS

Every scene shop requires a set of basic equipment necessary for the construction of scenery and properties. Tools come in two varieties, hand and power. A maxim for all work involving tools is: "The right tool for the right job."

Power Tools It is difficult to imagine producing the quantity and quality of work that has come to be associated with theatre technicians without the help of power tools. Although it may not be necessary to equip a scene shop with all the power tools described in the "Technician's Inventory," those descriptions of various tools will give the practitioner an estimate of their efficiency and capabilities.

Metalworking Tools In recent years the use of metal has become an extremely important technology, not only as a functional replacement for lumber structures and supports, but also for pure sculptural effect, emphasizing form, texture, and color. In this case the aesthetic concepts of the designer depend totally on the technician and the capabilities of the scene shop. If metal cannot be worked, then the potential visual impact of the setting is lost. Many scene shops now contain metalworking areas with welding equipment operated under the supervision of qualified technicians.

Welding The technician may choose from three kinds of welding—*gas, electric arc,* and *gas-metal arc.* All three need careful safety precautions, and any equipment operators must be thoroughly instructed in handling welding tools. Local fire regulations should be checked carefully before installation, and precautionary protective clothing and goggles must be worn while operating the equipment.

gas welding A method of metalworking using a mixture of oxygen and acetylene

Gas welding involves igniting a mixture of oxygen and acetylene in a torch to produce a flame that burns at 6,000° Fahrenheit. The flame is controlled by adjustable valves on the torch itself. The two gases are kept in steel storage tanks under pressure, and regulators on the tanks control the amount of gas flow into flexible hoses connected to the hand-held torch.

electric-arc welding A method of metalworking using an electric spark arcing between an electrode rod and the metal to be welded

Electric-arc welding uses an electric spark arcing between an electrode or rod and the metal to be welded. The electric arc generates an intense heat of approximately 13,000° Fahrenheit and comes from a welding transformer. A cable from the transformer is connected to the metal material; when the electrode is introduced to complete the circuit, a fusion results.

gas-metal-arc welding A method of metalworking using a wire-fed electrode and a flexible hose leading to a nozzle

Gas-metal-arc welding is a one-handed operation. This process uses a wire-fed electrode and a flexible hose leading to a nozzle. Some systems use a tungsten electrode in the nozzle instead of the wire electrode. This equipment is quite heavy and not particularly portable, which may present some problems in smaller shops.

Materials

Lumber Lumber has long been the staple material for construction of stage scenery. It is inexpensive, lightweight, readily available, and easily worked. Northern white pine and Douglas fir are the most practical for scenery

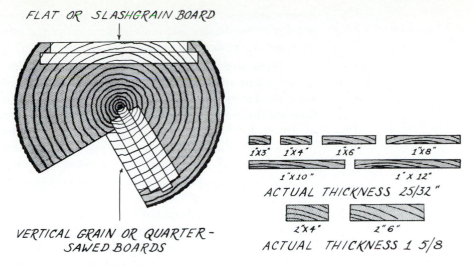

FLAT OR SLASHGRAIN BOARD

VERTICAL GRAIN OR QUARTER-
SAWED BOARDS

1"X3" 1"X4" 1"X6" 1"X8"

1"X10" 1"X12"

ACTUAL THICKNESS 25/32"

2"X4" 2"X6"

ACTUAL THICKNESS 1 5/8

Figure 11.15 Lumber.

(Fig. 11.15). Pine probably is the best because it is relatively soft, strong, and lightweight. Fir is heavier, harder, and splintery. Plywood and hardboard also are lumber products that play a useful role in construction of platforms and for floor coverings. By placing a hardboard covering on the stage floor, the designer can paint the floor area to look like wood, stone, or any other desired material. The result is an enhancement of the aesthetic look of the scene design—an enhancement not possible if the original stage floor (which normally cannot be painted) is left uncovered.

Fabric The scene designer and technician must also be familiar with various types and qualities of fabrics used for flat building, drops, curtains, draperies, floor coverings, upholstery, property construction, and other purposes. Again, a listing of the more popular types of cloth materials used for stage purposes can be found in the "Technician's Inventory" appendix.

Plastics Although the process of creating plastics was discovered before the turn of the century, the development of the plastic process industry did not begin until after World War II. Defined as a material that changes shape when pressure is applied and retains its new shape when the pressure is removed, plastic was originally an innovative chemical produced for industrial use. New items and uses are developed each year. Contemporary designers were quick to discover the advantages of plastics, which are strong, lightweight, inexpensive, and quickly and easily constructed. Plastics can also be transparent and reflective. They give the designer and technician a broad array of artistic and practical choices for making scenery that better meets a production's needs.

Many varieties of plastic materials are available to the contemporary technician and scene designer and offer almost unlimited opportunities for

Technical Production

experimentation. Today's artist must be aware of the possibilities for the use of plastics in the theatre and must make a concerted effort to keep informed of the most recent developments in the industry.

Paper and Paper Products   Although designers have resorted to using papier-mâché to produce properties and three-dimensional effects on stage since the 1800s, the increase in required realistic effects in the theatre since then and the low cost of paper materials has led to increased use. Products such as brown Kraft paper (a heavy, coarse paper product), fiberboard (a soft, porous material), paper tubing, corrugated board, and upson board (a hard surface board) all find frequent use in scene technology.

Metals   Metal is also increasing in importance as a material for stage scenery. Originally used as structural support for platforms, it is now replacing wood as the most substantial material in the construction of scenery. This practice has evolved because of the rising cost of lumber and the superior strength of metal, its nonflammable quality, and its delicate and decorative visual properties, which enhance its potential to contribute to aesthetic qualities of the production.

Shifting Scenery

Whenever a production requires more than one setting, consideration of the method by which scenery will be shifted becomes a major artistic and practical choice. The mechanics for executing scene shifting range from the ultrasimple to the fantastically sophisticated. Whatever method is chosen—a fifty cent furniture glide or an electronically driven wagon—each method is an elaboration on one of three basic concepts: *running, rolling,* or *flying.*

running *Shifting scenery essentially by human power*

Running   Running scenery employs only basic human power: Stagehands pick up and carry the units to be shifted. If one looks back over a career in the theatre, an amazing review emerges of what kinds of scenery can be run—for example, a bathtub full of water as well as twenty-foot-high flats.

rolling *Shifting scenery by means of some wheel or sliding device*

Rolling   Rolling scenery means pushing it from one place to another on some form of wheel or sliding device. The furniture glide—a smooth metal disc attached to the bottom of the unit—is the simplest device available and is useful on small items like sofas and tables. It is the same device used on household furniture. Because the glide does not rotate, its use is limited to rather light objects. Heavy, large units normally are rolled by attaching either swivel or rigid casters. The size of the unit dictates the size of the caster. In some cases—for example, complete stage-sized wagon stages with full settings on them—the stage may be equipped with permanent fixtures like railroad tracks embedded in the floor: These allow wagon stages to move in a straight line with ease. In such circumstances, the casters look like the wheels on a railroad car. Immense units can also be rolled with electronic controls. The movable seating areas in the Energy Pavilion at Epcot Center are examples of

Profile

Les Misérables: Designing the Human Spectacle

The Broadway production of *Les Misérables* is a musical version of Victor Hugo's 1862 novel of the same name depicting the struggle in nineteenth-century revolutionary Paris between the noble thief Jean Valjean and his relentless pursuer, the detective Javert. Much has changed since the musical's original creators, composer Claude-Michel Schönberg and lyricist Alain Boublil, mounted their original 1980 version in Paris. That production consisted of a dozen *tableau vivants* with incidental music during scenery changes. On hearing the record the next year, the English producer Cameron Mackintosh decided to go ahead with an English-language version.

In the next four years, various changes were made to create a fusion of drama, character, music, design, and movement. The result is an epic musical in which human relationships are not sacrificed to historical spectacle. To achieve this balance between private and public forces, codirectors Trevor Nunn and John Caird came up with a stunning staging device, using one huge revolving turntable inside another on which one set appears and is then replaced by the next as characters come and go. This device not only produces a fluid, cinematic effect but also suggests the inexorable movement of fate pushing the characters toward their individual destinies.

Working with Nunn and Caird from the start, designer John Napier also visually recreates Hugo's compassion for the downcast. For example, when the action moves to Paris, the set becomes an abstract representation of a slum bounded by shuttered windows, mirroring the city's refusal to recognize the existence of its poor. In another reflection of the outer and inner plight of the lower classes, Napier also limits his colors to earthy browns and the grays of city streets. Lighting designer David Hersey's use of hazy light is also suggestive of the fragility of human life.

Summing up the efforts of the production team, Caird reports, "As to which of the creators are responsible for what, it is always impossible to disentangle the complexities of a true collaboration . . . which is one of the most exciting things about the musical theatre."

such sophisticated arrangements. Another method of rolling, which really does not "roll" at all, is a system called an *air caster*. This device has a series of compressed-air jets that are located beneath the unit and lift it slightly above the stage floor; the unit is then easily moved on a cushion of air, more or less like a hovercraft.

fly loft Area over the stage from which scenery and instruments can be raised and lowered by a series of cables, ropes, and pulleys

Flying Well-equipped theatres contain high galleries over the stage called a **fly loft** in which a series of cables, ropes, and pulleys are arranged so that set pieces, drops, lighting instruments, and curtains can be lifted to a desired height (see Fig. 11.16). A well-designed fly loft has sufficient height to fly scenery out of sight of the audience. By pulling on a rope attached to a metal carriage filled with counterweights, a stage hand can easily control units or draperies weighing a ton or more. Mechanized versions of this counterweight system employ electric winches to fly scenery and other stage accoutrements. This concept of scene changing can be used in a variety of ways to do everything from flying curtains and drops to operating onstage elevators and flying people—as in, for example, the flying sequences in *Peter Pan* (Fig. 11.17).

No matter how simple or sophisticated the requirements of the play may be, whenever scenery or other stage units are moved, one of the three methods just noted will be used. Sometimes, the variation depends on budget—a small

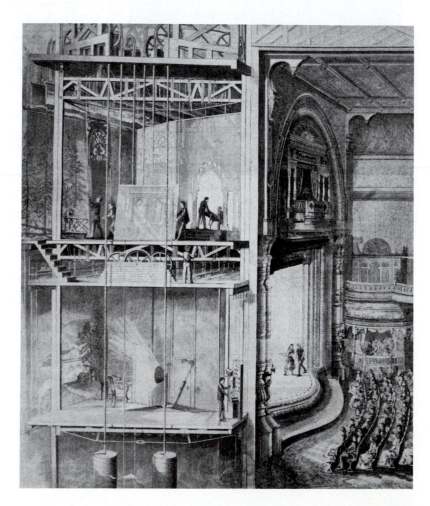

Figure 11.16 *Sectional drawing of the Madison Square Theatre, New York, 1884. Managed by David Belasco (1854–1931), the Madison Square Theatre, which opened in 1879, was the most elaborately equipped theatre in the country. This drawing of "the movable stage," which was considered sufficiently impressive for a report in the* Scientific American, *shows the theatre's two stages and the apparatus for flying drops and lighting instruments; placed one above the other, the elevators are operated by counterweights. Thomas Edison had a hand in designing and installing the theatre's lighting system.*

From *Scientific American,* April 5, 1884.

Technical Production

Figure 11.17 *Former medal-winning gymnast Cathy Rigby in* Peter Pan, *Lunt Fontanne Theatre, New York, 1991. The musical adaptation of James M. Barrie's 1904 fantasy about a boy who refuses to grow up calls for the title character (usually portrayed by an actress) to fly across the stage; in some productions, Peter is joined by young Wendy Darling and her brothers. The feat can be accomplished by adapting a scene-shifting method also called* flying, *which makes use of a system of cables and pulleys mounted over the stage in the* fly loft.

community theatre, for example, probably cannot afford air casters. Sometimes the theatre building itself creates the decision: Little or no fly space precludes certain options, and so on. The ultimate decision rests on the creativity of the technician coupled with the availability of practical resources: space, time, staff, and budget.

SUMMARY

- *Technical production* is the craft of turning the scene design into reality.

- In general, stage scenery has nine qualities:

  It is constructed to be used for a comparatively short time;

  It must be planned for rapid construction;

  It is often planned for possible alteration and reuse;

It is usually built in one place and used in another;

It is constructed in easily portable units and assembled onstage by temporary joining;

It is generally finished on one side only;

It must be light in weight and capable of compact storage;

It must be strong enough for safe use and handling;

It must be constructed as inexpensively as possible and still comply with the foregoing requirements.

- *Working drawings* transform the elevational drawings of the scene designer into a back view showing how each unit will be constructed.

- Stage scenery can be divided into two categories:

    Two-dimensional units, including *framed* and *unframed* scenery;

    Three-dimensional units, including *weight-bearing* and *non-weight-bearing units*.

- *Sculptured effects* give scenery a professional look and include:

    Wooden trims;

    Appliqué;

    Papier-mâché;

    Plastic foam;

    Vacuum-formed plastics.

- *Stage properties* fall into four basic types according to use:

    Set properties;

    Hand properties;

    Set decoration.

    Other properties not included in the previous three groups

- *Decor* items give final dressing to the set and consist of pictures, lighting fixtures, vases, flowers, clocks, and so on.

- The *scene shop* is as important to the effect of a production on an audience as the actors' performances and the director's concepts. A scene shop must be organized like a well-run factory.

- Vital to the scene shop's operation are its *space areas, tools,* and *materials.*

  Space areas include trial setup, construction, and storage spaces; tools include metalworking and power tools; materials include lumber, fabric, plastics, paper and paper products, and metals.

- All methods of shifting scenery are elaborations of three basic concepts:

  Running—moving units manually;

  Rolling—mounting units on wheels;

  Flying—lifting units off the floor and out of sight.

THE BEGGAR
(Mr. Arnold Pilbeam)

Chapter 12

Costumes *and* Makeup

*A*fter studying this chapter,
you should be able to:

- Characterize a *stage costume* and its relationship to an actor's presentation.
- Describe the purposes of stage costumes and their relationship to the production.
- Discuss the *costume-design procedure*.
- Identify and describe the characteristics and functions of the *costume shop*.
- Define *stage makeup* and discuss its relationship to stage costuming.
- Explain several processes of *makeup application*.

Costume drawing for The Beggar's Opera. *Performing Arts Research Center, New York Public Library at Lincoln Center.*

*T*he physical appearance of an actor tells us much about character and about the times and style of the production. In this chapter we will examine costumes and makeup—important tools for transforming the actor into a believable character and transmitting to the audience significant information about the production itself. Our examination will cover a variety of topics, beginning with a few comments on the history of costume in the theatre. Because costume is treated in some detail in the history chapters, this discussion will be brief. Next, we will discuss stage costumes and their various functions. As in Chapters 10 and 13, we will spend some time describing the design process, including how costumes are made and how a production is organized. Finally, we will look at the requirements and equipment of the costume shop. The chapter closes with a topic—stage makeup—that some individuals consider part of stage costuming and others consider a related but separate art. We will treat stage makeup as part of stage costume, thereby placing it on equal footing with the other aspects of stage costumes as opposed to dividing the chapter into two major headings, "Stage Costume" and "Stage Makeup."

The ultimate purpose behind the process of costume design, makeup design, and all the other artistic elements of the production is bringing to life an aesthetic design—a reflection of careful artistic choices stemming from production goals. For full-color illustrations of professional costume and makeup design, see the third insert in this book, "The Art of Costume and Makeup Design."

Stage Costumes *in* History

Stage costumes have played an important role in theatrical production from earliest times. In the theatre of Asia (see Chapter 14), costumes do not suggest time or place but have highly symbolic functions that call for sophisticated understanding from the audience. In the Western tradition, the ancient Greeks also used costumes to provide highly symbolic and sophisticated information through elaborate robes, boots, headgear, and masks. The tragic and comic masks of the ancient Greek theatre have come to symbolize theatre itself. Later—in Roman comedy, for example—grossly suggestive costumes created much of the bawdy character of this genre. During the Middle Ages, stage costuming paid great attention to detail—especially to the devils that inhabited Hell. At some times during the history of Western theatre, stage costumes took a secondary part—for example, during the English Renaissance of Shakespeare's time, when actors took the stage in what amounted to "street clothes." From that time until the mid-eighteenth century, stage costuming was a peripheral part of production, and our concepts of costumes as a communicator of historical and character details did not exist.

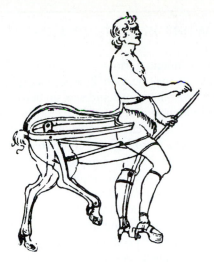

Figure 12.1   *The fascination of Italian Renaissance designers with new dimensions of spectacle made possible by advances in technology extended to ingenuity in costuming, especially in opera and court productions (see the excerpt from Joseph Furttenbach's handbook in Chapter 11). A contemporary drawing shows how the actor assigned to the role of a centaur might be outfitted with the creature's body and moving legs.*

Beginning with the eighteenth century, however, stage costumes emerged as devices for setting the play in its particular historic environment (see Fig. 12.2). From that time until today, stage costumes gained greater importance as elements that the production uses to communicate to the audience a wide variety of information—not only about time, place, and character, but about the style and fundamental nature of the production itself. In the contemporary theatre, we are likely to find the role of costume changing from production to production: In some plays it is a critical part of the production's visual elements, whereas in others it may be completely deemphasized. That is the nature of contemporary theatre: Each of the elements of production serves a production's specific needs, as the artistic choices of its personnel dictate.

Figure 12.2   François-Joseph Talma as Nero in Jean Racine's Britannicus (1661). *The social scene of seventeenth- and eighteenth-century French theatre (see Chapter 16) was dominated by great actors and actresses, culminating in the highly passionate performances of Talma (1763–1826). At the same time, Talma tempered his Romantic style with an insistence on the historical accuracy and naturalness of both dialogue and costuming. He is shown here in a Roman toga instead of the costuming—often contemporary dress—characteristic of his day.*

[New York Public Library, Lincoln Center.]

Costumes *and* Makeup

What Is *a* Stage Costume?

costume Everything about the actor that the audience sees but also including such items as foundation garments that give shape and underpinning to the clothing

"A costume is a 'magic garment'—a garment that enables an actor to become, for a time, someone else. Like Prospero's cape, which concentrated his supernatural powers over the winds and sea, an actor's costume helps concentrate the powers of imagination, expression, emotion, and movement into the creation and projection of a character to an audience." In this quotation, costume designer Rebecca Cunningham compares costumes to a "magic garment" like Prospero's cape in *The Tempest* by William Shakespeare. In the theatre, **costume** assumes a detailed, sophisticated, and wide-ranging definition. Certainly, stage costume is clothing: clothing allowing the actor "to become . . . someone else." Costume also includes hairstyle and makeup. Costume, then, comprises everything about the actor that the audience sees. *Costume is the actor's skin:* Everything visible about the actor—the outward appearance of the actor, as well as such hidden items as undergarments—is an element of costume.

To some degree, costume functions as a disguise for the actor's personality. It may be a complete disguise or merely a slight accentuation of character that is different from the actor's self. A costume aids the actor in moving in accordance with his or her character. Some costumes are designed specifically to enhance certain kinds of movement and to prohibit others. The hoop skirts of the nineteenth century, for example, definitely promote a graceful gait and sweeping movements. An actor who does not adapt to the style of movement appropriate to such a costume will present a ludicrous picture. Obviously, a costume should fit well and should be usable by the actor in the character he or she portrays. Costumes may enhance and/or inhibit certain movements; for example, the tendency of a hoop skirt to bounce unattractively can force an actress to adopt a smoother and more graceful gait, so that the costume's inhibiting role actually adds to the production. By contrast, a costume that fits poorly and causes chafing or inhibits motion in an actor who must turn somersaults is not acceptable and may even be dangerous.

The Functions *of* Stage Costume

It is helpful to divide the functions of costume into five categories: to accent relationships; to reflect time and place; to clarify character; to support purpose and style; and to create mood. Costume accents relationships by telling us how the personages on stage relate to each other.

Accenting Relationships   First, a well-designed costume clearly indicates the relative importance of characters by the use of color, contrast, and detail. The most important personages in a scene stand out because their costumes, for example, may use more brilliant or eye-catching colors than those of the other personages on stage at the time. One costume may stand in contrast to other costumes—for example, in *value* (light to dark) and/or in *texture*.

Detail in a costume design is often another indicator of emphasis. In crowd scenes on stage or in films, the less important characters seem to recede into the background because their costumes are far less detailed than those of the more important characters. Thus, costume helps the director, actor, and audience arrive at a communication relationship in which those things that need to stand out visually do so.

Second, costume shows us how characters relate to each other in terms of conflict or agreement. In Shakespeare's *Romeo and Juliet*, for instance, we find two large groups of individuals in conflict: the Capulets and the Montagues. In order for us to distinguish the characters, all the individuals in the Capulet camp usually are dressed in similar colors—ones that contrast with the unified color scheme of those in the Montague camp. An interesting accentuation of relationship also occurs in the design of the costumes of Romeo and Juliet themselves, who belong to opposing families as well as to each other. In accent, then, although Romeo must stand out as a major figure relative to other personages, he must also be "allied" both with his family and with Juliet. Each of these relationships can be clarified through costume.

Reflecting Time and Place Costume reflects not only character but time and place as well. To an important extent, time and place draw on one major characteristic of costume—**silhouette**, or the outline of the costume. Every historical period has a fairly distinct silhouette. The outline created by the bustle on the rear of a late-nineteenth-century woman's skirt, the high waist of an Empire gown, and the wide panniers of an Elizabethan skirt are all examples of how we can identify period by silhouette. In addition to historical period, moreover, the costumer also tells us the time of day, climate, season, and even the occasion of the play. The more sophisticated our own knowledge of history and fashion, the better we as audience members can discern what the visual design of the play tells us. Such details often do more than simply define historical time and place. Some periods carry a certain mystique or reputation, and setting the play therein may create a special ambience for the production—as for example, in Restoration comedies. Sometimes, a historical period different from the one normally associated with the play may be chosen—for example, setting Sophocles' *Oedipus Rex* in an Edwardian English setting. Sometimes, a totally neutral time and place can be indicated by costume, as occurred in the production of *Hamlet* starring the late Richard Burton, with actors costumed in black tights as opposed to historical garb. Whatever the time or place chosen for the production—and for whatever reasons—costume provides that reflection.

Clarifying Character In addition to reflecting time and place, costume also tells us about a character's social position, profession, personality, age, physique, and health. Hairstyle, for example, can give vital messages in creating age. Garment length, neckline shape, and sleeve type are other design choices used to indicate age, social status, and profession. The use of various

silhouette Outline of the *costume*

Figure 12.3 *Costume as an indicator of time and place in Louis O. Cox and Robert Chapman's Billy Budd. University of Arizona Theatre. Director, Peter R. Marroney; scene design by Robert Baker; costume design by Helen Workman Currie; lighting design by John E. Lafferty.*

textures, such as rich velour as opposed to coarse linen, can indicate social condition. Facial makeup and the condition of the garments can indicate a character's health and/or well-being. These are only a few examples of the many devices that costumers use to reflect the numerous important aspects of character to an audience.

Supporting Style As should be clear from discussions in previous chapters, costume, as one of the many parts of the overall production, also functions to support the overall goals and concepts of the production. Costume supports the style of the play and the director's interpretation of that style. If the style is realism, costume accents and reflects in the style of realism—that is, unless the director seeks deliberately to place costume in opposition to the style of some other element. Because of practical concerns like scene shifting in a multi-scene production, a unit setting (see Chapter 10) may be used, making it impossible to create a "realistic" scenic environment. If a sense of history and realism is important to the play, however, then communication of those details may rest on the costumes. In such a case, costume would be rendered realistically while the setting would reflect a nonrepresentational locale. Hundreds of

Costumes *and* Makeup

options exist for every production; whatever choice is made must be in support of the overall concept.

Creating Mood   Mood is another important supportive function for the costumer. Color and texture are the most frequently used tools in creating mood. For example, in support of a high comedy with a generally light, frivolous mood, the costumer will choose articulated textures and bright colors of high value—that is, light as opposed to dark tones. Mood also may call for some exaggeration of historical style. In order to create a lighthearted mood for a baroque comedy like Molière's *The Doctor in Spite of Himself*, the costumes may exaggerate details and ornamentation to give the production a slightly ridiculous slant.

The Design Process

PLAY AND CHARACTER ANALYSIS

The costume designer's choices, like those of the set and lighting designer, director, and actors, depend on the results of an extensive process of play and character analysis, as noted in Chapter 3. Without a thorough understanding of the play, the costume designer cannot make choices that will allow the costumes to accent, reflect, and support properly. Specifically, for each individual in the play, the costumer makes notes about character, based on questions like these:

1. What kind of character is this—major, minor, allegorical, and so on?
2. What are the physical characteristics—age, appearance, and so on?
3. What personality or mental traits are indicated?
4. What is the social status?
5. What is the character's *spine* (see Chapter 9)?
6. What specific references to clothing are made in the script?
7. How does the actor cast in the role fit the physical description?
8. When and with whom does the character appear on stage?

The costume designer charts the answers to these and other questions as part of the design process. Then, once a detailed analysis of the script has been made, the designer is ready to meet with the director and other designers in the first production conference.

PRODUCTION CONFERENCES

We will not restate the material on production conferences covered in previous chapters. Suffice it to say that the costume designer, as a member of a

Costume Plot

Play ☐ Musical ☐ Opera ☐

Title **Cabaret**

Author **Joe Masteroff**

NOTE: Under each act and scene mention time of year; time of day; interior or exterior; period and contry.

Name of Character	Act 1 Scene 1 Type of Costume	Act 1 Scene 2 Type	Act 1 Scene 3 Type	Act 1 Scene 4 Type	Act 1 Scene 5 Type	Act 1 Scene 6 Type	Act 1 Scene 7 Type
Sara Rose Martin	✓						
Sally Bowles	✓						
Brent Marty							
Emcee		✓	✓			✓	✓
Scott Payton							
Cliff Bradshaw		✓	✓	✓	✓	✓	
Susan Henderson							
Fraulein Schneider			✓			✓	
Paul Nickly							
Ernst Ludwig		✓				✓	
Bill Wikison			✓				
Herr Schultz			✓				
Holly Williamson			✓				
Fraulein Kost			✓				
Kit kat Girls							
Maria (Heather Baker)	✓			✓	✓		✓
Lulu (Holly Stultz)	✓			✓	✓		✓
Rosie (Cathy Cassaza)	✓			✓	✓		
Fritzie (Melissa Paris)	✓			✓	✓		
Texas (Jacey Frazier)	✓			✓	✓		
Frenchie (Heather McGee)	✓			✓	✓		
John Clark	Maitra D			Maitra D	Maitra D		
Jim Williams				Max	Max		
John Fitzgerald	Bartender	Customs off		Bartender	Bartender	Taxi Man	

Figure 12.4 *A basic costume plot.*

collaborative team, must be able to discuss concept, ideas, effects, images, schedules, and budgets from his or her particular point of view. The costumer's creativity will be called upon to add to the ideas and visions of the other participants. Because the costumes for a production must work within the creative context dictated by the set and lighting designers while enhancing the tasks of the actors, the costumer, like the other artists, must know enough about the tasks of these others to see costuming as part of the larger picture.

In addition, the costumer must be able to provide meaningful, accurate information about just what kind of costumes *can* be achieved given the available budget, shop workers, and construction time. From the outset, the costumer must know whether the costumes for a show can be built from scratch, taken from stock (using costumes in storage from previous productions), rented from a costume rental service, or provided from some combination of these sources. Such practical factors may influence the director's choices and concept. Typically, costume, scenic, and lighting designers work on more than one show at a time. They must let the director know how the current production relates to other productions in ways that will affect design, construction, and rehearsal time. Although preliminary production meetings may be scheduled months ahead of opening night, other shows on the season calendar may prevent the designer from beginning actual construction until just a few weeks before opening. If a large cast, a period show, a musical, or an opera must be costumed immediately prior to the current show, then the costumer may not be able to support an elaborate production concept by this director. The costumer needs to know that fact and make it known to the director immediately. Occasionally such conflicts get a production off to a rough start because directors may not respond well to having their concepts given a lower priority by design staffs responsible for several shows in a season. Nonetheless, trimming the concept at the beginning of the design process is a far better option than ending up at opening night with incomplete and unsatisfactory results due to overcommitment.

RESEARCH

Perhaps even before the first production conference, the costumer begins to research various elements about the play. The type and amount of research vary from play to play. If there is any question about the particular period to be chosen for the production, the costumer may wish to postpone in-depth research until after conferring with the director about that aspect of the concept. If, however, the designer has a preference for a particular period for the play, he or she should prepare for the first production conference with enough material on style and period to make that viewpoint clear and cogent. Some historical plays will require extensive research into social history, period fashion, literature, and visual art. Some plays may even require site visits. When the basic research is accumulated, the designer sifts through it, analyzes it, and chooses silhouettes, colors, hairstyles, accessories, and so on to meet the needs of each character and the overall production concepts and goals.

Susan Hilferty: You Don't Have to Draw Like Michelangelo

A painting and fashion-design student before she enrolled as a costume designer at the Yale School of Drama, Susan Hilferty then spent a year in London, where an active theatre culture enabled her to train her eye at three or four productions a week. Since returning to work in the professional theatre in the United States, she has created costumes both on and off Broadway, at the major resident theatres including The Guthrie, Goodman, A. C. T., LaJolla Playhouse, Center Stage, Yale Rep, Berkeley Rep, etc.; London, and South Africa. In this interview, she emphasizes the creative opportunities available in a highly collaborative medium and focuses on the imaginative freedom that she experienced in a 1988 production of Shakespeare's Comedy of Errors *at Lincoln Center. She currently teaches costume design in N.Y.U.'s graduate program, Tisch School of the Arts.*

When Sharon Ott decided to set the Berkeley Repertory's production of *Twelfth Night* in the 1920s, costume designer Susan Hilferty suggested the director read Roger Shattuck's *The Banquet Years*, a historical study of the period in France a few years prior to that roaring era. In the end, the book's surrealist style and sensibility set the tone for the production as a whole—costumes included.

"She was almost performing a dramaturgical function," Ott says of the designer's contribution to the play's shifted focus. "She doesn't just talk in terms of the line of the clothes. It's the idea we're trying to put across and how we can make it relate to now. There's no one I feel as comfortable with talking about the entire play. . . ."

More than a style or trademark, [Hilferty's] career seems to be based on close collaborative relationships with various directors. "The thing that attracted me to being a designer attracted me to being in theatre," she says. "It's a collaborative art. I find that my designs are completely integrated into a production and that I can never pull my clothes away and have them survive intact outside the production. . . ."

It's a collaborative art. I find that my designs are completely integrated into a production and that I can never pull my clothes away and have them survive intact outside the production.

Collaboration took full force in *Comedy of Errors* [Lincoln Center Theater Company, 1988], a production full of bizarre and imaginative images that featured the acrobatic antics of the Flying Karamozov Brothers. Initially, Hilferty says, "Nobody had a clue what we were doing. We literally built and designed throughout the rehearsal process. It was like being in this huge playpen."

Out of discussions between Hilferty, [director Robert] Woodruff, and set designer David Gropman two basic ideas emerged: a busy marketplace and Turkey. In the bold, exaggerated design that evolved, Hilferty sought to combine contemporary and Turkish images: a turban with baggy shorts, a paisley rayon shirt with leopard print shoes. "Since everybody plays at least three or four characters, with not a lot of time for changes," she told *Theatre Times*, "and since these are not performers who do big acting transitions between one character and the next, the costume choices were big." Thus, performers who were part of the band wore red clothing, fake noses, and dark glasses. Townspeople wore stripes and bright colors. Policemen dressed in pink costumes with reflective glasses, fake noses, and helmets with flashing lights. "We used the word 'stupid' as a compliment," Hilferty recalls, laughing, " 'Really stupid' was high applause."

As the production developed, one performer, Alec Willows, ended up with two roles, the Second Merchant and Angelo, the goldsmith. The team decided to split him down the middle, each half of his body representing one of the characters. Two separate costumes, one made of gold lamé for the goldsmith, the other of black leather for the merchant, were literally cut in half and sewn back together. Willows even permed one half of his hair while bleaching the other.

The extraordinary physical demands of the performance presented more practical challenges, Hilferty says. Juggling, for example, requires tight fitting sleeves; juggling of fire limits the range of fabrics that can be used. "In fittings," she adds, "this show was hilarious. Normally an actor comes to a fitting, lifts his arms and says, 'Yeah, that's okay, I can lift my arms, but I also have to turn around and sit on a chair.' These guys go, 'Well it feels okay,' but then they'll do a backflip, bring in a friend who stands on his shoulders, and cartwheel across the room."

The process by which the play developed, Hilferty says, is ideal. "That's the way I

like to work," she notes. "I spend a lot of time in rehearsal, with the actors, with the other designers. I find that's the key to the work I do. And I like that it builds slowly within the idea of the production. . . ."

Although her distinctive approach to designing costumes is hard to teach, design students at Parsons School of Design in New York, where Hilferty is an instructor, do learn about her views on more practical aspects of the craft, like drawing. "In costumes, I always start sketching," Hilferty says, "Whenever there's time I do a complete rendering.

"I tell my students you don't have to draw like Michelangelo," she says. "But if you don't put it down on paper, you don't really know what your ideas are. And for somebody else to know what you're talking about, you need to put it down on paper even if in the most crude manner."

Such details are secondary to the real thrust of Hilferty's work—immersing herself in a play's ideas and working with others to convey them visually. "A lot of times people ask me what plays I would like to design," she says. "That's an impossible question to answer. Probably the first question I would ask is 'Who is the director?' I work with specific directors and that's the thing that inspires me, because that is a relationship I depend on. I have to be part of a team."

From Beth Howard, "Designers on Design: Susan Hilferty," *Theatre Crafts*, January 1990.

TRANSLATING IDEAS INTO PICTURES

The Rough Sketch Now the costume designer is ready to translate images and ideas into pictures. Like the scene designer, the costumer begins with a series of quick pencil sketches called **roughs** (Fig. 12.5). These sketches are more conceptual than detailed. They give general impressions of silhouette, color, texture, and line to indicate character, relationships, and period. From these roughs the costumer works out a unified chart of the play's action, noting costume changes and how those reveal progress in conflict or character with

roughs Costume designer's quick *pencil sketches* that translate images and ideas into pictures

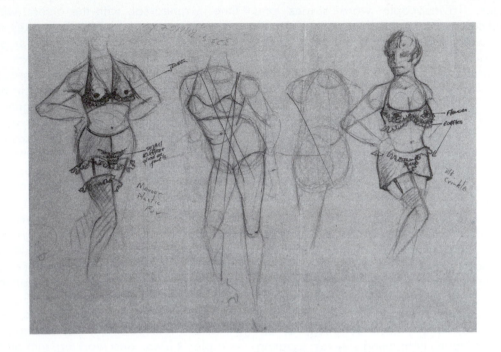

Figure 12.5 *Costume designer's rough sketch and production-conference presentation sketch. The color rendering will be based on this second draft.*

regard to the dramatic action and overall concept. When the roughs have progressed to the point that the designer is satisfied with the entirety, they are presented to the director and other designers at another production conference (see Fig. 12.5).

color rendering Colored drawing that provides a complete and accurate picture of *stage costumes*

The Color Rendering When the roughs have been approved, the next step requires a full **color rendering** of each costume in the production. A variety of media may be used for these renderings—pencil, ink, gouache, acrylics, and/or watercolors. Each designer has a favorite medium in which he or she works accurately and comfortably. The key is to pick a medium that best suits the effect required; for example, a dazzling evening dress made of gold lamé requires the addition of glitter to communicate the intent accurately. The color rendering must be an accurate picture: It represents the designer's contract with and sales pitch to the production team. At this point fabric swatches are usually appended to the rendering so that actual textures and colors may be examined. The costume designer's rendering, unlike that of the scene designer, ultimately differs considerably from the final product. Because the costume designer's actual medium is *fabric*, not paint, every effort must be made to give an accurate representation of the surface textures and details of the costume. This is important not only for the director and the scene designer but also for the lighting designer, whose effects will vary drastically if a costume is made of sateen as opposed to velvet of the same color. Because they may have a significant effect on lighting angles, any reflective materials, such as glitter, must be noted in the production meetings.

Focal Points and Physiques In developing the color renderings, the costume designer includes all important details. The first of these is *focal point* or emphasis. Because an actor's most expressive tool is his face, the focal area of a costume usually will be the head or face. Sometimes, however, other areas—hands, feet, or stomachs, for example—take focus.

The next important detail is the actor's *physicality*. Not only must each character's costume be designed with the ideal qualities of the character in mind—for example, a tall, muscular "heroic" physique—but the actor playing the role must have his actual physique tailored to the needs of the character and the costume. Several years ago in one of the popular women's magazines, two costume designers for the Metropolitan Opera shared their secrets on making obese singers look slim on stage. They indicated how they used line and recessive and attractive colors to create costumes that changed circular figures into apparently trim ones. At other times, costumes must be padded to create bulky figures on stage from small or slightly built actors.

accessories Details like scarves, jewelry, shirts, and shoes that complete a costume and give it individuality

Accessories Another important detail in the color rendering is **accessories**. Often the difference between an excellent costume and a mediocre one lies in the accessories. This concern is no different from many of the choices we make in everyday dress. Men and women alike often enliven basic garments with stunning accessories—for example, jewelry, scarves, shoes, ties, and shirts—to give a basic set of clothes an air of individuality. The costume designer thus takes time to consider hats, shoes, handbags, hairstyles, scarves, and jewelry—added details that give each costume its personality and tell the

Figure 12.6 *Costumes and accessories complete the illusion of time, place, style, and character in the University of Arizona production of* Hello Dolly *by Jerry Herman and Michael Stewart. Production directed by Peter R. Marroney with scenic design by Robert C. Burroughs, costumes by Helen Workman Currie, and lighting by John E. Lafferty.*

audience in vivid terms about the individual character who inhabits the costume.

Coordination   The color rendering of each costume is usually done on a single piece of paper or board to enable the costume designer to show the production team how each design coordinates with the others that will be on stage at the same time. This method makes it possible to be sure that each character has the right degree of emphasis and coordinates well. Here, the use of French scenes (see Chapter 3) is invaluable. Charting the play scene by scene in terms of who is on stage with whom plays a critical role developing the color renderings.

Figure Drawing   Because the proportions of the human figure play such an important role in the way a costume design communicates to an audience, the costume designer must pay close attention to the accuracy of figure drawing. The human figure—the fundamental form on which all costume must be based—is extremely difficult to draw, because it comprises such a complex arrangement of interrelated and articulated curvatures. That is why every visual artist begins his or her training with a course in figure drawing. The training, technique, and observation required to master the art of representing the human figure on a two-dimensional surface call for intense discipline and repetitive practice.

For the visual artist, figure drawing is analogous to practicing scales as part of the effort to become a masterful pianist. The costume designer who is

Costumes *and* Makeup

deficient in this skill will never reach the pinnacle of the art because the sketches that he or she uses to transmit images and ideas to the director and other designers will never truly capture what is intended. The slightest mistake in body proportions can change the style of a design to one that the designer does not intend at all.

Working Drawings   Although the final color rendering provides the basic model from which the actual costume is developed, there may be a need for additional **working drawings** to help clarify the design and its parts. These drawings constitute a specific step in the design process. Details of construction, trim, and other details are created in pencil or ink on separate sheets or boards and attached to the color rendering. Some details—for example, floral prints, buttons, hats, and trims—may require actual scaled mechanical drawings. In effect, the designer must put together whatever additional materials are necessary to make the intent of the sketch clear. Those who build the design must have detailed, accurate information available in order to do their work just as the technician and scene designer must create accurately scaled drawings for the construction of the scenery. Because support staff cannot expect the designer to be present every moment in order to answer questions, the designer must be sure to answer those questions in advance by providing clear drawings, fabric swatches, and so on.

working drawings
Detailed drawings used to help to clarify the costume design and its parts

Making *the* Costume

The next step in the design process involves making the costume. To execute this step, the costumer pays attention to *fabric*, *patterns*, and actual *construction*.

Fabric   As we mentioned earlier, the costumer works in fabric and must have an expert knowledge of this medium. The designer must be sensitive to how a fabric drapes and to its surface texture, how it moves on an actor, and how it acts under light.

Draping Qualities   In general, fabric can be divided into two groups based on its *draping qualities*: *limp fabrics*, which hang in soft folds, and *stiff fabrics*, which hang in angular folds. There are, of course, many variations between these two extremes; some fabrics near the middle of the spectrum might be classified as either soft or stiff. Nonetheless, these categories are helpful for understanding the costume designer's work.

surface texture
Particular surface of a fabric, either dull or shiny

Surface Texture   Fabrics also can be divided by **surface texture**—again, into two groups: *dull* and *shiny*. Dull fabrics absorb light, and shiny fabrics reflect it. Dull fabrics have a dense texture, shiny fabrics a smooth texture. At first glance, dealing with fabrics seems fairly straightforward. The untrained eye, however, does not know how to see a texture or a drape as it will actually look to an audience responding to the fabric from a distance of thirty to eighty feet. Many attractive fabrics actually carry an unattractive image across the distances present in the theatre, and vice versa. In addition, the inexperienced

Figure 12.7 *A variety of textures create interest and design focus in* Fulgens and Lucrece *by Henry Medwall, done as at a Tudor banquet, at the Washington and Lee University Theatre. The production was directed by Al Gordon and designed by Tom Ziegler. In the early sixteenth century, certain features of the medieval morality play (see Chapter 15) were adapted to the so-called interlude—an hour-long episode performed during or after meals in large private dining halls and often concluded by a prayer for the wealthy host. Surrounded by guests at table on three or four sides, actors performed essentially in the round, and—as here—the interlude is thus quite adaptable to the modern dinner theatre.*

designer may decide that a rich velvet provides just the right effect for a kingly gown only to discover that it takes a kingly budget to execute the design. Often, inexpensive fabrics can be substituted for expensive ones and may, in fact, carry the image of texture better than the original.

Composition   One of the first things a costume designer must learn about fabrics is their nature and **composition**—the ways in which fabrics are woven, treated, and finished. Cloth can be constructed in a number of ways. *Weaving* interlaces two sets of yarns at right angles. *Knitting* comprises rows of loops of yarn drawn through another series of loops by needles. *Crocheting* makes a looped fabric from a single yarn by creating a chain of loops with a hook. *Braiding* interlaces yarns at an angle of less than ninety degrees to form a flat, tubular fabric. *Knotting* produces an openwork fabric consisting of threads knotted together in a pattern. *Felting* presses fibers together by heat, steam, and pressure to form a matted fabric. *Laminating* presses fabrics together into a single sheet held together by adhesives. Fabrics made by one of these methods are called *textile fabrics* and consist of *natural* (cotton, linen, silk, and wool) and *synthetic* or man-made (rayon and nylon) fibers.

Patterns   The next step in making the costume requires the translation of the design onto the fabric by using a **pattern**. Sewing stores sell thousands of patterns for all sorts of different garments, for men and women, for all kinds of occasions. Unfortunately, such commercial patterns have only minimum application for stage costumers, who must turn elsewhere in order to create a pattern for most theatrical costumes. Many stage costume books contain pat-

composition In fabric, the way that *costume cloth* is constructed—for example, by knitting, crocheting, braiding, knotting, or felting

pattern Paper or canvas model from which the parts of a *costume* can be traced onto fabric

terns for period garments among their illustrations. These designs must be researched, blown up to size, and adapted to fit the needs of the production and the size of the actor. Once a pattern is made, it is kept on file for future reference. Every theatre costume shop has an elaborate file of home-made patterns developed over years. The designer, however, still must know how to draft a pattern from an actor's measurements so as to execute the design as it was intended in the rendering. In normal circumstances, standard drafting equipment does the job, and the pattern is drafted on heavy wrapping paper. The finished pattern is transferred to muslin, which can be readily laid out on the fabric, stands up to reuse, and stores easily.

Construction   Once the designs are finished, the fabrics chosen, and the patterns assembled, actual construction of the garment involves specially trained personnel working with special tools in a specifically designed facility. The costume designer has responsibility for supervising a shop foreman, seamstresses, cutters, and other personnel who may be assigned particular responsibilities, such as dyeing fabrics or constructing accessories and ornamentation. Throughout the construction process, the original intent of the production— and thus the costume—must be kept in mind.

fittings Series of appointments for the actor with the costumer in which the costume is measured and tested for fit and function

Fittings   In the process of construction comes a series of actor **fittings** through which the costume emerges. At the first fitting, the actor wears all the garments that he or she will wear *under* the costume—for example, padding, corsets, brassieres, and petticoats. With these in place, either the roughly assembled costume or its muslin pattern is put on and adjusted. By the second fitting, the costume should be near the finished state, including all accessories, and the actor runs through all stage actions that will occur in this costume to ensure that the costume will comfortably accommodate any required movements without tearing. Every seam, fastener, and opening must be checked for appearance and strength. When the costumes have passed this trial stage, they are finished. At the third fitting, finished costumes are tried on in sequence and checked again for movement and accessories. At this fitting, the actor receives a checklist with each costume so that no confusion arises in the dressing room concerning what is worn and when it is worn. Any necessary finishing—for example, reinforcement of seams and adding of lining—occurs immediately after the third fitting.

Production Organization

The next step in the design procedure consists of organizing the finished costumes for the entire production. For a large-cast musical, this step may involve hundreds of costumes with thousands of pieces. Lack of proper organization will lead to chaos. As each piece is finished, it is labeled and put on a rack; this practice prevents the confusion that would arise if finished and unfinished garments were stored together. Small items like gloves, tights, and handkerchiefs are kept in a bag hung on the same hanger. Very small items such as jewelry are kept in a box placed within the bag. When everything is finished, the entire lot is turned over to the wardrobe crew, whose responsibility is to maintain the costumes throughout the run of the show. This responsibility includes repair, cleaning, and pressing, as well as planning and supervising all changes: Each actor is checked by a "dresser" after each costume change to be sure the costume is complete and worn properly. Several weeks before the performance, the wardrobe master or mistress begins to go over all requirements and garments with the designer. All sequences and quick-change problems are discussed thoroughly. The wardrobe crew then organizes the backstage space allotted to costumes and plans every routine.

DRESS PARADE

An optional step in the design procedure is an event called a *dress parade*. Many designers and directors like to see all the costumes assembled, on stage, and under light just prior to dress rehearsals (see Fig. 12.8). This stage is the first time that all garments and accessories will have been assembled, and it

Figure 12.8 *The full cast assembled in costume. Richard Rogers and Oscar Hammerstein,* Carousel. *Music Theatre of Wichita (1990). Director, Wayne Bryan; scene designer, Charles O'Connor; costume designer, Peggy Kellner; lighting designer, David Neville. Photo by Charles O'Connor.*

Costumes *and* Makeup

serves as a final check to be sure that everything looks as it was intended to look, each item by itself and in relation to others, so that last-minute problems can be addressed before final dress rehearsals. During the **dress parade**, actors try doorways and stairways to be sure they can negotiate these spaces and to be sure that the set-construction crews have not left protruding nails or splinters that can snag or tear garments. Throughout the rehearsal period, actors should have been dressed in "rehearsal garments" approximating the finished costume so that they can get used to garments like robes, long skirts, and high-heeled boots. Thus, actors are given similar garments in which they can rehearse while the actual costume is being built. Rehearsal garments let actors practice moving in costume and while saving wear and tear on actual costumes—which may be finished before dress rehearsal.

dress parade Period, just prior to *dress rehearsal*, when all the costumes are assembled, on stage, and under light

Dress Rehearsals

The last phase of the design procedure is called a **dress rehearsal**. Ideally, everything is well in hand by the time when final dress rehearsals occur. At this time, near-performance conditions should be in effect. As noted earlier, the dress rehearsal is the moment when all elements, in their final form, are coordinated. Small final adjustments are made, and the actors gain a true sense of the time involved, for example, in quick changes. The costume designer sits through the dress rehearsal and takes careful notes on what he or she sees. The director and the lighting designer may also have suggestions. When dress rehearsals are finished, the production opens, and the design process comes to an end.

dress rehearsal *Production stage* at which all elements, including prepared costumes, meet near-performance conditions

The Costume Shop

In exactly the same sense as we noted in Chapter 11, the designer's artistic choices and execution depend directly on the quality of space and equipment available. Regardless of the skills of the personnel involved, much of a high-quality product depends on the tools and spaces in which the costume designer and costume staff must work. Paramount among the spaces in the costume process is the storage area. A large and varied **wardrobe stock** is crucial to any theatre organization. Aside from the cost, the amount of time required for the construction of individual garments makes it literally impossible to do new construction for most shows. A large, dry, easily accessible storage facility exceeds in importance even the construction space itself. Nonetheless, the workshop must meet certain basic conditions and must be equipped with the proper tools. Important major elements include cutting tables on which fabric is laid out, cut, and pinned; industrial-quality sewing machines, hem finishers, mirrors, ironing boards and irons; laundry facilities; dye vats; dress forms; and a mountain of buttons, threads, scissors, rivets, beads, and so forth.

wardrobe stock *Costumes* made for previous productions that are kept in storage for possible reuse

Stage Makeup

Our brief foray into the world of stage makeup gives us a sampling of yet another layer of the many that make up a theatre production. Our discussion, though limited, should reinforce how thoroughly every detail of a production is attended to and how every detail emerges from the production conferences and the director's concept.

Although stage makeup often is seen as a separate part of the production, it really falls under the broad definition of costume: Face, hair, hands (indeed, any visible portion of the actor's body) must function in conjunction with the rest of the actor's outward skin—that is, *costume*. Unless a particular production concept specifically ties makeup to costumes—for example, the use of masks—the job of designing makeup is assigned in a variety of ways to a variety of individuals, including a subordinate of the costume designer. Often, however, it falls to the actor to plan and execute his or her own makeup.

PURPOSE AND ANALYSIS

The purpose of all stage makeup is to help the actor reveal the character to the audience. Designing makeup begins with an analysis that yields a thorough understanding of character, history—for example, fashion makeup and hairstyles from the period of the play—and the style of the production. Ideally, the actor and director have made a thorough analysis of each character, and that information can provide much of the basis for the makeup. Just as other designers use artistic tools to communicate meaning to an audience, the makeup designer applies understanding of character to general stereotypes that help an audience *see* the character—for example, if the character is dishonest, the designer may call upon a stereotype such as small beady eyes to help communicate that aspect of character. Once the character has been analyzed, the makeup must be visualized.

Visualization Sketches Visualizing a makeup design involves the same sort of process used by the scenic and costume designers—translation of artistic visions into colored drawings called **visualization sketches.** In this step, what is known about the character is turned into a design of physical features. Questions of genetics, environment, health, disfigurement, fashion (including beard and hairstyles), age, and personality give rise to answers that are translated into kinds of eyes, noses, mouths, and chins. This process calls for creative imagination and investigation of choices that will attempt to play on an audience's general stereotypical responses.

Worksheets When the makeup sketch has been approved, the designer prepares a **worksheet** to guide the actor or crew member who applies the makeup (see Fig. 12.9). All specifications for application of base makeup, lining, facial hair, and or prosthetics (three-dimensional pieces) appear on the

worksheet
Designer-prepared guide for actors and crew members who apply makeup

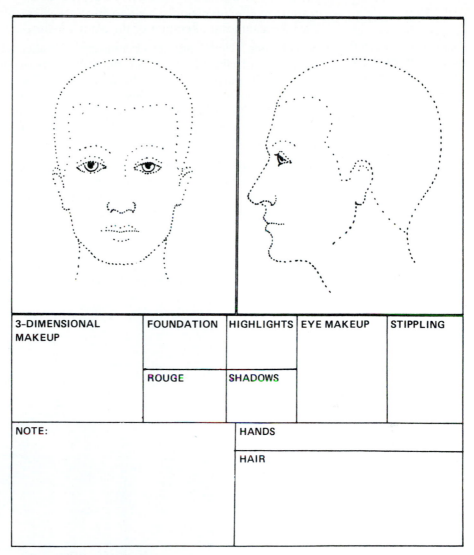

3-DIMENSIONAL MAKEUP	FOUNDATION	HIGHLIGHTS	EYE MAKEUP	STIPPLING
	ROUGE	SHADOWS		
NOTE:	HANDS			
	HAIR			

Figure 12.9 *A makeup worksheet.*

From Richard Corson, *Stage Makeup*, 8e, p. 34. Reprinted by permission of Prentice Hall, Englewood Cliffs, New Jersey.

worksheet, which must be prepared in detail. All the subtle highlights and shadows that will be part of the makeup must be carefully drawn.

   Execution   Makeup can be executed in two basic ways: by *painting* the effects on the face of the actor or by *building* the effects using three-dimen-

prosthetics
Three-dimensional pieces used for building makeup effects

straight makeup
Makeup used when the actor's features require no major changes to effect the character

character makeup
Makeup that provides significant alteration of the actor's features

greasepaint Common name of a stage makeup that comes in a tube

sional pieces known as **prosthetics.** The latter category includes beards and wigs as well as false noses and warts. Makeup is further divided into two categories: *straight* and *character*. **Straight makeup** is used when the actor's features require no major changes to effect the character. **Character makeup** is used for significant alteration of the actor's features.

Foundations Under normal circumstances, makeup begins with a base or *foundation* of cake makeup, creme makeup, or **greasepaint.** The base is applied sparingly. Its purpose is to tint the skin to the desired color—not to cover the skin. Once the base is applied, highlights and shadows are drawn with pencils or brushes. The technique of painting in highlights and shadows is very much like the work of the easel painter: The artist attempts to create a three-dimensional effect on a two-dimensional surface.

Special Effects Modern plastics and other synthetic materials make it possible to create makeup effects of fantastic proportion. The best examples of the range of makeup possibilities occur in film; effects as varied as Dustin Hoffman's age makeup in *Little Big Man* and the plethora of creatures in the *Star*

Figure 12.10   *Final makeup for Alice Robinson as "Woman" in* Rockaby *by Samuel Beckett. The Maryland Stage Company (1990). Production director, Xerxes Mehta; set and costume design by Richard Montgomery; and lighting design by Lewis Shaw. Photo by Bob Dold. Notice the attention to detail in the hair styling, which completes the effect of the makeup and costume. As a major figure in absurdist theatre, Beckett is discussed in Chapter 17.*

Wars series come to mind. All these effects and the materials from which they derive, however, can also be found in the theatre, when and if a production demands them. In many theatres, however, even if one assumes the presence of a trained professional capable of executing them, elaborate makeup designs prove too expensive to execute at the level displayed in most films.

Beards, mustaches, and eyebrows use a product called *crepe hair*, which is cut to roughly the desired length and applied to the skin with a liquid adhesive that remains flexible when dry. After the adhesive dries, the hair is trimmed to its desired length and shape.

Any number of products can be purchased for special effects, and sometimes the sheer inventiveness of the designer solves problems with producing certain effects. A soft, waxy substance called *nose putty*, for example, often suffices for three-dimensional changes to the actor's face. Such mundane products as crumpled facial tissue can be mixed with liquid latex to create texture in special makeups.

SUMMARY

- For most of us, in normal circumstances, the word *costume* means clothing. In the theatre, however, *costume* takes on a far more detailed definition, including:

    Clothing for the actor;

    Hairstyle and *makeup*.

- Costume is the actor's skin: *everything visible about the actor*—the outward appearance, as well as hidden items like undergarments.

- Costume functions as a *disguise for the actor's personality*.

- Costume aids the actor in moving *in accordance with his character*.

- Costume normally functions in three ways:

    To *accent relationships*;

    To *reflect character, time,* and *place*;

    To *support purpose, style,* and *mood*.

- For the costumer, as for other designers in the theatre, the *design procedure* begins with tools and skills that include the elements and principles of artistic composition.

- The design procedure also hinges on the costumer's ability to draw the *human figure*, the fundamental form on which all costume must be based.

- As in all artistic pursuits in a theatrical production, the costumer begins the design procedure with *play and character analysis*.

- In *production conferences*, the costume designer faces the same needs to communicate and function as a member of a collaborative team as do the other artists involved in the production. The costumer must be able to give meaningful, accurate insight into the kind of costumes that can be achieved for the production.

- The type and amount of *research* done by the costumer during the design process varies from play to play.

- When basic research and analysis are finished, the costumer prepares a *rough sketch*: a series of quick pencil drawings.

- After the rough sketches have been approved, the costumer prepares a detailed *color rendering* that should contain:

  A *focal point* or emphasis;

  A consideration of the actor's physicality and its relationship to the ideal characteristics of the character;

  Proper *accessories* like shoes, ties, jewelry, and so on.

- The next step in the design process is the completion of *working drawings* that tell the costume staff how to build the costume.

- The costume is then *constructed*, with careful attention to *fabric* and the use of *patterns*.

- Actual construction of the garment involves specially trained personnel working with special tools in a specially designed facility called a *costume shop*.

- The design process involves a careful *production organization* so that all the parts and details of the complete costume can be kept together without confusion.

- When all costumes are finished, they are assembled on the actors, on stage, and under light in a procedure just prior to dress rehearsals called a *dress parade*.

- The final phase of the design process, the *dress rehearsal*, simulates actual production circumstances and allows for final adjustments and acclimation by the actors to circumstances like quick changes.

- The *costume shop* plays an important role in making possible the execution of costumes for a theatrical production. Without a well-designed and organized facility, proper execution of costumes is impossible.

- *Stage makeup* is an important part of costume design that often is seen as a separate artistic part of theatrical production.

• The purpose of stage makeup is to help the actor reveal the character to the audience.

• By using *visualization sketches* and *worksheets*, the makeup designer decides how to transform the face and other affected areas of the actor's body into a visual representation of the character.

• Makeup is executed in two basic ways: by *painting* the effect on the actor or by *building* the effect using three-dimensional pieces called *prosthetics*.

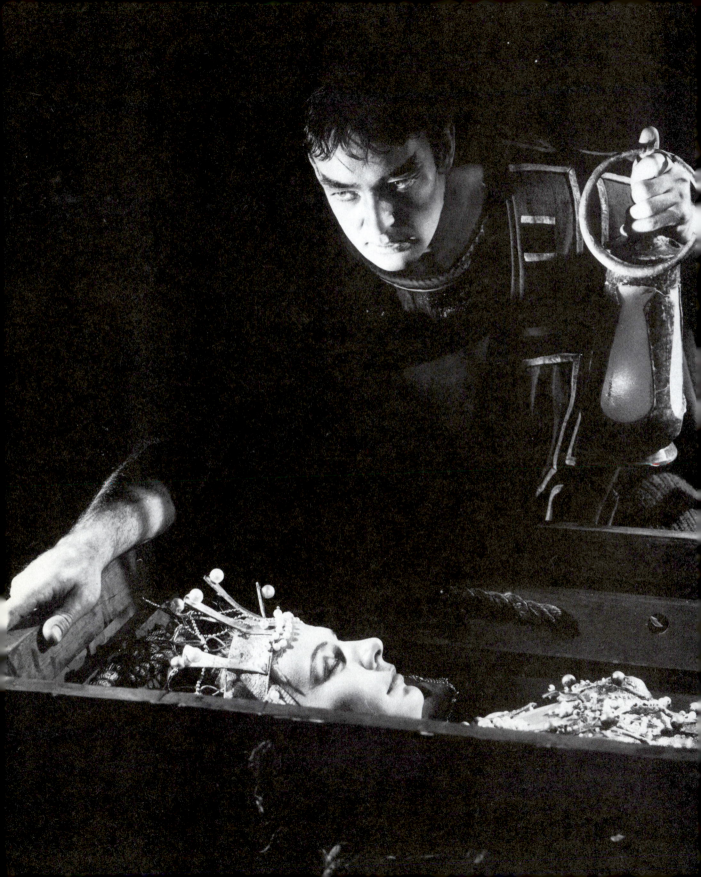

Lighting *and* Sound

*A*fter studying this chapter, you should be able to:

- Describe the development of modern *stage lighting*.
- Identify and explain the functions of stage lighting.
- Characterize the *properties of light*.
- Explain the *lighting design process*.
- Identify and describe basic lighting instruments.
- Explain *lighting control*.
- Evaluate a *lighting design*.
- Discuss the art of *sound design*.

Pericles. *Angus McBean/Harvard Theatre Collection.*

*A*s we saw in Chapter 2, the word *theatre* means *"a place for seeing."* Much theatre is visual, and what we see rests in the hands of the lighting designer. Common wisdom, however, states that good theatrical lighting is lighting that nobody notices. In this chapter, in addition to pointing out the fundamental principles and practices of lighting design, we may also dispel some of the misconceptions that surround this vital aspect of production art. Even in the brief treatment given here, it should become clear that stage lighting is the most technically intricate of the theatre arts, combining aesthetics, design, physics, optics, and even computer technology. It depends on a tremendously sophisticated arrangement of hardware. The lighting designer must be one part artist, one part electrician, one part administrator, and one part magician.

The second insert in this book, "The Art of Scene and Lighting Design," offers several full-color illustrations of the professional lighting designer's work.

The Development *of* Modern Lighting Design

The modern approach to stage lighting is probably the only art style in which theory preceded practice. As in our study of directing and acting, we can gain additional insight into the art of today if we see it in historical context.

Figure 13.1 *Performance of an* opéra comique *at the Hôtel de Bourgnogne, Paris, 1769. Drawing by P.A. Wille the Younger. The only permanent theatre in Paris in the first two decades of the 17th century, the Hôtel de Bourgnogne was originally the enclave of the* Confrérie *troupe (see Chapter 15), which turned to secular drama when religious drama was banned in 1548 and rented the theatre to other companies seeking exposure in the French theatrical center. Note the candle-powered footlights at the forefront of the stage.*

[From Bibliotheque Nationale, Paris.]

Lighting *and* Sound

From Candlelight to Gaslight   For some two thousand years, from its beginnings in ancient Greece until the Renaissance, theatre required no artificial lighting at all. Only when production began to move indoors was illumination required. The earliest indoor attempts at lighting, however, still sought to reflect "atmosphere"—at least in terms of using light for comedies and dark for tragedies. Nevertheless, although candles provided the only lighting source, some ingenious devices were invented to change lighting intensity and to create color. In the sixteenth century, for example, Sebastiano Serlio (see Chapter 10) suggested in his book *D'Architecttura* ways to create colored light by using colored liquids in bottles. An elementary spotlight was made by putting a barber's basin behind a torch, and candles were dimmed by lowering metal cylinders over them (see Fig. 13.2). Until the invention of the kerosene lamp in 1783, candles—in chandeliers, as footlights, in sconces behind the proscenium, or in various combinations—remained the tool of the lighting art.

The kerosene lamp was quickly eclipsed by the use of gaslight, which gave a light of greater intensity and also lent itself to more precise control. At the same time, the use of heated lime, which produces a strong, white light, came into the theatre. When carried in a box and moved by an attendant standing on the auditorium floor level at the front of the stage, limelight became an effective followspot. From this application came the phrase "in the limelight"—that is, being the center of attention.

The Advent of Electricity   Electricity first came to the theatre in the form of the *arc light,* variations of which still provide the light source for modern commercial movie projectors and theatre followspots. The invention of the incandescent lamp in the late nineteenth century ushered in the modern era—but not the modern *style*. Many problems remained to be solved before lighting could reach its potential. The first of these was solved when the technology was developed to dim the new lamps. The second, and perhaps more important, development was the technology to focus light from these lamps into controlled and useful beams.

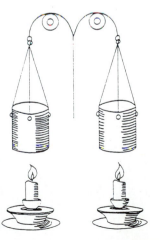

Figure 13.2   *A sixteenth-century dimming device consisting of metal cylinders that were lowered over candles.* (*From Sabbatini,* Practica de fabrica Scene e Machine ne Theatri, *1638.*)

[From Selden and Lesley, *Essentials of Stage Lighting.* Copyright © 1982, p. 12. Reprinted by permission by Prentice-Hall, Englewood Cliffs, New Jersey.]

Many devices for dimming light appeared almost immediately, but little progress was made in the development of controlled focus until nearly 1920, when the modern spotlight appeared. In the 1930s, a radical new technology called the *ellipsoidal spotlight* gave stage lighting just the tool it needed to put light where it was wanted and keep it away from where it was not wanted. The only major change in stage lighting instruments in the sixty intervening years has been the invention of the *tungsten-halogen lamp,* which gives greater candle power (amount of light) with a much smaller lamp.

During the late nineteenth century, lighting theory was shaped by a Swiss named Adolphe Appia. His insistence on controlled light, plasticity (three-dimensionality), and atmosphere shaped modern lighting practice and cast its theory before technology made its execution possible. The work of Appia is discussed in Chapter 17.

Functions *of* Stage Lighting

Lighting design serves four functions or purposes: It provides *selective visibility,* establishes *rhythm and structure,* evokes *mood,* and provides *motivation* or *illusion.*

SELECTIVE VISIBILITY

selective visibility One of the functions of *stage lighting*—providing the audience with the ability to see

The primary purpose of stage lighting, **selective visibility,** makes it possible for the audience to see. Obviously, however, there is more to it than that. Simply seeing the action on stage requires nothing more than some work lights turned on at the beginning of the play and turned off at the end. In fact, simple visibility could occur through general illumination, which is available when the audience enters the theatre and persists after the audience leaves—basically the way lighting was managed for centuries. Today, however, even the least sophisticated theatregoer expects more than *mere* visibility—as does the art of theatre. Therefore, when we observe that the primary function of stage lighting is *visibility,* we attach the modifier *selective* for good reason: The audience needs to see, but it also needs to see comfortably and clearly—and to see what the production artists want it to see. The lighting designer, therefore, creates visibility in which *proper focus* and *quality of form in space* result.

Visibility: Focus and Form. Lighting is the strongest device available in the theatre for drawing audience focus. In Chapter 9, for example, we noted that isolating an actor or part of the setting in light overpowers any other focusing device, including color and movement. Selective visibility, therefore, means *focused visibility.* It also means *quality of visible form.* In the painting *The Calling of St. Matthew* by the Italian baroque artist Caravaggio (Fig. 13.3), you will see *form* defined by strong highlights and shadows. The *quality of form* is made more dramatic not only by the strong contrast between what is lit and what is not lit but also by the fact that all the light comes from only one

Figure 13.3 *Carravaggio*, The Calling of St. Matthew, ca. 1596–1598. *Chiesa, S. Luigi de Francesi, Rome.*

[Alinari/Art Resource.]

chiaroscuro Use of light and shade to enhance three-dimensionality

direction. The forms in the painting stand out from the background and take on an intense three-dimensionality because of the contrasts of light and dark known as **chiaroscuro.** By using chiaroscuro, Caravaggio creates form that is highly plastic—that is, three-dimensional. Like the painter, the lighting designer must define form in a *qualitative* manner. For example, if the production goals require that form—that is, actors and scenery—appear three-dimensional, the lighting designer must achieve that effect (see Fig. 13.4). Conversely, by changing the lighting, the designer can make the same forms appear two-dimensional. The option lies in the hands of the lighting designer, guided by the director's production concept (see Chapter 8).

Figure 13.4 *Directional lighting from above and behind create a sense of three-dimensionality in* Terra Nova *by Ted Tally. Ball State University Theatre (1988). Directed by Jeff Cazazza with lighting design by Lisa K. Murphy, scenic design by Baron von Imhoof, and costumes by Kathy Jaremski.*

Lighting *and* Sound

Form and Depth Perception Another important factor in defining form on stage is controlling the ability of the audience to perceive *depth*. The relationship between the scenery and the actor contributes to this critical factor, and light establishes that relationship. For example, the illusion of deep space created when an actor stands in front of a panoramic backdrop will appear ludicrous if the actor's shadow falls on the background. Careful control of lighting angles and actor placement can keep shadows from falling in unwanted areas. Similarly, actors lit solely from the front tend to appear flat and also to fade into the background; plasticity, depth of space, and focus are all minimized under such conditions. The separation of actor from background, then, is an extremely important part of creating depth perception and, thereby, proper illumination of form.

Selective visibility, then, means using light to reveal proper focus and properly plastic form in space.

RHYTHM AND STRUCTURE

When we discuss lighting as a means of establishing *rhythm* and *structure,* we mean that lighting functions as a *design element* in the overall composition of the production. Lighting functions to cement the pictures formed by actors, costumes, and settings as they interrelate over the course of the production—that is, over time. Throughout this book, we have discussed the dynamic and dramatic structure of the play and the need for direction, acting, and design to accentuate that structure so that the audience can perceive meaning. The lighting designer also plays a role in emphasizing rhythm and structure.

Design and Plot Structure Recall, for example, the pyramidal structure of plot dynamics that we examined in Chapter 3. As a play progresses, it rises and falls in a developing series of *crises* until it reaches the *climax*. It is then resolved through the *denouement* to the end. Over time, the peaks or crises, as they occur relative to each other, make up the rhythmic structure of the play much as the notes and phrases create rhythmic structure in a musical composition. Well-designed lighting can help the audience understand the structure of the play by emphasizing moments of crisis and separating them from transitional or relaxed moments. The result is a "mobile" design created in space and moving over time so as to create meaning. A particularly effective aspect of lighting design is its ability to move with the demands of the play—theatre is an intensely dynamic medium (see Fig. 13.5). Appia called it "living light": "Without light," he reminds us, "design cannot exist; and without design, lighting is only illumination."

MOOD

Mood is a psychological and emotional impression. We can describe qualities of mood as "cheerful" or "sad," "bright" or "gloomy," and so on. In evoking the proper mood for a production, light plays a major role: It creates the overall *atmosphere* of the stage environment (see Fig. 13.6).

Figure 13.5 *Dynamic contrasts, focus, and enhanced three-dimensionality created through the use of directional lighting in Stephen Sondheim's* Sweeney Todd, the Demon Barber of Fleet Street *in a production of the Ball State University Theatre directed by Don Heady with scenic design by D. C. Shawger, costumes by C. Shawger, and lighting design by J. Koger.*

Atmosphere: Color and Intensity   Color and intensity are the lighting designer's chief tools in creating atmosphere. By varying these elements, the designer can change the atmosphere from moment to moment. Mood, of course, is an intangible factor; no theatre artist can predict with certainty how a given color or a particular level of lightness or darkness will affect individuals in the audience. In fact, all the production designers—that is, set, costume, and lighting designers—for whom color is a primary element of their art can do little more than guess how audiences will respond to color and/or the other compositional elements and principles of the designs. Does a given color—say,

Figure 13.6 *A mood of warmth and a sense of isolation are created in the lighting design for* The Diary of Anne Frank *by Frances Goodrich and Albert Hackett at the University of Arizona Theatre. The lighting surrounds the family and keeps them separated from their environment. Downlighting effectively makes the characters three-dimensional and simulates the motivated light provided by the overhead lamp which creates a soft circle of light on the floor around the table. The production was directed by Peter R. Marroney, with scenic design by Robert C. Burroughs, costumes by Fairfax P. Walkup, and lighting by John E. Lafferty.*

Lighting *and* Sound

primary red—trigger connotations of anger, passion, heat, or something else? In the Asian theatre, red has a specific philosophical and religious connotation. What would be its effect on a group of Chinese spectators in an otherwise Anglo audience attending an American production? Such questions run through the mind of every designer in the process of preparing a production, and the answers provide only vague, intuitive suggestions.

Mood in Context   The lighting designer works with the other designers and the director to try to set color and intensity for each scene that all agree are correct for eliciting the proper mood. Though most effectively established through variety and change, mood also must be controlled in proportion to a given moment. A dramatic lighting effect may be highly successful in motivating audience response, but if that response comes at the expense of an important line delivered by an actor, overall meaning may be sacrificed for a momentary impulse. Like every other aspect of the performance, lighting for mood must play its role within the larger context of the production.

MOTIVATION AND ILLUSION

The final function of stage lighting is that of providing motivation and illusion. This means that stage lighting must make the light appear to come from appropriate sources (*motivation*)—for example, lamplight—and make that appearance (*illusion*) look as natural as possible. One of the curious conventions of the theatre is that, whatever the source of light on the stage is supposed to be—sunlight, lamplight, firelight—the lighting designer must work from fairly fixed positions, most of which are on the audience side of the actors. Working from these positions while concerned with selective visibility, rhythmic intensity, and mood, the designer also must lend the *illusion* of *natural* or **source-motivated light** to most productions. Time of day, weather, season, location, sky, clouds, sunshine, and moonlight all must bear some relation to *verisimilitude*.

source-motivated light
Light that appears to come from a natural source

What color, for example, is moonlight? Perhaps your first inclination is to say "blue." That answer, of course, is wrong: Moonlight is fundamentally the same color as sunlight, which is white or slightly yellow/white. Moonlight is less intense because it is reflected from the surface of the moon, a gray/white surface, rather than from the yellow/orange surface of the sun. In any case, even though sunlight is not yellow/orange and moonlight is not blue, we *perceive* them in those colors. Thus, if verisimilitude calls for a sense of "blueness," the atmosphere might look reasonably credible in blue colored light, but then the actors will not.

In fulfilling the function of motivation and illusion, the lighting designer must decide how to make the light in each scene appear motivated by a source appropriate to the play and how to give that motivated light the illusion of plausibility. Some plays do not require natural sources such as the moon, sun, or lamplight; in fact, some plays place the stage lighting instruments in full view of the audience in order to create an atmosphere of *theatricality* rather than verisimilitude. In such cases, the lighting designer will choose different qualities of light to emphasize a motivation and illusion of stage light rather than natural light.

The Properties *of* Light

In general, we can isolate four properties of light that the designer can use to achieve the basic functions of the art: *intensity, color, angle,* and *movement.*

intensity Brightness and quality of light

Intensity   **Intensity,** the brightness and quality of the lighted area, comprises the amount and beam characteristics of light produced by the individual lighting instruments. Light is *cumulative;* that is, an object illuminated by two separate light sources will be brighter than if it were lit by only one. Light intensity on the stage thus reflects the cumulative effect of all the instruments that may be in use at any moment. By using a device called a **dimmer,** the lighting designer can set each individual instrument at a particular brightness level or intensity, thereby controlling the overall effect of all the instruments lighting the stage picture.

dimmer Device for controlling the *intensity of light*

The quality or *beam characteristics* of light depend on whether the rays of light from a particular instrument are *parallel* or *off-parallel.* Beams of light in parallel configuration create hard-edged shadows; conversely, the greater the deviation from parallel, the more diffuse the shadows. Naturally, the quality of light and shadow has a definite effect on the appearance of the actors, settings, and audience perception. Beam quality helps to create visibility and mood. When beams of light create sharp shadows, actors' features appear sharper and more distinct, whereas diffuse shadows make the atmosphere seem hazy. Thus, the appearance of hardness or softness in quality of light can render the mood of a scene either dynamic or passive, depending on degree.

color Complex visual phenomenon helpful to the lighting designer in setting the tone of a scene

Color   **Color,** a complex phenomenon in light as well as pigment, can change with the tone of the design and the intensity of illumination. Every color (hue) corresponds to a specific, measurable wavelength. The primary colors of light are blue, red, and green; in pigment, they are blue, red, and yellow. In the theatre, color is created by placing a transparent color medium or *filter* (usually plastic) in front of a lighting instrument. These filters also change the intensity of the light because they absorb and screen out a certain percentage of the light (that is, other wavelengths) emanating from the instrument. Controlling color in stage lighting means carefully considering the filter and the effect that it will have when the light passing through it mixes with light from other instruments that may have different colored filters.

In addition, the designer must consider the effects of colored light on the colors of the objects that light strikes—for example, costumes, makeup, and scenery. A simple lesson in the effects of colored light can be learned by observing what happens to red lipstick when the person wearing it stands under a streetlight. The greenish tint of the streetlight turns the lipstick black—or so it seems. The same kind of garish results can occur in the theatre if the lighting designer does not communicate with the scenic and costume designer.

Figure 13.7 *Engraving of a scene from Sheridan's* The School for Scandal, *Drury Lane Theatre, 1777. The influential scene painter Jacques de Loutherbourg (1740–1812), also exercised an interest in realistic lighting effects, using such devices as colored-glass lamp tubes to create illusions like fire and moonlight. Note in this production the dramatic use of sidelighting in the shaft of light coming from the wings. In 1781, Loutherbourg introduced the* Eidophusikon, *a panoramic device that complemented moving pictures with music and lighting effects.*

[New York Public Library.]

angle Direction chosen for *light* to strike an object

Angle **Angle,** as a property of light, means the direction chosen for the light to strike an object. *Front, back, top, side, high, medium,* and *low* angles, for example, each create a particular effect on an actor or a setting. Light coming directly from the front tends to flatten out the features of an actor's face, thus making the actor appear two-dimensional. Such an effect may be correct for a farce or a melodrama in which characters are stylized. In contrast, light from a high, side angle makes an actor appear three-dimensional because it creates strong highlights and shadows for the audience. That kind of angle creates a dramatic effect like the one in Caravaggio's *The Calling of St. Matthew*—an effect perhaps appropriate to a dramatic scene in a tragedy. By analyzing each scene and its demands, the lighting designer chooses angles in order to make the actors and the set appear the way the scene and the play demand that they appear.

movement Changes in any of the *properties of light*

Movement Finally, **movement** in lighting comprises *changes in any of the previous properties.* Changing intensities so that light goes out in one area and comes on in another creates a sense of movement on stage for the audience. Adding or deleting instruments with differing color media also creates a sense of movement, as does changing the angle of lighting sources within a scene. To a great extent, movement as a property of light makes light the dynamic factor that it is in theatre production.

The Design Process

As was the case in scene and costume design, the design process of the lighting designer is a more or less chronological procedure from the first reading of the script to the opening curtain of the production. It consists of script analysis, production conferences, designing the light plot, and setting and rehearsing cues.

ANALYZING THE SCRIPT

The lighting designer goes through exactly the same analysis process (outlined in Chapter 3) as the director, costume designer, and scene designer. In order to contribute fully to the production conferences and the collaborative effort, the lighting designer must understand character, dramatic action, theme, symbols, mood, atmosphere, style, genre, and the facts of the play.

Although each of these elements is important in conceptualizing the design, the lighting designer needs particularly to attend especially to character. Each character must be analyzed in terms of function, relationships with other characters, the character in focus at any given moment, and the impression made by the character on the audience. (See, for example, Figure 9.13, in which the dramatic impression in a production of *The Elephant Man* is reinforced by lighting designed to amplify mood and intensity.) In satisfying the demands of lighting design, the designer thus has potentially strong control over the working out of character. Traditionally—and in some contemporary musicals—the most important character has been identified for the audience by isolation in a followspot. Although most lighting is no longer obvious, the basic principle remains the same. Lighting design can play an active role in communicating the meaning of the production, and in some productions a perceptive audience member may be able to answer basic questions about character importance and relationships by watching the lighting.

THE PRODUCTION CONFERENCE

For designers, production conferences not only involve discussions about the play and the goals of the production but also constitute show-and-tell sessions in which they communicate by means of sketches with the director and with each other. Unlike the scene and costume designers, however, the lighting designer cannot adequately render the lighting for a production in a sketch. During production conferences, the lighting designer can often do little more than talk through ideas with the director and other designers. Thus, discussions of how the lighting will actually execute the director's concepts of rhythmic structure, character relationship, focus, and balance must be thorough and frequent. During production conferences, the lighting designer must also be sure that the set designer has planned adequately for the lighting. If the setting, for example, places actors in positions that light cannot reach, the lighting designer must be able to spot such problems from the scene designer's ground plan and sketch (see Chapter 10). For example, a realistic setting with a ceiling must contain some means whereby light can be thrown into the upstage areas. In response to the plans for the setting, the potential for serious problems, especially in theatres with limited facilities, must be addressed by the lighting designer at production meetings.

As noted in Chapter 8, production meetings give the lighting designer, director, and costumer opportunities to work through the play by means of *French scenes* in order to arrive at a consensus on how and when the light

Jean Rosenthal: A Bloody Electrician with Notions

A pioneer in lighting technique for the modern stage, Jean Rosenthal emphasizes here the element of the lighting designer's "notions"—that is, his or her contributions to the production concept. At the same time, she emphasizes the collaborative nature of her craft, in working not only with the visuals of the scene designer but with the words of the playwright, and explains the paradoxical virtues of expressive restraint.

I am a lighting designer. The profession is only as old as the years I have spent in it. This is astonishing when you consider the flexibility lighting by electricity had achieved before I was born. I think it simply never occurred to anyone until the 1930s that the lighting of anything should be the exclusive concern of a craftsman, let alone under the artistic aegis of a specialist.

Lighting design . . . is still considered for the most part somewhat less important than interior decoration. That attitude is scarcely justified because light remains primarily important in order for people to see what it falls upon. The lighting of it affects everything light falls upon: how you see what you see, how you feel about it, and how you hear what you are hearing.

Affect is the key word. Change the "a" to an "e" and you get lighting effects. Effects should be handled with all the care and used with the rarity of fireworks. The most successful and brilliant work a lighting designer does is usually the least noticeable.

The use of light for anything must remain primarily social and logical. A major design feature is that light is a necessity, and you use it as a necessity. The logical, basic function of light, of fixtures, of all artificial light, goes all the way back to the human demand and need for visibility in order to see in the dark.

On that firm basis, and when you have complete technical control of your tools, your medium, you can design lighting for infinite subtlety.

I have been called a "bloody electrician with notions." That is not a bad definition of a lighting designer. . . . In a time when equipment is becoming yearly more pliant, I should like to expose as clearly as possible what these "notions" are. Lighting design, the imposing of quality on the scarcely visible air through which objects and people are seen, begins with *thinking* about it.

Effects should be handled with all the care and used with all the rarity of fireworks. The most successful and brilliant work a lighting designer does is usually the least noticeable.

Writers and painters have always understood how light affects what it falls upon, how you see and how you feel (and how you hear). All literature is full of light. No novelist who controls the lighting of his lifelike universe is apt to set a tender proposal in a blaze. Or to present tragedy without appropriately shading it. If sad events are fictionally brightly lighted, the light falls subjectively on the scene, merciless and not benign.

Artists see the air they see through. Naturalistic painters, seeking the essence of what inspires them, may wait for months to catch the ideal light on a particular landscape. Portrait painters use light to reveal the character in faces. In the twentieth century painters began consciously to create arbitrary sources of light within their canvases, an important step in the direction of abstraction.

Dramatists, dependent on others to carry out their intentions, indicate appropriate light and weather to set their scenes. Shakespeare, whose stage was open to the arbitrary sky, filled his spoken words with subtle light. In the nineteenth century, when "special effects" were added to stage illumination, there were times when Shakespeare's poetic subtleties were lost against lurid, realistic sunsets or deluged by lightning.

In the twentieth century, Eugene O'Neill wrote his stage directions with as much care as his dialogue. For the opening of *Mourning Becomes Electra* he asks for a "luminous mist" and stipulates that "the windows of the lower floor reflect the sun's rays in a *resentful* glare [italics mine]."

What a challenge to designers who refrain from using steam for mist. It requires from us what the light-conscious scene designer Robert Edmond Jones pleaded for: "the artist's approach." Without it, we offer nothing. Yet the humble word "approach" should be kept in mind.

In the past thirty-odd years, during which I have designed the lighting for over three hundred shows, the separate program credit "Lighting by _____" or for those scene designers who prefer to do their own lighting, "Scenery and lighting by _____" has become a standard acknowledgment. It is important to remember that lighting is a contributory art, a high craft serving the creative purposes of other people. We need the artist's approach, but to impose a separate artist's ego through light on the artistic whole becomes destructive.

Only when you know that necessity remains the guiding factor, and when the techniques and functions of lighting are under your complete technical control, may you adopt even the artist's *approach* safely. The minute you fuss around with light, use it arbitrarily or egotistically, decoratively or in a tricky, arty manner, you get a kind of aggressiveness that is not only unattractive in a show and distracting, but equally annoying in a house or an office.

Why on earth, for example, are so many modern offices lit with downlight? Because it is a pretty design idea and it became the fashion to put a lot of fixtures in the ceiling and turn them on. The fact of the matter is that no office worker can stand downlights. They have headaches. They are always moving their desks around to get out of the direct light. We have the technical means now to reproduce natural light in most of its shadings and intensities and we live more and more of our lives by artificial light—but most of it is bad light.

There is no excuse for bad light. It is the result of poor thinking and impractical application. You must know what the lighting you choose will *do* before you install it. . . .

All the arts and crafts collaborate in the theatre. You light the stage exclusively with artificial light and can take no advantage of natural light, as films may do. All the conditions of life are reconstructed in the theatre, foreshortened and intensified in "scenes." All emotional states are encompassed. Ranging through drama, entertainment, music, and dance, you cover all that lighting may contribute to life.

should change to punctuate the changing relationships and crises that constitute the action. After the blocking is finished, the director and the lighting designer must work through the show so that the designer knows where actors will be and how special effects and cues can be executed. Before designing the light plot, the lighting designer should attend several full run-through rehearsals and plot actor movement scene by scene. The director must communicate with the lighting designer any changes in blocking done after such discussions and rehearsal attendance. When communication is thorough, final rehearsals—when lighting cues and actors are brought together for the first time—go smoothly. Faulty communication leads to frustration, tension, and wasted time and effort. For example, I once designed lighting for a production in which light changes were frequent because the production called for actors to be individually lit as they gave their lines. Having discussed the blocking carefully with the director and attended rehearsals to note where each actor was at every moment, I wrote the numerous cues into the elaborate charts necessary for the control board operators. In the technical rehearsals, we discovered that throughout the play light would go up on one area, but the actor speaking would be in another area—and unlit. The director had changed the blocking but had failed to tell me. As a result, an entire rehearsal was ruined, and I spent several hours rewriting cues.

THE LIGHT PLOT

Every lighting designer has a preference for organizing analysis, notes, and other materials from which a final design emerges. Some designers work entirely in their heads, conceptualizing moments as the play unfolds and jotting cryptic symbols only they can understand in the margins of their prompt books: symbols denoting placement of actors, ideas on mood, areas of focus, possible instrumentation, timing, motivation, and so on. Others work out elaborate **lighting scores** for charting the same materials (see Fig. 13.8).

lighting scores Lighting designer's preliminary charts for plotting actor placement, areas of focus, the timing of action, and other elements of the production

The Rough Plot   Once the designer believes that he has a good grasp of the details and ideas of the production, he prepares a **rough lighting plot.** Here the designer translates concepts and movements into stage space, mounting positions, and actual lighting instruments. Given the need for certain qualities of light, the distances from instruments to the stage, and available positions, the designer chooses specific kinds of lighting instruments. He also begins to address questions about the control of those instruments: Does the theatre facility allow each instrument to be controlled separately, or does it require that several instruments be "ganged together" for control?

rough lighting plot Preliminary drawing by which the designer draws together a variety of concepts and ideas into instrumentation and design

The rough lighting plot is a plan of action that combines ideas, problems, and solutions and works them out on paper. The rough plot takes different forms and may go through several phases. Early on, for example, the plot uses a ground plan of the stage and its settings, on which the designer draws circles representing acting areas and arrows representing angles from which light emanates. Later, an expanded ground plan of the entire theatre is used so that actual instruments can be drawn in according to actual mounting positions.

Inventory and Circuiting   At this point the lighting designer consults the inventory of available equipment. Are there enough instruments of a particular type to meet the needs of the show? If not, what accommodation needs to be made? How can each instrument be *circuited* (that is, supplied with electricity)

Lighting *and* Sound

Oedipus Rex	Opening	Woman holds child DC	Suppliants assemble	Priest enters	Oedipus enters	Oedipus US of altar
Overall Brightness	very dark	altar brightens	brighter	same	binding	Oed. bright
Use of Stage Floor		(symbol)	(symbols)	(symbols)	(symbols)	(symbols)
Key	vague	silhouette	side	shadowy	silhouette	bottom
Closure	closed	tight	low	same	vertical	same
Contrast	low ——————————————→				high ——————→	
Conflict	building ——————————————————————————→					
Tempo	slow ——————————————→				strong ——→	
Mood	eerie	grotesque	foreboding	expectant	surprising mystical	threatening
Color	grn/amb		add cool sd		wht back	amb bottom
Focus	vague	woman/child	suppliants	Priest	Oedipus	Oed/Priest
Time of day	predawn ——→		first glimmer ——————————————————→			
Altar fire	dim glow	some bright ——————————————→				light
Doorway	dark closed ——————————→			lighten	open/ brilliant	closed

Figure 13.8 A lighting score for the opening of Oedipus Rex before the beginning of the first speech. The production opens with a woman kneeling before a low altar on which a fire dimly burns. The suppliants enter from the sides, calling Apollo, followed by the entrance of the Priest, who redirects the calls to Oedipus. The king enters through the central doorway.

[From Richard H. Palmer, The Lighting Art: The Aesthetics of Stage Lighting Design © 1985 by Prentice Hall. Reprinted by permission.]

and eventually tied to the control board? In a complex show, roughing out the light plot is analogous to piecing together a jigsaw puzzle. At this point, organizational ability and discipline become key ingredients in the lighting designer's personal profile.

The Final Plot Once the rough plot has reached a satisfactory stage, the designer drafts a final lighting plot (Fig. 13.9). This is a mechanical drawing showing every lighting instrument, circuiting instructions, mounting positions, and dimmer connections. In addition, the plot contains a detailed instrument

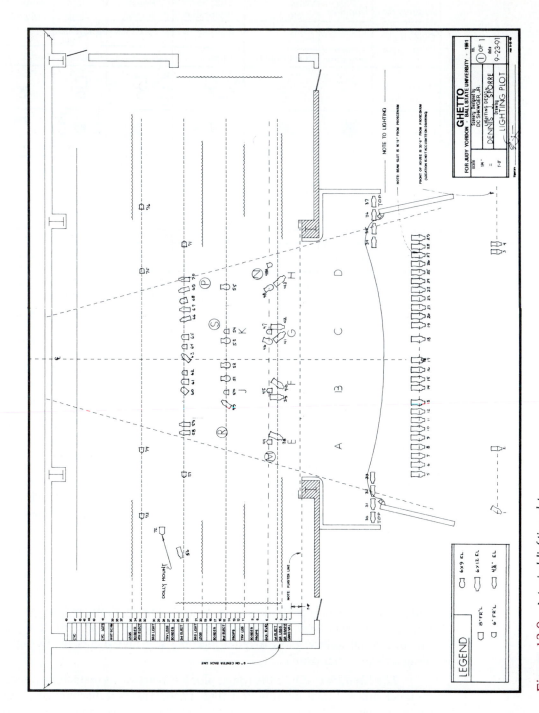

Figure 13.9 A typical lighting plot.

INSTRUMENT SCHEDULE
CARNIVAL

CHAN	CIR/DIM	POSITION	INSTRUMENT/LAMP	GEL	FOCUS	NOTES
1	20	13	6 x 9 EL 750	60	C – R	
2	21	17		—	C – C	
3	22	23		02	C – L	
4	23	15		60	D – R	
5	24	28		—	D – C	
6	25	19		02	D – L	
7	26	21		60	E – R	
8	27	30		—	E – C	
9	28	32		02	E – L	
10	29	26		60	F – R	
11	30	36		—	F – C	
12	31	34		02	F – L	
13	32	14	6" ELZM 1000	60	G – R	
14	33	18		—	G – C	
15	34	24		02	G – L	
16	35	16		60	H – R	
17	36	20		—	H – C	
18	37	27		02	H – L	
19	38	22		60	I – R	
20	39	29		—	I – C	
21	40	31		02	I – L	
22	41	25		60	J – R	
23	42	33		—	J – C	
24	43	35		02	J – L	
25	62	49	6" ELZM 1000	60	K – R	
26	66	52		—	K – C	
27	70	56		02	K – L	
28	65	51		60	L – R	
29	69	55		—	L – C	
30	75	61		02	L – L	
31	71	57		60	M – R	
32	74	60		—	M – C	
33	80	66		02	M – L	

Figure 13.10   *Instrument schedule.*

schedule (Fig. 13.10) that details each instrument, where it is hung, where it is focused, which circuit it uses, what dimmer it occupies, the color medium it utilizes, and any notes pertinent to its operation.

CUES

cues Instructions for the control-board operator indicating what, when, and how lights are changed during a performance

When decisions have been made and equipment put in place, a system of instructions must be organized to tell the lighting control operators what to do and when and how to do it. These instructions are called **cues.** In addition to giving the what, when, and how, cues also must reflect the designer's artistic intent: The operator must understand the subtleties of the lighting and be able to make occasional minor adjustments during the performance. In theatres that have computerized control boards, all aspects of a cue are programmed into the computer; the operator merely pushes a button at the proper time, and the computer executes the cue. Computer systems remove both the subtleties and the inconsistencies of manual control. They make cues easier to record and change and ensure that they will be consistent from performance to performance. On the other hand, however, they relegate the control board operator to a position of "button-pusher." Nevertheless, at any time, the operator can override the computer manually and make any adjustments that are necessary. In manual systems, cues need to have a form that will not distract the operator from his or her primary functions; that is, cues must be written clearly and simply. The operator must be able to concentrate on executing the cue—not on understanding its directions.

Normally, cues are set in three phases: (1) a preliminary phase that approximates intensity levels, execution timing, and starting point—thus saving time at the first technical rehearsal; (2) a *dry technical rehearsal* at which the director, designer, and stage manager meet to set cues in the stage manager's prompt book; and (3) a *technical rehearsal,* with actors present, at which cues are run as written and then changed to final status as need dictates. For example, if a cue begins too soon, it is set a line or two earlier in the script; if an instrument is too bright, the cue is changed to lower the intensity level; and so on. Changing cues occupies a great deal of time on some control systems because changing one part of one cue may require the rehearsal to stop while the designer and operators check previous settings to be sure the change does not affect either earlier or later cues. Computer control systems simplify the process immensely. By the time of final dress rehearsals, cues are set, and— like the other production artists—lighting personnel use this time for polishing and perfecting.

Lighting Instruments

Although it may seem somewhat technical, we cannot leave our discussion of lighting design without examining some of the basic equipment requisite to its execution. Lighting designers cannot control light in artistic ways without a set of technological tools called *lighting instruments.* These optical and mechanical devices come in many shapes and sizes, and each is designed for a specific purpose. Part of the creation of an artistic lighting design is the careful choice of instrument type for the desired effect. Mastery of instrumentation is an important aspect of the lighting designer's ability to put concepts into practice. A variety of other specialized equipment is used in theatrical lighting—for example, slide and film projectors, strobe lights, and miniature display lights. Equipment like smoke and fog machines is also used to help

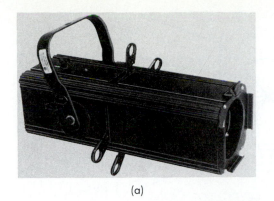

(a)

(c)

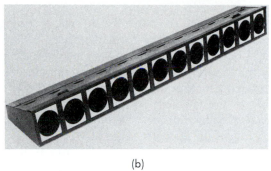

(b)

Figure 13.11 *Stage light-ing instruments: (a) ellipsoidal spotlight; (b) striplights; (c) fresnel spotlight.*

create lighting effects, such as fire and fireplace effects. In the theatre, whatever works to create the desired visual effect is used. In general, lighting instruments fall into three broad groupings: *spotlights, striplights* (see Fig. 13.11) and *floodlights.*

    Spotlights *Spotlights* are the workhorses of the modern theatre. They allow maximum control of light by producing controllable beams of light. Spotlights consist of metal housings, lamps, reflectors, color frame guides, and lenses. Two general types of spotlights see the most use in the contemporary theatre: *fresnel spotlights* and *ellipsoidal spotlights.*

Fresnel Spotlights In a **fresnel spotlight,** a spherical reflector gathers light from the lamp and reflects it forward to the lens, which gathers the light and shapes it into a controlled—though not parallel—beam (Fig. 13.12). The lamp in this type of spotlight can move backward and forward in the housing and can decrease or increase the size of the beam. The beam of a fresnel spotlight has a soft edge that is very useful for a variety of area sizes and effects. It produces a controllable and yet diffuse beam of light. Characteristic of the fresnel spotlight is the fresnel lens that gives it its name. The fresnel lens (Fig. 13.13) replaces the thick glass of a normal lens with concentric ribs of differing diameters cast into one flat disc that has the same optical characteristics of a normal lens. The beam of the fresnel spotlight may also be controlled by using a device called a **barn door.** The barn door contains four movable shutters for shaping the light.

fresnel spotlight
Lighting instrument with a spherical reflector that produces a controllable but soft-edged beam

barn door Device used in a *fresnel spotlight* to shape the beam of light

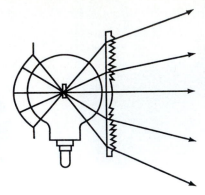

Figure 13.12   *Diagram of a fresnel spotlight.*

ellipsoidal spotlight
Lighting instrument
with an ellipsoidal
reflector that produces
a sharp, hard-edged
beam

Ellipsoidal Spotlights   A more efficient type of spotlight is the **ellipsoidal spotlight,** which takes its name from the shape of its reflector. Because of its efficient optics, this instrument is the most popular and useful lighting instrument in the theatre. The ellipsoidal reflector captures light and throws it forward through a focal point where it can be gathered by a lens and shaped into a very sharp and relatively parallel beam (Fig. 13.14). The beam can be precisely controlled by four movable internal shutters. Because of the evenness of its field of light, the instrument can also function as a projector when glass or metal slides are inserted at the "gate" between the shutters.

All spotlights are designated by their lens sizes—3″, 6″, 9″, 12″, and so on—and each is rated for a particular wattage of lamp—300, 500, 750, 1,000, and so on. Other types of spotlights exist, but the fresnel and ellipsoidal are the most common and useful in the lighting designer's inventory.

Floodlights   *Floodlights* are general-purpose instruments, without lenses, designed to throw highly intense light over a fairly large area. They allow the designer little control of their light, and thus they are used mostly for lighting large scenic units such as sky cycloramas and backdrops. A variety of instruments fall into this category—for example, *beam projectors,* whose light forms parallel rays: It is particularly effective in simulating sunlight or moon-

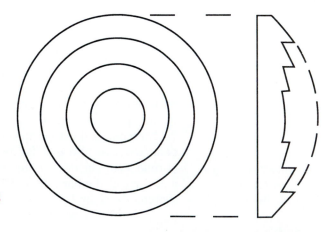

Figure 13.13
Fresnel lens.

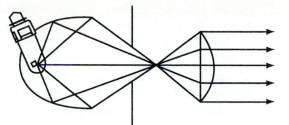

Figure 13.14 *Diagram of an ellipsoidal spotlight.*

scoop *Floodlight* used for broad washes of light

light. The most commonly used floodlight is the ellipsoidal floodlight or **scoop** (see Fig. 13.11), which is effective in lighting sky cycloramas and drops.

Striplights Striplights (see Fig. 13.11) were once a staple in the theatre. Today they are used in well-equipped theatres only for special needs—for example, lighting ground rows. In theatres that have limited instrumentation, however, striplights—hung above the stage—provide effective general illumination. Striplights usually contain three separate color circuits—red, blue, and green—that allow a variety of color mixes.

Lighting Control

The lighting designer must make all of the light-producing instruments perform in concert to create a balanced and changeable design. To achieve that result, the lighting designer uses an electronic technology called a *control system*. Control systems in the United States range from rudimentary electrical technologies to state-of-the-art computers. Whatever type of hardware exists in a theatre, its sole purpose is to allow the lighting designer to set every instrument or combination of instruments at specific levels of intensity and then to change those levels as desired. Most theatres contain some form of remote-control system: The operator is placed so that he or she can see the stage, and the dimmers and other bulky pieces of equipment that form the control system are placed in some noncritical part of the theatre building. The *control board* or console sends a low-voltage electrical signal to the dimming devices that control the lighting instruments. By using control systems, the lighting designer can make hundreds of lighting instruments respond precisely.

EVALUATING A LIGHTING DESIGN

In evaluating a lighting design, we can use five basic questions as a guideline:

1. How did the lighting blend with the other elements of production—that is, was the lighting an extension of the action or an end in itself?

2. Did the lighting contribute to an overall unified effect in a way that made what you saw more complete than if the production had taken place under work lights of adequate intensity by which to see?

3. Was the lighting technically smooth—that is, did it contribute to artistry or did it manifest awkwardness and abruptness?

4. Could you perceive changes in lighting that indicated or reinforced the movement of the play?

5. Overall, did the lighting meet the basic functions of the art—that is, selective visibility, establishment of rhythm and structure, evocation of mood, and providing motivation or illusion?

Sound Design

expository sound Sound required in the play—for example, doorbells, telephone rings, and gunshots

Sound design probably represents one of the theatre's less appreciated arts. Often assigned to whoever can be dragooned to do it, a production's sound lives a homeless life unbecoming to its importance. Without question, sound has a vital impact on the audience's perception of meaning and mood. Even before the curtain rises, sound begins to evoke audience response. *Music* reinforces tone and location throughout the performance. **Expository sound** consists of required sounds—ringing telephones, gunshots, breaking glass, doorbells, and so on. Properly executed, these sounds allow the production to proceed. Like every other facet of theatre performance, sound works best when it reflects careful analysis, artistic design, and precise execution. Whether live or recorded, sound serves functions almost identical to the functions of stage lighting—that is, *selective audibility*, establishment of *rhythm* and *structure*, evocation of *mood*, and providing *motivation* and *illusion*. Substitute "sound" for "light" in the discussion of the functions of stage lighting earlier in the chapter, and you will have a full description of the functions of sound in the theatre.

Sound in the theatre runs through a wide range of applications, from simple to sophisticated: Some theatres operate with a single tape recorder and one or two speakers, and other theatres use complex control systems with MIDI (Musical Instrumentation Digital Interface), multiple channels, and multiple speakers that would be the envy of a modern recording studio. Wireless microphones and sound reinforcement—in addition to integration of live and prerecorded voice and audio—give sound a potential prestige in the contemporary theatre. As a tool for creation of an artistic work and enhancement of audience enjoyment, sound stands as a viable partner in this collaborative and cooperative art.

SUMMARY

• The development of modern *lighting design* encompasses an art whose theory preceded its practice:

It developed from candlelight to gaslight;

It was enhanced by the advent of electricity.

- Lighting design serves four functions or purposes:

    Selective visibility—including focus and form and form and depth perception;

    Rhythm and *structure*—including design and plot structure;

    Mood—including atmosphere: color and intensity and mood in context;

    Motivation and *illusion*.

- The properties of light include *intensity, color, angle,* and *movement*.

- The lighting design process consists of *script analysis, production conferences, designing the light plot*—including the rough plot, inventory and circuiting, and the final plot, and *setting and rehearsing cues*.

- Cues are set in three phases: (1) a preliminary phase, (2) a dry rehearsal phase, (3) a technical rehearsal phase.

- Lighting instruments comprise a variety of specialized equipment, but in general lighting instruments fall into three broad groupings:

    Spotlights—including fresnel and ellipsoidal spotlights;

    Floodlights;

    Striplights.

- *Lighting control* allows the lighting designer to make all of the light-producing instruments perform in concert to create a balanced and changeable design.

- Evaluating a lighting design can be enhanced by asking five questions:

    How did the lighting blend with the other elements of production?

    Did the lighting contribute to an overall unified effect?

    Was the lighting technically smooth?

    Could you perceive changes that indicated or reinforced the movement of the play?

    Overall, did the lighting meet the basic functions of the art?

- *Sound design*, though not fully appreciated as an art, makes a vital impact on the audience's perception of meaning and mood through *music* and *expository sound*.

- Sound in the theatre runs through a wide range of applications, from simple to sophisticated.

Chapter 14

Asian Theatre

*A*fter studying this chapter,
you should be able to:

- Characterize the relationships between *drama and religion* in China, Japan, and India.

- Identify and describe the *dramatic forms* of China, Japan, and India.

- Explain the important relationship of *music* to the theatre of China, Japan, and India.

- Define the various approaches to *acting* among the theatres of China, Japan, and India.

- Describe the *physical theatres* of China, Japan, and India.

- Discuss the meaning and characteristics of *costume and makeup* in theatrical production in China, Japan, and India.

The Actor Otani Oniji III as Edohei, 1794, *by Toshusi Sharaku. Kirara over pearl gray.*
14 3/4 × 19 3/4 in. Courtesy of Art Institute of Chicago. Clarence Buckingham Collection.

Units I and II have expanded our ability to approach and enjoy theatre by providing us with a theoretical and practical base. Unit III fills in the details of how theatre has interacted with culture and society in both the Eastern and Western traditions (the insert entitled "The Expressions of International Theatre" offers a gallery of photographs reflecting the range of theatrical practices around the world). This chapter is dedicated to exploring the theatrical traditions and practices of the East—specifically, China, Japan, and India. The arts of Asia, of course, differ significantly from the arts of the West. Intuition, for example, plays a central role in Eastern art—an important goal of which is to grasp internal and eternal truths: The material world represents illusion rather than fact, truth rests in religion and philosophy rather than in science, and the human condition is but a small part of an overriding Nature animated by a common spirit that flows through the universe.

The Theatre *of* China

DRAMA AND RELIGION

Much of the theatre of China had its roots in the traditions of Buddhism and spread across Asia as Buddhist missionaries carried their religion from India to China and, finally, to Japan. However, just as the dogmas of Confucianism also shaped Chinese culture, the same ideas—which centered on a proposed return to the ancient order in which individuals played the roles assigned them and subjected themselves to proper authority—gave shape to early Chinese drama. (Tradition holds, in fact, that Confucius once put to death an entire troupe of actors who took part in a play that violated his teaching.) At the same time, however, Taoism, which preached the independence of the individual and resistance to rigid intellect schemes, provided important building blocks for the theatre in China, and "the origin of Chinese theatre," according to one scholar, "is represented by the mythological figure of Lan Ts'ai-ho, one of the Eight Immortals of Taoism and 'the patron saint of itinerant actors.'"* As a result, we can find in some Chinese drama the mystical leanings of Taoism, in which the exploration of reality—in this case, the relationship between individuals and society—reflects an intuitive and emotional tendency coupled with great flights of fantasy and imagination. Meanwhile, the Confucian influence maintained an emphasis on the realm of the practical intellect. Main characters, consequently, tend to shift from soldiers and priests to scholars. The Indian religion Buddhism—which influenced a theatre quite different from the Buddhist theatre of India—added such dimen-

* E. T. Kirby, *Ur-Drama: The Origins of the Theatre* (New York: New York University Press, 1975), p. 70. Quoted in Paul Kuritz, *The Making of Theatre History* (Englewood Cliffs, NJ: Prentice Hall, 1988), p. 84.

sions as self-denial and blissful meditation. In all three cases, however, a strong theme remained the "idea of intuitive communion with nature through art."*

One interesting characteristic of Chinese drama that emerged from these complex socioreligious roots concerned the roles of women on the stage. Because women in China were subjected to severe restrictions and forbidden to perform publicly, the roles of women in the theatre (at least until the twentieth century) were portrayed by men. These portrayals mimicked the teetering style of walking that resulted from the practice of foot-binding among the upper classes and employed a device called *tsai jiao* to keep the actor "on point" throughout the performance.

THE DEVELOPMENT OF THEATRE

Legend documents the presence of actors and clowns and a dramatic form known as the *Beijing play* as early as the nineteenth century B.C. By the Han Dynasty of the third century A.D., the court was entertained by dramatic presentations performed with masks, song, and dance. However, the traditional founding of Chinese theatre is dated from the seventh to tenth centuries A.D., during the Dang Dynasty, when the Emperor Minghuang established the Pear Garden Conservatory for the training of professional actors. During this era, theatre performances explored a number of themes, inluding satires of government officials. Acting, singing, costume, and makeup were prevalent.

The Sung Dynasty   The Sung Dynasty (tenth to thirteenth centuries) witnessed a flowering of drama, of which the titles to 280 plays survive. From this period came the *zaju* or variety play. It had three parts: a *prelude* of low comedy, a one- or two-scene *poetic play* featuring song and dialogue, and a musical *epilogue*. During festivals, families of professional players performed *zaju* on temporary booth stages open on three sides. Actors were known by such nicknames as "Orange Peel," "Dimples," and "Silver Fish." A company generally consisted of a leading male actor and producer-playwright, a director, a comedian, a secondary male actor, an official character, and a musician. Plays were included on variety bills with storytellers, balladeers, puppeteers, medicine men, and fortune tellers.**

The Yuan Dynasty   The era roughly equivalent to the Gothic period in Western history (the Yuan Dynasty, 1280–1368) witnessed a Chinese golden age of literature in which both literature and popular theatre flourished. At this time, the Mongols were in control of China, whose drama and literature enjoyed the political and economic prosperity of the relatively tolerant Mongol government. Written in the vernacular as opposed to the classical written form, Mongol-period drama sought to reach broader and less highly educated audiences than had Chinese literature of the past. In fact, the use of the vernacular reflected a general trend in Chinese society wherein all written materials sought to reach those who had not been classically educated.

* Kuritz, *The Making of Theatre History*, p. 85.
** Kuritz, *The Making of Theatre History*, p. 88.

Figure 14.1 *A dramatic performance during the Yuan Dynasty (1279–1368). From a wall painting, Shansi Province, 1324. The five men in the foreground are actors, the five in the background musicians. Songs served to structure the plot of the zaju, a popular period play of about ten acts, each punctuated by songs whose musical keys were their most distinctive elements. One of the most famous zaju, Li Jianfu's (The Story of the)* Chalk Circle, *was staged by Max Reinhardt in Berlin in 1935 (see Chapter 17) and partially inspired Bertolt Brecht's 1945 play* The Caucasian Chalk Circle.

Chung-kuo ku-tai yin-hueh t'u-pien (Pictures of Ancient Chinese Music, Peking, 1959) Plate 16.

As the Western world entered its Renaissance, China entered the Ming Dynasty (1368–1644). Although the Mongols had been deposed, in pursuit of social stability, the new rulers severely limited popular entertainment. Nothing could be produced, for example, that in any way criticized or offended the emperor, the establishment, or Confucius. The theatre that developed during this period was an aristocratic or court theatre and had little to do with the common people. The next dynasty, the Jing or Manchu, lasted for nearly 300 years, during which time popular theatre returned in a form called the *Beijing opera.*

A Western drift in Chinese theatre occurred after the 1912 revolution that made China a republic. Many Chinese had been educated in the West, and they sought to turn China away from Confucian philosophy. During this time, many Western plays, including Harriet Beecher Stowe's *Uncle Tom's Cabin,* were produced in China. The advent of communism in 1946, of course, sounded a death knell for the Beijing opera, and Chinese theatre soon became an educational tool in the hands of the state.

DRAMATIC FORMS

In its earliest forms, Chinese drama fell into two general categories, that of the North and that of the South. In the North, drama was based generally on a seven-tone musical scale and featured a lively and energetic quality,

Figure 14.2 *Chinese theatre performance. Although the first reference to Beijing opera dates from the Dang Dynasty (618–907), the designation was not specifically applied to the classical Chinese theatre until the Jing or Manchu Dynasty (1644–1912). During the Ming Dynasty (1368–1644), the zaju gave way to the gunzhu— long (up to forty or more acts) musical plays that were originally quite popular until they became aristocratic, intellectually oriented entertainments for an elite audience. The gunzhu then gave way to the growing popular appeal of the jing-xi, a staple of local theatres that eventually developed into Beijing opera.*

[New York Public Library Collection.]

colloquial dialogue, and free verse. Accompaniment for Northern drama came from stringed instruments. In the South, drama was based on a five-tone scale and featured a soft and gentle quality, poetic dialogue, and strict meter and verse. By the sixteenth century, Southern drama predominated and included theatrical types that comprised upwards of thirty acts, each of which was reasonably complete and could stand by itself. Each act had a separate title, and in general, the play opened with a minor character explaining the situation. In the second act, the plot began to develop, and before the play was over, numerous subplots and characters had appeared. The intricate complexity of plot development gave Southern drama a wealth of variety that appealed to audiences. Because of the relative independence of each act, performances could also be varied by rearranging or eliminating acts. Such rearrangement seemed to have little consequence in the overall effectiveness of the play.

The Beijing Opera   As we have noted, the major form of Chinese drama became the Beijing opera. This form had two major types—civil and military. In Beijing opera of the *civil* type, themes dealt with domestic and social issues; the *military* type explored the exploits of warriors and/or robbers. Beijing opera plays often were based on history, legend, or popular novels, and the action always ends happily. As theatre historian Oscar Brockett explains, "A Westerner sometimes has trouble following a Chinese play, for the dramas concentrate upon the high points and relegate the development of the story to narrative passages. Thus, interest is focused upon the climactic moments rather than upon a fully dramatized story. A play in the Chinese theatre, however, is essentially the outline for a performance; the audience goes to see a production rather than to hear a literary text."*

ELEMENTS OF PERFORMANCE

Music Chinese drama depends heavily on music to create its atmosphere, establish the pace of the production, provide accompaniment for the singers, and, in general, organize the production into a unified whole. Of particular interest is the relationship that musicians and actors must establish in putting the production together. We have seen how theatre works as a collaborative art, and because of the importance of music in the general scheme of things, collaboration in Chinese theatre production may be even more important than in Western theatre. The music of Chinese theatre comes from a variety of sources and, as we might guess, retains a highly traditional quality and relationship to every established element of the theatre. Unlike Western music, Chinese music has no precise notation system; the music chosen for a particular production must therefore be memorized by the players. Music in China is thus much like dance in the West: The primary method of transmitting artworks and their traditions from one generation to another is from performer to performer rather than by means of script or manuscript.

The tonal quality of music in Asia sounds quite unfamiliar to Western ears, and the same may be said of its melodies. Obviously, Asian music rests on a completely different set of conventions from that of the West and illustrates quite amply how cultural conditioning can influence concepts of what is enjoyable, "good," or even understandable. Chinese instruments have no Western counterparts, although they may be divided into groupings that Westerners might recognize, such as woodwinds, strings, and percussion. Most importantly, the tempo of Chinese drama is established by an orchestra leader who beats tempos and rhythms on a variety of drums. Other instruments in the orchestra include brass cups, gongs, cymbals, a kind of flute, and a variety of stringed instruments. Strings and flutes make up the *wen* section, percussion the *wu* section. Loud percussion passages signal every actor's entrances and exits. When the dialogue calls for singing, solo passages are accompanied only by flutes and strings. The action of the play, then, is very much shaped within the musical framework.

Quite specific symbolic conventions also indicate precise emotional meaning to the Chinese audience. For example, specific "keys" represent sorrow, freshness of spirit, loneliness, humor, sophistication, disappointment, recklessness, a languid mood, robustness, or calamity. We would perhaps find the criteria for acting in the Chinese theatre more like the criteria for opera in the Western tradition: That is, the most important characteristic for a Chinese actor is the singing voice rather than "acting ability." Every role in Chinese theatre is ascribed a specific musical timbre, pitch, and rhythm (see Chapter 9).

* Oscar Brockett, *The Theatre*, 2nd ed. (New York: Holt, Rinehart and Winston, 1969), p. 264.

Female roles require speaking in falsetto, although portrayals of old women use the natural masculine pitch range.

Acting Two aspects of acting present themselves for our attention. One is the *stage* aspect of acting, the other the *social*. Although the theatre—and thus the art and profession of acting—achieved an important role in Chinese culture, actors have always occupied a rather questionable place in the social order. As early as the Ming Dynasty, actors were in fact associated with prostitution and various other forms of immoral behavior. The association was so strong in the eighteenth century that all women were banned from the stage. That proscription, of course, mandated the use of men for all roles; as a result, boys assumed feminine roles. Actors held such low social status that, for nearly three generations, descendants of actors could not work in socially respectable occupations. Nonetheless, acting troupes and actors continued to thrive and, in fact, to have a significant impact on fashion and style, as well as remaining popular in their own right. The ban on female actors was lifted in 1911.

Acting style, as we have already noted, depended to a large extent on convention. Movements were formalized, and acting skills ranged from music and dance to acrobatics. The personal charisma of the individual actor formed a vital part of role creation. Convention and presentation far exceeded the script as the basis for Chinese theatrical production. Stage conventions in the Chinese theatre also differ from those in the Western theatre. "On stage," for example, means "center stage." When an actor "exits," he merely moves to an area away from center: Even though he remains in full view of the audience, he is by convention not there and so can perform whatever tasks need to be done, from drinking tea to adjusting his costume. All entrances occur from stage-left, all exits from stage-right.

In the Beijing opera, four *types* of roles occurred. The male role was

Figure 14.3 A *Chinese theatre,* ca. 1846.

[New York Public Library Theatre Collection]

sheng, the female role *dan,* the so-called "painted face" *jing,* and the comic *chou.* Each of these roles had its own rigidly specified speech patterns, musical accompaniment, movement, costume, and makeup. Each role also had several subdivisions—for example, soldiers and warriors, scholars and students, and patriarchs and politicians among the *sheng;* the concubine, wife, and comic shrew among the *dan.* The bizarrely painted *jing* represented a number of types and characteristics, including demons, bandits, and supernatural characters. The *chou* characters presented a stylistic counterpoint to the conventionalized characters we have just noted: They were acted in a very realistic style and portrayed a variety of subordinate characters who ad-libbed lines, made jokes, and entertained with acrobatic movements.

THE PHYSICAL THEATRE

The space in which Chinese drama is performed retains its strong religious orientation. In the same sense that the classic Greek theatre retained the vestiges of an altar at the center of the orchestra, the classic Chinese theatre retains the form of a temple porch with a roof (Fig. 14.4 shows the ground plan of a typical Chinese theatre). The stage is an open platform, nearly square, over which rests a roof supported by columns (see Figs. 14.5A and 14.5B). A wooden railing, approximately two feet high, surrounds the stage. At the back of the stage is a wall penetrated by two doors. The one on the right is for all entrances, the one on the left for all exits. A large embroidered curtain hangs between the doors, carpet covers the floor, and a wooden table and two chairs form the only stage decoration.

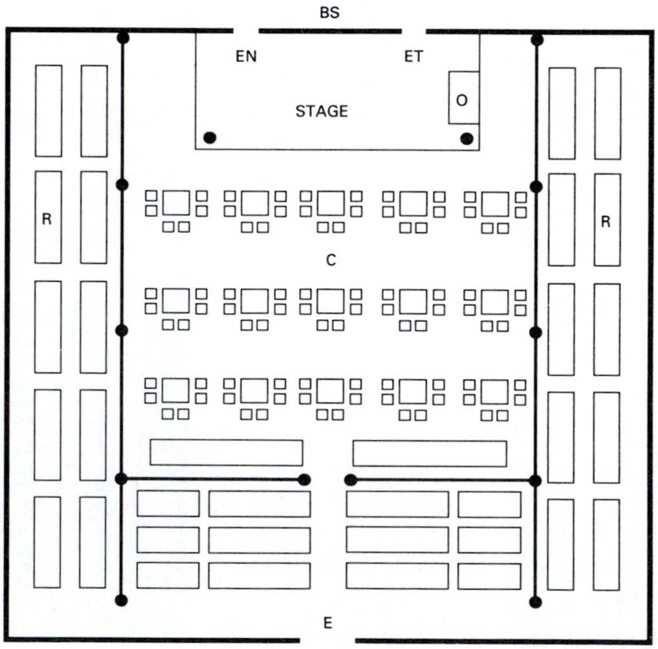

Figure 14.4 *Groundplan of a typical Chinese theatre.* BS = *backstage;* EN = *entrance to stage;* ET = *exit from stage;* O = *orchestra;* E = *main entrance to auditorium;* R = *raised seats;* C = *tables and stools for audience (see Fig. 14.5B).*

[Drawing by Douglas Hubbel, in Oscar Brockett, *The History of the Theatre,* 6E (Boston: Allyn and Bacon, 1991). Reprinted by permission.]

Asian Theatre

Figure 14.5A *A nineteenth-century private theatre on the grounds of a Beijing mansion. The earliest Chinese theatres—sometimes consisting simply of porches or even carpets—were often laid out in private gardens.*

[Performing Arts Research Center, New York Public Library at Lincoln Center.]

Figure 14.5B *Theatrical performance at a private house, Beijing, nineteenth century. Note the visible musicians and the detailed costuming that is emblematic of character type and motivation. The audience, meanwhile, smokes and drinks tea below the simple raised-platform stage.*

[From Globus, vol. 10, no. 2, (1866) p. 40.]

As in the Elizabethan theatre, location in the Chinese production is indicated by convention rather than depiction. Lyrics and dialogue may inform the audience of the location, or it may be indicated through pantomime. Actors also pantomime climbing stairs, knocking on gates, and entering doors. When an actor makes a large circle around the stage, he pantomimes a long journey. The placement of the furniture also indicates location—a law court, a banquet hall, and so on. Various set decorations—curtains, incense holders, and banners—can indicate palaces, tents, and offices. By convention, specific placement of the two chairs and the table also indicates walls, bridges, and hills. A banner with fish designs on it would represent water. We can see, therefore, how much communication in Chinese theatre depends on a reasonably knowledgeable audience. The entire effect of the theatre is to stimulate the imagination, not to recreate temporal reality. Nothing is hidden from the audience.

Property men, dressed in everyday clothing, add and remove items from the stage area as the action dictates. Musicians also remain in full view of the audience. The conventions are so firmly in place that none of these characteristics intrudes in the slightest on audience perception.

COSTUMES AND MAKEUP

Costume and makeup play significant symbolic roles in Chinese theatre. In particular, color reflects emotion and social standing. Red, for example, connotes individuals of high social standing; yellow means royalty. Dark crimson is reserved for military personages and for barbarians. Black symbolizes the poor and the fierce; green stands for virtue, white for the old, the very young, and the bereaved. Color also specifies character types. We can get an impression of the subtlety, complexity, and depth of Chinese drama and its audience relationships when we realize that costume is used to make very specific and detailed statements about character, with perhaps as many as three hundred combinations of headdresses, shoes, and other costume items per character—all of which are meant to be understood by the audience.

Like scenery, Chinese theatrical costume strives for no historically accurate depiction. Styles and periods mix freely in order to create a dramatic effect and reinforce subtle nuances. Nuance and subtle inflection form important parts of Chinese philosophy and language, and the same is true for the theatre. In addition to color and item, meaning also flows from design motifs. Animal and insect designs, for example, carry specific connotative values for the Chinese audience. The emperor was symbolized by a dragon; butterflies mean long life and happiness; tigers symbolize power, the phoenix good fortune. Flowers also have meaning: Spring and beauty are represented by the peony, while the plum blossom signifies wisdom and charm.

Frequently, flags appear appended to the shoulders of a character. Such characters represent generals, and the higher the general's rank, the more flags rise from his shoulders. Chinese costuming is similar to classical Greek costuming in that rank and station also are indicated through the use of padding and *kothurnoi,* or thick-soled boots (see Fig. 15.2). The melodramatic American movie form, the western, is not unlike Chinese drama in its use of costume. In the classic western, for example, the good guys wear white hats, the bad guys black ones. In Chinese theatre, the good guys wear square hats, the bad guys round ones.

Contemporary audiences in the Western tradition who are used to some variation on realistic performance may easily get lost in the barrage of symbols that are essential to the conventionalized drama of the Orient. A few more examples will suffice. The cut and style of garments, for instance, represent character type and station. Whether a garment buttons on the left or the right is also important, as is the style of collar, length of kimono, cut of the sleeves, texture of the fabric, and so on.

Asian Theatre

The pictorial effect of the actor receives its final effect from makeup. Actually, several character types, such as *sheng* and old women, wear very little makeup. Others, such as younger females and *jing*, wear elaborate and powerful makeup effects. Strong contrasts between red and white, for example, typify some female roles. The face is painted white and the eyes are surrounded with red. The clown typically has a white patch around the eyes. The *jing* features strong accents and bold patterns on the face, the effects of which are not only conventional but sometimes wild and ferocious as well (see Fig. 14.6). Each role employs a different design, and each design derives from a complex and subtle symbolism. Very clearly, an audience member cannot be a casual observer in Chinese drama. Tradition and convention make meaning a matter of informed participation.

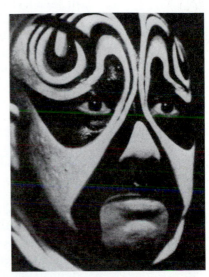

Figure 14.6 *Symbolic makeup patterns for* jing *characters in the Beijing opera: a "dragon" character (left) and a "hero." Like conventionalized dialogue delivery, highly codified gestures, and standardized costumes and accessories, the makeup employed by actors in the Beijing opera complements the elaborate representation of a character type. Although so-called "painted-face" roles range from soldiers and bandits to supernatural creatures, convention dictates certain common traits, such as great strength and exaggerated self-importance.* Jing *roles are also strictly subdivided into such categories as status (for example, soldier or civilian), personality (honest or deceitful), and physical requirements (fighting or singing). Actors begin their training (which may last more than ten years) by learning the general requirements of the art and then enter specialized training regimens when they demonstrate skills suited to certain character types.*

[Oscar Brockett, *The History of the Theatre*, 6E, (Boston: Allyn and Bacon, 1991) Reprinted by permission.]

The Theatre *of* Japan

DRAMA AND RELIGION

In Japan as in China, religion and drama have an interwoven history. Early Shinto religion, for example, produced a series of rhythmic movements set to music called *sangaku*. The introduction of Buddhism brought a series of masked dances, one of whose forms, *bugaku*, continues to be performed, although the term itself has come to mean any dance performed to classical court music. In all cases, the influences of Korea and, especially, China are prevalent. In addition to other ritualistic elements in music and dance, such dances originating from China and Korea are combined with traditions in acrobatics and elements of rural harvest-festival celebrations to form the basis of Japanese drama.

Shinto festivals used dance and pantomime in rituals and celebrations as ways of symbolizing or reenacting the discovery of the gods, and symbols of Shintoist faith eventually found their way into Japanese drama: Purity, courage, and charity, for example, are represented by a mirror, a sword, and a necklace, respectively. Japanese legend also suggests a mythological origin for the drama: Once, the sun goddess, Amaterasu o-mikami, offended by her brothers' teasing, hid herself in a cave to sulk and sealed the cave with a rock. When the world was plunged into darkness, the gods met to coax her out. Finally, Amano-uzume-no did a striptease on a soundingboard outside the cave. The gods laughed so hard at the dance that Amaterasu peeked out to see what was so funny. As she watched, she calmed down and returned to her place in the sky. In this way, song and dance rid the world of darkness.*

Japan's two great dramatic forms, *Noh* and *Kabuki*, both originated in religious ritual dating to the late eighth and early ninth centuries, when dramatic devices were used as teaching tools by Buddhist monks. In a fashion very similar to medieval miracle, mystery, and morality plays (see Chapter 15), the dramatizing of religious ritual in Buddhism slowly became more and more secularized, made its way out of the sanctuary, gained in popularity, and emerged as dramatic forms performed in markets as well as temples.

DRAMATIC FORMS

Two major forms of drama exist in Japan: *Noh* (or *No*) and *Kabuki*. Noh is austere, Kabuki flamboyant; Noh ritual, Kabuki spectacle; Noh offers spiritual consolation, Kabuki physical excitement; Noh celebrates chastity and contemplation while Kabuki delights in the eccentric, the extravagant, and the willfully perverse; Noh is gentle, Kabuki often cruel; Noh is concerned with the hereafter, Kabuki bound by the here-and-now.**

* Kuritz, *The Making of Theatre History*, pp. 96–97.
** Peter Arnott, *The Theatres of Japan* (New York: St. Martin's Press, 1969), p. 67.

Noh Drama   Japanese Noh drama, which emerged from the fourteenth century, represented the most significant and original literary and performing art development of the Ashikaga period, when Japan experienced intense religious activity. A highly conventionalized artform, Noh drama grew out of two sources: simple dramas based on symbolic dances performed to music at the imperial court and similar mimetic performances popular with the common people. Its final form is credited to a Shinto priest named Kan'ami (1333–1384) and his son Seami (1363–1443). They also founded one of the hereditary lines of Noh performers, the Kanze, which still perform today.

Noh drama is performed on a simple, almost bare stage and, like classical Greek tragedy, uses only two actors. Also as in Greek classical drama, actors wear elaborate masks and costumes, and a chorus functions as a narrator. Actors chant highly poetic dialogue to orchestral accompaniment. All actions *suggest* rather than *depict*—a convention that gives the drama its sense of stylization and conventionality; symbolism and restraint characterize both acting and staging. The subjects of Noh drama range from Shinto gods to Buddhist secular history and usually center on the more popular Buddhist sects. The tone of Noh plays tends to be serious, appealing largely to the intellect and focusing on the spirit of some historical person who wishes salvation but is tied to this earth by worldly desires. Plays tend to be short, and an evening's performance usually includes several plays interspersed with comic burlesques called *Kyogen* ("Crazy Words"). Although Noh drama is still extremely popular, it remains primarily a fourteenth-century form. Almost its entire canon of scripts (approximately 240 plays) comes from that period, with more than 100 written by Seami alone (see the synopsis of *Atsumori* below).

Atsumori

SEAMI

Atsumori, a three-character play, tells the story of the warrior, Kumagai, who has killed Atsumori, a nobleman, in battle. In his grief over the deed, Kumagai becomes a priest, now called Rensei, in order to pray for Atsumori's soul. While traveling to a shrine to pray, Rensei encounters, among a group of reapers, one of Atsumori's family and kneels immediately to pray. This ends the first act. Between the two acts, a narrator details the events surrounding Atsumori's death. At the beginning of the second act, the ghost of Atsumori appears in the form of a young warrior. He identifies himself to Rensei, and the remainder of the play details the battle in which Atsumori died. The play ends with a re-creation of the fight in the form of a dance accompanied in narrative by the chorus. At the climax, Atsumori's ghost rises above Rensei, and is about to deliver a death blow. However, Rensei's prayers deliver him. The play ends with a salutation from Atsumori asking Rensei to "pray for me again, oh pray for me again."*

---

* Brockett, *The Theatre,* p. 272.

In general, Noh plays can be classified into five types: plays about the gods, warriors, women, spirits or mad persons, and demons. Traditionally, an evening's performance included all five types, generally performed in the order noted. Contemporary practice, however, has shortened the program to two or three offerings.

Kabuki Kabuki theatre originated approximately 400 years ago and has changed significantly over the centuries because of its ability to adapt and incorporate aspects of other theatre traditions. It has borrowed freely from Noh drama and from the popular Japanese puppet theatre, whose plays and stage machinery it also has incorporated. Kabuki began as a middle-class theatre and, as such, was the object of contempt by the samurai and the court. The earliest Kabuki plays were simple sketches; two-act plays did not appear until the mid-seventeenth century. By the mid-eighteenth century, the plays of the popular writer Takeda Izumo (1691–1756) had reached eleven acts in length and required an entire day to perform. However, the most important Kabuki playwright was the legendary seventeenth-century writer Chikamatsu, whose poetic style and the scope of his subject matter have occasioned comparisons with Shakespeare.

Kabuki plays tend to be melodramas and fall into three types. Plays with a historical background are called *jidai kyogen;* those portraying domesticity are called *sewamono,* dance plays *shosagoto.* The focus of a Kabuki play tends to be the climactic moment as opposed to the overall plot, and in that sense, Kabuki has a strong parallel with the "sensation-scene" focus of the Western melodramas of the nineteenth century. However, the connections between scenes in Kabuki plays tend to be rather vague—much in contrast to the Western melodrama, whose development follows a causal scheme such as the "well-made play" form of Eugène Scribe (see Chapter 17). Productions continue to be lengthy, although the practice of the day-long performance of the eighteenth century has been pared back to two five-hour performances per day. Because actors do not sing, a narrator and chorus play predominant roles in Kabuki productions. The narrator describes the scene, comments on the action, and even speaks portions of the dialogue. The overall style of Kabuki drama tends to be somewhere between convention and depiction. Every location is portrayed scenically, and scenery is changed in full view of the audience.

ELEMENTS OF PERFORMANCE

Music The intricate relationship of music to drama in Noh theatre comes from the work of Kan'ami (1333–1384), who applied the rhythmical intonation of speech sounds to music. As a result, Noh has a complicated, expressive, and varied relationship to music. Drums and flutes provide the principal musical accompaniment. A chorus of six to eight singers chants an accompaniment to dance movements and also provides narration and commentary. Every dance gesture reflects a complex symbolism that gives ultimate meaning to the action.

In Kabuki, music is divided into three categories. The beginning and end of the performance comprises ceremonial music provided by drums. Special effects are accompanied by *samisens* (three-stringed banjo-like instruments), drums, and flutes played by performers hidden in a black box stage-right. Onstage music is played in full view of the audience by an orchestra whose location changes in relationship to the dance and whose music can symbolically portray snow, rain, wind, and waves (see Fig. 14.7).

Acting   All actors in Noh theatre are male. Characters are divided into primary (*shite*) and secondary (*waki*) levels. Many Noh plays contain only two characters, although it is common for each of the primary and secondary characters to have a companion. The primary characters and their companions wear wooden masks, which represent a variety of categories: aged, male, female, god, and monster. The other characters remain unmasked.

Kabuki acting centers on the conventionalized portrayal of such basic character types as courageous men, villains, young men, women, and children, all of whom are played by men or boys. Because training for the Kabuki actor begins in childhood, children's roles are filled by child actors in training. Acting in the Kabuki theatre tends to be limited to a small number of families and is passed from generation to generation. Each family has a strong sense of identity with the public, and names and roles tend to be unique to each family.

THE PHYSICAL THEATRE

Noh Drama   The stage of the Noh theatre represents a far larger reality than actual time and space—it represents the world beyond temporal reality. Because the Noh stage goes beyond physical reality, there exists no need for illusionistic scenery or scenic depiction. The purpose of the mise-en-scène in

Figure 14.7   *Performance at the Kabuki-za Theatre, Tokyo, 1962. The musicians on the upper level right are playing* samisens, *the most important instrument in the Kabuki orchestra. Rather than a mask (as in the Noh drama), the actor wears heavy makeup that creates a symbolic image designed to combine the effect of the mask with that of the human face. Although stage machinery was often used to satisfy the audience's desire for spectacle, the stage scenery, as here, usually centered on stylized decorative backgrounds which, like the actor's makeup, were designed to suggest a certain universal or symbolic dimension to earthly settings and earthly dramas.*

Sergei Eisenstein: A Grand Total Provocation of the Human Brain

Although he gained international renown as a film director, the Russian Sergei Eisenstein (1898–1948) began his career in the arts as a disciple of Vsevelod Meyerhold in the theatre (see Chapter 17). An early and influential theorist of the cinema, Eisenstein based his ideas on the key principle of montage: *the ability of the cinema to create a new third "image" through the artful combination or "collision" of two distinct images recorded on different strips of celluloid. When a Japanese Kabuki troupe visited the Soviet Union in 1928, Eisenstein took the occasion to explain not only the workings of the Kabuki performance but their importance to an understanding of how, in his mind, the new art of the cinema should be conceived. In particular, Eisenstein was fascinated by the Kabuki theatre's combination of sight and sound and by the possibilities of this practice for understanding the brand-new art form of the sound film.*

We have been visited by the Kabuki theatre—a wonderful manifestation of theatrical culture.

Every critical voice gushes praise for its splendid craftsmanship. But there has been no appraisal of what constitutes its wonder. . . . We come to the conclusion that there is nothing to be learned, that (as one of our most respected critics has announced) there's nothing new here: Meyerhold has already plundered everything of use from the Japanese theater!

Behind the generalities, there are some real attitudes revealed. Kabuki is conventional! How can such conventions move Europeans! Its craftsmanship is merely the cold perfection of form! And the plays they perform are *feudal!*

More than any other obstacle, it is this conventionalism that prevents our thorough use of all that may be borrowed from the Kabuki.

But the conventionalism . . . of Kabuki is by no means the stylized and premeditated mannerism that we know in our own theater, artificially grafted on outside the technical requirements of the premise. In Kabuki this conventionalism is profoundly logical—as in any Oriental theater, for example, in the Chinese theater.

Among the characters of the Chinese theater is "the spirit of the oyster"! Look at the makeup of the performer of this rôle, with its series of concentric touching circles spreading from the right and left of his nose, graphically reproducing the halves of an oyster shell, and it becomes apparent that this is quite "justified." This is neither more nor less a convention than are the epaulettes of a general. From their narrowly utilitarian origin, once warding off blows of the battle-axe from the shoulder, to their being furnished with little stars, the epaulettes are indistinguishable in principle from the blue frog inscribed on the forehead of the actor who is playing the frog's "spirit."

Another convention is taken directly from life. In the first scene of *Chushingura* (*The Forty-Seven Ronin*) (see Fig. 14.8), Shocho, playing a married woman, appears without eyebrows and with blackened teeth. This conventionalism is no more unreal than the custom of Jewish women who shear their heads so that the ears remain exposed, nor of that among girls joining the Komsomol who wear red kerchiefs, as some sort of "form." In distinction from European practice, where marriage has been made a guard against the risks of freer attachments, in ancient Japan (of the play's epoch) the married woman, once the need had passed, destroyed her attractiveness! She removed her eyebrows, and blackened (and sometimes extracted) her teeth. . . .

The Japanese have shown us another, extremely interesting form of ensemble: Sound—movement—space—voice here do not accompany . . . each other, but function as elements of equal significance.

We are familiar with the emotional ensemble of the Moscow Art Theatre—the ensemble of a unified collective "re-experience"; the parallelism of ensemble employed in opera (by orchestra, chorus, and soloists); when the settings also make their contribution to this parallelism, the theater [becomes an] . . . outmoded form where the whole stage [turns into] a naturalistic imitation of the life that is led by the "assisting" human beings.

The Japanese have shown us another, extremely interesting form of ensemble: Sound—movement—space—voice here do not accompany (nor even parallel) each other, but function *as elements of equal significance.* . . .

It is impossible to speak of "accompaniments" in Kabuki—just as one would not say that, in walking or running, the right leg "accompanies" the left leg, or that both of them accompany the diaphragm!

Here a single sensation of theatrical "provocation" takes place. The Japanese regards each theatrical element, not as [a separate] unit among the various categories of affect (on the various sense-organs), but as a single unit of theater. . . .

The Japanese in his, of course, instinctive practice, makes a fully one hundred per cent appeal with his theater. Directing himself to the various organs of sensation, he builds his summation to a grand *total* provocation of the human brain, without taking any notice *which* of these several paths he is following.

In place of *accompaniment,* it is the naked method of transfer that flashes in the Kabuki theater. Transferring the basic affective aim from one material to another, from one category of "provocation" to another.

In experiencing Kabuki one involuntarily recalls an American novel about a man in whom are transposed the hearing and seeing nerves, so that he perceives light vibrations as sounds, and tremors of the air—as colors: he *hears light* and *sees sound.* This is also what happens in Kabuki! We actually "hear movement" and "see sound."

An example: Yuranosuke leaves the surrendered castle. And moves from the depth of the stage towards the extreme foreground. Suddenly the background screen with its gate painted in natural dimensions is folded away. In its place is seen a second screen, with a tiny gate painted on it. This means that he has moved even further away. Yuranosuke continues on. Across the background is drawn a brown-green-black curtain, indicating [that] the castle is now hidden from his sight. More steps. Yuranosuke now moves out on the "flowery way." This further removal is emphasized by sound!

First removal—steps, i.e., a *spatial* removal by the actor.

Second removal—a flat *painting:* the change of backgrounds.

Third removal—an *intellectually*-explained indication: we understand that the curtain "effaces" something visible.

Fourth removal—*sound!*

Here is an example of pure cinematographic method from the last fragment of *Chushingura:*

After a short fight ("for several feet") we have a "break"—an empty stage, a landscape. Then more fighting. Exactly as if, in a film, we had cut in a piece of landscape to create a mood in a scene, here is cut in an empty nocturnal snow landscape (on an empty stage). And here after several feet, two of the "forty-seven faithful" observe a shed where the villain has hidden (of which the spectator is already aware). Just as in cinema, within such a sharpened dramatic moment, some brake has to be applied. . . . A brake is applied to the action, and the tension is screwed tighter.

The moment of the discovery of the hiding-place must be accentuated. To find the *right* solution for this moment, this accent must be shaped from the *same* rhythmic material—a return to the same nocturnal, empty, snowy landscape . . .

But now there are people on the stage! Nevertheless, the Japanese do find the right solution—and it is a *flute* that enters triumphantly! And you *see* the same snowy fields, the same echoing emptiness and night, that you *heard* a short while before, when you *looked* at the empty stage . . .

Occasionally the Japanese double their effects. With their mastery of the equivalents of visual and aural images they suddenly give *both* brilliantly calculating the blow of their sensual billiard-cue on the spectator's cerebral target. I know no better way to describe that combination of the moving hand of Ichikawa Ennosuke as he commits hara-kiri—*with* the sobbing sound off-stage, *graphically* corresponding with the movement of the knife.

There it is: "Whatever notes I can't take with my voice, I'll show with my hands!" But here it was taken by the voice and shown with the hands! And we stand benumbed before such a perfection of montage.

[In our thoughts about the sound film, we have suggested the need for a] method of combining visual and aural images. To possess this method one must develop in oneself a new *sense: the capacity of reducing visual and aural perceptions to a "common denominator."*

This is possessed by Kabuki to perfection. And we, too—crossing . . . [the bridge] between theater and cinema and between cinema and sound-cinema—must also possess this. We can learn the mastery of this required new sense from the Japanese.

From "The Unexpected." In *Film Form and the Film Sense*, Jay Leyda, ed. New York: World Publishing, 1957, pp. 18–27.

Noh theatre is to transport the audience, through its own imagination, into the spiritual world. This form of Japanese theatre thus hints at a particular level of reality—in this case, one that transcends the temporal. With little need for illusion, Noh theatre uses little scenery.

Properties, on the other hand, play a more important role, especially the fan. Fans can represent all manner of objects—for example, bottles, cups, and weapons. It is the stage itself, however, that takes on the most important role in the presentation of Noh drama. In its earliest forms, Noh drama used temporary stages and stands erected in dry river beds. Two ramps connected the stage with dressing areas set up to the side. The audience–stage relationship was three-sided and arranged in a 100-foot diameter. The aristocracy watched performances from raised boxes. Later, Noh drama moved into the palaces under the patronage of the nobility, and the traditional situation became that of a house and garden erected within a house and garden (see Fig. 14.9). Even after performances moved indoors, a gravel-covered space separated the audience from the stage.

Figure 14.8   Hokusai, *print (1798) depicting the famous brothel scene from* The Forty-Seven Loyal Ronin. *The story is about a troop of samurai who have been put out of work by the death of the nobleman to whom they have sworn loyalty. So well known is the story to Japanese audiences that companies regularly perform famous scenes from the play as part of Kabuki programs. This scene-in which a father sells his daughter into prostitution to raise money for the ronin-is a particular favorite of Japanese audiences, who sometimes weep openly at its theme of tragic inevitability.*

[Courtesy of Museum of Fine Arts, Boston]

Figure 14.9   Masanobu Okumura (1686–1764), *painting of a theatre in Tokyo. Noh performances, which were originally played on temporary outdoor stands, moved indoors—that is, to specially constructed garden areas on the grounds of sufficiently large houses—when the dramatic form became popular with the aristocratic classes. The raised seating area for nobles (right) derives from the practice whereby aristocratic theatregoers built elevated boxes from which to watch outdoor performances.*

[The Tsubouchi Memorial Theatre Museum, Waseda University, Tokyo.]

Asian Theatre

Figure 14.10A *Contemporary Noh stage and auditorium, Tokyo. Note the painted-design scenery. Noh scenic convention drew upon myths concerning the creation of nature: The stylized representation of the natural object is also a suggestion of that object as an ideal, and one function of the drama was to "prompt" the audience to experience or appreciate the link between the natural world and a higher level of reality.*

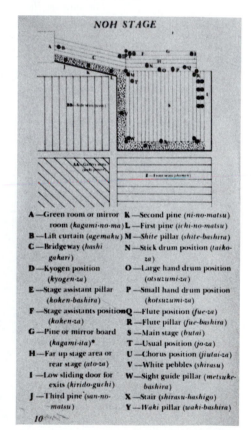

Figure 14.10B *Groundplan of a typical Noh stage.*

From *On Stage in Japan* (Tokyo: Shufuno-tomo Company, Ltd., 1974). Reprinted by permission © 1974.

NOH STAGE

A —Green room or mirror room (*kagami-no-ma*)
B —Lift curtain (*agemaku*)
C —Bridgeway (*hashi gakari*)
D —Kyogen position (*kyogen-za*)
E —Stage assistant pillar (*koken-bashira*)
F —Stage assistants position (*koken-za*)
G —Pine or mirror board (*kagami-ita*)*
H —Far up stage area or rear stage (*ato-za*)
I —Low sliding door for exits (*kirido-guchi*)
J —Third pine (*san-no-matsu*)
K —Second pine (*ni-no-matsu*)
L —First pine (*ichi-no-matsu*)
M —*Shite* pillar (*shite-bashira*)
N —Stick drum position (*taiko-za*)
O —Large hand drum position (*otsuzumi-za*)
P —Small hand drum position (*kotsuzumi-za*)
Q —Flute position (*fue-za*)
R —Flute pillar (*fue-bashira*)
S —Main stage (*butai*)
T —Usual position (*jo-za*)
U —Chorus position (*jiutai-za*)
V —White pebbles (*shirasu*)
W —Sight guide pillar (*metsuke-bashira*)
X —Stair (*shirasu-hashigo*)
Y —*Waki* pillar (*waki-bashira*)

The stage had a peaked roof in the style of a Shinto temple (Figs. 14.10A and 14.10B) and was supported by four fifteen-foot-square columns. Each column had a name according to its stage function. For example, on his entrance, an actor moved to the first column to state his name and function in the play. He then moved to the next appropriate column; the column upstage-right was the *shite*'s column. Additional columns were for the flute player, the *waki,* the "eye-fixing" column, and so on. A platform for the orchestra was located at the rear of the stage. At the left of the platform was a low door called the "hurry door," which was used by subordinate characters, stage assistants, chorus, and musicians. The main entrance to the stage was a bridge called *hashigakari,* a railed gangway connecting the stage to the dressing rooms. All important entrances came over this 33- to 52-foot-long, 6-foot-wide causeway. In front of the *hashigakari* appeared three small pine trees symbolizing man, earth, and heaven.

Acoustics in the Noh theatre are very carefully enhanced by specifically selected materials and devices. The floor of the 18-foot-square stage is made of seasoned and polished wood. Under the stage, twelve large jars, suspended strategically by copper wires under the floor, act as resonating chambers for voice, music, and dance.

Kabuki Theatre Kabuki stages represent a combination of Noh conventionalism and Western scenic illusionism. A long runway connects a dressing area at the rear of the audience to the square, roofed Kabuki stage. Four pillars support the roof, and the audience sits on one side, as in the proscenium or open-stage forms. However, the runway also can function as a stage extension or as an independent stage, and so the actor–audience relationship in Kabuki theatre can take a variety of forms. By the sixteenth century, and progressing into the nineteenth century, a number of developments in the Kabuki stage separated it from its Noh prototype and gave it a new complexity (see Fig. 14.11). A curtain, for example, revealed on-stage action; revolving stages, double revolving stages, trap doors, and elevators covered the stage and ramp areas and made possible a wealth of scenic effects. A two-dimensional scenic background comprising flats nailed side by side was used to emphasize the three-dimensional actor. By the mid-nineteenth century, the Noh-style roof had been removed, and the stage was widened to extend the full width of the auditorium (Fig. 14.12). Several conventions regarding stage areas continue: Stage-left, for example, holds socially important scenes and is reserved for high-ranking characters; stage-right has the opposite functions—that is, it serves for minor scenes and low-ranking characters. Because virtually all characters in Kabuki drama are seeking higher social standing, all entrances come from stage-right. Females walk one pace behind the men; male movement starts with the left arm or leg, female with the right.*

COSTUMES AND MAKEUP

Noh Drama Costumes in the Noh theatre are divided into four categories: outer garments, indoor garments or garments worn without an overdress, lower garments (for example, divided skirts), and headdresses and wigs. There

---

* Kuritz, *The Making of Theatre History,* pp. 106, 113–114.

KABUKI STAGE

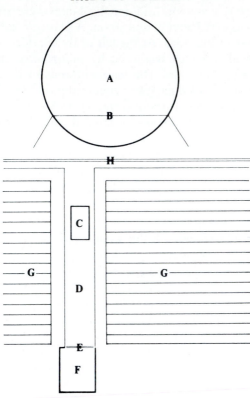

A —Revolving stage (*mawari-butai*)
B —Panel set (*kakiwari*)
C —Trap lift (*kiri-ana* or *suppon*)
D —Ramp (*hanamichi*)
E —Draw curtain at end of ramp (*hanamichi no age-maku*)
F —Room behind curtain (*toriya*)
G —Seating area (*kyakuseki*)
H —Draw curtain (*joshiki-maku*)

Figure 14.11 *Groundplan of a typical Kabuki stage. Note the* revolving stage (A) *and the* trap lift (C). *The Kabuki performance is mechanically much more complex than the Noh performance. Such apparatus as revolving stages and trap lifts appeared in the 18th century, and the Kabuki audience typically expects more spectacular action and effects.*

[From *On Stage in Japan* (Tokyo: Shufunotomo Company, Ltd., 1974). Reprinted by permission © 1974. Paul Kuritz, *The Making of Theatre History* (Prentice Hall, 1988), p. 113.]

are many variations within each category, and various combinations of garments may be used for a wide range of characterizations and effects. Costume in the Noh theatre has less conventional restriction than, for example, that of the Chinese theatre. The orchestra and chorus wear the traditional costume of the samurai. Although based on historic court dress, Noh costumes have been adapted so as to create an effect of enhanced size and grandeur. They are extremely rich and colorful, constructed of silk, and decorated with elaborate embroidery.

Kabuki Theatre Although Kabuki costuming does not call for masks, boldly painted makeup is common for most roles. Brown, red, black, and blue designs are painted over a white base. Each makeup pattern carries symbolic

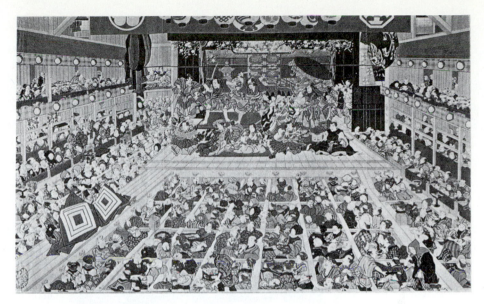

Figure 14.12 *Kabuki theatre at the end of the Edo period. Note that the runway or hanamichi now runs in front of the stage instead of to the side. The stage has also become larger than the Noh stage and is faced by all seats. Both stage and auditorium are wide and shallow.*

[New York Public Library Picture Collection.]

meaning relative to the character. Likewise, costumes are symbolic and conventionalized. Based for the most part on historic dress, period style nevertheless has no relationship to the particular play, and any number of styles may be mixed in a given production. Kabuki costumes tend to be quite elaborate and heavy, some weighing as much as fifty pounds. They must be rearranged frequently, and stage attendants accomplish this task in full view of the audience. In performing their duties, stage attendants wear black and, by convention, are therefore assumed to be invisible. Finally, costume bears a strong relationship to emotion in Kabuki theatre, and a novel technique called *bukkaeri* calls for a stagehand to pull a cord that holds the costume together at the shoulders. When this occurs, the old costume falls to the ground and a new one is revealed, signaling a change in emotion.

The Theatre *of* India

DRAMA AND RELIGION

The seeds of dramatic theatre in India occurred in the Vedic religion. *Veda* means knowledge, and this predecessor of Hinduism centered on the worship of nature—sky, sun, fire, light, wind, water, and sexual reproduction. Each of these elements was personified and so easily re-created as dramatized personages. Central to the Vedic religion were sacrifice and celebration, and

Figure 14.13 *Indian entertainers perform in the public streets during religious festivities. Note the tall staff, or jaraja, on which tightrope walkers perform above jugglers, acrobats, and musicians. The jaraja, which was first dedicated with music and decoration, was erected in a central location and became the center point of festivities that were highly religious in origin.*

[Museum fur Indische Kunst Staatliche Museen PreuBischer Berlin.]

acting out the mythology of these characters was a natural step in the establishment of formal drama. Vedic mythology contains some of the oldest literary canons in the Indo-European tradition, some of which date to as early as 6000 B.C. The philosophical system of Vedism, called the Upanishads, explains the relationship between the individual and the universal soul and constitutes a viewpoint that still forms the heart of Indian theatre.

As early as the fourth century B.C. professional actors appeared in dramatic rituals performed in honor of the gods. Written evidence from as early as the third century B.C. indicates that theatre events were prevalent at public festivals and other celebrations (Fig. 14.13). During the time when Buddhism spread throughout India and East Asia, approximately the fourth to the second centuries B.C., drama occupied an important and popular place as a device for spreading Buddhist doctrine. Religion, therefore, played a fundamental contextual role for all aspects of Indian culture. Particularly important during the first seven hundred years of the Christian era were Hindu festivals. Such festivities, according to one theatre historian,

continued as principal occasions for dramatic theatre. In February or March, fertility rituals, erotic games, comic operas, and folk dances marked the Holi festival. Men and women ran through the streets squirting colored water at one another, and theatrical troupes competed for prizes, as in the August through October festival of Indra's standard. A tree, shorn of branches, possibly representing the flagstaff used by Brahma to consecrate the first theatre, was

Asian Theatre

paraded to the main square, where it was decorated and adorned to music. Erected in the middle of the town, the *jaraja* (staff), through which the gods' spirits descended to Earth, became the focal point of popular celebrations, dances, poetic songs, juggling, and more ever-popular water squirting. Festivals continued dramatic presentations even after the rise of new religious ideas in India.*

DRAMATIC FORMS

Sanskrit Drama Sanskrit drama is the most important form in Indian drama. Sanskrit, of course, is an ancient language, and the classical drama of India appears in that language dating from the period between approximately 320 A.D. and the twelfth century. The word *sanskrit* means "prepared, pure, perfect, or sacred," and Sanskrit served as the scholarly language of Indian literati even after the language ceased to be used in common practice. Organized around nine basic moods, or *rasas,* Sanskrit drama focuses on the erotic, comic, pathetic, furious, heroic, terrible, odious, marvelous, and peaceful moods. Obviously, this approach stands in stark contrast to the practice in Western drama of organizing plays around character or theme. Sanskrit drama employs single central plots with a number of subplots. The object of the drama is to manipulate the audience's *rasa,* or state of aesthetic awareness, so that the spectator is drawn, as one student of Asian theatre puts it, "from the material of the play into consciousness of an enduring reality."**

Sanskrit plays resemble epic poetry in the Western tradition. Dialogue, for example, alternates with narrative in order to explain offstage events and lay the scene. Location changes freely, and the conventional time frame is limited to a twenty-four-hour period within a single act; no more than one year should elapse between acts. The number of acts varies from one to ten. Characterizations in Sanskrit drama can be diverse, with a variety of social orders represented, although the hero almost always represents the aristocracy. Language incorporates poetry and prose, both Sanskrit and the vernacular. The most important form of Sanskrit drama is the heroic, in which a mythic hero defends a moral cause. Love themes also are incorporated into the drama, with the lovers separated by evil until the end (all Sanskrit drama ends happily).

Two excellent plays exist among surviving examples, both dating from the second or third and late fourth or early fifth centuries. *Carudatta,* by Bhasa, tells of the love of a Brahmin and a courtesan and falls, according to traditional Hindu classification, into the category of "social plays." Its characters include a true prince, the Brahmin, courtesan, and an evil prince whose actions nearly cause the death of the Brahmin and the courtesan. In the end, the true prince regains his throne and the good characters "live happily ever after."

---

* Kuritz, *The Making of Theatre History,* p. 69.
** A. C. Scott, *The Theatre in Asia* (London: Weidenfeld & Nicolson, 1972), p. 36. Quoted in Kuritz, *The Making of Theatre History,* p. 72.

Figure 14.14 *Scene from Sha-kuntala by Kalidasa. Miniature from a Hindi manuscript, 1789. This drawing depicts the first en-counter between King Dushyanta (right) and the hermit's daughter Shakuntala.*

[New Delhi, National Museum.]

Shakuntala by the late-fourth-century playwright Kalidasa, is generally considered to be the finest Sanskrit drama ever written. A seven-act heroic drama, it tells, in beautifully crafted narrative passages, the story of King Dushyanta and his meeting with Shakuntala, the foster daughter of a hermit (Fig. 14.14). They fall in love, are separated (with complications resulting from a curse by a rejected suitor), and are reunited. Scenes shift between heaven and earth and the forest and the court, and the mood varies from serious to comic in an ambitious exploration of the breadth of human experience.

Kathakali Dance-Drama   Kathakali dance-drama is another important Indian dramatic form. The form itself developed in the seventeenth century in the southwestern part of India and remains localized to that region. Kathakali draws its subjects from Hindu mythology and presents them in a pantomimic style designed to exaggerate the characteristics of Sanskrit drama and to allow both death and violence to occur on stage. The plots of Kathakali dance-drama focus on the passions of gods and demons. Characters are superhuman, and conflicts inevitably involve the clash between good and evil (again, good triumphs over evil in the end). Actors use pantomime, makeup, costume, and dance to tell the story, with musicians singing and playing to assist in full communication. The gestures of Kathakali dance-drama include more than five hundred separate signs, with characterizations representing basic types rather than individuals. Female roles are played by boys. Costume and makeup are totally symbolic. Performances occur in temple courtyards and other open spaces on stages approximately sixteen feet square and covered by flowered canopies. Performances, which last all night, are lit by torches.*

ELEMENTS OF PERFORMANCE

Music   As we have noted, music plays an important role in Kathakali dance-drama. It not only provides accompaniment for the actor's pantomime and dance but conveys significant information to the audience in its own right.

* Oscar Brockett, *History of the Theatre* (Boston: Allyn and Bacon, 1987), pp. 316–317.

Sanskrit drama also employs music in fundamental ways. Intonation, pitch, and tempo play conventional roles relative to situation, mood, and character. Musical accompaniment, played on stringed instruments and drums, occurs throughout the drama. The drums accent the actors' voices and create rhythmic structure for the audience. Music also creates changes in mood, provides information about situation, and explains character motivation. Also important is the *raga*, or melodic line, which can communicate mood, personality traits, seasons, and times of day. Finally, music forms the bridge from the material to the spiritual world, from the drama on stage to the spiritual, internal peace of the audience.

Acting   Actors in India fared little better in the social order than those of ancient China or ancient Rome. In fact, so little were actors regarded in India that, by law, the penalty for adultery with an actor's wife was far less severe than for trespass with women married into other occupations. Nonetheless, a few actors were held in high esteem—at least on their artistic merits. Roles in Indian theatre could be played by both men and women, and cross-role situations—wherein women played effeminate men and men played more virile women—also occurred. In Kathakali dance-drama, all roles were played by men and boys.

In role performance, the actor needed to achieve a proper balance between inner and outer techniques. It was deemed most important that an actor not only represent the proper state or condition of the character but show through body language the feelings and emotions of the character. In the Kathakali dance-drama, five hundred separate signs made up the physical vocabulary, and characters fell into seven basic types. In Sanskrit drama, physical movement was detailed minutely in the classic manuals, which listed, for example, 36 different types of glances alone (Fig. 14.15). Every part of the body had its variety of attitudes for transmission of meaning to the audience. According to one Indian historian,

every inch of the human form, every joint of the human skeleton, is given significance, for it is not only the geometrical and physical possibility which is being explored, but its correlation to the meaning, to the attitude of the state the whole will evoke. . . . Character is thus portrayed through a knowledge of types in which particular qualities predominate, and by a systematic use of physical postures, movements, turns and thrusts of the body which correspond to the moods.*

The intricate sign language of the actor's body was complemented by an equally intricate vocal system in which particular pitches and tempos evoked specific *rasas* (that is, sentiments). The actor's symbolic tools also integrated costumes, makeup, and properties with bodily movement to suggest such themes as darkness, mourning, swimming, climbing, and so on.

However, the most important characteristic of acting was the psychologi-

* Kapila Vatsyayam, *Classical Indian Dance in Literature and the Arts* (New Delhi: Sangeet Natak Akademi, 1968), p. 14. Quoted in Kuritz, p. 74.

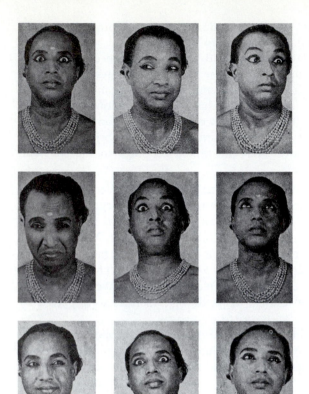

Figure 14.15 *Facial expression in the Sanskrit theatre. According to the gesture code called* abhinaya, *which refers to the presentation of theme to the audience, facial expression (*bhava*) may communicate nine principal emotions (*rasas*). Clockwise from top left, they are:* love, valor, pathos, wonder, laughter, fear, disgust, anger, tranquility. *It is absolutely essential to the success of the* abhinaya *that the* rasa *evoke the same essential sentiment in the spectator.*

cal. The classical Indian actor had to capture the character's mood in his or her own "being." Only by adhering to four crucial characteristics—sign language, voice, externalization (with costumes and properties), and psychological composition—could an actor become a part of the "inner school."

THE PHYSICAL THEATRE

Although no permanent theatres existed in India, temporary playhouses met very precise parameters (Fig. 14.16). An area approximately 48 by 66 feet was divided in half. The audience occupied one half, the stage the other. The area in front of the stage comprised the seats of honor and was reserved for the patron of the production. The stage area had two equal parts, the front half housing the acting area and the rear the dressing rooms and other offstage space. On occasion, the stage may have had a second level symbolizing places in heaven or other lofty abodes. The stage was strictly conventionalized. Location was indicated through narrative and pantomime, and no scenery was used, although the changing color of the background suggested various moods—for example, white for the erotic, yellow for heroic, and red for

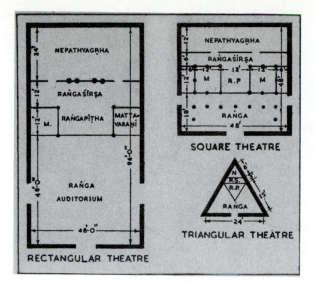

Figure 14.16 *Floorplans for Sanskrit theatres. Performances were first conducted on temporary platforms erected in front of city temples. Before a permanent theatre could be constructed, astrological readings had to be taken and offerings made; measurements could be taken only at specific times of certain days and were followed by commemorative celebrations. Once the structure was completed, it featured separate doors through which men and women entered, and the seating area was designed to accommodate the strict segregation of social classes. The stage (ranga) was composed of separate areas because it was believed that different deities presided over different stage spaces.*

Courtesy Birla Vishvakarma Mahavidyalaya. D. R. Mankad, *Ancient Indian Theatre* (Anand: Charotar Publishing House, 1960).

violence. The imagination of the audience, stimulated by the skillful work of the actor, created the scene. Kathakali dance-dramas occurred in temple courtyards or other open spaces. As we noted earlier, productions were staged by torchlight on stages approximately 16 feet square and covered with a flower-decked roof.

COSTUMES AND MAKEUP

The symbolism of Indian costume and makeup was as elaborate and intricate as every other part of the performance. Color symbolism dominated costuming, with religion, caste, and social station all indicated by color. Among female characters, white symbolized the divine, yellow the superhuman; black was for female demons. Male characters of various qualities wore multicolored costumes; harem chiefs wore red jackets. The dress of kings was highly colorful, and lack of color in a king's costume indicated ill omens. Ascetics wore black rags. Makeup covered the full body with the colors white, blue-black, red, and yellow were considered basic. An unhappy character had skin colored dark orange. Skin color and hairstyle also denoted various castes and subdivisions of castes.

Perhaps even more than the theatre of Japan and China, Indian theatre depended heavily on sophisticated audiences and was, therefore, largely a theatre of the elite. Even to begin to comprehend the drama, audience members must have been well read and perhaps even erudite in art and literature. Each audience member expected to participate in the theatre experience through emotional involvement in the laughing, crying, clapping, and screaming occasioned by the event. Ideally, the goal was to achieve a sublime self-realization—the great *rasa*. Any action that held the potential of distracting from such a response was strictly forbidden—for example, unhappy endings, murder, fights, eating, embraces, breast-fondling, and bathing.

SUMMARY

- The arts of Asia differ significantly from the arts of the West, relying on *intuition* and using the material world to represent illusion rather than fact.

- Much of the theatre of China had its roots in the traditions of Buddhism, but Confucianism also gave shape to early Chinese drama.

- The *golden age of Chinese drama and theatre* occurred at a time roughly equivalent to the Gothic period in Western history.

- In its earliest forms, Chinese drama fell into two general categories, that of the North and that of the South:

  In the North, drama was based on a seven-tone musical scale; it had a lively and energetic quality, colloquial dialogue, and free verse.

  In the South, drama utilized a five-tone scale, had a soft and gentle quality, poetic dialogue, and strict meter and verse.

- The major form of Chinese drama became the *Beijing Opera*.

- Chinese drama depends heavily on music to create its atmosphere, establish the pace of the production, provide accompaniment for the singers, and, in general, pull the production into a unified whole.

- Acting style in Chinese drama relies on *convention* and divides roles into various *types*.

- The space in which Chinese drama is performed maintains strong religious orientations and relies heavily on convention for establishing location.

- Chinese costumes and makeup play a significant and symbolic role in Chinese theatre:

  Color is especially important,

  Costume attempts to make no historically accurate depiction,

  Makeup provides an important identifying factor in character development.

- Religion and drama in Japan have an interwoven history, emerging from early rhythmic movements produced by the *Shinto religion*.

- Japan's two great dramatic forms, Noh and Kabuki, both originated from religious ritual dating to the late eighth and early ninth centuries:

  Noh drama emerged from the fourteenth century and represented the most significant and original literary and performing art development of the Ashikaga period.

  Kabuki theatre began approximately 400 years ago and has changed significantly over the centuries.

- Music has an intricate and important relationship to both Noh drama and Kabuki theatre.

- All of the actors in Noh theatre are male.

- Acting in the Kabuki theatre tends to be limited to a small number of families and is passed from generation to generation.

- The stage of the Noh theatre represents a far larger reality than actual time and space: It represents the supernatural world beyond temporal reality.

- Kabuki stages represent a combination between Noh conventions and Western scenic illusion.

- Costume in the Noh theatre has less conventional restriction than, for example, that of the Chinese theatre. Noh costumes are extremely rich and colorful.

- Kabuki costume does not use masks. Boldly painted makeup is common for most roles.

- The seeds of dramatic theatre in India occurred in the Vedic religion: As early as the fourth century B.C., professional actors appeared in dramatic rituals performed in honor of the gods.

- Sanskrit and Kathakali represent the two most important dramatic forms in India:

  Sanskrit drama, the most important dramatic form in India, is a classical drama using the scholarly language Sanskrit.

  Kathakali dance-drama draws its subjects from Hindu mythology and presents them in a pantomimic style.

- In role performance the actor needed to achieve a proper balance between inner and outer techniques:

  Every inch of the human form is given significance.

  The intricate sign language of the actor's body was complemented by an equally intricate vocal system.

- The most important characteristic of acting was the psychological characteristic.

- No permanent theatres existed in India, and the temporary playhouses met very precise parameters.

- The symbolism of Indian costume and makeup was elaborate and intricate. Color symbolism dominated costumes.

- Indian theatre depended on a sophisticated audience: Audience members must have been well read and erudite in Indian art and literature.

The Expressions of International Theatre

Plate 4.3 (Above)
Masks represent human types and surround one human individual in a carnival in Binche, Belgium.

Plate 4.1 (Left Above)
In Brazil, a Passion Play depicting the trial crucifixion, and resurrection of Jesus Christ uses period costume and spectacle in recreating a play form that dates to the Middle Ages.

Plate 4.2 (Below)
In a dramatic form much like traditional theatre, puppetry effectively brings alive the dramatic format using puppets rather than live actors. Here, Italy's Manteo Family puppets employ costumes, scenery, and script in their performance.

Plate 1.A

Plate 1.B

Plate 1.C

Plate 4.4
Ritual has formed the roots and often lies at the heart of theatre in many cultures. In these illustrations, colorful costumes, ritual, and mimetic behavior create a drama and theatre-like atmosphere in a Senegalese initiation rite (1A), a Peruvian festival (1B), a Balinese festival (1C), a Guatemalan "Dance of the Conquistadors" (1D), and a Nepalese Mani Rimdu festival (1E).

Plate I.D

Plate I.E

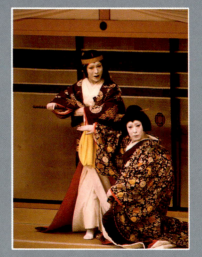

Plate 4.5 *(Left Above and Below)*
The elaborate and symbolic costumes of the Peking Opera can be seen
in these two illustrations.

Plate 4.6 *(Above Right)*
Japanese Kabuki actors (see Chapter 14) pantomime action at the
Kabukiza Theatre in Tokyo. Note the rich textures and layered effect
of the costumes.

Western Theatre *from* Ancient Greece *to the* Middle Ages

*A*fter studying this chapter you should be able to:

- Describe the production practices of the *classical Greek theatre*.
- Identify and discuss the major *tragedians* of the classical Greek theatre.
- Discuss *Old Comedy* and the approach of its major practitioner, Aristophanes.
- Explain the major dramatic forms of the *Roman theatre*.
- Identify and describe the physical theatre of Rome.
- Define *miracle, mystery,* and *morality* plays and their relationship to the *medieval theatre*.
- Characterize the production practices of the medieval period and compare them with those of Greece and Rome.

Actor Studying His Mask.

*I*n the next three chapters, we will survey the history of theatre in the Western tradition. In this chapter, we begin with the origins of Western theatre in ancient Greece and follow its changes as Greek and, later, Hellenistic influence was replaced by Roman political dominion and decline. Finally, we watch as theatre rises from semiobscurity to a position of importance in the Middle Ages. Throughout the chapter, our focus will fall on three general areas: *playwrights, dramatic forms,* and *production practices* (including, for example, the nature of the theatre facility).

Ancient Greece

Under the ruler Pericles, classical Greek culture reached its zenith. To that civilization and its works Western culture has returned for nourishment for over 2,000 years. In the brief span of time between approximately 600 B.C. and 200 B.C., Greek influence and civilization spread throughout the Mediterranean world until, under Alexander the Great, it stretched—for the space of a single lifetime—from Spain to the Indus River of India. All this was achieved by a people whose culture, at its height, took as its measure the human intellect. In society as in the arts, rationality, clarity, and beauty of form were the aim. The style that we call *Hellenistic* developed in the fourth century B.C., as artists increasingly sought to imbue their works with the expression of feeling.

PRODUCTION AND STYLE

The theatre of Periclean Athens was a theatre of convention, which, as we have noted, implies a style of production lacking in illusion or stage realism. For the Greek classicist, whose vision focused on form, structure, and idealism, a theatre of convention offered a better means to explore the ideal than did a theatre of illusion, in which scenic details are realistically portrayed. Because imagination is the key to theatre of convention, the level of reality portrayed is free to go beyond the world of the here and now. Nonetheless, although some plays from the era have survived, we are not sure, specifically, how they actually sounded or looked in production. In order to arrive at conclusions about Greek classical theatre production, scholars have extrapolated a picture of production from descriptions in the plays themselves, from other literary evidence, and from a few extant archeological examples.

Theatre productions in ancient Greece were part of three yearly religious festivals—the *City Dionysia, Rustic Dionysia,* and *Lenaea.* The first of these was a festival of tragic plays and the last of comic. In each tragic contest, the playwright was required to present four plays in succession—three tragedies and a *satyr play* (a genre whose characteristics have been lost in the dust of history). The City Dionysia was held in the Theatre of Dionysos in Athens (see

Figure 15.1

Detail, Dionysos and a comic actor, from a vase by Asteas, ca. 350 B.C. *The cult of the god Dionysos, which included frenzied rituals of sacrifice and celebration of the deity of joy and the grape, was ultimately absorbed into official yearly festivals at city-states like Athens, where drama was also a matter of religious and civic functions. Although certain details of the activities of dionysiac cults remain shrouded in prehistory, it is possible that worship of Dionysos, as a release into states of irrational exhiliaration, gave rise to the concept of drama as catharsis (see the excerpt from Aristotle in this chapter).*
[British Museum]

Fig. 5.2). The contests were begun in 534 B.C., before the classical era. Our knowledge of Greek theatre is enhanced somewhat by the fact that although we do not possess most of the plays, we do know the titles and the authors who won these contests from the earliest to the last. From the records (inscriptions in stone), we know that three playwrights figured prominently and repeatedly as winners in the contests of the era: Aeschylus, Sophocles, and Euripides. Our entire collection of complete tragedies is from these three playwrights—7 from Aeschylus, 7 from Sophocles, and 18 from Euripides. The only comic playwright whose works have survived is Aristophanes.

A playwright entering the contests for tragedy or comedy was required to submit his plays to a panel of presiding officers who selected three playwrights for actual production. The early plays of the classical style had only one actor plus a chorus. The *chorus* was a distinctive feature of Greek drama, portraying the dual function (in the same play) of narrator and a collective figure who responded to the actors. In the earliest tragedies, the chorus had 50 members. At the time of play selection, the playwright was assigned a chief actor plus a *choregus*—a patron who paid all the expenses for the production. The playwright was author, director, choreographer, and musical composer. He often played the leading role as well.

THE TRAGEDIANS

Aeschylus In the early fifth century B.C., Aeschylus (525–456 B.C.), the most famous playwright of ancient Greece began to write for the theatre. Clearly fitting the classic mold, he wrote magnificent tragedies of high poetic nature and lofty moral theme. In *Agamemnon,* the first play in the Oresteia trilogy (summarized in Chapter 5), Aeschylus' chorus warns us that success and wealth are insufficient without goodness:

> Justice shines in sooty dwellings
>   Loving the righteous way of life,
> But passes by with averted eyes
> The house whose lord has hands unclean.
> Be it built throughout of gold.
> Caring naught for the weight of praise
> Heaped upon wealth by the vain, but turning
> All alike to its proper end.

Aeschylus probed questions that we still ask: How responsible are we for our own actions? How much are we controlled by the will of heaven? His characters were larger than life; in accord with the idealism of the time, they were *types* rather than individuals. Aeschylus' early plays consisted of one actor and a chorus of 50, conforming to the convention of the time. He is credited with the addition of a second actor. By the end of his long career, a third actor had been added and the chorus reduced to 12.

In Aeschylus' plays, we find a strong appeal to the intellect. Aristophanes, the master of Greek comedy, has Aeschylus, as a character in the *Frogs,* defend his writing as an inspiration to patriotism, to make men proud of their achievements. This is inspiration in an intellectual, not a rabble-rousing, sense. Aeschylus lived through the Persian invasion, witnessed the great Athenian victories, and fought at the battle of Marathon. His plays reflect this experience and spirit.

Sophocles Contemporary with Aeschylus was Sophocles (496?–406 B.C.), who reached the peak of his career during the zenith of the Greek classical style with works like *Oedipus the King* (see Chapter 3; see also Fig. 10.5B).

Often cited as the greatest tragedy of all time, *Oedipus the King* rises in pyramidal structure to a tense climax. The action focuses on a single character, Oedipus, by unfolding his noble, if egotistical, pursuit of the truth about the situation. The terrible deeds that comprise the truth which Oedipus seeks are revealed in their consequence and not as they occur. The tragedy lies in the hero's understanding of his guilt rather than in the guilt itself. For Sophocles, such self-knowledge had the effect of freeing the individual in that humankind has free choice and cannot blame the gods or fate or the Oracle for his actions. As a result, there is a victory of a moral nature over the tragedy of the physical order.

Sophocles' plots and characterizations illustrate a trend toward increasing realism. The movement toward realism was not a movement into theatre of illusion; even Euripides' plays, the most realistic of the Greek tragedies, are not "realistic" in our sense of the word. Sophocles, however, was a less formal poet than Aeschylus. His themes are more humane and his characters more subtle, although his exploration of the themes of human responsibility, dignity, and fate is of the same intensity and seriousness that we see in Aeschylus.

Aristotle: The Form of Tragedy

Dating from the fourth century B.C., Aristotle's Poetics remains the Western world's single most influential work on the nature of art. As we saw in Chapter 2, Aristotle's thoughts about the nature of drama were inspired by the great works, especially those of Sophocles, that were produced in his own era, and he was concerned as much with the form of drama as with its ultimate purpose. In the famous sixth chapter of the Poetics, then, although he identifies the purpose of tragedy as "arousing pity and fear" and achieving "catharsis of such emotions," he concentrates his energies on describing the means by which, in both its ideal and very real forms, tragic theatre may accomplish its lofty intention of teaching us something about human experience.

A tragedy is the imitation of an action that is serious and also, as having magnitude, complete in itself; in language with pleasurable accessories, each kind brought in separately in the parts of the work; in a dramatic, not in a narrative form; with incidents arousing pity and fear, wherewith to accomplish its catharsis of such emotions. . . .

But further: the subject represented also is an action; and the action involves agents, who must necessarily have their distinctive qualities both of character and thought, since it is from these that we ascribe certain

qualities to their actions. There are in the natural order of things, therefore, two causes, Thought and Character, of their actions, and consequently of their success or failure in their lives. . . . Character is what makes us ascribe certain moral qualities to the agents; and Thought is shown in all they say when proving a particular point or, it may be, enunciating a general truth. . . .

Tragedy . . . is an imitation not only of a complete action, but also of incidents arousing pity and fear. Such incidents have the very greatest effect on the mind when they occur unexpectedly and at the same time in consequence of one another. . . . Even matters of chance seem most marvellous if there is an appearance of design.

Tragedy is essentially an imitation not of persons but of action and life, of happiness and misery. All human happiness or misery takes the form of action; the end for which we live is a certain kind of activity, not a quality. Character gives us qualities, but it is in our actions—what we do—that we are happy or the reverse. In a play accordingly they do not act in order to portray the Characters; they include the Characters for the sake of the action. So that it is the action in it that is the end and purpose of the tragedy; and the end is everywhere the chief thing. . . . We maintain, therefore, that the first essential, the life and soul, so to speak, of Tragedy is the Plot; and that the Characters come second. . . . We maintain that Tragedy is primarily an imitation of action, and that it is mainly for the sake of the action that it imitates the personal agents. Third comes the element of Thought, i.e. the power of saying whatever can be said, or what is appropriate to the occasion. . . .

Having thus distinguished the parts, let us now consider the proper construction of the Plot, as that is at once the first and the most important thing in Tragedy. Now a whole is that which has beginning, middle, and end. . . . A well-constructed Plot, therefore, cannot either begin or end at any one point. Again: to be beautiful, a living creature, and every whole made up of parts, must not only present a certain order in its arrangement of parts, but also be of a certain definite magnitude. . . .

The Unity of a Plot does not consist, as some suppose, in its having one man as its subject. An infinity of things befall that one man, some of which it is impossible to reduce to unity; and in like manner there are many actions of one man which cannot be made to form one action. . . . The truth is that, just as in the other imitative arts one imitation is always of one thing, so in poetry the story, as an imitation of action, must represent one action, a complete whole, with its several incidents so closely connected that the transposal or withdrawal of any one of them will disjoin and dislocate the whole. For that which makes no perceptible difference by its presence or absence is no real part of the whole.

From what we have said it will be seen that the poet's function is to describe, not the thing that has happened, but a kind of thing that might happen, i.e. what is possible as being probable or necessary. . . . Hence poetry is something more philosophic and of graver import than history, since its statements are of the nature rather of universals, whereas those of history are singulars. By a universal statement I mean one as to what such or such a kind of man will probably or necessarily say or do—which is the aim of poetry, though it affixes proper names to the characters. . . . In Tragedy, however, they still adhere to the historic names; and for this reason: what convinces is the possible; now whereas we are not yet sure as to the possibility of that which has not happened, that which has happened is manifestly possible, else it would not have come to pass. . . .

Tragedy, however, is an imitation not only of a complete action, but also of incidents arousing pity and fear. Such incidents have the very greatest effect on the mind when they occur unexpectedly and at the same time in consequence of one another; there is more of the marvellous in them then than if they happened of themselves or by mere chance. Even matters of chance seem most marvellous if there is an appearance of design as it were in them. A Plot, therefore, of this sort is necessarily finer than others. . . .

The tragic fear and pity may be aroused by the Spectacle; but they may also be aroused by the very structure and incidents of the play—which is the better way and shows the better poet. The Plot in fact should be so framed that, even without seeing the things take place, he who simply hears the account of them shall be filled with horror and pity at the incidents; which is just the effect that the mere recital of the story in *Oedipus* would have on one. To produce this same effect by means of the Spectacle is less artistic, and requires extraneous aid. Those, however, who make use of the Spectacle to put before us that which is merely monstrous and not productive of fear, are wholly out of touch with Tragedy; not every kind of pleasure should be required of a tragedy, but only its own proper pleasure.

His plots show increasing complexity, but with the formal restraints of the classical spirit. Sophocles lived and wrote beyond the death of Pericles in 429 B.C. and so experienced the shame of Athenian defeat. Even so, his later plays show nothing of the action that can be seen in Greek sculpture of that time and that signals a movement away from the restraint of the classical style. Classical Greek theatre was mostly discussion and narration. Themes often dealt with bloodshed, but even though the play led up to violence, blood was rarely shed on stage.

Euripides　　Euripides (480?–406 B.C.) was younger than Sophocles, although both men died in 406 B.C. They did compete with each other, but they do not share the same style. Euripides' plays carry realism to the furthest extent we see in Greek tragedy. Plays like *The Trojan Women* deal with individual emotions rather than great events, and his language, though still basically poetic, is higher in verisimilitude and much less formal than that of his predecessors. Euripides also experimented with, and ignored, many of the conventions of his theatre. He explored the mechanics of scenography and questioned in his plays the religion of his day. His tragedies are more tragicomedies than pure tragedies. Some critics have described many of his plays as melodramas. He was also less dependent on the chorus.

Plays like the *Bacchae* reflect the changing Athenian spirit and dissatisfaction with contemporary events, and show a trend toward the mundane. Euripides was not particularly popular in his time, perhaps because of his less idealistic, less formal, and less conventional treatment of dramatic themes and characters. His plays elicited much greater enthusiasm in later years and are unquestionably the most popular of the Greek tragedies today.

COMEDY

Aristophanes and Old Comedy　　Although no examples survive from the Periclean period, the Athenians were extremely fond of comedy. Aristophanes (450?–380? B.C.), of whose plays we have 11, was the most gifted of the comic poets, and his comedies of the postclassical period, such as the *Acharnians,* are highly satirical, topical, sophisticated, and often obscene. They represent a style and approach known as *Old Comedy.* Although translated productions of his comedies are still staged, the personal and political targets of his invective are unknown to us, and so modern productions are mere shadows of what took the stage at the turn of the fourth century B.C.

The characteristics of theatre of convention held sway over Aristophanic comedy. In fact, Aristophanes uses the conventions of his theatre to lay the groundwork for audience expectation. The obscenity present in Aristophanic comedy appears to serve two main functions: (1) to illustrate the moral theme of his work, that natural behavior produces more happiness than artificial systems of thought or action; and (2) to produce laughter for its own sake. Aristophones' *Lysistrata* is summarized in Chapter 1, *The Frogs* in Chapter 4; see also the commentary on *The Birds* at Fig. 1.7.

Figure 15.2 Roman statuette of a Greek tragic actor wearing a mask and a rich costume, ca. fourth century B.C. With theatres like the one at Dionysos (see Fig. 5.2A) seating between 14,000 and 17,000 spectators, it is obvious that Greek audiences expected conventional and easily communicated characterizations. Instantaneous changes of costume and character, of course, were also possible with masks and conventional costuming.

[The Archives of Photographiques, Pans.]

COSTUMES

If the plays of the Greek classical style treated lofty themes with language high in theatricality or poetic value, production style showed no less formality, idealism, and convention. Larger-than-life characters were portrayed by actors in larger-than-life, conventionalized costumes. Actors and chorus wore brightly colored robes whose colors gave specific information to the audience. The robes were padded to increase the actor's size, his height was increased by thick-soled boots called *kothurnoi*, and (after approximately 400 B.C.) large masks with fixed, conventionalized expressions were readily identified by the sophisticated and knowledgeable audience (Fig. 15.2). The actor's height was further increased by an *onkos*, a wiglike protrusion on top of the mask.

THE THEATRE FACILITY

Very little evidence exists concerning the actual architectural features of the early Greek theatres. Because the plays of the period were predominantly religious and involved a large chorus, we can assume that the theatre required a large acting area. Because the religious nature of the plays appealed to large masses of the population, we can also assume that the seating facilities of these theatres accommodated large audiences numbering more than 10,000 and provided them with a reasonably good view of the playing area. The natural slope of a hillside probably constituted the first seating arrangement for the audience. More important individuals most likely sat on wooden seats or benches. At the bottom of the hillside, a large circle, called the *orchestra*, provided performance space for the chorus. The wooden seats must have formed a semicircle around the orchestra. An altar, or *thymele*, occupied the center of the orchestra and served to honor the god of the particular festival (Fig. 15.3).

The scene building, or *skene*, was probably a one-story edifice containing three doors facing the audience. The practical roof may have been used as an additional acting area. A slightly raised platform may have run the length of the building between the structure and the orchestra. Many modern theatre terms come from the parts of this building. *Skene* is the basis for our word *scene*, and our term *proscenium* comes from the Greek *proskenion*, referring to the narrow porch or colonnade attached to the front of the skene (Fig. 15.4).

Figure 15.3 *Model of the theatre at Athens. Evidence indicates that when the platform stage and permanent* skene *appeared, the speaking actors performed there while the chorus remained in the orchestra, where all dramatic action had previously taken place. The separation of actors and chorus reflects the emergence of a more realistic theatre and its evolution away from its roots in ritual.*

[From Oscar G. Brockett, *The History of the Theatre*, 6th ed. Copyright © 1991 by Allyn and Bacon, Inc. Reprinted by permission.]

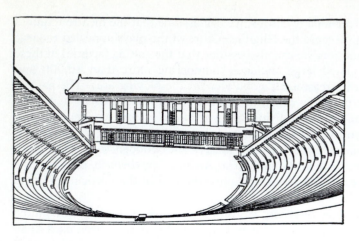

Figure 15.4 *Plan of the theatre at Epidaurus, showing the* proskenion, skene, *and* paradoi *(passageways for both the chorus and the audience). By this time, the skene was probably two stories high; as the stage eventually became larger, playwrights began incorporating both stage and skene as set locations.*

We do not know whether the theatres of this period enjoyed anything in the way of painted scenery, but some evidence both from the Roman historian Vitruvius and from Aristotle suggests that possibility. Aristotle attributes the use of painted scenery to Sophocles, and Vitruvius to Aeschylus. As we have suggested earlier, however, whatever form such scenery may have taken, if any, it undoubtedly was not the kind of illusionistic—that is, realistic—scenery that we are familiar with today.

THE HELLENISTIC PERIOD

New Comedy   In the period from the middle of the fourth to the middle of the third century B.C., comedy was the staple of the theatre. However, we have only the fragments of five plays from this entire period. All of these fragments, representing a style called *New Comedy*, are by the playwright Menander, but from them we can see some definite contrasts with the older style of Aristophanes. Although the action is still bawdy, for example, the biting political invective is gone. The situations of the plots are pleasant and domestic, as opposed to heroic, and, for the most part, are superficial and without satire. Religion no longer played a central role in the theatre, and the chorus had disappeared.

The Theatre Facility   This period witnessed great expansion for the theatre in Greece, and theatre building extended throughout the Mediterranean. Although the general plan of the theatres did not change, the *skene* was frequently two stories tall. When a low stage existed, it appears to have been connected to the *orchestra* by steps. However, after the chorus had disappeared, the stage in later Hellenistic times often went as high as 12 feet.

For us, the most fascinating aspect of this period of theatre came in the form of its stage machinery and scenic units. Many of our modern stage devices can be traced back to these. Among the most interesting units were revolving, three-sided columns called *periaktoi*. Placed on each side of the stage, they turned to present a different face when a change of scene occurred. The faces of the panels probably held nothing more than decorative designs or symbols applicable to a particular scene. *Periaktoi* functioned much as our revolving stages do, although *periaktoi* themselves occasionally serve in the modern theatre as a scene-changing device.

Another shifting mechanism enjoyed by the Greeks was the *eccyclema,* meaning "that which is rolled out." The *eccyclema* was a low wagon on which a tableau was arranged and rolled out from behind one of the three doors in the *skene.* The Greeks declined to show violence on stage and used this device to provide a bit of sensationalism in the form of gory scenes for tragedy. The *machine* or *crane* raised and lowered actors, suspending them in midair and moving them from the orchestra to the roof of the second story of the *skene.* It might even have swung them from one side of the playing area to the other. This device frequently lowered gods from the roof to the stage, as though they were descending from the heavens. When used in this fashion, it took the name *deus ex machina,* or "god from the machine." The Greeks also enjoyed other technical effects such as the sound of thunder, created by pouring bags of pebbles into brass containers.

Rome

The Romans were the conquerors of their world. By A.D. 70, they had destroyed the Temple of Jerusalem and colonized Britain, spreading their pragmatic and pluralistic version of Hellenistic Mediterranean civilization to peoples of the Iron Age in north and west Europe. Under Augustus, Roman culture turned again to Greek classicism and in that spirit glorified their city, its Emperor, and its Empire. The Augustan period, falling at the opening of the Christian era, represents the plateau between the Roman Republic and Empire of the preceding 150 years and the gradual but accelerating slide into chaos and ultimate extinction that was to follow over the next 300 years. Inventive and utilitarian, Roman culture left us roads, fortifications, viaducts, planned administration, and a sophisticated yet robust legal system—in contrast to the temples and ideas of the Greeks. The Greeks provided us with the foundations for our society and its culture.

The Romans loved entertainment, and particularly drama. For the most part, Roman drama occupied the opposite end of the intellectual spectrum from Greek classicism. Roman theatre was wild, unrestrained, lewd, and highly realistic. Accounts of stage events suggest that very little was left to the audience's imagination. Although we might find the Roman theatre buildings somewhat strange in their conventions, and although we would need to learn the conventions of various masks, we would for the most part have little difficulty understanding the events portrayed. Undoubtedly we would find the grotesquely padded costumes and farcical actions as comic as the Romans did.

Figure 15.5 Scenes from Roman phly-akes farces, from the Greek colonies of southern Italy, ca. 300 B.C. These popular comedies were essentially satiric. Sometimes, they focused their burlesque on everyday events: At the top, for example, exaggerated figures representing "youth" and "age" are having a generation-gap argument. Frequently, the phlyakes farce got its satiric edge from turning epic or mythic episodes into comedy: In the center, for example, Hercules tries to gain admittance to a house by banging on the door with his club, and at the bottom, the hero Achilles watches as his decrepit tutor is helped up to the stage in a bit of early slapstick.

[From Mantzius, A History of Theatrical Art in Ancient and Modern Times.]

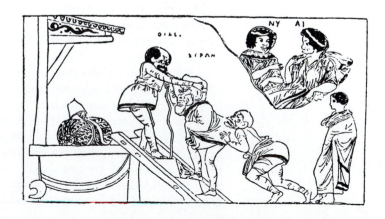

Three important dramatic forms were prevalent at various times in Roman history: *phlyakes farces, Roman comedy,* and the *mime.*

Phlyakes Farces   The earliest of these forms was the *phlyakes farce,* which some authorities trace to Grecian origin as early as the fifth century B.C. in Sicily (see Fig. 15.5). Whatever its sources, the *phlyakes* (from the word for "gossips") had an earthy style. Its themes first parodied mythology and, later, burlesqued tragedy. Very little literary evidence exists about the *phlyakes,* but numerous vase paintings testify to its existence and character. If such evidence can be taken at face value, the *phlyakes* were bawdy, with actors suggestively padded and extravagantly masked. Apparently, these farces used a raised stage consisting of a rough wooden platform containing a simple background and doors for entrances and exits by the actors. Curtains masked the area below the stage.

Roman Comedy   Roman comedy developed from third- and second-century B.C. influences of Hellenistic comedy, with the large theatres, high stages, and elaborate scene buildings that we noted earlier. The New Comedy of Menander was easily understood by the Romans and was assimilated quickly. Playwrights copied Greek originals and changed their settings to Rome and Roman domestic life. Character development dwelt on types. Farcical action formed the backbone of the comic "plot."

Mime   Although the third form of Roman theatre, the mime, was probably as old as or older than the other two forms, it did not achieve prominence in Rome until the time of the Empire. Mimes dealt with low life and appealed to all classes of Romans (Fig. 15.6). Some mimes were adventures, a style

Figure 15.6   *Roman mime. Terra cotta statuette, first century* A.D. *By the time of Constantine, about 310* A.D., *opposition by the Christian community of Rome, which regarded the mime shows as vestiges of paganism, had largely driven mimes from public performance. Companies of traveling mimes, however, survived as wandering minstrels and storytellers in the Middle Ages.*

[British Museum]

copied by some dramatists in Elizabethan England. Some mimes ridiculed Christianity, particularly the rite of baptism, and consequently were not well favored by the Christian community. Early Christian writers condemned the obscenities of the mimes, noting that adulteries actually took place on stage. The style of Roman theatre in general clearly was anticlassical. Idealization, formality, simplicity, and appeal to the intellect were not among its characteristics.

PLAYWRIGHTS

Plautus   Roman comedy produced two important playwrights—Plautus and Terence. Plautus (*ca.* 254–184 B.C.) was principally a translator and adaptor, and 20 of his plays have survived. He copied Greek originals, changing the locations to Rome and inserting details of Roman domestic life. His characters were types, not individuals: the braggart soldier (*miles gloriosus*), the miser, the parasite, and the wily but mistreated slave. These stock characters were extremely important in later developments like *commedia dell'arte* (see Chapter 16), influencing both Shakespeare and Molière. Plautus' plays depend on slapstick humor and "sight gags" for their effect. They are full of farcical energy and appeal directly to the emotions, not the intellect. They are not particularly well written and, as is the case with much theatre, play better than they read. Plautus' *The Menaechmi* is summarized in Chapter 5.

Terence   Terence (*ca.* 185–159 B.C.) was a more literary-minded writer and better educated than Plautus, and enjoyed the support of a wealthy patron. From his six extant plays, we find a dramatist capable of drawing universal situations and characters. Like Plautus, he had a tremendous influence on the theatre of later ages. However, perhaps because he did not make use of banality and buffoonery, he was not particularly popular with contemporary Roman audiences.

THE THEATRE FACILITY

Although the Roman theatre facility had its origins in the Greek theatre, it differed from the Greek in many ways. Although the Greek theatre was built into a hillside, the Roman counterpart was always constructed on level ground. On the outside, the Roman theatre buildings were covered with elaborate architectural detail. The shape of the auditorium, or *cavea,* was an exact semicircle, and the *cavea* was connected to the scene building, thereby closing the passageway found in the Greek theatre (Fig. 15.7). Because of the shape of the auditorium, the orchestra became a semicircle as well, connecting with the front edge of the stage and providing space for additional seating for spectators.

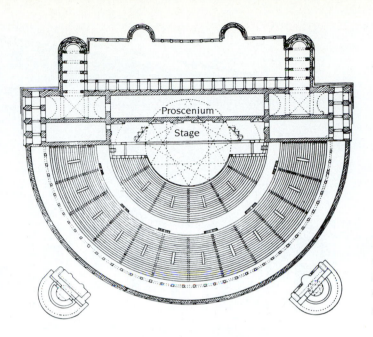

Figure 15.7 *Plan of the Theatre of Marcel-lus, Rome, 23–13* B.C. *Theatres like this also hosted the popular "scenic games"—festivities celebrating military victories and honoring generals and emperors.*

The stage itself was raised (though seldom over five feet), and its depth was increased from earlier theatres. The most impressive difference was in the façade of the scene building, or *scaenae frons*. Two and three stories high, this façade presented a series of elaborate porticoes, panels, niches, columns, capitals, and statues (see Fig. 15.8). Probably a roof frequently covered the stage area, protecting it from inclement weather. The audience, too, was often protected by an enormous awning covering the auditorium.

As a rule, Roman theatre auditoriums were smaller than their Greek counterparts. This was probably due to government censure in the early days of the Empire, to the competition supplied by other forms of public entertainment, and to the weakness of the plays presented in these playhouses. The first permanent theatre, built by Pompey in Rome, did not appear until 55 B.C.

The Romans made use of the scenic devices of the Greeks and added some of their own. The most interesting introduction was a curtain, or *auleum,* which was raised and lowered from a slot at the front at the stage. Scenery varied depending on the genre. Tragedy apparently utilized a background of columns and pediments appropriate for nobles and kings. Comedy had rows of houses, and satyr plays featured natural hills, trees, and foliage.

Roman theatre fulfilled an important social function in keeping the minds of the masses from their difficulties. It also served as a forum in which the general public could address grievances to the bureaucracy. When an official of the state had betrayed his trust, when a wrong had been suffered, or when an impropriety of state had become flagrant, the satirical bite of the Roman theatre was brought fully to bear, replete with grotesque masks, bright costumes, and penetrating directness.

Figure 15.8 *Reconstruction of the* scaenae frons *at Aspendos. The actual theatre flourished in the second century* A.D. *Because of widespread colonial garrisons manned by armies that demanded entertainment, the ruins of Roman theatres can be found from England to North Africa.*

[Victoria and Albert Museum/Art Resource.]

The Medieval Period

The Middle Ages is the name we have come to use for the thousand years centered upon the close of the first Christian millennium: the period that began with the fall of Rome and closed with the "reawakening" of the Renaissance in

Italy. The so-called Dark Ages make up the early part of this period, when it came to seem that humankind had crept into a barricaded world of mental and physical isolation and self-protection. It was for many a time of fear and superstition: a "vale of tears" for the Christian, who had little hope save the hope that beyond this life lay the possibility of heaven for those who followed the teachings of the Church. In monasteries and convents throughout Europe, however, literacy, learning, and artistic creativity were nurtured, and the works of the period are in many cases filled with intuitive vision of rare and deeply moving quality.

Humanity in the late Middle Ages seemed to experience a spiritual and intellectual revival that had a profound influence on the creative spirit. In the arts at least, the human spirit seemed to blossom as emphasis shifted from the oppressive wrath of God to the sweetness and mercy of the loving Savior and the Virgin Mary. Meanwhile, the vigorous growth of towns and cities accelerated the pace of life and turned the focus of wealth and power away from the feudal countryside, and the new universities replaced monasteries as centers of learning. Although some early scholars have argued that theatre ceased to exist in the Western world for a period of several hundred years after the fall of the Roman Empire, that viewpoint is no longer widely held. Throughout the Middle Ages troupes of mimists, jugglers, bear baiters, acrobats, wrestlers, and storytellers wandered throughout Europe. The mimetic propensity of human beings is too compelling to deny its existence amid the entertainments we know to have thrived in this era. However, "theatre" at this time may have consisted of simply miming a story or reading a play script, rather than the more formal presentations we prefer to call "theatre" (see Fig. 15.10).

Figure 15.9 *Scene depicting the three Marys at the tomb of Christ, from a twelfth-century ivory carving at Cologne, France. Such scenes, which were dramatized as part of the Mass, are among the origins of drama in the Middle Ages.*

[Drawing by Gerda Becker With, *Die Deutsche Dichtung des Mittelalters.*]

Figure 15.10   *Miniature showing the miming of a classical comedy by masked actors. Early fifteenth century, France. This miniature frontispiece faces the title page of the book, which, in the bottom figure, is being delivered to his patron by its author (probably the copyist who did the illustrations). At the top, the text of the play is being read to a large audience from a draped box.*

[Bibliothèque de L'Arsenal, Paris]

Evidence of Medieval Theatre

Writings from North Africa refer to the popularity of *ludi theatrici* at marriages and feasts, adding that members of the clergy should leave when these were performed. In the ninth century, the Council of Tours and the Council of Aix-la-Chapelle ruled that the clergy should not witness plays and the obscenities of actors. We can therefore infer that theatre existed from the fact that the Church railed against it. Charlemagne went so far as to declare that no actor could wear a priest's robe under penalty of corporal punishment or banishment.

LITURGICAL DRAMA

Charlemagne's edict has been taken by some not only as evidence of theatrical presentation but, perhaps inaccurately, as evidence of the beginnings of liturgical drama. If this were the case, the prohibition would imply the use of actors other than the clergy in church drama. In the tenth century, however, the German nun Hrosvitha is known to have written at least six plays based on the comedies of the Roman playwright Terence. We do not know if Hrosvitha's plays were performed; but if they were, the audience would have been restricted to the other nuns in the convent.

We are sure, however, that liturgical drama began as an elaboration of the Roman Catholic Mass, probably in France. These elaborations were called *tropes* and took place on special ceremonial occasions, usually Easter, the dramatic highlight of the Church year. Records at Winchester in the late tenth century tell of a trope in which priests acted out the discovery of the tomb on Easter morning. Thus theatre, along with the other arts—except dance—was adopted by the Church and became an instrument of God in an age of faith and demons.

Miracle, Mystery, and Morality Plays   Probably because of their relationship to the Church, major movements in the arts in the twelfth to fifteenth centuries were both reasonably unified and widespread. Although local diversity was common, styles were generally alike. The theatre was no exception. As the Middle Ages progressed, drama associated with the Church followed the example of painting and included more and more Church-related materials. Earliest Church drama (the trope) was a simple elaboration and illustration of the Mass. Later, drama included mystery, miracle, and morality plays. *Mystery plays* take their name from the Latin word meaning "service" or "occupation"

Figure 15.11   *Schematic of earthwork ruins where mystery plays were performed in Cornwall, England. Drawing from the manuscript of* The Castle of Perseverance, *about 1461 to 1483. According to the manuscript, the castle of the title stood in the center, over the "Bed of Mankind" below. The outer circle was supposed to be a ditch to restrain the audience, which sat on raised circular benches rimming the outside. There may have been scaffolding that served as mansions (see Figs. 10.2A and 10.2B) to house various symbolic figures or locales. Called "rounds," such theatres were up to 300 feet in diameter.*

[From Borlase, *The Natural History of Cornwall* and Albright, *The Shakespearean Stage.*]

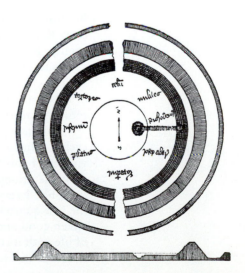

The Representation of Adam: *"Paradise Shall be Situated in a Rather Prominent Place"*

Dating from the twelfth century, The Representation of Adam *is the oldest known French mystery play. There were three parts, each with written dialogue: the Fall of Adam and Eve, the Murder of Abel, and the Prophecies of Christ. Latin instructions, which indicated scenery, costumes, and even actors' gestures, provide a fairly accurate example of the medieval concept of liturgical staging. (Compare these instructions with those given by Hamlet to the players at Fig. 16.2.)*

Paradise shall be situated in a rather prominent place, and is to be hung all around with draperies and silk curtains to such a height that the persons who find themselves in Paradise are seen from their shoulders upward. There shall be seen sweet smelling flowers and foliage; there shall be different trees covered with fruit, so that the place may appear very agreeable. Then the Savior shall appear, robed in [an outer vestment of the deacons]; Adam and Eve place themselves in front of him, Adam dressed in a red tunic, Eve in a white garment and white silk veil; both rise before [God], Adam nearest, bending his head, Eve lower down. Adam shall be trained well to speak at the right moment, so that he may come neither too soon nor too late. Not only he, but all shall be well practised in speaking calmly, and making gestures appropriate to the things they say; they shall neither add nor omit any syllable of the metre; all shall express themselves in a distinct manner, and say in consecutive order all that is to be said.

rather than from the word for "mystery." The designation probably refers to the production of religious plays by the occupational guilds of the Middle Ages rather than the "mysteries" of revelation. The name was given to any of the Biblical plays performed, usually in cycles, during the late Middle Ages and early Renaissance. A typical mystery play was the Adam play of early twelfth-century France. It was performed in the vernacular and began by reminding the actors to pick up their lines, to pay attention so as not to add or subtract any syllables in the verses, and to speak distinctly. The play told the biblical story of Adam and was probably played in squares outside churches, with the actors retiring into the church when not directly involved in the action.

Miracle plays were medieval religious plays, also usually performed in cycles, whose subject matter dealt with the lives of the saints, apocryphal visions of the Virgin, and so on. The *morality* play was a type of medieval religious drama in which the personages take the form of allegorical abstractions like Everyman, Good Deeds, Faith, and Mercy. The genre developed in the last quarter of the fourteenth century. Its themes portray the conflict between good and evil powers over people's souls and the journey or pilgrimage of life with its choice of eternal destinations. The most enduring morality play is called, not surprisingly, *Everyman.*

Everyman

Death summons Everyman to his final judgment. Everyman then seeks, as companions on his journey to judgment, the qualities (characters) of Fellowship, Kindred, Cousin, and Goods. Each refuses to join him. He finally asks Good Deeds, but Good Deeds is too weak from neglect to make the journey. Seeking advice from Knowledge, Everyman is told to do penance—an act that revives Good Deeds, who then takes up the journey with Everyman. Along the way, Strength, Discretion, Beauty, and the Five Wits also desert him as he nears the grave. Good Deeds, however, stays with him until the end.

This universal depiction unfolds in slightly less than one thousand verses. Its appeal has held strongly throughout the centuries, and it continues to be performed today.

Illustrative of the expanding subject matter of Christian drama was a play of the thirteenth century, *Le Jeu de Saint Nicholas* by John Bodel of Arras. The play is set in the Holy Land amid the battles between the Christian Crusaders and the infidels. In the battle, all the Christians are killed except one Monsieur Prudhomme, who prays to St. Nicholas in the presence of the Saracen king. The king is told that St. Nicholas will safeguard his treasure, and when St. Nicholas actually intervenes to foil a robbery attempt, the king is converted. Similar plays dealing with the conversion of historical figures (usually amid attempts to ridicule Christianity or vilify Christians) were very popular, as were plays about the lives of saints (see Fig. 15.12), and the intercession of Mary (called *Mary-plays*).

PRODUCTION PRACTICES

Theatrical development throughout Europe (including Germany, Italy, and Spain) appears to have followed a similar route, although the dates were different. Tropes were performed in the sanctuary, using niches around the church as specific scenic locations. On special occasions, cycles of plays were performed, and the congregation moved from niche to niche to see part of the cycle. Although it is difficult for us to pinpoint specific developments, even in specific churches, it is clear that these dramatizations quickly became very popular.

Over the years, production standards for the same plays changed drastically. At first, only priests performed the roles; later, laymen were allowed to act in liturgical drama. Female roles were usually played by boys, but evidence exists to suggest that women did participate occasionally. The popularity of church drama soon made it impractical, if not impossible, to contain the audience within the church building. Evidence also suggests that as laymen

Figure 15.12 Jean Fouquet,
miniature depicting The Martyr-
dom of St. Apollonia, *ca*. 1452–
1456. *Most such spectacles were
performed to celebrate the Feast of
Corpus Christi and were in effect
"epics" produced by the Church.*

[From Germain Bapst, *Essai sur l'histoire du
théâtre*, Paris, 1893.]

assumed a greater role, certain vulgarities were introduced. Comedy and comic
characters emerged, even as part of the Easter tropes. On their way to the tomb
of Jesus, for example, the three Marys stop to buy ointments and cloths from a
merchant. This merchant developed into one of the earliest medieval comic
characters. The most popular comic character of all was the Devil.

Mansion Stages Church drama eventually moved outside the sanctuary
and opened itself more widely to the common man and woman. As medieval
drama moved out of the Church, various production practices developed. In
France and Italy, the stationary stage decoration of the church interior became
a *mansion stage* (see Fig. 10.2A). The specific configuration of the mansion

stage differed from location to location. In Italy, it was rectangular and linear, designed to be viewed from one or two sides; in some parts of France, arena staging, in which the audience completely surrounded the stage area, was introduced. Whatever the specific application, the mansion stage had a particular set of aesthetic conventions that made its style unique. The individual mansions depicted their locations realistically. At the same time, areas between the mansions were treated conventionally and could serve as any location. The text of the play told the audience where the action was supposed to occur, and the audience then imagined that locale.

The most interesting depiction on the medieval stage was that of Hell or Hellmouth. If we knew more about exact dates, the development of Hellmouth could provide comparisons with other arts—for example, sculpture—in charting changing attitudes toward death, Hell, fear, and mercy. Audiences demanded more and more realism and complexity in Hellmouth, and descriptions of devils pulling sinners into the mouth of Hell (often depicted as the jaws of a dragon-like monster) amid smoke and fire are common. One source describes a Hellmouth so complicated that it took 17 people to operate it. Although some plays—for example, *Anticriste* and *Domesdaye*—were clearly intended to be frightening in the late Middle Ages, even vividly depicted Hellmouths seem to have been comic in their intentions. Plays such as *Abraham and Isaac* and the *Second Shepherd's Play* are humorous and compassionate, clearly reflecting the change in attitude of the age.

Pageant Wagons   In England and parts of France and the Netherlands, another staging style developed. Rather than move the audience or depict the entire set of locations on a multiscened mansion stage, theatre was brought to the audience on a succession of *pageant wagons* like the floats of a modern parade (Fig. 15.13). Each wagon depicted a specific part of the play cycle. Many of these wagons were quite elaborate, sometimes two stories tall, and curtained for entrances and exits like a modern theatre. In some cases, a flat wagon was combined with an elaborate background wagon to provide a playing area. This type of production was mostly used in cities, where narrow wagons were needed to negotiate narrow streets. At intersections where there was more space, wagons were coupled and crowds gathered to watch one segment of the play. When that segment was finished, the wagon moved on and was shortly replaced by another that served as the setting for another short play in the cycle.

As time progressed, theatrical production became both more elaborate and more realistic. Many productions were extremely complicated in detail and direction as well as in realistic depiction. Live birds, rabbits, and lambs gave life to the play, as did elaborate costumes that represented specific characters. Bloody executions, wounds, and severed heads and limbs were quite common in later medieval drama.

When drama moved out of the church, local guilds began to assume responsibility for various plays. The topic of the specific play usually dictated which guild was responsible. For example, the watermen performed the Noah play, and cooks presented *The Harrowing of Hell* because it dealt with baking,

Figure 15.13 *English pageant wagon showing an episode of a mystery play in a village square. The draped lower floor of this two-story wagon may have been used as a dressing room.*

[Drawing by Gerda Becker With, after Sharp, *A Dissertation on the Pageants or Dramatic Mysteries Anciently Performed at Coventry.*]

boiling, and putting things into and out of fires. Increasing secularization and fourteenth-century philosophical division of Church and state gave rise to a separate secular tradition, which led in the fifteenth century to French farce. Even religious drama came into professional secular control in France when, in 1402, King Charles VI granted a charter to the Confrèrie de la Passion, which gave the troupe a monopoly on all religious theatrical production.

SUMMARY

• Under the ruler Pericles, classical Greek culture reached its miraculous zenith: to that civilization and its works Western culture has returned for nourishment for over two thousand years.

- The theatre of Periclean Athens was a theatre of *convention*.

- Theatre productions in ancient Greece were part of three yearly religious festivals.

- The three major writers of tragedy in ancient Greece were Aeschylus, Sophocles, and Euripides.

- Although no examples of comedy survive from the Periclean period, the postclassical period witnessed *Old Comedy,* a form whose most famous practitioner was Aristophanes.

- In keeping with the lofty style of classical plays, costumes of the period were conventionalized and larger than life.

- Although very little physical evidence exists, the theatre facility of ancient Greece probably consisted of a large, circular acting area, a semicircular seating arrangement, and an architectural background called a *skene*.

- The Hellenistic period witnessed a dramatic form called *New Comedy* and expanded the size and significance of the skene.

- The major dramatic forms of the Roman theatre were *phlyakes farces, comedy,* and *mime*.

- The major playwrights of Rome were Plautus and Terence.

- Although originating from the Greek theatre, the Roman theatre building differed significantly:

    It comprised a free-standing building;

    Roman auditoriums were smaller;

    The Romans added new scenic devices.

- Theatre fell into semiobscurity during the early part of the Middle Ages and reemerged in dramatic elaborations of the Roman Catholic Mass.

- Three dramatic forms were important to early Medievel theatre:

    Miracle plays—depictions of lives of the saints and similar themes;

    Mystery plays—religious plays produced by occupational guilds;

    Morality plays—allegorical plays about Christian morality.

- Production practices changed significantly over the period of the Middle Ages. Plays were first produced in the sanctuaries of churches, later on the steps of church porches, and eventually on *mansion stages* in the countryside and on *pageant wagons* in cities.

Chapter 16

Western Theatre *from the* Renaissance *to* Romanticism

*A*fter studying this chapter
you should be able to:

- Describe the viewpoints of the *Renaissance* and how they affected theatre.

- Identify cultural subdivisions of the Renaissance and comment on the plays, playwrights, and production practices of those subdivisions.

- Discuss the *Baroque* age and its theatrical situations—including approaches like *French neoclassicism* and the *English Restoration*.

- Explain how the attitudes of the *Enlightenment* of the eighteenth century affected theatre, playwriting, and production in countries like Germany, England, and France, as well as in America.

- Identify and describe the characteristics of *Romantic philosophy and style* and how they affected theatre playwriting and production practice.

M. Garrick and Mrs. Pritchard in The Tragedy of Macbeth.

*T*he period from the Renaissance to the late nineteenth century represents the emergence and development of contemporary—that is, modern—Western civilization. The viewpoints of the Renaissance constituted a significant shift from those of the Middle Ages, and with changes in cultural viewpoints came changes in theatre as well. In this chapter, as we study the general historical periods of the Renaissance, the *baroque* age—that is, the seventeenth century—the *enlightenment* (the eighteenth century), and the *Romantic* period of the nineteenth century, we will lay a foundation for the subject of our next chapter, the modern theatre.

The Renaissance

The Renaissance was seen by its leading figures as a rebirth of our understanding of ourselves as social and creative beings. "Out of the sick Gothic night our eyes are opened to the glorious touch of the sixteenth-century sun" was how French writer François Rabelais expressed what most of his educated contemporaries felt. At the center of Renaissance concerns were the visual arts, whose new ways of looking at the world soon had their counterparts in the performing arts as well. Florence, the crucible of the Renaissance in Italy, was called the "New Athens," and it was here that there first emerged a redefinition of the fine arts as "liberal arts," in contrast to their lowlier status as "crafts" in the Middle Ages. Now accepted among the intellectual disciplines, the arts have since the Renaissance become an essential part of learning and literary culture. Artists, architects, composers, and writers gained confidence and independence both from their new status and from the technical mastery that they were achieving. For the first time, it seemed possible not merely to emulate the works of the Classical world, but to surpass them.

New Dramatic Forms

In the years corresponding to the Renaissance and High Renaissance in the visual arts—from approximately 1400 to 1525—theatre retained the characteristics that it had developed in the Middle Ages. Secular adaptation and production of mysteries and moralities flourished. The Confrèrie de la Passion, under license from Charles VI, continued to produce mystery plays in France throughout the fifteenth century. The company's cycle of plays representing *The Mystery of the Old Testament* consisted of 44,325 verses and took twenty performances to complete. *The Mystery of the New Testament* consisted of 34,574 verses. A third cycle, *The Acts of the Apostles*, rounded out the Confrèrie's repertoire and took forty days to present in its entirety.

Sottie The French also developed a new secular form, the *sottie*—short theatrical entertainments woven into the early festivals of the Feast of the Ass and the Feast of the Fools. These festivals originated partly in pagan rites and were bawdy burlesques of the Roman Catholic Mass. A person called the Bishop, Archbishop, or Pope of Fools celebrated a mock Mass with a great deal of jumping around, buffoonery, and noise. Participants wore strange costumes (or nothing at all), and the entire affair was accompanied by much drinking. One of the most popular of the sotties written for the Feasts, Pierre Gringoire's *Play of the Prince of Fools,* was produced in Paris in 1512 at the request of King Louis XII to inflame the populace against Pope Julius II.

Farce At the same time, a more substantial French theatrical form also emerged—the *farce.* Unlike the sottie, which was an entr'acte entertainment, the farce was fully developed as a play form and performed as an independent production. The most famous of the French farces of this period was *Maître Pierre Pathélin* (1470), which is still occasionally produced.

Commedia dell'arte Featuring the actor rather than the script, Italy's unique *commedia dell'arte* enjoyed tremendous popular support. Commedia dell'arte could be identified by four specific characteristics. The first was *improvisation*: Even though fully-fledged productions had plots and subplots, dialogue was completely improvised, depending only on a rudimentary plot outline or scenario. Although a few commedia works were serious and some were pastoral, most were comic. We assume from the information available that the acting style was highly naturalistic, calling for good entrance and exit lines as well as repartee. The second characteristic was the use of *stock characters*—for example, young lovers, old fathers, braggart soldiers, and comic servants (*zanni*) (see Fig. 16.1). All wore stock costumes that the audience could easily identify. Because much of the action was visual, actors required great skill, physical dexterity, and timing. The famous Scaramouche (Tiberio Fiorilli) could apparently still box another actor's ears with his foot at age eighty-three. Actors in the commedia also depended on skills in dancing, singing, and acrobatics. Somersaulting without spilling a glass of wine seems to have gained an actor great adulation among regular attendees. A third characteristic was the use of *mime* and *pantomime*: Masks were worn by those in all roles except the lovers and the serving maid, and attitudes were communicated through gesture.

Actors in the commedia dell'arte also traveled in companies, with each member of the company playing the same role over and over again. The practice was so pervasive and popular that actors often lost their own individuality to the roles they played. Many actors even changed their original name to those of the stage personages they portrayed. From the mid-sixteenth to the mid-seventeenth centuries, troupes of commedia actors traveled throughout Europe. Their influence and popularity were tremendous, but even though characters and situations found their way into the theatre of other nations, commedia remained an Italian form. By the end of the seventeenth century, commedia had to all intents and purposes disappeared. One final fact must be

Figure 16.1 *Stock characters of the commedia dell'arte. Except for unmasked lovers, the whole world of the commedia was populated by character types. At upper right, for example, the capitano—a cowardly braggart who is usually after the female lead—is recognizable by his mask (with its distorted long nose), moustache, sword, and feathered cap. (Compare these character types with those in the drawing of a seventeenth-century French troupe at Fig. 16.7.)*

[Courtesy of the Lilly Library, Indiana University, Bloomington, Indiana.]

noted. Commedia dell'arte introduced women into the theatre as equals. Their roles were as important as, and often more important than, those of men.

THE ENGLISH RENAISSANCE

England's drama in the mid- to late sixteenth century was national in character, influenced undoubtedly by the severance of Church and state under Henry VIII. Nevertheless, literary influences in sixteenth-century England were strongly Italian—fact that was reflected in the theatre. England, however, produced at this time a new theatre of convention and extraordinary playwrights.

The Elizabethans loved drama, and the theatres of London featured prince and commoner together among their audiences. Both sought and found—usually in the same play—action, spectacle, comedy, character, and intellectual stimulation so deeply reflective of the human condition that Elizabethan plays have found universal appeal through the centuries since their first production.

William Shakespeare William Shakespeare (1564–1616) was the preeminent Elizabethan playwright, and his sensitivity to and appreciation of the

William Shakespeare

Italian Renaissance can be seen in the Renaissance Italian locations of many of his plays. In true Renaissance expansiveness, Shakespeare took his audiences back into history, both British and classical, and far beyond, to the fantasy world of Caliban in *The Tempest*. We gain perspective on the Renaissance world's perception of its own condition when we compare the placid, composed reflections of Italian painting with Shakespeare's tragic portraits of Renaissance Italian intrigue in such plays as *Othello* and *Romeo and Juliet*.

Like most playwrights of his age, Shakespeare wrote for a specific professional company (of which he became a partial owner). The need for new plays to keep the company alive from season to season provided much of the impetus for his prolific writing. A robust quality exists in Shakespeare's plays. His ideas have universal appeal because of his understanding of human motivation and character and his ability to probe deeply into emotion. He provided insights dramatically equivalent to Rembrandt's visual probings. Shakespeare's plays body forth life and love, action and nationalism; moreover, they present those qualities in a magnificent poetry that explores the English language in unrivaled fashion. Shakespeare's use of tone, color, and complex new word meanings gives his plays a musical as well as dramatic quality that appeals to every generation.

Figure 16.2 *Von Czarclorski,* Hamlet and the Players. *Hamlet's instructions to one of the actors who will be performing in a play-within-a-play are sometimes taken to reflect his opinion on the proper means of acting in the Elizabethan theatre:*

> *Suit the action to the word, the word to the action, with this special observance, that you o'erstep not the modesty of nature. For anything so overdone is from the purpose of playing, whose end, both at the first and now, was and is, to hold, as 'twere, the mirror up to nature, to show virtue her own feature, scorn her own image, and the very age and body of the time his form and pressure (Act III, Scene 2).*

Compare these instructions with those given to the actors who will perform the medieval liturgical drama The Representation of Adam *(excerpt in Chapter 15).*

Margaret Webster: Shakespeare Our Contemporary (I)

A veteran actress of numerous English repertory companies, including the Old Vic, Margaret Webster first garnered attention as a Shakespearean director with her production of Richard II *on Broadway in 1937. As both lecturer and producer, she has specialized in popularizing Shakespeare among a variety of modern audiences. Also a scholar and critic, Webster has delved into such subjects as Shakespeare's biography, the texts of the plays themselves, and, here, the conditions under which he worked not only as a playwright but also as an actor and theatre owner.*

The Globe Company was in many respects radically different from the haphazard collection of actors from whom we, today, expect the same results in three or four weeks of work on a single production. . . . A parallel might well be found in Stanislavski's Moscow Art Theatre Company [see Chapter 17]. The methods of the two companies are as widely apart as the poles, but it is probable that Chekhov and Shakespeare would have found a common ground in the simultaneous and inseparable evolution of a dramatist and a company of actors.

The hierarchy at the Globe was intricate and exact. Certain members, including Shakespeare, were joint owners of the lease and property, and as such received among them a half share of the takings. They were also, with the other principal actors, actor-sharers and in this capacity divided among them the other half of the gross. The proportion of expenses borne by each category of sharers corresponds roughly to the front-stage and back-stage division still prevalent today between theater owners and the current producing company. The rest of the Lord Chamberlain's Men were made up of "hired men," paid on a salary basis, and boy apprentices for the female parts, who were often ex-members of the children's companies.

When there was a landlord, like [Phillip] Henslowe of the Rose and the Fortune, matters became more complicated. Henslowe, the first of the commercial managers, is an Awful Warning. He received at first half the gallery receipts from his tenant company; then, as they grew more and more deeply indebted to him, he took three-quarters, and finally the whole gallery receipts, part of which went to pay off the debts the company had contracted. . . .

But posterity may be grateful to [Henslowe] because, ironically enough, it is from his meticulous accounts that we draw much of our present knowledge of the Elizabethan theater. . . .

> *[Shakespeare] owned his share in the Burbage theaters and properties and his further share as an active member of the company. He was, in a sense, employer and employee, and his income was a steady one. . . . Shakespeare and his fellows were, by the standards of their day, pretty prosperous men.*

Such entries as "lane aperne wraght eaged with gowlde lace and creamson strings" and a black velvet cloak which cost as much as £20, so richly was it decorated, were presumably for theatre wear. . . .

Richard Jones gets a loan of £5, "to be payed me agayne," notes the cagey Henslowe, "by ten shillings a weake." We may be sure that ten shillings were stopped from Richard's salary until the debt was discharged. Even the sum of five shillings for the heartening purpose of "good cheer at the Tavern in Fish Street" is noted as a loan. We can almost hear a young actor's protesting "Look, Mr. Henslowe, my salary's sixpence short this week." "Your share of the party, dear boy, your share of my party. . . ."

The authors attached to his companies were paid something like £4 to £6 for an entire play, which would seem little enough, judging from the comparative munificence of the sums expended on props for their plays. The initial payment bought the play outright, and it became the property of the company. . . .

When, as was very frequently the case, a play was written by several authors in collaboration, they divided the fee among them. Chettle, Dekker, Heywood, Smith, and Webster must have done some unsatisfactory arithmetic over the £8 they jointly received for *The First Part of Lady Jane*.

Very often, too, an author earned a few shillings by revising an old play for revival, or adding a scene or two to someone else's script. The method is startlingly paralleled today in any Hollywood studio. It has caused commentators endless headaches in their diligent efforts to disentangle the early Shakespearean hand from that of his fellows, particularly in the *Henry VI*'s. . . .

There was no system of continuing royalties. But Shakespeare was not dependent on them, nor on such down payments as Henslowe's hack authors received. He owned his share in the Burbage theaters and properties and his further share as an active member of the company. He was, in a sense, employer and employee, and his income was a steady one. The shares were salable and could be left to the owner's heirs. In addition there were rewards for court performances and other miscellaneous remuneration. Shakespeare and his fellows were, by the standards of their day, pretty prosperous men.

From *Shakespeare Without Tears*. New York: World Publishing Co., 1955.

Christopher Marlowe Shakespeare, however, was not the only significant playwright of the English Renaissance stage. The plays of Christopher Marlow (1564–1593), for example, also bear witness to the astounding intellectual climate of the Elizabethan theatre. Marlowe's love of sound permeates his works, and if his character development is weak, his heroic grandeur has the classical qualities of Aeschylus and Sophocles (see the synopsis of *Doctor Faustus* below).

Marlowe's powerful poetic language was a breakthrough in drama of the time. His flexible use of blank verse and the brilliance of his imagery combined to stimulate emotion and rivet his audience's attention. The imagery of terror in the final scene of *Doctor Faustus* is among the most powerful in all of drama. In addition, Marlowe's language and imagery unify the play: The patterns in Faust's references to Heaven provide a subtle suggestion of the force from which Faust cannot escape and yet which he must, at the beginning, deny.

The Tragical History of the Life and Death of Doctor Faustus

Marlowe's most famous play is *Doctor Faustus* (or, more properly, *The Tragical History of the Life and Death of Doctor Faustus*), first published in 1604. The story resembles the plot of a morality play, narrating a man's temptation, fall, and damnation, in richly poetic language.

Marlowe's source appears to have been an English translation of the German legend of Faustus that appeared in England at that time. The plot centers on Faust, who is tired of the limitations of his own learning and even the scope of human knowledge. He turns to magic and makes a contract with Mephistopheles, a minor devil. They agree that Mephistopheles will be Faust's slave for twenty-four years, at the end of which term Faust will be damned for eternity. For twenty-four years, Faust uses his powers to the full, from playing practical jokes to summoning up Helen of Troy. On the last night of his contract, he waits in agony and terror; Mephistopheles comes and carries him off to Hell.

The central theme of *Doctor Faustus* is that life on this earth has meaning because it determines the nature of eternal life. The play harkens back to the medieval morality play, wherein the forces of good and evil battle for control of the human soul. At the same time, the play displays a typically Renaissance interest in the zealous quest for knowledge that characterized the times. Faust is a devoted student of classicism and science. His personality exhibits the new individualism. Classical allusions can be found throughout the play, from the appearance of Helen to the use of a chorus in the Greek tragic manner.

The tension of the drama comes from the conflict of the Renaissance desire for individual and unlimited power and the medieval philosophy of damnation for those who use Satanic means to gain those ends. However, the play goes far beyond those moralistic tensions, becoming a universal drama in which we can find personal identity. Here is the struggle between personal potential and personal limitation, between seeking those eternal goals stemming from the being that we are and enviously seeking those goals that seem to grant us power. In Christian terms, *Doctor Faustus* is about the difference between submitting to grace through repentance and, although regretting one's actions, failing to repent. In humanistic terms, the play is about the corruption of an individual to the point at which he destroys himself. In either case, the defiance of moral values eventually leads to catastrophe.

The complexity and depth of Faust's character makes the play a tragedy rather than a melodrama. Faust is a sympathetic human being with whom we can identify. He has the classical tragic flaw that leads to his tragic demise, and he is a universal symbol of humanity. In Aristotelian terms, he is a slightly larger-than-life figure, an identifiable tragic hero.

THE PLAYHOUSES

Italy   A contemporary account indicates that in 1486 the Roman comedy *The Menaechmi* by Plautus (see Chapter 15) was played in a courtyard upon "a wooden stage with five battlemented houses." Each of the houses had a door and a window; a ship also came in which was fitted with oars and a sail in "a most realistic manner." We know, then, that fairly elaborate illusion was employed in stage scenery as early as the 1480s. For the most part, Italian drama of the early and High Renaissance—that is, the early part of the sixteenth century—was produced at court, for the aristocracy, and with elaborate trappings in a scenic style reflective of the visual art of the time.

During the era, the staging of Roman plays was extremely popular, and a playhouse of great importance was built at the Olympic Academy in Vicenza. The Teatro Olimpico in Vicenza (Figs. 16.3A and 16.3B), designed for the Olympic Academy by the distinguished architect Andrea Palladio (1518–1580), was the first attempt to recreate a Roman theatre. It had thirteen rows of seats that followed the shape of an ellipse instead of a semicircle. This arrangement provided better sightlines than had its Roman prototypes. It also had a flat orchestra floor for the chorus and a raised stage backed by a long wall with three doorways. The long back wall was flanked by two shorter walls. The center doorway took the form of a triumphal arch. The other openings were probably intended to be covered with curtains.

Palladio died the same year that the work began, and his successor, Vicenzo Scamozzi, made several radical changes to the design. Scamozzi

Figure 16.3A *Andrea Palladio, interior, Teatro Olimpico, Vicenza, 1580–1584.*

[Scala/Art Resource, New York.]

Figure 16.3B *Palladio, stage, Teatro Olimpico.*

[Art Resource.]

slanted the stage floor and built short vistas of streets behind the five door-ways. From the central arch, the vistas radiated out like the spokes of a wheel. The theatre, finished in 1584, held about 1,000 people and is still used today for an occasional presentation of the classics.

The street vistas behind the archways of the Olympic Theatre caused some scholars to conclude that this was the first proscenium-style theatre (see Chapter 6). However, that theory has given way to the claim of the Teatro Farnese (see Fig. 6.14), which had a wide—and true—proscenium opening designed to frame the action on the stage itself. The auditorium took the shape of a horseshoe and seated 3,500 spectators. The orchestra floor could be flooded with water for various kinds of spectacles, but it is the true proscenium opening that made the Teatro Farnese a prototype for the future rather than a reconstruction of the past.

Framing the action on stage with a proscenium arch gave Italian scenery the look of its cousin, Renaissance painting, and the arch gave the scene designer the ability to do what his painterly colleagues also could do for the first time in the history of art—to display with accuracy the phenomenon known as *linear perspective,* the ability to render the third dimension rationally. When applied to the theatre, rational, linear perspective yielded a new style of scenery, described by one of its principal proponents, Sebastian Serlio, in his book *D'Architecttura* (see Chapter 10). He published drawings of the three types of classic scenery: the "tragic" set with lofty palaces and temples for the great lords; the "comic" set with ordinary city houses on a public square (see Figs. 6.13 and 10.3B); and the "satyr play" with a landscape of trees, hills, and cottages. Scene designers in Serlio's time combined false perspective with certain three-dimensional elements. The backing, for example, was flat, but the wings were splayed at an angle and featured cornices and architectural embellishments.

Serlio has also provided us with details of such effects as thunder and lightning, moving mechanical figures, and forms on wires. Another Italian designer, Nicolà Sabbatini, dealt in his *Manual for Constructing Theatrical Scenes and Machines* with the problem of creating stage effects such as descending clouds and rolling waves. He also described fast scene changes that utilized wing units sliding on tracks (see Chapter 6). Another scene-changing device, the chariot and pole, invented by Giacomo Torelli (see Fig. 11.12) modified the grooved-track system with slots in the floor of the stage. Cables, pulleys, and casters for sliding scenic units back and forth stayed hidden in the basement of the theatre.

Until the early nineteenth century, scene changing was done in full view of the audience—it was in fact considered part of the entertainment. No act curtain appeared in the theatre until 1800. The audience knew the scene was over when the actors left the stage. Illusion was the primary aim of the Renaissance designer, who depended on the wonders of perspective to rival reality.

The Elizabethan Playhouse Although we know more about the theatres in which Shakespeare played than we do about his life, even that information is far from complete. Most authorities believe that the Elizabethan theatre took a unique form. The only previous theatres that approach it are the Spanish *corrales* (see Fig. 16.4). Only a few sources of information about the Elizabe-

Figure 16.4 *Nineteenth-century reconstruction of the Corral del Principe, Madrid. Because northern Spanish cities like Madrid did not have patios like those where temporary theatres were located in southern cities, permanent* corrales *were built against the backs of houses surrounding courtyards. The* corrale *was open to the sky, and two or three galleries accommodated spectators on all four sides; above these were boxes on the first and second floors of the surrounding houses and areas called "attics" on their roofs.*

[Museo Municipal Madrid.]

than playhouse exist, and the one most frequently cited is a sketch drawn by a draughtsman named Johannes DeWitt of the interior of the Swan Theatre (see Figs. 5.4A and 5.4B). The basic elements of the Elizabethan theatre consist of a stage with a door at each side, a balcony above to be used by the actors, a flat floor, and galleries at the sides and rear to hold the audience.

The actual structure of the stage has troubled scholars for years. As best we can determine, the Elizabethan theatre appears to have had seven acting areas: (1) the main stage, (2) an inner stage on the same level, (3) the gallery, (4) an inner stage on the gallery level, (5–6) two windowed stages at the sides, and (7) a high platform for the musicians. Stairways served the various levels, including both the hut and the cellarage under the main stage.

The hut was the top of the tiring house and had room for cannons and other sound machines. From here, the actors could enter the "shadow," or heavens, which was actually the roof over the stage, and they could be let down into the scene through a trapdoor. The main stage also contained a number of trapdoors.

The forestage, or apron, was quite prominent. In most cases, it was wedge-shaped and extended well into the open pit or yard. Above this, there may or may not have been a porch-like structure supported by two columns. The inner-above and the inner-below were probably equipped with traverse curtains that could be opened or closed to divide the propertied inner stage from the unpropertied forestage.

When we examine the Elizabethan play, we soon realize how flexible the stage must have been. Shakespeare's *Antony and Cleopatra,* for example, has forty-three scenes. Only by means of a theatre of convention could that many

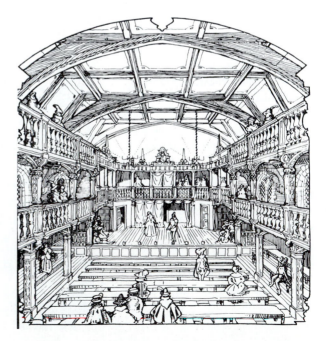

Figure 16.5 *Reconstruction of the second Black-friars Theatre, 1597. The Blackfriars was built by James Burbage, and its success as a private theatre inspired the construction of several similar theatres, many of which adapted indoor designs to satisfy the growing audience fascination with settings suitable for spectacle and sensationalism. As a member of the King's Men, Shakespeare performed at the second Blackfriars until about 1598, when he joined with Burbage and other actors to open the Globe Theatre (see Fig. 6.16). By about 1610, outdoor perform-ances in London were largely relegated to summer festivals.*

[Performing Arts Research Center, New York Public Library at Lincoln Center.]

separate scenes be handled efficiently; illusionistic scenery would have been unmanageable.

On the other hand, plays performed at court and in the inns appear to have used a great deal of scenery. By the time of James I (1603), Italianate scenery and scenic devices had definitely begun to invade court performances. Beginning in 1605, Italianate scenery was employed in the court masques staged by the Italian-influenced architect-designer Inigo Jones. Toward the end of the reign of Charles I (1649), scenery seems to have spread from the court masques to performances in private theatres.

The Baroque Period

In many leading minds in the decades following the close of the High Renaissance, there was a certain nervousness and unease. The Reformation had challenged institutional Christian faith and its authority. The proposal of a heliocentric universe threatened to knock humankind from its previously assured place at the center of all things. Harmony seemed once more to be an unattainable ideal, as Europe was torn by wars and as philosophers and a new breed of scientists cast doubt on the certainties of the Renaissance. In short, the modern age was in the making. *Baroque* meant opulence, intricacy, ornateness, and appeal to the emotions, and as a style reflecting an outlook, it surpassed its predecessors in reflecting the grandiose expectations of its patrons. Diverse and widespread, seventeenth-century Baroque art took Renaissance clarity of form and recast it into intricate patterns of geometry and fluid movement.

FRENCH NEOCLASSICISM

The years from 1550 to 1720 in France witnessed traveling commedia troupes and a cross-pollenization of theatre influences from France to England and vice versa. Within its own borders, France developed a unique and significant theatrical tradition that scholars have called *French neoclassicism*. Medieval religious drama had continued its strong traditions under the royal monopoly granted to the Confrèrie de la Passion. In 1548, however, a combination of Protestant and Catholic attitudes resulted in the abrupt legal suppression of all religious drama and the breaking of the monopoly on professional production. Secular professional drama, freed from its religious competition and the Confrèrie's monopoly, turned to Renaissance classicism. French rediscovery of Sophocles, Euripides, Aristophanes, and Menander provided even further impetus.

This turning back to the ancients had a tendency in the theatre and other arts to foster specific rules for acceptability in works of art. In the French theatre, such regulations, formulated by the Pleiade and the Académie Française—two groups of literary arbiters appointed by the king and the powerful prime minister, Cardinal Richelieu—forced plays to fit a structural and spatial mold called the Unities. As a result, the spirit and substance of classical drama was lost in attempts to bend it into artificial confines. The Unities became the masters of drama. No play was found acceptable by the Academy unless it conformed to specific rules—for example, that the action be singular and encompass no greater time span than 24 hours. All of these regulations were in fact based on errant judgments about the characteristics of Greek classical drama. Of course, had French antiquarians thoroughly studied actual classical Greek dramas, they would have discovered many "violations" of the Unities. Perhaps as a result of all this historically inspired rule making, little French tragedy of consequence was written during the period.

Corneille   Pierre Corneille (1606–1684) came to the stage via a Jesuit education and a career in the law. As a result of his initial playwriting attempts, including a comedy titled *Mélite* (*ca.* 1630), he was invited by Cardinal Richelieu to write for the Cardinal's personal theatre. From this invitation resulted the French neoclassic masterpiece *The Cid* (*ca.* 1636). Intended as a tragedy and hailed by the public, the play was nonetheless condemned by the French Academy. Labeled a "tragicomedy," it seemed outwardly to conform to the Unities but was criticized as straining the acceptable sense of decorum and credibility. The Academy quibbled further over the moral questions raised by the play and found that Corneille had destroyed credibility by crowding an impossibly huge amount of action into a twenty-four-hour period. Finally, the Academy charged, rather than meeting a tragic ending, the play's lovers emerge happy.

Corneille typically places his heroes in the dilemma of choosing between personal desires and societal mores. He calls upon them to become superheroes and to sacrifice all for their country, but as his career progressed, his plays reflected more and more dissatisfaction with the monarchy and tyranny.

Racine   Jean Racine (1639–1699) wrote in the preface to his play *Bérénice* (1670) that "the principal rule is to please and to stir; all others are simply means to arrive at that end." In other words, the playwright seeks to entertain and to teach—the latter occurring via the former: The playwright teaches via the act of entertaining. Racine was an orphan educated by the Jansenists, an extreme sect of Roman Catholicism. As a result, his characters, usually headstrong women, were frequently driven by original sin to a predetermined destiny. The conflict in Racine's plays usually occurs in the mind of a single person rather than between two individuals—as would be the case in the work of Corneille, for example. His plots retain a classical simplicity and focus on the destructive power of unbridled passion.

Molière   Molière (Jean Baptiste Poquelin) (1622–1673) provided a comic counterpoint to the achievements of the French tragedians. Early in his career, he joined a professional company, a family of actors named Béjart. His earliest productions took place in what has come to be known as a "tennis court theatre" because the shape and size of the indoor tennis courts of the time made them easily adaptable to theatre. For over thirteen years, the Béjarts and Molière toured France as an itinerant company (see Fig. 16.7). A fateful

Jean Racine

Molière

Figure 16.6 Engraving of a scene from Racine's Bérénice, 1678. Against the back-drop of a Rome designed to reflect both the grandeur that was the France of Louis XIV and the antithesis of private passions, the Emperor Titus is torn between his responsibility to the city and his passion for Bérénice. The sensitivity with which Racine's heroes responded to moral dilemmas sometimes put him at odds with his audience, which preferred passions to be romanticized. Presented in 1672, Racine's Bérénice was based on the same subject as Corneille's Titus and Bérénice (also 1672); such deliberate "contests" between major playwrights was not uncommon.

[Bibliotheque, Nationale, Paris.]

Figure 16.7 A sketch from 1670 depicts Molière (far left) among "French and Italian Farceurs." Molière's fondness for the commedia dell'arte made its way into what he later called "those little entertainments which had won him some reputation with provincial audiences" in the Illustre Théâtre, and the parts that he wrote for himself were often comic types—gullible old men and henpecked husbands. Note the similarity between these types and the commedia dell'arte types at Fig. 16.1—for example, "Le Capitan Matamore" as "Cap. Zerbino" with sword and flowered cap.

[Giraudon/Art Resource.]

Western Theatre *from the* Renaissance *to* Romanticism

447

appearance before Louis XIV launched Molière's career as a playwright, which he combined with his work as an actor and manager. *Tartuffe* (see the summary in Chapter 3), *The Misanthrope*, and *The Bourgeois Gentleman* brought French comedy to new esteem. For comedy to be so highly regarded is relatively rare in the history of the theatre. Molière's instincts for penetrating human psychology, fast-paced action, crisp language, and gentle but effective puncturing of human foibles earned him a foremost place in theatre history. His comedies were not only dramatic masterpieces but also weathered the potentially overpowering baroque scenic conventions of the court theatre at Versailles. His later plays challenged the painted backgrounds and elaborate machinery of Italian scene designers and again emerged unscathed.

In *Tartuffe,* Molière, though accused of attacking religion in general, satirizes religious hypocrisy. The play that we have is the third version; the previous two were suppressed because of the objections of religious interests. Religion was taken seriously, and numerous organizations existed to protect the faith from freethinking. It was in this light that Molière's comedy was seen, and it took five years of rewriting to bring *Tartuffe* to the stage. Molière reiterates continuously the difference between hypocrisy and true religious feeling and sets up his characters as careful counterbalances around the norm of acceptable behavior. The long didactic passages seem clearly directed toward reducing any confusion as to those at whom the force of the satire is directed.

The play contains stock characters derived from commedia—for example, the witty and wily maid Dorine—and it also ends with such contrivance in the intervention of the king that *Tartuffe* comprises a classic example of the deus ex machina conclusion.

FRENCH NEOCLASSIC PRODUCTION

Acting Style With its roots in the commedia dell'arte, the acting style of French comedy, especially that of Molière's Illustre Theatre during its years in the provinces, reflected broad improvisational techniques. When Molière returned to Paris, the acting style, perhaps of necessity, changed to one of restraint and subtlety. Whether in comedy or tragedy, as the seventeenth century progressed, acting style changed to accommodate a developing refinement in dialogue and increasing sophistication in the audience.

The Playhouses After 1650, the new trends and directions in theatre centered in France and Italy, where experimentation in theatrical structures and scenic design took on new meanings. Palladio and Serlio were out of date, and every production was rendered in a more spectacular and ostentatious fashion. In France around 1655, for example, the Salles des Machines was constructed in the Tuileries, the royal palace in Paris. This edifice consisted of a stage that was 32 feet wide at the proscenium arch and 132 feet deep. It could accommodate enormous machines as large as 40 feet wide by 60 feet long.

ITALY

The Italians, too, were active during this period. In the second half of the seventeenth century, the rage for Italian opera spread all over Europe, and every noble wanted to make it a part of his court festivities. Italian scene designers and painters migrated to other countries. The first great family of Italian scenic artists was the Mauri family, consisting of five brothers—three decorators and two machinists. The Mauris also had a young assistant who was to found another, even more famous family of designers—Ferdinando Galli da Bibiena (1657–1743). After designing for the opera house at Parma, Bibiena was invited to Barcelona to design the celebrations for the wedding of Charles and Elizabeth, later Holy Roman Emperor and Empress. He then moved to Vienna, where he remained for the greater part of his life. He is credited with the revolutionary departure in design that involved the use of diagonal perspective drawing (see Fig. 10.4B).

Since the Greeks, the tendency in auditoriums had been toward greater length, with the precise shape taking different forms in the hands of different architects. Some theatres had straight galleries running at right angles to the stage front; others had ovoid galleries, and still others horseshoe-shaped galleries. At this time, the proscenium arch began to move forward to the apron, placing the actors behind rather than in front of it. England, however, retained the apron stage for almost another 150 years.

THE ENGLISH RESTORATION

The return of Charles II and his court to England from France in 1660 gave rise to a monopolistic attempt to adapt theatre to the service of the king. Charles II authorized two dramatists, Thomas Killegrew and Sir William D'Avenant, to form two acting companies. These two companies held the only *patents*—that is, licenses—for the production of professional theatre in London, and their audiences comprised a small number of courtiers rather than the public at large.

Restoration Comedy The noteworthy accomplishment of the late-seventeenth-century English playwrights was a unique genre known as *Restoration comedy*. It focused on the adventures of "people of quality" and reflected their intrigues, manners, and "humours," or idiosyncratic dispositions. The staple of this "comedy of manners" was verbal wit, which playwrights used not only to lay bare the follies of this class but to satirize the morality of the bourgeoisie. Another favorite target was the boring and boorish life of the country gentleman.

Several outstanding playwrights emerged from this period, including Sir George Etheredge (*ca.* 1634–1691), William Wycherly (*ca.* 1640–1715), and William Congreve (1670–1729). Their comedies depict handsome, witty, well-dressed individuals who often seem to be concerned about nothing more than sexual liaisons and impressing each other with claims of wealth, wit, and sexual triumphs. The genre carried into the eighteenth century in the works of such playwrights as Richard Brinsley Sheridan (1751–1816) and Oliver Goldsmith (1730–1774). Goldsmith's works, especially *She Stoops to Conquer* (1773), exhibit excellent humor and exceptionally well drawn characters. Sheridan, probably the most famous British playwright of the period, created two masterpieces, *The Rivals* (1775) and the most brilliant comedy of the English stage, *The School for Scandal* (1777), a biting satire with crisp, fast-paced dialogue (see Fig. 16.8).

RESTORATION PRODUCTION

Actors and Acting The patents granted to Killegrew and D'Avenant specified that women be cast in feminine roles in order to avoid female impersonation. Acting schools were established by the patent holders, and plays were staged by the companies' leading actors or actor-managers. Contemporary style called upon the actor to stand full-front in the dominant stage position when speaking. During this period, actors developed greater realism in their presentation, although we probably would find their "realism" highly stylized by our own standards. Among the stars of the Restoration theatre were Thomas Betterton, Nell Gwynn, and Anne Bracegirdle. The supreme actor of the Restoration theatre, however, was David Garrick (1717–1779), whose breadth of feeling, natural style, and uncanny ability to transform him-

Figure 16.8 *Drawing of a scene from Sheridan's* The School for Scandal, *1783. Although Sheridan often distributed witty intelligence among his characters so democratically that they tended to be verbally indistinguishable, Lady Teazle is one of his most skillfull creations. Starting with the conventional figure of the country maid delighted by the sexual sophistication of high society, Sheridan made his heroine more complex by combining her sophistication with a certain innocence. The counterpoint furnished a basis not only for some basic comic business but for one of the best actress's roles of the period. A less stylized depiction of a performance of* School for Scandal *from a contemporary engraving can be found in Fig. 13.7.*

[Harvard Theatre Collection.]

Figure 16.9 *David Garrick as Richard III. Garrick's reputation as the greatest actor of his age was launched when he debuted as Richard III in 1741. Although he was known as an actor of restraint, noted for his ability to develop a broad range of feelings without unnecessary emoting, Garrick gained fame at a time when both spectacle and sentiment were considered proper for the "corrected" production of Shakespeare (see the report on eighteenth-century Shakespearean productions by Harold Child in this chapter).*

[Courtesy of the Lilly Library, Indiana University, Bloomington, Indiana.]

self into his characters made him the unquestioned "star" of the age (see Fig. 16.9).

Playhouses and Production Style   The scenic simplicity of Elizabethan theatre (all acting was done in front of an unchanging architectural facade) stood in strong contrast to the opulent spectaculars of English court masques during the reign of Charles I in the early years of the seventeenth century. Essentially, the court masque was a toy for the nobility—an indoor extravagance that had developed earlier in the sixteenth century, probably influenced by its visually resplendent cousins in Italy. Short on literary merit, the English masque was nevertheless a dramatic spectacle par excellence and a reflection of monarchial splendor.

Banqueting halls in palaces were often redesigned to accommodate the scenic complexities of the masques. Stages often exceeded 35 feet in width and 25 feet in depth. Six feet high in front and seven feet at the rear, these stages allowed the manipulation of scenery from below and used a form of staging called *forestage-façade*, in which the actors played on a protruding area in front of (as opposed to amid) drops and wings. What is important about the English court masque is its direct tie to the scenic style of Serlio in Italy. Inigo Jones (1573–1652), the most influential English stage designer of the time, freely imitated Italian perspective, using elaborate stage machines and effects. All this baroque finery, however, came to an end in 1642, when Oliver Cromwell's Puritan revolution overthrew the monarchy. Theatres were closed and productions forbidden (at least publicly) until the Restoration of the Stuarts under Charles II in 1660. Opera, however, provided a handsome substitute. When Charles II returned from exile in France, he brought to the English theatre the continental style current in the French court.

Western Theatre *from the* Renaissance *to* Romanticism

Harold Child: Shakespeare Our Contemporary (II)

"I lov'd the man," said Ben Jonson of Shakespeare, "and doe honour his memory (on this side Idolatry) as much as any." Here, the critic and historian Harold Child describes some typical Restoration practice in rendering Shakespeare in production. In the process, he raises the question of just what side of "idolatry" such renowned seventeenth-century producers as William D'Avenant and Thomas Betterton stood in their admiration for Shakespeare. Although D'Avenant, he observes, may have had "a true reverence for Shakespeare," one might be hard put, based on contemporary accounts of his productions, to say just what he considered most indispensable in the Bard's originals.

Before the closing of the playhouses the public stage had been learning from the masques about spectacle and the decoration of drama; and [William] D'Avenant produced some time in 1656 his 'opera,' *The Siege of Rhodes,* which had 'scenes in prospective.' These scenes consisted of permanent side-wings painted to represent rocks and cliffs, and of shutters, or flats, which could be run together and changed, in sight of the audience, to make different backgrounds. There was no attempt at creating the illusion that what the audience saw was not a stage setting but a real place. The stage still projected a long way in front of the proscenium; and . . . the art of acting was still largely the art of declamation and gesture on an open platform with the audience on three sides of it. The implications of the change were important. [For example] . . . the idea of scenery and of spectacle as things to be cultivated for their own sakes was transferred from the masques to drama that had been written for very different purposes; and the implication was that that drama might be sacrificed at pleasure to the claims of scenery and spectacle.

> *There was some rearrangement of scenes to make room for all the music, dancing and spectacle, in which monkeys and Chinese persons and properties had a place. . . . The show . . . tipped the scales heavily against simplicity in the production of Shakespeare's comedies.*

It was, however, by no means only the new toys they had to play with—actresses, painted scenes and mechanical devices—which induced the men of the Restoration to tamper with the drama of Shakespeare. . . . [To D'Avenant] Shakespeare was an author who needed not coarsening but refining, especially in his comedies. Let us agree at once that some of the Restoration refinement can make our own stomachs turn; but there is evidence that Shakespeare's comedies seemed to that age 'silly'; and that in comedy and tragedy alike, they believed that could improve him. . . . D'Avenant and his followers strove for symmetry of plot and balance of persons and consistency of character; they tried to make the action easy to follow, and every word of the dialogue . . . strictly to the point. They tried to polish and to regulate; and Shakespeare, himself a valiant adapter, would probably have admitted them right in principle, and laughed, or sworn, at the havoc they made of his poetry, his fancy, the range and freedom of his thought and knowledge. It was scarcely their fault they did not know when to let well alone. . . .

[D'Avenant's] *Macbeth* shows his desire for balance and for consistency. Macbeth and Lady Macbeth are both more whole-heartedly and simply evil than in Shakespeare; and to balance the evil pair there must be a consistently good pair, Macduff and Lady Macduff. At the end all the poetry is cut out of Macbeth's part; and as for the diction, it is hard to say whether D'Avenant's rhymed couplets or his blundering blank verse are less like the Shakespeare they replace. But they are certainly more refined. . . .

Yet the play would doubtless go with a bang in performance; and it was not at first all overlaid with spectacle, as it was to be in 1672. There was, indeed, a good deal of trap-door and flying-machine stuff for witches and ghosts, and the supernatural part was, in general, purged of mystery and revealed in the clear light of acrobatics. . . . D'Avenant, no doubt, loved spectacle and the devices of stagecraft. His production of *King Henry VIII* was splendid with costumes, processions and "shows" (or tableaux, as we might call them) of massed figures—some of them, no doubt, painted in perspective. . . .

[In 1692, Thomas] Betterton went further than D'Avenant had ever done in making a fine show of music and machines. *The Fairy Queen* was a version of *A Midsummer Night's Dream* produced at the Dorset Garden house in 1692. . . . If this "opera"

achieved only half that it aimed at, it must have been a triumph of ingenuity in the use of shutters or flats, cut-out wings and scenes, back cloths, running water and much else. The dialogue was tamed a little, and there was some rearrangement of scenes to make room for all the music, dancing and spectacle, in which monkeys and Chinese persons and properties had a place. Though too costly to make such profit, the show was a great success; and it tipped the scales heavily against simplicity in the production of Shakespeare's comedies. . . .

The age had set an example of altering Shakespeare, and that example was pretty consistently followed till within living memory. But in the next era, a physical change was made of an importance which few can have then foreseen. In order to make the pit bigger, the manager of Drury Lane, cut off some of the fore-stage. The more open the platform, the more chance there was for a drama of a free and fluid structure. The more the play was pushed back towards and behind the proscenium arch, the more need there was for a new technique in production; and henceforth there was a continuous series of attempts to fit Shakespeare not (as D'Avenant had) into new critical rules, but into a stage for which his plays were not written.

From *A Companion to Shakespeare's Studies*. Edited by H. Granville Barker (with G.B. Harrison). Reprinted by permission of Cainbridge University Press.

During the Restoration period, the theatre building became a link between the earlier Elizabethan playhouse and the modern proscenium. The Restoration theatre borrowed not directly from its immediate predecessor, but from a combination of two Renaissance forms: the proscenium arch from the Italians and the French, and the enormous apron or forestage and a form of the inner-above from the English public theatre. In general, the Restoration playhouse included a proscenium and a stage with movable flats and backdrops; a deep apron or forestage for most of the acting; entrances for the actors in the

Figure 16.10 *Title page of the Commonwealth law suppressing English plays and playhouses, 1647. When the Puritan Commonwealth collapsed, a permissive backlash quickly became apparent in the fashionable arts, especially literature. Such subjects as masochism (Thomas Otway's* Venice Preserved*) and tranvestism (Colley Cibber's* The Careless Husband*) were suggested in the theatre, and when actresses first appeared on the English stage, numerous plot devices called for them to dress as men—the better to display more bare leg.*

walls of the proscenium (Fig. 16.11); chandeliers in the auditorium and over the forestage; footlights consisting of candles; a raked stage slanting upward from the footlights; and a "pit," or main floor, with benches. The floor of the auditorium was raked, and one row of boxes rose above the pit. Two large galleries were above the boxes.

Production techniques were comparatively simple. Backdrops could be

Figure 16.11 *Drury Lane Theatre, 1808. Although the features of the Restoration theatre are still evident, by the dawn of the nineteenth century, the actress Sarah Siddons was to call this immense auditorium "a wilderness place" where performing technique was compromised by the need to amplify voice and gesture. Originally built in 1663, Drury Lane burned in 1672 and was rebuilt by the architect Christopher Wren. The most important scene designer of the era, Phillippe Jacques De Loutherberg, worked there with Garrick for ten years beginning in 1771. Garrick comanaged the theatre from 1746 until his retirement.*

[Prints Division, New York Public Library, Astor, Lenox, and Tilden Foundations.]

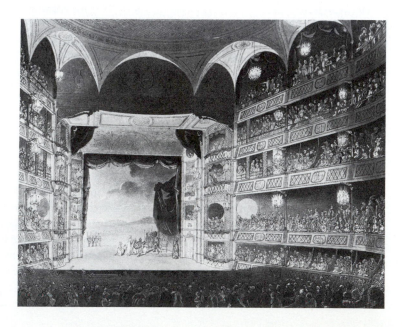

raised or lowered, and a front curtain was often painted with a scene. Between the backdrops and the front curtain stood rectangular painted flats or wings arranged in groups of four or five, which ran in grooves. The outer flat in each group could be pulled back to reveal a new one. A flat on one side and a flat on the other could be pushed to the middle of the stage to form the back wall of a set. Such flats were called "shutters" when used in place of a backdrop. Although this arrangement did not produce much in the way of illusion, the method was simple and quite economical and did not require the raising or lowering of the front curtain to change scenes.

The Enlightenment

The eighteenth century was an age of change and revolution in some areas and prosperous stability in others. The idea of the absolute monarch was challenged—though with varying success. The middle class rose to demand its place in social and economic life, and humanitarianism—social philosophy in action—attempted to make a place for all classes in the scheme of things. Knowledge was regarded as a transcendent and universal goal. The aristocracy found itself in decline and in an increasingly superficial and delicate condition—a fact reflected in the *rococo* style in the visual arts. The pendulum then swung back—at least temporarily—from exquisite refinement and artifice to intellectual seriousness. The structural clarity of classicism returned in painting, sculpture, architecture, and, above all, in music, which found the culmination of a remarkable century in works of emotional depth and formal inventiveness. The century closed amid the turmoil caused by the French Revolution and the upheavals of *Sturm und Drang* or "Storm and Stress" in literature and drama that ushered in the era of the Romantics.

ENGLISH SENTIMENTAL DRAMA

As more and more of the merchant class began to attend the theatre, the tone of drama shifted from the bawdy comedy of the Restoration to a more bourgeois sensibility and sentiment. "The purpose of sentimental comedy," observes theatre historian Paul Kuritz, "was neither laughter nor ridicule, but the arousal of 'a pleasure too exquisite' for laughter." *Sentimental comedy* rejected verbal wit and focused on middle- and upper-class characters: The lower classes vanished from its pages. "Goodness" became the denouement in this approach to drama, and "bad" characters were reformed through emotional appeals.

Undoubtedly the most popular theatre form in early-eighteenth-century London was the *ballad opera,* and the best of these unquestionably was John Gay's *The Beggar's Opera* (1728) (see Fig. 16.12). It caricatured the corruption of the English government, and the play created a social scandal. *The Beggar's Opera,* however, was not the only theatrical piece to burlesque gov-

Figure 16.12 *Painting of a scene from John Gay's* The Beggar's Opera. *Alternating dialogue and song in the story of Macheath, a celebrated highwayman, and various denizens of the London underworld, Gay's satire of the English political scene proved immensely successful. In 1928, Bertolt Brecht (see Chapter 17) updated* The Beggar's Opera *as* The Threepenny Opera, *also a raucous political commentary that used the underworld as an ironic mirror held up to the values of capitalist society. For a contemporary production of* The Beggar's Opera *see Fig. 2.9.*

[Harvard Theatre Collection.]

ernmental corruption, and partially as a result of public theatrical attacks, Prime Minister Robert Walpole successfully convinced Parliament to institute the Licensing Act of 1737, which limited legal theatrical production to three theatres—Drury Lane, Covent Garden, and Haymarket—and gave the Lord Chamberlain the right to censor any play.

Tragedy had been virtually nonexistent in England since 1640, when all public theatres were closed by the Commonwealth. By the early eighteenth century, however, the neoclassical traditions of seventeenth-century France and the pseudoclassical theories of essayist, critic, and poet Alexander Pope (1688–1744) had made some inroads into British tragedy. A number of plays and playwrights followed these precepts. The foundation was, again, sentimentality. George Lillo's (1693–1739) *The London Merchant, or The History of George Barnwell* (1731) exemplified the sentimental movement, and, in fact, became the best known play in the world. Audiences came and cried. The hero of the play, a London apprentice, becomes involved with a prostitute and murders his favorite uncle. True to the genre, however, by play's end, he has repented.

The Georgian Playhouse   Theatre structure in England did not change radically during the early part of the eighteenth century. Several new theatres were built and old ones altered. Even on the continent, examples of the fore-stage-façade style could be found well into the century (Fig. 16.13). Several characteristics distinguished the Georgian theatre from that of the Restoration. Seating capacity, for example, increased in many cases. Architectural treatment of the side boxes was simplified, creating a lighter architectural atmosphere and a more unified structure. A number of spiked railings were placed around the stage and auditorium to prevent members of the audience from climbing onto the stage or into more expensive seats. The number of boxes or galleries increased, with some theatres boasting as many as five tiers of boxes towering above the pit. Eventually, a definite division existed between the side boxes and the front boxes, and, during this period, the private box appeared. Private boxes were frequently called *lattices* or *lettices* because of the presence of a lattice across the front.

Although the stage itself showed little change until the next century, scenery witnessed some interesting developments. Rejecting the heavy Baroque style, designers turned toward a more classical style and began creating what is known as the "landscape style." A new theory, championed by Philippe Jacques de Loutherbourg (1735–1810), suggested that a stage setting need not be architectural. His invention of transparent scenery, moonshine, fire, volcanoes,

Figure 16.13 Interior of the Hôtel de Bourgogne, Paris, ca. 1765. *See comments at* Fig. 13.1.

[Bibliotheque Nationale, Paris.]

Western Theatre *from the* Renaissance *to* Romanticism

and cutout scenery produced spectacular effects. Near the end of the century came William Capon's "romantic architectural settings" for Shakespearean revivals, and these designs, based on authentic documents, constituted the first attempts to emphasize research and historical accuracy.

AMERICA

In eighteenth-century America, theatre came up squarely against Puritan austerity. Sometime between 1699 and 1702, however, Richard Hunter gained permission from the acting governor of the province of New York to present plays in the city of New York. In 1703, an English actor named Anthony Ashton landed at Charlestowne, South Carolina. He was, according to one contemporary account, "full of lice, Shame, Poverty, Nakedness, and Hunger," and so to survive recreated himself in the image of "Player and Poet." Eventually, he found his way to New York, where he spent the winter "acting, writing, courting, and fighting." Perhaps as a consequence, the province forbade "play acting and other forms of disreputable entertainment" in 1709.

Notwithstanding this inauspicious start, however, American theatre struggled forward. The first recorded theatre was built in Williamsburg, Virginia, in 1716 and housed a performing company for the next several years. For the most part, theatre in America was merely an extension of the British stage, and English touring companies provided most of the fare. Theatres themselves appear to have been small and closely modeled on provincial English theatres with their raked stages, proscenium arches, painted scenery, and apron forestages flanked by entrance doors. Four hundred seats seems to have been about average. The front curtain rose and fell at the beginning and end of each act, and numerous scene changes within the acts were executed in full view of the audience.

Plays and Companies Companies from London, usually comedy troupes, came to Williamsburg annually for an eleven-month season. By 1766, touring British companies played the entire eastern seaboard from New York and Philadelphia to Charleston, South Carolina. A milestone was passed on April 24, 1767, when the "American Company" (which was in fact British) presented Thomas Godfrey's *The Prince of Parthia*—the first play written by an American to receive a professional production. As the American Company prepared for its 1774–1775 season, the Continental Congress passed a resolution discouraging "exhibitions of shows, plays, and other expensive diversions and entertainments."

During the years of the American Revolution, numerous American plays were written, most of which were never performed. Because there were no American professional actors, and because all the British professionals had fled back to England, the war years saw a flurry of amateur production throughout the colonies, including performances staged by the American troops themselves with the approval of George Washington.

The century closed with eighteen postwar years of production by the American Company, which returned from England in 1782. In 1787, Royall

Tyler's *The Contrast* successfully launched a firm tradition of American theatre. Tyler was a Boston lawyer and American army officer who had seen his first play only a few weeks before writing *The Contrast*. His play presented a lively picture of New York society, with facile dialogue and well-drawn characters. *The Contrast* satirizes Dimple, a young New Yorker who has turned into a fop because of his admiration of all things British. Although he is engaged to Charlotte, the daughter of a wealthy merchant, Dimple considers himself a European rake and makes advances to two of his fianceé's friends. One of these friends has a brother, Colonel Manly, who is the aptly named epitome of American plain manners, high principles, and patriotism. Manly falls in love with Charlotte, exposes Dimple, saves both Charlotte and his own sister from Dimple's duplicity, and ends up united with Charlotte. In the midst of this delightful comedy are two additional characters of extreme importance—Jessemy, Dimple's servant, every inch the mirror of his master, and Jonathan, Manly's servant, the prototypical "country bumpkin." The subplot of scenes between these two provides hilarious fun even for contemporary audiences.

Although *The Contrast* was successful, the first American playwright was really British-trained William Dunlap, who wrote *The Father, or American Shandyism* (1789), which combined sentiment, wit, comic humor, and "the finer things of the human heart."

Playhouses In 1794, the focus of American theatre turned to Philadelphia with the opening of the Chestnut Street Theatre (Fig. 16.14). This new

Figure 16.14 *Interior of the Chestnut Street Theatre, Philadelphia. The first American theatre to install gas lighting (1816), the Chestnut was once known affectionately by local citizens as "Old Drury of Philadelphia" after London's Drury Lane Theatre (see Fig. 16.11). Many native playwrights and stars made their debuts at the Chestnut, and Philadelphia rivaled New York as the major theatre city until the 1820s.*

[Harvard Theatre Collection.] •

playhouse had a handsome interior with boxes set in a semiellipse and a total seating capacity of either 1,200 to 2,000 (sources vary). The auditorium was gray with gold trim, including elegant gilt railings. The orchestra pit held thirty musicians, and the large forestage was flanked by walls representing the façades of handsome buildings. The large stage was lit by oil lamps, the auditorium by candles. A French traveler, whose descriptions detailed the theatre, indicates that the circumstances were noisy and even indecent.

FRANCE

Plays and Playwrights   Although ripples of the comic style of Molière and the neoclassicism of Racine extended well into the eighteenth century, the theatre of France underwent a stagnant period after the death of Molière. The recently established Comédie-Française produced fine actors and actresses in both comedy and tragedy, but management appeared overly aware of its state patronage and harbored a regressive philosophy of production that stifled new directions. The Comédie-Française slipped into sentimental and melodramatic tragedies and comedies that were caught up in contemporary triviality. A rival company at the Hôtel de Bourgogne was called the Comédie-Italienne both to distinguish itself from the Comédie-Française and to reflect the Italian nationality of the actors (although they played in French). Success for this company had begun in the closing years of the seventeenth century. Plays of the early years of the century often show a combination of neoclassicism, popularism, and rococo niceties. Tearful comedies called *comédies larmoyantes* satisfied the tastes of the salon set as well as an ever-increasing middle-class audience that demanded emotional plays in recognizably contemporary situations. The egalitarianism of the Enlightenment brought tragedy to a curious state—the increasing numbers of women in theatre audiences seemed determined to cry, even at comedies, and they flocked to the well-equipped theatres in pursuit of such release. By the time of the French Revolution, serious drama had become *drames bourgeois*—middle-class drama of melodramatic proportion.

A few undistinguished tragedies of neoclassical bent were written, only to fall justifiably by the wayside. Of interest in this vein are the works of Jolyot de Crébillon (1674–1762), who wrote popular horror plays. His intention was to move an audience to pity and terror while never offending its sense of refinement or propriety. The plots of Crébillon's plays speak for themselves: A father kills his son (*Idoménée,* 1705); a father drinks his son's blood (*Atrée et Thyeste,* 1707); a man kills his mother (*Électra,* 1709). Crébillon continued to write tragedies well into the middle of the century.

The shifting character of French drama of the first half of the century can also be seen in the plays of Pierre de Marivaux (1688–1763). Although Marivaux's style is difficult to classify, it is certainly more in the rococo style than anything else—sentimental and a little too concerned with plot embellishments. For the most part, however, Marivaux's plays are charming, sentimental, and meticulously written. *Les Fausses Confidences* (1732) described the efforts of a poor but handsome young man who sets out to make his rich mistress fall in love with and marry him. The questionable morality of his duplicity is balanced somewhat by irony when, in the end, the young man actually falls in love himself. Marivaux had his eye on the neoclassical "Unities"—the entire action of the play occupies less than a day.

Voltaire

Voltaire Perhaps nothing summarizes the first three-quarters of the eighteenth century better than the theatrical ventures of its most dominant personality, François Marie Arouet, known as Voltaire (1694–1778). His plays were diverse in style and genre. Curiously, given his critical, antiestablishment propensities, early plays like *Oedipe* follow fairly closely the rules of the French Academy (actually *Oedipus* is a rather slavish imitation of Racine). An admirer of Shakespeare, Voltaire once called the English dramatist an "inspired barbarian" because Shakespeare's dramatic structures were far too untidy for neoclassical tastes. In *Mérope* (1741), Voltaire declared that he had returned to first Greek principles. Most critics agree that what he meant by this was that he had eliminated any love scenes. His last play, *Nanine* (1778), had a gala premiere attended by most of the royal family, and by the time of his death two months later, he had received the greatest acclaim ever bestowed on anyone in the French theatre.

Beaumarchais In the plays of Pierre de Beaumarchais, French drama enjoyed one final blaze of brilliance before the Revolution. His two most famous plays, *The Barber of Seville* (1775) and *The Marriage of Figaro* (1784), are entertaining comedies built on the traditions of neoclassicism dating back to *The Cid*. In fact, at the last moment Beaumarchais expanded *The Barber of Seville* into a neoclassical five-act structure, adding only ponderousness to an otherwise fine play. Opening-night criticism caused him to rewrite it into a four-act structure—a revision that restored the sparkle and brilliance. In a sense, the circumstances surrounding *The Barber of Seville* and *The Marriage of Figaro* prefigured the French Revolution, and the nine years between the two works saw a dramatically changed audience perception of the forecast. While *The Barber of Seville* was enjoyed and received calmly, by 1784 France was well aware of its circumstances. The criticisms directed against the character of Figaro—the archetypal common man easily perceived as representative of the French citizenry—were taken seriously as an indictment of society as a whole. The horrors and chaos of the Revolution left the French stage barren during the final ten years of the eighteenth century.

GERMANY

Plays and Playwrights The mid-eighteenth century in Germany marked a determined attempt to develop a significant national theatre, even if the political concept of "Germany" remained somewhat nebulous. Chaos and a lack of any stable national boundaries or capital cities to act as cultural centers had previously prevented the development of a strong national theatre such as England, France, Italy, and even Spain had enjoyed.

However, seeds planted by touring English, French, and Italian compa-

Voltaire: Shakespeare Our Contemporary (III)

Although interspersed with occasional praise, Voltaire's comments on Shakespeare over the course of some forty years (1735 to 1775) consisted primarily of attacks on such items as Shakespeare's "barbaric" disregard for decorum and his gross laziness in plagiarizing the plots of others. Here, he observes that although Shakespeare no doubt "created" the English theatre, he can rightly be considered the primary factor in its "ruin." The English Romantic poet and critic Samuel Taylor Coleridge dismissed Voltaire's criticism of Shakespeare as "vulgar abuse"; other English defenders of the Bard pointed to Voltaire's reliance on poor translations and suggested that his blindness to Shakespeare might somehow be related to his own moral failures as a writer and a man.

The English as well as the Spaniards were possess'd of theatres, at a time, when the French had no more than moving, itinerant stages. Shakespeare, who was consider'd the Corneille of the first mention'd nation created, as it were, the English Theatre. Shakespeare boasted a strong, fruitful genius: he was natural and sublime but had not so much as a single spark of good taste or knew one rule of the drama. I will now hazard a random, but, at the same time, true reflection, which is, that the great merit of this dramatic poet has been the ruin of the English Stage.

There are such beautiful, such noble, such dreadful scenes in this writer's monstrous farces, to which the name of *tragedy* is given, that they have always been exhibited with great success. Time, which only gives reputation to writers, at last makes their very faults venerable. Most of the whimsical, gigantic images of this poet, have, through Length of time (it being a hundred and fifty years since they were first drawn) acquir'd a right of passing for sublime. Most of the modern dramatic writers have copied him; but the touches and descriptions which are applauded in Shakespeare are hiss'd at in these writers; and you'll easily believe that the veneration in which this author is held, increases in proportion to the contempt which is shown to the moderns. Dramatic writers don't consider that they should not imitate him; and the ill success of Shakespeare's imitators produces no other Effect, than to make him be consider'd as inimitable.

Shakespeare . . . was natural and sublime but had not so much as a single spark of good taste or knew one rule of the drama.

You remember that in *Othello* (a most tender piece), a man strangles his wife on the stage; and that the poor woman, whilst she is strangling, cries aloud, that she dies very unjustly. You know that in *Hamlet*, two gravediggers made a grave, and are all the time drinking, singing ballads, and making humourous Reflexions on the several skulls they throw up with their spades; but a circumstance which will surprize you is, that this ridiculous incident has been imitated. In the Reign of King Charles the Second, which was that of politeness and the Golden Age of the Liberal Arts, Otway, in his *Venice preserv'd*, introduces Antonio the Senator and Naki his courtesan in the midst of the horrors of the Marquis of Bedemar's Conspiracy. Antonio, the decrepit Senator, plays, in his mistress's presence, all the apish tricks of a lewd, impotent debauchee who is quite frantic and out of his senses. He mimicks a bull and a dog; and bites his mistress's leg, who kicks and whips him. However, the players have struck these buffooneries (which indeed were calculated merely for the dregs of the people) out of Otway's tragedy; but they have still left in Shakespeare's *Julius Caesar* the jokes of the Roman shoemakers and coblers who are introduc'd in the same scene with Brutus and Cassius.

nies had provided the basis for a "German" theatre. Johann Christoph Gottsched (1700–1766) began a small literary renaissance at the University of Leipzig by translating numerous French neoclassical plays into German.

Gotthold Ephraim Lessing

Lessing   The literary values prominent in German theatre in the mid-eighteenth century were strengthened by the work of a superb playwright, Gotthold Ephraim Lessing (1729–1781). Lessing became part of the newly established Hamburg National Theatre. He was offered the position of "stage poet," whose responsibilities included writing new plays, making translations, and composing prologues and epilogues for special occasions. Lessing refused the position, indicating that he could not complete plays as frequently as required for such a position. Nevertheless, the Hamburg National Theatre was so eager to be associated with Lessing that he was hired without this condition.

Lessing's first tragedy, written before his association with the Hamburg National Theatre, was *Miss Sara Sampson* (1755), a reworking of the Medea story in a middle-class English setting. A typical *tragédie bourgeoise*, it had great influence in Germany and replaced French neoclassical drama as a standard. His most memorable play, *Minna von Barnhelm* (1767), a tender, serious comedy about womanhood, is often called the first German contemporary drama. Lessing's final, and perhaps best, play was *Nathan the Wise* (1779), which preached religious toleration, introduced blank verse, employed strong symbolism, and generally exemplified enlightened thought. In addition to his plays, Lessing provided important theoretical advancement in German theatre. He argued that all art is but a reflection of nature, and that pseudoclassical rules interfering with that perception were false. Lessing considered Sophocles and Shakespeare the dramatic models by which all playwrights should be measured.

Johann Wolfgang von Goethe

Goethe   German theatre changed direction around 1770, and the years that follow introduced the *Romantic movement* that was to dominate the nineteenth century. Both Lessing's interest in Shakespeare and his concern for unbroken action were shared by Johann Wolfgang von Goethe (1749–1832). Goethe and others in Germany turned to Shakespeare, chivalry, and Elizabethanism for inspiration. In 1771, Goethe produced his *Goetz von Berlichingen*, a Shakespearean historical drama of German thought and concept. Complete with typically Shakespearean comic interludes amid the tragedy, *Goetz von Berlichingen* told the story of a Robin Hood–like robber-knight of the sixteenth century. Four years after the play, Goethe helped change the course of the next century with two monumental works—the novel *The Sorrows of*

Faust Part I

The play begins with a poetic dedication followed by a "Prelude in the Theatre" and a "Prologue in Heaven," in which, after a long debate about the nature of humankind, God agrees to allow Mephistopheles to set about tempting Dr. Faust. God is the creative, divine force, Mephistopheles the destructive force. God maintains that humankind will go astray as long as it strives. However, humankind cannot be misled forever because it has at its heart an "instinct of the one true way." What follows is a series of 26 scenes ranging from Faust's study to a final prison scene. After striking a bargain with Mephistopheles, according to which the devil will possess Faust's soul when his longings and strivings are complete, Faust is led to a student drinking party and a witch's kitchen, finally to meet Gretchen. With Mephistopheles' help, Faust falls in love and seduces Gretchen. Gretchen kills their child and is sent to prison. Half-mad, she refuses the help for escape offered to her by Faust and Mephistopheles. As a result, her soul goes to heaven. As Faust witnesses her agony of sin and punishment, he recognizes his role in her predicament and so his guilt. Thereafter, Mephistopheles fights a losing battle in the effort to tempt Faust because sensual and material temptations no longer hold interest for the hero.

Young Werther and the first draft of the play *Faust* (see synopsis). These two works, along with Friedrich von Klinger's play *Sturm und Drang* (*Storm and Stress*) (1776), began a new revolt against classicism. Drawing much of its inspiration from the American Revolution, *Sturm und Drang* became associated with a movement attracting young and free spirits everywhere, Goethe among them.

Goethe's *Faust* was certainly the masterpiece of the age. Part I is actually the theatrical masterpiece. Goethe began and partially completed it around 1774–1775 but continued to rework it until 1801. Part II occupied the remaining 30 years of his life and was not actually published until 1833, the year after he died. Although the Faust story, of course, was not original to Goethe, his treatment of it was. There is some doubt whether Goethe even intended Part I to be a stage presentation as opposed to a dramatic poem. Nowhere, for example does Goethe enumerate the scenes or give a list of characters; he does not even indicate passage of time. Rather, he provides absorbing speeches illustrating the struggles in Faust's mind and his commentary on life. The work is a dramatic mixture of passion and wisdom. Part II reflects idealism removed from the "conflict of conscience and love" of Part I. Part II is so formless that it is virtually impossible to stage. Goethe's *Faust* was a poet-dreamer and idealist seeking the divine and the ability to understand the workings of nature and the mystery of life. He is the prototypical romantic hero—a figure of great significance in the years to come.

Acting and Production Christoph Gottsched turned from literary works to production efforts when he met and became enamored of the acting

Figure 16.15 *Drawing of a scene from Goethe's* Iphigenia in Tauris. *Depicting the premiere of Goethe's final version of the play, this drawing shows Goethe, as Orestes, in the center. Goethe's version of the classical story (1787) is anchored in some of the great themes of Romanticism—for example, the power of mankind to free itself from myths that are revealed as projections of its own powerful imagination. As such,* Iphigenia *is one of the clearest expressions of early Romantic humanism.*

[Nationale Forschungs-und Gedenkstatten der Klassischen deutschen Literatur.]

talents of Carolina Neuber (1697–1760). In 1724, when the troupe of which Neuber was a member came to Gottsched's attention, playwright and actress joined forces. Their later collaborations to reform the theatre of Germany did much to improve circumstances and establish traditions. Konrad Ekhof (1720–1778) followed Neuber's tradition with an acting style of earnestness, sincerity, and honest restraint that set the production standard of the era.

Lessing also made a further contribution of consequence to German and Western theatre: He wrote plays that allowed for scene changes at the act break rather than between scenes so as not to impede the movement of the action. This change was significant. In a theatre using depictive scenic background—as opposed to theatre of scenic convention like the Greek or Elizabethan—pauses at any point in the dramatic action break the rhythmic and emotional flow of the production; elaborate scene changes thus disturb the audience's involvement and attention. Clearly, Lessing was a playwright of the theatre for which he wrote. His plays were written for the stage with theatre aesthetics and effective production in mind.

The Romantic Era

With its roots in the eighteenth century, the Romantic movement entered the nineteenth with a force that matched the new engines of industrial progress. In the arts, the pendulum had swung once again. Classical formality and restraint gave way to a relentless questioning and self-questioning—and, in some cases, to escapism—as the artist, a moral hero now liberated from patronage, was on his or her own, to rise or fall, to experiment and to protest. Caught between the institutionalized expectations of the Academy, the tastes of the public, and the artist's own vision of individual expression, each generation reacted more and more strongly against the style of its predecessor. The pace of change—social, technological, artistic—was quickening, and artists began to feel themselves increasingly on the margin of a materialistic society.

PLAYS AND PLAYWRIGHTS

In the theatre, Romanticism, as a philosophy, was perhaps its own worst enemy. Artists sought new forms to express great truths and strove to free themselves from neoclassical rules and restraints. Significantly, Shakespeare was seen as both exemplary of new ideals and symbolic of freedom from structural confinement. Intuition reigned, and "genius," transcending everyday humankind, placed its holder above or beyond normal constraints. As a result, the Romantic writer had little use for any guide but his or her own imagination. Unfortunately, however, the theatre operates within some rather specific limits. So many nineteenth-century playwrights penned scripts that were unstageable that the era justly gained its reputation for dramatic barrenness. It seemed that great writers could not constrain themselves to the practicalities of the stage, and hacks, yielding to popular taste, could not restrain themselves from overindulgence in phony emotionalism, melodrama, and stage gimmickry. As a result, the best Romantic theatre came from the pen of William Shakespeare, brought out of his Elizabethan "theatre of convention" into nineteenth-century antiquarianism —the sanctioning of the past as fashionable. Be that as it may, the Romantic period succeeded in shaking loose the arbitrary rules of neoclassicism, thus paving the way for a new era in the later years of the century.

Goethe's *Faust* Part I was basic to Romantic drama. Unfortunately, it was also virtually unstageable. In Romantic philosophy, art and literature were thoroughly entwined. Plays often were seen and studied as literature. The theatre–literature link of the nineteenth century thus brought writers to the theatre who were not of the theatre. Their inexperience was complicated by Romantic disregard for practicality, and the result was problematic, to say the least.

Victor Hugo

Victor Hugo The novelist Victor Hugo (1802–1885) attained an almost godlike position in the artistic community of Paris. After two abortive attempts (one at the hands of the state censor), he finally succeeded in producing his play *Hernani* in 1830. An earlier diatribe directed by Hugo against the neoclassicists succeeded in filling his audience with revenge-seekers who were determined that the play would fail. Their disruptions during the performance on opening night made a shambles of the production (see Fig. 5.1). In the play itself, characters violate their own integrity, honor is carried to ridiculous extremes, and the ending is completely contrived. The poetry remains nonetheless lyrical and charming, and Hugo's brave assault on the bastions of French neoclassicism did open a few doors for Romantic dramatists, not least of whom was the novelist Alexandre Dumas, père (1802–1870). His work *Henry III et sa Cour* (1829) enjoyed success at the Comédie-Française and did much to popularize the Romantic movement through its introduction of justified illicit love.

The English Romantics   In England, revivals of Shakespearean plays enjoyed more success than contemporary works. The Romantic poets Coleridge, Wordsworth, Byron, Keats, and Shelley attempted to write plays, and although a few of their works were produced, all suffered from the difficulties endured by poets who ventured into theatre in the Romantic era. James Sheridan Knowles (1784–1862), an actor, enjoyed some success as a playwright, mingling Shakespearean verse with melodramatic stories in plays like *Virginius* (1820), *William Tell* (1825), and *The Hunchback* (1832).

Von Kleist and Büchner   Along with Goethe and Schiller, Heinrich von Kleist (1777–1811) helped to carry the German theatre into the nineteenth century. His *Prince of Homburg* (1811) tells the story of a young officer so desirous of fame that he defies orders in an attempt to win a victory. His success does not excuse his endangering the entire army, and he is condemned to death. Only after realizing that his ego must be subordinate to service and the good of all is he spared. Another German playwright, Georg Büchner (1813–1837), illustrates in *Danton's Death* (1835) the pessimistic side of Romanticism. The dashing of hopes resulting from Napoleon's despotism and defeat is reflected in this story of idealism crushed by pettiness. *Woyzek* (1836) also expresses disillusionment, but in a remarkably modern and expressionistic psychological study.

MELODRAMA

The popular side of theatre production in the nineteenth century developed a romantically exaggerated form called *melodrama* (see Chapter 4). Typically, this form or genre is characterized by sensationalism and sentimentality. Characters tend to be stereotyped, and problems, solutions, and people all tend to be entirely good or entirely evil. Plots are sentimental and the action is exaggerated. A strict moral code must also be observed: Regardless of circumstances, good must be rewarded and evil punished. Melodrama also often employs some form of comic relief, usually through a minor character. The action usually progresses at the whim of the villain, and the hero is forced to endure episode after episode of superhuman trial. Suspense is imperative and reversal at the end obligatory. The term *melodrama* implies music and drama, and in the nineteenth century, melodramatic plays were generally accompanied by musical scores tailored to the emotional or dynamic character of given scenes. Actual practice was quite similar to the use of contemporary film and television scores, but the music of the melodrama also often included incidental songs and dances used as curtain raisers and entr'acte entertainment.

Melodrama was popular throughout Europe and the United States, and playwrights like August von Kotzebue (1761–1819) and Guilbert de Pixérécourt (1773–1844) enjoyed great success. *Uncle Tom's Cabin,* based on the novel by Harriet Beecher Stowe (1852), took the stage by storm. The stage version was opposed by Mrs. Stowe, but copyright laws did not exist to protect her. Although the play does represent the same complex themes of slavery,

Figure 16.16 *Uncle Tom's Cabin, 1901. Eliza prepares to cross the frozen river. By the late nineteenth century, the onstage presence of dogs and horses was no longer unusual in American melodramas. The ice-laden trees are elaborately cut wings. Compare this production with both the earlier staging of the popular play depicted at Fig. 4.12 and Donald Oenslager's modern production design at Fig. 17.8.*

[Harvard Theatre Collection.]

religion, and love found in Stowe's original novel, the action involves a number of additional episodes, some of which are rather loosely connected. As is characteristic of melodrama, *Uncle Tom's Cabin* places considerable emphasis on spectacle, the most popular of which at the time was Eliza's crossing a raging ice-filled river, with mules, horses, and bloodhounds in pursuit (see Fig. 16.16). (For a plot synopsis of *Uncle Tom's Cabin,* see Chapter 4.)

AUDIENCES

The audiences of the nineteenth century played a significant role in what took place on the stage. Royal patronage, of course, was significantly diminished and box-office receipts were necessary to pay the bills. A rising middle class also swelled the eighteenth-century audience and shaped its changing character. In addition, the nineteenth century witnessed the admission of the lower classes to theatres. The Industrial Revolution created larger urban populations, expanded public education, and sent feelings of egalitarianism throughout European and American social orders. All of these developments enlarged theatre audiences and prompted widespread theater building. Audience diversity and capitalist entrepreneurial spirit caused theater managers to program for the popular as well as sophisticated taste. In order to offer something for everyone, therefore, an evening's theatre program might contain several types of fare and last upwards of five hours. The consequence was predictable: Fewer and fewer sophisticated patrons chose to attend, and the quality of the productions declined in direct proportion.

By 1850, however, a semblance of order had returned, and theatres began to specialize, thus attracting the sophisticated playgoer to the theatre with productions designed to suit the level of audience expectation. Nevertheless, the multiproduction evening remained typical until nearly the turn of the twentieth century. Audience demand was high, and theatre continued to expand. Although theatre in continental Europe was silenced during the Napoleonic Wars and the depression that followed, prosperity had revived it considerably by 1840.

REPERTORY COMPANIES

The nineteenth-century theatre was typified by the *repertory company*. These companies comprised a set group of actors, including stars or leading actors, and performances arranged around a season of plays. Unlike our contemporary Broadway theatre, in which each play is produced and cast independently and runs for as long as it shows a profit, repertory companies staged several productions each season. Gradually, better known actors began to capitalize on their reputations (and were sometimes exploited by the same) and began to tour, starring in local productions that featured their most famous roles. A virtual craze for visiting stars developed, and the most famous began to make world tours. Along with the increase in touring stars came an increase in touring companies; and, in the United States especially, these companies, with their star attractions and complete sets of costumes and scenery, became regular features of the landscape. By 1886, America could boast 282 touring companies. At the same time, local *resident companies* became significantly less popular—except in Germany, where a series of local state-run theaters was established.

The Playhouse and Mise-en-Scène In the nineteenth century, theaters both increased in number and decreased in size. Lighting moved slowly through the era of the candle, gaslight, limelight, and finally to the incandescent lamp. In scenery, a change appeared not only in a tendency toward historical accuracy and realism, but also in its physical arrangement. For example, the wing and drop set that were so popular in the eighteenth century gave way to the *box set* with its three realistic walls. Definite and imaginative theories of staging were also developed and put into practice. With the increase in the number of theaters in England, a new and bourgeois type of program emerged. Theatre programs frequently centered on pantomimic and musical shows (a forerunner of American vaudeville of the late 1920s). Melodramas, burlettas, and reviews also became popular, and such productions required elaborate scenic devices and effects—horses, fire engines, ships, and wild animals were fairly common props. Burnings, floods, and snowstorms could be seen every season. These effects were not limited to the minor and less dignified theatres. Drury Lane, for example, spent £5,000 to mount an exotic extravaganza called *Cataract of the Ganges*; the Old Vic installed a curtain of mirrors.

For two centuries, the pit or ground floor of the auditorium had provided the cheapest admission price. Until 1660, there were no benches in this area, which consisted only of "standing room." Although benches—hard, uncomfortable, and without backs—were finally introduced in the eighteenth century, this entire part of the theater had neither aisles nor reserved seats. Finally, at the beginning of the nineteenth century, new or rebuilt theaters began to reduce the size of the apron, and theater managers filled the extra space with a row of "stalls" with backs and, eventually, upholstery and armrests. Because these seats could bring as much as six times the amount for ordinary "pit" benches, managers began adding more and more "orchestra" seats, and the pit was pushed farther and farther back until it was eliminated altogether in most theatres. Next, the four or five rows of large boxes on the side walls and at the back of the theaters were raised and the pit extended under them. This arrangement transformed boxes into balconies (Fig. 16.17) and increased the seating capacity of the particular house. In addition, the proscenium doors, which opened onto the apron, were eliminated despite objections from the actors, who found it necessary to revise many of their techniques and simple stage rules.

Figure 16.17 *Interior of the State Opera House, Tbilisi, Georgia, USSR. Nineteenth century, restored.*

Figure 16.18 *Charles Kean's production of Shakespeare's* Richard II, 1857. *Interpolated between Acts III and IV. The entry of Bolingbroke into London with Richard II as captive. Contemporary watercolor by Thomas Grieve. Grieve's rendering of other scenes from Kean's staging of Richard II can be found at Figs. 4.9 and 8.2.*

[Victoria and Albert Museum, London/Art Resource.]

A trend toward historical accuracy in settings and costumes began in Germany around 1810. In England, Shakespearean revivals began to be produced with reasonably accurate costumes and sets. This trend, called *antiquarianism*, peaked in the mid-nineteenth century in the spectacular productions of the actor-manager Charles Kean. In every Kean revival, the settings came sharply into focus. Kean's spectacular climax scenes followed the trend toward the so-called sensation scene, which was the chief attraction of every melodrama. Kean contended that "historical accuracy might be so blended with pictorial effect that instruction and amusement would go hand in hand" (Fig. 16.18).

It is difficult to determine exactly when the *box set* came into being. Some eighteenth-century plans show wings hinged so that they could be aligned from the proscenium to the backdrop. In 1834, when Drury Lane produced a new play, one reviewer reported that "the stage was entirely enclosed" and even suggested that there was a ceiling rather than the traditional hanging borders.

Before development of the box set, scene changes were made in full view of the audience. The front curtain did not mark the ends of the acts in England until 1800. In 1817, gaslight was introduced to the London stage. Whether or not this was an improvement is debatable: Between 1800 and the coming of electricity, nearly four hundred theaters burned in America and Europe. Gas did have two advantages, however: the flow could be controlled and, consequently, dimmed and it could even be extinguished and relit. For the first time, therefore, the auditorium could be darkened and all light concentrated on the stage, thereby creating an isolated and self-contained stage world. A final, important scenic development took place in the early part of the century in the use of the *simultaneous set* (see Chapter 6). Unlike the use of simultaneous stages in the medieval theatre, the nineteenth-century practice consisted of showing a complete cross-section of a house on stage. For example, in London in 1817, the setting for *The Actor of All Work; or the First and Second Floor* showed two rooms at the same time, one above the other. This practice continues in the contemporary theatre in settings for plays like *Brighton Beach Memoirs* and *Broadway Bound*.

SUMMARY

- The *Renaissance* was seen by its leading figures as a rebirth of our understanding of ourselves as social and creative beings.

- Theatre in the Renaissance, while retaining some of the characteristics it had developed in the Middle Ages, produced some new dramatic forms:

  sottie—a secular form of short theatrical entertainments

  farce—a fully developed play form of low comedy

  commedia dell'arte—a unique Italian form characterized by improvisation, stock characters, mime and pantomime, and traveling companies.

- England's drama during the Renaissance was national in character and featured the plays of William Shakespeare, Christopher Marlowe, and Ben Jonson.

- The playhouses of the time took different forms in different countries:

  Italy, while renovating Roman theatres, gave birth to the *proscenium form*.

  England featured architectural stages in public theatres such as Shakespeare's Globe Theatre as well as Italianate style production in the *court masques* of the aristocracy.

- The *Baroque* age produced theatrical styles like *French neoclassicism*:

  Playwrights of the *neoclassical era* in France included Pierre Corneille, Jean Racine, and Moliere.

  The acting style of neoclassicism reflected the broad improvisational heritage of *commedia dell'arte*.

  The playhouses witnessed experimentation in structures and new meanings in scene design.

- The Baroque age also produced an extravagant style of stage scenery—especially for the widely popular dramatic form, the *opera*.

- During the Baroque period, the English Restoration produced a unique style of comedy, called *Restoration comedy*. It focused on the machinations of "people of quality" and reflected their manners and intrigues.

Contemporary acting style of the Restoration called for the actor to stand "full front" in the dominant stage position when speaking.

The scenic simplicity of the Elizabethan theatre stood in contrast to the indoor extravagance of *court masques,* which were staged in the banqueting halls of palaces.

The Restoration playhouse developed a new form of staging called the *"forestage façade"* that combined the Italianate scenery of the masque with the open stage of the Elizabethan public theatre.

• The eighteenth century was an age of change and revolution in some areas and prosperous stability in others. Out of this period came *English sentimental drama,* modifications to the forestage-façade type of theatre, and an emerging theatre in America.

• In France, the plays of Voltaire and Beaumarchais proved preeminent.

• Eighteenth-century Germany produced playwrights like Johann Gottshed and Gotthold Lessing, but is most remembered for the emergence of Johann Wolfgang von Goethe and the beginnings of *Romanticism.*

• With its roots in the eighteenth century, the Romantic movement entered the nineteenth century with a force that matched the new engines of the industrial revolution.

Romanticism proved problematical in the theatre because playwrights tended to ignore the practical limitations of the theatre.

The period produced a number of notable playwrights—for example, Victor Hugo, Georg Büchner, and Edmond Rostand.

It also produced a romantically exaggerated play type called *melodrama.*

• Audiences in the nineteenth century played a more important role in determining the style and nature of theatrical plays and performance.

• The period also saw an increase in the use of *repertory companies.*

• In the nineteenth century theatres increased in number and decreased in size:

New technologies such as gaslight and electricity changed theatre production significantly.

A trend toward historical accuracy also changed production style—eventually leading to the *"box set"* as a scenic type.

Chapter 17

The Modern Theatre

*A*fter studying this chapter
you should be able to:

- Describe *realism* and *naturalism* and the impact that these two styles had on playwrights and production practices.

- Discuss major styles and individuals whose works can be categorized as "antirealistic" and "theatrical"—for example *symbolism, eclecticism, expressionism, social action, epic theatre,* and *absurdism.*

- Characterize several movements and individuals associated with *pluralism* in contemporary theatre—for example, Peter Brook, New Theatre, Living Theatre, Black Liberation movement, Performance Group, and Theatre of Images.

- Identify and describe the trends and designers characteristic of *theatrical scene design since World War II.*

Stage set. New York Public Library.

What is past may be prologue, but the theatre of our times balances precariously between traditional approaches on the one hand and practices and experiments that deny the validity of these approaches on the other. In this chapter, we will survey the twentieth century and a variety of the styles and movements that it has given us in the theatre. Although the focus of previous chapters on plays and playwrights, dramatic forms, and production practices remains the same in this chapter, that approach gives way here to larger divisions that draw to our attention wider and more inclusive topics. The chapter has four main divisions: (1) *Realism and Naturalism*; (2) *Antirealism and Theatricalism*; (3) *Pluralism*; and (4) *Scenic Design since World War II*. Within each of these sections reside important individuals and movements—for example, symbolism, expressionism, epic theatre, New Theatre, Living Theatre, the Black Liberation movement, and so on.

Realism *and* Naturalism

PLAYS AND PLAYWRIGHTS

Realism   In line with trends in philosophy and the other arts, a conscious movement toward realism in the theatre emerged around the middle of the nineteenth century. This movement brought significant change, and by 1860 one could find in dramatic literature a striving for verisimilitude—the more or less faithful portrayal of a real world of human personal and social activities. Objectivity was stressed, and knowledge of the real world was seen as possible primarily through direct observation. As a result, contemporary life—or at least life with which the playwright was directly familiar—became the subject matter of drama. Representation turned from the utopian past and exotic places to an investigation—and, to a large extent, idealization—of human motives. Exposure to such topics on the stage, however, was not particularly pleasant for many playgoers, and objection to turning the theatre into a "sewer or a tavern" came from many quarters. Playwrights responded by arguing that the way to avoid such ugly depiction on the stage was to change it in society—that the fault lay in the model and not in the messenger.

The Well-Made Play   Translating contemporary life into realistic dramatic form required a thorough knowledge of theatre practicality and presentation. At least one workable solution came from the French playwright Eugène Scribe (1791–1861). Scribe was a master of plot manipulation who, as a playwright, was better able to mold a dramatic structure than most of his Romantic predecessors. His early success came through well-plotted comedies of intrigue, and although his characterizations were typically weak, his ability to coordinate comprehensible action made him quite influential, both in his own time and later. Scribe perfected a form that came to be known as the *well-made play*, and his formulaic approach allowed Scribe (and his factory of collaborators) to turn out plays in great numbers. The formula was fairly straightforward: Present a clear exposition of the situation; carefully prepare events that will happen in the future; provide unexpected but logical reversals; build suspense continuously; bring the action to a logical and believable resolution. The crux of the well-made play was logic and cause-and-effect relationships.

Henrik Ibsen The acknowledged master of realist drama was the Norwegian Henrik Ibsen (1828–1906). Ibsen took the format of Scribe's well-made play, eliminated many of its heavy-handed devices, and built powerful, realistic "problem-dramas" around the careful selection of detail and plausible character motivations. His exposition is usually meticulous, and in Ibsen the play itself tends to bring to a conclusion—however tragic or melodramatic—events that began well in the past. Ibsen's concern for realistic detail carries into his mise-en-scène, and his plays contain detailed descriptions of settings and properties, all of which are essential to the action.

Vehicles for social criticism as well as psychological investigation, many of Ibsen's plays were controversial. Most present still-pertinent and significant questions concerning social and moral issues and personal relationships—for example *The Pillars of Society, A Doll's House* (1879), and *Ghosts* (1881) (see the synopsis in Chapter 4). Ibsen's late plays like *The Master Builder* (1892) abandoned realism in favor of a symbolist quality; others, such as *Peer Gynt* (1867) (see Fig. 2.7) display highly poetic content.

Anton Chekhov Realism found complex and often innovative expression in many quarters, perhaps especially in the Russian playwright Anton Chekhov (1860–1904). Although Chekhov, like Ibsen, departs from realism to incorporate symbolic overtones, he is regarded by many critics as fundamental to modern realism. His themes and subject matter were drawn from Russian daily life, and they are realistic portrayals of frustration and the often depressing qualities of everyday existence. His plots often flow in the same apparently aimless manner as do the lives of his characters; theatricalism and compact structure are noticeably absent. Nonetheless, Chekhov's plays are skillfully constructed to give the appearance of reality. For example, in his last and perhaps greatest play, *The Cherry Orchard* (1904), we find an almost overriding resignation toward the inability of the older generation to accept change or abandon personal possessions in favor of overall societal good. At the same time, a play like *Uncle Vanya* (1899) (see Fig. 17.1) expresses an underlying compassion for characters seemingly lost in the throes of day-to-day existence. (A synopsis of *The Three Sisters* can be found in Chapter 4.)

George Bernard Shaw The spirit of realism in England found its most distinctive voice in the socially critical wit of George Bernard Shaw (1856–1950), who was, despite the keenness of his insight into personal foibles and social inadequacies, a humanist. Sometimes considered a heretic and subversive because of his devotion to socialism, Shaw nevertheless maintained his oft-taxed trust and faith in humanity and its infinite potential.

To many readers and theatregoers, Shaw's plays often appear inconsis-

Henrik Ibsen

Anton Chekhov

George Bernard Shaw

Figure 17.1 *Chekhov's Uncle Vanya. Moscow Art Theatre, 1899. Directed by Constantin Stanislavski and Vladimir Nemirovich-Danchenko. The story of a meek and gullible man who slaves away on his niece's estate and invests everything in the work of a parasitic scientist, Uncle Vanya is a distinctly unromantic tragedy with several sub-plots involving unrequited loves. However, although everyone is doomed to boredom and unhappiness, Stanislavski, Nemirovich-Danchenko, and the theatre's well-established repertory company managed to capture the inherent warmth of Chekhov's characters through the subtle humor with which he endowed them. Although it is a subdued drama centering on conflicting human needs and desires, Uncle Vanya was an immediate success for the Moscow Art Theatre and entered the fairly exclusive repertory (only three to five new plays per year) on which, in part, Stanislavski and his famous company came to rely.*

tent—and even contradictory—in characterization and structure. His favorite device is to construct a pompous notion only to destroy it. In *Man and Superman* (1901) for example, a respectable Victorian family learns that their daughter is pregnant—a situation to which they react with predictable indignation. To the girl's defense comes a character who obviously speaks for the playwright—he attacks the family's hypocrisy and defends her. The girl, however, explodes in anger—not against her family but against her defender: She has been secretly married all the time and, as the most respectable of the lot, rejects not only her defender's pompous freethinking but that of the audience, who have been led to sympathize with what they thought to be the playwright's point of view.

Convinced that a play was a more effective means of transmitting social messages than speakers' platforms and pamphlets, Shaw nonetheless insisted that art should have a purpose. His pursuit of message through dramatic device is exceptionally skillful, as in the philosophical history play *Saint Joan* (1923) (see the synopsis in Chapter 4), and he succeeds—often despite careless characterizations—in pointing out life's problems through a chosen character in each play who acts as the playwright's mouthpiece. Shaw, however, does

Figure 17.2 *Shaw's* Candida. *North Carolina School of the Arts, 1980. A satirist and social philosopher, Shaw perfected a comic formula for designing middle-class drawing-room skirmishes as reflections of much larger battles fought on the moral front. In* Candida *(1893), the central figure in the struggle is the heroine of the title, who must decide whether to run off with a young poet or remain with her husband. In a play that presents the theme of passion in the context of a comedy of manners, the great moral decision reveals a very basic practical (and human) component: She stays because her husband needs her more.*

more than sermonize: His plays show deep insight and understanding as characters typically probe the depths of the human condition and often discover themselves—albeit through crisis—in logical, reasonable, and realistic portrayals of life. (A synopsis of *Major Barbara* [1905], one of Shaw's most representative comedies, can be found in Chapter 4.)

Eugene O'Neill

Eugene O'Neill   The Independent Art Theatre Movement produced one of America's greatest playwrights, Eugene O'Neill. In the United States, the first two decades of the twentieth century saw an intense struggle for control of the commercial theatre. Meanwhile, unions formed, the movies drained theatre audiences, and little attention was paid to nurturing any vital theatre. One independent theatre, however, showed the way. The Provincetown Players consisted of a group of young actors and writers who spent their summers together on Cape Cod, in Massachusetts. After mounting original productions in Provincetown, they moved to New York, where their commitment to American plays and playwrights led to productions of the young O'Neill (1888–1953). Son of the famous actor James O'Neill, Eugene knew the theatre well and was influenced especially by the expressionist works of August Strindberg (see the profile in this chapter) as well as the sea stories of the English novelist Joseph Conrad. O'Neill's prolific output covered wide-ranging subjects, and he tried a number of different styles, including expressionism (see the synopsis of *The Hairy Ape* [1922] in Chapter 3), in his restless search for new approaches. It was in psychological realism, however, that he found his most profound success. Arguably, he is America's first (and perhaps only) great playwright. The posthumously performed *A Long Day's Journey into Night* (1956—see synopsis) is widely considered not only O'Neill's greatest play but the finest work in American dramatic literature. (A synopsis of *Desire under the Elms* can be found in Chapter 4.)

Robert Lewis (I): You Can't Play Anything if You Can't Play the Piano

For Robert Lewis, "the piano" here is the basics of acting, "anything" roles in plays by everyone from Shakespeare to Samuel Beckett. One of the original founders of the Group Theatre in 1931, Lewis was nevertheless given to straying from the party line: Whereas "hardliners" like Harold Clurman and Lee Strasberg propounded the rigorous virtues of psychological and social realism and the "Method" of Stanislavski, Lewis experimented with a broader range of nonnaturalistic means of expression. In this interview, conducted by fellow director Charles Marowitz in 1986, Lewis looks back on the ideology and influence of the Method and the Group. Lee Strasberg, who championed the Stanislavski Method through the celebrated Actor's Studio, is profiled in Chapter 9. By the time the Group disbanded in 1941, Clurman, who had been responsible for staging many of its plays over the course of ten years, went on to direct numerous Broadway successes.

CHARLES MAROWITZ: FOR A LOT OF PEOPLE OF MY GENERATION, THE LEGACY OF THE GROUP THEATRE IS A THEATRE GLUTTED WITH PSYCHOLOGY AND NATURALISM; ROOM-SIZED DRAMAS AND AUTHORS WHOSE WORKS ARE ONLY A FEW NOTCHES UP FROM SOAP OPERA; A THEATRE . . . FIXATED AT THE LEVEL OF THE '30S AND ONE WHICH DOES NOT REFLECT THE DYNAMIC CURRENTS OF LATE 20TH-CENTURY EXPERIENCE. IS THIS A FAIR ASSESSMENT?
ROBERT LEWIS: What they said in the '30s was, "We are going to have a theatre that reflects 'the life of our times.'" So naturally, they did plays by new and contemporary playwrights.

They couldn't take classical plays or revivals and make *them* reflect "the life of our times" [because] the directors of the Group—especially Harold Clurman and Lee Strasberg—were psychologically oriented. They weren't interested in language. They weren't interested in movement. They *were* interested in psychology. They wanted to do plays where people's feelings and relationships were important, and that's why they did those plays. . . .

All the "means of expression"—that is, the way characters dress and so on, the behavioral things—they paid no attention to at all. All they were interested in was "true feeling." Their definition of truth (which was the catchword at the Group Theatre and subsequently at the Actors' Studio) was a very limiting definition, because what they meant was the truth of *their* feeling. We were told the question you were always to ask yourself was: What would I do if I were in that situation? Which is a lot of bunk because *I'm* not Hamlet, *I'm* not Macbeth, *I'm* not Hedda Gabler. What you really have to ask yourself is: What would I do if I were *that* character, in *that* play, in *that* period, *that* class, etc. And then you use your sense of truth to transform yourself into that character. People in those days never played more than five minutes away from their own daily behavior.

One of the things that worried [Clurman] most was that people would think that the Actor's Studio was just stuck in the '30s—because they're still doing their emotional memories and private moments and all the rest of that stuff, and here we are in the '80s.

ONE HAS NO GREAT COMPLAINT AGAINST THE GROUP THEATRE AND THE SOCIAL-REALISTIC WORK THAT CAME OUT OF IT BECAUSE, AS YOU RIGHTLY SAY, IT WAS A THEATRE THAT REFLECTED ITS TIME. BUT WE'RE NOW LIVING IN THE '80S, AND THE LEGACY OF THE GROUP APPEARS TO BE NATURALISTIC WRITING AND NATURALISTIC ACTING. DOES THAT PUT A POOR CONSTRUCTION ON THE GROUP THEATRE AS AN INFLUENCE? No, I don't think so. I mean people have gone on from Freud—that doesn't mean Freud was a stinker. In his time, those were the things that people believed. Now people have developed further. In its day, the Group was a departure from the star system that prevailed at the time. . . .

IT SEEMS TO ME THAT THE METHOD HAS CRIPPLED MORE ACTORS THAN IT EVER HELPED PRECISELY BY INSTILLING THE IDEA THAT THE PARAMETERS OF CHARACTER ARE IDENTIFIED TO THOSE OF THE ACTOR. IT ENCOURAGES ACTORS TO TAKE EPIC CHARACTERS AND CUT THEM DOWN TO DIMENSIONS THEY CAN PERSONALLY HANDLE. IS THIS ONE OF THE THINGS FOR WHICH WE MUST REALLY INDICT THE METHOD? You have to indict all of the people who put into practice only one portion of it. Because, after all, Stanislavski did all kinds of plays. He did Shakespeare, Molière; he even did Gilbert and Sullivan. But some people got stuck in the '30s. I remember when Harold Clurman was dying, one of the things that worried him most was that people would think that the Actors' Studio was just stuck in the '30s—because they're still doing their emotional memories and private moments and all the rest of that stuff, and here we are in the '80s, a half-century later. Harold felt that Lee Strasberg had "ghettoized" the American stage. That was Harold's own word. . . .

CLURMAN USED TO TALK ABOUT THE METHOD AS BEING SYNONYMOUS WITH ACTING GRAMMAR. IT WAS NEITHER GOOD NOR BAD, BUT SIMPLY NECESSARY IN CREATING A ROLE. IS THAT TOO SWEEPING A GENERALIZATION? IS THERE A BODY OF TECHNIQUE AND TRAINING WHICH EXISTS AS AN ALTERNATIVE TO THE STANISLAVSKI SYSTEM AND ITS DERIVATIVES? I don't think anybody has really taught the Stanislavski system in its entirety. If you look at the chart Stella Adler brought back in 1934 from Stanislavksi himself, you will see that one half of it has to do with the means of expression—right down to punctuation, movement, plastique, fencing, etc. All of these things are in the Stanislavski system but not observed in any of the Stanislavski schools. . . .

THE METHOD, INTELLIGENTLY APPLIED, ENABLES ACTORS TO UNCOVER PSYCHOLOGICAL SUBTEXT; THAT IS, THE STEW OF LIVING MEANING DIRECTLY UNDERNEATH THE TEXT. BUT IS THAT THE END OF THE LINE? ARE THERE MEANINGS AND PERTINENCES IN A PLAY THAT NESTLE BELOW PSYCHOLOGICAL SUBTEXTS, AND IF THERE ARE, HOW CAN THE ACTOR FIND THESE OUT? That's where the means of expression comes in. There's not only *what* one does or *why* one does it, there's also *how* one does it—not only what one thinks or feels but the behavior that emanates from one's character.

BUT THAT'S ALSO PSYCHOLOGICAL, ISN'T IT? BEHAVIOR CORRESPONDS TO PSYCHOLOGICAL STATES. It has to do with all sorts of things. It has to do with costume, with language, not only psychology. That's exactly my point. You cannot stop at psychology.

WOULD YOU SAY THE METHOD DOES NOT APPLY IN THE WORKS OF WRITERS SUCH AS BECKETT, IONESCO OR GENET? No, it's basic. It's like asking, is there any music where you don't have to practice scales? You have to practice your scales in order to play the piano. That doesn't mean that all you have to play is Mozart sonatas. You can play Schoenberg; you can play Stockhausen. You can play everything, but you can't play *anything* if you can't play the piano.

THEREFORE, IN YOUR VIEW, THE METHOD IS A KIND OF BASIC GRAMMAR; THE MEANS BY WHICH YOU FORM THE MORE COMPLICATED SENTENCES OF THE MODERN THEATRE? I think it is basic to having a sense of truthful communication on the stage—to be able to speak and listen and feel yourself within the truth of a situation. That's what it's all about. Now there are all kinds of situations. If they are realistic situations, then fine, you're home free. But the theatre is not always limited to that. Therefore, if you have problems with language—abstruse language, poetic language, rhythmic language, or movement that is more than just lighting cigarettes and drinking wine and has to do with physical transformation of character—then you have to work to achieve that. I don't mean it must be done *only* physically. You always have to find some kind of inner justification for doing it—which in a way, brings us back to our old friend Stanislavsky—because, after all, our behavior does not come from the outside, but from the inside.

Excerpted by permission from the Charles Marowitz interview with Robert Lewis in the April 1986 issue of *America Theatre.* Published by Theatre Communications Group.

African American Playwrights and the Black Experience   The realistic tradition in modern theatre gave also rise to a number of black playwrights, such as W. E. B. Du Bois, who was to become a motivating force in the movement known as the Harlem Renaissance of the 1920s. Garland Anderson wrote the first black play to open on Broadway, *Appearances*, in 1925. The list continues with such major writers as Langston Hughes (1902–1967), Paul Green (1894–1981), and Lorraine Hansberry (1930–1965), whose 1959 play *A Raisin in the Sun* (see Chapter 4) presented the tribulations of a family from Chicago's South Side as they struggle to make their way in a white society. (Also see the excerpt from August Wilson's *Fences* in Chapter 2 and the Wilson interview in Chapter 5.)

Psychological and Symbolic Realism: Tennessee Williams and Arthur Miller
Realism continued its strong tradition throughout the postwar era and owed much of its strength to the works of the American playwrights Tennessee Williams and Arthur Miller. Williams (1912–1983) skillfully blended the qualities of realism with whatever scenic, structural, or symbolic devices were

Figure 17.3   *Robert Edmond Jones, setting for Eugene O'Neill's* Mourning Becomes Electra, *1931. Transporting Aeschylus' three-play* Oresteia (*see Chapter 3) to New England at the close of the Civil War, O'Neill's trilogy (which runs some seven hours) overlays the Greek tragedy of a doomed family with often heavy Freudian analysis, with such staple themes of Greek tragedy as intense passion, murder, adultery, and incest resolving (perhaps too easily) into psychotic motivation: In essence, the curse on Aeschylus' House of Atreus becomes the curse of repressed sins and secrets in O'Neill's Mannon family.*

[Performing Arts Research Center, at New York Public Library at Lincoln Center.]

Long Day's Journey into Night

Over a day and an evening, the pretensions and illusions of the Tyrone family (which is based on O'Neill's own) are torn apart. Each member of the family confronts the others with their most private sufferings. As the play progresses, Mary Tyrone, the mother, begins to relapse into the morphine addiction that her family hoped she had conquered. The addiction, apparently, was caused by improper treatment by a hotel doctor during the time her husband was touring as an actor. Father James Tyrone suffers from miserliness—a prominent factor in the inept treatment that led to his wife's addic-

tion. When he discovers that his younger son Edmund has tuberculosis, Tyrone again reverts to spiritual selfishness by suggesting treatment in a state sanitorium (it is cheaper). Contempt for their father increases in the two sons. Over the course of the evening, they become increasingly drunk, and in their stupor they reveal the various loves and hates they have for each other. Through it all, Mary remains blissfully oblivious, fondling her wedding gown and remembering the good times of the early days of her marriage.

---

necessary to meet his goals. Plays like *The Glass Menagerie* (1945), *A Streetcar Named Desire* (1947—see Chapter 8), *Cat on a Hot Tin Roof* (1955), and *Night of the Iguana* (1961), dealt sensitively and poignantly with the power of psychological trauma in the lives of vividly drawn characters. His character development is thorough and occupies the principal focus in dramas that also explore the emotional ills of a troubled society. Miller (*b.* 1915) probed the social and psychological forces that destroy contemporary men and women in plays like *All My Sons* (1947), *Death of a Salesman* (1949—see the synopsis in Chapter 3), and *The Crucible* (1953).

Naturalism   A style closely related to realism, naturalism emerged and flourished in the nineteenth century and can be clearly identified in the writings of the French novelist-playwright Emile Zola (1840–1902), who was more a theoretician and novelist than a dramatist. The essential differences between realism and naturalism are often debated. Both insisted, for example, in "the truthful" depiction of life, but naturalism went on to insist on *scientific methodology* in the pursuit of art and the basic principle that behavior is largely determined by heredity and environment. Absolute objectivity, then, tended to dominate naturalistic theories of art.

Naturalism in the theatre found inspiration in the Théâtre Libre of André Antoine in France, the Moscow Art Theatre under Stanislavski and Nemirovich-Danchenko in Russia, and the Broadway plays of the American director-manager David Belasco (1859–1931). Belasco's passion for exact reproductions of reality were often carried to extremes. In *The Governor's Lady* (1912), for example, Belasco faithfully reproduced New York's well-known Child's Restaurant on stage, complete with frying pancakes; his production of *The Easiest Way* (1909) used materials taken from tenement buildings in lower

Manhattan, including the wallpaper. Belasco, however, also heightened otherwise naturalistic productions with elaborate electrical effects calculated not only to intrigue and fascinate his audiences but to reinforce the elevated mood of melodramatic plots.

Between Realism and the Absurd: Luigi Pirandello   Sitting as a pivot-point between realism, naturalism, and the nonrealist directions of the later twentieth century, the Italian dramatist Luigi Pirandello (1867–1936) spread new roots, out of which would grow the Theatre of the Absurd. Pirandello wrote essentially realistic plays that questioned the very nature of reality. The product of disillusionment in Europe between the wars, Pirandello had lost faith in religion, realism, science, and humanity itself. Searching in frustration for some meaning or basis for existence, he found only chaos, complexity, grotesque laughter, and perhaps insanity. Plays like his famous *Six Characters in Search of an Author* (1921) (see Fig. 17.4) are obsessed with the question "What is real?" and Pirandello pursued the riddle with brilliant variations. *Right You Are (If You Think You Are)* (1916) presented a situation in which a wife, living with her husband in a top-floor apartment, is not permitted to see her mother. The neighbors' curiosity, however, soon demands an explanation

Figure 17.4   *Pirandello's Six Characters in Search of an Author, 1931. The characters grouped at the far right are (a) members of the theatre company performing the play in progress and (b) members of the theatre company comprising the characters whom the play is about. Abandoned by the playwright who created them, six characters take on lives of their own in a complex, humorous quest to find the meaning of those "lives." Six Characters (1921) is Pirandello's most famous effort to explore the hidden realities of life by complicating otherwise realistic plays with distinctly unrealistic premises. To meet the world, Pirandello suggests, we put on masks (become "characters"), and when reality strips those masks away, we become naked masks—characters, as it were, seeking the meaning of the life stories that have been written for us.*

from the husband. A satisfactory answer is forthcoming, but the mother has an equally plausible—though radically different explanation. Finally, the wife—who is the only principal who can clear up the mystery—is approached. Her response, as the curtain falls, is simply loud laughter. Although Pirandello cried bitterly at a world that he could not understand, he did so with mocking laughter directed at those who purported to have the answers or were sure that they soon would.

Realist Directing Practice: The Duke of Saxe-Meiningen In 1866, "the Theatre Duke" took the leadership of the Saxe-Meiningen players and became the first director to practice ensemble playing. Production unity thus became a principal aesthetic concern, and the director was assigned the over-riding responsibility of ensuring the coherence of the production. That consideration remains fundamental to modern theatre practice and owes its emergence principally to Georg II, Duke of Saxe-Meiningen (who is profiled in Chapter 8). The concern for production unity grew in part out of the theories of the great German opera composer Richard Wagner, who had called for a totally integrated artwork—the famous *Gesamtkunstwerk*. Saxe-Meiningen further refined directing practice by changing the convention of having the speaker actor assume the downstage-center position to the principle of organizing all actors into a carefully composed picture in which the most important actor came into focus through the confluence of line or some other visual or compositional device. The play was also broken down into moments of important crisis, each of which had its carefully composed "picture" of actors that then dissolved to make room for the next important stage composition.

The Independent Theatre Movement The so-called Independent Theatre Movement actually consisted of a series of theatres throughout Europe and the United States whose purpose was to produce theatre of high quality that was free from the demands and expectations of the mass audience. Their significance lay in the fact that they were mostly private, open only to members. They thus avoided the censorship that plagued numerous public theatres and were able to nurture experimentation and artistic development, thereby laying the foundations for a truly modern theatre. From this movement, for example, came France's Théâtre Libre and Berlin's Freie Buhne, both champions of realism and naturalism; London's Independent Theatre, organized to produce plays of "literacy and artistic rather than commercial value; and the Moscow Art Theatre, founded by Constantin Stanislavski, the most influential figure in acting and actor training in the twentieth century (see Chapter 9).

Realist Mise-en-Scène The onset of realism as a standard for production led to three-dimensionality in settings and away from drop and wing scenery to the box set (see Chapter 10). The stage floor was leveled, new methods of shifting and rigging were devised to meet specific staging problems, and distraction of scene changes was alleviated by closing the curtain to hide stage hands. Over a period of years, all elements of the production became more thoroughly integrated into a total aesthetic unity, much in the spirit of Wagner's *Gesamtkunstwerk*. In addition, stage space itself became clearly defined and separated from the audience: Rather than playing on the forestage between audience-occupied stage boxes, the actors moved upstage, still within the confines of the scenery.

In America—which at this time had more than 5,000 playhouses in at least 3,500 cities and between 50,000 to 70,000 actors—new ways of lighting the stage, changing scenery, and making theatregoing more pleasant emerged. In 1869, for example, the actor-manager Edwin Booth had excavated under his new theatre in New York and installed hydraulic machinery to raise and lower sets through slots and traps in the floor. In 1880, Steele Mackaye built an elevator stage in the rebuilt Madison Square Theatre in New York: One stage could be lowered into the basement and changed, and the other could be raised to a second floor and changed there (see Fig. 11.16). In the same theatre Mackaye also installed gas footlights in 1874 and became the first manager to use indirect lighting for the auditorium itself. Another innovative practice placed the orchestra above the proscenium arch, much as in the Elizabethan theatre. Other innovations introduced by Mackaye for the first time in America included illuminating the stage with electricity, air-cooling the theatre, and using an elevator in the orchestra pit to lower musicians out of sight during performances.

Antirealism *and* Theatricalism

Symbolism   Very briefly in the nineteenth century, an antirealistic movement called *Symbolism*, which was also known as *neoromanticism, idealism,* or *impressionism,* erupted in France. Symbolism held that truth can be grasped only by intuition, not through the five senses or rational thought. Ultimate truth, according to the Symbolists, could be suggested only through symbols, which evoke various states of mind corresponding vaguely with an artist's feelings. A principal dramatic Symbolist, Maurice Maeterlinck (1862–1949), believed for example, that every play contains a second level of dialogue that seems superficial but actually speaks to the "soul." He argued that great drama contains not only verbal beauty, contemplation, and the passionate portrayal of human nature and sentiments, but an intuitive idea that the poet forms of the unknown. Therefore, plays (which contain human actions) only suggest through symbols those higher truths gained through intuition. Not surprisingly, the Symbolists did not follow the realists' path in dealing with social problems: Rather, they turned to the past, and, like the neoclassicists, tried to suggest universal truths independent of time and place. Maeterlinck's *Pelléas and Mélisande* (1892) and *The Blue Bird* (1905) (see Fig. 17.5) are excellent examples.

ANTIREALISM: THE NEW STAGECRAFT

Adolphe Appia and Gordon Craig   Two important theorists in theatre production and design bridged the turn of the century. The Swiss designer Adolphe Appia and the Englishman E. Gordon Craig (1872–1966), both with

Figure 17.5 *Stage design for Maurice Maeterlinck's The Bluebird, Paris, 1923. According to the Symbolist Manifesto issued by Jean Moreas in 1866, realism itself was one of the problems in properly perceiving reality: Whereas reality consists of much more than just what we normally perceive, realism simply represents just what we normally perceive. For Maeterlinck, then, art had to make a "detour" around everday perceptions in the direction of the symbol, which, unlike realistic apparatus, "does not tolerate the presence of man." Costumes in Symbolist drama often look as if they are designed for puppets; settings often consist of simply detailed drawings designed—as in dreams—to give vague outlines to a mysterious void. (See the discussion of symbols in Chapter 2.)*

[Bibliotheque de l'Arsénel, Paris.]

Symbolist leanings, tried to articulate new ideas and ideals about stagecraft and theatre art. Appia (1862–1928) attempted to find a new means for unifying theatre action among the diverse visual forms and conditions of the theatre—moving actors, horizontal floors, and vertical scenery. In 1899, Appia set forth his suggested reforms in his influential work *Music and Staging.* Beginning with the actor, he maintained that stage design must be in harmony with the living presence of the performer. Realistic depiction of scene was unnecessary: Rather, there should be a human atmosphere for each setting, and the audience's attention should be focused on the character, not on scenic details. Appia believed that two-dimensional painted scenery was incompatible with the live actor because of the extreme contrast between flat scenic elements and the three-dimensional human form. For Appia, the human body was reality itself, and the stage floor should merely set the human body in relief. Scenic reality was the living presence of the actor, and the stage should be cleared of everything that is "in contradistinction with the actor's presence."

The Englishman Craig, who is profiled in Chapter 10, was more a visionary and a theorist than an actual man of the theatre. He sought to replace scenic imitation with suggestion and insisted on a coherent conceptual relationship between setting and action. For Craig, moving figures, light and shadow, and dramatic color all had a tremendous potential (see Fig. 17.6). Although Craig's actual designs often proved impractical, he enjoyed some influential successes and managed to convince many theatre artists of the significance of his viewpoint.

Eclecticism Both Appia and Craig were proponents of a movement called *eclecticism* (sometimes *artistic realism*, sometimes *organic unity*), which radically changed theatre style at the turn of the twentieth century. Previously, virtually all plays had been held to a single standard—generally, whatever was the vogue of the day. For example, in the mid-nineteenth century when antiquarian realism was the fashion, all varieties plays—melodramas, Greek trage-

Figure 17.6 E. *Gordon Craig, scene design for* King Lear. Act III. Scene II. The Storm. *Woodcut reproduction of a drawing from* The Mask, *1924. Insistent that every aspect of a production should be part of a carefully unified whole, Craig preferred simple sets that could be easily harmonized with other elements of a director's concept. He also argued that, for simplicity's sake, much of the emotional activity normally suggested by the literal movements and gestures of actors could be captured on a larger symbolic scale by such design elements as lighting and color.*

dies, or Shakespearean comedies—were staged in the same prevailing style. Eclecticism, however, held that the stage environment must be appropriate to the given play and that theatrical style should reflect the style of the period in which the play was written. Therefore, the twentieth century became—and still is—an era of stylistic diversity in which each play and each production of each play determines the actual style that the audience witnesses.

Max Reinhardt

Max Reinhardt The organic approach to theatre was championed in the work of the German producer-director Max Reinhardt (1873–1943). Reinhardt treated each play as an aesthetic problem and saw the physical environment of the production (the mise-en-scène) as a vital part of stylistic communication. In addition, in order to ensure organic unity when numerous different artists contributed to a single production, Reinhardt cast the director as the supreme theatre artist who was ultimately responsible for all aspects of production—actors, lighting, costumes, scenery, props, sound, and even the final version of the script itself. Although artistic realism has remained the principal approach to the theatre in the twentieth century, when Reinhardt's approach finally reached the United States around 1910, it gave impetus to the important movement called the "New Stagecraft" which was carried forward primarily by the efforts of two influential designers—Robert Edmond Jones (see Fig. 17.3) and Lee Simonson (Fig. 17.7).

Scene Design of the New Stagecraft: Jo Mielziner and Donald Oenslager Jo Mielziner (1901–1976) was a dominant force in the professional design field for more than forty years (see the PROFILE in Chapter 10). He designed more than 300 settings for some of the most successful plays produced in the

The Modern Theatre

American theatre. Nor was he limited to set designing, frequently designing the lighting as well. He was also involved in the architectural design of more than fifteen theatre plants, including the Vivian Beaumont and Forum theatres at Lincoln Center in New York. His designs are characterized by a strong poetic feeling emphasized by expressive lighting, skeletal scenic forms, and a liberal use of scrim and gauze (see Fig. 10.10).

Donald Oenslager (1902–1975) shared with Mielziner the design leadership in the New Stagecraft. He designed his first Broadway production in 1925, the same year that he joined the faculty of the new Yale Drama School, where he is credited with establishing the first professional course in stage design to be taught at an American university. Oenslager was responsible for the training of several generations of exceptional Broadway designers, and he influenced the formation of visual-design courses in American colleges and universities for the next four decades.

Figure 17.7 *Lee Simonson, constructivist set for Eugene O'Neill's* Dynamo, 1929. *Compare this design with the expressionist design for O'Neill's* The Hairy Ape *in Figure 3.12 and the stage design for Kaiser's expressionist play* Gas *in Figure 17.9. Whereas expressionism generally treated images based on technology as symbolic of both the innovative power of the human imagination and the grotesque distortions of modern life, constructivist design (especially in the early Soviet Union) reflected the conviction that the images of technology showed the way to a new postbourgeois art.*

Robert Lewis (II): There Must Be Something Different About the Way Jackson Pollack Throws Paint

Briefly pursuing his train of thought about the Method and modern acting, Lewis, who eventually became head of the acting department at the Yale School of Drama and then a teacher and director in Los Angeles, also expresses his opinion about the role of the director as theatre artist and concludes with a note on actors who are trained in media other than the stage.

DIRECTORS TALK A LOT ABOUT "DIRECTORIAL CONCEPTION," IMPLYING THEY ALWAYS SEEM TO BE PROCEEDING FROM SOME KIND OF MASTER PLAN. DO YOU ALWAYS BEGIN WORK WITH A CLEAR-CUT CONCEPTION OR DO YOU SOMETIMES EVOLVE ONE AS YOU GO ALONG?

Unconsciously every artist has a concept. It's almost the definition of an artist, isn't it? But the good artist, I think, solves the conceptual problems in *writing* the book, *composing* the symphony, *painting* the picture or whatever. Now in the back of his head, if he is an artist, he is being subconsciously guided by something that he sees there. Jackson Pollock is throwing paint along that canvas. Now if that's all there were to it, we'd all be millionaires, because I can throw paint, too. But there must be something different about the way Jackson Pollock throws the paint. . . .

SOME OF THE GREATEST PRODUCTIONS OF THE NINETEENTH AND EARLY TWENTIETH CENTURIES WERE THE WORK OF WHAT WE DISPARAGINGLY CALL "AUTOCARATIC DIRECTORS": THE MEYERHOLDS, THE REINHARDTS. IS THERE A CASE TO BE MADE FOR THE AUTOCRAT-DIRECTOR AS OPPOSED TO THE GENIAL DEMOCRAT WHO SEEMS TO HAVE TAKEN HIS PLACE TODAY?

. . . I don't think democracy has any place in art, I'll tell you that right off the bat.

Democracy is fine if you want to vote about clean toilets or pay or rehearsal hours and things like that. You can vote from morning to night but nobody can vote anything artistic; that must come from the creative source. And in the theatre, the creative source for all departments—the acting, the text, the scenery, the costumes, the lighting, the make-up, the music and so on—must have the same center. And that center is the director. . . .

Remember in Sunset Boulevard *Gloria Swanson says, "In those days, we had faces"? Well in those days, we had voices.*

YOU ACTUALLY SAW THE PERFORMANCES OF ACTORS SUCH AS JEANNE EAGELS, LAURETTE TAYLOR, DUDLEY DIGGES, WALTER HAMPDEN, JOHN BARRYMORE. WHAT DISTINGUISHED THOSE ACTORS FROM COMPARABLE ACTORS OF OUR PRESENT GENERATION? First of all, they could speak English. They all had voices. Remember in *Sunset Boulevard* Gloria Swanson says, "In those days, we had faces"? Well, in those days, we had voices. I remember . . . John Barrymore, certainly. Walter Hampden made a kind of nineteenth-century Shakespearean sound. Each one of them had a distinctive voice. Then Strasberg came along and said, "All of that is shit—the only thing that is important is emotion, 'true feeling.'" That was the collapse of theatre in this country, and I think it's going to take us a long time to get over it.

DOES IT HAVE ANYTHING TO DO WITH THE FACT THAT THESE ACTORS WERE, IN A SENSE, BORN AND BRED ON THE STAGE, NOT CONDITIONED BY MEDIA WORK LIKE

CONTEMPORARY ACTORS? Absolutely. I go mad in my own workshop because people work all week with microphones. In films and television, they don't want actors to speak up. There's this little man sitting there with a knob who doesn't want the needle to flick past some point on his dial. If you get too loud, they just turn you down. If you're too soft, they turn you up. Also, film and television actors don't have to be able to think clearly the way good stage actors do. If they can't tell what you're thinking, they just zoom in and give the audience a close-up of your eyes so that everyone can see that you are or aren't happy. The machine is doing all the acting for you.

Today we have a whole series of actors who work in films. Very few of them have tackled the great parts—and when they do, they just mangle them.

THEY'RE SMALLER THAN LIFE RATHER THAN LARGER THAN LIFE. Right—but given the choice, I'd rather be larger than life.

Excerpted by permission from the Charles Marowitz interview with Robert Lewis in the April 1986 issue of *American Theatre*. Published by Theatre Communications Group.

Designing both settings and lighting, Oenslager worked in opera, ballet, musicals, and straight dramas. His designs always reflected his conviction that the designer is "essentially an artist/craftsman." He believed that the designer's knowledge must include a history of architecture, painting, and engineering; the designer must always remain flexible and allow the freedom of his or her imagination to guide design development. The visual details of his designs reflect his academic dedication to historical accuracy and research (Fig. 17.8). Oenslager was also a consultant on many noted theatre structures, including Avery Fisher Hall and the State Theatre at Lincoln Center and the John F. Kennedy Center for the Performing Arts in Washington, D.C.

MAJOR ANTIREALIST MOVEMENTS

Expressionism Expressionism actually brought to the theatre ideas that reflected disillusionment more than realism. Here, however, we must tread carefully and remind ourselves that the theatre is both visual and dramatic. On the one hand, the painter's revolt against naturalism came to the theatre in visual form in scenic design, and designs that followed expressionism in painting became extremely influential. For the playwright, on the other hand, expressionism was merely an extension of realism and naturalism that allowed playwrights more flexible means to express their reactions to specific items observed in the course of human experience. The Swedish playwright-novelist August Strindberg, for example, had turned inward to the subconscious in such expressionistic plays as *A Dream Play* (1902) and *The Ghost Sonata* (1907). In so doing, he had created a presentational rather than representational style. (See the profile of Strindberg in this chapter.)

Figure 17.8 *Donald Oenslager, scene designs for* Uncle Tom's Cabin 1933. *Compare these designs with the designs for the conventional nineteenth century productions of* Uncle Tom's Cabin *in Figures 4.12 and 16.16. The realistic visual detail suggested by Oenslager's design reflects his conviction that imagination can be inspired by research into such fields as architectural and social history.*

[Courtesy of the New York Public Library.]

The dissillusionment of German expressionism after World War I is typified by the plays of Ernst Toller (1893–1939) and Georg Kaiser (1878–1945). Toller's personal struggles, his communistic idealism, and his opposition to violence and revolution are reflected in the heroine of *Man and the Masses* (1921). Sonia, a product of the upper class, leads a strike for peace. Her desire to avoid violence and bloodshed is opposed by the mob Spirit (the Nameless One), which seeks just those results and the destruction of the peace that the strike is intended to achieve. For leading the disastrous strike, Sonia is imprisoned and sentenced to death. Kaiser's *From Morn until Midnight* (1916) traces its way through the nightmarish life of a bank clerk whose pursuit of happiness is shattered at every turn; *Gas* (Fig. 17.9) is about the universal destructiveness of technology and the doomed idealism of the younger generation.

Expressionism also found its way to America. Elmer Rice's *The Adding Machine* (1923), for example, features Mr. Zero as a cog in the great industrial machinery of twentieth-century life. He stumbles through a pointless existence until he finds himself replaced by an adding machine, goes berserk, kills his employer, and is executed. Adrift even in the hereafter, he is too narrow-

August Strindberg: From Naturalism to Expressionism

After an unhappy childhood that doubtless contributed to the deep pessimism of his work, the Swedish dramatist August Strindberg (1849–1912) began his theatrical career as an actor. His first major play, *Master Olof* (1872), was not produced in Sweden until 1881. The lack of success of his early dramas propelled him to spend much of the years between 1883 and 1896 abroad. Influenced by the naturalism of the French author Émile Zola (1840–1902), Strindberg's plays of this period, especially *The Father* (1887), *Miss Julie*, and *The Creditors* (both 1888), as well as the one-act play *The Stronger* (1889), focused on sin, crime, pathological behavior, and a deadly battle between the sexes (Strindberg married three times, each disastrously).

In 1895–1897, following a severe nervous breakdown, Strindberg took up alchemy and occultism. The naturalism of his early works subsequently developed into *realism* (or, as he called it, "neonaturalism"), through which he explored his version of spiritual reality in four historical dramas completed in 1899 and *The Dance of Death* (1901), among other works.

In his later life, Strindberg's plays became increasingly experimental, heavily symbolic, and dreamlike in structure. Such works as *The Crown Bride* (1901), *Dream Play* (1902), and *The Great Highway* (1909) anticipate some of the major trends of twentieth-century drama: expressionism, surrealism, and the theatre of the absurd.

Always involved in the production of his plays, Strindberg cofounded the Intimate Theatre in Stockholm in 1907. For it he wrote his last group of plays, including his expressionist masterpiece, *The Ghost Sonata* (1907).

Figure 17.9

Emil Pirchan, stage design for George Kaiser's Gas. *Schillertheatre, Berlin, 1928. Expressionist drama often uses machines of destruction as images in technocratic nightmares to distort and emphasize a vision of the direction in which the modern world is headed:* Gas *is actually a trilogy about a son and daughter's idealistic rebellion against everything that their industrialist father stands for, including the conviction of a demented engineer that devastating "explosion after explosion" is the way to conquer the universe.*

The Modern Theatre

minded to understand the happiness offered to him there. He becomes an adding-machine operator in heaven and finally returns to earth to begin his tortured existence all over again.

Social Action   In response to worldwide political and social upheaval, the early twentieth-century theatre, witnessed numerous production experiments aimed at encouraging social action. Typical of the devices used by social-action advocates were interpretive approaches to subject matter of a social, and even political, nature, including fragmentary scenery and generally distorted visual elements. For the most part, such artists sought to combine the traditional goals of theatre—to entertain and to teach—hoping that through entertainment they could motivate spectators to action in the larger world of social interaction outside the theatre.

Vsevelod Meyerhold

Vsevolod Meyerhold   An excellent example came from the Moscow Art Theatre in the person and work of the producer-director Vsevolod Meyerhold (1874–1942). Meyerhold's plays were a direct product of the Russian Revolution and its attempts to transform a vast and backward society: For Meyerhold, a revolutionized society required a revolutionized theatre. His approach, however, led him to difficulty on two counts. First, his schematic treatment of the actor was not acceptable to Stanislavski, still the dominant force in the Moscow Art Theatre. Second, Meyerhold was considered too "formalistic"—that is, more concerned with the experimental form of the production than its "message"—to appeal to the masses. Nevertheless, by the time he was removed from his post in the 1930s, he had earned fame and influence throughout Europe and America.

Meyerhold shared the belief that the director was the supreme artist in the theatre and freely rewrote scripts to suit his own ends. He devised a system of actor training called "biomechanics," the object of which was to make an actor's body an efficient "machine" for carrying out the instructions of its operator (the director). Meyerhold's actors were often required to swing from trapezes, do gymnastic stunts, spring up through trap doors, and even transport scenery across the stage on rollerskates.

Central to Meyerhold's viewpoint was the concept of *theatricalism*: Rather than striving to imitate or depict life, he wished the audience to be fully aware that they were in a theatre, never to confuse theatre with life. Desiring to inspire in his audience the need for social action outside the theatre, Meyerhold removed many of the devices that theatre typically uses to hide its theatricality—curtains for example, were removed so that backstage areas and lighting instruments were fully visible (see Fig. 17.10). He also introduced a practical and theatrical style of staging called *constructivism*. Settings, called "constructions," consisted of various levels and playing areas of a completely nonobjective nature; scenery functioned not as background but rather as a series of structures on which actors could perform and with which they could be totally integrated. Ultimately, the stage, the actor, and all aspects of the performance were conceived as parts of a machine to be manipulated by the director.

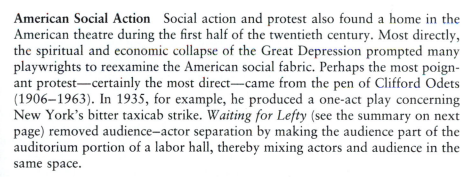

Figure 17.10 *Scene from Meyerhold's production of* Don Juan, *1910. Ostensibly mounting a production of a play by Molière, Meyerhold "redesigned" both the play and its performance to remind the audience that they may function as central participants in the theatrical experience. Playfully extinguishing the boundaries among auditorium, stage space, and backstage, he dropped chandeliers from the ceilings over both stage and auditorium. The proscenium and front curtain have been removed; screens for prompters are clearly visible at either side of the stage, and stage hands dressed in period costume as "proscenium servants" stand ready to maneuver scenery in full view.*

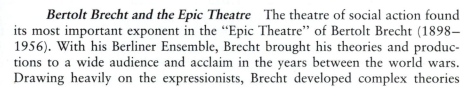

Bertolt Brecht

American Social Action   Social action and protest also found a home in the American theatre during the first half of the twentieth century. Most directly, the spiritual and economic collapse of the Great Depression prompted many playwrights to reexamine the American social fabric. Perhaps the most poignant protest—certainly the most direct—came from the pen of Clifford Odets (1906–1963). In 1935, for example, he produced a one-act play concerning New York's bitter taxicab strike. *Waiting for Lefty* (see the summary on next page) removed audience–actor separation by making the audience part of the auditorium portion of a labor hall, thereby mixing actors and audience in the same space.

    Bertolt Brecht and the Epic Theatre   The theatre of social action found its most important exponent in the "Epic Theatre" of Bertolt Brecht (1898–1956). With his Berliner Ensemble, Brecht brought his theories and productions to a wide audience and acclaim in the years between the world wars. Drawing heavily on the expressionists, Brecht developed complex theories

The Modern Theatre

Waiting for Lefty

A bare stage occupies the front of the room. Members of a labor-union the strike committee debate the wisdom of a strike for higher wages. The final decision hinges on the opinion and arrival of Lefty Costello. As the debate proceeds in the interim, four scenes depicting corruption and poverty in American society are interspersed. A fiery taxi driver named Agate urges the union members to strike and stands up to the abusive, crooked union leaders. When news comes that Lefty, the union's champion, has been murdered, the cry rises to a fever pitch: "Strike! Strike! Strike!"

In the first (and in subsequent) production, the mixing of actors and audience in the auditorium created such an electric atmosphere that members of the audience actually began shouting "Strike! Strike! Strike!" with the actors.

---

about theatre and its relationship to life, and he continued to mold and develop those theories until his death. Brecht called his approach "epic" because he wanted to characterize it as a revolt against "dramatic" theatre. Essentially, he strove to move the audience out of the role of passive spectator and into a more dynamic relationship with the play. Toward this end, Brecht postulated three circumstances—historification, alienation, and epic. In order to make the actions presented seem unfamiliar, *historification* removed events from the lifelike present to the past. According to Brecht, the playwright should make the audience feel that if they had lived under the historical conditions presented onstage, they would have taken some positive action. Moreover, because the audience could also see that things have in fact changed, they should also be inspired to make changes in their own present conditions as well. *Alienation* was part of the goal of making things unfamiliar. Many devices could be used, such as calling the audience's attention to the make-believe nature of the production or inserting songs and film sequences.

Like Meyerhold, Brecht believed that the audience should never confuse the theatre with reality: Rather, the audience should see the play as a comment on life that must be watched critically. Alienation, therefore, meant that spectators should judge what they see in the theatre and apply it to life outside—although they will no doubt become emotionally involved on some level, spectators must be "alienated" from the play's events. Brecht did not subscribe to the unified approach to production. Rather, he saw each element as independent and, thereby, as a device to be employed for further alienation. Theatricality characterized the production elements of scenery, lighting, costumes, and properties (see Brecht's comments on scene design in Chapter 10).

Finally, Brecht called his theatre *epic* because he believed that his plays resembled epic poems more than traditional dramas. His plays presented a story from the point of view of a storyteller and frequently involved narration and changes of time and place—changes that might be accomplished with nothing more than an explanatory sentence. *The Good Woman of Setzuan* (Fig. 17.11A), *The Caucasian Chalk Circle* (1945) (Fig. 17.11B), *The*

Figure 17.11A
Brecht's The Good Woman of Setzuan.

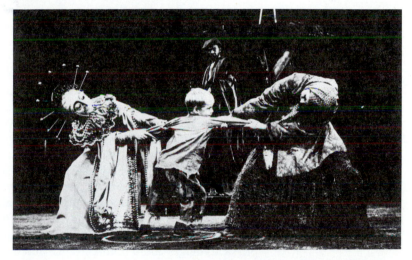

Figure 17.11B   Brecht's The Caucasian Chalk Circle. *Brecht argues that dependence on instincts and emotions only leads to a certain passive acceptance that hardly encourages revolutionary thinking. Later plays like* The Good Woman of Setzuan (1940) *and* The Caucasian Chalk Circle (1945) *feature a new Brechtian character—the female revolutionary—whose central importance seems to dictates a modification in the formula. The Good Woman is a prostitute with maternal instincts who must fight with equal ruthlessness to win both her property and her offspring. In Chalk Circle, the heroine is split as two women who seek custody of the same child: a real mother who tries to get the boy through law as property and a foster "spiritual" mother who wins the boy because she is willing to give him up rather than hurt him. Although the law is normally on the side of property rights and "reason," emotion triumphs even over maternal instincts that have been corrupted by the ways of the commercial world.*

Threepenny Opera (1928—see Fig. 10.15), *Mother Courage* (1939—see the summary in Chapter 2), and *Galileo* (1939/1947) are some of Brecht's more important works.

Following in the Brechtian tradition were such German playwrights as Max Frisch, whose works deal with the general question of guilt, and Friedrich Dürrenmatt, who emphasized the interplay of social and moral responsibility. Later came Peter Weiss, whose *The Persecution and Assassination of Jean-Paul Marat as Performed by the Inmates of the Asylum of Charenton under the Direction of the Marquis de Sade* (1964), an elaborately theatricalized vision of history and revolution in the making in an insane asylum, has become one of the century's most celebrated plays.

Antonin Artaud

Antonin Artaud and The Theatre of Cruelty   Antonin Artaud's collected essays, entitled *The Theatre and Its Double* (1931–1937), provided tremendous challenge to practitioners and theorists of the modern theatre. Although Artaud (1896–1948) had very little practical experience in the theatre, his ideas proved to be extremely influential in charting the course that modern theatre was to take. Preferring Eastern religious and metaphysical theatre over the psychological and intellectual bias that he found in Western theatre, Artaud attacked the latter and urged its disciples to return to what he perceived to be the roots of Western theatre—that is, magic, myth, ritual, and dance.

Artaud's writings appeared shortly after he had witnessed the performance of a Balinese dance troupe at the Paris Exposition of 1931. What he saw was a dancer who, having entered a trance, became possessed by the dance itself and seemed to exert a mysterious power over the audience. The Eastern preoccupation with the "inner theatrical life" captivated Artaud, who found that preoccupation vastly superior to Western logic and dramatic materialism. Artaud thereafter sought a theatre of sensory experience in which human characters communed with the forces of the universe. He sought a theatre that could exorcise the emotional, psychological, and moral demons of modern Western man. Because it would do so at any cost, Artaud's approach has become known as *theatre of cruelty:* It would be a theatre in which violent physical images could both entrance and assault the sensibility of a spectator "seized by the theatre as by a whirlwind of higher forces." He wanted to free the repressed unconscious. Cruelty, however, was not physical, and violence was not to be used for its own sake: Rather, Artaud envisioned a process of purification that, ultimately, would rid society of institutionalized violence.

Finding the language of the traditional theatre unresponsive to contemporary needs, Artaud also rebelled against the customary use of language. He wanted instead a new theatricalism in which communication went beyond the words of the actors to a "subterranean current of impressions, correspondences and analogies." The language that he envisioned encompassed sounds used for their "vibratory quality"—onomatopoeia, cries, and intonations. Everything that took the stage was intended to create an effect on the senses. Artaud wanted people to take the theatre seriously as a means of looking at the hypocrisy of society, facing themselves honestly, and realizing their own deepest, latent powers. His answer lay in the cruelty of absolute honesty in facing oneself.

Absurdism Pirandello's departures from realism helped to create the mold from which emerged a movement called *absurdism*. By placing a meaningless present somewhere between a guilt-ridden past and an unknowable future, the philosophical movement known as *existentialism* also contributed to the absurdist approach to theatre. From such antecedents came numerous dramas, probably the best known of which were written by the French philosopher and playwright Jean-Paul Sartre (1905–1980). Sartre's existentialism held that there were no absolute or universal moral values and that humankind inhabited a world without purpose; men and women, therefore, were responsible only to themselves. Dramatizing the logical conclusions to be drawn from "a consistent atheism," plays like *No Exit* (1944) and *The Condemned of Altona* (1959) translate Sartre's existential viewpoint into dramatic form. *The Flies* (1943) re-creates Aeschylus' Orestes as an existential hero seeking the meaning of his life in social and political engagement.

Albert Camus (1913–1960) was the first playwright to use the term *absurd*—a state that he considered to be a result of the gulf between humankind's aspirations and the meaninglessness of the universe in which individuals live. Finding one's way in a chaotic universe, then, became the theme of such plays as *Caligula* (1945).

Samuel Beckett

Beckett and Ionesco After these two playwrights came a series of theatrical innovators who differed quite radically from Sartre and Camus, both of whom—at least in their approach to theatrical form—strove to bring order out of absurdity. The plays of Samuel Beckett and Eugène Ionesco, for example, tend to point only to the absurdity of existence and to reflect the chaos that these playwrights perceive in the universe. Their plays are chaotic and ambiguous, and the absurd nature of these plays tends to make analysis a matter of interpretation. *Waiting for Godot* (1958—see the synopsis below), the most

Waiting For Godot

A barren landscape populated only by a withered tree surrounds two tramps who wait for a mysterious person named Godot. Their major goal seems to be only to pass the time. In so dong they tell stories, relive the past, argue with each other, and eat scraps of food. Into the scene comes Pozzo with a slave, Lucky, held like a dog on a rope. Pozzo chats with the two tramps and Lucky "performs" by thinking out loud. Then they leave. At the end of Act I a boy enters to tell them that Godot will not come today—but certainly he will come tomorrow. In Act II the landscape is the same, but the tree has grown a few leaves. The two tramps again are faced with the task of passing time, which they do in similar fashion to Act I. Pozzo returns with Lucky only this time Pozzo is blind and Lucky does the leading. The boy reappears to tell them that Godot will not come today either.

popular work of Samuel Beckett (*b.* 1906), has been interpreted in so many ways to suggest so many different meanings that it has become an eclectic experience in and of itself. Beckett left it to the audience to draw whatever conclusions they wished about the work confronting them. The works of Ionesco (*b.* 1912) are perhaps even more baffling, using nonsense syllables and cliches for dialogue, endless and meaningless repetition, and plots that have no development. Ionesco called *The Bald Soprano* (1950), for example, an "anti-play," and his other works reflect virtually the same approach (see Fig. 17.12). The absurdist movement has influenced other playwrights and production approaches, including those of English and American playwrights like Harold Pinter, Edward Bond, Caryl Churchill, David Hair, Edward Albee (see Chapter 4), David Mamet, Sam Shepherd (see the PROFILE below), and David Rabe (see the interview in this chapter).

Pluralism

The great social turmoil of the late 1960s and early 1970s made a distinct impression on the arts. "Happenings," "group gropes," and "participatory performances" all contributed to a new kind of theatre which, as often as not, was performed not in traditional theatre buildings but in streets, parks, garages, and vacant lots. Convention was ignored, and traditional theatre split at the sides. In an era of global and domestic strife, life began to imitate art, and scenes of ritualized madness seemed more like a synthesis of Pirandello, Brecht, Artaud, and Ionesco than a response to real life. Theatre since the 1960s has remained vital largely because of its diversity. Unfortunately, that diversity also makes it impossible to do more than scan the landscape.

Figure 17.12 Ionesco's The Chairs. *Paris, 1957. An elderly couple prepares to host an important speech on the secrets of existence, welcoming invisible guests who take their places at a proliferation of empty chairs. The old people jump out the window just before the speaker makes his pronouncement, but then he turns out to be deaf and dumb anyway. In order to assist future directors of* The Chairs *(1952), Ionesco jotted down some notes on the play's purpose:*

> To express the void by means of language, gesture, acting and props. To express absence. To express regret and remorse. The unreality of the real. Original chaos. The voices at the end, the noises of the world, mutterings, the world in ruins. . . . the voices at the end: the sound of the world, of us, the audience.

The theme of the theatre of the absurd, says Ionesco, is the "theme of man astray in the labyrinth, without a guiding thread."

Sam Shepard: Varieties of the Real

Moving from the surreal to the realistic, Sam Shepard (*b.* 1943), one of America's most prolific living dramatists and probably the most critically acclaimed, has written more than forty plays as well as a number of screenplays. His first play, *Cowboys,* was produced off-Broadway in 1964. From the start, Shepard's work, recognizable by its inventive language and revolutionary structure, has resisted easy categorization, in part because he not only explores a wide range of subjects but relies on a variety of sources. His subjects include American stereotypes and myths, the disintegration of the family, the betrayal of the American dream, and the search for roots. Among his influences are rock and roll, the graphic arts and dance, the pop and countercultures, Hollywood's version of the American West, and hallucinatory experiences. Yet, as one critic suggests, Shepard's plays "constitute a series of facets of a single continuing act of imagination."

Eleven of Shepard's plays have earned Obies (off-Broadway awards) for distinguished writing, including his first full-length work, *La Turista* (1967). Other well-known plays are *The Tooth of Crime* (1972), a rock drama that is also a critique of American social values and mythologies; the first play in a trilogy, *Curse of the Starving Class* (1976), about a lower-middle-class family whose interactions symbolize the chaos of American society; the second play in the trilogy, *Buried Child* (1978), for which he won the 1979 Pulitzer Prize; the third play in the trilogy, *True West* (1980), a tragicomic updating of the Cain-and-Abel story set in contemporary California; and *A Lie of the Mind* (1985, New York Drama Critics Circle Award), depicting the aftermath of a husband's brutal beating of his wife. In addition to his writing, Shepard has also acted in a number of films (*Days of Heaven* and *The Right Stuff*), his screenplay for the film *Paris, Texas* won the Golden Palm Award at the 1985 Cannes Film Festival.

Jerzy Grotowski   Jerzy Grotowski (*b.* 1933) provided the moving spirit for the Polish Laboratory Theatre. His goal was to provide dramatic experiences of serious nature linked with the primary experiences of myth. His focus lay on the actors whom he called upon to use every power and tool available to them in order to create a fusion of movement and meaning (Fig. 17.13). These powers and tools have included mime, gesture, intonation, and association of ideas. At the center of Grotowski's theory lies the concept of a "poor theatre," in which all nonessentials would be stripped away, leaving the performer alone with the audience. Grotowski espoused his ideas in the book *Towards a Poor Theatre,* from which he has gained tremendous influence in Europe, England, and America.

Grotowski typically rearranged scripts and actor–audience relationships

Figure 17.13   *Grotowski's production of* Akropolis (1966): The Prisoners Think They See the Savior. It Is a Headless Doll. *Grotowski relocated a 1904 Romantic play by the Polish poet-playwright Stanislaw Wyspiański at the concentration camp in Auschwitz. The obviously appropriate sense of space as a prison is achieved by means of a claustrophobic boxlike set; properties double as the apparatus necessary for building gas chambers. Wyspiański's original takes place in a Polish city on Easter and romanti- cizes contemporary history by drawing parallels with biblical and classical ancient his- tory. Working in Poland in the aftermath of a very different episode in history, Grotowski constructs parallels of a much different sort: Headless corpse of the Savior in hand, the procession of prisoners descends at the end in the chambers that they have built.*

for each production. In order to develop their abilities, his actors lived commu- nally as ascetics. His experiments drew on a variety of sources, from the Moscow Art Theatre of Stanislavski to the Indian *kathakali* and the Japanese Noh (see Chapter 14). Grotowski eventually became more and more interested in psychodrama and therapeutic theatre, and in America, his Theatre of Sources thus became involved in private psychological and physical confronta- tions.

Peter Brook   Peter Brook (*b.* 1925) gained a reputation as an innovative director through startling theatrical productions of Shakespeare, such as *A Midsummer Night's Dream* (see Fig. 5.5). His career began in the traditional theatre, but he abandoned that direction to pursue innovations that would place him at the forefront of the avant garde. He became a close ally of both Grotowski, whom he brought to London, and Artaud, whose theatre of cruelty was the conceptual base for Brook's production of Weiss' *Marat/Sade* in 1964. Brook's lasting influence also stems from his book *The Empty Space,* which attacks contemporary theatre practice and points to his vision of theatricalism based on four kinds of theatre:

Figure 17.14   *Peter Brook's Orghast Part II. Founder of the International Center for Theatre Research and, with Charles Marowitz (who conducts the interview with Robert Lewis in this chapter), the Theatre of Cruelty Workshop, Brook has experimented not only with the design of the Western theatre but with the idea of a theatre whose design is inspired by cross-cultural sources and techniques. Orghast, based on an ancient Persian source, was created by the International Center for an Iranian theatre festival. The Mahabharata, first staged in a rock quarry in France, was adapted from an epic Sanskrit novel. A theatrical marathon running for some nine hours, The Mahabharata actually centered on the theme of a universal quest: the search for meaning in a world in which destructive forces cut across ages and cultures.*

1. The *deadly theater* is the sterile, conventional one that acts as a museum for the "classics," particularly Shakespeare, Molière, and opera.
2. The *rough theater* is close to the people; down-to-earth; natural and joyous; without style; antiauthority; and filled with noise, vulgarity, and boisterous action. Examples are the Elizabethans and Meyerhold's productions.
3. The *holy theater* is one of revelation and ceremony. Its rituals are the genuine ones that affect people's lives, not the pseudorituals injected in much of the contemporary theater. Artaud is the prophet of the holy theater and Grotowski its chief disciple for such productions as *The Constant Prince.*
4. The *immediate theater* is an eclectic one, vigorous, restless, full of joy—a combination of the rough and the holy. It is dynamic, not rigid.

Brook's own productions demonstrate his commitment to the immediate theater.*

* Peter Brook, "Introduction to *Marat/Sade* by Peter Weiss," from the introduction to *The Persecution and Assassination of Jean-Paul Marat as Performed by the Inmates of the Asylum of Charenton under the direction of the Marquis de Sade,* by Peter Weiss. Copyright © 1965 by John Calder Ltd. New York: Atheneum Publishers, 1965. Reprinted by permission of Atheneum Publishers.

Jan Kott: Shakespeare Our Contemporary (IV)

The Polish poet-critic Jan Kott focuses here on what, after all, is not a startlingly new argument: namely, that the themes to which Shakespeare gives voice are quite similar to those that occupy both contemporary playwrights and contemporary Shakespearean interpreters like producer-director Peter Brook and actor-director Laurence Olivier. Kott uses the occasion of Brook's 1957 production of Titus Andronicus *to argue for the similarities between the Elizabethan staging of Shakespeare and modern staging strategies borrowed from the most contemporary of the arts—the cinema.*

Brook and Olivier have both declared that they were encouraged to produce *Titus* on realizing that this play contained—though still in a rough shape—the seed of all great Shakespearean tragedies. Watching *Titus Andronicus,* we come to understand—perhaps more than by looking at any other Shakespeare play—the nature of his genius: he gave an inner awareness to passions; cruelty ceased to be merely physical. Shakespeare discovered the moral hell. He discovered heaven as well. But he remained on earth.

Peter Brook saw all this in *Titus Andronicus.* But Mr. Brook did not discover *Titus.* He discovered Shakespeare in *Titus.* Or rather—in this play he discovered Shakespearean theatre. The theatre that had moved and thrilled audiences, terrified and dazzled them.

If we were to ask the question who in our time was the first to show the true Shakespeare convincingly, there would be only one answer: Sir Laurence Olivier [see the Profile in Chapter 9]. The living Shakespeare of our time has been presented, first and foremost, in film. Film has discovered the Renaissance Shakespeare. In the [Brook] production it is the return to the true Shakespeare in the theatre through the experiences of film that amazes us most. Above all I have in mind Olivier's films: *Henry V* and *Richard III.*

The beginnings of Elizabethan tragedy were very similar to the beginnings of film. . . . Just as films do now, it fed on and digested crime, history and observation of life. Everything was new, so everything could be adapted.

IN WHAT SETTINGS AND COSTUMES SHOULD SHAKESPEARE BE PERFORMED? I have seen Shakespeare played on a huge staircase and with a background of cubist prisms . . . [and] in so-called fantastic settings with fish scales, floating gauze and armour hired from the Opera. . . . Only film has shown that one way to transmit Shakespeare's vision could be the great paintings of the Renaissance and the Baroque; or tapestries, as in *Richard III.* Of course, this had to be a starting point for gesture, visual composition, costume. In Shakespearean tragedies, Romans . . . must be Romans as seen and painted by the Renaissance.

This is the way chosen by Mr. Brook. Like a true artist, he does not copy, or impose an artificial unity. He has freely taken a full range of yellows from Titian, dressed his priests in the irritating greens of Veronese. . . . What matters is that it is painting as seen through film experience. . . . The scenes are composed like film shots and follow each other like film sequences.

Once Shakespeare's plays began to be filmed, action became as important as speech. All Shakespeare's plays are great spectacles. . . . Elizabethan theatre was a theatre for the eyes. Everything in it was really happening. The audience believed that they were watching a tempest, a sinking ship, a king with his retinue setting out for a hunt, a hero stabbed by hired assassins.

The beginnings of Elizabethan tragedy were very similar to the beginnings of film. Everything that was at hand could be included in a tragedy. Everyday events, tales of crime, bits of history, legends, politics and philosophy. It was a news-reel and an historical chronicle. Elizabethan tragedy did not follow any rules; it snapped at any subject. Just as films do now, it fed on and digested crime, history and observation of life. Everything was new, so everything could be adapted. The great Elizabethans often remind one of film producers looking, above all, for an attractive subject.

When the theatre abandoned Elizabethan convention, it also lost the spectacular quality and full-bloodedness of Shakespeare. It lacked technical means, or had too many of them. . . . Theatre has alternated between illusionism and convention. Illusionism has been flat, naturalistic or childish and operatic; convention has been abstract and formalistic, or obtrusive. Illusionism and convention alike have managed to deprive Shakespeare of awe and poetry. . . .

Shakespeare is truer than life. And one can play him only literally. Olivier's films have achieved this literal meaning and supertruth more than any theatre has. They have created a new Shakespearean language where no word is meaningless. . . .

The fact that the action of Shakespeare's plays is so condensed requires a particular kind of acting. The text is intense, metaphorical. Like a film director, Shakespeare makes frequent use of close-ups. Soliloquies are spoken directly "to the camera," i.e., on the apron stage, directly to the audience. Shakespearean soliloquy is like a close-up. A stage actor of the old school stands helpless in such moments. In vain does he try to give the soliloquy some probability. He continues to be conscious of the whole stage around him, while in fact he is meant to be alone with the audience.

Shakespeare's plays have been divided in the theatre into a number of scenes according to the places of action. After the theatre had abandoned the Elizabethan convention, it tried in vain to put the scenes together to form some sort of entity. A scenario is not divided into scenes, but into shots and sequences. Shakespeare's plays are also composed of shots and sequences.

Mr. Brook has [thus] composed his *Titus Andronicus* not of scenes, but of shots and sequences. In his production tension is evenly distributed, there are no "empty places". He has cut the text but developed the action. He has created sequences of great dramatic images. He has found again in Shakespeare the long-lost thrilling spectacle. . . .

From *Shakespeare Our Contemporary* by Jan Kott. Copyright © 1964 by Pantswowe Wydawnictwo and Doubleday, a division of Bantam Doubleday Dell Publishing Group, Inc. Used by permission of Doubleday, a division of Bantam Doubleday Dell Publishing Group, Inc.

AMERICAN ALTERNATIVE THEATRE

The New Theatre   The social distress of the 1960s spawned a reaction against the traditional commercial theatre in the United States. For example, a somewhat limited movement called the New Theatre appeared in coffee houses and off-off-Broadway theatres. Participants stressed creativity and nontraditional standards and forms and sought new kinds of theatrical materials. They mounted anti-illusionistic productions and were avowedly antitheater in their choices of performance locations. The movement was neither organized nor particularly widespread. It was the product of several highly visible groups whose talent for theatricalism made its mark. In the early days, performers worked for little or no pay and production budgets were minuscule. The New Theatre put into practice both the earlier ideas of Meyerhold, Brecht, and Artaud and those of contemporaries like Grotowski, Brook, and the absurdists.

The Living Theatre   A very visible part of the New Theatre was a group formed by Judith Malina and Julian Beck called the Living Theatre. Their work freely mixed actor and audience so that often the audience was not entirely sure what was real and what was theatrical. In the 1959 production of Jack Gelber's *The Connection,* for example, actors circulated through the audience at intermission demanding handouts. Forced to abandon its theatre because of failure to pay taxes, the group moved to Europe. On its return in 1965, it gained national attention with its production of *Frankenstein.* Highly propagandistic, the purpose of the Living Theatre was to stir the audience to social action. Its aims were Marxist and its means frenetic. Audience members were insulted and obscenities rained from every quarter as the group sought to move the audience to respond not only to the performance but to the ills of capitalism and bourgeois society.

The Black Liberation Movement   The Black Liberation movement emerged in the 1960s, when many black artists turned toward militancy, espousing such causes as "black consciousness" and even separatism. This movement found an inescapable hostility between whites and blacks, and many longed for a completely separate black nation. The rise of radical groups designed to destroy Western society was joined by a rise in black conversions to the religion of Islam. The anti-Christian and anti-Western thrust of these movements turned many blacks toward Africa and a new identity in the Third World—an attitude that turned in the 1980s to a new self-descriptive change from black to African-American.

Black artistry in the theatre continued in the works of playwrights such as LeRoi Jones (Imamu Amiri Baraka), whose visions dramatize the dangers that occur when blacks allow whites into their private lives and call for black racial integrity. In Charles Gordonne's *No Place to Be Somebody,* that cause is renewed, and violence is espoused as a legitimate means to an end in the penetrating drama of a fair-skinned black searching for his own racial identity.

The same period and philosophy also witnessed the emergence of many new black theatre companies, such as the Negro Ensemble Company, a New

Home

[*Home*] traces the life of a Southern black, Cephus, from his farmboy youth, through escape to the big city, draft evasion and jail, joblessness and welfare, disease and despair, to his return to the honest labor and creative values on the farm. What makes *Home* more than a typical change-of-fortune melodrama are the poetic language and the conventions of its production format. Cephus is played by a single actor, but all the other roles—old, young, male, female, black, white—are played by two women who take on whatever role they wish by a simple costume addition. . . . Sometimes they are characters in Cephus's odyssey; at other times they act as a chorus, helping the audience to collapse time and space and see the whole of Cephus's life from the larger viewpoint of American black history and culture. . . . The fact that the place itself never changes, although Cephus is constantly on the move, and the fact that the actors never change, although they play multitudes of different roles, suggest that *Home* is right there all the time, ready to be grasped once the inner yearning is acknowledged, ready to be offered once others are willing to help, to extend themselves, to choose roles of grace instead of confrontation.*

York voice of liberation founded by Douglas Turner Ward. From that company came the moving portrayal of Samm-Art Williams' *Home* (1979—see the synopsis above).

August Wilson (*b.* 1945) is the son of a white father and a black mother. Comfortable with the description of himself as a black nationalist, he writes with an ear attuned to the rhythms and patterns of blues and of the speech of the black neighborhoods (see the interview in Chapter 5). Wilson was founder of the Playwrights Center in Minneapolis, and his plays range from *Jitney* (1982) to a planned series of ten plays beginning with *Ma Rainey's Black Bottom* (1984) based on the black American experience. Wilson believes that the American black has the most dramatic story of all humankind to tell. A winner of the Pulitzer Prize and the New York Drama Critics Circle Award, Wilson explores important African traditions, religious rituals, and highlights of the African heritage in his plays. His concern lies with the stripping away of that heritage from blacks by whites. In plays like *The Piano Lesson* (1987), he portrays the complexity of Afro-Americans' attitudes toward themselves and their past. The conflicts between black and white cultures and attitudes form the central core of Wilson's work. (An excerpt from Wilson's *Fences* appears in Chapter 2.)

The Performance Group—Environmental Theatre   Moving out of his experiences with Grotowski's Workshop, Richard Schechner founded New York City's Performance Group. The avowed purpose of the group was to eliminate

---

* Richard Schechner, *Public Domain*. Copyright © 1969 by Richard Schechner. Indianapolis: Bobbs-Merrill, 1969, p. 146. Used by permission of the publisher, Bobbs-Merrill Company, Inc.

Martha Clarke: From the Dance to the Visual Image

Performance artist and director Martha Clarke (*b.* 1944) is one of the most original and challenging artists currently working in the American theatre. The creator of dreamlike theatre pieces that are sometimes called "moving paintings" because they are inspired by the works of famous painters. Clarke began her professional career as a dancer. In 1972, she and her teacher Alison Chase joined four male Dartmouth undergraduates who had recently formed the collaborative Pilobolus Dance Company.

Clarke's transformation from dancer to performance artist and director began in 1977 (two years before she left Pilobolus), when she worked with the actress Linda Hunt to create *Portraits,* a show composed of Hunt's dramatic monologues and Clarke's dance solos for New Haven's famed Long Wharf Theatre. The two women followed this with *A Metamorphosis in Miniature* (Obie, 1982), an adaptation with music of Kafka's *Metamorphosis.* Clarke's next work, *The*

Garden of Earthly Delights—a series of sketches derived mainly from the surreal religious allegories of the fifteenth-century Flemish painter Hieronymus Bosch—opened off-off-Broadway to great critical acclaim in 1984. Clarke's first collaboration with composer Richard Peaslee and lighting designer Paul Gallo, *Garden* showed the trademarks of her later work: an elegant minimalist yet intensely personal style coupled with a surrealistically visual imagination that sacrifices narrative logic in order to create a mood through nonliteral images and dramatic vignettes treated with cinematic fluidity.

Since then, Clarke has conceived *Vienna: Lusthaus* (Obie, 1987), whose increasingly nightmarish tableaux attempt to capture a civilization on the verge of collapse as Europe moves toward World War I. More recent works include *Miracolo d'Amore* (1988), an exploration of love combining dance, opera, and theatre, and *Endangered Species* (1990), in which Clarke employs grand scenic effects and a cast of humans and circus animals to recycle some of her favorite themes—sex, death, oppression, and genocide.

the sentimentalism of the contemporary theatre by eliminating the barriers between audience and actor. Performance was seen as a sort of communal celebration. The work of the Performance Group grew out of exercises derived from Grotowski and from the collective dynamics of rehearsals. The Group's first major production was *Dionysus in '69* (1968–1969), based partly on Euripides' *The Bacchae* and partially on rituals originating in the group's exercises and rehearsals (see Fig. 17.15). Language was distorted, and the chorus chanted and wailed in frenetic rituals involving amplified sound and nudity.

This outburst of expressive freedom exemplified a new cooperation and collaboration among the members of the group. Schechner's approach is often

Figure 17.15 *The Performance Group,* Dionysus in '69 *(the Birth Ritual). See the comment on Dionysian ritual and the birth of theatre at Figure 15–1. The cult of the god Dionysus is the subject of Euripides'* The Bacchae, *which is the basis for the Performance Group's version. The actor at center-right is the god emerging from the birth canal formed by the rest of the company as the chorus. Founded by proponents of off-off-Broadway experimental theatre, the Performance Group was leftist in its politics and confrontational both as a matter of political strategy and as a means of using the techniques of* environmental theatre *to propose radically new ways of perceiving human activity. The choice of subject matter in* Dionysus in '69, *then, suggests the theme of seeing the "rebirth" of the theatre experience in primitive—and theoretically shocking—terms (hence the nudity).*

called *environmental theatre* because he argued that society itself should move in the direction of collaborative and cooperative approaches like those pioneered in the theatre. In pursuit of his ends, Schechner created a chart of differences between traditional and "new" theatre:

Traditional	*New*
plot	images/events
action	activity
resolution	open-ended
roles	tasks
themes/thesis	no preset meaning
stage distinct from house	one area for all
script	scenario or free form
flow	compartments
single focus	multifocus
audience watches	audience participates, sometimes does not exist
product	process*

* Richard Schechner, *Public Domain* (Indianapolis: Bobbs-Merrill, 1969), p. 146.

Profile

David Rabe: Everybody is Sane in Realism

Along with Lanford Wilson, David Mamet, and Sam Shepherd (see the PROFILE in this chapter), David Rabe (b. 1940) is one of this country's foremost contemporary playwrights. A Vietnam veteran, Rabe has treated, sometimes controversially, themes of physical and emotional violence in plays that use the war as a backdrop: in Sticks and Bones *(1969), for example, David Nelson, the elder son of Ozzie and Harriet, returns from Vietnam blind and enraged. (Rabe also wrote the screenplay for the film* Casualties of War.*) In this 1991 interview, he discusses both Vietnam and television, as well as his devotion to language as a dramatic tool for combining his seemingly paradoxical interest in brutality and physicality on the one hand and psychological introspection on the other. The mix, he suggests finally, is not entirely suitable for realistic treatment.* Hurlyburly *(1984) is about drug- and people-abuse in Hollywood.*

MANY OF THE MALE CHARACTERS YOU WRITE HAVE THIS HOODLUM, DEMENTED QUALITY. WHY IS THAT? RABE: *I like to have a world in which a particular lingo exists that people are restrained by—an idiom that is a kind of vision of the world. Jargon is, by both the values it espouses and those it prohibits, a defining vision. In* Streamers *and* Pavlo Hummel, *there's the language of the army, the melting pot of all those different neighborhoods and slang, plus the army jargon. It's a very masculine vision. The way they speak very much makes them who they are. It's a choice, a dramatic strategy of some kind. In* Hurly-*

burly the characters all talk the language of high tech and Hollywood and then also wherever they're from, and in the amalgam of all this, a kind of stage poetry can be found. I like to use these things kind of metaphorically or stylistically, not trying to be like the realistic play where everything is proportionate and where the statements or the characters are reflecting a reality that already exists, physically and emotionally. Rather, the words are inventing the stage, and character reality and event, as they go.*

YOU'RE KNOWN AS A, MAYBE THE, VIETNAM PLAYWRIGHT, AND IT'S OBVIOUS THAT VIETNAM IS BACK AS A DOMINANT TOPIC IN THE POPULAR CULTURE. WHAT DO YOU MAKE OF THIS? There is no overview about the war. . . . Nothing ever seemed to capture the arc and divergence of the whole thing, the unique tone of it. Each guy who went to Vietnam seemed to come back from his own particular Vietnam. . . .

I feel that a lot of what's on TV is a dissolving of the experience. It's just America eating the reality of Vietnam, the real phenomenon; it's being consumed and transformed into something in people's minds, something quite unreal, I think. The end result is that it's increasingly difficult to have any real impact anymore. Everything is just part of the vast entertainment field. The conventional is overwhelming people's ability to perceive that which is original. A kind of sentimental, high-tech sheen has been glossed over it all—not just over the war, but over everything.

ISN'T THIS WHAT EDDIE [THE CENTRAL FIGURE IN HURLYBURLY] RAILS AGAINST WHEN HE RANTS AT THE TV? I always thought that once the audience began to see Eddie's distress—the brilliance of his mind and the waste of it, the burning virtue in him turned in on itself—I always felt that the

510　　　　　　　　　　　　　　　　The Modern Theatre

Everything is just part of the vast entertainment field. . . . A kind of sentimental, high-tech sheen has been glossed over it all—not just over the war, but over everything.

recognition of his ideas, a kind of sympathetic chord in his sensibility being heard and responded to by the audience, would draw them to him. He has a kind of innocence and gullibility, Eddie does. He's very open, really, I felt that by the end you would be with him completely. But somehow that never happened. The play does not get interpreted as if there was a questionable society around it, a sociological context, materialistic and deluded, that might in some way be conditioning and directing the characters. The New York production tried to isolate the play, to make it eccentric, so that the audience would feel that this is some odd Hollywood group, rather than that these people can be found anywhere, in a wide variety of occupations.

WHAT'S IN THIS PLAY THAT'S DIFFERENT FROM THE BEHAVIOR OF CERTAIN WHEELER-DEALERS ON WALL STREET OR THE TEXAS S&L GUYS, OR WASHINGTON, D.C. POLITICIANS, OR FOOTBALL PLAYERS, ATHLETES? The only common denominator to all these groups is this time and this country. Everybody's addicted, and in the Los Angeles pro-duction I tried to make it clear that cocaine and TV are both drugs. . . .

WHAT ABOUT THE QUESTION OF REALISM, IN TERMS OF WHAT YOU'VE DONE WITH IT OR TO IT? I've never written a realistic play. . . . What I'm saying is that it's not where a play is set or whether the language appears contemporary that creates "realism" as I mean it. Realism is an underpinning construct, which declares the validity of a strict cause-and-effect being always at work in human events, a proportionate relationship between events and the forces that create them and which they create. I yell at you, so you yell at me. Your response, in this system, is dictated by the nature of my attack—you react proportionately to my stimulus. It's a Newtonian, clockwork, mechanistic view, and it's very comforting to us, but in our souls we know it's not true. . . .

Realism excludes from experience the unconscious. The unconscious makes people behave in ways that are not strictly dictated by their present circumstances. Something happens and this whole other thing shows up, this agenda in action. Realism doesn't allow for that. It's sane—everybody is sane in realism, no matter how crazy they are.

Excerpted with permission from the January 1991 issue of *American Theatre Magazine.* Published by Theatre Communications Group.

Theatre today is a mix of "modernists," who still believe that theatre requires a representation of an action, and "postmodernists," who, in Robert Palmer's words, believe that theatre represents "an archeological shift in the presuppositions of our thinking." Playwrights as such seem unnecessary to the postmodernists. Rather, they are makers of theatre—people such as Richard Foreman and Robert Wilson, who call performance art "the theatre of images." Theatre, like the other arts, has entered an age of pluralism.

The Theatre of Images: Robert Wilson   Visual appeal rather than the written script forms the basis for Robert Wilson's experimental work. His imaginative productions have earned him the reputation of a "seer genius" and a "feeler genius." Sensual imagery forms the focus of such works as *Einstein on the Beach* (1976), produced at the Metropolitan Opera House in New York. The visual emphasis of his productions (which are often collaborative efforts) stems from the fact that Wilson was trained as a painter and uses a painter's eye to form what the audience responds to.

Numerous other "groups" and approaches have filled the theatre and other places with what, arguably, may be termed "theatrical" production. Mime troupes, puppet theatre, and "happenings," or performance art, all have made their claim to inclusion in the annals of theatre experience (see Figs. 17.16A and 17.16B). Some quickly fade away after bright bursts of energy, while some demonstrate considerable staying power amid a limited following. More and more often in recent years, locations other than traditional theaters have witnessed these performances. Art galleries, open public places, and streets have become performance locations. Mixtures of live and recorded images occur. Improvisation in the tradition of the commedia dell'arte often finds its way to the fore. Frequently, although these nontraditional performances have explicit political messages to transmit, at the same time, many have no clear didactic purpose. Applying Aristotelian analysis to these diverse applications simply does not work.

To the degree that one's own preconceptions of what constitutes "theatre" apply to such performances they may or may not be seen as "theatre," but rather as some entirely different art form or some interdisciplinary, mixed-media form: valid as expressions of art though not within the unfolding tradition of the theatre.

Figure 17.16A *The Bread and Puppet Theatre,* Domestic Resurrection Circus 1971.

The Modern Theatre

Figure 17.16B   *The San Francisco Mime Troupe, L'Amant Militaire, 1967. The Bread and Puppet Theatre, which is located in Vermont, was founded by producer-puppeteer Robert Schumann in 1961; the San Francisco Mime Troupe first appeared in the parks and streets of San Francisco in 1962. The Puppet Theatre typically uses outsized puppets (actors on stilts) to lend proper dimension to performances, parades, and pageants on such themes as the colossal danger of modern war. More overtly political in its origins, the Mime Troupe often uses interactive techniques to enlist spectators as social activists in the war on racism, militarism, and other modern evils. Both favor collective production and outdoor performances.*

Scenic Design Since World War II

Although the 1930s were marked by notable experimentation in scenic design, the Depression and war years slowed development in the commercial theatre. With the advent of the 1950s, the American theatre saw many experimental and progressive activities disappear, and a more mature and established style of design began to emerge. The profession was reinforced by strong unions and the construction of new theatre buildings at educational institutions as well as in most major metropolitan communities in America. New audiences were created, many of whom would never view a Broadway show, and regional theatre became as important to the urban scene as parks and museums.

Television also began to provide visual staging—something that, of course, had not been necessary in the radio industry. In addition, colleges and universities began creating theatre training programs designed to graduate professionally oriented designers. Experimentation in design was encouraged by the new theatre buildings themselves, with their multiform stages and electronic equipment. Newly available plastic materials also allowed for new solutions to old problems. The proscenium arch no longer separated the actor from the audience, and the two now became more integrated into a "theatrical experience."

The Broadway theatre was graced with the vitality and talents of such designers as Lemuel Ayers (1915–1955) whose designs displayed his fresh, colorful approach to musical comedies with a sense of poetic realism (Fig. 17.17). Award winning Oliver Smith (*b.* 1918) has been one of the most active of contemporary designers, with over three hundred productions to his credit. Smith moved easily among genres, designing for musical comedy, drama, ballet, and opera, as well as film (Fig. 17.18). Originally a student of architecture, he quickly moved into the professional design field, where his versatility as well as his colorful palette made him the top American designer of the 1950s and 1960s. The husband-and-wife team of William (*b.* 1920) and Jean (*b.* 1921) Eckart also divided their time among musical comedy, drama, and films until moving to university teaching at the decline of the Broadway theatre in the 1970s. All of their designs displayed a strong sense of delicacy and color. Each of these designers is a product of university and professional school training.

By 1960, rising costs due to increased salary and material expenses began to create problems for live performances. Electronic shifting devices, required to eliminate backstage salaries, added to initial production design costs. Designers with graduate degrees in theatre began to establish themselves in television, film, and theatre. With the advent of the new regional theatres throughout America, young scene designers, no longer confined to Broadway productions, accepted assignments in Dallas, San Francisco, Minneapolis, Atlanta, and Washington. Veteran designers like Mielziner, Oenslager, and Alswang took on the additional chores of theatre consulting, assuring that new theatre buildings would be functional as well as architecturally inspirational.

Howard Bay (1912–1987) is probably best remembered for his startling design for *Man of La Mancha* (1965) at the ANTA Washington Square Theatre. The setting consisted of a breathtaking, floating thrust stage with sus-

Figure 17.17 *Lemuel Ayers, scene design for* Cyrano de Bergerac.

[New York Public Library.]

The Modern Theatre

Figure 17.18 *Oliver Smith, scene design for* Brigadoon.

[New York Public Library.]

pended stairs. The design dramatically changed the old-fashioned concept of pictorial design so long associated with commercial postwar musicals. Bay taught scene design at Brandeis University for fourteen years and was noted for using many innovative materials in his productions.

Boris B. Aronson (1900–1980) began designing on Broadway in the early 1930s, after some years of work with New York Yiddish Theatre. He spent the next forty years as one of the American theatre's most prolific and respected scenic designers. He was the designer for some of Broadway's most successful productions, but truly hit his stride starting in the mid-1960s with his wonderful and imaginative settings for the musicals *Fiddler on the Roof* (1964), *Cabaret* (1966), and *A Little Night Music* (1975), among others.

Peter Wexler (*b.* 1936) drew the attention of audiences with his inventive organic setting for the Association of Producing Artists' production of *War and Peace* (1962). He quickly moved to become resident designer for Los Angeles' new Mark Taper Theatre after designing its initial offering of *The Devils* (1967). He followed this assignment with an extraordinary design for revolving stages for the Broadway musical *The Happy Time* (1968). In 1973, he designed the scenery, costumes, and visual effects for the Metropolitan Opera's huge production of *Les Troyens* (Fig. 17.19). Wexler was one of the designers who responded to the appeal of new advances in materials and

Figure 17.19
Peter Wexler, scene design for Les Troyens, 1973.

Figure 1.38   Peter Wexler, scene design for *Les Troyens.* Metropolitan

mechanics in the 1960s. His designs captured the atmosphere essential to an environment for the play, rather than limiting themselves to time and space aspects alone.

The 1980s witnessed a definite decline in commercial Broadway productions but a distinct rise in regional theatre production and an increase in the number of working artists in the field of design. The training in education centers across the country has resulted in increased strength in the level of creativity, experimentation, technical skills, imagination, and sheer artistry on the part of American designers. No longer is the design just the environment of the play: It is now frequently the essence of the play, insinuating a mood or suggesting an atmosphere coupled with a rhythm inherent in the script and the total production. In musicals like *Starlight Express* and *Phantom of the Opera,* one can argue that the design *is* the production. Today's designers work easily among the various media of theatre, opera, ballet, and television and strive for flexibility in adapting to various theatre locations and stage requirements. Currently, productions like *Cats, Starlight Express, Les Misérables,* and *Phantom of the Opera* all are graced by lavish and innovative settings.

As in any aspect of the modern theatre, many more individuals deserve mention than the scope of this text allows. In closing, two designers must also be mentioned. Josef Svoboda, a Czechoslovakian whose experiments and teaching grew out of his association with Prague's Laterna Magica in the 1950s, has undertaken frequent workshops and design assignments in Europe and North America up to the present time (see Fig. 10.5B). Ming Cho Lee also emerged as a major name in theatrical design, creating fresh use of space, form, and forging an important link between theatrical design and contemporary visual art.

The Modern Theatre

SUMMARY

A conscious movement toward *realism* in the theatre sought an objective and truthful portrayal of the real world—with the result that contemporary life became the principal subject matter for playwrights of the time.

• Among the playwrights who exemplified realism in the theatre were Henrik Ibsen, Anton Chekhov, George Bernard Shaw, Eugene O'Neill, Tennessee Williams, and Arthur Miller.

• The realistic approach also involved a number of black playwrights—especially those associated with the *Harlem Renaissance* movement of the 1920s.

• *Naturalism,* a style closely associated with realism and one that is dominated by objectivity rather than personal opinion, found adherents in theatre personalities like David Belasco. Luigi Pirandello emerged as a bridge between realism, naturalism, and the *nonrealist directions* that were soon to emerge.

• Realism and naturalism also affected directing practice and movements such as the *Independent Theatre Movement.*

• Late in the nineteenth century, *antirealism* and *theatricalism* took an opposite direction from realism and naturalism:

> *Symbolism* held that truth could be grasped only through symbols;
>
> *The New Stagecraft* emphasized avoidance of depictive scenery and harmony between actor and setting;
>
> *Eclecticism* held that the stage environment must be appropriate to a specific play;
>
> *Expressionism* turned inward toward the subconscious;
>
> *Social action* sought to motivate the spectator into action outside the theatre;
>
> *Epic theatre* drew on expressionism and sought social action;
>
> *Absurdism* took Luigi Pirandello's departures from realism and drew on existentialism to create a new direction.

• The great social turmoil of the 1960s turned the arts and theatre in new directions that reflected the *pluralism* of contemporary society:

> The *New Theatre*—which stressed creativity and nontraditional standards for performance;
>
> The *Living Theatre*—which freely mixed actors and audience members at the intersection of the real and the theatrical;
>
> The *Black Liberation Movement*—which moved African-American playwrights in new directions;
>
> The *Performance Group*—which sought to eliminate the sentimentalism of contemporary theatre by breaking down the barriers between audience and actor;
>
> The *Theatre of Images*—which hinges on visual appeal rather than the written script.

• *Scenic design since World War II* has been marked by experimentation and the emergence of a number of outstanding scenic artists.

A Timeline

Theatre and General World Events

	Theatre	General Events
600 BC		
532	City Dionysia organized in Athens	
525	Aeschylus born (*d.* 456)	
500 BC		
496	Sophocles born (*d.* 406)	
493	Theatre of Dionysos	
486	Comic competition introduced at City Dionysia	
480?	Euripides born (*d.* 406)	
ca. 468	Third actor introduced in Greek theatre by Sophocles	
458	Aeschylus' *The Oresteia*	
449	Acting competition introduced at City Dionysia	
448?	Aristophanes born (*d.* 388?)	
445–31		Pericles, beginning of the Athenian "Golden Age"
431	Euripides' *Medea*	
ca. 430	Sophocles' *Oedipus the King*	
428?		Plato born (*d.* 348?)
411	Aristophanes' *Lysistrata*	
400 BC		
384		Aristotle born (*d.* 322)
ca. 365	First Roman theatrical performance	
300 BC		
204?	Plautus' *Miles Gloriosus*	
200 BC		
161	Terence's *Phormio*	
100 BC		
55	First permanent Roman theatre built	
29		Beginning of Roman Classicism—the Age of Augustus
15	Vitruvius' *De Architectura*	
0		
33 AD	Death of Jesus	
80	Colosseum completed (Rome)	
100		
117		Roman Empire at its greatest extent
200		
286–93		Diocletian divides Roman Empire
300		
ca. 300	Sudraka's *The Little Clay Cart* (India)	
309		Christianity legalized in the Roman Empire
400		
ca. 400	Kalidasa's *Sakuntala* (India)	
476		Fall of Rome
500		
ca. 595		Buddhism introduced to Japan
600		
637		Moslems conquer Jerusalem
700		

	Theatre	General Events
800		
900		
ca. 925	"*Quem quaeritis*" trope (Switzerland)	
ca. 999-1002		Leif Ericson explores North America
1000		
1095		First Crusade begins
1100		
ca. 1100		First universities founded in Europe
ca. 1125	Mansion stages appear in Europe	
ca. 1192 (-1338)		Kamakura period begins (Japan)
1200		
1215		Magna Carta
1279 (-1368)		Yuan Dynasty begins (China)
1300		
ca. 1313		Gunpowder introduced in Europe
1368 (-1644)		Ming Dynasty begins (China)
ca. 1375	*Second Shepherd's Play*	
1398	Confrèrie de la Passion founded (France)	
1400		
ca. 1400-1550	Morality plays flourish in Europe	
1438		Gutenberg begins experiments in printing
1452		Leonardo da Vinci born (*d.* 1519)
1475		Michelangelo born (*d.* 1564)
1492		Columbus lands in the New World
1500		
1500	*Everyman*	
ca. 1515		The Protestant Reformation begins
1519-22		Magellan circumnavigates the globe
1545	Serlio's *De Architettura*	
1564	William Shakespeare born (*d.* 1616)	
1609-18		Johannes Kepler publishes laws of planetary motion
1585	Teatro Olimpico (Vicenza)	
1588	Marlowe's *Dr. Faustus*	
1590-1610		Development of the microscope
1595	Shakespeare's *Romeo and Juliet*	
1600		
1601	Shakespeare's *Hamlet*	
1605	Shakespeare's *King Lear*	
1609		Galileo constructs his first telescope
1610	Jonson's *The Alchemist*	
1611		King James Bible issued
1618	Teatro Farnese (Parma)	
1622	Molière born (*d.* 1673)	
1636	Corneille's *The Cid*	Harvard College founded
1649-60		English Commonwealth
1653	Chikamatsu Monzaemon born (Japan) (*d.* 1724)	
1660		Restoration of Charles II to English throne
1664	Molière's *Tartuffe*	
1665-66		Newton formulates the laws of gravitation

	Theatre	General Events
1675	Wycherley's *The Country Wife*	
1679	Comédie Française founded	
1688		"The Glorious Revolution" in England
1688-1703		Genroku period (Japan)
1694	Voltaire born (*d.* 1778)	
1700		
1700	Congreve's *The Way of the World*	
1728	Gay's *The Beggar's Opera*	
1732	Covent Garden Opera House (London)	
1737	Licensing Act (England)	
1748	Izumo's *Chushingura* (Japan)	
1749	Johann Wolfgang von Goethe born (*d.* 1832)	
1765	*Autos sacramentales* banned in Spain	
1769		James Watt patents the steam engine
1773	Goldsmith's *She Stoops to Conquer*	Boston Tea Party
1775-83		American Revolution
1777	Sheridan's *The School for Scandal*	
1784	Beaumarchais' *The Marriage of Figaro*	
1787	Tyler's *The Contrast*	First steamboat launched
1788		U.S. Constitution ratified
1789		French Revolution begins; George Washington becomes President
1794	Chestnut Street Theatre (Philadelphia)	
1800		
1802	Victor Hugo born (*d.* 1885)	
1803-15		Napoleonic Wars
1808-32	Goethe's *Faust,* Parts I and II	
1813	Richard Wagner born (*d.* 1883)	
1816	Gaslight introduced at the Chestnut Theatre; limelight invented	
1826	Duke of Saxe-Meiningen born (*d.* 1914)	
1828	Henrik Ibsen born (*d.* 1906)	
1836	Büchner's *Woyzeck*	
1839		Daguerre demonstrates his photographic process
1844		Samuel Morse demonstrates his telegraph
1859		Darwin's *On the Origin of Species*
1861-65		U.S. Civil War
1863	Constantin Stanislavski born (*d.* 1938)	
1870		Electric arc lighting introduced
1872	E. Gordon Craig born (*d.* 1966)	
1873	Max Reinhardt born (*d.* 1943)	
1874	Vsevelod Meyerhold born (*d.* 1940)	
1877		Bell patents the telephone
1878		Edison introduces the phonograph
1879	Ibsen's *A Doll's House*	
1887	Théâtre Libre (Paris)	
1890	Ibsen's *Hedda Gabler*	
1891	The Independent Theatre (London)	
1893	Strindberg's *Miss Julie;* Shaw's *Candida*	
1895	Wilde's *The Importance of Being Earnest*	X-rays discovered
1896	Antonin Artaud born (*d.* 1948); Jarry's *Ubu Roi*	Olympic games revived
1897	Rostand's *Cyrano de Bergerac*	
1898	Moscow Popular Art Theatre; Bertold Brecht born (*d.* 1956)	

	Theatre	General Events
1900		
1903		Wright brothers demonstrate power-driven airplane
1904	Chekhov's *The Cherry Orchard*	
1905	Maeterlinck's *The Blue Bird*; Shaw's *Major Barbara*	Einstein publishes special theory of relativity
1907	Strindberg's *Ghost Sonata*	
1912	Actor's Equity Association formed; Sorge's *The Beggar*	
1914-18		World War I
1915	Provincetown Playhouse	
1917-20		Russian Revolution
1920	O'Neill's *The Emperor Jones*	League of Nations founded
1921	Pirandello's *Six Characters in Search of an Author*	
1926		First successful television demonstrated
1924	O'Neill's *Desire under the Elms*	Union of Soviet Socialist Republics established
1927	Kern and Hammerstein's *Showboat*	
1929		Penicillin discovered
1931	The Group Theatre	
1933		Franklin Roosevelt becomes president; Adolf Hitler comes to power
1935	Gershwin's *Porgy and Bess*	
1935-40		Radar developed
1936-39		Spanish Civil War
1938	Artaud's *The Theatre and Its Double*; Wilder's *Our Town*; Brecht's *Mother Courage*	
1939-45		World War II
1943	Rodgers and Hammerstein's *Oklahoma!*	
1944	Brecht's *The Caucasian Chalk Circle*	
1945		United Nations founded
1948		Transistor invented
1946	O'Neill's *The Iceman Cometh*	First all-electronic digital computer goes on-line
1947	Williams' *A Streetcar Named Desire*; Actors' Studio	
1949	Miller's *Death of a Salesman*	
1953	Beckett's *Waiting for Godot*	DNA structure described
1954	New York Shakespeare Festival	
1956	Osborne's *Look Back in Anger*	
1962	Albee's *Who's Afraid of Virginia Woolf?*	Cuban missile crisis
1963		Assassination of John F. Kennedy
1964	Weiss' *Marat/Sade*; Jones' *Dutchman*; The Open Theatre	
1967	MacDermot and Ragni's *Hair!*	
1968	Performance Group	Martin Luther King, Jr., assassinated
1969		Men land on the moon
1970	Brook's *A Midsummer Night's Dream*	
1975	*A Chorus Line* opens	
1978		First test-tube baby
1981		AIDS diagnosed
1983	Mamet's *Glengarry Glen Ross*	
1988	Webber's *Phantom of the Opera*	
1989		Berlin Wall falls
1991	*A Chorus Line* closes	War in the Persian Gulf; collapse of the Soviet Union and the Soviet bloc

Glossary

Accessories Details like scarves, jewelry, shirts, and shoes that complete a *costume* and give it individuality

Acoustics The qualities of a theatre that affect how clearly sounds can be transmitted in it

Actor-manager Nineteenth-century actors who performed the role of producer and director and from whose concentration of duties emerged the concept of the modern director

Actors Equity The national actors' union

Aesthetic distance The proper psychological and physical separation between the audience and the action that enables the audience to become involved at a level appropriate for understanding and meaning

Angle Direction chosen for *light* to strike an object

Apron The part of the stage that extends out in front of the curtain line

Arena form/theatre-in-the-round A physical arrangement in which the audience completely surrounds the stage or playing area

Artifact The *function* of art as the product of the ideas and/or technology of a specific time and place

Aural elements (or sound) That aspect of the *production* that communicates through what the audience hears, including music, actors' voices, and sound effects produced both on and off the stage

Barn door Device used in a *fresnel spotlight* to shape the beam of light

Body tone The energy conveyed by the body and its movements

Business manager. *See* House manager/business manager

Casting The process of choosing actors to play specific roles in a play

Ceiling units Large, *framed scenic units* designed to form a ceiling over an interior setting

Character Aspect of the play consisting of the psychological motivations of the persons in it

Character makeup *Makeup* that provides significant alteration of the actor's features

Chiaroscuro Use of light and shade to enhance three-dimensionality

Classicism Play and production *style* that focuses on intellect and structure and concentrates on restraint and control

Climax End of the *complication* and turning point in the series of *plot crises* the conflicts bring to an end

Color Complex visual phenomenon helpful to the lighting designer in setting the tone of a scene

Color rendering Colored drawing that provides a complete and accurate picture of *stage costumes*

Comedy Highly complex play *type* embracing a wide range of theatrical approaches—from intellectual wit to slapstick

Comedy of manners *Type* of dialogue-centered, "high" comedy popular in the seventeenth century and characterized by intellectual wit

Communication The process through which the artist *shares* a perception of human thought or interaction with a *respondent*

Communication model A model of theatre that emphasizes the *process* of *experience* and *response* on the part of the audience that comes into contact with the production

Community theatres Generally nonprofit local producing organizations staffed by nonsalaried amateurs and supported by local funding

Complication Part of the *plot* comprising a series of conflicts or *crises* that increase in intensity

Composition In fabric, the way that *costume cloth* is constructed—for example, by knitting, crocheting, braiding, knotting, or felting

Construction head (or **shop foreman** or **master stage carpenter**) Staff member responsible for scene construction, rigging, and assembly

Contextual criticism *Criticism* that sees the artwork as the result of several forces and functions, including such related materials as the artist's biography and philosophy, prevailing social and political conditions, and so forth

Costume Everything about the actor that the audience sees but also including such items as foundation garments that give shape and underpinning to the clothing

Crisis Point in the *plot* at which events or forces require of characters that decisions be made or actions taken

Criterion of communication Criterion for *judgment* that focuses on the interpretation of what the artist is trying to achieve and evaluating the success of the effort

Criterion of craftsmanship Criterion for *judgment* that focuses how well the work is made as a touchstone for evaluating the success or effect of an artwork

Criticism A detailed process of analysis performed in order to gain enhanced understanding and appreciation of an artwork in one or more of its aspects

Cues Rehearsed signals, such as spoken dialogue, stage business, or lighting changes by which the stage manager communicates to actors and technicians some transition in the production

Cues (lighting) Instructions for the control-board operator indicating what, when, and how lights are changed during a performance

Denouement Final resolution of the *plot*, lower in intensity than the *climax*

Dimmer Device for controlling the *intensity of light*

Director's concept The director's overall vision of the play and the production—its meaning and goals

Discovery Aspect of the *plot* in which information is revealed about characters, their relationships, and so forth

Downstage area Those parts of the stage closest to the audience

Downstage center The center portion of the stage closest to the audience

Draperies Large pieces of fabric hung to mask the backstage areas from the audience's view

Dress parade Period, just prior to *dress rehearsal*, when all the costumes are assembled, on stage, and under light

Dress rehearsal *Production stage* at which all elements, including prepared costumes, meet near-performance conditions

Drop *Scenery*, framed or unframed, equipped with a bottom weight for raising and lowering

Educational theatres *Producing* organizations located at and sponsored by educational institutions, often with professional equity associations

Electric-arc welding A method of metalworking using an electric spark arcing between an electrode rod and the metal to be welded

Ellipsoidal spotlight Lighting instrument with an ellipsoidal reflector that produces a sharp, hard-edged beam

Empathy Our immediate emotional, mental, and physical *response* to events that we witness or situations in which we are not direct participants

Ensemble effect Effect of variety and coordination achieved by casting actors of different but complementary types or voices

Entertainment The *function* of art that offers a means of escape from everyday activities or concerns; the artistic function of amusing or giving pleasure to respondents

Exposition Aspect of *plot* in which the playwright provides background information

Expository sound Sound required by the play—for example, doorbells, telephone rings, and gunshots

Expressionism Play and production *style* that tries to evoke in the audience responses to experience similar to the artist's by expressing the underlying reality of the play's subject matter rather than its surface appearance

Extended stage A variation of the open-stage or proscenium forms in which the action wraps around the audience

Facial expression Use of facial muscles and features to convey meaning

Farce Kind of "low comedy" involving exaggerated physical actions, mistaken identities, and pratfalls

Fittings Series of appointments for the actor with the costumer in which the costume is measured and tested for fit and function

Flat. *See* Plain flat

Floor plan. *See* Ground plan

Fly loft Area over the stage from which scenery and instruments can be raised and lowered by a series of cables, ropes, and pulleys

Force The intensity of sound, regardless of its volume

Foreshadowing Preparation for subsequent action that keeps the audience clear about *plot* development

Formal criticism *Criticism* that attempts to analyze an artwork with no external conditions or information applied to it

Framed scenery Two-dimensional *scenic units* constructed with rigid supporting members

French scenes A method of dividing the play into parts that change each time a person enters or leaves the stage

Fresnel spotlight Lighting instrument with a spherical reflector that produces a controllable soft-edged beam

Front elevation A scaled drawing designed to show the actual details of the audience side of scenic units

Gas-metal-arc welding A method of metalworking using a wire-fed electrode and a flexible hose leading to a nozzle

Gas welding A method of metalworking using a mixture of oxygen and acetylene

Gesture Hand and arm movements

Greasepaint Common name of a stage makeup that comes in a tube

Ground plan (or floor plan) A scaled drawing showing the dimensions and placement of the setting as seen from above

Half-blackout A convention indicating a break in the action in which stage lights are left on dimly so that actors and stagehands can see to move about the stage without running into furniture

Hand properties A category of properties used by the actors

House manager/business manager One or two individuals with managerial responsibility for all audience-related and business-office activities

Humanities The field of study concerned with the expression and perception of human thought and interaction

Inciting incident Moment in the *plot* at which an action or decision upsets the current state of affairs

Inflection A change of pitch on a single syllable

"In one" technique Method of changing scenes by shifting smaller or larger components of a single set to create multiple sets

Intensity Brightness and quality of light

Irony Device, often in *plot*, marked by such a deliberate contrast that the apparent or literal meaning and the intended meaning are just the opposite of one another

Language The essential aspect of the script through which the playwright communicates overall tone and style and reveals character, theme, and level of *verisimilitude*

Lighting score Lighting designer's preliminary charts for plotting actor placement, areas of focus, the timing of action, and other elements of the production

Low comedy Comedy that depends on action and situation, usually involving a trivial theme

Master stage carpenter. *See* Construction head

Medium of expression The vehicle, such as painting, sculpture, music, literature, or the theatre, through which the artist expresses a perception of human thought and interaction

Melodrama Mixed *type* characterized by stereotypical characters involved in serious situations portraying the forces of good and evil battling in exaggerated circumstances

Mise en scène The setting and arrangement of all the *visuals* of the production

Models Three-dimensional replicas of the stage setting

Movement Changes in any of the *properties of light*

Multiple setting *Scenic form* in which complete separate sets are designed for different locations

Musical Play *type* in which dialogue is interspersed with songs and dances, but characterized by more serious subjects and treatments than "musical comedy"

Musical comedy Play *type* in which dialogue is interspersed with songs and dances

Nonrestrictiveness A definition of art that includes among artworks anything that tries to communicate a perception of human thought and interaction through means traditionally associated with the arts

Off-Broadway theatre Collectively, professional *producing organizations* initially founded as a commercial and artistic alternative to the commercial theatre of Broadway

Open audition Audition in which actors are chosen for roles on the basis of short presentations and prior experience

Open stage A physical arrangement in which the audience is placed on one side of the action but is not separated from the actors by an archway or raised stage

Opéra comique Opera that, in addition to musical solos and ensembles, has dialogue that is spoken rather than sung

Operetta Theatrical production that has many of the musical elements of opera, but is lighter and more popular in subject and style, and contains spoken dialogue

Paint details Scaled drawings designed specifically for scene painters and presenting the units as they will be painted

Pattern Paper or canvas model from which the parts of a *costume* can be traced onto fabric

Pitch The measurable frequency of sound

Plain flat (or **flat**) The basic unit of two-dimensional *framed scenery* for the theatre

Platform A three-dimensional *scenic unit* designed to raise floor areas of the stage

Playwright Maker of plays; the theatre artist whose vision is transmitted through characterizations described by dialogue in a script

Plot The *structure* of the play, which determines its story movement, its conflict development, and its resolution

Point of attack Aspect of *plot* in which background *exposition* gives way to the development of the story

Political (or **social**) **commentary** The *function* of art that encourages political change or the modification of social behavior

Posture The manner in which the body is carried by the actor

Producer Individual, usually in the commercial theatre, with varying degrees of authority in managing the overall project of mounting a production

Production conferences Meetings between the director and other members of the artistic, craft, and business staffs during which collaborative efforts affect decisions relating to the production

Production goal An artistic vision involving the entire production and its effect on an audience

Production The actual *theatre artwork* that combines *script*, *character*, *thought*, and *visual and aural elements* into a finished single entity

Professional theatre Any *producing organization* that pays its staff, usually those with some formal relationship to

Actors Equity and *United Scenic Artists*

Profile flat A version of the *plain flat* with irregular edges added

Prompt book Stage manager's record of script changes, scene-shifting instructions, actor movements, and light, sound, and special-effects *cues*

Properties Items used on stage that are not scenery or costumes

Property manager/property head Staff member responsible for constructing and organizing all properties and items of scenic decor

Proscenium arch An opening through which the audience, sitting on one side of the stage, views the action

Proscenium stage A physical arrangement in which the audience is placed on one side of the stage and views the action through an opening called a *proscenium arch*

Prosthetics Three-dimensional pieces used for building *makeup* effects

Rate The speed at which speech is uttered

Realism Play and production *style* holding that art should depict life with complete honesty, trying to paint pictures of life as we actually experience its commonplace, often brutal aspects

Regional theatres Professional *producing organizations*, usually repertory companies, located in and supported by local venues and groups

Repertory company A permanent acting company that prepares several productions during a yearly season

Respondent Any person with whom the artist enters into communication for the purpose of sharing a perception of human thought and interaction

Reversal Any turn of fortune during the development of the *plot*

Rolling *Shifting scenery* by means of some wheel or sliding device

Romanticism Play and production *style* that focuses on an appeal to emotion, experimenting with form and language and glorifying the individual

Rough lighting plot Preliminary drawing by which the light designer draws together a variety of concerns and ideas into instrumentation and design

Roughs Costume designer's quick *pencil sketches* that translate images and ideas into pictures

Running *Shifting scenery* essentially by human power

Satire Use of derisive wit to attack folly or wickedness

Scene design The art of creating the proper visual environment for a play

Scene painting The art of theatrical painting by which two-dimensional surfaces are transformed into representations—for example, of wood, brick, foliage, and so on

Scene shop A specially designed location used for the construction of *stage scenery*

Scoop *Floodlight* for broad washes of light

Script The text through which the playwright uses *language* to communicate a play's structure and meaning

Selective visibility One of the functions of *stage lighting*—providing the audience with the ability to see

Set decoration A category of *properties* used to dress the setting

Set properties A category of properties used as parts of the setting

Setting As a *fact* of the play, the playwright's use of time and place to communicate theme and tone through the play's environment

Shop foreman. See *Construction head*

Showcase theatres Professional *producing organizations* operating in small theatres and generally offering limited-run productions

Sightline drawings Scaled drawings showing the horizontal or vertical plan of the theatre and projecting imaginary lines from the furthest seats right or left to the back of the setting

Silhouette Outline of the *costume*

Simultaneous setting The provision, in one production, of several settings that remain totally within view of the audience at all times

Social commentary. See Political (or social) commentary

Sound. See Aural elements

Source-motivated light Light that appears to come from a natural source

Spectacularism Use of lavish settings and costumes to add sensational qualities to a dramatic production

Spine The single drive that motivates the character in making decisions and taking action

Stage business Actor movements used to reinforce character

Stage manager Technical staff member in control of all performance elements requiring the coordination of actors and production technicians

Straight makeup *Makeup* used when the actor's features require no major changes to effect the character

Strength of focus The relative ability of a character to draw the attention of the audience

Style The identifying characteristics in the manner of expression, design, or execution of an artwork

Subtext The meaning that lies beneath the actual dialogue

Surface texture Particular surface of a fabric, either dull or shiny

Symbol A thing, often an object, that *represents* some other thing, whether an object, a quality, or a process, whose *meaning* is abstract or not immediately apparent

Sympathy Sensitivity to the condition of others in a deep and meaningful way

Technical director Staff member responsible for all aspects of technical production, including budgets and schedules

Technical production The craft of *turning the scene design* into reality

Theatre Aesthetic communication through an experience of the art, process, and production of works of dramatic expression

Theatre form The physical relationship of audience space to stage space

Theatre-in-the-round. *See* Arena form/theatre-in-the-round

Therapy (or **psychodrama**) The *function* whereby such artistic activities as role playing are used to treat or communicate with individuals suffering from a variety of physical and mental illnesses

Thought The aspect of the *theatre artwork* that communicates its intellectual content—its themes, ideas, and perceptions about human experience

Three-quarter stage. *See* Thrust/three-quarter stage

Thrust/three-quarter stage A physical arrangement in which the audience encircles three sides of the stage or playing area, leaving one side open to act as a scenic background or entrance to backstage areas

Thumbnail sketches Rough, rapidly drawn, basic conceptions concerned more with feelings than details

Timbre The tonal color or identifying characteristics of a single voice

Tragedy Complex theatre *type*, typically described as a play with an unhappy ending with a hero who makes a free choice that brings about suffering, defeat, and, sometimes, triumph as a result of defeat

Tragic flaw Some defect that causes the hero of a tragedy to participate in his or her own downfall

Tragicomedy Mixed *type* originally characterized as a serious play involving reversals, language appropriate to both tragedy and comedy, and ending free of disaster for the characters

Type *Character* who is larger than life—as opposed to a "real" or life-like individual

Unit set A single *setting* that serves as a scenic location for a multi-scene play; it provides a means for staging the play without the need for shifting scenes

Upstage areas Those parts of the stage furthest from the audience

Variety Any *change* in the ordered presentation of the elements of a work of art

Verisimilitude The playwright's or the production team's intended level of faithfulness to truth or reality

Visual elements That aspect of the *production* that communicates through what the audience sees, including stage settings, lighting, costumes, and properties, as well as the actors, their movements, and the *physical relationships* between the actors and the audience

Wagons *Platforms* mounted on wheels

Wardrobe stock *Costumes* made for previous productions that are kept in storage for possible reuse

Willing suspension of disbelief Ability of an audience member to accept, without condition or distraction, the *conventions* and *artifices* of the theatrical environment

Working drawings Detailed drawings used to help to clarify the *costume design* and its parts

Work of art The *process*, *product*, and *experience* in which one person's perception of human thought and interaction is expressed in a particular medium and shared with others

Worksheet Designer-prepared guide for actors and crew members who apply *makeup*

Further Reading

Antoiné, Andre. *Memories of the Théâtre-Libre*. Coral Gables, FL: University of Miami Press, 1964.

Appia, Adolphe. *Music and the Art of the Theatre*, edited by Bernard Hewitt. Coral Gables, FL: University of Miami Press, 1962.

Arnott, Peter D. *An Introduction to the Greek Theatre*. Bloomington, IN: Indiana University Press, 1963.

——. *The Theatre in Its Time*. Boston: Little, Brown, & Company, 1981.

——. *The Theatres of Japan*. New York: St. Martin's Press; 1969.

Artaud, Antonin. *The Theater and Its Double*. Trans. Mary C. Richards. New York: Grove Press, Inc., 1958.

Barranger, Milly S. *Theatre, A Way of Seeing*, 2nd ed. Belmont, CA: Wadsworth Publishing Company, 1986.

Beck, Julian. *The Life of the Theater*. New York: 1972.

Beckerman, Bernard. *Dynamics of Drama: Theory and Method of Analysis*. New York: Alfred A. Knopf, Inc., 1970.

Bellman, Willard F. *Lighting the Stage: Art and Practice*. San Francisco: Chandler Publishing Co., 1967.

Benedetti, Robert L. *The Actor at Work*, 4th ed. Englewood Cliffs, NJ: Prentice-Hall, Inc., 1986.

——. *The Director at Work*. Englewood Cliffs, NJ: Prentice-Hall, Inc., 1985.

Bentley, Eric. *The Life of the Drama*. New York: Atheneum Publishers, 1967.

Bieber, Margarete. *The History of the Greek and Roman Theater*. Princeton, NJ: Princeton University Press, 1961.

Bigsby, C. W. E. *Twentieth Century American Drama*, 3 vols. New York: Cambridge University Press, 1982–85.

Blau, Herbert. *The Impossible Theater: A Manifesto*. New York: Macmillan, Inc., 1964.

Booth, Michael. *Victorian Spectacular Theatre 1850–1910*. Boston: Routledge and Kegan Paul, 1981.

Brockett, Oscar G. *The Essential Theater*, 3rd ed. New York: Holt, Rinehart & Winston, 1984.

——. *History of the Theatre*, 6th ed. Boston: Allyn and Bacon, Inc., 1991.

——. *Modern Theater: Realism & Naturalism to the Present*. Boston: Allyn & Bacon, Inc., 1982.

——. *The Theatre*, 2nd ed. New York: Holt, Rinehart & Winston, 1969.

Brook, Peter. *The Empty Space*. London: MacGibbon and Tree, 1968.

——. "Introduction to *Marat/Sade* by Peter Weiss." New York: Atheneum Publishers; 1965.

Burris-Meyer, Harold, and Edward Cole. *Theaters and Auditoriums*, 2nd ed. New York: Van Nostrand Reinhold Company, 1964.

Carlson, Marvin, and Yvonne Shafer. *The Play's the Thing*. New York: Longman, 1990.

Carnovsky, Morris. *The Actor's Eye*. New York: Performing Arts Journal Publications, 1984.

Cheney, Sheldon. *The Theatre: Three Thousand Years of Drama, Acting, and Stagecraft* (rev. ed). New York: Longmans, Green, 1952.

Cole, Toby, and Helen Krich Chinoy. *Actors on Acting*. New York: Crown Publishers, 1980.

——. *Directors on Directing*. Indianapolis: The Bobbs-Merrill, Co., Inc. 1964.

Corrigan, Robert. *The Making of the Theatre*. Glenview, IL: Scott, Foresman, & Company, 1981.

Cunningham, Rebecca. *The Magic Garment*. New York: Longman, 1989.

Dean, Alexander, and Lawrence Carra. *Fundamentals of Play Directing*. New York: Holt, Rinehart and Winston, 1965.

Delattre, Edwin J. "The Humanities can Irrigate Deserts," *The Chronicle of Higher Education* (October 11, 1977), p. 32.

Esslin, Martin. *An Anatomy of Drama*. New York: Hill and Wang, 1976.

Fergusson, Francis. *The Idea of a Theatre*. Princeton, NJ: Princeton University Press, 1949.

Freedley, George, and John A. Reeves. *A History of the Theatre*. New York: Crown Publishers, Inc., 1968.

Gassner, John, and Ralph G. Allen. *Theatre and Drama in the Making*, 2 vols. Boston: Houghton Mifflin Company, 1964.

Gillette, Arnold S. *Stage Scenery: Its Construction and Rigging*, 2nd ed. New York: Harper and Row, Publishers, 1972.

Grotowski, Jerzy. *Towards a Poor Theatre*. New York: Simon & Schuster, Inc., 1968.

Hatlan, Theodore W. *Orientation to the Theatre*, 3rd ed. Englewood Cliffs, NJ: Prentice Hall, Inc.; 1981.

Huerta, Jorge A. *Chicano Theater*. Ypsilanti, MI: Themes and Forms, 1982.

Izenour, George C. *Theater Design*. New York: McGraw-Hill Book Company, 1977.

Jones, Robert E. *The Dramatic Imagination*. New York: Duell, Sloan, and Pearce; 1941.

Kazan, Elia. "Notebook for *A Streetcar Named Desire*" in Cole, Toby and Helen Krich Chinoy. *Directors on Directing*. Indianapolis: The Bobbs-Merrill Company, Inc; 1963.

Kernodle, George, Portia Kernodle, and Edward Pixley. *Invitation to the Theatre*, 3rd edition. San Diego: Harcourt, Brace, Jovanovich, Publishers, 1985.

Kirby, E. T. *Ur-Drama: The Origins of the Theatre*. New York: New York University Press; 1975.

Kuritz, Paul. *Playing: An Introduction to Acting*. Englewood Cliffs, NJ: Prentice-Hall, Inc., 1982.

——. *The Making of Theatre History*. Englewood Cliffs, NJ: Prentice-Hall, Inc., 1988.

Malpede, Karen, ed. *Women in the Theater: Compassion and Hope*. New York: Drama Book Publishers, 1981.

Matthews, Brander. *The Principles of Playmaking*. Freeport, NY: Books for Libraries Press, 1970.

Molière, Tartuffe. In Morris Bishop, trans. *Eight Plays by Molière*. New York: Random House, Inc., 1957.

Nagler, Alois M. *Source Book in Theatrical History*. New York: Dover Publications, Inc., 1952.

Nicoll, Allardyce. *The Development of Theatre*. New York: Harcourt Brace Jovanovich, Inc., 1966.

———. *The Theatre and Dramatic Theory*. New York: Barnes & Noble Books, 1962.

Palmer, Richard H. *The Lighting Art: The Aesthetics of Stage Lighting Design*. Englewood Cliffs, NJ: Prentice-Hall, Inc., 1985.

Rowe, Kenneth Thorpe. *The Theatre in Your Head*. New York: Funk and Wagnalls, Inc., 1960.

Rowell, George. *The Victorian Theatre*, 2nd ed. Cambridge, Eng.: Cambridge University Press, 1978.

Russell, Douglas A. *Stage Costume Design*. Englewood Cliffs, NJ: Prentice-Hall, Inc., 1973.

Saint-Denis, Michael. *Training for the Theater, Promises and Promises*. New York: Theater Arts Books, 1982.

Schechner, Richard. *Public Domain*. Indianapolis: The Bobbs-Merrill Co. Inc., 1969.

Scott, A. C. *The Theatre in Asia*. London: Weidenfeld & Nicolson, Ltd; 1972.

Sellman, Hunton D., and Merrill Lessley. *Essentials of Stage Lighting*, 2nd ed. Englewood Cliffs, NJ: Prentice-Hall, Inc., 1982.

Sontag, Susan. *Against Interpretation*. New York: Farrar, Straus & Giroux, Inc., 1966.

Southern, Richard. *The Seven Ages of the Theatre*. New York: Hill and Wang, 1961.

Sperry, Roger. *Science and Moral Priority: Merging Mind, Brain, and Human Values*. New York: Columbia University Press, 1983.

Spolin, Viola. *Improvisation in the Theater*. Evanston, IL: Northwestern University Press, 1963.

Sporre, Dennis J. *Perceiving the Arts*, 4th ed. Englewood Cliffs, NJ: Prentice-Hall, Inc., 1992.

———. *Reality Through the Arts*. Englewood Cliffs, NJ: Prentice-Hall, Inc., 1991.

———. *The Creative Impulse*, 2nd ed. Englewood Cliffs, NJ: Prentice-Hall, Inc., 1991.

———. *The Literary Spirit*. Englewood Cliffs, NJ: Prentice-Hall, Inc., 1988.

Sporre, Dennis J., and Robert C. Burroughs. *Scene Design in the Theatre*. Englewood Cliffs, NJ: Prentice-Hall, Inc., 1990.

Stanislavski, Constantin. *An Actor Prepares*. New York: Theater Arts Books, 1963.

———. *Creating a Role*, trans. E. R. Hapgood. New York: Theater Arts Books, 1961.

———. *My Life in Art*. New York: Theater Arts Books, 1924.

Styan, J. L. *Elements of Drama*. Cambridge, Eng.: Cambridge University Press, 1960.

———. *Drama, Stage and Audience*. Cambridge, Eng.: Cambridge University Press, 1975.

———. *The Dramatic Experience*. Cambridge, Eng.: Cambridge University Press, 1965.

Vatsyayam, Kapila. *Classical Indian Dance in Literature and the Arts*. New Delhi: Sangeet and Natak Akademi; 1968.

Vinson, James, ed. *Contemporary Dramatists*. New York: St. Martin's Press, 1977.

Walker, Ethel Pitts. *The Theatre of Black Americans*. Englewood Cliffs, NJ: Prentice-Hall, Inc., 1980.

Williams, Raymond. *Drama in Performance*. London: F. Muller, 1954.

Photo and Figure Credits

Chapter 1 22 Wolfgang Volz

Chapter 2 34 National Tourist Organization of Greece 36 Friedman-Abeles Collection, Performing Arts Research Center, NYPL at Lincoln Center 40 Wide World Photos 44 Ball State University of Muncie Indiana 47 Donald Cooper/Photostage 49 Utah Shakespearean Festival 49 Robert C. Burroughs 50 Victoria and Albert Museum 50 Victoria and Albert Museum 51 Victoria and Albert Museum 51 University of Arizona Theatre 54 Will Rappaport 56 Friedman-Abeles Collection, Performing Arts Research Center, NYPL at Lincoln Center

Chapter 3 62 Martha Swope 62 Donald Cooper/Photostage 63 Photo courtesy of Utah Shakespearean Festival 64 NYPL at Lincoln Center 65 Photo courtesy of Utah Shakespearean Festival 66 Western Ways Photo 67 Western Ways Photo 76 Stratford Shakespearean Festival 76 Guthrie Theatre 77 Mark Donnelly 78 W. E. Smith, Life Magazine, © Time Warner Inc. 80 Margot Berthold, Weltgeschichte des Theatres Alfred Kroner Verlag, Stuttgart 1968. 83 Photo courtesy of Utah Shakespearean Festival 88 Charles O'Connor

Chapter 4 96 Peggy G. Kellner 98 World Wide Photos 99 Vandamm Collection, Performing Arts Research Center, NYPL at Lincoln Center 99 NYPL at Lincoln Center 102 Robin Platzer/Images 103 NYPL at Lincoln Center 104 Christopher Briscoe 104 Courtesy of the Lilly Library, Indiana University, Bloomington, Indiana 104 Arena Stage 107 Christopher Briscoe 109 Vandamm Collection. Performing Arts Research Center, NYPL at Lincoln Center 110 Arena Stage 112 Photograph by Byron. The Museum of the City of New York, The Theatre Collection 112 Ball State University 114 Friedman-Abeles Collection, Performing Arts Research Center, NYPL at Lincoln Center 116 Joan Marcus

Chapter 5 118 Courtesy of the Art Institute of Chicago, Gift of Emily Crane Chadbourne, 1922.4790 123 Photograph courtesy of the Cleveland Museum of Art, Cleveland State University Theater Arts 129 Donald Cooper/Photostage 130 Joan Marcus 131 David Burnett, Contact Press/Woodfin Camp & Associates 135 Joan Marcus 140 Richard Howard 142 Tom Arntsen

Chapter 6 148 Loeb Drama Center, Harvard 150 Tony Rivenbark 162 Robert Ashley Wilson 163 Robert Ashley Wilson 164 Carol Spector Associates 165 Molinari, *Theatre through the Ages*, p. 128, by permission of F. Arborio Mello, Studio dell-illustrazione, Milano 165 Rockefeller Collection, Yale School of Drama Library 172 Dwaine Smith, Oregon Shakespearean, Ashland, OR 173 NYPL

Chapter 7 178 The Guthrie Theatre 180 Ball State University, Muncie, Indiana 183 UPI/Bettmann Newsphotos 184 Vic De Lucia/New York Times Pictures 185 Ken Regan/Camera 5 187 David S. Talbott 190 NYPL at Lincoln Center 191 Victoria and Albert Museum/Art Resource 192 Courtesy of the Lilly Library Indiana University, Bloomington, Indiana 194 © 1982 Martha Swope 195 Washington and Lee University Theatre 196 George Tarbay, Northern Illinois Theatre

Chapter 8 202 James Nachtwey/Magnum Photo 209 NYPL at Lincoln Center 210 Martin Harris/Pix Inc. 211 Edie Catto 213 © United Artists 215 Free Library of City of Philadelphia 215 Free Library of City of Philadelphia 219 Martine Franck/Magnum Photos 220 Ball State University, Muncie, Indiana 220 Peter Balestrero 225 George Tarbay 228 Christopher Briscoe

Chapter 9 232 Vandamm Collection, Performing Arts Research Center, NYPL at Lincoln Center 236 Christopher Briscoe 239 Moscow, Bakhrishin Theatre Museum 240 Christopher Brisco 241 Friedman-Abeles Collection, Performing Arts Research Center, NYPL at Lincoln Center 243 Costa Manos/Magnum Photos 244 Boyd Redinton, Photo courtesy Southern Utah University Theatre, Cedar City, Utah 84720 245 Christopher Briscoe 246 Ball State University, Muncie, IN 47306 248 Ball State University, Muncie, IN 47306 249 Western Ways Photo by Balestrero 251 Edie Catto 254 Boyd Redington, photo courtesy of Southern Utah University Theatre, Cedar City, Utah 84720 254 Christopher Briscoe 255 Christopher Briscoe 257 Courtesy of the Lilly Library, Indiana University, Bloomington, Indiana 253 White Studio Collection, Performing Arts Research Center, NYPL at Lincoln Center

Chapter 10 268 Bibliotheque Nationale, Paris 271 Margot Berthold, Weltgeschichte des Theaters, Alfred Kroner Verlag, Stuttgart. 273 Performing Arts Research Center, NYPL at Lincoln Center 275 White Studio, Performing Arts Research Center, NYPL at Lincoln Center 280 NYPL at Lincoln Center 280 Performing Arts Research Center, NYPL at Lincoln Center 289 Vandamm Collection, Performing Arts Research Center, NYPL at Lincoln Center (PH files)

Chapter 11 301 Vandamm Collection, Performing Arts Research Center, NYPL at Lincoln Center 319 Michael Le Poer/Bob Marshak (Photo courtesy of NYPL at Lincoln Center) 321 Carol Rosegg/Martha Swope Associates

Chapter 12 342 Charles O'Connor 346 Bob Dold

Chapter 13 357 Ball State University of Muncie, IN 357 Department of Drama, University of Arizona, Tucson, AZ 369 Altman 369 Altman 369 Altman

Chapter 14 389 Japan Tourist Association 1 Marunouchi, Tokyo, Japan 390 World Wide Photos 394 The NYPL Picture Collection 402 Mohan Khokar

Chapter 15 411 Alinari/Art Resource

Chapter 16 437 NYPL at Lincoln Center 454 From "The Old Book Collectors' Miscellany" 461 Metropolitan Museum of Art, New York 463 Presse-und Informationsamt der Bundesregierung 463 Presse-und Informationsamt der Bundesregierung

Chapter 17 474 NYPL 477 Performing Arts Research Center NYPL at Lincoln Center 477 Keystone View Company 478 Moscow, Bakrushin Theatre Museum 479 NYPL Theatre Collection 480 Performing Arts Research Center NYPL at Lincoln Center 484 Vandamm Collection, Performing Arts Research Center, NYPL at Lincoln Center 489 Courtesy of the NYPL 493 Giraudon/Art Resource 494 Performing Arts Research Center NYPL at Lincoln Center 495 Gerela Goedhart 495 University of Bristol Theatre Collection 497 © 1992 Martha Swope 497 The Guthrie Theatre 498 editions du Seuile 499 Bruce Davidson/Magnum Photos 500 Agnes Varda 501 AP/Wide World Photos 502 Teatr-Laboratorium 503 Nicolas Tikhomiroff 508 Mimi Cotter/People Weekly © 1986 509 Max Waldman 510 Thomas Victor/Time Magazine 512 Ron Levin 513 San Francisco Mime Group, Photo by Gerhard E. Gscheidle 516 Metropolitan Opera, New York

Line Drawings

Dennis J. Sporre, *Perceiving the Arts*, 4e. Prentice Hall, Englewood Cliffs, New Jersey. Pages 68 and 96.

Dennis J. Sporre and Robert C. Burroughs *Scene Design in the Theatre*. Prentice Hall, Englewood Cliffs, New Jersey. Pages 154, 155, 162, 163, 165, 166, 167, 169, 171, 182, 301, 302, 303, 306, 307, 308, 309.

Color Plates

2.1 Marc Bryan-Brown 2.2 Giraudon/Art Resource 2.3 Scala/Art Resource 2.4 Martha Swope 2.5 Bob Marshak 2.6 George E. Joseph 2.7 George E. Joseph 2.8 Martha Swope 2.9 Martha Swope 2.10 Martha Swope

3.1 Clive Barda/Woodfin Camp 3.2 Terry O'Neill/Sygma 3.3 Martha Swope 3.4 (top) George E. Joseph 3.4 (bottom) George E. Joseph 3.5 George E. Joseph 3.6 Bridgeman Art Library/Art Resource 3.7 Giraudon/Art Resource 3.8 (top) Martha Swope 3.8 (bottom) Martha Swope

4.1 S. Gutierrez/Viesti Associates, Inc. 4.2 Martha Cooper/City Lore 4.3 Viesti Associates, Inc. 4.4 (1A) Viesti Associates, Inc. 4.4 (1B) Robert Frerck/Woodfin Camp 4.4 (1C) Lindsay Hebberd/Woodfin Camp 4.4 (1D) Viesti Associates, Inc. 4.4 (1E) Andy Selters, Viesti Associates Inc. 4.5 (top) Lauren Freudmann/Woodfin Camp 4.5 (bottom) Michael S. Yamashita/Woodfin Camp 4.6 Mike Yamashita/Woodfin Camp

Note: New York Public Library has been abbreviated NYPL throughout the photo and figure credits.

Index

Absurd, Theatre of the, 484, 499–500
Accessories, 337–38, *cp* 3.3
Acoustics, 156, 395
Acting, 233–63
 approaches to, 237–42
 in Asian theatre, 381–82, 389, 401–2
 creating role, 242–52
 in French neoclassic theatre, 448
 in German Enlightenment, 464–65
 in life and art, 234–36
 in Restoration period, 450–51
Action, analyzing, 214–15
Actor-audience spatial relationships, 158–68, 222–23
Actor-manager, 205
Actors, 195–96, 236
 auditioning and casting, 211–14
 equipment of, 252–59
 rehearsing, 214–18
Actors Equity, 181, 186
Actors' Studio, 241, 481
Actors Theatre of Louisville, 187*f*
Act without Words II (Beckett), 142*f*
Adding Machine, The (Rice), 492–94
Aeschylus, 50*f*, 70, 121, 122–24, 409–10
Aesthetic distance, 134–36
Agamemnon (Aeschylus), 122, 123, 410
Aiken, George L., 113
Air caster, 319, 321
Ajax (Sophocles), 34*f*, 35
Akalaitis, JoAnne, 173
Albee, Edward, 102
Aldredge, Theoni V., 56*f*, *cp* 2.6, 3.3
All My Sons (Miller), 140*f*, 140–41
America, theatre in, 458–60, 495, 506
American Company, 458
American Gothic (Wood), 24, 25*f*
Anderson, Garland, 482
Androcles and the Lion (Shaw), 191*f*
Angle (light), 360
Angles-of-vision perception, 154–55, 157
Antirealism, 486–500
Antoine, André, 205–6, 207, 238, 483
Appia, Adolphe, 354, 356, 486–87
Appliqué, 310
Apron, 221
Architectural units, 310
Architecture. *See* Theatre forms and architecture
Arc light, 353
Arena form, 162, 162*f*, 168, 169–70, 171*f*, 429
Aristophanes, 26, 26*f*, 101–3, 103*f*, 105, 410, 413
Aristotle, 37, 39, 53, 96, 98, 411–12
Aronson, Boris B., 515
Artaud, Antonin, 166, 219, 498–99
Artifact, 29, 54–56
"Art of the Theatre, The" (Craig), 275
Arts, the, 16–31
 defining, 20–24
 functions of art, 24–29
 humanities, humanity and, 16, 17–20

Ashton, Anthony, 458
Asian theatre, 375–405
 in China, 376–85
 in India, 397–403
 in Japan, 386–97
Atkinson, Brooks, 86
Atmosphere, lighting and, 357–58
Atsumori, 387
Attention, 136–39
Audience, 119–47
 actor-audience spatial relationships, 158–68, 222–23
 in ancient Greece, 122–24
 in ancient Rome, 124–25
 communication and theatre, 130–33
 as critic, 145–46
 in Elizabethan England, 125–28
 in English Restoration, 128
 experience and response, 133–39
 individual and group reactions in, 143–46
 in modern times, 128–30
 as participant, 145
 perception of, enhancing, 140–42
 perception of visuals, control of, 219–26
 in Romantic era, 468–69
Auditions, 211–12
Auleum, 421
Aural elements, 41–42, 72
Ayckbourn, Alan, 228*f*, 240*f*
Ayers, Lemuel, 514, 514*f*

Bacchae, The (Euripides), 132, 171*f*, 413
Bakst, Léon, *cp* 2.2
Balcony, The (Genet), 251*f*
Bald Soprano, The (Ionesco), 500, 500*f*
Ballad opera, 455–56
Baraka, Imamu Amiri (LeRoi Jones), 506
Barber of Seville, The (Beaumarchais), 461
Barn door, 369, 371*f*
Baroque period, theatre of, 445–55
Barretts of Wimpole Street, The (Besier), 66, 66*f*, 249*f*
Bay, Howard, 266, 514–15
Beam projectors, 370–71
Beaumarchais, Pierre de, 461
Beckmann, Max, 79, 79*f*
Beckett, Samuel, 83*f*, 83–84, 142*f*, 220*f*, 499–500
Beethoven's Tenth, *cp* 3.2
Beggar's Opera, The (Gay), 53–54, 54*f*, 455–56, 456*f*
Beijing opera, 378, 379–80, 381–82, *cp* 4.5
Belasco, David, 483–84
Bérénice (Racine), 446, 447*f*
Berne, Eric, 242
Bernhardt, Sarah, 257
Besier, Rudolf, 66, 66*f*, 249*f*
Betterton, Thomas, 452, 453
Bibienas, the, 269, 270*f*, 449
Big River, *cp* 2.4
Birds, The (Aristophanes), 26, 26*f*

Björnson, Maria, 47*f*, 116*f*, 135*f*, 136, *cp* 3.1
Black Liberation movement, 506–7
Blocking, 204, 214–15, 215*f*, 364
Body, actor's use of, 252–55
Body position, 224, 224*f*
Body tone, 255
Book ceiling, 303, 303*f*
Booth, Edwin, 143*f*, 486
Boublil, Alain, 319
Boucicault, Dion, 192*f*
Box set, 469, 471
Brando, Marlon, 210, 259
Brecht, Bertolt, 43, 44*f*, 53, 219, 227*f*, 288, 495–98, 497*f*
Brighton Beach Memoirs (Simon), 175–76
Brisson, Frederick, 194
Broadway theatre, 181, 183–86, 514–16
Brockett, Oscar, 379–80
Brook, Peter, 49*f*, 96*f*, 129*f*, 209*f*, 502–3, 504
Büchner, Georg, 467
Burgess, Anthony, 76*f*
Burn This (Wilson), 39–41
Burris-Meyer, Harold, 161
Burroughs, Robert C., 49*f*, 67*f*, 220*f*, 227*f*
Burton, Richard, 329
Business manager, 199

Cage aux Folles, La, *cp* 3.3
Caird, John, 319, *cp* 2.5
Calling of St. Matthew, The (Caravaggio), 354–55, 355*f*, 360
Camus, Albert, 499
Candlelight lighting, 352–53, 353*f*
Capon, William, 458
Cariou, Len, 76*f*
Carnival, 44–45
Carudatta (Bhasa), 399
Casting, 212–14
Cats, 144, *cp* 2.10, 3.8
Caucasian Chalk Circle, The (Brecht), 496, 497*f*
Ceiling units, 303, 303*f*
Character, 39, 61–64, 70–71, 329–30, 331, 411–12
Character makeup, 346
Charlemagne, 424, 425
Chekhov, Anton, 110, 110*f*, 111, 162*f*, 239*f*, 241, 256, 477
Cherry Orchard, The (Chekhov), 477
Chestnut Street Theater (Philadelphia), 459*f*, 459–60
Chiaroscuro, 355, 355*f*
Chikamatsu, 388
Child, Harold, 50*f*, 452
China, theatre in, 376–85
Chorus (Greek), 409
Chorus Line, A, 184*f*
Chou, 382
Christ and the Woman Taken in Adultery (Beckmann), 79, 79*f*
Christo, 22, 22*f*

Chronegk, Ludwig, 207
Cid, Le (Corneille), 38, 446
Circuiting, 364–65
City of Angels, cp 2.9
Cixous, Hélène, 219
Clarke, Martha, 508
Classicism, 75–76
Climax, 38, 39f, 68, 69, 70, 356
Clurman, Harold, 86, 480, 481
Cobb, Lee J., 78f
Cocteau, Jean, cp 3.7
Cole, Edward, 161
Coleridge, Samuel Taylor, 462
Color (light), 357–58, 359
Color rendering, 337–39, cp 3.6
Color symbolism, 403
Comédie Française, 460
Comédie-Italienne, 460
Comedy, 53, 100–107, 413, 419, 449–50, 455
Comedy of Errors (Shakespeare), 334–35
Comedy of manners, 100
Commedia dell'arte, 189, 420, 435–36, 436f
Commercial theatre, 181, 183–86, 276, 514–16
Communication, 23–24, 89–90, 130–33, 180–81, 218–26
Communication model, 42
Community theatre, 188
Company (Sondheim), 175f, 194
Complication, 38, 39f, 68f, 69
Composition, 223–24, 226
Composition (fabric), 340
Concept musicals, 194
Conference, production, 209–11, 331–33, 361–64
Confrèrie de la Passion, 430, 434
Congreve, William, 128, 211, 211f, 449
Construction head, 198
Constructivism, 494
Contextual criticism, 88–89
Contrast, The (Tyler), 459
Conventions, 94, 134, 383–84, 390–91
Corneille, Pierre, 38, 98, 446
Corner blocks, 300, 301f
Corrales, 443, 443f
Costume of the Chinese (Picasso), cp 3.7
Costume plot, 332f
Costumes, 326–43, cp 3.1–3.8
   in Asian theatre, 384–85, 395–97, 403
   costume shop, 343
   design process, 331–39
   functions of, 328–31
   in history, 326–27, 327f, 414, 414f
   makeup, 344–47, 384–85, 385f, 403, 395–97, cp 3.2
   making, 339–41
   production organization, 341–43
   research, 333
Court masque, 451
Craig, E. Gordon, 275, 486–87, 488f
Crawford, Cheryl, 241
Crébillon, Jolyot de, 460
Crisis, 38, 39f, 69, 356
Criterion of communication, 89–90
Criterion of craftsmanship, 89
Criticism, 73–74, 80, 81–91
Cromwell, Oliver, 451

Cronyn, Hume, 253
Cruelty, Theatre of, 498–99
Cuba and His Teddy Bear (Povod), 193
Cues, 196–97, 197f, 367–68
Cunningham, Rebecca, 328
Curved movements, 248
Cyrano de Bergerac (Rostand), 77f, 77–78

Dan, 382
D'Architecttura (Serlio), 272, 353, 443
Dark of the Moon (Richardson and Berney), 220f
D'Avenant, William, 449, 450, 452–53
Davidson, Gordon, 190
Death of a Salesman (Miller), 78f, 78–79
Decor items, 314, 314f
Delsarte, François, 238
Denouement, 38, 39f, 68, 68f, 69, 356
Depth perception, form and, 355–56
Design. *See* Lighting design; Scene design
Design of space and time, 218–26
Desire under the Elms (O'Neill), 99, 99f, 100
DeWitt, Johannes, 127f, 444
Diaghilev, Sergei, cp 3.7
Diction, 37
Dimmer, 359
Dionysos in '69 (Schechner), 508, 509f
Director, 203–31
   emergence of modern, 204–6
   evaluating work of, 228–29
   as manager, 226–27
   responsibilities of, 208–18
   role of, 194–95, 206–8
   utilization of time and space, 218–26
Director's concept, 208
Discovery, 38, 39f, 70
Doctor Faustus (Marlowe), 261, 439, 440
Doll's House, A (Ibsen), 55, 56, 56f
Domestic comedy, 100–101
Downstage areas, 221
Downstage center, 221–22
Dramatic forms
   in Asian theatre, 378–80, 386–88, 399–400
   in Renaissance, 434–36
   in Rome, 419–20
   See also Production
Draperies, 305
Drawing(s)
   figure, 338–39
   scene design, 278–84
   working, 297, 298–99f, 339
   See also Sketches
Dress parade, 342f, 342–43
Dress rehearsals, 218, 343
Drops, 305
Dry technical rehearsal, 368
Du Bois, W.E.B., 482
Duke's Theatre, 151f, 152f
Duncan, Isadora, 275
Dunlap, William, 459
Dürrenmatt, Friedrich, 498
Duse, Eleonora, 275

Eccyclema, 417
Eckart, William and Jean, 514
Eclecticism, 487–88
Educational theatre, 181, 187–88, 276, 286

Edwin Drood, cp 2.7
Eisenstein, Sergei, 390–92
Ekhof, Konrad, 465
Electric-arc welding, 316
Elephant Man, The (Pomerance), 244f, 254f
Elizabethan England, theatre of, 125–28, 436–40, 443–45, 444f
Ellipsoidal spotlights, 354, 370, 371f
Empathy, 44–46, 139
Enemy of the People, An (Ibsen), 27, 40
English Renaissance, 326, 436–40
English Restoration theatre, 128, 449–55
English Romantics, 466–67
English sentimental drama, 455–58
Enlightenment, theatre of, 455–65
Ensemble effect, 213
Entertainer, The (Osborne), 256
Entertainment, 24, 24–25, 52
Environmental theatre, 509
Epic Theatre, 53, 227f, 288, 495–98, 497f
Escape, theatre as, 145
Etheredge, George, 449
Eumenides, The (Aeschylus), 50f, 121, 122, 123
Euripides, 132, 171f, 413
Everett, Jeanne Henderson, 3
Everyman, 54–56, 71, 426–27
Existentialism, 499
Experience, 20
   audience, 133–39
   theatre as, 43–51
Exposition, 38, 39f, 68f, 69
Expository sound, 372
Expressionism, 79–80, 491–94
Extended stage, 166, 167f

Fabric, 317, 339–40
Facial expression, 254–55
Facts about character, 242
Facts of play, understanding, 64–65
Farce, 100, 418f, 419, 435
Fausses Confidences, Les (Marivaux), 460–61
Faust (Goethe), 464, 466
Fences (Wilson), 37–38, 131
Figure drawing, 338–39
Firebird, The (Stravinsky), cp 2.3
Fittings, 341
Flats, 300–303, 301f, 302f, 303f, 455
Floodlights, 369f, 370–71
Floor space, 221f, 221–22
Flying, 320–21, 321f
Fly loft, 320, 320f
Focus, 141–42, 354–55
Folding platform, 306, 306f
Folk opera, 159
Force of voice, 259
Foreman, Richard, 511
Foreshadowing, 38, 39f, 70
Forestage-façade, 451, 457
Form, 354–56. *See also* Theatre forms and architecture
Formal criticism, 87–88
Forrest, Edwin, 235f
Framed scenery, 300
Freeman, Morgan, cp 3.4
French neoclassicism, 445–48
French scenes, 214, 215, 361

Fresnel spotlights, 369, 370*f*
Friedman, Gary, 3
Frisch, Max, 498
Frogs, The (Aristophanes), 101–3, 103*f*, 105, 410
From Morn Until Midnight (Kaiser), 492
Front elevations, 284, 287*f*
Front-of-house operations, 199
Frye, Northrop, 101
Furniture, 313
Furttenbach, Joseph, 304–5

Gallo, Paul, 508, *cp* 2.7, 2.9
Garrick, David, 450–51, 451*f*
Gas (Kaiser), 492, 493*f*
Gaslight, 353
Gas-metal-arc welding, 316
Gas welding, 316
Gay, John, 53–54, 54*f*, 455–56, 456*f*
Gelber, Jack, 506
Genet, Jean, 173, 251*f*
Georgian playhouse, 456–58, 457*f*
Gershwin, Ira, 195*f*
Gesamtkunstwerk, 204–5, 485
Gesture, 254
Ghetto (Sobol), 2–13, 174, 183, *cp* 1.1–1.8
Ghosts (Ibsen), 97, 99, 99*f*
Gielgud, John, 256
Glass Menagerie, The (Williams), 246*f*, 261–62
Globe Theatre, 166, 167*f*, 438
Godfrey, Thomas, 458
Goethe, Johann Wolfgang von, 89–90, 463–64
Goldsmith, Oliver, 450
Good Woman of Setzuan, The (Brecht), 227*f*, 496, 497*f*
Gordonne, Charles, 506
Gottsched, Johann Christoph, 463, 464–65
Graham, Martha, 190
Grand opera, 160
Grazzo, Michael, 241
Grease (Jacobs and Casey), 225*f*
Greasepaint, 346
Greek theatre, 34–35, 95, 122–24, 268, 269*f*, 326, 408–17
Green Coca Cola Bottles (Warhol), 21
Grieve, Thomas, 206*f*
Grotowski, Jerzy, 501–2, 502*f*
Ground plans, 284, 285*f*
Group Theatre, 86, 480–82
Guthrie, Tyrone, 76*f*

Hairy Ape, The (O'Neill), 79, 80, 80*f*
Half-blackout, 157
Hamlet (Shakespeare), 46–48, 47*f*, 51*f*, 256, 275, 462
Hand properties, 311
Hansberry, Lorraine, 111, 114–15, 482
Hart, Moss, 215*f*
Hatful of Rain, A (Grazzo), 241
Hedda Gabler (Ibsen), 249*f*
Hellenistic period, 416–17
Hellman, Lillian, 111, 112*f*, 113
Henry V (Shakespeare), 108*f*
Henslowe, Philip, 438–39
Hernani (Hugo), 120, 120*f*
Hersey, David, 319, *cp* 2.5
Hilferty, Susan, 334–35

Historification, 496
History plays, 107–9
Holistic approach to acting, 242
Home (Williams), 507
House manager, 199
Hrosvitha, 425
Hugo, Victor, 120, 120*f*, 319, 466
Humanities 16, 17–20
Hurlyburly (Rabe), 510–11
Hwang, Henry David, 129–30, 130*f*

Ibsen, Henrik, 27, 40, 48, 49*f*, 55, 56, 56*f*, 97, 99, 99*f*, 249*f*, 275, 477
Iceman Cometh, The (O'Neill), 223*f*
I Do, I Do (Merrick), 183*f*
Illusion, lighting and, 358–59
Images, Theatre of, 511–13
Importance of Being Earnest, The (Wilde), 51*f*, 65, 65*f*, 67, 70
Improvisation, 435
Inciting incident, 69
Independent Art Theatre Movement, 479, 485
India, theatre in, 397–403
Indians (Kopit), 66, 67*f*
Inflection, 257–58
In-one technique, 174
Intensity (light), 357–58, 359
Interaction approach to acting, 242
International Alliance of Theatrical Stage Employees (IATSE), 277
Ionesco, Eugène, 499–500
Irony, 107
Irving, Henry, 104*f*, 192, 247*f*

Japan, theatre in, 386–97
Jaremski, Kathleen M., 5, 6, 7–8, 246*f*
Jeu De Saint Nicholas, Le (John Bodel of Arras), 427
Jing, 382, 385
John Bodel of Arras, 427
Jones, Inigo, 451
Jones, James Earl, 62*f*
Jones, LeRoi (Imamu Amiri Baraka), 506
Jones, Robert Edmond, 363, 482*f*, 488
Jonson, Ben, 101, 125–26
Judgment, criticism and, 81, 84, 85, 89–90
Julia, Raul, *cp* 3.4
Julius Caesar (Shakespeare), 207*f*

Kabuki theatre, 386, 388, 389, 390–92, 395, 396*f*, 396–97, 397*f*, *cp* 4.6
Kaiser, Georg, 492
Kalidasa, 400
Kan'ami, 387, 388
Kathakali dance-drama, 400, 401, 403
Kaufman, George, 195*f*
Kazan, Elia, 78*f*, 210, 216–17, 243, 244
Kean, Charles, 50*f*, 192, 192*f*, 205, 206*f*, 207*f*, 471
Kennedy, Arthur, 78*f*
Keystones, 300, 301*f*
Killegrew, Thomas, 449, 450
King Henry VIII (Shakespeare), 453
King Lear (Shakespeare), 96, 96*f*, 97
Kirby, E.T., 376*n*
Kitchen (Wesker), 219
Klinger, Friedrich von, 464
Knowles, James Sheridan, 467

Kook, Edward K., 280
Kopit, Arthur, 66, 67*f*
Kott, Jan, 49*f*, 504
Kotzebue, August von, 192*f*, 467
Kritzanc, John, 164
Kuritz, Paul, 455
Kyogen ("Crazy Words"), 387

Lan, David, 2
Landesman, Heidi, *cp* 2.1, 2.4
Language, 37–38, 46–48, 71–72
Last Supper, The (Leonardo da Vinci), 222, 223*f*
Learning experience of audience, 144–45
Lee, Ming Cho, 516, *cp* 2.6
Legitimate drama, 159
Lekain, Henri-Louis, 237*f*
Leonardo da Vinci, 222, 223*f*
Leroux, Gaston, 136
Lessing, Gotthold Ephraim, 463
Lewis, Robert, 480–82, 490–91
Libation Bearers, The (Aeschylus), 70, 122, 123
Licensing Act of 1737, 456
Light, properties of, 359–60
Lighting design, 352–73, *cp* 2.1–2.10
   design process, 360–68
   development of modern, 352–54
   evaluating, 371–72
   functions of, 354–59
Lighting instruments, 368–71, 369–71*f*
Lighting scores, 364, 365*f*
Light plot, 364–67, 365–67*f*
Lillo, George, 456
Limited-run, 184
Linear perspective, 442
Little Foxes, The (Hellman), 111, 112*f*, 113
Liturgical drama, 425–27, 428*f*
Living Theatre, 506
London Merchant, or The History of George Barnwell (Lillo), 456
Long Day's Journey into Night (O'Neill), 483
Loquasto, Santo, 56*f*
Loutherbourg, Philippe Jacques de, 457–58
Low comedy, 100
Lysistrata (Aristophanes), 26–27

Macbeth (Shakespeare), 61–64, 62*f*, 63*f*, 64*f*, 258, 453
Mackaye, Steele, 486
Mackintosh, Cameron, 319
Macready, William, 234*f*
Maeterlinck, Maurice, 486
Major Barbara (Shaw), 101, 107, 107*f*, 191*f*, 245*f*
Makeup, 344–47, 384–85, 385*f*, 403, 395–97, *cp* 3.2
Man and Superman (Shaw), 478
Man and the Masses (Kaiser), 492
Mann, Klaus, 219
Mansion stages, 428–29
Manteo puppets, *cp* 4.2
Manual for Constructing Theatrical Scenes and Machines (Sabbatini), 443
Ma Rainey's Black Bottom (Wilson), 131, 507
Marat/Sade (Weiss), 196*f*
Marivaux, Pierre de, 460–61

Marlowe, Christopher, 261, 439–40
Mason, James, 76f
Masque, court, 451
Master stage carpenter, 198
Materials, 316–18, 317f
Mauri family, 449
Mayhew, Richard, 18, 28
M Butterfly (Hwang), 129–30, 130f
Medea (Earipides), *cp* 3.4
Medieval theatre, 268, 269f, 270f, 326, 422–30
Medium of expression, 22–23
Meininger Court Theatre, 207
Melodrama, 110–15, 467–68
Menaechmi, The (Plautus), 124–25, 440
Menander, 416
Mencken, H.L., 86
Merchant of Venice, The (Shakespeare), 104, 104f, 105, 247f, 255f
Merrick, David, 183f
Meyerhold, Vsevolod, 494–95, 495f
Middle Ages, theatre of, 268, 269f, 270f, 326, 422–30
Midsummer Night's Dream, A (Shakespeare), 129, 129f, 209f, *cp* 3.6
Mielziner, Jo, 78f, 280, 488–89, 514
Miller, Arthur, 40, 55, 78f, 78–79, 86, 95, 98, 140f, 140–41, 482–83
Mime, 419f, 419–20, 435
Miracle plays, 426
Mise en scène, 46, 469–72, 485–86
Misérables, Les (Hugo), 319, *cp* 2.5
Mitchell, Cameron, 78f
Mnouchkine, Ariane, 219
Models, 283f, 283–84
Modern theatre, 475–519
 antirealism, 486–500
 audience in, 128–30
 naturalism, 483–85, 493
 pluralism, 500–513
 realism, 78–79, 280, 476–83, 485–86, 493, 510–11
Molière (Jean Baptiste Poquelin), 87–89, 88f, 104, 104f, 106, 446–48
Mood, creating, 331, 356–58
Morality plays, 426–27
Moscow Art Theatre, 239, 275, 438, 483, 485, 494
Mother Courage (Brecht), 43, 44f
Motivation, 144–46, 358–59
Mourning Becomes Electra (O'Neill), 363
Movement, 168–70, 214–15, 223–26, 247–48, 249f
Movement (lighting), 360
Multiple settings, 172–74
Musical comedy, 116, 159
Musicals, 116, 159, 194
Music and Staging (Appia), 487
Music in Asian theatre, 380–81, 388–89, 389f, 400–401
Mystery plays, 425–26, 434

Napier, John, 319, *cp* 2.5, 2.10, 3.8
Nathan, George Jean, 86
National Endowment for the Arts, 186–87
Naturalism, 483–85, 493
Nazimova, Alla, 99f
Neher, Caspar, 288

Nemirovich-Danchenko, Vladimir 483
Neoclassicism, 77, 445–48
Neorealism, 78
Neuber, Carolina, 465
New Comedy, 416
New Stagecraft, 488–91
New Theatre, 506
New York reviewers, 86
New York Shakespeare Festival, 185
Nijinsky, Vaslav, 83
Nobel Mirror of Art, The (Furttenbach), 304
Noh drama, 386, 387–88, 389–95, 393f, 394f, 395–96
Nonartistic staff, 196–98
Noncommercial theatre, 181, 187–88
Nonrestrictiveness, 20–21
Not-for-profit regional theatre, 181, 186–87
Nudity, use of, 138–39
Nunn, Trevor, 319, *cp* 2.5, 2.10, 3.8

Observation, 245–46
Odets, Clifford, 53, 495, 496
Oedipus the King (Sophocles), 70, 75, 76f, 259–60
Oenslager, Donald, 489–91, 492f, 514
Off-Broadway theatre, 186
Of Mice and Men (Steinbeck), 180f
Of Thee I Sing (Gershwin and Kaufman), 195f
Old Comedy, 413
Olivier, Laurence, 256, 504
Olympic Theatre (Vicenza), 441–42, 442f
O'Neill, Eugene, 79, 80, 80f, 86, 99, 99f, 100, 223f, 363, 479, 483
One (Number 31, 1950) (Pollack), 17f
Open audition, 212
Open stage, 166–68
Opéra comique, 116
Operetta, 116, 159
Orchestra, 415, 416f
Oregon Shakespeare Festival, 172, 172f
Oresteia, The (Aeschylus), 122–24
Osborne, John, 256
Othello (Shakespeare), 61, 62f, 462
Ott, Sharon, 334
Our Town (Wilder), 236f, 254f

Page, Geraldine, 241
Pageant, 160
Pageant wagons, 429–30, 430f
Paint details, 284
Painting, scene, 284–91, 290f
Palladio, Andrea, 441
Palmer, Robert, 511
Pantomime, 383, 435
Paper and paper products, 318
Papier-mâché, 310
Papp, Joseph, 185, 193, *cp* 2.6
Passion Play, *cp* 4.1
Patterns, costume, 340–41
Peaslee, Richard, 508
Peer Gynt (Ibsen), 48, 49f
Perception, 133–42
 angles-of-vision, 154–55, 157
 of visuals, control of, 219–26

Performance Group, 507–9
Performance elements in Asian theatre, 380–82, 388–89, 400–402. *See also* Production
Periaktoi, 417
Personality of play, 72–80
Personal space, 132–33, 135
Phantom of the Opera (Webber), 116, 116f, 135f, 135–36, *cp* 3.1
Phlyakes farces, 418f, 419
Physical presence, casting for, 213–14
Physical response, 44–46
Physical space, 132–33
Physical theatre. *See* Theatre forms and architecture
Physique, costume design and, 337
Piano Lesson, The (Wilson), 507
Picasso, Pablo, *cp* 3.7
Picture-frame stage, 164
Pippin (Schwartz), 142f
Pirandello, Luigi, 484–85, 499
Pitch, 257
Pixérécourt, Guilbert de, 467
Place, use of, 65–66, 329, 330f
Plain flat, 300–303, 301f, 302f, 303f
Plastic foams, 310–11
Plastics, 317–18
Platforms, 306f, 306–7, 307f, 308
Plautus, 420, 440
Play, analysis of, 59–91
 approach for, 60–61
 characters, 61–64
 costume design and, 331
 criticism and, 73–74, 80, 81–91
 facts of play, 64–65
 first impressions, 60, 61
 parts of play, 67–72
 play's personality, 72–80
 setting, 65–66
Playhouses. *See* Theatre forms and architecture
Play of the Prince of Fools (Gringoire), 435
Plays, types of, 95–117
 comedy, 53, 100–107, 413, 419, 449–50, 455
 history plays, 107–9
 melodrama, 110–15, 467–68
 musicals, 116, 159, 194
 tragedy, 36, 37–42, 53, 95–100, 411–12
 tragicomedy, 110
Playwright, 94, 189–91, 208. *See also specific playwrights*
Plot, 38–39, 39f, 41, 68f, 68–70, 356, 412 light, 364–67, 365f, 366f, 367f
Pluralism, 500–513
Poetics (Aristotle), 37, 53, 96, 411–12
Point of attack, 38, 39f, 69
Political commentary, 25–27, 53–54
Pollock, Jackson, 17f
Pomerance, Bernard, 244f, 254f
Posture, 255
Povod, Ray, 193
Presentation sketches, 278–82, 281f, 282f
Pretenders, The (Ibsen), 275
Prince, Harold, 86, 116f, 135f, 136, 194, *cp* 3.1
Prince of Parthia, The (Godfrey), 458
Producer, 183, 184, 191–94
Producing organization, 181–88

Production, 35–42
 experiencing play as, 60
 organizing costumes for, 341–43
 parts of, 37–42
 practicalities of, theatre spaces and, 168–71
 See also Technical production
Production conferences, 209–11, 331–33, 361–64
Production goal, 208
Production team, 180–81, 189–99
Profanity, use of, 138–39
Professional theatre, 181–83
Profile flat, 303
Prompt book, 197, 197f, 215
Properties, 311–13, 392
Property manager/head, 198
Proscenium arch, 164, 170–71
Proscenium stage, 151, 164, 165f, 168–71, 169f, 415, 416f
Prosthetics, 346
Provincetown Players, 479
Proximity, 132–33
Psychodrama, 27–29, 52–53
Psychological motivation, 39, 71, 128

Rabe, David, 510–11
Rabelais, François, 434
Racine, Jean, 98, 446
Radcliffe, Philip, 73, 82–83
Rails, 300, 301f
Rate of speech, 258
Realism, 78–79, 280, 476–83, 485–86, 493, 510–11
Red River, 213f
Regional theatres, 186–87, 516
Rehearsal, 214–18, 250–52, 368
Reinhardt, Max, 275, 488
Religion, drama and, 376–77, 386, 397–99, 425–27, 428f
Renaissance, theatre of, 326, 434–45
Repertory company, 212, 469–72
Representation of Adam, The, 426
Respondent, 23
Response, audience, 133–39
Response, theatre as, 43–51
Restoration comedy, 449–50
Reversal, 38, 39f, 70
Rice, Elmer, 492–94
Rich, Frank, 86
Richard II (Shakespeare), 50f, 108f, 109, 206f
Richard III (Shakespeare), 504
Richardson, Ralph, 256
Richelieu, Cardinal, 446
Ricketts, C., 50f, 121f
Rigid platforms, 306–7, 307f
Rite of Spring (ballet), 83
Role, creating, 242–52
Rolling, 318–19
Romanticism, 77–78, 463, 465–72
Rome, theatre of ancient, 124–25, 417–22
Romeo and Juliet (Shakespeare), 250, 256, 329, cp 2.6
Rosenthal, Jean, 190, 362–63
Rostand, Edmond, 77f, 77–78, 467
Rough lighting plot, 364
Roughs, 335–37, 336f

Running, 318
Running Fence (Christo), 22f

Sabbatini, Nicolà, 153, 170, 443
Saint Joan (Shaw), 109, 109f, 478
Sangaku, 386
Sanskrit drama, 399–400, 401
Sartre, Jean-Paul, 499
Satie, Erik, cp 3.7
Satire, 101
Saxe-Meiningen, Georg II, Duke of, 205, 207, 207f, 485
Scaenae frons, 421
Scamozzi, Vicenzo, 441–42
Scaramouche, 435
Scene design, 265–93, cp 2.1–2.10
 design process, 278–91
 of New Stagecraft, 488–91
 since World War II, 513–17
 traditions, 266–78
 See also Technical production
Scene designer, 274–78
Scene painting, 284–91, 290f
Scenery. *See* Technical production
Scene shop, 314–16
Schechner, Richard, 507
Schönberg, Claude-Michel, 319
School for Scandal (Sheridan), 450, 450f
School for Wives, The (Molière), 104, 104f, 106
Schroder, Friedrich, 237f
Scoop, 369f, 371
Screens, The (Genet), 173
Scribe, Eugène, 476–77
Script, 37–39, 60, 94, 361
Sculptured effects and textures, 310–11
Seating comfort, 157–58
Secret Garden, The, cp 2.1
Selective visibility, 354–56, 355f
Sensory response, 46–51
Sentimental drama, English, 455–58
Serlio, Sebastiano, 165f, 269, 269f, 272–73, 353, 442–43, 451
Set decoration, 311
Set properties, 311
Setting(s), 65–66
 multiple, 172–74
 simultaneous, 175–76, 471–72, cp 2.9
 unit, 174–75
Seurat, Georges, cp 2.8
Shakespeare, William, 46–48, 47f, 49f, 50f, 51f, 61, 62f, 96, 101, 103–4, 104f, 105, 107, 108f, 129, 129f, 206f, 207f, 247f, 255f, 256, 329, 334, 363, 436–37, 438, 439, 452–53, 462–63, 466, 504–5
Shakuntala (Kalidasa), 400
Shaw, George Bernard, 101, 107, 107f, 109, 109f, 191f, 245f, 247f, 477–79
Shawger, David C., Jr., 4–5, 44f, 112f, 180f, 220f, 246f, 249f
Sheen, Martin, cp 2.6
Shéhérazade (ballet), cp 2.2
Sheng, 382, 385
Shepard, Sam, 501
Sheridan, Richard Brinsley, 450
She Stoops to Conquer (Goldsmith), 450
Shop, costume, 343

Shop, scene, 314–16
Shop foreman, 198
Showcase theatre, 186
Sightline drawings, 284, 286f
Signs, symbols vs., 23f, 23–24
Silhouette, 329
Simon, Neil, 175–76
Simonson, Lee, 482f, 488
Simultaneous settings, 175–76, 471–72, cp 2.9
Skene, 415, 416f
Sketches
 presentation, 278–82, 281f, 282f
 roughs, 335–37, 336f
 thumbnail, 278, 279f
 visualization, of makeup, 344
Smith, Oliver, 514, 515f
Sobol, Joshua, 2–13
Social action, 53–54, 494–95
Social commentary, 25–27
Sondheim, Stephen, 86, 175f, 194
Sophocles, 20, 34f, 35, 259–60, 410–13
Sottie, 435
Sound (aural elements), 41–42, 72
Sound design, 372
Sound effects, 72
Source-motivated light, 358
Spatial relationships, 224
 actor-audience, 158–68, 222–23
Special effects (makeup), 346f, 346–47
Spectacularism, 111
Spine, 242–44, 331
Sporre, Dennis J., 9–11, 51f, 67f, 132f, 175f
Spotlights, 354, 369f, 369–70, 370f, 371f
Streep, Meryl, cp 3.4
Stage
 arena form, 162, 162f, 168, 169–70, 171f, 429
 central staging, 162
 mansion, 428–29
 open, 166–68
 proscenium, 151, 164, 165f, 168–71, 169f, 415, 416f
 thrust, 163, 163f, 168, 169, 169f
 See also Theatre forms and architecture
Stage business, 225, 248–50
Stage manager, 196–98
Stage space, 221f, 221–22
Stanislavski, Constantin, 205–6, 207, 239, 275, 438, 483
Stanislavski Method, 239–41, 480, 481–82
Stein, Doug, 334
Steinbeck, John, 180f
Steps and stairs, 308–9, 309f
Stiles, 300, 301f
Stock characters, 435, 436f
Stowe, Harriet Beecher, 111, 112f, 113, 378, 467–68
Straiges, Tony, cp 2.8
Straight makeup, 346, cp 3.2
Straight movements, 247, 248
Stranger, The (Kotzebue), 192f
Strasberg, Lee, 241, 480
Stravinsky, Igor, 83, cp 2.3
Streetcar Named Desire, A (Williams), 210, 216–17, 243
Strength of focus, 221
Strindberg, August, 491, 493

Index

Striplights, 369f, 371
Sturm and Drang (Klinger), 464
Style, 66, 74, 210
    in ancient Greece, 408–9
    costume to support, 330–31
    of play, character's relationship to,
        244–45, 245f
    Restoration production, 451–55
Subtext, 245
Sunday in the Park, cp 2.8
Surface texture (fabric), 339–40, 340f
Svoboda, Josef, 516
Swan Theatre (London), 125, 126f, 444
Symbol, 23f, 23–24, 35
Symbolism, 486
Sympathy, 139
Szajna, Jozef, 5

Takeda Izumo, 388
Tamara (Kritzanc), 164
Taming of the Shrew, The (Shakespeare),
    cp 3.4
Tandy, Jessica, 210, 243, 253
Tartuffe (Molière), 70, 87–89, 88f, 448
Teatro Farnese (Parma), 165f, 442, 441f,
    441–42, 442f
Technical director, 198
Technical production, 295–323
    defined, 296
    materials, 316–18, 317f
    scenery, characteristics of, 297–99,
        298–99f
    scenery units, types of, 299–314
    scene shop, 314–16
    shifting scenery, 318–21
    See also Scene design
Technical rehearsal, 368
Terence, 420, 425
Terkel, Studs, 114–15
Terry, Ellen, 64f, 247f
Thalian Hall (Wilmington, NC), 150f, 151
Theatre, 35
    as art, 35–51
    drama and, 34
    functions of, 51–56
Théâtre du Soleil, 219
Theatre form, 158, 222–23
Theatre forms and architecture, 149–77
    actor-audience spatial relationships,
        158–68, 222–23
    in ancient Greece, 414–17, 415f, 416f
    in Asian theatre, 382f, 382–84, 383f,
        389–95, 393f, 394f, 396f, 397f,
        402–3, 403f
    in English Restoration, 451–55, 454f
    in French neoclassic theatre, 448
    general considerations for, 151–58
    options within, 171–76
    production practicalities and, 168–71
    production types and, 158, 159–61
    of Renaissance, 440–45
    Roman, 420–22, 421f, 422f
    in Romantic era, 469–72, 470f
Theatre-in-the-round, 162, 162f
Théâtre Libre, 238, 483, 485

Theatre of Dionysos (Athens), 123f
Theatricalism, 358, 494, 495f, 502–3
Therapy, 27–29, 52–53
Thought, 39–41, 71, 411
Three-dimensional scenic unit, 306f,
    306–10, 307f, 308f, 309f
Three-quarter stage, 163, 163f
Three Sisters, The (Chekhov), 110, 110f,
    111, 162f, 241
Thrust Stage, 163, 163f, 168, 169f
Thumbnail sketches, 278, 279f
Thymele, 415, 415f
Timbre of voice, 258–59
Time process for rehearsing actors, 217–18
Titus Andronicus (Shakespeare), 49f, 504,
    505
Toller, Ernst, 492
Tools for scene shop, 315–16
Torch Bearers, The, 142f
Torelli, Giacomo, 443
Torn, Rip, 241
Tragedians, ancient Greek, 409–13
Tragédie bourgeoise, 463
Tragedy, 36, 37–42, 53, 95–100, 411–12
Tragic flaw, 95
Tragicomedy, 110
Tribute Money, The (Masaccio), 205f
Trojan Women, The (Euripides), 413
Trollope, Anthony, 121
Trollope, Frances, 121, 138
Tropes, 425, 427
Troyens, Les, 515, 516f
Tungsten-halogen lamp, 354
Twelfth Night (Shakespeare), 334
Two-dimensional scenic unit, 300–305,
    301f
Tyler, Royall, 458–59
Type (character), 95
Tyrone Guthrie Theatre (Minneapolis), 163,
    163f
Tyspin, George, 173

Ullman, Liv, 56f
Ullman, Tracy, cp 3.4
Uncle Tom's Cabin (Stowe), 111, 112f,
    113, 378, 467–68, 468f
Uncle Vanya (Chekhov), 239f, 256, 477,
    478f
Unframed scenery, 303–5
Unions, 181, 186, 276–77
Unistrut channel, 307, 308f
United Scenic Artists, 181
Unities, 446
Unit set, 174–75
Upanishads, 398
Upstage areas, 221
Ustinov, Peter, cp 3.2

Vacuum-formed plastics, 311
Value judgments, making, 89–90
Variety, 140–41, 226
Vatsyayam, Kapila, 401n
Vaudeville revue, 161
Vaughn, Brian, 244f, 253, 254f
Verisimilitude, 37, 358

Visibility, selective, 354–56, 355f
Vision, ease of, 152–55, 154f, 155f
Visual elements, 41, 48–51, 72
Visualization sketches of makeup, 344
Voice, 212–13, 255–59
Volpone (Jonson), 125–26
Voltaire (François Marie Arouet), 461,
    462–63
von Kleist, Heinrich, 467

Wagner, Richard, 204–5, 485
Wagons, 308, 309f
    pageant, 429–30, 430f
Waiting for Godot (Beckett), 83f, 83–84,
    220f, 499–500
Waiting for Lefty (Odets), 53, 495, 496
Ward, Douglas Turner, 507
Wardrobe stock, 343
Warhol, Andy, 21
Waterston, Sam, 56f
Wayne, John, 213f
Way of the World, The (Congreve), 128,
    211, 211f
Webber, Andrew Lloyd, 116f, 136, cp 3.1
Webster, Margaret, 62f, 438–39
Weiss, Peter, 196f, 498
Weist, Diane, 62f
Wesker, Arnold, 219
Western theatre, 407–73
    ancient Greece, 34–35, 95, 122–24, 268,
        269f, 326, 408–17
    Baroque period, 445–55
    Enlightenment, 455–65
    Middle Ages, 268, 269f, 270f, 326,
        422–30
    Renaissance, 326, 434–45
    Romantic era, 77–78, 463, 465–72
    Rome, 124–25, 417–22
    See also Modern theatre
Wexler, Peter, 515–16
Who's Afraid of Virginia Woolf? (Albee),
    102–3
Wilde, Oscar, 51f, 65, 65f, 67
Wilder, Thornton, 236f, 254f
Williams, Samm-Art, 507
Williams, Tennessee, 36, 45, 210, 243,
    246f, 261–62, 482–83
Willing suspension of disbelief, 133–34
Willows, Alec, 334
Wilson, August, 37–38, 131–32, 482, 507
Wilson, Lanford, 39–41
Wilson, Robert, 511–12
Woman in Mind (Ayckbourn), 228f, 240f
Wood, Grant, 24, 25f
Wooden trims, 310
Woodruff, Robert, 334
Working drawings, 297, 298–99f, 339
Work of art, 20–24
Worksheets of makeup, 344–45, 345f
Wycherly, William, 449

Yeats, William Butler, 275
Yordon, Judy E., 2–4, 11–13, 246f
You Can't Take It with You (Hart), 215f

Zaju (variety play), 377
Zola, Émile, 483, 493